Microsoft® Win32™

Application Programming Interface

The Programmer's Reference

Volume 1

Overview
Guide to Programming
Reference A-G

PRE-RELEASE

Microsoft
PRESS

PUBLISHED BY
Microsoft Press
A Division of Microsoft Corporation
One Microsoft Way
Redmond, Washington 98052-6399

Library of Congress Cataloging-in-Publication Data pending.

Printed and bound in the United States of America.

1 2 3 4 5 6 7 8 9 FGFG 7 6 5 4 3 2

Distributed to the book trade in Canada by Macmillan of Canada,
a division of Canada Publishing Corporation.

Distributed to the book trade outside the United States and Canada by
Penguin Books Ltd.

Penguin Books Ltd., Harmondsworth, Middlesex, England
Penguin Books Australia Ltd., Ringwood, Victoria, Australia
Penguin Books N.Z. Ltd., 182-190 Wairau Road, Auckland 10, New Zealand

British Cataloging-in-Publication Data pending.

VMS® is a registered trademark of Digital Equipment Corporation. IBM® is a registered trademark of International Business Machines Corporation. Microsoft® and MS-DOS® are registered trademarks and *Information at Your Fingertips*,™ NT,™ Win32,™ Windows,™ Windows NT,™ and the Windows logo are trademarks of Microsoft Corporation. OS/2® is a registered trademark and Presentation Manager™ is a trademark licensed to Microsoft Corporation.

Contents

Volume 1

An Overview... viii

Guide To Programming
Introduction... 1

    1.1 Overview... 3

    1.2 Constraints and Goals... 3

    1.3 Win32 API Design... 4

Basic Specification 5

    2.1 Overview... 7

    2.2 Win32 Extensions 7

    2.3 Overview of Base Functionality 8

Win32 Network APIs 31

    3.1 Overview... 33

    3.2 Interprocess Communication 33

    3.3 Network Object Connection 34

    3.4 Network Support of Win32 APIs 35

Windows 32-Bit GDI Design Specification.. 37

    4.1 Introduction 39

    4.2 Enhancements to GDI.. 39

    4.3 Changes to GDI.. 40

    4.4 Summary of GDI Functionality 47

User 32-Bit Design Overview.. 59

    5.1 Overview... 61

    5.2 Enhancements to User in the Windows 32-Bit API............................ 61

    5.3 Overview of User Functionality 78

Memory.. 101

    6.1 About Memory 103

    6.2 Global and Local API... 104

    6.3 Standard C library 104

    6.4 Heap API... 104

    6.5 Virtual API.. 104

6.6 About Shared Memory 105

6.7 Summary 111

Synchronization Objects 113

7.1 Introduction 115

Console Functions 131

8.1 Introduction 133

Communications 157

9.1 Introduction 159

9.2 Summary 166

Pipes Overview 169

10.1 Anonymous Pipes 171

10.2 Named Pipes 171

Overview of Structured Exception Handling 177

11.1 Structuring Exception Handling 179

Windows Debugging Support 187

12.1 Introduction to Win Debug Support 189

12.2 Debug APIs 191

User Security 199

13.1 Goals 201

13.2 Users32 Securable Objects 201

13.3 Objects Handles 204

13.4 Opening an Object 208

13.5 Object Access 208

13.6 Closing an Object 208

13.7 Window Classes 209

13.8 SM-SECURE System Metric 209

13.9 ES_PASSWORD Style Edit Controls 209

13.10 Window Enumeration 209

13.11 Accessing Screen Contents 209

13.12 Clipboard Access 210

13.13 DDE Security 210

13.14 Auditing 211

13.15 Server Initialization 212

13.16 Client Initialization 212

13.17 Logon Processing 213

13.18 System Shutdown 214

Unicode Support 215

14.1 Overview 217

14.2 Unicode Support in the Windows 32 API 217

14.3 Data Types 217

14.4 API Prototypes 218

14.5 Basic Steps 219

14.6 Window Classes 220

14.7 Messages 220

14.8 Resources 220

14.9 C Run Times 221

14.10 Filenames 222

14.11 Special Characters 222

14.12 Unicode Plain Text Format 225

14.13 Special Topics 226

14.14 Workarounds 227

Programming Reference A-G

Windows Interfaces and Application Callbacks: A-G 229

Volume II

Programming Reference H-Z

Windows Interfaces and Application Callbacks: H-Z 679

Other Information

DDE Transaction Types 1086

Messages 1097

Notifications 1208

Structures 1216

Types and Macros 1387

The Win32™ Application Programming Interface: An Overview

Since its original release in 1985, Microsoft® Windows™ graphical environment has become the leading graphical system for personal computers. Microsoft Windows version 3.0, released in May 1990, was a milestone that broke the 640K barrier of the Microsoft MS-DOS® operating system by running applications in protected mode, thus making it possible to develop much more sophisticated applications. This innovation spawned myriad applications and is responsible for the huge success of the Windows environment in the marketplace, showcased by the volume of graphical applications sold (see Figure 1).

Market Perspective

	12/91 Installed base	Forecast [1] annual run rate 1992	YTD 1991 [2] application volume
Windows 3.0	7.9M	9.2M	$711M
MS-DOS	96.0M	24.3M	$2,148M
Macintosh	6.5M	2.2M	$457M
PC UNIX	1.0M	.4M	n/a
OS/2	1.2M	.7M	$29M

Sources: 1) IDC, October 1991; 2) Software Publishing Assoc., September, 1991

Figure 1

Between May 1990 and October 1991, more than 7 million personal computer users worldwide have licensed version 3.0. International Data Corporation estimates that an additional 9.2 million users will adopt it during 1992. In addition, more than 70 thousand Microsoft Windows version 3.0 Software Development Kits have been shipped, a clear indication of the number of applications likely to appear during the next 12 to 18 months. By fall 1991, more than 4,900 Windows-based applications were shipping.

Building on this achievement and on the success of independent software developers, Microsoft is extending and expanding the Windows environment so that Windows-based applications can run on a broad range of computing platforms — from battery-operated portables to high-end RISC workstations and multiprocessor servers.

We are expanding Windows to make it fully 32-bit and are adding additional operating system services. Microsoft Windows for Pen Computing and Microsoft Windows with Multimedia Extensions will also take advantage of new hardware technologies.

Windows Today

Today many people think of Windows as a graphical add-on to the familiar MS-DOS operating system they have used for years. This perception took much of the fear out of upgrading to Windows for the end user. But, in fact, Windows is not limited by MS-DOS.

Windows is a complete operating system that provides extra features on top of MS-DOS and replaces certain MS-DOS features. Windows version 3.0 does not use MS-DOS screen or keyboard I/O, does not use MS-DOS memory management, and can even bypass MS-DOS file I/O with new Windows-specific device drivers. Windows version 3.0 enhanced mode can handle 32-bit device drivers that are not limited by the infamous 640K MS-DOS barrier. These drivers talk through Windows to applications that are also not limited by the constraints of MS-DOS.

The advantage of being able to work with MS-DOS is that it preserves the value added by the MS-DOS long life span (in computer years). Windows can run with MS-DOS TSRs, MS-DOS device drivers, and of course, it can run MS-DOS applications. Future versions of Windows will continue to be available on MS-DOS.

The Windows Architecture

Since the IBM® PC was introduced in 1981, personal computers have become much more diverse in capability and in configuration. This diversity will increase in the next few years as personal computers based on RISC processors and multiprocessor systems are introduced.

These diverse systems have different operating system needs. For example, a battery-operated portable requires minimal memory and hard disk footprint to minimize weight and cost. It also requires power management to extend battery life. In contrast, network servers and mission-critical desktops require sophisticated security to ensure the integrity of data. RISC-based systems require portability for both the operating system and the applications.

Some vendors feel that the diverse range of hardware requires totally different operating systems with incompatible applications. They sell different operating systems for personal computers, workstations, servers, and in the future, pen-based systems. Each of their operating systems requires unique, incompatible applications. Connectivity between these divergent platforms is complicated.

Microsoft is focused on a much simpler solution. We're extending Windows into multiple, fully compatible implementations. Different implementations of Windows will be optimized for different classes of hardware. Customer investment in Windows development and Windows applications will be protected. Windows applications will run across the spectrum of hardware, from notepad-sized pen systems, to mission-critical desktops, to multiprocessor and RISC-based systems.

Microsoft Windows is evolving into a complete operating system architecture that addresses diverse requirements by supporting different modes of operation. Today Windows has three modes: real mode, standard mode, and enhanced mode. Real mode provides compatibility with previous versions of Microsoft Windows. Standard mode is optimized for an 80286 processor and provides access to the full 16 MB of memory supported by that chip. Enhanced mode takes advantage of the 80386 and 80486 processors by providing support for multiple MS-DOS applications and, through a technique called demand paging, provides applications with access to more memory than is physically present in the machine. All three modes support both MS-DOS and Windows applications.

Building upon the success of Windows version 3.0, Microsoft will introduce version 3.1 in early 1992. Version 3.1 incorporates significant customer feedback. It includes TrueType™, an advanced scalable fonts technology; it improves performance, introduces a newly designed file manager, improves network connectivity, and improves system reliability. Version 3.1 will support Windows standard mode and enhanced mode.

Also during 1991, Microsoft will enhance Windows standard mode and enhanced mode by providing extensions for sound, animation, and CD-ROM access, called Windows with Multimedia Extensions. We will also release an operating environment for clipboard and pen-style computing, called Microsoft Windows for Pen Computing.

Windows NT

In 1992, Microsoft will introduce a new product called Windows NT™ (New Technology). Windows NT is built on a 32-bit operating system kernel. Windows NT will deliver an extremely robust client environment for mission-critical applications, a high-end desktop platform, and a portable, scalable server environment (see Figure 2). Windows NT will also transform Windows into a Microsoft LAN Manager server platform, thus adding a fourth server platform to the three currently supported by LAN Manager: OS/2®, UNIX®, and VMS®.

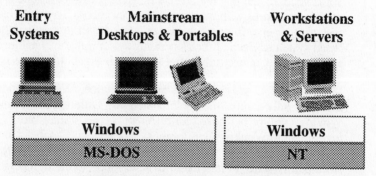

Windows:
Scalable and Evolutionary

| Entry Systems | Mainstream Desktops & Portables | Workstations & Servers |

Single User Interface
Single Programming Model

Figure 2

Windows NT does not require MS-DOS to function. It is, however, compatible with the large installed base of MS-DOS and Windows applications. In addition to providing compatibility with these existing applications, Windows NT includes the features required to meet the needs of the high-end desktop and server marketplace in the 1990s and beyond.

To support large server applications, Windows NT provides symmetric multiprocessor support, with tasks symmetrically distributed between processors on a per-thread basis. This design provides maximum utilization of each processor in a multiprocessor system and simplifies the development of multiprocessor applications.

Network servers and many mission-critical applications require security. To meet this need, Windows NT has been designed as a secure operating system. Microsoft is working with the U.S. government to certify Windows NT as "C2-level" secure. In addition, the internal design of Windows NT can be enhanced in future releases to "B-level" security.

Windows NT is a key component of the Advanced Computing Environment (ACE) initiative announced in April 1991, by Microsoft, Compaq Computer Corp., Digital Equipment Corp., MIPS Computer Systems, The Santa Cruz Operation, and others. It now includes more than 200 members.

The goal of the ACE initiative is to provide an open, standards-based advanced computing environment for microprocessor-based systems as they become increasingly powerful. The ACE initiative provides full support for two platforms: 386/486-based PCs and MIPS RISC-based systems. As a portable operating system that spans both these environments, Windows NT is a crucial element of the ACE standard. With Windows NT, existing MS-DOS and Windows programs will run unchanged on MIPS-based computers.

In addition to these advanced capabilities, the kernel-based design of Windows NT can be thought of as a nucleus that is compatible with different operating system environments. The kernel design provides Windows NT compatibility with MS-DOS and Windows applications. It also provides the foundation for Windows NT to support the OS/2 and POSIX application program interfaces, both of which are under development at Microsoft and will be available as add-on toolkits. This design also allows Windows NT to support applications written to the new Win32 application programming interface.

Win32 API

Developers and end users have made enormous investments in Windows programming and Windows applications. Most of these applications have been developed to run on both the 16-bit 80286 processor and the 32-bit 80386 and 80486 systems. Although highly capable, programs written to the Windows 16-bit API, which is supported by Windows 3.0, are constrained by the memory limits inherent in a 16-bit architecture. Code must be divided into segments that cannot exceed 64K (65,536 bytes). This makes programming more difficult. It also imposes a performance penalty on high-performance 80486 and RISC-based systems.

The Win32 API (Win32) has been designed to make the transition from the Windows 16-bit API (Windows 16) to 32-bit as easy as possible. Only minimal changes have been made to the syntax of the Win32 API. The API names are the same as Windows 16. The semantics are identical. The message order is identical. In fact, it is possible to keep a single source code base and compile that source code into both 16-bit and 32-bit programs. The changes that are necessary are detailed in "Portable Programming Considerations for 32-Bit Windows Operating Systems," later in this overview.

Although the Win32 API is extremely compatible with the Windows 16 API, it also contains significant new features. These features include preemptively multitasked processes that use separate address spaces, preemptive threads, semaphores, shared memory, named pipes, mailslots, and memory-mapped file I/O. Graphic device interface (GDI) improvements include Bézier curves, paths, and transforms.

The Win32 API is fully supported in both MS-DOS Windows and Windows NT. The Win32 API will first be available in the Windows NT product during 1992. It will be added to MS-DOS Windows in 1993. Programs written to the Win32 API will run binary code compatibly on both Windows NT and MS-DOS Windows. All Win32 features will be supported by both MS-DOS Windows and Windows NT, including preemptive multitasking. Win32 programs will be fully source-compatible between x86 and MIPS processors. Software Development Kits for the Win32 API will be available in the first half of 1992.

In addition, Microsoft Languages is developing a Windows extender product that implements a compatible subset of the Win32 API on Windows 3.1. This product will provide a 32-bit programming environment for all Windows 3.1 features but will not include advanced capabilities present in the full Win32 API such as preemptive multitasking. Programs written to this subset will run unmodified as Win32 applications on Windows NT and MS-DOS Windows. Additional information on this product will be released during the first half of 1992.

The following section highlights some key features of the Win32 API.

Kernel: The Base Operating System

The Win32 API on both Windows NT and MS-DOS Windows provides preemptive, thread-based multitasking. It also runs all Win32 and MS-DOS applications in separate address spaces so that they cannot corrupt one another.

The Win32 API is designed to be portable beyond the 80386 and 80486 processors and in particular to be portable to RISC architectures. All these processors have different features but have in common 32-bit addressing and paged virtual memory architectures. Paged virtual memory is more efficient to implement and executes faster than segmented virtual memory. Memory management in Win32 is secure because the operating system places different memory objects in different pages of memory and allows an application to control access permissions (read, write, read/write, execute) to memory objects.

Given a large 32-bit address space, the operating system can conveniently and efficiently optimize file I/O because processes treat the file as a very large memory object and randomly access that object. The operating system, through page faulting, can detect read access to a file and bring in that data. It can detect when a shared file is written to and then write out that data. With process-configurable access permissions and sparse allocation of physical memory pages, processes can implement very efficient data access, even when access patterns are entirely unpredictable.

GDI Improvements: Béziers, Paths, Transforms

GDI, the drawing API for Windows versions 3.0 and 3.1, provides a useful device-independent drawing set for applications. As output devices have become more sophisticated, so have drawing needs; hence, GDI has been improved.

Some Windows applications for versions 3.0 and 3.1 have needed to implement high-level graphics functions using the low-level drawing primitives of the Windows environment. Although this capability has provided application vendors flexibility in extending the Windows GDI, it has not allowed them to take seamless advantage of advances in printer and display technology. Application developers have had to code their own algorithms for displaying graphics such as Bézier curves and paths. With the Win32 API, developers can call new high-level graphics features that will take advantage of the built-in drawing capabilities in advanced output hardware. Under Win32, displaying Bézier curves can be handled by the graphics engine or by output devices that have implemented Bézier optimizations.

The Win32 GDI is a complete and general-purpose drawing package. Bézier curves are a general-purpose curve primitive from which a straight line can also be derived. This function combined with the PolyBézier functionality makes it possible to draw any combination of continuous lines and curves.

Win32 adds a Path API, making it easy for an application to manage multiple shapes efficiently. These shapes can consist of an arbitrary combination of lines, arcs, ellipses, and Bézier curves. A path is started by calling BeginPath. Subsequent calls to drawing primitives define the shape and size of the path. A call to EndPath closes the path. Applications can then draw, clip through, fill, and transform these defined shapes.

The Win32 Transform API maps the virtual two-dimensional surface on which you draw to the two-dimensional output surface. This API, combined with the TrueType font technology first available with Windows version 3.1, makes it possible to draw truly device-independent graphics that the system can map to the display surface, including the rotation of bitmaps, fonts, and metafiles.

The Windowing System and System Classes

The most significant change to the Windows windowing system is the desynchronization of the per-window message queue from the system message queue. This change prevents errant, looping applications that, when they stop processing their messages, block the computer system's entire user interface and thus make other applications unavailable.

From an end-user perspective, desynchronization means that they can do other things while one application is busy. For example, if a word processing program is busy printing a 100-page document, a user can click on another application's window or bring up the Task Manager to begin working in another application. This effectively minimizes the time the user waits with an hourglass on their screen.

The desynchronization of the message queue is completely compatible with the Windows versions 3.0 and 3.1 message models. The message ordering is the same. If WM_xyz came after WM_abc, it still does. This compatibility is necessary because, in Win32 systems, existing Windows applications run on top of the Win32 message system. The messages are simply copied from the 32-bit stack to the 16-bit stack and passed onto the application; therefore, message order cannot change.

Networking Extensions

Each time the APIs are further standardized in a particular area, it becomes easier to write significant new applications. Because of the variety of networking layers, ranging from network card interfaces and protocol stacks to the wide array of network interprocess communications (IPC) mechanisms, networking is probably the most confusing interface for developers today. Win32 will include standard network APIs that can replace those that network providers have previously needed to supply. Win32 will expose driver-style interfaces similar to the WinNet APIs provided by Windows version 3.0 so that third-party vendors can plug their network services into the Windows open architecture.

Some of the new, 32-bit WinNet APIs being defined are file, print, named pipes, mailslots, server browsing, and machine configuration. This means applications can rely on a consistent programming interface regardless of the underlying network. Even if a network is not present, the APIs are still available and will return appropriate error codes.

The Win32 API includes peer-to-peer named pipes, mailslots, and APIs to enable (RPC) remote procedure call compilers. With Win32, a mail-server vendor can build a messaging service on named pipes and asynchronous communication that will run on top of any network operating system, protocol stack, or network card - each of which could come from a different network vendor.

Compatibility with Windows 16-Bit APIs

Windows version 3.0 and 3.1 applications will be able to run on MS-DOS Windows and Windows NT. To be compatible with versions 3.0 and 3.1, all Windows 16 applications will run as one process in one address space. They will be nonpreemptive with respect to one another but preemptive with respect to the rest of the system, which mirrors their behavior under Windows version 3.0 enhanced mode. Windows 16 applications run against the Win32 APIs without a "layer" and without any state mapping or message reordering.

Windows executables will also run on RISC-based Windows NT machines (see Figure 3). Excellent performance is expected on this platform because, although some code will be run against 80286 emulator technology, all Windows calls will be mapped directly to the Windows NT software.

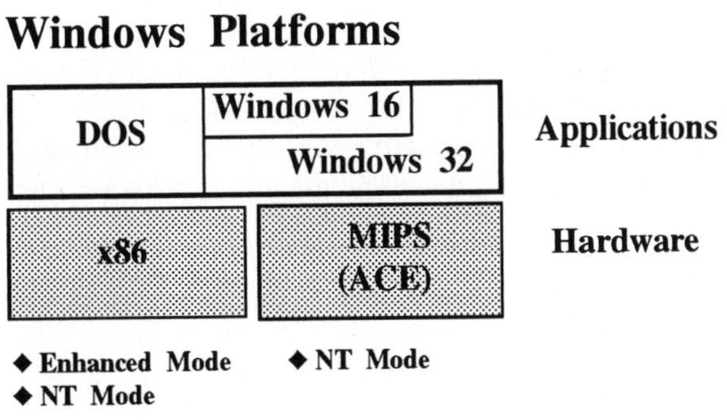

Windows Platforms

◆ Enhanced Mode   ◆ NT Mode
◆ NT Mode

Figure 3

Win32 APIs: The Future of Windows

Millions of people are actively using Windows version 3.0 today. Corporations and independent software vendors are making major commitments to Windows and investments in Windows applications.

To protect this investment, Microsoft is evolving Windows into a complete architecture. Through separate implementations, Microsoft Windows will run on vastly different types of hardware, from pen-based notepad computers to multiprocessor and RISC systems.

Windows NT and future versions of MS-DOS Windows will support the Win32 APIs. Designed to simplify migration of Windows applications from 16-bit to 32-bit, these APIs will also make it easy to develop new Win32 applications. They contain significant new features that will enable a new generation of powerful Windows applications.

In addition, the Win32 APIs will be used as the foundation for future versions of Windows under development at Microsoft. This technology, often called Information at your fingertips, will make it even easier to use personal computers and will provide significant new functionality to Windows users.

Portable Programming Considerations for Win32 Operating Systems

Abstract

The first prerelease Microsoft Win32 Software Development Kit will be available soon. During the beta testing of Windows 3.1, developers can update application source code and make changes that will result in a robust Windows 3.1 application as well as prepare the application for transition into the full 32-bit environment provided by the Win32 API. This paper is not a call to start creating 32-bit source code but rather a highlight of the changes that will benefit updating source code for Windows 3.1 now and Win32 applications later.

Goals of Microsoft Win32 API

The creation of the Win32 application programming interface (Win32 API) focused on six goals:

1. Provide a 32-bit migration path for existing Windows applications.

2. Make porting a Windows application to Win32 as easy as possible.

3. Create an efficient mapping layer to run Windows 3.x binaries on Win32 systems.

4. Support a single source code base for creating Windows 3.x and Win32 binaries.

5. Offer an identical Win32 API on both Windows NT and a future release of MS-DOS Windows.

6. Add a new API for advanced operating system features such as preemptive multitasking, IPC mechanisms, sophisticated memory management, and graphics capabilities while maintaining compatibility by simply widening the existing Windows API.

To achieve these goals, Microsoft derived the Win32 API from the existing Windows 3.1 API, disallowing arbitrary name changes of data types, functions, and structures. At first glance, a Win32 application is indistinguishable from an existing Windows 3.0 or 3.1 (hereafter referred to as Windows 3.x) application, both from an end-user's perspective and from a quick inspection of the source code. A native Win32 application (unlike its cousin, which uses the Windows 3.x API) can take full advantage of large linear memory allocation, multiple threads for background tasks and calculations, local and remote IPC via named pipes, and other features detailed in "The Win32 API: An Overview."

The Win32 API first appears in Windows NT for uniprocessor and multiprocessor 386 and 486 systems and for new RISC-based systems. A future version of MS-DOS Windows will also support the Win32 API. All Win32 features are supported by both Windows NT and the future release of MS-DOS Windows, including linear address space, threads, and preemptive multitasking. Win32 applications running on MS-DOS Windows or Windows NT will be binary-compatible with Intel 386/486 processors and source-compatible with Windows NT running on RISC processors.

This paper concentrates on two aspects of Windows application portability:

1. Steps that developers can take today while working on Windows 3.1 applications to better support binary compatibility of these applications on Windows NT

2. Techniques that developers can use to create Windows code that is more portable and that will make it easier to create Win32 versions of the application when Win32 Software Development Kits are available

Binary Compatibility

Win32 systems will be able to run existing Windows 3.x applications with interoperability via dynamic data exchange (DDE), object linking and embedding (OLE), metafiles, and the Clipboard with other Windows 3.x applications and with native Win32 applications. Windows 3.x applications and Win32 applications will exist side-by-side on the same display rather than running in separate screen groups. Windows 3.x applications will be fully compatible with Windows NT if developers follow these rules:

- Ensure that Windows 3.x applications run in standard/enhanced mode.

- Use published Windows 3.x APIs, messages, and structures.

- Do not modify WIN.INI directly; use a profile string API (for example WriteProfileString).

- Use QUERYESCSUPPORT to determine whether particular printer driver escapes are implemented.

The ability to run Windows 3.x binaries on Windows NT is not restricted to 386 and 486 systems; these binaries will also run on RISC-based Windows NT systems. This is accomplished with a very high-performance PC emulator and the same efficient mapping layer technology used to seamlessly integrate Windows 3.x applications on Windows NT systems running on 386 and 486 systems.

Design Requirements

Mapping-layer technology has been offered in the past to allow Windows-based applications to run on OS/2. Past solutions such as Windows Libraries for OS/2 (WLO) required special run-time libraries and DLLs before Windows-based applications could run on OS/2. ISVs must ship WLO mapping-layer DLLs along with their applications, which complicates distributing and installing the product. This approach is unacceptable on Win32 systems.

To achieve binary compatibility and high performance on Win32 systems, developers of Windows version 3.x applications do not need to recompile the source code, use special run-time libraries, or develop or acquire special tools to make executables compatible.

The ability to run Windows 3.x binaries allows an end-user to update to Win32 systems and continue to use existing Windows 3.x applications as well as native Win32 applications as they become available. This protects investments in existing Windows 3.x applications and allows users to update to new Win32 applications as they are released. Native Win32 applications will take advantage of the higher performance, linear 32-bit addressing and enormous capacity increase for data processing.

Microsoft will encourage Windows developers to test their current Windows 3.x products on prerelease versions of Windows NT by means of a Windows NT beta test program to assure that binary compatibility is thorough and efficient.

Supported Features

The following is a list of many of the Windows 3.x features supported on Win32 systems. This list shows that existing Windows applications can be binary-compatible with future Win32 systems with little work on the part of developers. It also illustrates that complex windowing, graphics, and low-level operating system reliance by Windows 3.x binaries will be completely supported.

Examples of major user interface features that are fully supported (no modifications needed) include:

- Multiple document interface messages and default message handling
- Resource files (for example, dialog boxes, menus, accelerator tables, and user-defined resources)
- DDE messages and the DDE manager library (DDEML) API
- Windows-compatible OLE
- Metafiles
- Clipboard data exchange

Major graphical interface features that are fully supported include:

- TrueType and TrueType APIs
- Windows 3.x icons and cursors in existing format
- Bitmaps (BMPs) and device-independent bitmaps (DIBs)
- Printing by means of native Win32 printer drivers

Base system functionality includes support for:

- Shared memory for IPC
- NetBIOS and Microsoft LAN Manager for MS-DOS named pipe support
- MS-DOS 5.0 interfaces (called with DOS3Call or INT21)

Methods to Achieve Binary Compatibility

The Win32 API will employ a registration database that will maintain all system and application configuration information. Files such as WIN.INI will no longer exist in the file system; instead, calls to the profile API (for example, GetProfileString) will be routed to the database. Therefore, applications should not attempt to create or modify *.INI files directly by means of file I/O. The Windows 3.x profile APIs should be used to manipulate all profile information. Installation programs that create private installation files should be modified to use the profile API or Windows 3.1 registation database API.

Windows NT ships with a set of printer drivers similar to Windows 3.x. This has been accomplished by sharing printer minidrivers. However, Windows NT also includes native Win32 printer drivers to take advantage of high-end printing capabilities present on such devices as Postscript® printers. Windows applications should always use QUERYESCSUPPORT before using any extended printer driver escape. Applications should not assume that printer drivers of a certain class (LaserJet® or Postscript for example) are guaranteed to provide specific driver escapes. Querying for support guarantees that an application will not be affected by subsequent Windows 3.x or Win32 printer driver updates.

Applications must be compatible with Windows 3.x standard or enhanced mode. Win32 systems will not support Windows real mode. Applications should use only published Windows 3.x APIs, messages, and structures.

Portable Coding Techniques

With the release of Windows 3.1, many applications are being updated to add support for features such as OLE and to take advantage of TrueType. Because Windows programmers are already scrutinizing their applications' sources, now is a convenient time to prepare the code for the future: a future that offers a 32-bit environment with powerful new features.

The discussion concentrates on the important issues that affect the portability of existing Windows source code to Win32. Although this list may seem long and detailed, all the recommendations are useful for creating robust Windows 3.1 applications. In addition, applications will be more portable, and it will be easier to create native Win32 applications when Win32 Software Development Kits are available.

To assist in creating portable source code, the Win32 SDK will provide tools to automate the porting process. One of the tools is an editor with a table-driven search capability that can be used to search source code for API, messages, and certain C constructs that are nonportable. Once an item is found, the code is highlighted for review. Online help is available to assist in making portable source code modifications.

Rules for Writing Portable Windows 3.x/Windows 32-Bit Source Code

- Parse wParam and lParam immediately in WndProc routines.
- Use portable API forms (for example, MoveToEx instead of MoveTo).
- NULL is a valid return value from GetFocus and GetActiveWindow.
- Use FindWindow (or IPC) instead of hPrevInstance to find other running instances.
- GlobalLock and malloc will not return 64K aligned pointers.
- Use Windows 3.x DIB functions to initialize color bitmaps.
- Do not use GetInstanceData; replace with supported IPC mechanism.
- Do not share GDI object handles (for example, pens and bitmaps) between processes.
- Compile warning level -W2 or higher (-W3 recommended).
- Create function prototypes for all functions.
- Review structure member alignment and data types.
- Remove hard-coded buffer sizes (for example, filenames and path names).
- Do not extract private copies of WINDOWS.H definitions.
- Use unique typedefs (HPEN, HWND, not generic types such as HANDLE or int).
- Use portable integer typedefs (UINT, WORD).

A Brief Look at Win32

If you start with Windows 3.x source code, creating a native Win32 application using the Win32 API is straightforward and requires minimal source changes. In general, the Win32 API simply involves widening parameters and return values to 32 bits. Over the course of a few months, a Windows NT development team ported a range of Windows 3.x source code to Win32, including the complete Windows 3.0 and Beta 3.1 software development kit sample code and relatively complex Windows 3.1 applets--Program Manager, File Manager, Cardfile, and so on. This porting effort has validated the design of the Win32 API and proven that it is possible to create Win32 applications quickly from Windows 3.x sources. The Windows software development kit samples and system applet source code was modified to be fully portable, allowing Windows 3.1 and Win32 binaries to be created from the same code base.

The Windows 3.1 system applets contain more than 100,000 lines of source code. File Manager in particular contains approximately 20,000 lines of code; yet within one day, it was compiling as a native Win32 application. Within a week, File Manager could execute and display directory listings. Changes included recoding several assembler routines in C so that the sources can be compiled for both x86 and RISC processors. Few changes to the original Windows 3.x C code were required, which is indicated by the short time needed to create a functional, portable version of File Manager.

An important porting factor is that Windows 3.x resource files containing menus, dialog boxes, icons, accelerator tables, and so on are directly compatible with the 32-bit resource compiler. You need not modify the resource files for Win32: This is not surprising, since the resource file is simply a script with no information that is 32-bit sensitive.

Win32 Sample Source Code

The following code fragment is from the Windows 3.0 software development kit sample, GENERIC. Only one minor change to the entire GENERIC sample is required; the fragment builds completely as either a Windows 3.x or Win32 binary. Although the GENERIC sample is not particularly sophisticated, it does contain a menu and a dialog box, indicating that more complex Windows functionality is easily supported.

If we look at the code fragment through the eyes of Win32, we see a true 32-bit application. Function parameters, pointers, and structure members are all widened from 16 to 32 bits. This widening is accomplished "under the covers" by means of typedefs in WINDOWS.H (Win32 version). For example, the typedef LPSTR is a linear 32-bit pointer. The variable *hInst* is defined as a 32-bit HANDLE. The window handle, *hWnd,* returned by **CreateWindow**, is a 32-bit window handle. The window class structure contains 32-bit handles to icons, 32-bit linear pointers to string constants, and a 32-bit stock brush handle.

Generic Sample Application from Windows 3.0 SDK

```
#include "windows.h"    /* required for all Windows applications*/
#include "generic.h"    /* specific to this program      */

HANDLE hInst;            /* current instance      */

int PASCAL WinMain(hInstance, hPrevInstance, lpCmdLine, nCmdShow)
HANDLE hInstance;         /* current instance      */
HANDLE hPrevInstance;     /* previous instance     */
LPSTR lpCmdLine;          /* command line      */
int nCmdShow;             /* show-window type (open/icon) */
{
    MSG msg;              /* message      */
    if (!hPrevInstance) /* Other instances of app running? */
if (!InitApplication(hInstance)) /* Initialize shared things */
    return (FALSE);       /* Exits if unable to initialize      */

    /* Perform initializations that apply to a specific instance */

    if (!InitInstance(hInstance, nCmdShow))
        return (FALSE);

    /* Acquire and dispatch messages until a WM_QUIT message is
received. */

    while (GetMessage(&msg,  /* message structure      */
    NULL,                    /* handle of window receiving message */
    NULL,                    /* lowest message to examine      */
    NULL))                   /* highest message to examine      */
{
TranslateMessage(&msg);  /* Translates virtual key codes      */
DispatchMessage(&msg);   /* Dispatches message to window      */
    }
    return (msg.wParam);  /* Returns the value from PostQuitMessage */
}

BOOL InitApplication(hInstance)
HANDLE hInstance              /* current instance      */
{
    WNDCLASS  wc;

 /* Fill in window class structure with parameters that describe the */
    /* main window.        */

    wc.style = NULL;                 /* Class style(s).      */
    wc.lpfnWndProc = MainWndProc; /* Function to retrieve messages for
*/
                                     /* windows of this class.      */
    wc.cbClsExtra = 0;               /* No per-class extra data.   */
    wc.cbWndExtra = 0;               /* No per-window extra data. */
    wc.hInstance = hInstance;     /*  Application that owns the class. */
    wc.hIcon = LoadIcon(NULL, IDI_APPLICATION);
    wc.hCursor = LoadCursor(NULL, IDC_ARROW);
    wc.hbrBackground = GetStockObject(WHITE_BRUSH);
    wc.lpszMenuName =  "GenericMenu";  /* Name of menu resource in .RC
file. */
```

```
wc.lpszClassName = "GenericWClass"; /* Name used in call to
CreateWindow. */

    /* Register the window class and return success/failure code. */
    return (RegisterClass(&wc));
}

BOOL InitInstance(hInstance, nCmdShow)
    HANDLE          hInstance;       /* Current instance identifier. */
    int             nCmdShow;     /* Param for first ShowWindow()call.*/
{

    HWND            hWnd;             /* Main window handle.       */

    /* Save the instance handle in static variable, which will be used
in */
    /* many subsequent calls from this application to Windows.   */

    hInst = hInstance;

    /* Create a main window for this application instance.   */
    hWnd = CreateWindow(
        "GenericWClass",              /* See RegisterClass() call.  */
"Generic Sample Application",        /* Text for window title bar.  */
        WS_OVERLAPPEDWINDOW,      /* Window style.         */
        CW_USEDEFAULT,            /* Default horizontal position. */
        CW_USEDEFAULT,            /* Default vertical position.   */
        CW_USEDEFAULT,            /* Default width.            */
        CW_USEDEFAULT,            /* Default height.          */
        NULL,                   /* Overlapped windows have no parent. */
        NULL,                   /* Use the window class menu.      */
        hInstance,              /* This instance owns this window.  */
        NULL                    /* Pointer not needed.          */
    );

    /* If window could not be created, return "failure" */
    if (!hWnd)
        return (FALSE);

    /* Make the window visible; update its client area; and return
"success" */
    ShowWindow(hWnd, nCmdShow);  /* Show the window              */
    UpdateWindow(hWnd);          /* Sends WM_PAINT message        */
    return (TRUE);               /* Returns the value from PostQuitMessage
*/
}
```

User Interface Code

Message Parameter Packing

With the widening of handles to 32 bits, both *wParam* and *lParam* (the additional message parameters) must be 32 bits wide. If, in Windows 3.x applications, a handle and another value were packed into the high and low 16 bits of *lParam*, widening to 32 bits requires repacking. A 32-bit handle occupies *lParam* completely, requiring the previously packed second parameter to be moved to *wParam*. Several messages have been affected by handle widening, including WM_COMMAND:

```
WM_COMMAND

    Win 3.x:        wParam == window id
                    lParam == hwnd, command

    Win 32-Bit:     wParam == window id, command
                    lParam == hwnd
```

The WM_COMMAND *window id* and *command* parameters remain 16-bit values in Win32 and can therefore be packed in the widened 32-bit *wParam*. The 32-bit *hwnd* value is now fully contained in *lParam*. Therefore, the notification code has been moved from the high word of *lParam* to the high word of *wParam*.

Code that tests for a message identifier should be modified:

```
Existing code:
    switch (message) {
        :
        case WM_COMMAND:
            switch (wParam) {
                case ID_OK:
                    :
            }
    }

Portable code:
    switch (message) {
        :
        case WM_COMMAND:
            switch (LOWORD(wParam)) {
                case ID_OK:
                    :
            }
    }
```

In this case, the change can be made portably and continue to compile for either Windows 3.x or Win32. LOWORD(wParam) extracts the correct low -order 16-bit message identifier on Windows 3.x and Win32.

In extracting window handles from the WM_COMMAND message parameters, existing Windows code often uses constructs such as the following:

```
hwnd = LOWORD(lParam);
notification = HIWORD(lParam);
```

The portable method for extracting a window handle from the WM_COMMAND *lParam* is as follows:

```
hwnd = (HWND)(UINT)lParam;
```

UINT is a new data type discussed later in this document. (UINT) casts *lParam* to a 16-bit value on Windows 3.x (extracting the window handle) and a 32-bit value on Win32.

Handling the extraction of the WM_COMMAND notification code portably requires explicit coding.

```
#ifdef WIN32
   notification = HIWORD(lParam);
#else
   notification = HIWORD(wParam);
#endif
```

To minimize the affect of parameter packing differences, a set of macros that parse message parameters has been created . In this way, you can compile source code either as a Windows 3.x application or as a Win32 application without unique message-handling code or C compiler #ifdef directives. Some programmers prefer macros, others #ifdef statements. Both methods can be used to create portable code. Examples of macros used to parse WM_COMMAND information are as follows:

```
GET_WM_COMMAND_ID   (wParam, lParam) // Parse control ID value
GET_WM_COMMAND_HWND(wParam, lParam) // Parse control HWND
GET_WM_COMMAND_CMD (wParam, lParam) // Parse notification
command
```

The underlying macro definitions are Windows 3.x and Win32-specific, parsing the information from *wParam* or *lParam* as appropriate for each implementation. The important point is that you can easily create readable source code that can be compiled for Windows 3.x or Win32.

Summary:

For messages that have changed their packing, extract the *wParam/lParam* information immediately upon handling the message. Use local variables to hold this information, and refer to the data using these variables not via continued references but via *wParam* or *lParam* manipulations. Pass values extracted from *wParam* and *lParam*, not the *wParam* or *lParam* itself, to worker routines.

LOWORD and HIWORD are always suspect, and each should be verified (search for them in an editor). Locating each occurrence will quickly highlight nonportable code. Study the target data type of these macros and the data type receiving the result.

The proper use of casts and/or macros can be used to handle many porting issues.

Fortunately, there are few message differences, and most of these messages are used infrequently. The following table lists affected messages:

```
MESSAGE
Win 3.x: (Existing form)
     wParam: 16-bits
     lParam: Least Significant 16-bits, Most Significant 16-bits
Win 32:  (Widened form)
     wParam: Least Significant 16-bits, Most Significant 16-bits
     lParam: 32-bits
```

The following list can be used for quick reference. Similar approaches in handling packing differences with each message can be used as discussed for WM_COMMAND in the text above:

```
WM_ACTIVATE
Win 3.x:
     wParam: state
     lParam: fMinimized, hwnd
Win 32:
     wParam: state, fMinimized
     lParam: hwnd


WM_CHARTOITEM
Win 3.x:
     wParam: char
     lParam: pos, hwnd
Win 32:
     wParam: char, pos
     lParam: hwnd


WM_COMMAND
Win 3.x:
     wParam: id
     lParam: hwnd, cmd
Win 32:
     wParam: id, cmd
     lParam: hwnd


WM_CTLCOLOR
Win 3.x:
     wParam: hdc
     lParam: hwnd, type
Win 32:
     WM_CTLCOLORBTN
     WM_CTLCOLORDLG
     WM_CTLCOLORLISTBOX
     WM_CTLCOLORMSGBOX
     WM_CTLCOLORSCROLLBAR
     WM_CTLCOLORSTATIC
     WM_CTLCOLOREDIT
       wParam: hdc
       lParam: hwnd
```

Note: Porting WM_CTLCOLOR requires handling the specific control class
color message. Portable code should use #ifdefs to handle this
difference.

WM_MENUSELECT
Win 3.x:
      wParam: cmd
      lParam: flags, hMenu
Win 32:
      wParam: cmd, flags
      lParam: hMenu

WM_MDIACTIVATE (when message is sent to the MDI client window)
No change.

WM_MDIACTIVATE (when client window sends message to MDI child)
Win 3.x:
      wParam: fActivate
      lParam: hwndDeactivate, hwndActivate
Win 32:
      wParam: hwndActivate
      lParam: hwndDeactivate

WM_MDISETMENU
Win 3.x:
      wParam: 0
      lParam: hMenuFrame, hMenuWindow
Win 32:
      wParam: hMenuFrame
      lParam: hMenuWindow

WM_MENUCHAR
Win 3.x:
      wParam: char
      lParam: hMenu, fMenu
Win 32:
      wParam: char, fMenu
      lParam: hMenu

WM_PARENTNOTIFY (also has two cases)
Win 3.x case #1:
      wParam: msg
      lParam: id, hwndChild
Win32 case #1:
      wParam: msg, id
      lParam: hwndChild

Win 3.x case #2:
      wParam: msg
      lParam: x, y
Win32 case #2:
      wParam: msg
      lParam: x, y

WM_VKEYTOITEM
Win 3.x:
      wParam: code
      lParam item, hwnd

```
Win 32:
     wParam: code, item
     lParam: hwnd


EM_GETSEL
Win 3.x:
      returns (wStart, wEnd)
     wParam: NULL
     lParam: NULL
Win 32:
     returns (wStart, wEnd)
     wParam: lpdwStart or NULL
     lParam: lpdwEnd or NULL


EM_LINESCROLL
Win 3.x:
     wParam: 0
     lParam: nLinesVert, nLinesHorz
Win 32:
     wParam: nLinesHorz
     lParam: nLinesVert


EM_SETSEL
Win 3.x:
     wParam: 0
     lParam: wStart, wEnd
Win 32:
     wParam: wStart
     lParam: wEnd


WM_HSCROLL:
WM_VSCROLL:
Win 3.x:
     wParam: code
     lParam: pos, hwnd
Win 32:
     wParam: code, pos
     lParam: hwnd
```

Window and Class Extra Words

The following APIs have nonportable implementations:

```
GetClassWord
GetWindowWord
SetClassWord
SetWindowWord
```

These APIs have two uses: to manipulate system information and to manipulate user-defined data. System data is modified by index values. The portability problem is that these APIs manipulate 16-bit data, but the data may need to widen to 32-bit on Win32. This is especially true for handle data accessed via predefined index values. For portability, these index values are now supported via the Windows extra long API:

```
GetClassLong
GetWindowLong
SetClassLong
SetWindowLong
```

The index values used to manipulate data that has widened to 32-bit are mapped as follows:

```
GCW_CURSOR          --> GCL_CURSOR
GCW_HBRBACKGROUND   --> GCL_HBRBACKGROUND
GCW_HICON           --> GCL_HICON
GWW_HINSTANCE       --> GWL_HINSTANCE
GWW_HWNDPARENT      --> GWL_HWNDPARENT
GWW_ID              --> GWL_ID
GWW_USERDATA        --> GWL_USERDATA
```

Therefore, to modify code that can compile on either Win3.x or Win32, #ifdefs are recommended:

```
#ifdef WIN32
hwndParent = (HWND)GetWindowLong( hWnd, GWL_HWNDPARENT );
#else
hwndParent = (HWND)GetWindowWord( hWnd, GWW_HWNDPARENT );
#endif
```

Alternatively, a named API already exists that obtains a parent Windows handle and is portable.

```
Non-portable:
hwndParent = (HWND)GetWindowWord( hWnd, GWW_HWNDPARENT );

Portable:
hwndParent = GetParent( hWnd );
```

Additional named APIs are being considered to address the remaining values only accessible via indexes in the current API. The named API will be available on Windows 3.x and Win32.

The Windows extra word APIs are also used to manipulate user-defined data that may consist of private handles, pointers, or data that also must widen to 32-bit. Therefore, review all uses of these APIs in existing code to ensure that the data stored in Windows extra words remains 16-bit. Otherwise, use Windows extra long API to manipulate this data on both Windows 3.x and Win32 even though the data may only be 16-bit on Win3.x.

Profile String Use

Win32 systems will provide a registration database. All system and application configuration data will be stored in the database on a per-user basis with appropriate security controls to ensure that applications cannot corrupt one another's data or the system's configuration data. A centralized database has a number of advantages, including simpler installation, remote administration of workstation software, remote software updating, and error logging.

Win32 versions of the Windows 3.x profile API (for example, **GetProfileString and WriteProfileString**) route profile string requests, including private profiles (that is, *.INI files) to the registration database transparently. Therefore, do not attempt to manipulate *.INI files directly with file I/O functions. These files will not exist, and the data contained in them is not accessible via file I/O calls; only the profile string API will be supported.

Localized Input

The Win32 model is different from Windows 3.x in that input ownership is assigned at user input time--when the input is created--instead of when the input is read out of the system queue. For this reason, each thread has its own input-synchronized state information. In other words, each thread has its own input-synchronized picture of the mouse capture and the active window and is aware of which window has the focus.

This change adds tremendous benefit to programmers and users alike: It is no longer possible for an application that fails to process messages to bottleneck the system. Unlike Windows 3.x and OS/2 Presentation Manager, no applications will be affected by other applications that process their messages slowly or that otherwise fail to check their message queue.

The following APIs are affected by localized input state:

```
SetFocus( HWND )
GetFocus( VOID )
SetActiveWindow( HWND )
GetActiveWindow( VOID )
GetCapture( VOID )
SetCapture( HWND )
ReleaseCapture( VOID )
```

In general, the **Get** APIs query only local current thread state. The **Set** APIs set state local to the window creator thread. If the current thread did not create the window, the current thread's related input state is set to NULL as if the input related state were being transferred between threads.

Thus, the Windows 3.x semantics of APIs that return input-synchronized states are changed slightly. For example, **SetFocus** can be called with an hwnd and a return value of TRUE for success, but a follow-up call to **GetFocus** might return NULL. More substantially, **GetFocus** now returns NULL if the calling thread does not have a focus window. Under Windows 3.x, **GetFocus** never returns NULL because a window in the system always has the keyboard focus.

Therefore, code applications expect that functions such as **GetFocus** can return NULL as a legal value. The return value should be tested against NULL before being used in subsequent function calls.

Mouse capture is affected in an added dimension. The Win32 server input thread cannot know ahead of time when an input thread will set the capture. Also, regardless of the input state of any application, the system must allow the user direct input to any other application at any time. Therefore, the semantics of mouse capture change slightly.

The semantics of how and when the capture changes are not affected; how and when an application gets mouse input is affected. The Win32 server will send all mouse input between a mouse down operation and a mouse up operation to the queue of the thread that created the window into which the original mouse down went. Thus, the input thread processes mouse capture as the input is read out of the queue. If the mouse button is down during the mouse capture, the capture window sees all input generated by the mouse, no matter where the mouse is on the screen, until the mouse button goes up or the mouse capture is released. If a thread sets the mouse capture while the mouse button is up, the mouse capture window sees mouse events only as long as the mouse is over a window that thread created.

Graphics Interface Code

Portable Solutions for Win32 API Changes

The Windows API consists of several hundred API; all are widened to 32-bits with minimal impact on existing source code, except for approximately two dozen API (generally GDI related). Unfortunately, these specific API could not be supported as-is in the Win32 API but had to be modified. Most of these API fall into a specific class. Previously, they returned a packed x/y value in a DWORD return value. Since graphics coordinates are now 32-bit, rather than 16-bit, an extra parameter has been added to these functions, a pointer to a POINT structure. To simplify porting, the Win32 forms for these functions are shipping with Windows 3.1. Windows 3.1 will support the old and new form. The Win32 API names are based on the original with an Ex suffix added. Win32 will support only the new form. Writing to the new form will allow compiling for either Win32 or Windows 3.x.

Windows 3.1 will implement the API via a static library, so that code compiled with the new API will also function on Windows 3.0.

Modifying code to use the new forms of these APIs is straightforward in most cases. Half of the APIs are used to get coordinates from GDI. The other half set GDI coordinates and return the previously set value.

```
MoveToEx
OffsetViewportOrgEx
OffsetWindowOrgEx
ScaleViewportExtEx
ScaleWindowExtEx
SetBitmapDimensionEx
SetMetaFileBitsEx
SetViewportExtEx
SetViewportOrgEx
SetWindowExtEx
SetWindowOrgEx
```

In general, most Windows applications ignore the return value from the above functions. Therefore, modifying an existing application to use the new forms of these API is straightforward:

```
Original:
MoveTo( hDC, x, y );

Portable:
MoveToEx( hDC, x, y, NULL );
```

For cases where the return value is used, code must be modified to use a structure rather than the packed DWORD in the original API. This is identical to the matching APIs that are used explicitly to obtain x/y information.

```
GetAspectRatioFilterEx
GetBitmapDimensionEx
GetBrushOrgEx
GetCurrentPositionEx
GetTextExtentPoint
GetTextExtentPointEx
GetViewportExtEx
GetViewportOrgEx
GetWindowExtEx
GetWindowOrgEx
```

Of these APIs, GetTextExtent is the most common API to be encountered. In the case of GetTextExtent, the Point suffix has been used since GetTextExtent already has a Windows 3.1 extended function GetTextExtentEx. Therefore, the mapping of related functionality is as follows:

```
GetTextExtent        ---> GetTextExtentPoint
GetTextExtentEx      ---> GetTextExtentPointEx
```

Since the Win32 API form now relies on a structure, the typical coding change requires a temporary (local) structure to be created:

```
Non-portable:
dwXY = GetTextExtent( hDC, szFoo, strlen( szFoo ) );
rect.left = 0; rect.bottom = 0;
rect.right = LOWORD(dwXY); rect.top = HIWORD(dwXY);
InvertRect( hDC, &rect );

Portable:
{
SIZE sizeRect;

GetTextExtentPoint( hDC, szFoo, strlen( szFoo ), &sizeRect );
rect.left = 0; rect.bottom = 0;
rect.right = sizeRect.cx; rect.top = sizeRect.cy;
InvertRect( hDC, &rect );
}
```

Another class of necessary Win32 changes concerns a handful of Windows APIs that do not provide a parameter for specifying buffer sizes of buffers receiving data. This an API design error that is corrected in Win32. The functions affected are as follows:

```
DlgDirSelectEx
DlgDirSelectComboBoxEx
```

And the changes for portability are minor:

```
Win3.x:
DlgDirSelect( hDlg, lpString, nIDListBox );

Portable:
DlgDirSelectEx( hDlg, lpString, sizeof( lpString ),
nIDListBox );
```

As noted previously, all of the functions listed in this section have equivalent, portable versions defined in Windows 3.1. Therefore, converting to the Win32 forms is not a one-way street.

DIBs vs. DDBs

Beginning with Windows 3.0, device-independent bitmaps (DIBs) have been the recommended format for creating and initializing bitmap data. This format includes a header with bitmap dimensions, color resolution, and palette information supporting portability between Windows 3.x and Win32. Device-dependent bitmaps (DDBs), as originally offered in Windows 1.x and 2.x, are not recommended.

Because DDBs lack complete header information, applications that directly manipulate DDB data are not portable to Win32. Developers are encouraged to write to the Windows 3.x DIB API (for example, **SetDIBitmapBits**); these calls are portable. Win32 does provides, however, a subset of functionality for DDB API, such as **SetBitmapBits**:

- Monochrome DDBs are fully supported.
- Caching color bitmaps with **GetBitmapBits** and **SetBitmapBits** is supported.

Caching implies that **GetBitmapBits** is used to save bitmap data on disk. Under low memory situations in Windows versions 1.x and 2.x, the bitmap in memory could be freed and easily restored with **GetBitmapBits**. This implies that the DDB data is never manipulated; it is simply backed up and restored on disk in its original form. While caching is not needed in Windows 3.x or Win32, source code employing this technique will still be supported.

Win32 does not support initializing color DDBs with **CreateBitmap**. Such code is also not portable among Windows 3.x systems with different display drivers because DDB data is device-driver dependent.

Sharing Graphical Objects

Windows 3.x runs all Windows applications in a shared address space. Data can be directly manipulated, and other Windows processes can directly access per-process objects that the system created. This architecture has been exploited by some applications that create a single graphical object, such as a pen or a bitmap, and allow separate processes to use the pen or draw on the bitmap.

Win32 applications run in separate address spaces, and graphical objects are owned by the process that creates them. Only its owner can manipulate a graphical object. A handle to a bitmap passed to another process cannot be used by that process because the original process retains ownership of the bitmap.

Pens and brushes should be created by each process. A cooperative process may access the bitmap data in shared memory (via standard IPC) and create its own copy of the bitmap. Alterations to the bitmap must be communicated between the cooperative processes via IPC and a proper protocol. One such protocol is DDE. Win32 may add an explicit ownership transfer API for graphical objects to allow cooperative applications to share graphical objects.

Base System Support

Instance Initialization

The first release of Windows (version 1.01) was designed to run on 8088-based systems, which assumed limited installed memory (512K RAM). Functions such as **GetInstanceData** and knowledge about other instances of an application already running allowed efficient data sharing and initialization using data belonging to other running instances. On protected systems in which applications run in separate address spaces, these functions are no longer appropriate.

Therefore, applications that want to share data among several instances must replace calls to **GetInstanceData** with standard IPC techniques such as shared memory and/or DDE.

A Win32 version of **WinMain** supports the same parameter list as does Windows 3.x:

```
int WinMain(hInstance, hPrevInstance, lpCmdLine, nCmdShow)
```

However, the parameter *hPrevInstance* always returns NULL, indicating that this is the first instance of the application, regardless of any other already running instances. Although this situation would appear to be a problem, the initialization of most applications is handled correctly. Under Windows 3.x, multiple instances can share private window classes registered by the first instance. Under Win32, each instance is required to register it own window classes.

Applications usually test *hPrevInstance* to see if they must register their window class. This test is guaranteed to work optimally under Win32, always indicating the first instance of the application, and Win32 requires that every instance register its own window classes.

Some applications, however, must know if other instances are running. Sometimes data sharing is required, but typically applications that care about multiple instances are interested in ensuring that only one instance of the application runs at any time. An example is the Control Panel; another is the Task Manager.

Applications such as these cannot use *hPrevInstance* in Win32 to test for previous instances. These applications must use an alternative method, such as creating a unique named pipe, creating/testing for a named semaphore, broadcasting a unique message, or calling **FindWindow**. If another instance is found, the application determines which instance should be terminated.

Memory Manipulation

Under the Windows 3.x segmented memory architecture, globally allocated memory always aligns on segment boundaries. Both **GlobalAlloc** and the C run-time **malloc** family of functions allocate global memory in a way that causes the 16-bit offset of the 32-bit segmented pointer that references the base address of this data always to be 0.

This behavior is not portable to linear memory. Memory allocation is not guaranteed to align on 64K boundaries. Memory is allocated with a 4K page granularity, but some objects may be packed to fit within a single page to maximize memory efficiency. (Pointer manipulation is discussed later in this document.)

Win32 API Replacements for Int 21

Direct **INT21** calls or the use of the Windows 3.x **DOS3Call** API to request MS-DOS to perform file I/O operations must be replaced by the appropriate Win32 file I/O calls. Win32 offers a complete set of named APIs to replace nonportable **INT21** calls:

INT 21H Function	MS-DOS Operation	Win32 API Equivalent
0EH	Select Disk	SetCurrentDirectory
19H	Get Current Disk	GetCurrentDirectory
2AH	Get Date	GetDateAndTime
2BH	Set Date	SetDateAndTime
2CH	Get Time	GetDateAndTime
2DH	Set Time	SetDateAndTime
36H	Get Disk Free Space	GetDiskFreeSpace
39H	Create Directory	CreateDirectory
3AH	Remove Directory	RemoveDirectory
3BH	Set Current Directory	SetCurrentDirectory
3CH	Create Handle	CreateFile
3DH	Open Handle	OpenFile
3EH	Close Handle	CloseHandle
3FH	Read Handle	ReadFile
40H	Write Handle	WriteFile
41H	Delete File	DeleteFile
42H	Move File Pointer	SetFilePointer
43H	Get File Attributes	GetAttributesFile
43H	Set File Attributes	SetAttributesFile
47H	Get Current Directory	GetCurrentDirectory
4EH	Find First File	FindFirstFile
4FH	Find Next File	FindNextFile
56H	Change Directory Entry	MoveFile
57H	Get Date/Time of File	GetDateAndTimeFile
57H	Set Date/Time of File	SetDataAndTimeFile
59H	Get Extended Error	GetLastError
5AH	Create Unique File	GetTempFileName
5BH	Create New File	CreateFile
5CH	Lock	LockFile
5CH	Unlock	UnlockFile
67H	Set Handle Count	SetHandleCount

In most situations, the standard C run-time libraries are sufficient for normal file I/O. The C run-time has the advantage of being portable across many platforms.

Dynamic Link Libraries

DLL initialization and termination functions behave differently in Windows 3.x and Win32 in terms of how they are defined, when they are called, and the information that is made available to them. Win32 DLLs are easier to create and have functionality not currently available in Windows 3.x. In Windows 3.x, initialization and termination functions must be provided, the termination function must be named WEP, and the initialization function is the DLL entry point written in master. Initialization and termination functions are optional in Win32 DLLs.

In Windows 3.x, the DLL initialization function is called once, when the DLL is first loaded in the system. The function is not called again, even if other applications that use the DLL are invoked. Likewise, the DLL termination function is not called until the DLL is unloaded from the system, when the last application using it terminates or frees the library. The initialization and termination functions are distinct. The startup code for the initialization function must be in assembly language, to allow access to parameters that are passed in machine registers.

In Win32, the DLL initialization function is the same as the termination function, and its name is specified at link time. Initialization or termination functionality is selected by a Boolean parameter, *bAttaching*, passed to the initialization function. The DLL initialization function is called each time a process attaches to the DLL for the first time or detaches from the DLL for the last time. Thus, if five processes access the same DLL, the DLL's initialization function is invoked five times with the *bAttaching* parameter set to TRUE. When these five processes terminate, detaching the DLL from each process causes five calls to the DLL initialization function, with the *bAttaching* parameter set to FALSE.

Windows 3.x DLLs are typically implemented completely in assembly language or in C and linked to the standard LIBENTRY.ASM function. This function calls **LibMain** after initializing the heap and saving appropriate registers. In porting to Win32, DLLs implemented in assembly language should be rewritten in C so that they are portable to RISC-based systems.

Windows 3.x DLL initialization functions are passed the following information:

- the DLL's instance handle
- the DLL's data segment (DS)
- the heap size specified in the DLL's .DEF file
- the command line

Win32 DLL initialization functions are passed the following information:

- the DLL's module handle
- the *bAttaching* Boolean, indicating initialization or termination

The Win32 module handle is analogous to the Windows 3.x instance handle. In Win32, the data segment is irrelevant because declared DLL data is either private to each process accessing the DLL or shared among cooperative processes accessing the DLL. The DLL's module definition file controls whether DLL data is shared or private. The heap size is not passed to the Win32 DLL initialization function because all calls to local memory management functions operate on the default heap, which is provided to each process. The command line does not need to be passed as a parameter since it can be obtained under Win32 through an API function.

Although the Windows 3.x LIBENTRY.ASM routine contains nonportable assembly routines, it isolates the assembly language initialization and supports writing additional DLL-specific initialization in C via the **LibMain** routine. For portability to Win32, DLL initialization code should be added to the LibMain routine and written in C. (For further information on LIBENTRY.ASM, see the Windows 3.x Software Development Kit documentation.).

C Coding Guidelines

The Win32 API was designed to simplify the creation of Win32 applications from Windows 3.x sources. Specific API differences have been discussed above. Creating portable Windows code also involves writing portable C. Fortunately, the similarity of Windows 3.x and Win32 requires only that a concise set of portable C guidelines be followed. Windows programs have generally been optimized to operate with the segmented x86 architecture. Therefore, the change from segmented to linear memory is the most significant issue in creating portable C code.

Pointer Manipulation

Win32 supports a compatible set of memory management functions, such as **GlobalAlloc** and **GlobalLock**, and a new set of advanced linear memory APIs. Therefore, existing Windows applications can easily be converted to Win32 and continue to use the Windows 3.x memory allocation and handle dereferencing API.

As mentioned previously, memory allocations are not aligned on 64K boundaries. Therefore, any pointer arithmetic based on assumptions of segment:offset encoded pointers will fail in Win32. When computing offsets to arrays of structures, do not create pointers by combining a computed 16-bit offset with the high-order 16 bits of an address pointer. This type of pointer arithmetic depends on segment:offset encoded addresses.

Several other pointer characteristics should be observed:

- All pointers (even pointers to objects in the local heap) grow to 32 bits.
- Code that takes advantage of 16-bit pointer address-wrapping is not appropriate with linear addresses.
- Structures that hold NEAR pointers in Windows 3.x will grow from 2 bytes to 4 bytes in Win32.

Promotions and Ranges

Expressions involving the C integer data types (int and unsigned int) should be reviewed for portability, especially if the compiler already generates warnings about signed/unsigned mismatches or conversion warnings. The int data type grows from 16 to 32 bits, which can subtly affect applications compiled for Win32. Typical problems encountered are sign extensions and assumptions (sometimes unintentional) about ranges. Loops that take advantage of 16-bit ints and of the fact that integer loop counters will wrap at 32767 or 65535 will experience problems when the integer loop counters grow to 32-bit and wrapping occurs at 2 GB or 4 GB.

Structure Member Alignment

Data accesses to unnaturally aligned data elements are expensive on some hardware architectures and are illegal on others. For example, on the 80386, accessing a DWORD that is not 4-byte aligned results in a performance penalty. When the same code is moved to a MIPS RISC processor, the misaligned access generates a fault. The system handles the fault, and system software decodes the data. Although the code is portable, it is not efficient. Therefore, all data elements should be aligned consistently with their type. Alignment rules vary with architecture, but the following guidelines are appropriate for the Intel and MIPS processors targeted by Win32:

Win32 Structure Member Alignment

char:	Align on byte boundaries
short (16-bit):	Align on even byte boundaries
int/long (32-bit):	Align on 32-bit boundaries
float/double:	Align on 32-bit boundaries
structures:	Align on 32-bit boundaries

Creating a portable structure that is both efficient in memory usage (without packing) and aligned properly is possible.

Unique Typedefs

As illustrated in the GENERIC code fragment listed earlier in this document, unique typedefs are useful in creating portable code. Even though the typedefs can have different underlying definitions in Windows 3.x and Win32, Windows source code can remain unchanged.

Windows offers unique typedefs for most objects defined in WINDOWS.H. Unique typedefs such as HPEN, HBRUSH, and HWND better support portability to Win32 than generic typedefs such as HANDLE. Although all handles in Windows 3.x are interchangeable with HANDLE or unsigned int, using these basic data types affects porting to Win32 because various objects require different typedefs under Win32 than under Windows 3.x.

Just as using unique typedefs is recommended when defining (or casting) Windows objects, creating a complete set of unique typedefs for application-specific objects is also strongly recommended. As with the Windows objects, the underlying application-specific data types and structures can be modified and minimally affect source code that uses these data types.

UINT vs. WORD

Win32 relies on existing Windows 3.x WINDOWS.H typedefs to automatically widen parameters and structure members to 32-bits as well as retain 16-bit data types for compatibility. All handles (HWND, HANDLE, HPEN, HBRUSH, etc.) grow to 32-bits. Data types such as LONG and DWORD are 32-bit on both the Windows 3.x and Win32 API.

In creating the Win32 API, it was recognized that a new flexible typedef was required. The data type, UINT, is defined to be an unsigned int. This data type is 16-bits on Windows 3.x and 32-bits on Win32. Therefore, this is a portable data type that also takes advantage of 32-bit mode. 32-bit data is more efficient to access than 16-bit data, especially by RISC processors. The WORD typedef is generally considered a 16-bit quantity and remains a 16-bit data type in Win32. UINT and WORD data types are defined as follows:

```
typedef unsigned int UINT;
typedef unsigned short WORD;
```

Therefore, WORD remains 16-bit on Win32 and should be used to specify only objects that should exist as 16-bit unsigned types. UINT should be used to define objects that naturally widen in 32-bit mode.

Structures and API prototypes in the Windows 3.1 header files have replaced WORD with UINT for structure members and API parameters that should widen to 32-bit. While UINT and WORD are interchangeable (for compatibility) in the Windows 3.1 headers, they are not interchangeable on Win32. Therefore, applications should review the following typedefs and update source code to use the proper data types for portability:

Flexible data types:

int	; 16-bit signed integer on Windows 3.x, 32-bit signed integer on Win32
UINT	; 16-bit unsigned integer on Windows 3.x, 32-bit unsigned integer on Win32

Fixed-size data types:

WORD	; 16-bit unsigned integer in Windows 3.x and Win32
DWORD	; 32-bit unsigned integer in Windows 3.x and Win32
LONG	; 32-bit signed integer in Windows 3.x and Win32

Portable Use of the WORD Data Type

Historically, Windows programs have used the various typedefs interchangeably: WORD, HWND, HANDLE, and so forth. It is not uncommon to see (WORD) casts being used to assign values to variables holding handles to windows:

```
Non-portable:
 HWND hWnd;
hWnd = (WORD)SendMessage( hWnd, WM_GETMDIACTIVE, NULL, NULL
);

Portable:
 HWND hWnd;
hWnd = (HWND)SendMessage( hWnd, WM_GETMDIACTIVE, NULL, NULL
);
```

In porting the Windows 3.x system applets, games, and sample code, most (WORD) casts were found to be nonportable.

Review all (WORD) casts in existing Windows 3.x code. All such references should be reviewed to determine the data type/size of the original value and result.

General Recommendations

The following coding recommendations are well known but are occasionally ignored. Reviewing your code and addressing the following issues will create more robust Windows 3.1 code and will create code that is more easily ported to Win32.

Review hard-coded buffer sizes for filenames and environment strings. Although dynamically allocating buffers to hold strings is not necessary, Win32 supports FAT 8.3 and long filenames (256 characters). Therefore, buffers hard-coded assuming FAT 8.3 format will not take advantage of long filename support. Using a #define to define sizes for array allocations will assist portability of the source code to Win32.

Compile all sources at warning level 2 (-W2); warning level 3 (-W3) is recommended. Warning level 3 has been a problem in the past because WINDOWS.H included non-ANSI C-compliant bit-field definitions that did not pass at this level. The latest release of the Microsoft C compiler (C 6.00a) moves this fatal error to -W4, allowing the strict type-checking of -W3.

Create function prototypes for all functions. Relying on default C compiler handling is often (but not guaranteed to be) portable. In addition to parameter assumptions, the Microsoft C compiler supports various calling conventions (_cdecl, _pascal, and so on), and the default calling convention may change because of future C compiler implementations. Using function prototypes helps isolate source code from default compiler behavior and changes in the ANSI C definition.

Until recently, the size of WINDOWS.H has been a problem for the Microsoft C compiler, causing out-of-heap space problems in Pass 1 and/or Pass 2 of the compiler. This problem is corrected in the MS-DOS extender version of the MS C compiler (C 6.00ax). ISVs have worked around this previous limitation by extracting specific WINDOWS.H definitions into their source code. This could cause portability problems if these WINDOWS.H definitions are not updated with Win32 definitions when the source is compiled under Win32. Therefore, either remove extracted header information and rely on WINDOWS.H, or clearly highlight extracted information for modification when building a Win32 version.

Conclusion

This overview has concentrated on the most common issues that will be encountered in creating a portable Windows application. While there may appear to be a significant number of changes required for portability, in practice, creating a portable Windows application that will run on Win32 systems (either native 32-bit or via binary compatibility) is straightforward. Porting tools help automate the process.

With the compatible changes being made in the Windows 3.1 SDK, there is truly one Windows API with 16-bit segmented and 32-bit linear forms. While the Win32 API offers new advanced features, this is accomplished without breaking the semantics of the existing Windows API. Only a small percentage of API and messages were affected by 32-bit widening. In these situations new, portable solutions have been provided in the Windows 3.1 API.

Summary of Compatibility Rules

Rules for Windows 3.x binary compatibility on Windows NT:

- Ensure that Windows 3.x applications run in standard/enhanced mode.
- Use published Windows 3.x APIs, messages, and structures.
- Do not modify WIN.INI directly; use a profile string API.
- Use QUERYESCSUPPORT to determine whether particular printer driver escapes are implemented.

Rules for Portable Windows 3.x/Win32 source code:

- Parse wParam and lParam immediately in WndProc routines.
- Use portable API forms (for example MoveToEx instead of MoveTo).
- NULL is a valid return value from GetFocus and GetActiveWindow.
- Use FindWindow instead of hPrevInstance to find other running instances.
- GlobalLock and malloc will not return 64K aligned pointers.
- Use Windows 3.x DIB functions to initialize color bitmaps.
- Do not use GetInstanceData; replace with supported IPC mechanism.
- Do not share GDI object handles (for example, pens and bitmaps) between processes.
- Compile warning level -W2 or higher (-W3 recommended).
- Create function prototypes for all functions.
- Review structure member alignment and data types.
- Remove hard-coded buffer sizes (for example, filenames and path names).
- Do not extract private copies of WINDOWS.H definitions.
- Use unique typdefs (HPEN, HWND, not HANDLE or int).
- Use portable integer typdefs (UINT, WORD).

Chapter 1 | Introduction

1.1 Overview 3
1.2 Constraints and Goals 3
1.3 Win32 API Design 4

1.1 Overview

The Windows 32-bit API set is a portable API set that exposes a flat 32-bit address space. The API set is implemented in two products:

Win32 on DOS	Available on Intel i386 and i486 processors running DOS 3.x and above. This environment does not include security features or other high end/robustness features but does implement the entire Win32 API set. Memory requirements for this environment are expected to be 2Mb.
Windows NT	Available on Intel i386 and i486, and MIPS-based computers. This environment implements all security features exposed by the Win32 API set. Memory requirements for this environment are expected to be 8Mb.

Win32 makes a clear distinction between 32-bit applications and 16-bit applications. Mode mixing is not allowed (i.e. a 32-bit application may only use Win32 APIs and may not make calls into 16-bit DLLs). This design encourages portability. The portability goals for Win32 are very simple: an application that calls the Win32 API set should only have to recompile in order to run on Windows NT for MIPS.

1.2 Constraints and Goals

Win32 has several explicit goals and constraints:

- The API set is upward compatible with the current 16-bit Windows 3.0 API set. APIs have only been changed where there is an absolute need to do so.

- Porting an existing 16-bit Windows 3.0 application to Win32 is simple and straightforward.

- Absolute source level compatibility exists between Win32 on x86 and Win32 on MIPS. Absolute binary compatibility exists between Win32 on DOS and Win32 on Windows NT.

- Processes execute in separate address spaces.

- Multiple concurrent threads of execution are available within a process. Scheduling is preemptive. The API is designed with symetric multiprocessing in mind.

- The memory addressing scheme is flat 32-bit addressing.

- The Win32 API set is portable across all platforms.

1.3 Win32 API Design

The Win32 API set has been designed with portability and security in mind. In addition, the single biggest factor influencing the API set is to preserve the functionality, style, and interfaces of the existing Windows API set. Wherever possible, existing APIs are expanded to 32-bits and classified as a Win32 API. If a security, or portability problem exists with an API, a new Win32 API was added that provides similar functionality as the existing API, but accomodates the security/portability concerns.

2.1   Overview 7

2.2   Win32 Extensions 7

     2.2.1   Multi-threaded process structure 7

     2.2.2   Flat address space 8

     2.2.3   Portable 32-Bit API 8

2.3   Overview of Base Functionality 8

     2.3.1   Atom Management Functions 8

     2.3.2   Communication Device Functions 9

     2.3.3   Character Mode Application Support 10

     2.3.4   Debugger support 12

     2.3.5   Dynamic Link Library Support 12

     2.3.6   Environment 13

     2.3.7   Event Logging 13

     2.3.8   Exception Handling 14

     2.3.9   File I/O Functions 14

     2.3.10   Handle/Object Management 16

     2.3.11   Mapped Files 16

     2.3.12   Ini-File Functions 17

     2.3.13   Install/Compression 18

     2.3.14   Memory Management Functions 19

     2.3.15   Module-Management Functions 21

     2.3.16   Pipes 22

     2.3.17   Processes and Threads 23

     2.3.18   Registration 24

     2.3.19   Resource Management Functions 24

     2.3.20   Security 25

     2.3.21   Segment Management Functions 27

     2.3.22   Sound 27

2.3.23 Synchronization 28

2.3.24 Time 29

2.3.25 Thread-Local Storage 29

2.3.26 Version Management 30

2.1 Overview

This document describes the base components of the Windows 32-bit APIs.

2.2 Win32 Extensions

To be a fully functional 32-bit operating system, the base API set present in Windows 3.0 needs several extensions. The motivation for the extensions is very precise. Extensions are required to:

- Support multiple threads of execution within a process with each process executing in a seperate address space

- Support a flat 32-bit address space

- Expose security on all objects that can be shared between processes

- Promote a portable 32-bit API interface

Note that the focus of the Win32 effort is to extend the current Windows 3.0 technology to allow easy migration from of Windows 3.0 apps to Win32 on x86 and MIPS platforms.

2.2.1 Multi-threaded process structure

A significant feature of Win32 is the introduction of a multi-threaded process structure. A Win32 process has:

- An address space that is protected and that has access to up to 2GB of virtual memory.

- Multiple threads of execution exist within the process. Each thread has its own stack and machine state. On MP systems running Windows NT, multiple threads may execute at the same time but on different processors.

In order to support the Win32 process structure a small set of extensions must be added to Win32. The extensions can be classified as:

- Support for process and thread creation and manipulation.

- Support for synchronization between threads within a process and synchronization objects that can be shared by multiple processes to allow synchronization between threads whose processes have access to the synchronization objects.

- A uniform sharing mechanism that provides security features that limit/control the sharing of objects between processes.

2.2.2 Flat address space

The single biggest extension to Win32 is the introduction of a flat 32-bit memory manager. Designed to supplement the 16-bit selector based memory manager (Local and Global APIs), the new APIs are much easier to use and document. Wherever possible equivalent capabilities have been preserved. There are some features in the 16-bit memory manager that have not been propagated into the 32-bit environment. This was only done when the feature was not portable or not required using the 32-bit model.

2.2.3 Portable 32-Bit API

The last major area where extensions were provided focused on applications portability. This area has two main goals:

- Limit an applications exposure to x86 constructs not present on MIPS platforms (EMS memory APIs...)
- Remove an applications dependency on DOS (int 21h) APIs.

Wherever possible, APIs that expose x86 contructs have been removed or replaced. Examples of this include:

- **SwitchStackBack** and **SwitchStackTo**
- **Catch** and **Throw**
- **LimitEmsPages**

The current versions of Windows require that applications call underlying DOS services to perform file management functions, at a minimum. The Win32 API set has been extended to provide a complete set of services. This promotes application portability across Win32 on DOS and Win32 for MIPS.

2.3 Overview of Base Functionality

The following gives a high level overview of the functionality available in the base component of Win32.

2.3.1 Atom Management Functions

Atom Tables are hash tables that are an efficient means of representing character strings as 16-bit integer values. There is one global atom table that is used for storing DDE atom values. Each application process can create one or more private atom tables that are visible only to their process.

The atom functions include:

Function	Description
AddAtom	Creates an atom for a character string
DeleteAtom	Deletes an atom if the reference count is zero
FindAtom	Retrieves an atom associated with a character string
GetAtomHandle	Retrieves a handle (relative to the local heap) of the string that corresponds to a specified atom
GetAtomName	Copies the character string associated with an atom
GlobalAddAtom	Creates a global atom for a character string
GlobalDeleteAtom	Deletes a global atom if the reference count is zero
GlobalFindAtom	Retrieves a global atom associated with a character string
GlobalGetAtomName	Copies the character string associated with a global atom
InitAtomTable	Initializes an atom hash table

2.3.2 Communication Device Functions

The communications functions have been enhanced based on feedback from applications developers.

For additional information on how to use the communications functions, see Chapter 9, "Communications."

The communications functions include:

Function	Description
BuildCommDCB	Fills a device control block with control codes
ClearCommBreak	Clears the communication break state from a communication device
ClearCommError	Clears a comm error and reenables the device for communcations.
EnableCommNotification	Enables message posting for comm events.
EscapeCommFunction	Directs a device to carry out an extended function
ExtendedProviderFunction	Allows access to provider-specific functionality.
GetCommConfig	Get the device-specific comm information.
GetCommMask	Retrieves the comm event mask.
GetCommModemStatus	Retrieves the status of a modem.
GetCommProperties	Retrieves the properties associated with a comm device.

Function	Description
GetCommState	Sets the state of a communications device.
GetCommTimeouts	Retrieves the current timeout settings for a comm device.
PurgeComm	Flushes the input and/or output queues.
SetCommBreak	Sets a break state on the communication device
SetCommConfig	Sets device-specific comm information.
SetCommMask	Sets the mask of events of interest to the caller.
SetCommState	Sets a communication device to the state specified by the device control block
SetCommTimeouts	Sets the timeouts for a comm device.
SetupComm	Sets the queue sizes for communications.
TransmitCommChar	Places a character at the head of the transmit queue
WaitCommEvent	Waits for a comm event to occur.

2.3.3 Character Mode Application Support

Win32 supports a character mode API set. The purpose of this API set is to provide a processor-independent mechanism that allows character-mode applications to be ported easily to the Windows environment, This API set includes limited support for:

- Standard Input, Output, and Error I/O operations.

- Re-direction of standard I/O handles through pipes and files.

- Direct manipulation of console state

For additional information on how to use the console functions, see the Console Overview.

The character-based functions include:

Function	Description
AllocConsole	Creates a new console for the calling process
CreateConsoleScreenBuffer	Allocates a new screen buffer.
FillConsoleOutputAttribute	Writes an attribute n times to the screen buffer
FillConsoleOutputCharacter	Writes a character n times to the screen buffer
FlushConsoleInputBuffer	Empties the console input buffer
FreeConsole	Removes the calling process's console

Function	Description
GetConsoleCursorInfo	Returns the cursor size and visibility for a console screen buffer
GetConsoleMode	Returns the console input or output mode
GetConsoleScreenBufferInfo	Returns information about a console screen buffer
GetConsoleTitle	Returns the window title of a console
GetLargestConsoleWindowSize	Returns the current font for a console screen buffer
GetNumberOfConsoleInputEvents	Returns the number of events in a console input buffer
GetNumberOfConsoleMouseButtons	Returns the number of mouse buttons
PeekConsoleInput	Reads events from a console input buffer without removing them
ReadConsoleInput	Reads events from a console input buffer
ReadConsoleOutput	Reads a rectangular region of a console screen buffer
ReadConsoleOutputAttribute	Reads a string of attributes from a console screen buffer
ReadConsoleOutputCharacter	Reads a string of characters from a console screen buffer
ScrollConsoleScreenBuffer	Copies a region from one part of a console screen buffer to another
SetConsoleActiveScreenBuffer	Sets the visible screen buffer for a console
SetConsoleCtrlHandler	Sets a ctrl handler for the calling process
SetConsoleCursorInfo	Sets the cursor size and visibility for a console screen buffer
SetConsoleCursorPosition	Sets the cursor position for a console screen buffer
SetConsoleMode	Sets the console input or output mode
SetConsoleScreenBufferSize	Sets the screen buffer size for a console screen buffer
SetConsoleTextAttribute	Sets the background and text color for a console screen buffer
SetConsoleTitle	Sets the window title of a console
SetConsoleWindowInfo	Sets the dimensions of the window relative to the console screen buffer
WriteConsoleInput	Writes events to a console input buffer

Function	Description
WriteConsoleOutput	Writes a rectangular region to a console screen buffer
WriteConsoleOutputAttribute	Writes a string of attributes to a console screen buffer
WriteConsoleOutputCharacter	Writes a string of characters to a console screen buffer

2.3.4 Debugger support

Services are provided for people implementing Windows-based debuggers to access processes being debugged.

For additional information on how to use the debugger functionality, see chapter 12, "Windows Debugging Support."

The debugger functions include:

Function	Description
ContinueDebugEvent	Continues a thread that previously reported a debug event
DebugActiveProcess	Allows a debugger to attach to a process.
DebugBreak	Forces a break to the debugger
GetThreadContext	Gets the context of the specified thread
ReadProcessMemory	Reads memory within the specified process
SetThreadContext	Allows debugger to set thread context.
WaitForDebugEvent	Waits for a debug event to occur in a debuggee process
WriteProcessMemory	Writes memory within the specified process

2.3.5 Dynamic Link Library Support

Dynamic link library initialization and termination has changed with respect to the 16-bit Windows environment. DLL's are called at process and thread initialization and termination. In addition, instance-data is now supported for DLL's, i.e. DLL's can have one instance of their data for each calling process.

The dll initialization function is:

Function	Description
DllEntryPoint	Initialization and termination routine for DLLs.

2.3.6 Environment

Win32 provides functions for Windows applications to get command line parameters and get and set environment variables.

These functions include:

Function	Description
GetCommandLine	Returns the application command line parameters
GetDOSEnvironment	Retrieves the environment string of the currently running task
GetEnvironmentStrings	Returns the address of the environment block for the current process
GetEnvironmentVariable	Returns the value of the specified environment variable
GetStartupInfo	Returns the startup information for the current process
GetVersion	Returns the current version number of Windows
SetEnvironmentVariable	Sets an environment variable for the current process.

2.3.7 Event Logging

Event logs are used to store records of interesting events on behalf of the system components and third-party applications. The general guideline for what events should be stored in the logs is that the information should be restricted to that which would be useful in diagnosing a hardware or software problem.

To allow all applications to easily log events, Win32 provides a general API for writing events into the log. To aid an administrator or support personnel in diagnosing a problem, Win32 systems will provide a general purpose Event Viewer.

Events are classified as Informational Notes, Warnings, or Errors. The informational notes may include facts such as an assertion that a service has started. Warning events may include information such as disk space is getting low. Error events would be used to record both recoverable and unrecoverable errors. All event types will have well-defined common data and may optionally include event-specific data.

The event logging functions include:

Function	Description
ClearEventLog	Clears an event log and optionally saves it.
CloseEventLog	Closes an event log.
OpenEventLog	Creates an event log.
ReadEventLogEntry	Reads an entry from an event log.

Function	Description
WriteEventLogEntry	Writes an entry to an event log.

2.3.8 Exception Handling

Win32 provides a sophisticated exception mechanism which allows applications to handle unexpected errors in a structured fashion.

For additional information on exception handling and the way it is implemented in Microsoft C, see the Structured Exception Handling Overview.

The exception functions include:

Function	Description
RaiseException	Raises a software exception.

2.3.9 File I/O Functions

The current Windows product contains a minimal set of file I/O functions that are just procedural versions of the corresponding DOS INT 21h functions. These functions are not portable and lack many of the necessary file system APIs an application might need.

Lacking a set of file system APIs, the current Windows environment requires that applications call DOS for some file I/O needs. Win32 has been extended in this area so that the DOS dependency can be removed from applications. The APIs are similar to their DOS counterparts and provides the minimum services required to portably access the file system from a Win32 application.

When a process is created, it inherits the current directory from the application that starts it. An application can determine which directory is current by using the **GetCurrentDirectory** function. An application can change the current directory using the **SetCurrentDirectory** function. When accessing a file, filenames may be either absolute or relative to the current directory.

The file functions include:

Function	Description
_lclose	Closes a file
_lcreat	Creates a new file or opens and truncates an existing file
_llseek	Positions the pointer to a file
_lopen	Opens an existing file
_lread	Reads data from a file

Function	Description
_lwrite	Writes data in a file
CompareFileTime	Compares two 64-bit file times.
CopyFile	Copies a file
CreateDirectory	Creates a directory
CreateFile	Creates or opens a file
DeleteFile	Deletes a file
FindClose	Finishes a file enumeration
FindFirstFile	Finds the first file matching the specified name
FindNextFile	Finds the next file after a FindFirstFile
FlushFileBuffers	Flushes buffered file i/o
GetCurrentDirectory	Returns the current directory
GetDiskFreeSpace	Returns the current disk free space
GetDriveType	Determines whether a disk drive is removeable, fixed, or remote
GetFileAttributes	Gets the attributes of the specified file
GetFileSize	Returns the size of a file.
GetFileTime	Gets the creation, last access, and last modified times of a file
GetFileType	Determines the file type (disk,pipe,char)
GetFullPathName	Returns the fully qualified pathname for the file
GetLogicalDrives	Returns a bitmask of available drives.
GetLogicalDriveStrings	Returns the names of available drives.
GetOverlappedResult	Returns the result of the previous overlapped i/o
GetStdHandle	Returns the handles for stdin, stdout, and stderr
GetSystemDirectory	Retrieves the pathname of the Windows system subdirectory
GetTempFileName	Creates a temporary filename
GetTempPath	Returns the pathname for the temp directory
GetVolumeInformation	Returns information for the specified volume
GetWindowsDirectory	Retrieves the pathname of the Windows directory
LockFile	Locks a file
MoveFile	Renames a file
OpenFile	Creates, opens, reopens, or deletes the specified file
OpenSystemFile	Opens a system file.
ReadFile	Reads from a file

Function	Description
RemoveDirectory	Deletes a directory
SearchPath	Searches for a file along the specified path
SetCurrentDirectory	Sets the current directory
SetEndOfFile	Sets the end of file location
SetFileAttributes	Sets the attributes of a file
SetFilePointer	Seeks to a new location in a file
SetFileTime	Sets the time for a file
SetHandleCount	Changes the number of file handles available to a task
SetStdHandle	Sets the handles for stdin, stdout, and stderr
UnlockFile	Unlocks a file
WriteFile	Writes to a file

2.3.10 Handle/Object Management

A set of API have been added that may be used on any of the following objects:

- Process Object
- Thread Object
- Mutex Object
- Event Object
- Semaphore Object
- File Object
- File Mapping Object
- Console Objects

These functions include:

Function	Description
CloseHandle	Closes a base object handle.
DuplicateHandle	Creates a duplicate handle for the specified base object.

2.3.11 Mapped Files

Win32 provides APIs that allow an application to map files into the address space of a process. Data within the file can then be accessed using memory read/write instructions rather than I/O system functions such as **ReadFile** and **WriteFile**.

The APIs are best suited to applications that need to read a file and parse the information contained within the file. This includes editors that map and parse the input file, compilers that map and parse source files, spreadsheets that map and parse the input spreadsheet... Mapping a file to read and parse the file allows an application to manipulate the file using memory operations rather than having to do reads and writes and seeks all over the file. Operations such as "unreading" a character are much easier to do with mapped files. All the application has to do is decrement a pointer. Doing this operation with regular reads and writes requires a much more complicated approach usually requiring an application to write its own buffering layer.

Another application for mapped files is to use them to support persistent named shared memory. An application could create a file, map it, then others could use this as shared memory by opening and mapping the file.

While file mapping can be used to write into memory causing a data file to be written, this is a more complicated use of file mapping and is not as easy to use.

Mapping a file occurs in two stages:

- The potential for mapping a section of the file is created by creating a file mapping object.

- A view of the mapping object may be mapped into the address space of the process allowing data in the file to be manipulated.

For more information on file mapping, see the Memory Overview.

The file mapping functions include:

Function	Description
CreateFileMapping	Creates a file mapping object.
FlushViewOfFile	Flushes a mapped file to disk.
MapViewOfFile	Maps part of a file into memory.
OpenFileMapping	Opens a file for mapping.
UnmapViewOfFile	Unmaps a file.

2.3.12 Ini-File Functions

The existing win.ini functions have been preserved. However, developers are encouraged to take advantage of the registry functionality.

The .ini file functions include:

Function	Description
GetPrivateProfileInt	Returns an integer value in a section from a private initialization file
GetPrivateProfileSection	Returns all the key name and value pairs for a section of a private initialization file
GetPrivateProfileString	Returns a character string in a section from a private initialization file
GetProfileInt	Returns an integer value in a section from the WIN.INI file
GetProfileSection	Returns all the key name and value pairs for a section of the WIN.INI file
GetProfileString	Returns a character string in a section from the WIN.INI file
WritePrivateProfileSection	Writes all the key name and value pairs for a section of a private initialization file
WritePrivateProfileString	Copies a character string to a private initialization file, or deletes one or more lines in a private initialization file"
WriteProfileSection	Writes all the key name and value pairs for a section of the WIN.INI file
WriteProfileString	Copies a character string to the WIN.INI file, or deletes one or more lines from WIN.INI"

2.3.13 Install/Compression

Win3.1 provides functions for application install programs to compress and decompress their files. These are provided in the 32-bit API as well.

These functions include:

Function	Description
CopyLZFile	Copies a file, decompressing if necessary.
GetExpandedName	Retrieves the original name of a compressed file.
LZClose	Closes a file opened with LZOpenFile.
LZCopy	Copies a compressed file.
LZDone	Frees buffers allocated by LZStart.
LZInit	Allocates structures for file compression.
LZOpenFile	Opens a file.

Function	Description
LZRead	Reads from a compressed file.
LZSeek	Seeks in a compressed file.
LZStart	Allocates buffers for CopyLZFile.

2.3.14 Memory Management Functions

Under Windows 3.1, there are two forms of memory management calls, Local and Global. The Global memory manager allocates segments from physical memory and returns a handle value that can be converted into a far pointer using the GlobalLock function. Global memory is globally visible to all applications, either by explicit request or implicitly because that is the way Windows 3.1 is implemented with all processes running in the same address space. The Local memory manager allocates objects from within a 64KB segment and returns a 16-bit offset to the allocated memory.

Under Win32, the local and global memory manager API calls are kept relatively intact, with moveable and discardable options supported along with the lock and unlock functions. The major difference is that local memory objects have a 32-bit handle instead of a 16-bit handle and the handle is an actual pointer instead of an offset relative to a segment. These changes will not affect most portable 16-bit code, which treated local memory handles as either char * or char **.

The other major difference between Win32 and 16-bit Windows is that global memory is no longer visible to all Windows applications. Since each application has its own address space, memory allocated by one process is not visible outside of the address space of that process. Memory used in DDE transactions will transparently be made available to the receiving process. Applications which need shared memory for other purposes should use named shared memory (available via **CreateFileMapping**).

Since the local and global memory manager API calls were designed specifically for a segmented environment and we did not want to change the API calls in any significant way, two new memory manager API sets have been added to the Win32 API set. The API calls are designed for use in a 32-bit linear address space. The Heap Manager API calls are analogous to the local memory manager, except that they operate on an explicit heap object instead of the heap object associated with the current process. This allows DLL code that used a private heap to be written for the Win32 environment. The Virtual Memory manager API calls are analogous to the global memory manager, except that they allow the sparse allocation of large contiguous objects.

For additional information on memory management, see the Memory Management overview.

The memory management functions include:

Function	Description
GetFreeSpace	Retrieves the number of bytes available in the global heap
GetFreeSystemResources	Gets information about system memory. GlobalAlloc Allocates memory from the global heap
GlobalCompact	Compacts global memory to generate free bytes
GlobalDiscard	Discards a global memory block if the lock count is zero, but does not invalidate the handle of the memory block
GlobalFix	Prevents a global memory block from moving in linear memory
GlobalFlags	Returns the flags and lock count of a global memory block
GlobalFree	Removes a global memory block and invalidates the handle of the memory block
GlobalHandle	Retrieves the handle of a global memory object
GlobalLock	Retrieves a pointer to a global memory block specified by a handle
GlobalLRUNewest	Moves a global memory object to the newest least-recently-used (LRU) position
GlobalLRUOldest	Moves a global memory object to the oldest least-recently-used (LRU) position
GlobalMemoryStatus	Returns information on current availability of memory
GlobalNotify	Installs a notification procedure for the current task
GlobalReAlloc	Reallocates a global memory block
GlobalSize	Returns the size (in bytes) of a global memory block
GlobalUnfix	Unlocks a global memory block previously fixed by the GlobalFix function
GlobalUnlock	Invalidates the pointer to a global memory block previously retrieved by the GlobalLock function
HeapAlloc	Allocates memory from the specified heap
HeapCreate	Creates a memory allocation heap
HeapDestroy	Destroys a memory allocation heap
HeapFree	Frees memory allocated from the specified heap

Function	Description
HeapSize	Returns the size of the specified allocated object
LocalAlloc	Allocates memory from the local heap
LocalCompact	Compacts local memory
LocalDiscard	Discards a local memory block if the lock count is zero, but does not invalidate the handle of the memory block
LocalFlags	Returns the memory type of a local memory block
LocalFree	Frees a local memory block from memory if the lock count is zero and invalidates the handle of the memory block
LocalHandle	Retrieves the handle of a local memory object
LocalInit	Initializes a local heap in the specified segment
LocalLock	Locks a block of local memory by increasing its lock count
LocalNotify	Installs a notification procedure for current task.
LocalReAlloc	Reallocates a local memory block
LocalShrink	Shrinks the local heap
LocalSize	Returns the size (in bytes) of a local memory block
LocalUnlock	Unlocks a local memory block
LockData	Locks the current data segment in memory
UnLockData	Unlocks the current data segment
VirtualAlloc	Reserves and/or commits a region of the virtual address space
VirtualFree	Releases and/or decommits a region of the virtual address space
VirtualProtect	Changes the protection of a region of the virtual address space
VirtualQuery	Returns information about a region of virtual address space

2.3.15 Module-Management Functions

Win32 module management functionality is similar to that of the Windows 16-bit API.

The module management functions include:

Function	Description
FindExecutable	Retrieves the handle of an executable file.
FreeLibrary	Decreases the reference count of a library by one and removes it from memory if the reference count is zero
FreeModule	Decreases the reference count of a module by one and removes it from memory if the reference count is zero
GetModuleFileName	Returns a module filename
GetModuleHandle	Returns the module handle of a module
GetProcAddress	Returns the address of a function in a module
LoadLibrary	Loads a library module
LoadModule	Executes a separate application

2.3.16 Pipes

Both anonymous and named pipes are provided in Win32. In the case of named pipes, both client- and server-side pipes are supported. Named pipes will work transparently across the network, regardless of the network implementation.

For additional information on how to use pipes, see the Pipes Overview.

The pipe functionality includes:

Function	Description
CallNamedPipe	Equivalent to CreateFile, TransactNamedPipe, CloseFile series
ConnectNamedPipe	Used on server side to wait for a client to connect
CreateNamedPipe	Used to create first and ensuing instances of a named pipe
CreatePipe	Used to create an anonymous pipe
DisconnectNamedPipe	Used on server side to force a client to disconnect
GetNamedPipeHandleState	Retrieves information about a named pipe handle
GetNamedPipeInfo	Retrieves information about a named pipe
PeekNamedPipe	Copies named pipe data without removing it from the pipe
SetNamedPipeHandleState	Sets the read and blocking mode of a named pipe
TransactNamedPipe	Writes data to and reads data from a named pipe
WaitNamedPipe	Waits for a named pipe to become available

2.3.17 Processes and Threads

Win32 exposes processes and threads of execution within a process as objects. APIs exist to create, manipulate, and delete these objects.

A process object represents a virtual address space, a security profile (Windows NT only), a set of threads that execute in the address space of the process, and a set of resources or objects visible to all threads executing in the process. A thread object is the agent that executes program code. Each thread is associated with a process object which specifies the virtual address space mapping for the thread. Several thread objects can be associated with a single process object which enables the concurrent execution of multiple threads in a single address space (possible simultaneous execution in a multiprocessor system running Windows NT).

The process and thread functions include:

Function	Description
CreateProcess	Creates process and thread objects
CreateThread	Creates an additional thread in an existing process
ExitProcess	Exits the current process
ExitThread	Exits the current thread
GetCurrentProcess	Gets a process handle for the current process
GetCurrentProcessId	Gets the process id for the current process
GetCurrentThread	Gets a thread handle for the current thread
GetCurrentThreadId	Gets the thread id for the current thread
GetProcessExitCode	Gets the termination status for a process
GetThreadExitCode	Gets the termination status for a thread
GetThreadPriority	Gets the priority for a thread
GetThreadSelectorEntry	
OpenProcess	Returns a handle to the process with the specified id
ResumeThread	Resumes execution of a thread
SetThreadPriority	Sets the priority for a thread
ShellExecute	Executes a program.
Sleep	Delays execution of the current thread for a specified time
SuspendThread	Suspends execution of a thread
TerminateProcess	Kills a process
TerminateThread	Kills a thread
WaitForInputIdle	Waits for a child process to reach GetMessage.

Function	Description
WinExec	Executes a program.

2.3.18 Registration

Win32 provides a centralized configuration database, which is accessible remotely. The registry is designed to solve the problem of multiple, unmaintainable configuration files. This is an extension of the Win3.1 registration functions.

The registry functions include:

Function	Description
RegCloseKey	
RegCreateKey	
RegCreateKeyEx	
RegDeleteKey	
RegDeleteValue	
RegEnumKey	
RegEnumKeyEx	
RegEnumValue	
RegFlushKey	
RegNotifyChangeKeyValue	
RegOpenKey	
RegOpenKeyEx	
RegOpenRegistry	
RegQueryInfoKey	
RegQueryValue	
RegQueryValueEx	
RegRestoreKey	
RegSaveKey	
RegSetValue	
RegSetValueEx	

Information to come

2.3.19 Resource Management Functions

All Windows 3.1 resource functionality has been preserved, with the exception of calculated resources.

The resource functions include:

Function	Description
EnumResourceNames	Enumerates resource names.
EnumResourceTypes	Enumerates resource types.
FindResource	Determines the location of a resource
FreeResource	Removes a loaded resource from memory
LoadResource	Loads a resource
LockResource	Retrieves the absolute memory address of a resource
SizeofResource	Supplies the size (in bytes) of a resource
UnlockResource	Unlocks a resource

2.3.20 Security

Win32 has been designed with B-level security in mind, and Windows NT will initially be certified as C2 secure.

For additional information on the security design, see the Security Overview.

The security functions include:

Function	Description
AbsoluteToSelfRelativeSD	
AccessCheck	
AccessCheckAndAuditAlarm	
AddAccessAllowedAce	
AddAce	
AdjustTokenGroups	
AdjustTokenPrivileges	
AreAllAccessesGranted	
AreAnyAccessesGranted	
CloseWindowStation	
CopySid	
CreateUserObjectSecurity	
DdeImpersonateClient	
DdeRevertToSelf	
DeleteAce	
DestroyUserObjectSecurity	

Information to come

Function	Description
EnumDisplayDevices	
EnumWindowStationFunc	
EnumWindowStations	
EqualSid	
GetAce	
GetAclInformation	
GetFileSecurity	
GetInputDesktop	
GetLengthSid	
GetObjectSecurity	
GetProcessWindowStation	
GetSecurityDescriptorControl	
GetSecurityDescriptorDacl	
GetSecurityDescriptorGroup	
GetSecurityDescriptorLength	
GetSecurityDescriptorOwner	
GetSecurityDescriptorSacl	
GetSidIdentifierAuthority	
GetSidLengthRequired	
GetSidSubAuthority	
GetSidSubAuthorityCount	
GetTokenInformation	
GetUserObjectSecurity	
GetWindowStationAttrs	
ImpersonateNamedPipeClient	
InitializeAcl	
InitializeSecurityDescriptor	
InitializeSid	
IsValidAcl	
IsValidSecurityDescriptor	
IsValidSid	
MapGenericMask	
NamedPipeRevertToSelf	
ObjectCloseAuditAlarm	

Information to come

Function	Description
ObjectOpenAuditAlarm	
ObjectPrivilegeAuditAlarm	
OpenProcessToken	
OpenThreadToken	
OpenWindowStation	
PrivilegeCheck	
PrivilegedServiceAuditAlarm	
SelfRelativeToAbsoluteSD	
SetAclInformation	
SetFileSecurity	
SetObjectSecurity	
SetProcessWindowStation	
SetSecurityDescriptorDacl	
SetSecurityDescriptorGroup	
SetSecurityDescriptorOwner	
SetSecurityDescriptorSacl	
SetTokenInformation	
SetUserObjectSecurity	

Information to come

2.3.21 Segment Management Functions

All of the Windows 3.x segment management functions are x86 specific and therefore have not been included in the 32-bit API.

2.3.22 Sound

The Win3.1 sound functions have been replaced by the PlaySound function from the Multimedia Extensions for Windows.

The sound functions include:

Function	Description
Beep	Beeps.
PlaySound	Plays waveforms.

2.3.23 Synchronization

Along with multi-threading and preemption in the Win32 system, a set of synchronization objects have been included. These objects provide the tools necessary to build reliable and robust multi-threaded applications.

The Win32 synchronization objects are:

- Critical sections. This object may only be shared by threads within a single process. It provides a very fast mechanism for controlling mutual exclusive access to a resource.

- Events. This object is used to record the occurrence of an event and synchronize it with some action.

- Mutexes. Like critical sections, this object provides a mechanism for controlling mutual exclusive access to a resource. Mutexes are not restricted to threads within a single process, but are slightly slower.

- Semaphores. A semaphore object is used to control access to a resource, but not necessarily in a mutually exclusive fashion. A semaphore object acts as a gate through which a variable number of threads may pass concurrently, up to a specified limit. The gate is open (Signaled state) as long as there are resources available. When the number of resources specified by the limit are concurrently in use, the gate is closed (Not-Signaled state).

For additional information on how to use the synchronization functionality, see the Synchronization Overview.

The synchronization functions include:

Function	Description
DeleteCriticalSection	Deletes a critical section object
EnterCriticalSection	Used to gain exclusive access to a resource
InitializeCriticalSection	Initializes a critical section
LeaveCriticalSection	Releases exclusive access to a resource
CreateEvent	Creates an event object
OpenEvent	Opens a event object
PulseEvent	Sets the event to signaled state and then resets it
ResetEvent	Sets the event to the not-signaled state
SetEvent	Sets the event to the signaled state
CreateMutex	Creates a mutex object
OpenMutex	Opens a mutex object
ReleaseMutex	Releases ownership of a mutex object

Function	Description
CreateSemaphore	Creates a semaphore object
ReleaseSemaphore	Releases ownership of a semaphore object
OpenSemaphore	Opens a named semaphore object
InterlockedDecrement	Subtracts 1 from a count.
InterlockedIncrement	Adds 1 to a count.
MsgWaitForMultipleObjects	Blocks waiting for an object or message
WaitForMultipleObjects	Blocks on multiple waitable objects
WaitForSingleObject	Blocks on a single waitable object

2.3.24 Time

Win32 provides a number of services for getting and converting times.

These functions include:

Function	Description
DosDateTimeToFileTime	Converts file time/date from DOS format to 64-bit format
FileTimeToDosDateTime	Converts file time/date from 64-bit format to DOS format
FileTimeToSystemTime	Converts file time/date from 64-bit format to system format
GetCurrentTime	Retrieves the current Windows time
GetSystemTime	Returns the current time and date
GetTickCount	Retrieves the elapsed time since the system started
KillTimer	Kills the specified timer event
SetSystemTime	Sets the current time and date
SetTimer	Creates a system-timer event
SystemTimeToFileTime	Converts system time to a 64-bit file time

2.3.25 Thread-Local Storage

Thread-Local Storage (TLS) allows an application or DLL to store data on behalf of a thread. APIs exist to allocate and free a TLS index, and to locate a TLS slot using its index.

Additional support provided by Win32 includes calling DLLs each time a thread begins execution, and each time a thread exits. This gives a DLL an opportunity to initialize and free its thread local storage slots.

The TLS APIs operate on the calling thread/processes TLS data structures. Each process contains a minimum number of garunteed thread local storage indexes. Once an index is allocated, it can be used to address a TLS slot in each thread.

- Each process contains a bitmap of TLS indexes. The bitmap has a fixed minimum size. The minimum size is 64 (TLS_MINIMUM_AVAILABLE).

- Each thread has an array of pointers. The array is indexed by a TLS index.

- Indexes are allocated by an application or DLL. An index is valid within the calling process. Indexes are typically allocated during application initialization or during DLL initialization. Once allocated, an application or DLL may use the TLS index to locate a per thread TLS slot. TLS indexes are not valid across process boundries. A DLL can not assume that an index assigned in one process is valid in another process.

These Thread-Local Storage include:

Function	Description
TlsAlloc	Allocates thread-local storage
TlsFree	Frees thread-local storage
TlsGetValue	Gets a thread-local value.
TlsSetValue	Sets a thread-local value.

2.3.26 Version Management

Win3.1 provides functions for an application to handle version management of files. These functions will be included in Win32.

The version functions include:

GetSystemDir
GetFileResource
GetFileResourceSize
GetFileVersionInfo
GetFileVersionInfoSize
VerFindFile
VerInstallFile
VerLanguageName
VerQueryValue

Chapter	**Win32 Network APIs**
3	

3.1	Overview	33
3.2	Interprocess Communication	33
	3.2.1 Mailslot APIs	33
	3.2.2 Netbios APIs	34
3.3	Network Object Connection	34
3.4	Network Support of Win32 APIs	35

3.1 Overview

This chapter describes the services available on all Win32 systems when a network provider is present. These are are "client" API, typically used by client components of distributed, client-server applications.

The services are provided uniformly across different types of networks. Note that they are only present when at least one network provider is installed. If no network provider is present, calls to the API will return indicating so.

The corresponding network provider mechanisms and interfaces are described in a separate document.

Network services include the following:

- Interprocess communication
- Network Object Connection
- Network Object Browsing

In the future, other API will be added to support network functions such as mail and messaging, directory services, software distribution and licensing.

3.2 Interprocess Communication

In addition to the Named Pipe IPC of the base, Win32 provides additional network IPC mechanisms. The Mailslot APIs provide a general purpose "mailbox" mechanism capable of many-to-one communication. As well, a one-to-many capability is provided utilizing the datagram delivery mechanism of the underlying provider.

The Netbios APIs provide an interface to a block-oriented transport service. The Netbios service provides both connection-oriented (virtual circuit) and connectionless (datagram) services with simple name-based addressing. It is based on the interrupt-based Netbios interface provided originally in DOS. The high degree of similarity eases the porting of applications using the DOS Netbios interface. This interface is reccommended primarily for migration of such applications, with the preferred services being the higher-level IPC or Remote Procedure Call (RPC) facilities.

3.2.1 Mailslot APIs

Mailslots provide a unidirectional interprocess communication mechanism. Mailslot messages can be sent locally to a single mailslot. Messages can also be sent remotely to a single machine or to multiple machines.

Two types of processes are involved in mailslots, the server process and the client process. A server process creates a local mailslot by calling CreateMailslot and obtains a server- side handle to the mailslot. Only a process with a server side handle can read messages from the mailslot, by calling ReadFile. Any number of client processes can open an existing mailslot and obtain a client-side handle. The client-side handle can be used to write messages to the mailslot by calling WriteFile. All received messages are appended to the mailslot and read by the server process in FIFO order.

A process may not read a mailslot without a server-side mailslot handle, nor may it write to a mailslot without a client-side mailslot handle. However, a single process may own both a types of mailslot handles. A useful feature of mailslot is broadcast. Cooperating server processes on machines in a single domain can participate by each creating a mailslot of the same name on their local machine.

The Mailslot functions include:

Function	Description
CreateMailslot	Creates a mailslot.
GetMailslotInfo	Gets information about a mailslot
SetMailslotInfo	Sets information about a mailslot.

3.2.2 Netbios APIs

Win32 provides a high level interface for Windows applications to access netbios functionality, if it is available. The **Netbios** function interprets and executes the specified NCB. This function contains extensions from the standard Netbios 3.0 specification to allow POST routines to be called from C and to operate efficiently in the Windows environment.

Function	Description
NetBios	High-level Netbios functionality

3.3 Network Object Connection

The Network Object Connection services provide a mechanism for local binding of objects such as logical drives or devices to network objects, such as files, directories or devices on file servers.

The Network Object functions include:

Function	Description
WNetAddConnection	Connect to a network resource
WNetAddConnection2	Connect to a network resource
WNetCancelConnection	Close a network resource
WNetCloseEnum	Finish enumerating network resources.
WNetEnumResource	Enumerate network resources
WNetGetConnection	Gets the network resource associated with a local name.
WNetGetUser	Gets the name to use to connect to the network.
WNetOpenEnum	Begins a network enumeration.

3.4 Network Support of Win32 APIs

In addition to the Network services, certain of the base and extended services are available remotely when a network provider is present. These include:

- Named Pipes

- File Services

- Printing

- Communications

- Security

- Error Logging

The remote support of these services is logically transparent to the application.

Chapter 4

Windows 32-bit GDI design Specification

4.1	Introduction		39
4.2	Enhancements to GDI		39
4.3	Changes to GDI		40
	4.3.1	Changes Across All Calls	40
		4.3.1.1 Widening to 32-bits	40
	4.3.2	Functional Changes	41
		4.3.2.1 Bitmap Changes	41
	4.3.3	Detailed Description of Changes	41
		4.3.3.1 Changed	41
		4.3.3.2 Compatibility Calls	44
		4.3.3.3 Deleted	44
	4.3.4	New Calls	45
		4.3.4.1 Drawing	45
		4.3.4.2 Fonts and Text	45
		4.3.4.3 BitBlts	45
		4.3.4.4 Path	45
		4.3.4.5 Transforms	46
		4.3.4.6 Miscellanious	46
		4.3.4.7 Minor Variations of existing calls	46
4.4	Summary of GDI Functionality		47
	4.4.1	Bitmaps	47
	4.4.2	Drawing Tools	48
	4.4.3	Clipping	48
	4.4.4	Color	49
	4.4.5	Curve Output	49
	4.4.6	Device Context Functions	50
	4.4.7	Fonts	50
	4.4.8	Line Output	51
	4.4.9	Mapping	52

4.4.10 Metafiles 53

4.4.11 GDI Objects 53

4.4.12 Palette Management 54

4.4.13 Paths 55

4.4.14 Position 55

4.4.15 Printing 56

4.4.16 Regions 57

4.4.17 Text Output 57

4.1 Introduction

This document discusses enhancements to GDI, and how the 16-bit GDI APIs have changed in being expanded to 32-bits. It also contains a high-level overview of the functionality available in 32-bit GDI.

4.2 Enhancements to GDI

The Windows 32-bit API includes a significantly improved GDI. It incorporates significant improvements based on feedback from software vendors who found 16-bit GDI lacking. While much of the feedback refers to new functionality, a significant amount addresses rough edges in the existing functionality.

Specific improvements to address rough edges or holes in existing Win3.1 functionality include:

Wideline support	Win32 provides improved wideline functionality, including brushed widelines, a selection of line joins, and multiple line styles.
Fractional character widths	This is critical for word processors and other applications whose ultimate goal is to provide perfect correspondence between what is displayed on the screen and what will appear on the printer. If the application can not find out the fractional component of a character width, it is difficult to achieve full WYSIWYG.
Metafiles	16-bit metafiles have a number of problems which make them sub-optimal in their role as a graphics interchange format. GDI32 provides a revamped 32-bit metafile format that provides device/configuration-independence across machines. In addition we provide APIs to allow applications to convert to/from the 16-bit metafile format.
Improved font mapping	We provide a new, Panose-based font mapper which will do a much better job of finding a good substitute if the requested font is not available.
Brushed Text	We will add the ability to specify a brush for filling text.

We also add new functionality:

Paths	The system provides support to make it easy for applications to manage multiple shapes (consisting of lines and curves) efficiently. Applications can draw, fill, and clip through these shapes.

Bezier curves	These curves are fast and predictable.
Additional transforms	We provide an additional transform layer to allow rotation and shearing of objects.
Device independent color	RGB today has little or no meaning. For applications with very simple dependencies on color this is ok, but it is inadequate for applications interested in high-quality picture output. We will provide a solution to this problem.
Improved bitmap support	We provide additional options for blending and halftoning on stretchblt, bitmap rotation/distortion, and masking.

4.3 Changes to GDI

The following summarizes API changes at a high level.

4.3.1 Changes Across All Calls

The changes made to the APIs can be broken down into several major categories. The first group are mainly mechanical changes that affect most of the Win32 GDI API. These changes are the result of widening the API to 32 bits or changes in pointers. By and large these changes are handled by the compiler, and application developers will not have to edit their code. These changes include:

4.3.1.1 Widening to 32-bits

The vast majority of changes made are the results of widening the APIs to 32-bits. These are simple conversions from 16 bit to 32 bit data. They affect most of the APIs in the system. The widening can be broken down into subcategories.

4.3.1.1.1 All Coordinates are 32-bits

In Win3 all coordinates were signed 16 bit integers. In the Win32 GDI all coordinates are signed 32 bit integers.

There are devices today that required more that 16 bits to span the device space. In the future we expect more devices to require the larger coordinate space. Applications also are running up against the 16 bit coordinate barrier (eg. CAD applications).

This change affects a small number of APIs which return a packed x, y value. These functions now take an additional pointer to a structure to receive the return value.

4.3.1.1.2 All handles are 32-bits

In Win3 handles were 16 bit quantities. In the new GDI all handles are 32 bit quantities. This is done in the type and structure definitions in the include files. A hDC stays a hDC. No change is required by applications developers.

4.3.1.1.3 Limits are 32-bit

A number of API calls pass in counts. As applications grow these limits will be hit. These limits are now 32 bit quantities.

4.3.1.1.4 All pointers are 32-bit flat

Pointers that were segment:offset are now flat 32 bits.

4.3.2 Functional Changes

One general class of APIs were changed beyond those listed above. They are bitmap functions. These calls contained some features that were not supportable under Win32.

4.3.2.1 Bitmap Changes

Applications are encouraged to use DIBitmaps. The old bitmap formats from GetBitmapBits contained no tags indicating the format. On reading them, we have no way to find out what version of Windows wrote them. The old Bitmap calls are included for compatiblity purposes. Applications are encouraged to use the newer DIB calls.

Bitmaps contain palettes just like device surfaces do. On CreateDiBitmap the palette is set to the given color table. The palette may be changed with RealizePalette.

4.3.3 Detailed Description of Changes

4.3.3.1 Changed

The following set of calls were changed as indicated. These changes may require resource code changes.

AddFontResource	This calls was split into AddFontResource and AddFontModule. The first call takes a filename. The second call takes a module handle. Applications that use the module handle feature of AddFontResource must now use AddFontModule.
CloseMetaFile	Widen to 32 bits. Returns handle to metafile HMF, not handle.
CopyMetaFile	Widen to 32 bits. Takes and returns a hMF not a HANDLE.
CreateMetaFile	Widened to 32 bits. Changed Handle to HMF.

DeleteMetaFile	Widened to 32 bits. Changed Handle to HMF.
DeviceCapabilities	Widened to 32 bits. Rather than calling LoadLibrary/GetProcAddress, the application now supplies the driver name to the system, which in turn will call these functions.
DeviceMode	Now returns a boolean. Rather than calling **LoadLibrary/GetProcAddress**, the application now supplies the driver name to the system, which in turn will call these functions.
EnumFonts	Widened to 32 bits. Callback function must be declared APIENTRY.
EnumMetaFile	Widened to 32 bits. Callback function must be declared APIENTRY.
EnumObjects	Widened to 32 bits. Callback function must be declared APIENTRY.
ExtDeviceModeApplication	Does not load driver. Rather than calling **LoadLibrary/GetProcAddress**, the application now supplies the driver name to the system, which in turn will call these functions.
GetAspectRatioFilter	Widened to 32 bits. Return value is now the lpAspectRatio parameter.
GetBitmapDimension	Widened to 32 bits. Return value is now the lpDimension parameter. Now returns boolean.
GetBrushOrg	Widened to 32 bits. Return value is now the lpPoint parameter. Now returns boolean.
GetCurrentPosition	Widened to 32 bits. Return value is now the lpPoint parameter. Now returns boolean.
GetDIBits	Widened to 32 bits. Return value is now a boolean, not the number of scan lines returned.
GetMetaFileBits	Widened to 32 bits. Call no longer returns a global memory handle. Now the application passes in a buffer to get the information. Added the nSize and lpData parameters.
GetMetaFile	Widened to 32-bits. Changed HANDLE to hMF.
GetTextExtent	Widened to 32-bits. Change return value to lpSize parameter.
GetTextFace	Widened to 32-bits. Permitted lpFacename to be NULL.
GetViewportExt	Widened to 32-bits. Change return value to lpSize parameter.

GetViewportOrg	Widened to 32-bits. Change return value to lpPoint parameter.
GetWindowExt	Widened to 32-bits. Change return value to lpSize parameter.
GetWindowOrg	Widened to 32-bits. Change return value to lpPoint parameter.
LineDDA	Widened to 32 bits. Callback function must be declared APIENTRY.
MoveTo	Widened to 32-bits. Change return value to lpPoint parameter.
OffsetViewportOrg	Widened to 32-bits. Change return value to lpPoint parameter.
OffsetWindowOrg	Widened to 32-bits. Change return value to lpPoint parameter.
PlayMetaFile	Widened to 32-bits. Changed HANDLE to HMF
ScaleViewportExt	Widened to 32-bits. Change return value to lpSize parameter.
ScaleWindowExt	Widened to 32-bits. Change return value to lpSize parameter.
SetBitmapDimension	Widened to 32-bits. Change return value to lpSize parameter.
SetBrushOrg	Widened to 32-bits. Change return value to lpPoint parameter. Win32 GDI will automatically track the origin of all window-managed device contexts and adjust their brushes as necessary to maintain alignment of patterns on the surface.
SetDIBits	Widened to 32 bits. Allows DIB without color table.
SetDIBitsToDevice	Widened to 32 bits. Allows DIB without color table.
SetMetaFileBits	Widened to 32 bits. Call no longer takes a global memory handle. Now the application passes in a buffer and a size.
SetViewportExt	Widened to 32-bits. Change return value to lpPoint parameter.
SetViewportOrg	Widened to 32-bits. Change return value to lpPoint parameter.
SetWindowExt	Widened to 32-bits. Change return value to lpPoint parameter.
SetWindowOrg	Widened to 32-bits. Change return value to lpPoint parameter.

4.3.3.2 Compatibility Calls

The following calls are included for compatibility only. We strongly recommend applications do not make these calls but rather the replacement calls.

CreateBitmap	We are discouraging applications from using the CreateBitmap calls. Applications should use CreateDIBitmap instead. CreateBitmap does exist for compatibility. It has been widen to 32 bits.
CreateBitmapIndirect	The call has been widened to 32-bits. Applications should use CreateDIBitmap.
CreateDIBPatternBrush	This call takes a memory handle. We recommend that applications use CreateDIBPatternBrushPt. The new call takes a pointer to the brush rather than a memory handle. This is the only difference between the two calls.
CreateDiscardableBitmap	This call is mapped to **CreateCompatibleBitmap** inside Win32 GDI.
FloodFill	This is the exactly same as **ExtFloodFill** with wFillType set to FLOODFILLBORDER. Applications should use ExtFloodFill.
GetBitmapBits	The "bits" returned by this call are device driver specific. The bits for a device on Win32 are not guaranteed to be the same as for previous versions of Windows. Do not do a GetBitmapBits on an old version of Windows, save the bits to file, then use those bits in a SetBitmapBits in a new version of windows. Preferable, application should use **GetDIBits.**
SetBitmapBits	Same caveats as GetBitmapBits. Preferable, applications should use SetDIBits

4.3.3.3 Deleted

The following calls were deleted from the GDI.

GetDCOrg	The GDI now does automatic brush tracking. Applications do not have to realign their brushes after the DC moved. This call was used for that purpose.
GetEnvironment	This calls was used by device drivers, not applications. It has been removed from the application API.
SetEnvironment	This calls was used by device drivers, not applications. It has been removed from the application API.

4.3.4 New Calls

This summarizes the additional functionality in GDI.

4.3.4.1 Drawing

The number of extensions were made to the drawing calls. The largest change is the addition of bezier curves.

AngleArc	Draws an arc of a circle.
ArcTo	Draws a arc starting from the current position.
CloseFigure	Close a drawing figure.
ExtCreatePen	Improved line styles and joins.
PolyBezier	Bezier drawing call.
PolyBezierTo	Bezier drawing call.
PolylineTo	Draw multiple lines starting from current position.
PolyDraw	Draw multiple lines and beziers.
PolyPolyline	Draw multiple sets of lines.

4.3.4.2 Fonts and Text

Font improvement include better font mapping and more information on fonts.

DiffFonts	Improved font enumeration
ExtCreateFontIndirect	Improved Font creation (panose).
GetCharWidthFloat	Fractional character widths.
GetFontMapperControls	Improved font mapping
GetKerningPairs	Get kerning information.
SetFontMapperControls	Improved font mapping
SetTextBrush	Brushs for text

4.3.4.3 BitBlts

A few extensions were made to blting.

CreateDibSection	New Dib creation call.
MaskBlt	Blt through a mask.
PlgBlt	Rotated blts.

4.3.4.4 Path

Win32 GDI has a complete set of path calls.

BeginPath	Start a path
EndPath	End a path

FillPath	Fill a path.
FlattenPath	Flatten a path to a series of lines
PathToRegion	Convert a path to a region.
SelectClipPath	Select a path as a region.
SetFlat	Set parameter for path flattening.
StrokeAndFillPath	Stroke and fill a path.
StrokePath	Stroke a path
WidenPat	hWiden a path.

4.3.4.5 Transforms

Win32 GDI has a new set of transform calls. These permit an application to specify arbitrary transforms.

GetWorldTransform	Get the current transform.
ModifyWorldTransform	Change the transform.
SetWorldTransform	Set the new transforms.

4.3.4.6 Miscellanious

A few miscellanious calls were added.

CancelDC	Stop long operations on a DC.
GetClipRgn	Get the current clipping region.

4.3.4.7 Minor Variations of existing calls

Three calls fall into this category. Two are split off from **AddFontResource** and **RemoveFontResource**. One is a slight variation of **CreateDIBPatternBrush**.

AddFontModule	This calls was split from **AddFontResource**. This call takes a module handle. **AddFontResource** takes a filename. Previously **AddFontResource** too both types of parameters.
CreatDIBPatternBrushPt	The **CreatDIBPatternBrush** calls takes a GLOBALHANDE to memory. We strongly recommend applications convert to the new **CreateDIBPatternBrushPt** call. This call takes a pointer to the brush rather than a GLOBALHANDLE. Other than that the functionality is identical.
RemoveFontModule	This calls was split from **RemoveFontResource**. This call takes a module handle. **RemoveFontResource** takes a filename. Previously **RemoveFontResource** too both types of parameters.

4.4 Summary of GDI Functionality

4.4.1 Bitmaps

Bitmap functions display bitmaps. A bitmap is a matrix of memory bits that, when copied to a device, defines the color and pattern of a corresponding matrix of pixels on the device's display surface. Bitmaps are useful in drawing, charting, and word-processing applications because they let you prepare images in memory and then quickly copy them to the display. The following list briefly describes each bitmap function:

Function	Description
BitBlt	Copies a bitmap from a source to a destination device
CreateBitmap	Creates a bitmap
CreateBitmapIndirect	Creates a bitmap described in a data structure
CreateCompatibleBitmap	Creates a bitmap that is compatible with a specified device
CreateDIBitmap	Creates a device-independent bitmap
CreateDIBSection	Creates a bitmap that application has direct access to.
CreateDiscardableBitmap	Creates a discardable bitmap that is compatible with a specified device
ExtFloodFill	Fills the display surface within a border or over an area of a given color
GetBitmapBehind	Gets cached bits behind a window.
GetBitmapBits	Retrieves the bits in memory for a specific bitmap
GetBitmapDimension	Retrieves the dimensions of a bitmap
GetBitmapDimensionEx	Retrieves the dimensions of a bitmap
GetDIBits	Retrieves the bits in memory for a specific bitmap in device-independent form
GetROP2	Retrieves the current drawing mode
GetStretchBltMode	Retrieves the current stretching mode
LoadBitmap	Loads a bitmap from a resource file
MaskBlt	Draws a bitmap through the specfied mask
PatBlt	Creates a bit pattern
PlgBlt	Distorts a bitmap into the specified parallelogram
SetBitmapBits	Sets the bits of a bitmap
SetBitmapDimension	Sets the height and width of a bitmap
SetBitmapDimensionEx	Sets the height and width of a bitmap

Function	Description
SetDIBits	Sets a memory bitmap's bits from a DIB This function is similar to SetBitmapBits
SetDIBitsToDevice	Sets bits on a device surface directly from a DIB
SetROP2	Sets the current drawing mode
SetStretchBltMode	Sets the stretching mode
StretchBlt	Copies a bitmap from a source to a destination device (compresses orstretches, if necessary)
StetchDIBits	Stretches device-independent bits.

4.4.2 Drawing Tools

Drawing-tool functions create and delete the drawing tools that GDI uses when it creates output on a device or display surface. The following list briefly describes each drawing-tool function:

Function	Description
CreateBrushIndirect	Creates a brush with specified attributes
CreateDIBPatternBrush	Creates a logical brush that has a pattern defined by a device-independent bitmap (DIB)
CreateDIBPatternBrushPt	Creates a brush from a DIB
CreateHatchBrush	Creates a hatched brush
CreatePatternBrush	Creates a logical brush that has a pattern defined by a memory bitmap
CreateSolidBrush	Creates a solid brush with a specified color
GetBrushOrg	Retrieves the origin of the current brush
GetBrushOrgEx	Retrieves the origin of the current brush
SetBrushOrg	Sets the origin of the current brush
CreatePen	Creates a logical pen
CreatePenIndirect	Creates a pen using a LOGPEN structure
ExtCreatePen	Creates a pen with style, width and brush

4.4.3 Clipping

Clipping functions create, test, and alter clipping regions. A clipping region is the portion of a window's client area where GDI creates output; any output sent to that portion of the client area which is outside the clipping region will not be visible. Clipping regions are useful in any Windows application that needs to save one part of the client area and simultaneously send output to another. The following list briefly describes each clipping function:

Function	Description
ExcludeClipRect	Excludes a rectangle from the clipping region
GetBoundsRect	Gets the bounding rectangle of a drawing.
GetClipBox	Copies the dimensions of a bounding rectangle
GetClipRgn	Returns the current clipping region
IntersectClipRect	Forms the intersection of a clipping region and a rectangle
OffsetClipRgn	Moves a clipping region
SelectClipPath	Selects a clipping path
SelectClipRgn	Selects a clipping region

4.4.4 Color

Color functions control the color used by the output primitives.

The color functions include:

Function	Description
GetBkColor	Returns the current background color
GetBkMode	Returns the current background mode
GetNearestColor	Returns the RGB color that will be displayed for the given color
GetPixel	Retrieves the RGB value for a pixel
ResizePalette	Changes the size of a logical palette
SetBkColor	Sets the background color
SetBkMode	Sets the background mode
SetPixel	Sets the RGB value for a pixel

4.4.5 Curve Output

Curve-output functions create simple and complex curves with the selected pen. The following list briefly describes each line-output function:

Function	Description
AngleArc	Draws the specified portion of a circle
Arc	Draws an arc
ArcTo	Draws an arc, updating the current position
Chord	Draws a chord

Function	Description
Ellipse	Draws an ellipse
Pie	Draws a pie
PolyBezier	Draws one or more bezier curves
PolyBezierTo	Draws one or more bezier curves using current position
SetFlat	Sets the flatness of curves

4.4.6 Device Context Functions

Device-context functions create, delete, and restore device contexts (DC). A device context is a link between a Windows application, a device driver, and an output device, such as a printer or plotter. Windows maintains a cache of special DCs for the system display. The functions **GetDC** and **ReleaseDC** obtain and release these special DCs.

Any Windows application can use GDI functions to access an output device. GDI passes calls (which are device independent) from the application to the device driver. The device driver then translates the calls into device-dependent operations.

The Device Context functions include:

Function	Description
CreateCompatibleDC	Creates a memory device context
CreateDC	Creates a device context
CreateIC	Creates an information context
DeleteDC	Deletes a device context
GetDCOrg	Retrieves the origin of a specified device context
ResetDC	Updates a device context
RestoreDC	Restores a device context
SaveDC	Saves the current state of the device context
WindowFromDC	Returns the window associated with the DC.

4.4.7 Fonts

Font functions select, create, remove, and retrieve information about fonts. A font is a subset of a particular typeface, which is a set of characters that share a similar fundamental design.

The following list briefly describes each font function:

Function	Description
AddFontModule	Adds the font resources from the specified module
AddFontResource	Adds a font resource in the specified file to the system font table
CreateFont	Creates a logical font that has the specified characteristics
CreateFontIndirect	Creates a logical font that has the specified characteristics
CreateScalableFontResource	Creates a font resource file.
EnumFontFamilies	Enumerates fonts by family.
EnumFonts	Enumerates the fonts available on a given device
ExtTextOut	Draws series of characters based on an array of points.
GetAspectRatioFilterEx	Returns the current aspect ratio filter
GetCharABCWidths	Retrieves the widths of characters in a font.
GetCharWidth	Retrieves the widths of individual characters
GetFontData	Gets font metrics data from a font file.
GetGlyphOutline	Retrieves the outline for a character.
GetOutlineTextMetrics	Retrieves metric data for TrueType fonts.
GetRasterizerCaps	Returns whether TrueType fonts are available.
GetTextExtentPoint	Retrieves the extent of a string.
GetTextExtentPointEx	Retrieves an array of sub-string lengths
GetTextMetrics	Fills the buffer with metrics for the selected font
RemoveFontModule	Removes the fonts loaded from the specified module
RemoveFontResource	Removes a font resource from the font table
SetMapperFlags	Alters the algorithm the font mapper uses
SetTextAlign	Positions a string of text on a display or device
SetTextCharacterExtra	Sets the current intercharacter spacing
SetTextColor	Sets the text color
SetTextJustification	Justifies a text line
TextOut	Writes a character string using the current font

4.4.8 Line Output

Line-output functions create simple and complex line output with the selected pen. The following list briefly describes each line-output function:

Function	Description
LineDDA	Computes successive points on a line
LineTo	Draws a line with the selected pen
PolyDraw	Draws a series of lines and beziers.
Polygon	Draws a polygon
Polyline	Draws a set of line segments
PolylineTo	Draws one or more connected lines, updating the current position
PolyPolygon	Draws a series of closed polygons that are filled as though they were a single polygon
PolyPolyline	Draws a series of lines segments, which may not be connected
SetMiterLimit	Sets the limit for miter joins of lines

4.4.9 Mapping

Mapping functions alter and retrieve information about the GDI mapping modes. In order to maintain device independence, GDI creates output in a logical space and maps it to the display. The mapping mode defines the relationship between units in the logical space and pixels on a device. The following list briefly describes each mapping function:

Function	Description
DPtoLP	Converts device points (that is,points relative to the window origin) into logical points
GetMapMode	Retrieves the current mapping mode
GetViewportExtEx	Retrieves a device context's viewport extents
GetViewportOrgEx	Retrieves a device context's viewport origin
GetWindowExtEx	Retrieves a device context's window extents
GetWindowOrgEx	Retrieves a device context's window origin
GetWorldTransform	Returns the current world tranform
LPtoDP	Converts logical points into device points
ModifyWorldTransform	Changes the current world tranform
OffsetViewportOrgEx	Modifies a viewport origin
OffsetWindowOrgEx	Modifies a window origin
ScaleViewportExtEx	Modifies the viewport extents
ScaleWindowExtEx	Modifies the window extents
SetMapMode	Sets the mapping mode of a specified device context
SetViewportExtEx	Sets a device context's viewport extents

Function	Description
SetViewportOrgEx	Sets a device context's viewport origin
SetWindowExtEx	Sets a device context's window extents
SetWindowOrgEx	Sets a device context's window origin
SetWorldTransform	Sets the current world tranform

4.4.10 Metafiles

Metafile functions close, copy, create, delete, retrieve, play, and return information about metafiles. A metafile is a collection of GDI commands that creates desired text or images. Metafiles provide a convenient method of interchanging graphical data.

The following list briefly describes each metafile function:

Function	Description
CloseMetaFile	Closes a metafile and creates a metafile handle
CopyMetaFile	Copies a source metafile to a file
CreateMetaFile	Creates a metafile display context
DeleteMetaFile	Deletes a metafile from memory
EnumMetaFile	Enumerates the GDI calls within a metafile
GetMetaFile	Creates a handle to a metafile
GetMetaFileBitsEx	Stores a metafile as a collection of bits in a global memory block
PlayMetaFile	Plays the contents of a specified metafile
PlayMetaFileRecord	Plays a metafile record
SetMetaFileBitsEx	Creates a memory metafile

4.4.11 GDI Objects

The object functions are used to select and delete pens, brushes, fonts, bitmaps, and regions. The object functions include:

Function	Description
DeleteObject	Deletes a logical pen, brush, font, bitmap, or region
EnumObjects	Enumerates the available pens or brushes
GetObject	Copies the bytes of logical data that define an object
GetObjectType	Gets the type of a GDI object.
GetStockObject	Retrieves handle of a stock pen, brush, or font
IsGDIObject	Determines if an object is a GDI object.

Function	Description
SelectObject	Selects an object as the current object
UnrealizeObject	Directs GDI to reset the origin of the given brush

4.4.12 Palette Management

Many color graphic displays are capable of displaying a wide range of colors. In most cases, however, the actual number of colors which the display can render at any given time is more limited. For example, a display that is potentially able to produce over 262,000 different colors may be able to show only 256 of those colors at a time because of hardware limitations. In such cases, the display device often maintains a palette of colors; when an application requests a color that is not currently displayed, the display device adds the requested color to the palette. However, when the number of requested colors exceeds the maximum number for the device, it must replace an existing color with the requested color. As a result, if the total number of colors requested by one or more windows exceeds the number available on the display, many of the actual colors displayed will be incorrect.

Windows color palettes act as a buffer between color-intensive applications and the system, allowing an application to use as many colors as needed without interfering with its own color display or colors displayed by other windows. When a window has input focus, Windows ensures that the window will display all the colors it requests, up to the maximum number simultaneously available on the display, and displays additional colors by matching them to available colors. In addition, Windows matches the colors requested by inactive windows as closely as possible to the available colors. This significantly reduces undesirable changes in the colors displayed in inactive windows.

The following list briefly describes the functions an application calls to use color palettes:

Function	Description
AnimatePalette	Replaces entries in a logical palette; Windows maps the new entries into the system palette immediately
CreatePalette	Creates a logical palette
GetNearestPaletteIndex	Retrieves the index of a logical palette entry most nearly matching a specified RGB value
GetPaletteEntries	Retrieves entries from a logical palette
GetSystemPaletteEntries	Retrieves a range of palette entries from the system palette
GetSystemPaletteUse	Determines whether an application has access to the full system palette

Function	Description
RealizePalette	Maps entries in a logical palette to the system palette
SelectPalette	Selects a logical palette into a device context
SetPaletteEntries	Sets new palette entries in a logical palette; Windows does not map the new entries to the system palette until the application realizes the logical palette
SetSystemPaletteUse	Allows an application to use the full system palette
UpdateColors	Performs a pixel-by-pixel translation of each pixel's current color to the system palette This allows an inactive window to correct its colors without redrawing its client area

4.4.13 Paths

Paths are a collection of lines and beziers which can be used to draw, fill, or clip. The path functions include:

Function	Description
BeginPath	Begins definition of a path object
CloseFigure	Closes the specified object
EndPath	Ends recording of a path object
FillPath	Fills a path object
FlattenPath	Turns curves in a path into sequences of lines
PathToRegion	Converts a path to a region
StrokeAndFillPath	Draws and fills the specified path
StrokePath	Draws the specified path
WidenPath	Transforms the path into that which would be painted with a wide pen

4.4.14 Position

The position functions are used to set where drawing should occur. They include:

Function	Description
GetCurrentPosition	Returns current position in logical coordinates
GetCurrentPositionEx	Returns current position in logical coordinates
MoveToEx	Moves the current position to the specified point

4.4.15 Printing

Printer-control functions retrieve information about a printer and modify its initialization state. The printer driver, rather than GDI itself, provides these functions. The following list briefly describes each printer-control function:

Function	Description
AbortDoc	
AbortSpooler	
AddJob	
AddPrinter	
AddPrinterDriver	
AddPrintProcessor	
CloseSpooler	
DeletePrinter	
DeviceCapabilitiesEx	
DeviceModeEx	
EndDoc	
EndPage	
EnumJobs	
EnumPrinterDrivers	
EnumPrinters	
Escape	
ExtDeviceModeEx	
ExtEscape	
GetJob	
GetJobFromHandle	
GetPrinter	
GetPrinterDriver	
OpenSpooler	
ReadSpooler	
SetAbortProc	
SetJob	
SetPrinter	
StartDoc	
StartPage	
WriteSpooler	

Information to come

4.4.16 Regions

Region functions create, alter, and retrieve information about regions. A region is an elliptical or polygonal area within a window that can be filled with graphical output. An application uses these functions in conjunction with the clipping functions to create clipping regions. For more information about clipping functions, see "Clipping Functions." The following list briefly describes each region function:

Function	Description
CombineRgn	Combines two existing regions into a new region
CreateEllipticRgn	Creates an elliptical region
CreateEllipticRgnIndirect	Creates an elliptical region
CreatePolygonRgn	Creates a polygonal region
CreatePolyPolygonRgn	Creates a region consisting of a series of closed polygons that are filled as though they were a single polygon
CreateRectRgn	Creates a rectangular region
CreateRectRgnIndirect	Creates a rectangular region
CreateRoundRectRgn	Creates a rounded rectangular region
EqualRgn	Determines whether two regions are identical
FillRgn	Fills the given region with a brush pattern
FloodFill	Fills the display surface within a border
FrameRgn	Draws a border for a given region
GetPolyFillMode	Retrieves the current polygon-filling mode
GetRgnBox	Retrieves the coordinates of the bounding rectangle of a region
InvertRgn	Inverts the colors in a region
OffsetRgn	Moves the given region
PaintRgn	Fills the region with the selected brush pattern
PtInRegion	Tests whether a point is within a region
RectInRegion	Tests whether any part of a rectangle is within a region
SetPolyFillMode	Sets the polygon-filling mode
SetRectRgn	Creates a rectangular region

4.4.17 Text Output

Text functions retrieve text information, alter text alignment, alter text justification, and write text on a device or display surface. GDI uses the current font for text output. The following list briefly describes each text function:

Function	Description
SetTextBrush	Sets the fill pattern for text
DrawText	Draws characters of a specified string
GetTabbedTextExtent	Computes the width and height of a line of text containing tab characters
GrayString	Writes the characters of a string using gray text
TabbedTextOut	Writes a character string with expanded tabs, using the current font
GetTextAlign	Returns a mask of the text alignment flags
GetTextCharacterExtra	Retrieves the current intercharacter spacing
GetTextColor	Retrieves the current text color
GetTextFace	Copies the current font name to a buffer

Chapter	# User 32-bit Design Overview
5	

5.1   Overview 61

5.2   Enhancements to User in the Windows 32-bit API 61

    5.2.1   Input in User32 61

        5.2.1.1   Win3 and PM's input processing problems 61

        5.2.1.2   Goals for input processing under Win32 62

        5.2.1.3   Multiple threads of execution 62

        5.2.1.4   Input pipeline 63

        5.2.1.5   Localized Input State 63

        5.2.1.6   Apis affected by localized input state 64

        5.2.1.7   Activation related z-order 65

        5.2.1.8   Erasing and Drawing a window frame or icon
                    of hung applications 66

    5.2.2   National Language Support (NLS) 66

        5.2.2.1   Unicode 66

        5.2.2.2   Compiling Unicode or Ansi ascii, or mixing 67

        5.2.2.3   Unicode and Ansi ascii type independence 67

        5.2.2.4   Unicode and Ansi ascii window classes and
                    window messages 67

        5.2.2.5   Unicode and Ansi ascii subclassing and
                    hooking 68

    5.2.3   Desktop Objects 68

    5.2.4   Notification messages 69

    5.2.5   Hot Keys 69

    5.2.6   Windows Hook Changes 70

    5.2.7   Misc USER32 api changes 70

        5.2.7.1   String counts 70

        5.2.7.2   Misc deletions 71

        5.2.7.3   wParam is now a DWORD instead of a WORD 71

        5.2.7.4   GetClassWord and GetWindowWord 77

5.3   Overview of User Functionality 78

5.3.1   Accelerators 78

5.3.2   Carets 78

5.3.3   Clipboard 79

5.3.4   Common Dialogs 79

5.3.5   Cursor 80

5.3.6   DDE Manager Libary 80

        5.3.6.1   Desktop apis 82

5.3.7   Dialog Boxes 83

5.3.8   Drag/Drop 84

5.3.9   Error 85

5.3.10   Hook 85

5.3.11   Icon 85

5.3.12   Keyboard 86

5.3.13   MDI 86

5.3.14   Menu 87

5.3.15   Message 88

5.3.16   Mouse 90

5.3.17   Object Linking and Embedding 90

5.3.18   Paint 92

5.3.19   Properties 93

5.3.20   Rectangles 93

5.3.21   Scrolling 94

5.3.22   String 95

5.3.23   Window Management 96

5.1 Overview

This chapter describes the User component of Win32, including changes relative to the Windows 16-bit APIs. Enhancements available in the 32-bit version of User are described first, followed by a high level overview of the functionality available in User32.

The User component consists of the user interface functionality, including window management, dialog box management, and input handling.

5.2 Enhancements to User in the Windows 32-bit API

This section describes the design enhancements made in the 32-bit version of User.

5.2.1 Input in User32

5.2.1.1 Win3 and PM's input processing problems

Windows3 is non-preemptive. Its input system was designed around this fact; only one app is allowed to process input at one time. This makes synchronization of input related state very easy – there is only one copy of the state and it is globally shared throughout the system. It also makes input-ahead (mouse and keyboard) straight forward – input is assigned to an application as it is read out of a shared 'system input queue'; that way who it is assigned to reflects the up-to-the-moment system state, thereby getting perfect 'type-ahead'.

In order to read messages out of this queue in an orderly way and process them one at a time in a serialized fashion, the Win3 system only lets one application read from this system queue at a time – either the application which has the keyboard focus (for key messages), or the application the mouse event is for (for mouse messages). This model is simple, but the down side is that the input system essentially hangs if that choosen application is not reading input for some reason (internally hung, recalcing, repaginating, printing, floodfilling, saving a file, reading a file, waiting on device timeouts, etc). This means the user is cut off, cannot switch to other applications or use any other applications in any way.

This worked ok for Windows since it was non-preemptive. Apps that went into loops needed to call Yield anyway to let other apps run, so as long as they also check for and processed input in these loops, the system would run/ hobble along. Unfortunately the exact same input model was ported to PM, a preemptive environment, where it didn't hold up to user expectations of a true multitasking environment – it turned out to be unacceptable to expect developers to carry the brunt of this problem for the system by writing their apps so their input thread would *always* be ready to read input. Apps commonly aren't written this way, and certainly Windows apps are not.

5.2.1.2 Goals for input processing under Win32

Input processing under Win32 will fix these problems. The goals for input processing under Win32 are:

1. Any app's activity should not affect the user's ability to direct input to any application. This means:

   ■ Apps are allowed to hang and/or do lengthy tasks with any thread that also is the primary processor of input.

   ■ Users can direct input to any application at any time (without being affected by hung applications in the system)

2. Stay semantically compatible with Win16.

5.2.1.3 Multiple threads of execution

Windows apps can painlessly create new threads of execution and operate user interfaces from within those threads of execution. There are no special demands on this type of thread in order to process hardware events and/or window messages.

Under win3, one application essentially represents one thread. Each thread had an input queue created for it automatically as part of the application initialization sequence. This thread would create windows; this thread would process window messages to those windows.

Under Win32, one application may represent many threads. Any thread will be allowed to create a window; the creator thread will be the recipient of window messages sent or posted to windows it created.

PostMessage(hwnd, ...) will post window messages to a queue associated with the thread which created hwnd. This means that each thread that creates a window can potentially have a message queue. This queue is an implied handle to many functions; the 'message queue' is bound to a thread and can be called the 'thread message queue'.

Thread message queues are created *on demand* in the api. This retains the semantics and parameters of the existing apis; thread message queues are not present as external object types.

The apis GetMessage/PeekMessage, which normally return messages from the application queue, now return messages with the thread queue. Threads that call GetMessage/PeekMessage return messages from their own thread message queue.

5.2.1.4 Input pipeline

In an abbreviated sense, here is the order of processing for any input:

1. Hardware device detects input and interrupts the processor

2. Hardware input gets queued.

3. A user mode thread wakes up and gets the next raw hardware event (in a time ordered manner)

4. The user mode thread does some quick checks to determine which application should get the input.

5. The input is put in the appropriate thread input queue. The thread owning the queue is woken up if necessary.

6. The thread reads the input out of the message queue. The thread determines which window it goes to. It creates the finished product – a window message.

7. The window message is returned back to the application, the application processes the input.

Although abbreviated, this is the normal sequence for input processing under Win32. Any application can have multiple threads. Each thread potentially has a message queue associated with it (as mentioned in the section on 'multiple threads of execution'). These threads can read input out of their input queues in a leisurely manner without affecting the performance of any other app or thread and without affecting the user's ability to redirect input to any other window.

5.2.1.5 Localized Input State

The only differing point in this model over win3 or pm is that input ownership is assigned at user input time – when the input is created – instead of when the input is read out of the system queue (win3's model). This change in the order of event processing affects the api significantly, mostly because multiple apps may be processing input simultaneously (input backlog, for example). This means all those input-synchronized states (like keyboard state, focus state, mouse capture state, active state, etc) can no longer be input-synchronized globally. It'd be worthless for one of the applications if two applications called **SetCapture** simultaneously, for example. There are much better examples.

For this reason, each thread has its own input-synchronized state information. In other words, each thread has its own input-synchronized picture of what the mouse capture is, what the active window is, which window has the focus, etc.

The input system splits up input states into two camps (and they are different kinds of state):

■ Local thread based state (thread synchronized state) This state reflects this thread's current input synchronized state, and refers to objects owned by this thread only.

■ focus window

■ active window

■ capture window

■ key state table, etc.

■ User synchronized state. This state reflects what the user sees, which is:

■ Which window is on top

■ Which window is active

■ Which window is receiving input

These are very different kinds of state. 'User synchronized state' is simply which application the user has told the system to direct input to. Thread synchronized state is that state local to that thread only. Thread states change as that thread processes its own input.

The user's job is to direct input at any application on the screen. The system's job is to ensure that the user can do this. An application itself is usually only concerned with its localized state (whether it has the focus, whether it is active, etc). An app is almost never interested in which window the user is directing input to. Therefore, the current host of apis will set/return thread specific input-synchronized state *only*.

5.2.1.6 Apis affected by localized input state

These apis are affected by localized input state. Please refer to the programmers reference for complete descriptions of these apis.

```
HWND APIENTRY SetFocus(HWND);
HWND APIENTRY GetFocus(VOID);
HWND APIENTRY SetActiveWindow(HWND);
HWND APIENTRY GetActiveWindow(VOID);
HWND APIENTRY GetCapture(VOID);
HWND APIENTRY SetCapture(HWND);
VOID APIENTRY ReleaseCapture(VOID);
```

As a general description, the 'get' apis will query only local current thread state. The 'set' apis set state local to the window creator thread. If the current thread did not create the passed window, then the current thread's related input state will get set to NULL as if the input related state where being transferred between threads.

This slightly changes the Win3 semantics of apis that return input-synchronized state. For example this means **SetFocus** can be called with a *hwnd* and return TRUE for success, but a followup call to **GetFocus** might return NULL. More substantially, **GetFocus** will now return NULL if the calling thread does not have a focus window, where under Win3 **GetFocus** almost never returns NULL because some window in the system usually has the keyboard focus.

Mouse capture is affected in an added dimension. The Win32 server input thread cannot know ahead of time when an input thread is going to set the capture and when it isn't. Also, regardless of the input state of any application, the system must allow the user to direct input to any other application at any time. Therefore, the semantics of mouse capture change slightly.

The semantics of how and when the capture changes are not affected; how and when an application gets mouse input is affected. The Win32 server will send all mouse input between a mouse down operation and a mouse up operation to the queue of the thread that created the window the original mouse down went into. This will allow the input thread to perform mouse capture processing as the input is read out of the queue. This means that if the mouse button is down during the mouse capture, the capture window will see all input generated by the mouse, no matter where the mouse is on the screen, until the mouse button goes up or the mouse capture is released. This also means that if a thread sets the mouse capture while the mouse button is up, the mouse capture window will see mouse events only as long as the mouse is over a window that thread created.

5.2.1.7 Activation related z-order

The stage has been set for applications to hang without affecting system performance. Internally the stage has also been set for multiple applications to process input simultaneously. Much input synchronized state has been made thread specific – except for window z-order (overlapping order). Bringing a window to the top, i.e. changing its z-order, is most often associated with a mouse click or some other user inspired operation, thereby being associated with input.

This is *not* thread specific state, but is state related to the global state of the window tree internal to the window manager. A user would not want to feed a mouse click to a hung app, only to have that app process that click later and bring itself on top, covering what work the user was currently doing.

So activation related z-order will not change z-order the application relative to other applications. For example, an activation related z-order would bring a dialog on top of its application, but not on top of all applications.

In most cases only the user can change the z-order of applications, and this is done simply to redirect input to the application of choice. In rare cases applications actually want to cause input to switch to a predetermined window and have that window come to the top. These are cases for 'hard-error' alert windows, application startup, application shutdown, etc. For these cases a special api will be created, called **SetForegroundWindow**.

5.2.1.8 Erasing and Drawing a window frame or icon of hung applications

If a thread or process is hung, the system not provide a user interface for that application. The system will however, erase and frame a hung window in a "not responding color". That may be a new color for the window frame or simply a "disabled" look (halftoned). This is a visual aid to the user that the application is not responding. Additionally, the mouse cursor will change to some shape indicating that the application is not resposive. Additional user interface hints may be employed, such as informing the user when he or she is clicking on an unresponsive application (to be determined). Hung applications cannot be sized or moved, and the system menu is inaccessible. Closing a hung application can be achieved by going to the task manager and clicking the "Close" button for that particular application.

5.2.2 National Language Support (NLS)

Win32 provides a model where applications can display and interact with multi-lingual data, which impacts the api, and multi-lingual users, which impacts the user interface. Win32 will allow a developer to create one application which serves multiple international markets. An application can be created to understand and manipulate multi-lingual data, string sorting, date and currency formatting. Making new international versions of a product should be reduced to replacing language specific strings. In addition, Win32 will allow an isv to ship a product with multiple sets of resources, each keyed off of a locale id. With this mechanism, developers can ship one executable that can be sold into multiple international markets.

5.2.2.1 Unicode

Unicode represents a 16 bit character set – each individual character is 16 bits – these are often called "wide characters". All the modern characters of the world can be fit within this range of 65,536 characters. Only displayable strings need be unicode – those that the user is going to see or edit on the screen. Strings which represent internal identifiers – such as object names, window class names, resource names, etc., do not need unicode equivalents.

Win32 allows 32 bit applications to be either Unicode or Ansi ascii applications, or even mix Unicode and ansi ascii calls. A strict Unicode or Ansi ascii "mode" approach was not taken because of the problems this approach implies. Therefore every api that can take a displayable string has two counterparts – a unicode and an ansi ascii version of that api.

5.2.2.2 Compiling Unicode or Ansi ascii, or mixing

To keep this straightforward, and to allow applications to share code between 16 bit ansi ascii Win3 and 32 bit Win32, a new type was defined TCHAR. This is a compile-dependent type that can refer to an ansi ascii char or a unicode char. Developers using this type can optionally compile for unicode or ansi by #define-ing the UNICODE label. Additional types are LPTSTR, for pointer to a string, a LPTCH for a pointer to a character. The programmers reference currently uses these types for displayable strings and characters.

In addition, ansi ascii apis end with the character "A", and unicode apis end with the character "W". Based on the UNICODE compile switch, apis are #define-ed to link to the "A" or "W" versions of the apis. In addition, applications that want to specifically call unicode or ansi versions of the apis can directly reference the "A" or "W" versions of the apis. For example:

SetWindowText – type independent version (macro)

SetWindowTextA – ansi ascii specific version

SetWindowTextW – unicode specific version

5.2.2.3 Unicode and Ansi ascii type independence

This approach allows existing ansi ascii apps to use existing apis without compile change. It allows developers to share code between 16 and 32 bit platforms when that code is ansi ascii on the 16 bit platform and unicode on the 32 bit platform. It also allows developers to mix types. The full range of string types is therefore:

Character Set	String Pointer	Char Pointer	Char
Win 3	LPSTR	LPCH	CHAR
UNICODE	LPWSTR	LPWCH	WCHAR
Either	LPTSTR	LPTCH	TCHAR

The programmers reference always refers to displayable characters as of the TCHAR type, and non-displayable characters (object names, for example) as the CHAR type. Additionally, the programmers reference does not specifically refer to the "W" or the "A" versions of the apis.

5.2.2.4 Unicode and Ansi ascii window classes and window messages

Window classes can be either ansi ascii or unicode. An app can determine if a window is unicode or ansi ascii by calling the api **IsWindowUnicode**. See the programmers reference for more detail on these.

Window messages also follow the "W" and "A" conventions. If an application sends an ansi ascii winow message to a unicode application, that message will be translated in route so the receiving window procedure understands that message. This will probably not be too common since applications are likely to be all unicode or all ansi ascii, but this does allow mixing. It also allows for the transparent communication between the windows of different applications.

5.2.2.5 Unicode and Ansi ascii subclassing and hooking

This brings up problems with window subclassing. If an ansi ascii subclass proc subclasses a unicode window, automatic translation of text sensitive messages will occur. Likewise, if an ansi ascii application sets a "windows hook" which a unicode application calls, automatic translation of text sensitive messages will occur.

5.2.3 Desktop Objects

The concept of 'desktops' will be added to the api. Desktops are objects which represent a physical display with certain physical display characteristics:

- the name of the physical device
- screen resolution
- color resolution
- hardware mode (like hardware 'text' mode vs 'graphics' mode)

These features will primarily be used for text mode console i/o and for the logon screen, which will run in a separate desktop. The shell may also use this construct and export multiple desktops as a general user interface construct (tbd).

In addition, the desktop api will be exported so applications can control the use of desktops to provide:

- 'desktops' of differing screen/color resolution tradeoffs to take advantage of hardware capabilities. A 3 D rendering program or a entertainment package might tradeoff for more color, where a CAD package might tradeoff for higher resolution.

- 'desktops' on different display devices. This is useful for page monitors (as the mac supports), and other diverse uses such as currency traders' workstations. There have been many requests for this through the years. Applications will be able to use the window management services to produce a consistent user interface on *almost* any desktop.

Desktops on the same display device can be switched between. When an application is selected from the task manager, the desktop that app is running in will be brought forward.

5.2.4 Notification messages

In the USER api there are many functions that send window messages; window messages constitute a very significant part of the available api. All messages in the Win3 api that are sent are synchronous. This means that the sender of the message does not continue executing until the receiver creates a reply to the message. This can cause problems – if a message is sent to a hung application, the sender will hang waiting on the receiver – a condition to be avoided where possible.

USER32 will differentiate between messages that need to be synchronous and messages that don't. Messages that need to be synchronous are messages that return specific values or messages that need to be executed before the sender can continue.

Messages that don't need to be synchronous are usually notification messages. These are messages sent to a window proc so it knows what is going on – no return value expected. For example, this would be the WM_ENABLE message to tell the app it is being disabled, the *WM_SIZE* message to tell the app it has just been sized, etc.

A new api is being introduced for these type of messages, called **SendNotifyMessage** (see programmers reference for in-depth detail). It is very similar to SendMessage except the sender returns immediately rather than waiting for a message reply. The receiver receives this message just as it always had – its window procedure is called directly.

Every message sent from USER32 that has a void return value will be sent as a notification message. This will not affect the receiver of these messages at all. It will affect the sender in that the sender will return right away; possibly before the receiver has processed the message.

5.2.5 Hot Keys

Win32 introduces a set of apis which will allow developers to identify "hot keys", which are key combinations that deserve special attention by the system. When one of these keys is hit, and recognized by the system, a **WM_HOTKEY** message is placed at top of a given thread's input queue, bypassing existing queued input.

Apps use these apis if they want notification of an event independent of their input queue. For example, this api will allow an app to recognize a control-c hot key (a keyboard based cancel or stop action) independent of existing queued key strokes. See **RegisterHotKey, UnregisterHotKey, and the WM_HOTKEY** window message in the programmers reference.

5.2.6 Windows Hook Changes

Windows hooks have a few changes but will basically operate as they do today under win3. First, these are the existing hook calls:

FARPROC SetWindowsHook(int, FARPROC);

BOOLUnhookWindowsHook(int, FARPROC);

DWORD DefHookProc(int, WORD, DWORD, FARPROC FAR *);

Under win3, these calls will set callback procs that the system calls in *any* context. For example, if app B sets an 'input' hook to point to a .dll routine, when app A calls GetMessage this hook will be called *in app A's context*.

Under win3 a .dll doesn't 'attach' to processes – it's just visible. Under Win32, attaching is required. This means if app A needs to call a hook in a .dll not visible to it, the hook code must 'attach' that .dll to that process (call LoadModule on that module in app A's context). Two points come up:

1. The hook code needs a module handle to do this, which is not part of the current api.

2. Most hooks are set for local processing, meaning when app B sets a hook, usually app B is only interested in app B calling that hook. As a result, the existing hook calls will set hooks that are sensitive to only the process that set them. This means these sort of hooks don't need to be put in .dlls but can be put in private code.

Two new apis are being introduced which allow finer control over hooking. They are **SetWindowsHookEx, UnhookWindowsHookEx, and CallNextHookProc**. They allow control over which input queue needs to be hooked. The Win3 apis are macroed on top of these calls, but only allow the calling thread is allowed to hook itself (a difference from Win3). To hook globally or hook other independent input queues, **SetWindowsHookEx** must be used. See the programmers reference for more details.

5.2.7 Misc USER32 api changes

This section documents other miscellaneous changes in the USER api.

5.2.7.1 String counts

Two existing win3 apis take string pointers but do not have maximum string length parameters. These are being added.

- *BOOL* DlgDirSelectComboBox(HWND hDlg, *LPSTR* lpString, int nIDComboBox)

- *BOOL* DlgDirSelect(HWND hDlg, *LPSTR* lpString, int nIDComboBox) these both change to:

- *BOOL* DlgDirSelectComboBoxEx(HWND hDlg, *LPSTR* lpString, *WORD nLength,* int nIDComboBox)

- *BOOL* DlgDirSelectEx(HWND hDlg, *LPSTR* lpString, *WORD nLength,* int nIDComboBox)

5.2.7.2 Misc deletions

These apis will no longer be supported:

- EnableHardwareInput (no replacement)

- SetMessageQueue (not needed since msg queues size dynamically)

- SetSysModalWindow (no replacement)

- GetSysModalWindow (no replacement)

- GetKBCodepage (no replacement)

- GetKeyboardType (no replacement)

- GetWindowTask (being replaced by GetWindowThreadProcessID)

5.2.7.3 wParam is now a DWORD instead of a WORD

This needs to change to allow more information to be passed through window messages. Now that handles are 32 bit entities, more room is needed. This also affected the packing of some messages, which needed rearranging:

WM_ACTIVATE

Old:

- *wParam:* state

- *lParam:* fMinimized, *hwnd*

New:

- *wParam:* state, fMinimized

- *lParam:* hwnd

WM_CHARTOITEM

Old:

- *wParam:* char

- *lParam:* pos, *hwnd*

New:

- *wParam*: char, pos
- *lParam*: hwnd

WM_COMMAND

Old:

- *wParam*: id
- *lParam*: hwnd, cmd

New:

- *wParam*: id, cmd
- *lParam*: hwnd

WM_CTLCOLOR

Old:

- *wParam*: hdc
- *lParam*: hwnd, type

New:

WM_CTLCOLORBTN

WM_CTLCOLORDLG

WM_CTLCOLORLISTBOX

WM_CTLCOLORMSGBOX

WM_CTLCOLORSCROLLBAR

WM_CTLCOLORSTATIC

WM_CTLCOLOREDIT

- *wParam*: hdc
- *lParam*: hwnd

WM_MENUSELECT

Old:

- *wParam*: cmd
- *lParam*: flags, *hMenu*

New:

- *wParam*: cmd, flags
- *lParam*: *hMenu*

WM_MDIACTIVATE (when the message is sent to the MDI client window)

no change.

WM_MDIACTIVATE (when the client window sends this message to the MDI child)

Old:

- *wParam*: fActivate
- *lParam*: hwndDeactivate, hwndActivate

New:

- *wParam*: hwndActivate
- *lParam*: hwndDeactivate

WM_MDISETMENU

Old:

- *wParam*: 0
- *lParam*: hMenuFrame, hMenuWindow

New:

- *wParam*: hMenuFrame
- *lParam*: hMenuWindow

WM_MENUCHAR

Old:

- *wParam*: char
- *lParam*: *hMenu*, fMenu

New:

- *wParam:* char, fMenu
- *lParam: hMenu*

WM_PARENTNOTIFY (also has two cases)

Old case #1:

- *wParam: msg*
- *lParam: id,* hwndChild

New case #1:

- *wParam: msg, id*
- *lParam:* hwndChild

Old case #2:

- *wParam: msg*
- *lParam: x, y*

New case #2:

- *wParam: msg*
- *lParam: x, y*

WM_VKEYTOITEM

Old:

- *wParam:* code
- *lParam* item, *hwnd*

New:

- *wParam:* code, item
- *lParam: hwnd*

EM_GETSEL

Old:

- returns (wStart, wEnd)
- *wParam:* NULL

- *lParam*: NULL

New:

- returns (wStart, wEnd)
- *wParam*: lpdwStart or NULL
- *lParam*: lpdwEnd or NULL

EM_LINESCROLL

Old:

- *wParam*: 0
- *lParam*: nLinesVert, nLinesHorz

New:

- *wParam*: nLinesHorz
- *lParam*: nLinesVert

EM_SETSEL

Old:

- *wParam*: 0
- *lParam*: wStart, wEnd

New:

- *wParam*: wStart
- *lParam*: wEnd

WM_HSCROLL:

WM_VSCROLL:

Old:

- *wParam*: code
- *lParam*: pos, hwnd

New:

- *wParam*: code, pos
- *lParam*: hwnd

WM_DDE_ACK (Posted form only – Sent form is unchanged)

Old:

- wParam:hwnd

- lParam:wStatus, aItem or wStatus, hCommands

New:

- wParam:hwnd

- lParam:hDdeAck

```
typedef   struct DDEACKSTRUCT {
    UINT   wStatus;
    UINT   aItemORhCommands;
}   DDEACKSTRUCT;
```

WM_DDE_ADVISE

Old:

- wParam: hwnd

- lParam: hOptions, aItem

New:

- wParam: hwnd

- lParam: hDdeAdvise

```
typedef struct _DDEADVISESTRUCT {
    HANDLE hOptions;
    UINT#ATOM aItem;
} DDEADVISESTRUCT;
```

WM_DDE_DATA

Old:

- wParam: hwnd

- lParam: hData, aItem

New:

- wParam: hwnd

- lParam: hDdeData

```
typedef struct _DDEDATASTRUCT {
    HANDLE hData;
    UINT#ATOM aItem;
}   DDEDATASTRUCT;
```

WM_DDE_POKE

Old:

- wParam: hwnd

- lParam: hData, aItem

New:

- wParam: hwnd

- lParam: hDdePoke

```
typedef struct _DDEPOKESTRUCT {
    HANDLE hData;
    UINT#ATOM aItem;
} DDEPOKESTRUCT;Callback Function:
```

LPSTR WordBreakFunc(
   LPSTR *lpchEditText*,
   DWORD *ichCurrentWord*,
   DWORD *cbEditText*);

Description

This is the callback function that edit controls call in order to determine where to break words apart from other words.

Parameter	Description
lpchEditText	points to the text string in question.
ichCurrentWord	Specifies the starting position of the current word.
cbEditText	Specifies the length of the buffer in bytes pointed to by *lpchEditText* .

Return Value

Returns a pointer to the next word position.

5.2.7.4 GetClassWord and GetWindowWord

GetClassWord / GetWindowWord under Win3 return handles to these return types:

GCW_HBRBACKGROUND
GCW_HCURSOR
GCW_HICON
GCW_HMODULE
GWW_HINSTANCE
GWW_HWNDPARENT

Handles are 32 bits under Win32. This is a place where Win3 has hardwired these types to words. Under Win32, these GWW_ and GCW_ types that return handles are no longer valid – they have been changed to GWL_ and GCL_ with the same name suffix.

5.3 Overview of User Functionality

This section describes the functionality available in User.

5.3.1 Accelerators

Accelerators are keyboard fast-paths to menu commands.

The Accelerator functions include:

Function	Description
CopyAcceleratorTable	Duplicates an accelerator table
CreateAcceleratorTable	Creates an accelerator table
DestroyAcceleratorTable	Destroys an accelerator table
LoadAccelerators	Loads an accelerator table
TranslateAccelerator	Processes keyboard accelerators for menu commands

5.3.2 Carets

Caret functions affect the Windows caret, which is a flashing line, block, or bitmap that marks a location in a window's client area. The caret is especially useful in word-processing applications to mark a location in text for keyboard editing. These functions create, destroy, display, hide, and alter the blink time of the caret. The following list briefly describes each caret function:

Function	Description
CreateCaret	Creates a caret
CreateCaretEx	Creates carets without horizontal/vertical restrictions.
DestroyCaret	Destroys the current caret
GetCaretBlinkTime	Returns the caret flash rate
GetCaretPos	Returns the current caret position
HideCaret	Removes a caret from a given window
SetCaretBlinkTime	Establishes the caret flash rate
SetCaretPos	Moves a caret to the specified position
ShowCaret	Displays the newly created caret or redisplays a hidden caret

5.3.3 Clipboard

Clipboard functions carry out data interchange between Windows applications. The clipboard is the place for this interchange; it provides a place from which applications can pass data handles to other applications. The following list briefly describes each clipboard function:

Function	Description
ChangeClipboardChain	Removes a window from the chain of clipboard viewers
CloseClipboard	Closes the clipboard
CountClipboardFormats	Gets the number of formats in the clipboard.
EmptyClipboard	Empties the clipboard and reassigns clipboard ownership
EnumClipboardFormats	Enumerates the available clipboard formats
GetClipboardData	Retrieves data from the clipboard
GetClipboardFormatName	Retrieves the clipboard format
GetClipboardOwner	Retrieves the window handle associated with the current clipboard owner
GetClipboardViewer	Retrieves the handle of the first window in the clipboard viewer chain
GetOpenClipboardWindow	Retrieves the handle of the window that has the clipboard open.
GetPriorityClipboardFormat	Retrieves data from the clipboard in the first format in a prioritized format list
IsClipboardFormatAvailable	Returns TRUE if the data in the given format is available
OpenClipboard	Opens the clipboard
RegisterClipboardFormat	Registers a new clipboard format
SetClipboardData	Copies a handle for data
SetClipboardViewer	Adds a handle to the clipboard viewer chain

5.3.4 Common Dialogs

Common dialog-boxes are dialog boxes that applications display by calling a single function rather than by creating a dialog template resource and a corresponding dialog procedure.

In addition to simplifying the development of Windows applications, common dialog boxes assist users by providing a standard set of controls for performing certain operations. As Windows developers begin using the common dialog boxes in their applications, users will find that once they master using the dialog in one application, they will have little trouble performing the same operations in other applications.

The common dialog functions include:

Function	Description
ChooseColor	Creates a standard dialog box for choosing colors.
ChooseFont	Creates a standard font selection dialog box.
FindText	Creates a standard dialog box for text searches.
GetFileTitle	Gets the file title from a file's pathname.
GetOpenFileName	Creates a standard dialog box for opening a file.
GetSaveFileName	Creates a standard dialog box for saving a file.
PrintDlg	Creates a standard dialog box for printing.
ReplaceText	Creates a standard dialog box for text search and replace.

5.3.5 Cursor

Cursor functions set, move, show, hide, and confine the cursor. The cursor is a bitmap, displayed on the display screen, that shows a current location. The following list briefly describes each cursor function:

Function	Description
ClipCursor	Restricts the cursor to a given rectangle
CreateCursor	Creates a cursor from two bit masks
CreateDIBCursor	Creates a cursor from a device-independent bitmap.
DestroyCursor	Destroys a cursor created by the CreateCursor function
GetClipCursor	Gets the rectangle that the cursor has been constrained to.
GetCursor	Retrieves the handle of the current cursor.
GetCursorPos	Stores the cursor position (in screen coordinates)
LoadCursor	Loads a cursor from the resource file
SetCursor	Sets the cursor shape
SetCursorPos	Sets the position of the cursor
ShowCursor	Increases or decreases the cursor display count

5.3.6 DDE Manager Libary

Dynamic data exchange is a form of interprocess communication that uses shared memory to exchange data between applications. Applications can use DDE for

one-time data transfers and for ongoing exchanges in which the applications send
updates to one another as new data becomes available.

Dynamic data exchange differs from the clipboard data-transfer mechanism that is
also part of the Windows operating system. One difference is that the clipboard is
almost always used as a one-time response to a specific action by the user—such as
choosing the Paste command from a menu. Although DDE may also be initiated by a
user, it typically continues without the user's further involvement.

The DDEML provides a set of application programming interface (API) elements that
simplifies the task of adding DDE capability to a Windows application. Instead of
sending, posting, and processing DDE messages directly, an application uses the
functions provided by the DDEML to manage DDE conversations. (A DDE
conversation is the interaction between client and server applications.) The DDEML
also provides a facility for managing the strings and data that are shared among DDE
applications. Instead of using atoms and pointers to shared memory objects, DDE
applications create and exchange string handles, which identify strings, and data
handles, which identify global memory objects. DDEML provides service that makes
it possible for a server application to register the service names that it supports. The
names are broadcast to other applications in the system, which can then use the names
to connect to the server. The DDEML also ensures compatibility among DDE
applications by forcing them to implement the DDE protocol in a consistent manner.

Existing applications that use the message-based DDE protocol are fully compatible
with those that use the DDEML. That is, an application that uses message-based DDE
can establish conversations and perform transactions with applications that use the
DDEML. Because of the many advantages of the DDEML, new applications should
use it rather than the DDE messages.

The DDEML functions include:

Function	Description
DdeAbandonTransaction	Cancels an assync transaction
DdeAccessData	Converts a data handle to a pointer
DdeAddData	Adds data to/reallocs, data handles
DdeCallback	Application provided callback for DDEML.
DdeClientTransaction	Starts a DDE transaction from the client side
DdeCmpStringHandles	Compares two strings
DdeConnect	Initiates a DDE conversation
DdeConnectList	Initiates multiple DDE conversations
DdeCreateDataHandle	Creates/initializes a data handle
DdeCreateStringHandle	Atomizes a string

Function	Description
DdeDisconnect	Terminates a conversation
DdeDisconnectList	Terminates a list of conversations
DdeEnableCallback	Turns on/off interruptable callbacks
DdeFreeDataHandle	Releases interest in a data handle
DdeFreeStringHandle	Frees an atom
DdeGetData	Copies data from a data handle to a buffer
DdeGetLastError	Retrieves last DDEML error
DdeInitialize	Sets up DLL, delcares callback function address
DdeKeepStringHandle	Increments atom use count
DdeNameService	Registers/unregisters runtime DDE services
DdePostAdvise	Updates server's links
DdeQueryConvInfo	Extracts conversation/transaction information
DdeQueryNextServer	Enumerates conversations in a list
DdeQueryString	Retrieves string from string handle
DdeSetUserHandle	Ties a 32 bit value to a conversation/transaction
DdeUnaccessData	Releases pointer retrieved by DdeAccessData()
DdeUnitialize	Shuts down DDEML instance
FreeDDElParam	Frees a structure associated with lParam packing.
PackDDElParam	Creates a structure for lParam packing
UnpackDDElParam	Unpacks a structure for lParam packing.

5.3.6.1 Desktop apis

These apis create, destroy, set, query, desktops and their attributes. Included are apis to query available device names and device attributes. The enumeration apis are prototyped in the Windows object enumeration style (callbacks). For a detailed look at these apis look at the USER ammers reference.

Function	Description
CloseDesktop	Closes a desktop object.
CreateDesktop	Creates a desktop object.
EnumDesktops	Enumerates desktop objects.
GetDesktopAttrs	Gets information about a desktop.
GetDesktopTypes	Gets information about desktop types.
GetThreadDesktop	Gets the desktop associated with the current thread.
OpenDesktop	Opens a desktop.

Function	Description
SetDeskWallpaper	Sets the background bitmap for the desktop.
SetThreadDesktop	Sets the desktop for the current thread.
SwitchDesktop	Switches to a different desktop.

5.3.7 Dialog Boxes

Dialog-box functions create, alter, test, and destroy dialog boxes and controls within dialog boxes. A dialog box is a temporary window that Windows creates for special-purpose input, and then destroys immediately after use. An application typically uses a dialog box to prompt the user for additional information about a current command selection. The following list briefly describes each dialog function:

Function	Description
CheckDlgButton	Places/removes a check, or changes the state of the three-state button
CheckRadioButton	Checks a specified button and removes checks from all others
CreateDialog	Creates a modeless dialog box
CreateDialogIndirect	Creates a modeless dialog box from a template
CreateDialogIndirectParam	Creates a modeless dialog box from a template and passes data to it when it is created
CreateDialogParam	Creates a modeless dialog box and passes data to it when it is created
DefDlgProc	Provides default processing for those dialog-box messages that an application does not process
DialogBox	Creates a modal dialog box
DialogBoxIndirect	Creates a modal dialog box from a template
DialogBoxIndirectParam	Creates a modal dialog box from a template and passes data to it when it is created
DialogBoxParam	Creates a modal dialog box and passes data to it when it is created
DlgDirList	Fills the list box with names of files matching a path
DlgDirListComboBox	Fills a combo box with names of files matching a path
DlgDirSelectComboBoxEx	Copies the current selection from a combo box to a string
DlgDirSelectEx	Copies the current selection from a list box to a string

Function	Description
EndDialog	Frees resources and destroys windows associated with a modal dialog box
GetDialogBaseUnits	Retrieves the base dialog units used by Windows when creating a dialog box
GetDlgCtrlID	Returns the ID value of a control window
GetDlgItem	Retrieves the handle of a dialog item from the given dialog box
GetDlgItemInt	Translates the control text of an item into an integer value
GetDlgItemText	Copies an item's control text into a string
GetNextDlgGroupItem	Returns the window handle of the next item in a group
GetNextDlgTabItem	Returns the window handle of the next or previous item
IsDialogMessage	Determines whether a message is intended for the given dialog box
IsDlgButtonChecked	Tests whether a button is checked
MapDialogRect	Converts the dialog-box coordinates to client coordinates
MessageBoxEx	Creates a message box using resources for a specific language.
SendDlgItemMessage	Sends a message to an item within a dialog box
SetDlgItemInt	Sets the caption or text of an item to a string that represents an integer
SetDlgItemText	Sets the caption or text of an item to a string
MessageBox	Creates a window with the given text and caption

5.3.8 Drag/Drop

The Drag/Drop functions allow the user the drag files from the file manager to an application. These functions include:

Function	Description
DragAcceptFiles	Used to accept dropped files.
DragFinish	Signifies the end of a drag operation.
DragQueryFile	Gets the name of a dropped file.
DragQueryPoint	Retrieves the mouse position where a file was dropped.

5.3.9 Error

Error functions display errors and prompt the user for a response. The following list briefly describes each error function:

Function	Description
FlashWindow	Flashes the window by inverting its active/inactive state
FormatMessage	Formats an message for display.
GetLastError	Gets the error information for the previous error
MessageBeep	Generates a beep on the system speaker
SetLastError	Sets the current error information

5.3.10 Hook

Hook functions manage system hooks, which are shared resources that install a specific type of filter function. A filter function is an application-supplied callback function, specified by the **SetWindowsHook** function, that processes events before they reach any application's message loop. Windows sends messages generated by a specific type of event to filter functions installed by the same type of hook. The following list briefly describes each hook function:

Function	Description
CallMsgFilter	Passes a message and other data to the current message-filter function
CallNextHookProc	Calls the next hook in the chain
CallWndProc	Filters messages sent by SendMessage
SetWindowsHook	Installs a system or application filter function
SetWindowsHookEx	Installs a system or application filter function
UnhookWindowsHook	Removes a Windows filter function from a filter-function chain
UnhookWindowsHookEx	Removes a system or application filter function

5.3.11 Icon

The icon functions are used to manipulate icons. They include:

Function	Description
CreateDIBIcon	Creates and icon from a device-independent bitmap.
CreateIcon	Creates an icon with the specified attributes
CreateIconFromResource	Creates an icon based on a resource.

Function	Description
CreateIconIndirect	Creates an icon based on a structure.
DestroyIcon	Destroys an icon
DrawIcon	Draws an icon
ExtractIcon	Retrieves the handle of an icon from a file with resources.
GetIconInfo	Gets information about an icon.
LoadIcon	Loads an icon resource
LookupIconFromDirectory	Loads the most appropriate icon from a set of icons.

5.3.12 Keyboard

The keyboard functions allow an application to get/set keyboard state.

These functions include:

Function	Description
GetAsyncKeyState	Returns interrupt-level information about the key state
GetKeyboardState	Copies an array that contains the state of keyboard keys
GetKeyNameText	Retrieves a string containing the name of a key from a list maintained by the keyboard driver
GetKeyState	Retrieves the state of a virtual key
MapVirtualKey	Accepts a virtual-key code or scan code for a key and returns the corresponding scan code, virtual-key code, or ASCII value
OemKeyScan	Maps OEM ASCII codes 0 through 0x0FF into the OEM scan codes and shift states
SetKeyboardState	Sets the state of keyboard keys by altering values in an array
VkKeyScan	Translates an ANSI character to the corresponding virtual-key code and shift state for the current keyboard
ToAscii	Translates a virtual-key code to the corresponding ANSI character or characters

5.3.13 MDI

Windows multiple document interface (MDI) provides applications with a standard interface for displaying multiple documents within the same instance of an application. An MDI application creates a frame window which contains a client window in place of its client area. An application creates an MDI client window by calling **CreateWindow** with the class MDICLIENT and passing a **CLIENTCREATESTRUCT** data structure as the function's *lpParam* parameter.

This client window in turn can own multiple child windows, each of which displays a separate document. An MDI application controls these child windows by sending messages to its client window.

The MDI functions include:

Function	Description
ArrangeIconicWindows	Arranges minimized (iconic) child windows
DefMDIChildProc	Provides default processing those for MDI child window messages an that application does not process
TranslateMDISysAccel	Processes multiple document interface (MDI) child window command accelerators

5.3.14 Menu

Menu functions create, modify, and destroy menus. A menu is an input tool in a Windows application that offers users one or more choices, which they can select with the mouse or keyboard. An item in a menu bar can display a pop-up menu, and any item in a pop-up menu can display another pop-up menu. In addition, a pop-up menu can appear anywhere on the screen. The following list briefly describes each menu function:

Function	Description
AppendMenu	Appends a menu item to a menu
ChangeMenu	Changes a menu.
CheckMenuItem	Places or removes checkmarks next to pop-up menu items
CreateMenu	Creates an empty menu
CreatePopupMenu	Creates an empty pop-up menu
DeleteMenu	Removes a menu item and destroys any associated pop-up menus
DestroyMenu	Destroys the specified menu
DrawMenuBar	Redraws a menu bar
EnableMenuItem	Enables, disables, or grays a menu item
GetMenu	Retrieves a handle to the menu of a specified window
GetMenuCheckMarkDimensions	Retrieves the dimensions of the default menu checkmark bitmap
GetMenuItemCount	Returns the count of items in a menu
GetMenuItemID	Returns the item's identification

Function	Description
GetMenuState	Obtains the status of a menu item
GetMenuString	Copies a menu label into a string
GetSubMenu	Retrieves the menu handle of a pop-up menu
GetSystemMenu	Accesses the System menu for copying and modification
HiliteMenuItem	Highlights or removes the highlighting from a top-level (menu-bar) menu item
InsertMenu	Inserts a menu item in a menu
IsMenu	
LoadMenu	Loads a menu resource
LoadMenuIndirect	Loads a menu resource
ModifyMenu	Changes a menu item
RemoveMenu	Removes an item from a menu but does not destroy it
SetMenu	Specifies a new menu for a window
SetMenuItemBitmaps	Associates bitmaps with a menu item for display when an item is and is not checked
TrackPopupMenu	Displays a pop-up menu at a specified screen location and tracks user interaction with the menu

5.3.15 Message

Message functions read and process Windows messages in an application's message queue. Messages are the input to the application. They represent events that the application may need to respond to. A message is a data structure that contains a message identifier and message parameters. The content of the parameters varies with the message type. The following list briefly describes each message function:

Function	Description
CallWindowProc	Passes message information to the specified function
DefFrameProc	Provides default processing for those multiple document interface (MDI) frame window messages that an application does not process
DefWindowProc	Provides default processing for those window messages that an application does not process
DispatchMessage	Passes a message to the window function of the specified window
EnumQueueMessages	Enumerates all messages in thread's message queue

Function	Description
GetMessage	Retrieves a message from the specified range of messages
GetMessageExtraInfo	Retrieves information about a hardware message
GetMessagePos	Returns the position of the mouse at the time the last message was retrieved
GetMessageTime	Returns the time at which the last message was retrieved
GetQueueStatus	Returns information about what messages are in the queue
InSendMessage	Determines whether the current window function is processing a message passed to it through a call to the SendMessage function
InsertQueueMessage	Inserts a message into the message queue
PeekMessage	Checks the application queue and places the message appropriately
PeekMessageEx	Peeks for messages with finer filtering
PostAppMessage	Posts a message to the application
PostMessage	Places a message in the application queue
PostQuitMessage	Posts a WM_QUIT message to the application
PostThreadMessage	Posts a message to a thread.
RegisterHotKey	Registers a hot key for the current thread
RegisterWindowMessage	Defines a window message that is unique throughout the system
ReplyMessage	Replies to a message
SendMessage	Sends a message to a window or windows
SendNotifyMessage	Sends a message synchronously to the same thread and asynchronously to other threads
SetMessageQueue	Creates a new message queue of a different size
SetQueueMsg	Sets the contents of the specified message
TranslateMessage	Translates virtual key-stroke messages into character messages
UnregisterHotKey	Unregisters a hot key previously registered for the current thread
WaitMessage	Yields control to other applications

5.3.16 Mouse

The mouse functions allow an application to get information about mouse state.
These functions include:

Function	Description
GetCapture	Returns a handle to the window with the mouse capture
GetDoubleClickTime	Retrieves the current double-click time for the mouse
ReleaseCapture	Releases mouse input and restores normal input processing
SetCapture	Causes mouse input to be sent to a specified window
SetDoubleClickTime	Sets the double-click time for the mouse
SwapMouseButton	Reverses the meaning of left and right mouse buttons
GetInputState	Returns TRUE if there is mouse or keyboard input

5.3.17 Object Linking and Embedding

An application that uses OLE can cooperate with other OLE applications to produce a
document containing different kinds of data, all of which can be easily manipulated
by the user. The user editing such a document is able to improve the document by
using the best features of many different applications. An application that implements
OLE gives its users the ability to move away from an application-centered view of
computing and toward a document-centered view. In application-centered computing
the tool used to complete a task is often a single application; whereas, in
document-centered computing, a user can combine the advantages of many tools to
complete a job.

A document that uses linked and embedded objects can contain many kinds of data in
many different formats; such a document is called a compound document. A
compound document uses the facilities of different OLE applications to manipulate
the different kinds of data it displays. Any kind of data format can be incorporated
into a compound document; with little or no extra code, OLE applications can even
support data formats that have not yet been invented. The user working with a
compound document does not need to know which data formats are compatible with
one another or how to find and start any applications that created the data. Whenever
a user chooses to work with part of a compound document, the application
responsible for that part of the document starts automatically.

The OLE functions include:

Function	Description
OleActivate	
OleBlockServer	

Information to come

Function	Description
OleClone	
OleClose	
OleCopyCompleted	
OleCopyFromLink	
OleCopyToClipboard	
OleCreate	
OleCreateFromClip	
OleCreateFromFile	
OleCreateFromTemplate	
OleCreateLinkFromClip	
OleCreateLinkFromFile	
OleDelete	
OleDraw	
OleEnumFormats	
OleEnumObjects	
OleEqual	
OleExecute	
OleGetData	
OleGetLinkUpdateOptions	
OleLoadFromStream	
OleLockServer	
OleMarkForCopy	
OleObjectConvert	
OleQueryBounds	
OleQueryClientVersion	
OleQueryCreateFromClip	
OleQueryLinkFromClip	
OleQueryName	
OleQueryOpen	
OleQueryOutOfDate	
OleQueryProtocol	
OleQueryReleaseError	
OleQueryReleaseMethod	
OleQueryReleaseStatus	

Information to come

Function	Description
OleQueryServerVersion	
OleQuerySize	
OleQueryType	
OleReconnect	
OleRegisterClientDoc	
OleRegisterServer	
OleRegisterServerDoc	
OleRelease	
OleRename	
OleRenameClientDoc	
OleRenameServerDoc	
OleRequestData	
OleRevertClientDoc	
OleRevertServerDoc	
OleRevokeClientDoc	
OleRevokeObject	
OleRevokeServer	
OleRevokeServerDoc	
OleSavedClientDoc	
OleSavedServerDoc	
OleSaveToStream	
OleSetBounds	
OleSetColorScheme	
OleSetData	
OleSetHostNames	
OleSetLinkUpdateOptions	
OleSetTargetDevice	
OleUnblockServer	
OleUnlockServer	
OleUpdate	

Information to come

5.3.18 Paint

Painting functions prepare a window for painting and carry out some useful general-purpose graphics operations. Although all the paint functions are specifically intended for the system display, some can be used for other output devices. The following list briefly describes each painting function:

Function	Description
BeginPaint	Prepares a window for painting
EndPaint	Marks the end of window repainting
ExcludeUpdateRgn	Prevents a region from being painted.
GetDC	Retrieves the display context for the client area
GetDCEx	Gets a dc with control over clipping
GetUpdateRect	Copies the dimensions of a window region's bounding rectangle
GetUpdateRgn	Copies a window's update region
GetWindowDC	Retrieves the display context for an entire window
InvalidateRect	Marks a rectangle for repainting
InvalidateRgn	Marks a region for repainting
ReleaseDC	Releases a display context
ValidateRect	Releases the specified rectangle from repainting
ValidateRgn	Releases the specified region from repainting

5.3.19 Properties

Property functions create and access a window's property list. A property list is a storage area that contains handles for data that the application wishes to associate with a window. The following list briefly describes each property function:

Function	Description
EnumProps	Passes the properties of a window to an enumeration function
EnumPropsEx	Enumerates properties, passing data to the callback.
GetProp	Retrieves a handle associated with a string from the window property list
RemoveProp	Removes a string from the property list
SetProp	Copies a string and a data handle to a window's property list

5.3.20 Rectangles

Rectangle functions alter and obtain information about rectangles in a window's client area. In Windows, a rectangle is defined by a **RECT** data structure. The structure contains two points: the upper-left and lower-right corners of the rectangle. The sides of a rectangle extend from these two points and are parallel to the *x*- and *y*-axes. The following list briefly describes each rectangle function:

Function	Description
CopyRect	Makes a copy of an existing rectangle
EqualRect	Determines whether two rectangles are equal
InflateRect	Expands or shrinks the specified rectangle
IntersectRect	Finds the intersection of two rectangles
IsRectEmpty	Determines whether the specified rectangle is empty
OffsetRect	Moves a given rectangle
PtInRect	Indicates whether a specified point lies within a given rectangle
SetBoundsRect	Controls bounds accumulation.
SetRect	Fills in a rectangle data structure
SetRectEmpty	Sets a rectangle to an empty rectangle
SubtractRect	Subtracts one rect from another.
UnionRect	Stores the union of two rectangles
DrawFocusRect	Draws a rectangle in the style used to indicate focus
FillRect	Fills a given rectangle by using the specified brush
FrameRect	Draws a border for the given rectangle
InvertRect	Inverts the display bits of the specified rectangle
Rectangle	Draws a rectangle
RoundRect	Draws a rounded rectangle

5.3.21 Scrolling

Scrolling functions control the scrolling of a window's contents and control the window's scroll bars. Scrolling is the movement of data in and out of the client area at the request of the user. It is a way for the user to see a document or graphic in parts if Windows cannot fit the entire document or graphic inside the client area. A scroll bar allows the user to control scrolling. The following list briefly describes each scrolling function:

Function	Description
EnableScrollBar	Enables or disables scroll-bar arrows
GetScrollPos	Retrieves the current position of the scroll-bar thumb

Function	Description
GetScrollRange	Copies the minimum and maximum scroll-bar positions for given scroll-bar positions for a specified scroll
ScrollDC	Scrolls a rectangle of bits horizontally and vertically
ScrollWindow	Moves the contents of the client area
ScrollWindowEx	ScrollWindow with additional functionality.
SetScrollPos	Sets the scroll-bar thumb
SetScrollRange	Sets the minimum and maximum scroll-bar positions
ShowScrollBar	Displays or hides a scroll bar and its controls

5.3.22 String

The string functions allow an application to manipulate strings, and convert between various character sets.

The string functions include:

Function	Description
AnsiLower	Converts a character string to lowercase
AnsiLowerBuff	Converts a character string in a buffer to lowercase
AnsiNext	Returns a long pointer to the next character in a string
AnsiPrev	Returns a long pointer to the previous character in a string
AnsiToOem	Converts an ANSI string to an OEM character string
AnsiToOemBuff	Converts an ANSI string in a buffer to an OEM character string
AnsiUpper	Converts a character string to uppercase
AnsiUpperBuff	Converts a character string in a buffer to uppercase
CharLower	Converts the given string to lower case
CharLowerBuff	Converts the given string to lower case
CharNext	Moves to the next character in a string
CharPrev	Moves to the previous character in a string
CharToOem	Translates the given string to an OEM character set
CharToOemBuff	Translates the given string to an OEM character set
CharUpper	Converts the given string to upper case
CharUpperBuff	Converts the given string to upper case
IsCharAlpha	Determines whether a character is alphabetical
IsCharAlphaNumeric	Determines whether a character is alphanumeric

Function	Description
IsCharLower	Determines whether a character is lowercase
IsCharUpper	Determines whether a character is uppercase
LoadString	Loads a string resource
lstrcat	Concatenates two strings identified by long pointers
lstrcmp	Performs a case-sensitive comparison of two strings identified by long pointers
lstrcmpi	Performs a case-insensitive comparison of two strings identified by long pointers
lstrcpy	Copies one string to another; both strings are identified by long pointers
lstrlen	Determines the length of a string identified by a long pointer
OemToAnsi	Converts an OEM character string to an ANSI string
OemToAnsiBuff	Converts an OEM character string in a buffer to an ANSI string
OemToChar	Translates the given string from an OEM character set
OemToCharBuff	Translates the given string from an OEM character set
wsprintf	Formats and stores a series of characters and values in a buffer
wvsprintf	Formats and stores a series of characters and values in a buffer

5.3.23 Window Management

The window management functions allow an application to create, display, move, size, destroy and otherwise manage windows.

The window functions include:

Function	Description
AdjustWindowRect	Computes the size of a window to fit a given client area
AdjustWindowRectEx	Computes a required size for a window.
AnyPopup	Indicates whether any pop-up window exists
CloseWindow	Hides the specified window or minimizes it
EnableWindow	Enables and disables mouse and keyboard input throughout the application
EnumChildWindows	Enumerates the child windows that belong to a specific parent window

Function	Description
EnumThreadWindows	Enumerates windows for a thread.
EnumWindows	Enumerates windows on the display
FindWindow	Returns the handle of a window with the given class and caption
GetActiveWindow	Returns a handle to the active window
GetClassInfo	Retrieves information about a specified class
GetClassLong	Retrieves window-class information from a WNDCLASS structure
GetClassName	Retrieves a window-class name
GetClassWord	Retrieves window-class information from a WNDCLASS structure
GetClientRect	Copies the coordinates of a window's client area
GetDesktopHwnd	
GetDesktopWindow	Gets the current desktop window handle.
GetFocus	Retrieves the handle of the window that currently owns the input focus
GetLastActivePopup	Determines which popup window owned by another window was most recently active
GetNextWindow	Returns a handle to the next or previous window
GetParent	Retrieves the handle of the specified window's parent window
GetTopWindow	Returns a handle to the top-level child window
GetWindow	Returns a handle from the window manager's list
GetWindowLong	Retrieves information about a window
GetWindowRect	Copies the dimensions of an entire window
GetWindowRgn	Gets the window clipping region.
GetWindowTask	Returns the handle of a task associated with a window
GetWindowText	Copies a window caption into a buffer
GetWindowTextLength	Returns the length (in characters) of the given window's caption or text
GetWindowThreadProcessIdnew	Retrieves the ids of the thread and process for a window.
GetWindowWord	Retrieves information about a window

Function	Description
IsChild	Determines whether a window is the descendent of a specified window
IsIconic	Specifies whether a window is open or closed (iconic)
IsWindow	Determines whether a window is a valid, existing window
IsWindowEnabled	Determines whether the specified window is enabled for mouse and keyboard input
IsWindowUnicode	Determines whether the window is ANSI or Unicode
IsWindowVisible	Determines whether the given window is visible
LockWindowUpdate	Enables drawing in a window.
OpenIcon	Opens the specified window
PtVisible	Tests whether a point lies in a region
RectVisible	Determines whether part of a rectangle lies in a region
RedrawWindow	Updates the specified area.
RegisterClass	Registers a window class
SetActiveWindow	Makes a window the active window
SetClassLong	Replaces information in a WNDCLASS structure
SetClassWord	Replaces information in a WNDCLASS structure
SetFocus	Assigns the input focus to a specified window
SetInputFocus	Sets the input focus to the specified thread or window
SetParent	Changes the parent window of a child window
SetSysModalWindow	Makes the specified window a system modal window
SetWindowLong	Changes a window attribute
SetWindowText	Sets the window caption or text
SetWindowWord	Changes a window attribute
ShowOwnedPopups	Shows or hides all pop-up windows
ShowWindow	Displays or removes the given window
UnregisterClass	Removes a window class from the window-class table

Function	Description
UpdateWindow	Notifies the application when parts of a window need redrawing
CreateWindow	Creates overlapped, pop-up, and child windows"
CreateWindowEx	Creates overlapped, pop-up, and child windows with extended styles"
DestroyWindow	Destroys a window
BeginDeferWindowPos	Initializes memory used by the DeferWindowPos function
BringWindowToTop	Brings a window to the top of a stack of overlapped windows
DeferWindowPos	Records positioning information for a window to be moved or resized by the EndDeferWindowPos function
EndDeferWindowPos	Positions or sizes several windows simultaneously based on information recorded by the DeferWindowPos function
IsZoomed	Determines whether a window is maximized
MoveWindow	Changes the size and position of a window
SetWindowPos	Changes the size, position, and ordering of child or pop-up windows
WindowFromPoint	Identifies the window containing a specified point
ScreenToClient	Converts screen coordinates into client coordinates
ChildWindowFromPoint	Determines which child window contains a specific point
ClientToScreen	Converts client coordinates into screen coordinates

Chapter	Memory
6	

6.1	About Memory	. . . .	103
6.2	Global and Local API	. . . .	104
6.3	Standard C library	. . . .	104
6.4	Heap API	. . . .	104
6.5	Virtual API	. . . .	104
6.6	About shared memory	. . . .	105
	6.6.1 Using the Virtual API	. . . .	105
	6.6.1.1 Using file mapping for shared memory	. . . .	108
6.7	Summary	. . . .	111
	6.7.1 Virtual API	. . . .	111
	6.7.2 Heap API	. . . .	112
	6.7.3 File Mapping API	. . . .	112

6.1 About Memory

In Win32, each process has a unique 32-bit linear virtual address space that allows it to address up to 4 gigabytes of memory. The 2 GB in low memory are available to the user, and the 2 GB in high memory are reserved for the kernel. The virtual addresses used by a process do not represent the actual physical location of an object in memory. Instead, the kernel maintains a map for each process that translates virtual addresses into the corresponding physical addresses.

The virtual address space of each process is much larger than the total physical memory available to all processes. To increase the size of physical storage, the kernel uses the disk for backing storage. The total amount of storage available to all executing processes is the sum of physical memory (RAM) and the free space on disk available to the paging file. Physical storage and the virtual (or logical) address space of each process are organized into pages of 4 KB each. To maximize its flexibility in managing memory, the kernel can move the pages of physical memory to and from a paging file on disk. When a page is moved in physical memory, the kernel updates the page maps of the affected processes. Each process is guaranteed a minimum number of pages in physical memory, but the kernel has complete flexibility to move any page of memory to the paging file according to a least recently used algorithm. It is not possible for a process to lock a page so it cannot be swapped out to the paging file. Manipulation of physical memory by the kernel is completely transparent to applications, which deal only in their virtual address spaces.

The pages of a process' virtual address space can be in one of three states: free, reserved, or committed.

Free   Free pages are those that are available to be committed or reserved.

Reserved   A reserved page is one where the logical page has been allocated but no physical storage has been allocated for the page. The effect of this is to reserve a range of virtual addresses that then cannot be used by other allocation operations (i.e ., by malloc, **LocalAlloc**, etc.) without first being released. Attempting to read or write a free page or a reserved page results in a page fault exception. A reserved page may be freed or committed.

Committed   A committed page is one for which physical storage (in memory or on disk) has been allocated. It may be protected to allow no access or read only access, or it may have read and write access. A committed page may be decommitted to release its storage, at which point it becomes a reserved page.

6.2 Global and Local API

A process can allocate memory using the Global and Local API, or using the functions of the standard C library. Memory allocated by any of these functions is in private, committed pages with read/write access. Private means that the memory cannot be accessed by other processes. The GMEM_DDESHARE flag with **GlobalAlloc** is ignored. Applications that need shared memory for DDE must use the DDE functions which have their own internal mechanisms for creating DDE shared memory objects. Applications that require shared memory for other purposes must use file mapping to provide named shared memory as described below.

The Global and Local API allow you to allocate a block of memory of any size (limited only by the available physical memory including backing store). However, the change from a 16-bit segmented memory model to the 32-bit virtual memory model has made some of the functions and their options unnecessary or meaningless. For instance, there are no longer near and far pointers, since both local and global allocations return 32-bit virtual addresses.

6.3 Standard C library

Memory can also be manipulated using the functions of the standard C library (malloc, free, etc.). With previous versions of Windows, these functions had potential dangers that do not exist for Win32. For example, malloc allocates a fixed pointer that did not allow the memory management advantages of moveable memory. With virtual memory, this is no longer a problem. Similarly, the confusions around near and far pointers are no longer relevant. So unless you want to allocate discardable memory, it is reasonable to use the standard C library functions.

6.4 Heap API

The Heap API provides another way to allocate memory. A process can create a private heap and then use a separate set of functions to manage the memory in that heap. The heap has an initial size of committed pages and additional reserved pages of the virtual address space. The heap grows automatically as memory is allocated from it (up to the limits of available physical storage and the reserved address space). There is no difference between memory allocated from a private heap and that allocated using the Global, Local, and C library functions.

6.5 Virtual API

The Virtual API allows a process to manipulate or determine the status of pages of its virtual address space. For example, using **VirtualAlloc** , you could reserve or commit a block of pages; and if committing pages, you could specify read/write, read only, or no access. The API also allows you to specify the desired base address of the allocated pages. Pages committed by **VirtualAlloc** can be accessed (if they are not protected) using normal pointer references. Other functions enable querying or modifying the access protection of any page in the process' virtual address space. This allows you, for example, to allocate read/write pages to store sensitive data, and then change the access to read only or no access to protect against accidental overwriting.

6.6 About shared memory

All memory allocated by the methods described above (**GlobalAlloc, LocalAlloc**, malloc, **HeapAlloc**, or **VirtualAlloc**) is inaccessible to other processes. Note that memory allocated by DLL code is in the address space of the process that invoked the DLL, and is not accessible by other processes using the same DLL.

Shared memory is implemented by file mapping, which is a two step process. First a file mapping object must be created; and then using that object, a view of the file can be mapped into the virtual address space of a process. A file mapping object can be created to map a named file in the file system or to map a portion of the system's paging file. You can specify the size in bytes of the mapped region, and the read and write access to the region. The mapping object is referred to by a handle, which is used to map a view of the file. This handle can be inherited by child processes or communicated to other processes to be duplicated. Alternatively, a name can be associated with a file mapping object. This name can then be used by other processes to obtain a handle to the object. To implement shared memory, each process must use a handle to the same file mapping object to map a view of the file into its virtual address space. Each view may consist of all or any part of the file. If multiple processes map views of a single mapping object, the views are guaranteed to be coherent. However, if multiple mapping objects are created for the same file, the views are not guaranteed to be coherent.

6.6.1 Using the Virtual API

Many applications will be able to satisfy their memory needs using the standard allocation functions (**GlobalAlloc, LocalAlloc** , malloc, etc). However, the additional functionality of the Virtual API makes it useful in some situations. One useful feature is the ability to reserve a contiguous block of address space from which pages can be committed as needed. This allows you to create dynamic data structures that can grow to the limits of the reserved region without committing pages until they are needed.

VirtualAlloc allocates pages of memory that are aligned on page boundaries. You can reserve or commit one or more free pages, or you can commit one or more previously reserved pages. Reserved pages have no physical storage, and committed pages are backed by storage that is visible only to the allocating process. Reserved pages are always allocated with a protection status of PAGE_NOACCESS; while committed pages may be allocated with read/write, read only, or no access. When pages are committed, backing storage is allocated in the paging file, but each page is initialized and loaded into physical memory only at the first attempt to read or write that page. The storage for committed pages will be released automatically when the process terminates. To free storage (MEM_DECOMMIT) or to release reserved pages (MEM_RELEASE) prior to termination, you would use **VirtualFree** as follows:

Release   Reserved or committed pages can be released only by freeing the entire block that was initially reserved by **VirtualAlloc**. The state of all pages in the block must be the same (either all committed or all reserved). If all of the pages in the block are committed, you can specify MEM_DECOMMIT | MEM_RELEASE to release them. If only part of the pages in the block are committed, these pages must first be decommitted before the entire block can be released. Once released, the pages are free and inaccessible.

Decommit   Committed pages can be decommitted to release their storage so it available for other uses and other processes. Any page or block of pages that was committed by **VirtualAlloc** can be decommitted. Decommitting changes the state of the page to reserved, unless the page was both decommitted and released, in which case the state of the page is free.

The following code fragments illustrates the use of **VirtualAlloc** and **VirtualFree** in reserving and committing as needed memory for a dynamic array. The first time **VirtualAlloc** is called, it is used to reserve a block of pages. In this case, NULL is passed as the base address parameter to allow the kernel to determine the location of the block. When **VirtualAlloc** is called to commit a page from this reserved region, the address parameter specifies the base address of the newly committed page. The example uses the *try-except* structured exception handling syntax to commit additional pages when a page fault exception occurs. The *except* block is executed only if an exception occurs while executing the *try* block. As an alternative to this dynamic allocation, the process could have simply committed the entire region instead of only reserving it, in which case, the committed pages would not be initialized or loaded until they are accessed. But this would reduce the total storage available to this and other processes. Notice that in freeing the pages, the committed pages are decommitted first, and then the entire region is released.

```
#define PAGELIMIT 80
#define PAGESIZE 0x1000

int pages = 0;
```

```
char *page_alloc(char *base) {
    char *pg;
    base += pages*PAGESIZE;
    pg = VirtualAlloc(base, PAGESIZE, MEM_COMMIT, PAGE_READWRITE);
    assert(pg);
    pages++;
    return pg;
}

BOOL free_pages(char *base) {
    BOOL bResult;

    // first decommit the committed pages

    bResult = VirtualFree(base, pages*PAGESIZE, MEM_DECOMMIT);

    // then release the entire buffer

    if (bResult)
        bResult = VirtualFree(base, 0, MEM_RELEASE);

    return bResult;
}

main() {
    char *base, *newpage;
    BOOL bRes;

    // reserve pages

    base = (char *) VirtualAlloc(NULL, PAGELIMIT*PAGESIZE,

    MEM_RESERVE, PAGE_NOACCESS);

    assert (base);

    // commit one page

    newpage = page_alloc(base);

    // use structured exception handling when accessing the pages

    while (1) {

        try {

            // read or write to buffer that begins at base

            base[5000] = 'a';
            break;

        }
        except (EXCEPTION_EXECUTE_HANDLER) {

            // if page fault occurs,
            // commit another page and try it again

            if (pages \< PAGELIMIT) {
                newpage = page_alloc(base);

            }
            else {

                /* reserved pages used up: time to panic */
            }
```

```
            }

        }

        bRes = free_pages(base);
}
```

VirtualQuery returns information about a region of pages beginning at any specified address in the address space of a process. The region is bounded by the specified address rounded down to the nearest page boundary, and extends through all following pages with the same state (free, reserved, committed) and protection (read/write, read only, or no access). The information returned includes the state, protection, size in bytes, and type (shared or private). In the example above, this information could have been used to determine the number of committed pages that needed to be decommitted before being released.

VirtualProtect allows you to modify the access protection of any committed page in the address space of a process. This is typically used with pages allocated by **VirtualAlloc** , but will work with pages committed by any of the other allocation functions. Remember, however, that **VirtualProtect** changes the protection of entire pages, and that pointers returned by the other functions are not necessarily aligned on page boundaries. The following code fragment uses **VirtualQuery** to determine the number of pages committed in the previous example, and then uses **VirtualProtect** to change their protection to read only:

```
MEMORY_BASIC_INFORMATION MemInfo;
DWORD buflen;
char *base;
BOOL bResult;
DWORD dwOldProtect;

buflen = VirtualQuery(base, &MemInfo,
    sizeof(MEMORY_BASIC_INFORMATION));

if (MemInfo.State == MEM_COMMIT)
    bResult = VirtualProtect(base, MemInfo.RegionSize,
        PAGE_READONLY, &dwOldProtect);
```

6.6.1.1 Using file mapping for shared memory

Named file mapping provides an easy way to create a block of shared memory. One process creates a file mapping object, specifying a name that can be used by other processes to obtain a handle to the mapping object. Then each process uses the mapping object to map a view of the file into its own address space. The views of all processes for a single mapping object are mapped into the same sharable pages of physical storage. However, the virtual addresses of the mapped views can vary from one process to another. And although sharable, the pages of physical storage are not global since they are not visible in the address space of processes that have not mapped a view of the file.

CreateFileMapping creates a file mapping object, but does not map the file. The file to be mapped is specified by a handle to an open file as returned by **CreateFile** . If the handle is 0xFFFFFFFF, the system's paging file will be used. Mapping a named file in the file system is useful if you want to share the data in an existing file, or if you want use the file to save the data generated by the sharing processes. The paging file should be used if you are only interested in creating a block of shared memory. If you map a named file, you should open it for exclusive access and keep the handle open until you are finished with the shared memory. This will prevent other processes from opening another handle on the file to use **ReadFile, WriteFile** , or to create additional mapping objects for the same file, any of which could lead to unpredictable results.

CreateFileMapping allows you to associate a name with the file mapping object. This name can be used by other processes to open a handle to the same object using the **OpenFileMapping** call. The name could include any character except for NULL and the path name separator character "\"; and would be limited to MAX_PATH bytes (MAX_PATHW for Unicode). The file mapping object names exist in their own flat name space, so they will not collide with the names of other objects (files, events, semaphores, etc.). Note that the process of setting up shared memory using named file mapping requires synchronization to ensure that the creating process creates the mapping object before the other processes try to open it. If no object name is specified in the **CreateFileMapping** call, the handle can still be shared with other processes by the less convenient means of handle duplication or inheritance.

When a process uses **MapViewOfFile** to map a view of a file, it allocates shared, committed pages with read/write or read only access. The access specified in **MapViewOfFile** (FILE_MAP_READ or FILE_MAP_WRITE) must be compatible with the access specified in **CreateFileMapping** or **OpenFileMapping**, and in the case of named files, when the file was opened with **CreateFile** . If more than one process has write access to the shared memory, a mutex object should be used to prevent simultaneous writing. The maximum size specified in the **CreateFileMapping** call limits the size of the views that can be mapped. A process may map the entire file or a portion of it, and the view may start at the beginning of the file or at any 64KB aligned offset in the file. Any pages committed by mapping a view will be released when the last process with a view on the mapping object either terminates or unmaps its view by calling **UnmapViewOfFile** . At this time, the named file (if any) associated with the mapping object will be updated. Updating a named file can also be forced by calling **FlushViewOfFile**.

The following example shows how two processes would use named file mapping to create a block of shared memory. Note that when the system's paging file is mapped (by using 0xFFFFFFFF instead of a file handle), the **CreateFileMapping** call must explicitly specify the size in bytes of the mapping. For named files, the mapping size can default to the current size of the file, if both high order and low order size parameters are 0. Each process has read/write access to the memory.

```
/****************************************************************/
/* creating process creates the mapping object */
/****************************************************************/

char *mapview;

HANDLE hMapObj;

// create named mapping object, size 4KB

hMapObj = CreateFileMapping((HANDLE) 0xFFFFFFFF,
    NULL, // not inherited
    PAGE_READWRITE,
    0, // buffer size, hi order
    0x1000, // buffer size, lo order
    "shared_mem_map_obj" // object name
    );

assert(hMapObj);

// map view of 4KB shared buffer

mapview = (char *) MapViewOfFile(hMapObj,
    FILE_MAP_READ | FILE_MAP_WRITE,
    0, // view offset, hi order
    0, // view offset, lo order
    0 // view size = max file size
    );

assert(mapview);

/****************************************************************/
/* other processes use name to open handle to mapping object */
/****************************************************************/

char *mapview;
HANDLE hMapObj;

// open named mapping object for read/write access

hMapObj = OpenFileMapping(FILE_MAP_WRITE, // read/write access
    FALSE, // no handle inheritance
    "shared_mem_map_obj"); // object name

assert(hMapObj);

// map view of 4KB shared buffer

mapview = (char *) MapViewOfFile(hMapObj,
    FILE_MAP_READ | FILE_MAP_WRITE,
    0, // view offset, hi order
    0, // view offset, lo order
    0 // view size = max file size
    );

assert(mapview);
```

6.6.1.1.1 Using the Heap API

HeapCreate creates and returns a handle to a private heap. The handle is used to identify the heap in the other functions of the Heap API. The **HeapCreate** function specifies an initial size which determines the number of committed, read/write pages that are initially allocated for the heap. The maximum size determines the number of additional reserved pages that are allocated to reserve a contiguous block of the virtual address space. Additional pages are automatically committed from this reserved space if allocation requests exceed the initial size (assuming that the physical storage is available). However, once the pages are committed, they are not decommitted until the process terminates or the heap is destroyed by calling **HeapDestroy** . The memory of the heap is visible only to the process that created it. If a DLL creates a private heap, each process that links to the DLL will cause a separate instance of the private heap to be created that is not visible to the other DLL users.

HeapAlloc allocates blocks of memory from a private heap and returns a pointer to the allocated block. The pointer can be used in **HeapFree** to release the block, or in **HeapSize** to determine the size of the block. Memory allocated by the Heap API is not moveable (except for normal paging at the granularity of 4KB pages). So if you are allocating and freeing many small blocks, it is possible for a private heap to become fragmented.

If **HeapAlloc** fails because the request exceeds either the available space in the heap or the available physical memory, an exception is raised. This allows the *try..except* structured exception handling to be used (refer to the example above in the section on the Virtual API). Typically, the exception handler in this case would just clean up the application and exit, since the heap cannot be grown or reallocated. If the *except* block handles the exception but does not exit, **HeapAlloc** will return NULL.

A possible use for the Heap API would be to create a heap when a process starts up, specifying an initial size sufficient to satisfy the memory requirements of the process. If the **HeapCreate** call failed, the process could terminate or issue some sort of memory warning; but if it succeeded, the process is assured of having the memory when it needs it.

6.7 Summary

6.7.1 Virtual API

Mlist	Description
VirtualAlloc	Reserves and/or commits a region of pages in virtual address space.

Mlist	Description
VirtualFree	Releases and/or decommits a region of pages in virtual address space.
VirtualProtect	Changes the access protection of a region of pages.
VirtualQuery	Returns the base address, size, state and access protection of a region of pages.

6.7.2 Heap API

Mlist	Description
HeapCreate	Creates a private heap with an initial block of committed pages and an additional block of reserved pages into which the heap can grow.
HeapDestroy	Decommits and releases the pages of a private heap.
HeapAlloc	Allocates a block of memory from a private heap.
HeapFree	Frees a block of memory allocated by **HeapAlloc**.
HeapSize	Returns the size of a block of memory allocated by **HeapAlloc**.

6.7.3 File Mapping API

Mlist	Description
CreateFileMapping	Creates a named or unnamed file mapping object, but does not map a view of the file.
OpenFileMapping	Opens a handle to an existing file mapping object that is identified by name, but does not map a view of the file.
MapViewOfFile	Maps a view of a file identified by a file mapping object into the virtual address space of the calling process.
FlushViewOfFile	Forces a block of bytes from a mapped view of a file to be written to the representation of the file on disk.
UnmapViewOfFile	Unmaps a view of a file and updates any dirty pages to the representation of the file on disk.

Chapter	**Synchronization Objects**
7	

7.1	Introduction	115
	7.1.1 About Synchronization Objects	115
	7.1.2 Interprocess synchronization	115
	7.1.3 Synchronizing threads of a single process	117
	7.1.3.1 Using Interprocess Synchronization objects	118
	7.1.3.2 Handles to Synchronization Objects	118
	7.1.3.3 Using named objects	118
	7.1.3.4 Inheriting Handles by a Child Process	119
	7.1.3.5 Duplicating Handles for an Unrelated Process	120
	7.1.3.6 Waiting for Objects	121
	7.1.3.7 Using an Event Object	123
	7.1.3.8 Using a Mutex Object	125
	7.1.3.9 Using a Semaphore Object	126

7.1 Introduction

In a multitasking environment, it is sometimes necessary to coordinate th
of multiple processes or multiple threads within a process. Win32 provides a set of
synchronization objects for this purpose. These objects give threads a mechanism for
signalling to each other, enabling the development of reliable and robust
multithreaded applications. The signals can be used to indicate that an event has
occurred or that a shared resource is being used. This chapter describes how to create
and use Win32 synchronization objects. The following topics are related to the
information in this chapter:

- Shared memory

- Shared resources

- Processes, threads, and sessions

7.1.1 About Synchronization Objects

A synchronization object is a data structure whose current state—either Signalled or
Not-Signalled—can be used to coordinate the execution of two or more threads. A
thread can interact with one of these objects either by modifying its state or by
waiting for it to be in a Signalled state. When a thread waits for an object, the
execution of the thread is blocked as long as the state of the object is Not-Signalled.
Typically, a thread will wait for a synchronization object before using a shared
resource or performing an operation that must be coordinated with other threads.

There are four types of synchronization objects: Mutex (mutual exclusion) objects,
Semaphore objects, Event objects, and Critical Section objects. The features of each
type enable a different functionality. A Mutex object is used to prevent simultaneous
use of a shared resource, such as a file, shared memory, or a peripheral device. A
Semaphore object is used as a resource gate that limits the use of a resource by
counting threads as they pass in and out of the gate. An Event object is used to notify
a waiting thread that an event has occurred. A Critical Section object is similar to a
Mutex except that it can only be used by the threads of a single process.

7.1.2 Interprocess synchronization

The Mutex, Semaphore, and Event types may be used by the threads of one or more
processes. Each type has its own set of functions for creating an object or modifying
its state; but they share the same functions— **WaitForSingleObject** and
WaitForMultipleObjects—to implement the wait operation. Both wait functions
allow you to wait indefinitely for the object or objects to be Signalled; or
alternatively, you can specify a timeout interval after which the wait is aborted. The
two generic wait functions may not be used with Critical Section objects. When an
application creates one of the three interprocess synchronization objects, space is

allocated in system memory, the object is initialized, and a handle to it is returned to the creating process. This handle can be inherited by child processes or passed to unrelated processes to be duplicated. Or, the creating process can associate a name with the object to be used by other processes in opening a handle to the object. An object is garbage-collected by the system when the last handle to the object is closed. Note that open handles are closed when a process exits.

A Mutex object is either owned (Not-Signalled) or unowned (Signalled). When a thread waits for a Mutex object, it is requesting ownership. If it is currently owned by another thread, the waiting thread will be blocked until the ownership is released. For example, two or more threads that communicate through a shared memory segment could use a Mutex object to avoid simultaneously writing to the memory. Before executing the sections of code in which the shared memory is accessed, each thread would use one of the wait functions to request ownership of the Mutex. And when finished using the memory, the thread would release its ownership. So any other thread requesting ownership of the Mutex would be blocked if the memory was currently in use. The thread that owns a Mutex can make additional wait calls on the same Mutex object without blocking, but it must release ownership once for each time that a wait was satisfied.

A Semaphore object maintains a count; and its state is Signalled as long as its count is greater than zero. A maximum count is specified when a Semaphore object is created, and each time that a wait operation is satisfied by the object, its count is decremented. When a thread releases the object, its count is incremented. This is useful in controlling a shared resource that can support a limited number of multiple users. Suppose, for example, that an application launches multiple child processes to evaluate a problem. To avoid performance degradation, the application limits the number of processes at any one time. It creates a Semaphore object with a count initialized to some maximum number of processes, and before a child process is executed, the parent process calls a wait function to see if the Semaphore is Signalled. As each child is started, the count is decremented; and if the maximum number of child processes are executing, the count is zero, the Semaphore state is Not-Signalled, the wait function blocks, and no more processes are launched. As each child terminates, it releases the Semaphore object (which it inherits from the parent). This increments the count, so additional processes can be started.

An Event object provides a signalling mechanism to notify one or more threads that an event has occurred. The Event API allow you to set (to a Signalled state) or reset (to a Not-Signalled state) an Event object. You can also pulse an Event, which sets the Event briefly and then automatically resets it. Two types of Event objects can be created:

Manual Reset	When a Manual Reset Event is set to Signalled, all waiting threads will be released until the Event is explicitly reset to Not-Signalled. A Manual Reset Event might be used by a process with several threads, where one thread writes to a region of shared memory and the other threads read from it. The writing thread could reset the Event to Not-Signalled when it is writing, to temporarily block the readers. When through writing, it could set the Event to Signalled to allow all the other threads to read freely until the next write operation occurs. Pulsing a Manual Reset Event will release all waiters before the automatic reset.
Auto Reset	When an Auto Reset Event is set to Signalled, a single waiting thread is released and then the Event is automatically reset to Not-Signalled, blocking other waiters until the Event is again set to Signalled. This can be used for releasing one of several waiting threads. For example, a master thread could distribute tasks to several worker threads using a loop that prepares the data for one task and then signals an Auto Reset Event to release one of the waiting workers to process it. An Auto Reset Event would also be used by a monitor thread to signal the occurrence of an interesting event. For example, an application could have several threads each of which monitors a device. When an event occurs, the monitor signals its Auto Reset Event to notify the application, and the Event object automatically resets so the monitor can use it again the next time an event occurs. Pulsing an Auto Reset Event will release a single waiter before the automatic reset.

7.1.3 Synchronizing threads of a single process

Critical Section objects are visible only to the threads of a single process. The other types of synchronization objects may also be used in a single process application; however, the Critical Section type provides a faster mechanism for mutual exclusion synchronization. A separate API implements the initialize, modify, and wait operations for Critical Section objects. These objects exist in memory allocated by the process, and are garbage-collected when the process terminates. You can, however, delete a Critical Section object when it is no longer needed, to release the system resources allocated for it.

Like a Mutex object, a Critical Section object can only be owned by one thread at a time, which makes it useful for protecting a shared resource from simultaneous access. For example, a Critical Section object could be used to prevent more than one thread at a time from modifying a global variable. A thread must enter the Critical Section to request ownership, and leave the Critical Section to release ownership. A thread can repeatedly enter a Critical Section without blocking, but it must leave once for each time that it entered. The **EnterCriticalSection** function is the equivalent to the wait functions for the other synchronization objects, with the limitations that you cannot wait for more than one object and you cannot specify a timeout interval at which to abandon the wait. If this functionality is needed, you will have to use the other object types.

7.1.3.1 Using Interprocess Synchronization objects

Each of the interprocess synchronization objects is designed to handle a particular type of synchronization. This section describes the use of each type. Also covered are the wait functions and the procedures for manipulating the object handles that are common to all three types.

7.1.3.2 Handles to Synchronization Objects

Any thread that wants to use an Event, Mutex, or Semaphore object needs an open handle to the object. If the thread will be waiting for the object, the handle must have synchronization access. If the thread will be modifying the state of the object, the handle must have modify state access. The handle returned by the creation function always has both synchronization and modify state access. All threads of the creating process can share the same handle. If the handle was created with an object name, other processes can use the name to open a handle. For unnamed objects, the creating process must transmit information to any other processes that need to access the synchronization object. This can be done by passing the handle through inheritance to a child process, or by duplicating the handle for an unrelated process.

7.1.3.3 Using named objects

Named objects provide an easy way for processes to share object handles. The object name specified by the creating process is limited to max_path bytes (max_pathw for Unicode); and it can include any character except for null and the path name separator character '\ '. The names for each type of object exist in their own flat name space, so an Event object could have the same name as a Mutex object without collision. After one process has created a named object, other processes can use the name in the appropriate Open function to get a handle to the object. Each opening process must specify the desired access to the object. The following code fragments illustrate this procedure for a Mutex object:

```
/********** creating process **********/

HANDLE hMutex;

hMutex = CreateMutex(NULL, // no security descriptor
    FALSE, // mutex not owned
    "NameOfMutexObject" // object name
    );

if (!hMutex) {
    /* check for error */
}

    .
    .
    .
```

```
/********* other processes *********/

HANDLE hMutex;

hMutex = OpenMutex(MUTEX_ALL_ACCESS, // synchronize, modify access
    FALSE, // handle not inherited
    "NameOfMutexObject" // object name
    );

if (!hMutex) {
    /* check for error */
}

    .
    .
    .
```

The next two sections show how to pass object handles to other processes without using named objects. This can be useful in situations where you want to ensure that a name collision does not occur.

7.1.3.4 Inheriting Handles by a Child Process

A child process can inherit an open handle to a synchronization object if the *InheritHandle* attribute (in the security_attributes parameter) was set when the handle was created. The handle inherited by the child process has the same access as the parent's handle. The parent can pass the value of the handle to the child as a command line argument via the **CreateProcess** function. The following code fragments illustrate this procedure:

```
char CommandLine[80];
HANDLE hEventObj;
SECURITY_ATTRIBUTES SecurityAttributes;

/* create event object that can be inherited */

SecurityAttributes.bInheritHandle = TRUE;
SecurityAttributes.lpSecurityDescriptor = NULL;
SecurityAttributes.nLength = sizeof (SECURITY_ATTRIBUTES);
hEventObj = CreateEvent(&SecurityAttributes,
    FALSE, // auto reset event
    FALSE, // initial state = not signalled
    NULL   // no name
    );

/* pass handle as a string in command line for child process */

sprintf(CommandLine, "\%s \%d",
    "childproc", /* pathname of executable file */
    hEventObj /* object handle */
    );

/*
 *spawn child; pass handle in command line;
 *set inherit handles to true
 */

Success = CreateProcess( NULL,
    CommandLine, /* args with handle string */
    NULL,
    NULL,
```

```
TRUE, /* inherit handles */
0,
NULL,
NULL,
&StartupInfo,
&ProcessInfo
);
```

The child process can then use the **GetCommandLine** function to retrieve the command line string and convert the handle argument back into a useable handle.

```
char *CommandLine, *ChildProcName;
HANDLE hEventObj;

CommandLine = GetCommandLine();
sscanf(CommandLine, "\%s \%d", ChildProcName, &hEventObj);
```

7.1.3.5 Duplicating Handles for an Unrelated Process

To share an unnamed object between unrelated processes, the creating process must communicate the information necessary for the other process to duplicate the handle. The duplicating process will need handles to the creating process and to the object to be duplicated. Any of the methods of interprocess communication described in other chapters can be used (e.g., named pipe, shared file, shared memory). The duplicating process can open its handle with the same access as the original handle by specifying duplicate_same_access in the **DuplicateHandle** call. Or it can specify a subset of the original handle's access.

The following code fragment shows the steps to be taken by the creating process:

```
HANDLE hMutexObj;
DWORD dwCreatingProcessID;

/* create a mutex object */

hMutexObj = CreateMutex(NULL, FALSE, NULL);

/* get handle to creating process */

dwCreatingProcessID = GetCurrentProcessID();

    .
    . /* communicate pid and Mutex handle to other process */
    .
```

Then the duplicating process opens its handle with the same access as the creator:

```
HANDLE hMutexSrcHandle, hCreatingProcess;
HANDLE hMutexDupedHandle;

    .
    . /* get communicated handle and pid from creating process */
    .

hCreatingProcess = OpenProcess(PROCESS_DUP_HANDLE,
    FALSE, /* not inherited handles */
    dwCreatingProcessID);

DuplicateHandle(hCreatingProcess,
    hMutexSrcHandle,
```

```
GetCurrentProcess(),
&hMutexDupedHandle,
0,
FALSE, /* not inherited */
DUPLICATE_SAME_ACCESS);
```

7.1.3.6 Waiting for Objects

Two generic functions, **WaitForSingleObject** and **WaitForMultipleObjects** , are used by threads to wait for the state of a waitable object to be Signalled. In addition to Event, Mutex, and Semaphore objects, these functions may be used to wait for process and thread objects. The process must have an open handle with synchronize access to any object for which it is waiting. These functions are not used to wait for Critical Section objects.

The **WaitForSingleObject** function waits for a single instance of any of these object types. If the state of the object is Signalled (or becomes Signalled before a timeout period has elapsed), the function returns zero and the calling process may continue its execution. If the timeout interval elapses before the object is Signalled, a non –zero value is returned. If a Mutex object is being waited for, the function may return WAIT_ABANDONED, indicating that the Mutex had been owned by another thread that terminated without releasing its ownership. In most situations, **WaitForSingleObject** also modifies the object: the count of a Semaphore object is decremented; an Auto Reset Event object is reset to Not-Signalled; and a Mutex object becomes owned (Not-Signalled). The state of a Manual Reset Event object is not changed by this function. If the waitable object is not Signalled, the function blocks until some other thread changes the state of the object, or the timeout period has elapsed. Note that if the timeout interval is set to –1, the function will wait indefinitely.

The **WaitForMultipleObjects** function allows a thread to wait on more than one object at the same time. The objects may be a mixture of different types of waitable objects. For example, you could wait for an Event to be signalled and for a Mutex to be unowned. The function may be used to wait for any one or for all of the objects to be Signalled.

If the function's *WaitAll* parameter is true , the wait is not successful unless all of the objects attain the Signalled state at the same time. For example, suppose a thread requires access to several Mutex-protected regions of shared memory at the same time. The function will block until all of the Mutex objects are unowned, at which time, the thread will acquire ownership of them all and the function will return zero. The thread can then access the shared memory while access by other threads is prevented. If one of the objects is an abandoned Mutex, the function will return WAIT_ABANDONED.

If the *WaitAll* parameter is false , the wait is satisfied when any one of the objects is Signalled. A process could use this to wait on a group of Event objects so that the function blocks until an event of interest occurs, at which time, the function returns (WAIT_OBJECT_0 + index) where *index* is the array index of the object that satisfied the wait. If more than one object is Signalled when the wait function is called, the one with the lowest array index will satisfy the wait. If the object that satisfied the wait is an abandoned Mutex, the function will return (WAIT_ABANDONED_0 + index).

The following code fragment creates five Event objects and then waits for one of them to be Signalled.

```
HANDLE hEventObjs[5];
ULONG i;
DWORD event;

// create 5 event objects

for (i = 0; i < 5; i++) {
    hEventObjs[i] = CreateEvent(NULL, FALSE, FALSE, NULL);

    if (!hEventObjs[i]) {
        /* deal with error */
    };
}


    .
    .
    .

while (TRUE) {
    event = WaitForMultipleObjects(5, // number of objects
        hEventObjs, // array of objects
        FALSE, // wait for any
        500L); // wait for 1/2 sec

    switch (event) {

        case WAIT_OBJECT_0 + 0: // hEventObj[0] was signalled

        case WAIT_OBJECT_0 + 1: // hEventObj[1] was signalled

            .
            .
            .

        case WAIT_TIME_OUT: // deal without timeout

    }
}
```

In general, you should be aware of the danger of deadlocking a process due to a wait that is never satisfied. For example, if one thread fails to release its ownership of a Mutex, another waiting thread could be blocked indefinitely if the timeout interval is infinite.

7.1.3.7 Using an Event Object

You can use an Event object to trigger execution of other processes or of other threads within a process. This is useful if one process provides data to many other processes. Using an Event object frees the other processes from the trouble of polling to determine when new data is available. For example, the Comm API uses an Event object to notify a thread that an event of interest has occurred on a device that is being monitored.

The **CreateEvent** function creates either a Manual Reset Event or an Auto Reset Event, depending on the value of its *bManualReset* parameter. **CreateEvent** also sets the initial state of the Event to either Signalled (true) or Not-Signalled (false). When an event's state is Not-Signalled, any thread waiting on the Event will block.

An Event may be set to the Signalled state by calling **SetEvent**. For Manual Reset Events, this releases all threads that are waiting on the Event; and the Event remains Signalled until it is explicitly reset to the Not-Signalled state by calling **ResetEvent**. For Auto Reset Events, the **SetEvent** function causes the Event to remain Signalled until one waiting thread is released, at which time the Event is automatically reset to the Not-Signalled state. **PulseEvent** sets the Event to the Signalled state and then immediately resets to the Not-Signalled state. **PulseEvent** resets even if there were no waiting threads to be released; otherwise, it releases one thread for Auto Reset Events and all waiting threads for Manual Reset Events. If an Event is pulsed, the Event will remain set long enough for a thread using **WaitForMultipleObjects**(*WaitAll*=true) to determine if the other objects are Signalled.

In the following code fragments, a master thread repeatedly writes new data to a shared memory buffer; and several worker threads wait for their turn to process a batch of data. The master process creates two Auto Reset Event objects to synchronize access to the shared memory. The *WriteEvent* object blocks the workers while the master writes; and the *ReadEvent* object notifies the master that a worker has read the data and it is safe to write again.

```
HANDLE hWriteEvent, hReadEvent;
DWORD waitresult, errcode;

/* create event object to notify workers when writing is done */

hWriteEvent = CreateEvent(NULL, // no security attributes
    FALSE, // auto reset (release one waiter)
    FALSE, // initial state = Not-Signalled
    "WriteEvent" // object name
    );

if (!hWriteEvent) {
    /* error exit */
}

/* create event object to notify master that reading is done */

hReadEvent = CreateEvent(NULL, // no security attributes
```

```
            FALSE, // auto reset (release one waiter)
            FALSE, // initial state = Not-Signalled
            "ReadEvent" // object name
            );

if (!hReadEvent) {
    /* error exit */
}

while (TRUE) {

    .
    . /* write new data to shared memory */
    .

    // set hWriteEvent to Signalled state to release one worker

    // hWriteEvent is automatically reset
    // when a worker thread is released

    if (!SetEvent(hWriteEvent)) { // error exit
        errcode = GetLastError();
        break;

    }

    /* wait on hReadEvent for data to be read; break if error */

    if (waitresult = WaitForSingleObject(hReadEvent, 500L))
        break;
}
```

Using the **WaitForSingleObject** function, the workers wait for the *WriteEvent* to be signalled. When the Event is signalled, one worker is released while the others continue to wait. When a worker is released to process the data, it first reads from shared memory and then signals the master before going on to complete its task.

```
HANDLE hWriteEvent, hReadEvent;
DWORD waitresult;

hWriteEvent = OpenEvent(EVENT_ALL_ACCESS, FALSE, "WriteEvent");
hReadEvent = OpenEvent(EVENT_ALL_ACCESS, FALSE, "ReadEvent");

while (TRUE) {

    /* wait indefinitely on hWriteEvent for data to be written */

    if (waitresult = WaitForSingleObject(hWriteEvent, -1))
        break;

    .
    . /* read data from shared memory */
    .

    /*
     * set hReadEvent to Signalled state
     * to release master process
     *
     * hReadEvent is automatically reset
     * after master process released
     */

    if (!SetEvent(hReadEvent)) {
```

```
        /* error exit */
    }

    .
    . /* process data */
    .

}
```

7.1.3.8 Using a Mutex Object

You can use a Mutex object to protect a shared resource from simultaneous access by multiple threads or processes. It does this by requiring each thread to wait for ownership of the Mutex before it can execute the code in which the shared resource is accessed. For example, if several processes need to write to the same disk file, the Mutex object can be used to permit only one process at at time to write to the file.

The **CreateMutex** function creates a Mutex object and sets its initial state to either unowned or owned by the creating process. The handle returned to the creating process has synchronize and modify access to the Mutex object.

Before entering the section of code that accesses the shared resource, you need to request ownership of the Mutex by calling either **WaitForSingleObject** or **WaitForMultipleObjects** . If another thread already owns the Mutex, these functions will block until the Mutex has been released or the timeout period has elapsed. If the Mutex is currently unowned, the system grants ownership to the requesting thread and it can execute the protected code. When it has finished using the shared resource, the thread uses the **ReleaseMutex** function to relinquish ownership of the Mutex, thereby allowing another thread to become owner. While a thread has ownership of a Mutex, it can make additional wait calls on the same Mutex object without blocking. However, to relinquish ownership of the Mutex, **ReleaseMutex** must be called once for each time that a wait was satisfied.

The following code fragment shows how a thread creates a Mutex object, requests ownership, and after writing to a shared file, releases ownership:

```
HANDLE hFileMutex;
DWORD waitresult;

/* create an initially unowned mutex */

hFileMutex = CreateMutex(NULL, FALSE, NULL);

if (!hFileMutex) {
    /* check for error */
}

    .
    .
    .

/* request ownership of Mutex */

waitresult = WaitForSingleObject(hFileMutex, 5000L);
```

```
switch (waitresult) {

    case 0:
        try {

            .
            . /* write data to shared file */
            .

        }

        finally {

            /* release ownership of Mutex */

            if (ReleaseMutex(hFileMutex)) {
                /* deal with error */
            }

            break;
        }


    case WAIT_TIME_OUT:

        /* unable to get ownership of mutex due to timeout */

    case WAIT_ABANDONED:

        /* got ownership of abandoned mutex */

}
```

The example uses the *try...finally* structured exception handling syntax to ensure that a thread properly releases a Mutex. The *finally* block of code is executed no matter how the *try* block terminates (unless the try block includes a call to TerminateThread). This prevents the Mutex from being inadvertantly abandoned. Either of the wait functions can return wait_abandoned if a Mutex has been abandoned, which occurs if a thread terminates without releasing its ownership of the Mutex. Only Mutex objects can be abandoned, since Event and Semaphore objects cannot be owned. The waiting thread will be given ownership of the abandoned Mutex, but you should probably assume that an abandoned Mutex means that the shared resource is in an undefined state and the process should terminate. If the thread proceeds normally as though the Mutex had not been abandoned, the wait_abandoned flag is cleared so future waits are satisfied normally.

7.1.3.9 Using a Semaphore Object

A Semaphore object is useful in controlling the number of threads that are simultaneously using a shared resource. It acts like a gate that counts the threads as they enter and exit the controlled area.

The **CreateSemaphore** function creates a Semaphore object, specifying the initial count and the maximum count. The handle returned to the creating process has synchronize and modify access to the Semaphore object. Processes that open, inherit, or duplicate the Semaphore should duplicate this access so they will be able to wait for the object (synchronize access) as well as release it (modify access).

When a thread wants to pass through a Semaphore gate, it calls either **WaitForSingleObject** or **WaitForMultipleObjects** . If the count of the Semaphore is greater than 0, the count is decremented and the wait function returns so the thread can execute the protected code. If the count of the Semaphore is 0, the thread will block until the timeout period has elapsed or some other thread increments the count by releasing the Semaphore. When it has finished using the shared resource, the thread exits the gate with the **ReleaseSemaphore** call. This increments the count of the Semaphore by a specified amount. Typically, you would use an increment of 1 when releasing the Semaphore, but you could specify a larger increment as long as the resulting count is not greater than the maximum count. For example, a Semaphore might be created with an initial count of 0 to block access during an initialization phase of the program. Then after the initialization, the creating process could use **ReleaseSemaphore** to increment the count to the maximum.

There is no ownership of Semaphore objects, so if a thread repeatedly enters the Semaphore gate, the count will be decremented each time and the thread will block when the count gets to 0. If a thread wants to decrement a Semaphore's count more than once, it must do multiple waits rather than calling **WaitForMultipleObjects** with multiple occurrences of the same handle.

The following code fragment creates a Semaphore object, waits for it, and then releases it:

```
HANDLE hSemaphore;
LONG lMaxCount = 10;
LONG PreviousCount;

/* create a semaphore with initial and max counts = to 10 */

hSemaphore = CreateSemaphore(NULL, lMaxCount, lMaxCount, NULL);

if (!hSemaphore) {
    /* check for error */
}

    .
    .
    .

/* enter the semaphore gate */

switch (WaitForSingleObject(hSemaphore, 5000L)) {
    case 0:

        . /* use shared resource */
        .

        /* exit the semaphore gate */

        if (ReleaseSemaphore(hSemaphore, 1, &PreviousCount)) {
```

```
                              /* deal with error */
            }
            break;
         case WAIT_TIME_OUT: /* deal without timeout */
    }
```

7.1.3.9.1 Using a Critical Section Object

You can use a Critical Section object to protect a shared resource from simultaneous access by multiple threads of a single process. For example, if several threads need to use a global variable, a Critical Section object could be used to control execution of the code in which the variable is accessed.

Typically, the Critical Section object would be declared as a global variable and the main thread of the process would use the **InitializeCriticalSection** function to initialize it. This function initializes the object's state to unowned, leaving it ready to be used by the threads of the process. When a thread needs to access the resource that is protected by the Critical Section, it calls the **EnterCriticalSection** function to request ownership of the object. If another thread already owns the Critical Section, this function will block until the Critical Section has been released. If the Critical Section is currently unowned, the system grants ownership to the requesting thread and it can access the resource. When it has finished executing the protected code, the thread uses the **LeaveCriticalSection** function to relinquish ownership of the Critical Section, thereby allowing another thread to become owner. While a thread has ownership of a Critical Section, it can make additional **EnterCriticalSection** calls on the same Critical Section object without blocking. However, to relinquish ownership of the Critical Section, **LeaveCriticalSection** must be called once for each time that the Critical Section was entered. Refer to the section above on Mutexes for a discussion of using the *try...finally* structured exception handling syntax. This is a good idea with Critical Sections as well, to ensure that a thread properly leaves the Critical Section.

The following code fragment shows a thread initializing, entering, and leaving a Critical Section:

```
CRITICAL_SECTION GlobalCriticalSection;
      .
      .
      .

/* initialize the critical section */

InitializeCriticalSection(&GlobalCriticalSection);

/* request ownership of the critical section */

EnterCriticalSection(&GlobalCriticalSection);
```

```
.
. /* access the shared resource */
.
/* release ownership of the critical section */

LeaveCriticalSection(&GlobalCriticalSection);
```

When an application is through using a Critical Section object, it may delete the object using the **DeleteCriticalSection** function. This function deallocates all system resources stored in the Critical Section object. A Critical Section can only be deleted when it is unowned; and once deleted, it can not be used in **EnterCriticalSection** or **LeaveCriticalSection.**

7.1.3.9.1.1 Summary

The following are the Win32 functions used with synchronization objects.

7.1.3.9.1.2 Event Object Functions

HANDLE CreateEvent(LPSECURITY_ATTRIBUTES lpEventAttributes,
    BOOL bManualReset, BOOL bInitialState, LPSTR lpName);
BOOL PulseEvent(HANDLE hEvent);
BOOL ResetEvent(HANDLE hEvent);
BOOL SetEvent(HANDLE hEvent);

7.1.3.9.1.3 Mutex Object Functions

HANDLE CreateMutex(LPSECURITY_ATTRIBUTES lpMutexAttributes,
    BOOL bInitialOwner, LPSTR lpName);
BOOL ReleaseMutex(HANDLE hMutex);

7.1.3.9.1.4 Semaphore Object Functions

HANDLE CreateSemaphore(
    LPSECURITY_ATTRIBUTES lpSemaphoreAttributes,
    LONG lInitialCount, LONG lMaximumCount, LPSTR lpName);
BOOL ReleaseSemaphore(HANDLE hSemaphore, LONG lReleaseCount,
    LPLONG lpPreviousCount);

7.1.3.9.1.5 Wait Functions

DWORD WaitForMultipleObjects(DWORD nCount,
    LPHANDLE lpHandles, BOOL bWaitAll, DWORD dwMilliseconds);
DWORD WaitForSingleObject(HANDLE hHandle,
    DWORD dwMilliseconds);

7.1.3.9.1.6 Critical Section Object Functions

VOID DeleteCriticalSection(LPCRITICAL_SECTION lpCriticalSection);
VOID EnterCriticalSection(LPCRITICAL_SECTION lpCriticalSection);
VOID InitializeCriticalSection(LPCRITICAL_SECTION lpCriticalSection);

```
VOID LeaveCriticalSection(LPCRITICAL_SECTION lpCriticalSection);
```

Chapter 8

Console Functions

8.1   Introduction 133

   8.1.1   About the Console 133

   8.1.2   Input and output via File API 133

   8.1.3   Input and output via console API 134

      8.1.3.1   Using the Console 135

      8.1.3.2   Getting Handles to Console Input and Output 135

      8.1.3.3   Console modes 137

      8.1.3.4   Modes for the File API 137

      8.1.3.5   Modes for the Console API 138

      8.1.3.6   Using the Console via the File API 139

      8.1.3.7   Moving and hiding the cursor 141

      8.1.3.8   Input using the Console API 141

      8.1.3.9   The Input Buffer 142

      8.1.3.10 Key events 143

      8.1.3.11 Mouse events 144

      8.1.3.12 *bBuffer *bresize events 145

      8.1.3.13 Output using the Console API 146

      8.1.3.14 Window and Screen Buffer Sizes 146

      8.1.3.15 Writing strings of characters to a screen buffer ... 147

      8.1.3.16 Writing strings of color attributes to a screen buffer 148

      8.1.3.17 Writing blocks of characters and attributes 149

      8.1.3.18 Reading from the screen buffer 150

      8.1.3.19 Scrolling the Screen Buffer 151

      8.1.3.20 Control Handlers 153

      8.1.3.21 Summary 153

8.1 Introduction

This chapter describes the console functions that allow character-based applications to execute in a window environment.

8.1.1 About the Console

The console provides input and output to character-based applications. The console displays output in a console window that acts like a terminal display. The system creates the console window and provides the input and output to the program just as if it were running in a full-screen session.

A console, consisting of an input buffer and one or more screen buffers, is shared by a group of processes. It is first created when an application without a parent application , such as CMD.EXE, is started. It is also possible for a detached process to create a console. Handles to Standard Input, Standard Output, and Standard Error files are created and are inherited by child processes. An application can get console input by reading from the input buffer which is referred to as "CONIN$". StdIn is a handle to "CONIN$". An application can write to a console by writing to a console screen buffer. StdOut and StdErr are handles to console screen buffers. The active screen buffer is referred to as "CONOUT$".

8.1.2 Input and output via File API

Limited access to the input and output buffers of a console is available through the API for File I/O. The application can use **ReadFile** with a handle to StdIn to get keyboard input; and it can use **WriteFile** with a handle to a screen buffer to write from a character buffer to the specified screen buffer at its current cursor location. Other API that support the use of console handles include **DuplicateHandle** and **CloseHandle** which can be used with either input or output handles. **CreateFile** can be used to open a handle to console input, "CONIN$". **CreateFile** can also be used to return a handle to the active screen buffer, "CONOUT$", if the process has an open handle to it (via inheritance or duplication).

The form of input and output for applications using the File API is affected by console modes which may be enabled or disabled. The following modes may be enabled for the input handle: line input, processed input, echo input. In line input mode, applications using **ReadFile** will not get console input until a carriage return has been input. In processed input mode, control characters are handled by **ReadFile** . This means that editing keys such as backspace and tab are handled appropriately, and Ctrl-C is passed on to the handler routines. In echo input mode, characters read by **ReadFile** are echoed to console output. Echoing only occurs if line input is also enabled. The following modes may be enabled for the output handle: wrap at EOL, processed output. The File API can send output to the screen buffer by writing using **WriteFile** or when using **ReadFile** if echoing is enabled. Wrap at EOL output mode determines whether long output lines will wrap to the beginning of the next line or be discarded beyond the end of the line. Processed output mode enables the output characters to be parsed for ASCII control sequences and the correct action performed.

Applications using **ReadFile** and **WriteFile** to write output to a console screen buffer can specify the color attribute with which subsequent characters will be written.

8.1.3 Input and output via console API

Expanded access to input and output is possible through the Console API. Through the Console API, the application can use a handle to StdIn to directly access the input buffer. The console input buffer consists of input records that contain information about keyboard, mouse, and window size events. The File API discard all but the keyboard input, but the Console API provide direct access to the input buffer so the application can receive mouse and window resize events, in addition to keyboard input. Console input modes may be manipulated to filter mouse and screen buffer size events if the application is not interested in them. It is also possible using the Console API to write input records to the input buffer; to read input records without removing them from the input buffer; to determine the number of pending events; or to flush the input buffer.

An application controls output to the screen by manipulating the contents of one or more screen buffers, and by selecting the active screen buffer which is the one that is currently displayed. Each TEXTMODE screen buffer is a two-dimensional array of character information records. The data for each character includes the UNICODE or ASCII value of the character and an attributes field that controls the foreground and background colors in which that character is displayed. The Console API provide direct access to TEXTMODE screen buffers to enable the following functionality:

- Strings of characters or character attributes (colors) can be read from or written to any location in a screen buffer, not just at the current cursor location (**ReadConsoleOutputCharacter, ReadConsoleOutputAttribute, WriteConsoleOutputCharacter, WriteConsoleOutputAttribute**).

- Rectangular blocks of characters and attributes can be read from or written to any location in a screen buffer (**ReadConsoleOutput, WriteConsoleOutput**).

- Any portion of a screen buffer can be filled with a single character or character attribute (**FillConsoleOutputCharacter, FillConsoleOutputAttribute**).

- A sub-block of a screen buffer can be copied from one part of the screen buffer to another to allow scrolling of the sub-block within the console window (**ScrollConsoleScreenBuffer**).

- The size of a screen buffer can be queried or set, although a screen buffer cannot be made smaller than the current size of the console window (**SetConsoleScreenBufferSize, GetConsoleScreenBufferInfo**).

- The character attributes (color) with which subsequent characters will be written can be set (**SetConsoleTextAttribute**).

- The location, appearance, and visibility of the cursor can be queried or set (**GetConsoleCursorInfo, SetConsoleCursorInfo, SetConsoleCursorPosition**).

- The visible portion of a screen buffer can be changed by changing the origin of the buffer with respect to the window or by changing the width and height of the window (in character cells to be displayed). This can have the effect of scrolling the contents, resizing the window, or both. (**SetConsoleWindowInfo**)

Applications using the Console API always receive raw character input, regardless of the line input and processed input modes. The File API modes that affect output to the screen (echo input, processed output, wrap at EOL output) affect only applications that use **ReadFile** and **WriteFile**. The two console modes that affect input for applications using the Console API (mouse aware and window aware) have no affect on applications using the File API.

8.1.3.1 Using the Console

An application receives input from the console and displays characters on the screen through either the File I/O API or the Console API. With either API, the console buffers are accessed through handles to Standard Input and Standard Output. The File API allow you to read keyboard input and write characters to the screen or console window at the current cursor location. The Console API enable direct access to the input buffer to read and write keyboard, mouse, and window size events. They also provide direct access to output buffers to enable expanded capabilities for reading, writing, scrolling, and highlighting characters at any location in the console window.

8.1.3.2 Getting Handles to Console Input and Output

A character-based application receives input from the input buffer, "CONIN$". StdIn is a handle to "CONIN$". The application writes to the console window by writing to a screen buffer. StdOut and StdErr are screen buffer handles (TEXTMODE). To access console input and output through either the File API or the Console API, you must have open handles to these buffers.

The application may retrieve the StdIn, StdOut, and StdErr handles by calling **GetStdHandle**. These handles will not be 0–2. **GetStdHandle** returns an open input handle with read/write access and read/write sharing mode, which may be used with any of the Console or File I/O API that access the input buffer. The same function returns an open output handle with read/write access and read/write sharing mode, which may be used with any of the Console or File I/O API that access a TEXTMODE screen buffer. If you use **GetStdHandle** to get an output screen buffer handle, remember that this is an inherited handle. Consequently, you should avoid changing any of the attributes associated with a screen buffer (e.g., screen buffer size, cursor appearance, scroll position, etc.), or you should save the state of the screen buffer and restore it when your application terminates. Another alternative is to create a new screen buffer for use by your application, leaving the inherited screen buffer unchanged. The following lines show the use of **GetStdHandle** to open the inherited console handles.

HANDLE hStdIn = GetStdHandle(STD_INPUT_HANDLE);

HANDLE hStdOut = GetStdHandle(STD_OUTPUT_HANDLE);

HANDLE hStdErr = GetStdHandle(STD_ERROR_HANDLE);

You could use **CreateFile** to open an input handle with different access or sharing modes, as shown in the following code fragment:

```
hReadWriteInput = CreateFile("CONIN$",
    GENERIC_READ | GENERIC_WRITE,
    0, // exclusive access
    NULL,
    OPEN_EXISTING,
    0,
    NULL
    );
```

Any handle to console input, whether created by **GetStdHandle** or by **CreateFile**, can be used in either **WaitForSingleObject** or **WaitForMultipleObjects** . The handle will be signalled when the input buffer is non-empty and reset when the buffer is empty.

CreateConsoleScreenBuffer is used to create additional screen buffers. This is used if you want more than one screen buffer. Typically, applications that use the Console API will use this function to create a private screen buffer, rather than using the StdOut. Creating a new screen buffer has no affect on StdOut or StdErr. The new screen buffer can be made the active screen buffer by calling **SetConsoleActiveScreenBuffer** which selects it as the screen buffer to display in the console window. Access to a screen buffer may be limited by restricting the file share access or by using the security attributes to set an ACL. This code fragment show the creation of a private TEXTMODE screen buffer to which the application has exclusive access and which will not be inherited by child processes:

```
SECURITY_ATTRIBUTES SecurityAttributes;

SecurityAttributes.bInheritHandle = FALSE;
SecurityAttributes.lpSecurityDescriptor = NULL;
SecurityAttributes.nLength = sizeof (SECURITY_ATTRIBUTES);
hPrivateScrnBuf = CreateConsoleScreenBuffer(
    GENERIC_READ | GENERIC_WRITE,
    0, /* no file sharing */
    &SecurityAttributes, /* no inheritance */
    CONSOLE_TEXTMODE_BUFFER,
```

```
NULL
) ;
```

When a TEXTMODE screen buffer is created, it contains blanks; its cursor position is at the buffer's origin (0,0), which is displayed at the upper left corner of the window. The initial size of the screen buffer (in character rows and columns) is determined by the user or by system defaults. Use **GetConsoleScreenBufferInfo** to determine the actual size; and use **SetConsoleScreenBufferSize** if you want to change its size. Note that the size of a screen buffer may not be made smaller than the size of the console window.

8.1.3.3 Console modes

The form of input and output for console applications depends on the current modes for the console handles being used. There are several I/O modes that may be set independently. The modes apply individually to input and output handles and must be set separately for each handle and handle type. The following modes are relevant only to applications that are accessing the console via the File I/O API: line input, processed input, echo input, processed output, and wrap at EOL output. The other modes are relevant only to those using the Console API: mouse aware input, and window aware input. All modes can be set with the **SetConsoleMode** function or queried with the **GetConsoleMode** function.

8.1.3.4 Modes for the File API

For the File API, the relevant input modes are line input, processed input and echo. All input handles are created with these three modes enabled by default. The following table lists the effects of these input modes:

line	In line mode, **ReadFile** does not return to the caller until the Enter key is pressed. If disabled, **ReadFile** returns when one or more characters are available in the input buffer; and the only key combination not passed on to the caller is Ctrl-Break.
processed	Any system editing or control keys are processed by the system and are not passed on to the user. If line input is also enabled, tab, backspace, carriage returns, and bell will be handled correctly. Tabs cause the cursor to move to the next tab stop, which occurs every 8 characters. Backspace causes the cursor to move back one space without affecting the character at the cursor position. Bell causes a short tone to be sounded. Carriage returns are converted to carriage return/linefeed. Ctrl-C and Ctrl-Break will be passed on to the appropriate handler regardless of whether line input is enabled. This mode affects the buffer that is returned by ReadFile. If echoing is enabled and you want the output to reflect the system editing, processed output must be enabled for the output handle.

echo
If echo is enabled in conjunction with line input mode, characters are echoed to the screen as they are read by **ReadFile**. Characters are echoed only if the **ReadFile** caller has an open handle to the active screen buffer. Echo mode may not be used with character input mode.

For the File API, the relevant output modes are processed output and wrap at EOL, both of which are enabled by default. Applications using the Console API are not affected by either of the output modes.

processed
If processed output is enabled, the characters written by **WriteFile** or echoed by **ReadFile** are parsed for ASCII control sequences and the correct action is performed. This is equivalent to the processed input mode, except that it affects the characters written to the screen buffer.

wrap at EOL
If wrap at EOL is enabled, the current output position (cursor position) moves to the first column in the next row when the end of the current row is reached. If the bottom of the window region is reached, the window origin is moved down one row. This has the effect of scrolling the contents of the window up one row. If the bottom of the screen buffer is reached, the contents of the screen buffer are scrolled up one row, discarding the top row of the screen buffer. If wrap at EOL is disabled, the last character in the row is overwritten with any subsequent characters. The effects of wrap or no wrap occur when the application calls **WriteFile** with a handle to the active screen buffer or when output is echoed during a call to **ReadFile**.

Typically, applications using the File API will choose to either enable or disable all of the above modes as a group. When all are enabled, you are in "cooked" mode, where most of the processing is handled for you. And when all are disabled, you are in "raw" mode, in which case, the input is unfiltered and the processing is up to you. By default, all input and output handles initially have all of the above modes enabled.

8.1.3.5 Modes for the Console API

For the Console API, the relevant input modes are mouse aware and window aware. By default, input handles are created with both modes enabled. With one exception, line, processed, and echo input modes have no effect on applications using the Console API, since the console input buffer always receives all keyboard input (raw mode) and input is only echoed when applications call **ReadFile**. The exception is that if processed input is enabled, Ctrl-C characters are passed to the control handler functions; if disabled, they are placed as ASCII characters into the input buffer. Mouse aware and window aware modes have no effect on applications using the File API, since **ReadFile** returns only keyboard input, discarding any mouse or buffer size events.

The following code fragment gets the current console mode and then modifies it to filter out mouse events:

```
ULONG Mode;
HANDLE hStdIn = GetStdHandle(STD_INPUT_HANDLE);
BOOL bSuccess;

/* get the current mode */

bSuccess = GetConsoleMode(hStdIn,&Mode);
if (!bSuccess) {
    /* handle error */
}

/* turn off mouse input */

Mode &= ~ENABLE_MOUSE_INPUT;
bSuccess = SetConsoleMode(hStdIn,Mode);

if (!bSuccess) {
    /* handle error */
}
```

8.1.3.6 Using the Console via the File API

For character-based applications that only want to do simple reading from Standard Input and writing to Standard Output, the console is accessible via the File API. This means that you use **ReadFile** with a handle to StdIn to get keyboard input or to read input from a file or a pipe if StdIn has been redirected. To write to the console window, you use **WriteFile** with a handle to StdOut or StdErr.

Using **ReadFile** with a handle to StdIn, the application can receive input from the keyboard. **ReadFile** only returns keyboard events that can be translated into ASCII characters, including control key combinations. The application does not receive keyboard events involving the function keys or direction keys; it has no access to mouse input; and it is not aware of window resize events.

If line input is enabled (the default), **ReadFile** does not return to the caller until the Enter key is pressed. In character mode (line input disabled), **ReadFile** does not return until at least one key is available. In either input mode, **ReadFile** transfers all available characters to the caller until either no more keys are available, or the caller's buffer is filled. In this case, the remaining characters are buffered until the next call to **ReadFile** . The total number of bytes actually read is returned to the caller.

Using **WriteFile** with a handle to StdOut or StdErr, the application can write to the console window. Characters are transferred from a buffer and written to the active screen buffer at the current cursor location, advancing the cursor to the next position.

Output for applications using the File API is affected by the echo mode of the input handle, and by the processed output and wrap at EOL modes of the output handle. Refer to the section above on console modes for a discussion of the effects of these modes.

Use the **SetConsoleTextAttribute** call to set the foreground and background colors with which subsequent characters will be written to the screen buffer. This call affects only characters written by **WriteFile** or echoed by **ReadFile**. Characters written by any of the Console API either explicitly specify their attributes or leave the attributes at the positions written unchanged. The current text attributes may be determined by calling **GetConsoleScreenBufferInfo**.

The following code fragment uses the File API for console input and output:

```
#define FOREGROUND_WHITE \
    (FOREGROUND_RED | FOREGROUND_GREEN | FOREGROUND_BLUE)

CHAR prompt1[] = "Type something and press Enter:\\n.";
CHAR prompt2[] = "Type any key: ";
CHAR Buffer[100];
DWORD dwBytesRead, dwBytesWritten, dwMode;
BOOL bSuccess;
HANDLE hInput = GetStdHandle(STD_INPUT_HANDLE);
HANDLE hOutput = GetStdHandle(STD_OUTPUT_HANDLE);

if (!hInput || !hOutput) {
    /* NULL handle, process error */
}

// draw white characters on a red background

bSuccess = SetConsoleTextAttribute(hOutput,
    FOREGROUND_WHITE | BACKGROUND_RED);

if (!bSuccess) {
    /* process error */
}

// default input modes: line, processed, echo

// default output modes: processed, wrap at EOL

// prompt user to enter a line

bSuccess = WriteFile(hOutput, prompt1, strlen(prompt1),
    &dwBytesWritten, NULL);

if (!bSuccess) {
    /* process error */
}

// wait for input which is echoed to the screen

bSuccess = ReadFile(hInput, Buffer, 100, &dwBytesRead, NULL);

if (!bSuccess) {
    /* process error */
}

// get the console mode, so we can change it

bSuccess = GetConsoleMode(hInput, &dwMode);

if (!bSuccess) {
    /* process error */
}
```

```
// turn off line input and echo

dwMode &= ~(ENABLE_LINE_INPUT | ENABLE_ECHO_INPUT);

bSuccess = SetConsoleMode(hInput, dwMode);

if (!bSuccess) {
    /* process error */
}

// prompt user to type any key

bSuccess = WriteFile(hOutput, prompt2, strlen(prompt2),
    &dwBytesWritten, NULL);

if (!bSuccess) {
    /* process error */
}

// wait for input which is not echoed to the screen

bSuccess = ReadFile(hInput, Buffer, 100, &dwBytesRead, NULL);

// write input and carriage return to the screen

Buffer[dwBytesRead] = '\\n';

bSuccess = WriteFile(hOutput, Buffer, dwBytesRead+1,
    &dwBytesWritten, NULL);

if (!bSuccess) {
    /* process error */
}
```

8.1.3.7 Moving and hiding the cursor

If you use **WriteFile** to write text to the screen buffer, characters are always written at the current cursor location. You can determine the current cursor position in the coordinate system of the screen buffer by calling **GetConsoleScreenBufferInfo**. Using the **SetConsoleCursorPosition** function, you can set the cursor position, and thereby control the placement of text by **WriteFile**. If you move the cursor, text at the new cursor location will be overwritten.

The cursor may be visible or hidden. When it is visible, its appearance may vary from completely filling the cell to a horizontal line at the bottom of the cell. You can query the appearance and visibility of the cursor using **GetConsoleCursorInfo**. This call returns the appearance of the cursor line as a percentage of a character cell that is filled by the cursor. The appearance and visibility of the cursor may be set using **SetConsoleCursorInfo**.

The state of the cursor (position, appearance, and visibility) is set independently for each screen buffer.

8.1.3.8 Input using the Console API

The Console API provide the tools for character-based applications that want to receive input about mouse events, window resize events, and unfiltered keyboard events; or that want to have greater control of the screen display.

Each console group has its own input buffer. When a console group has the keyboard focus, it receives information about input events which it formats as input records and places in its input buffer. Any process in the console process group can read from the input buffer of its group if it has an open handle to "CONIN$".

More than one process (or thread) in the same screen group can read at the same time from the shared input buffer. There is no guarantee that the correct process will receive the key strokes intended for it. The only way to control this is for applications to spawn child processes that do not inherit handles to StdIn, or alternatively, allow only one child to inherit keyboard access with the parent refraining from keyboard access until the child has terminated.

8.1.3.9 The Input Buffer

The particular set of keyboard, mouse, and window resize event messages that are stored in the input buffer depends on the current console input modes. Only the processed input mode that affects the key events placed in the input buffer. If enabled, processed mode filters the Ctrl-C combination and passes it to the functions registered with **SetConsoleCtrlHandler**. If mouse aware mode is enabled, mouse events are placed in the input buffer whenever the pointer is within the console window and the user moves the mouse or one of the mouse buttons is pressed or released. If window aware mode is enabled, an event is placed in the input buffer whenever the user changes the size of the screen buffer.. The modes that affect the input buffer can be queried using **GetConsoleMode** and set using **SetConsoleMode** . The different event types are placed into the single input buffer so that the application will receive the events in the order in which they occur. Except for the modes mentioned above, the effects of the other console modes (echo, wrap at EOL, and the line-editing features of the processed input and output modes) are not seen when using the Console API. These modes are intended primarily for controlling the way **ReadFile** reads from the input buffer or writes to the screen buffer, and the way **WriteFile** writes to the screen buffer.

Applications may read from the input buffer by using **ReadConsoleInput**, which blocks until at least one event is available to be read. Then all available events are transferred to the caller's buffer until either no more events are available, or the caller's buffer is filled. Unread events remain in the input buffer for the next read call. The total number of events read is indicated to the caller.

You may also read from the input buffer without removing events by using **PeekConsoleInput** which copies available events into the caller's buffer until all events have been read or the caller's buffer is full. If no events are available, the call returns immediately. The total number of events peeked at is indicated.

GetNumberOfConsoleInputEvents can be used to determine the number of events in the input buffer. Or you could use a handle to console input as an object to wait for in either **WaitForSingleObject** or **WaitForMultipleObjects**. The input handle becomes Signalled when the input buffer becomes not empty. The handle is reset to Not-Signalled when the input buffer becomes empty.

WriteConsoleInput and **FlushConsoleInputBuffer** can be used if the input handle was opened with write access. **WriteConsoleInput** places input records into the input buffer behind any pending events in the buffer. The input buffer grows dynamically, if necessary, to hold as many events as are written. **FlushConsoleInputBuffer** empties the input buffer.

The console places events of any type into the input buffer in the form of input records. Input records have the following structure:

typedef struct _INPUT_RECORD { WORD EventType; union { KEY_EVENT_RECORD KeyEvent; MOUSE_EVENT_RECORD MouseEvent; WINDOW_BUFFER_SIZE_RECORD WindowBufferSizeEvent; } Event; } INPUT_RECORD, *PINPUT_RECORD;

The EventType field of an input record indicates whether the event contains a keyboard, mouse, or buffer size event.

8.1.3.10 Key events

Key events are generated when any key, including control keys, is pressed. However, Alt when pressed and released without combining with another character has special meaning to Windows and is not passed through to the application. Also, Ctrl-C is not passed through if the input handle is in processed mode. If the event is a keystroke, the *Event* field of the input record will be a key event record with the following fields:

bKeyDown	TRUE if key is being pressed; FALSE if key was released
wVirtualKeyCode	The virtual key code that identifies the given key in a device-independent manner.
wVirtualScanCode	The virtual scan code that represents the value generated by the keyboard hardware for the given key. This value indicates in a device-dependent manner the identity of the physical key pressed.
uChar	The translation of the key into either an ASCII or Unicode character. The translation depends on whether the wide-character (Unicode) or ANSI version of the function was used

dwControlKeyState   A flag indicating the state of the control keys (Alt, Ctrl, Shift, Num Lock, Scroll Lock, Caps Lock). Constants defined in WINCON.H can be ANDed with this flag to determine if specific control keys were pressed. The flag also indicates if the pressed key was one of the keys on an enhanced keyboard, in which case, the specific key can be determined from the virtual key code. Enhanced keys for the IBM 101- and 102-key keyboards are: the insert, delete, home, end, page up, page down, and direction keys in the clusters to the left of the numeric key pad; and the divide (/) and ENTER keys in the numeric key pad.

8.1.3.11 Mouse events

Mouse events are placed in the input buffer when the console is in mouse mode. This is the default mode when a console is created, but it may be switched on or off by using **SetConsoleMode** . Changing the mouse mode only affects input that occurs after the mode is set, and pending mouse events in the input buffer are not flushed. The mouse pointer is displayed regardless of the mouse mode.

Mouse events are generated whenever the user moves the mouse or presses or releases one of the mouse buttons. Mouse events are placed in a console's input buffer only when the console group has the keyboard focus. If the mouse pointer is not within the borders of the window, mouse events are not reported.

For mouse events, the *Event* field of the input record will be a mouse event record with the following fields:

dwMousePosition   The coordinates of the mouse relative to the screen buffer. The coordinates are in terms of the row and column character cells of the screen buffer. Note that because the screen buffer may have been scrolled with respect to the window, the upper left corner of the window is not necessarily the 0,0 coordinate of the screen buffer. To determine the coordinates of the mouse relative to the coordinate system of the window, subtract the window origin coordinates from the mouse position coordinates. The window origin coordinates are the Left, Top fields of the srWindow rectangle returned by calling **GetConsoleScreenBufferInfo**. Refer also to the section below on window size and screen buffer size.

dwButtonState	A flag indicating status of mouse buttons. The least significant bit corresponds to the leftmost mouse button. The next least significant bit corresponds to the rightmost mouse button. The next bit indicates the next-to-leftmost mouse button. The bits then correspond left-to-right to the mouse buttons. The number of buttons on the mouse can be determined by calling **GetNumberOfConsoleMouseButtons**.
dwControlKeyState	A flag indicating the state of the control keys (Alt, Ctrl, Shift, Num Lock, Scroll Lock, Caps Lock). Constants defined in WINCON.H can be ANDed with this flag to determine if any of these keys were pressed.
dwEventFlags	Constants defined in WINCON.H can be compared with this flag to determine the type of mouse event. MOUSE_MOVED indicates a change in the mouse position. DOUBLE_CLICK indicates a double-click. For button press or release events that are not double-click events, this flag is set to 0.

8.1.3.12 *bBuffer *bresize events

If the input handle is in window aware mode, the console window's menu allows the user to change the size of the active screen buffer, generating a buffer size event. If not in window aware mode, the screen buffer resize menu option is disabled. Changes to the screen buffer size due to application calls to **SetConsoleScreenBufferSize** are not reported as events in the input buffer. In a buffer size event, the *Event* field of the input record will be a WINDOW_BUFFER_SIZE_RECORD containing the new size of the active screen buffer. The *X* coordinate of the new size is the number of characters per row and the *Y* coordinate is the number of rows. If the user reduces the size of the screen buffer, any data in the discarded portion is lost.

The following code fragment might be used by a thread whose purpose was to continuously read input from the input buffer and dispatch the events to the appropriate handlers:

```
DWORD NumRead;
BOOL bResult;
INPUT_RECORD InputBuffer[100];
HANDLE hStdIn = GetStdHandle(STD_INPUT_HANDLE));
int i;

while (1) {

    /* wait for events */

    bResult = ReadConsoleInput(hStdIn, InputBuffer,
        100, &NumRead);
    if (!bResult) { /* handle error */ }

    /* dispatch the events to the appropriate handler */
```

```
                    for (i=0; i<NumRead; i++) {

                        switch(InputBuffer[i].EventType) {
                            case KEY_EVENT:
                                doKeyEvent(InputBuffer[i].Event.KeyEvent);
                                break;

                            case MOUSE_EVENT:
                                doMouseEvent(InputBuffer[i].Event.MouseEvent);
                                break;

                            case WINDOW_BUFFER_SIZE_EVENT:
                                rows =
        InputBuffer[i].Event.WindowBufferSizeEvent.dwSize.Y;
                                cols =
        InputBuffer[i].Event.WindowBufferSizeEvent.dwSize.X;
                                AdjustScreenDisplay(rows, cols);
                                break;

                            default:
                                /* error: unknown event type */
                                break;
                        }

                    }

                }
```

8.1.3.13 Output using the Console API

Console output is displayed in a console window. An application writes to this display area by writing to a screen buffer which maps the window into a grid of character cells. When a console is first created, a default sized screen buffer is created. This buffer is initially the active screen buffer, the one that is displayed. Additional screen buffers may be created by calling **CreateConsoleScreenBuffer**, as described above in the section above on getting handles to console output. Use **SetConsoleActiveScreenBuffer** to change the currently displayed screen buffer. Any of the calls that read from or write to a screen buffer may be used to access active or inactive screen buffers.

There are a number of properties that are associated with a screen buffer and that may be set independently for each screen buffer. This means that changing the active screen buffer may have a dramatic effect on the appearance of the console window. The per screen buffer properties include: screen buffer size, text attributes, window size, window origin; cursor position, appearance, and visibility; and output modes (processed output and wrap at end of line).

8.1.3.14 Window and Screen Buffer Sizes

Console window and screen buffer sizes are expressed in terms of a coordinate grid based on character cells. The width is the number of characters in each row, and the height is the number of rows. The screen buffer may be of any size, limited only by available memory. The dimensions of a console window may not exceed the corresponding dimensions of either the screen buffer or the maximum window that could fit on the display using the current font.

Call **GetConsoleScreenBufferInfo** to determine the current size of the screen buffer or the console window associated with it. The *dwSize* field contains the screen buffer size. The *srWindow* field contains the coordinates of the topleft and bottomright corners of the window in terms of the screen buffer's coordinate system. The *srWindow* rectangle can be modified and then passed in to **SetConsoleWindowInfo** to scroll the screen buffer in the window and/or to change the size of the window. The *dwMaximumWindowSize* field returned by **GetConsoleScreenBufferInfo** is the maximum size of the console window given the current screen buffer size, the current font, and the display size. The size returned by **GetLargestConsoleWindowSize** is based only on the the current font and display, and does not consider the size of the screen buffer.

If the mode of the screen buffer is windows aware, the screen buffer size can be changed by the user as discussed above in the section on buffer size events. In any mode, the application can change a screen buffer's size by calling **SetConsoleScreenBufferSize**; and it can change the size of the console window by calling **SetConsoleWindowInfo**. If you change the size of the screen buffer such that it is smaller than the window, the window size will be automatically reduced. If you attempt to change the window size so that it exceeds the limits of the screen buffer or the display, **SetConsoleWindowInfo** will fail and return FALSE.

Typically, applications that are not in windows aware mode will either use the inherited window and screen buffer sizes, or set them to the desired size at initialization. Window aware applications will probably want to use **GetConsoleScreenBufferInfo** to query window and screen buffer size at start up. This information can then be used to determine the way data is displayed in the window. If the user changes the screen buffer size, the event will be reported and the application may want to respond by changing the way data is displayed. For example, you could adjust the way text wraps at the end of the line if the number of characters per row changes. Applications that change screen buffer attributes should either create their own screen buffer or save console state during startup and restore it at exit.

8.1.3.15 Writing strings of characters to a screen buffer

A program can write individual characters or strings to the screen at the current cursor location using the **WriteFile** call as described above in the section on File API. Using the Console API, you can write characters or attributes at specified character cells in the screen buffer. **WriteConsoleOutputCharacter** writes a specified number of ASCII or UNICODE characters from the caller's buffer to a specified location in the screen buffer. For example, the following code fragment writes a string of characters beginning at row 25, column 30 of the screen buffer.

```
HANDLE hOutput;
CHAR CharString[] = "Character String";
DWORD dwCharsWritten;
BOOL bSuccess;
COORD Coord;

Coord.X = 30;
Coord.Y = 25;
bSuccess = WriteConsoleOutputCharacter(hOutput,
    CharString,
    strlen(CharString),
    Coord,
    &dwCharsWritten
    );
```

The coordinates specify the location of the character string in the screen buffer. The actual location in the console window at which these characters would be written depends on the current window origin. For a discussion of the window origin, refer to the section below on scrolling the screen buffer.

You can write the same ASCII or UNICODE character to the screen repeatedly by calling **FillConsoleOutputCharacter**. For example, the following code fragment clears a 25 x 80 screen buffer:

```
HANDLE hOutput;
BOOL bSuccess;
DWORD dwCharsWritten;
COORD Coord;

Coord.X = 0; // start at 0,0
Coord.Y = 0;
bSuccess = FillConsoleOutputCharacter(hOutput,
    ' ', // fill with blanks
    80*25, // number of chars
    Coord, // starting coords
    &dwCharsWritten
    );
```

In any of the calls that write characters or attributes to consecutive screen buffer cells, writing wraps around to the beginning of the next row when the end of the current screen buffer row is encountered. This occurs regardless of the state of the wrap at EOL output mode. When the end of the last row of the screen buffer is encountered, all characters or attributes remaining to be written are discarded.

8.1.3.16 Writing strings of color attributes to a screen buffer

Calls similar to those for writing text are available to set the color attributes of any character cell in a screen buffer. **WriteConsoleOutputAttribute** writes a string of attributes to the screen buffer at a specified location. This call might be used to highlight a string of characters by drawing them with a different color. **FillConsoleOutputAttribute** writes the same attribute for a specified number cells, beginning at a specified location in a screen buffer. This call might be used to set the color attributes for the entire screen buffer prior to writing text. The color attributes determine the foreground (text) and background colors in which the character will be drawn. The attributes may be set individually for each character cell. Refer to

WINCON.H for the attribute constants that can be used in specifying attributes. The attributes may be ORed to achieve different colors. For example, the following combination results in bright cyan text:

```
FOREGROUND_BLUE | FOREGROUND_GREEN | FOREGROUND_INTENSITY
```

8.1.3.17 Writing blocks of characters and attributes

WriteConsoleOutput provides another way to write characters and attributes to a screen buffer. This functions copies from the caller's buffer to a screen buffer, but the source buffer is treated as a two dimensional array rather than a string, and copying is done from a rectangular block in the source buffer to a destination block in the screen buffer. The source buffer's array elements contain both the ASCII or UNICODE character and the color attributes to be written.

A destination rectangle in the screen buffer is specified. The size of this rectangle and the coordinates of the first element in the source buffer determine the portion of the source that will be copied. Only those parts of the destination rectangle that are within the boundaries of the screen buffer can be written to. So any sections in the source buffer that correspond to the part of the destination that is outside the screen buffer boundaries are not copied. Similarly, if the source rectangle extends outside the boundaries of the source buffer, the corresponding portion of the screen buffer is not written to.

The following code fragment reads a block of characters and attributes from the top two rows of one screen buffer, and then writes them into the middle rows of another screen buffer:

```
HANDLE hOutput_1, hOutput_2;
SMALL_RECT ReadRegion; // region of screen buf to read from
SMALL_RECT WriteRegion; // region of screen buf to write to
CHAR_INFO Buffer[160]; // buffer to read into
COORD BufferSize; // size of buffer in character rows and cols
COORD BufferCoord; // starting row/col to read or write from
BOOL bSuccess;

// read from top rows of source screen buffer

ReadRegion.Left = 0;
ReadRegion.Right = 79;
ReadRegion.Top = 0;
ReadRegion.Bottom = 1;
BufferSize.Y = 2; // dest buffer is 2 rows x 80 columns
BufferSize.X = 80;
BufferCoord.X = 0; // read and write from first cell of buffer
BufferCoord.Y = 0;
bSuccess = ReadConsoleOutput(hOutput_1,
    Buffer,
    BufferSize,
    BufferCoord,
    &ReadRegion
    );

// write from Buffer to middle rows of dest screen buffer
```

```
WriteRegion.Left = 0;
WriteRegion.Top = 10;
WriteRegion.Right = 79;
WriteRegion.Bottom = 11;
bSuccess = WriteConsoleOutput(hOutput_2,
    (PCHAR_INFO) Buffer,
    BufferSize,
    BufferCoord,
    &WriteRegion);
```

Note that if the destination screen buffer in this example is only 60 characters wide, the last 20 characters of the rows would be discarded. The current window size or origin does not affect writing to a screen buffer. It only determines which portion of the screen buffer is visible.

8.1.3.18 Reading from the screen buffer

Using **ReadConsoleOutputCharacter**, you can read a string of UNICODE or ASCII characters from a screen buffer by specifying the row and column of the character cell at which to begin and the number of characters to read. Using **ReadConsoleOutputAttribute** , you can read a string of attributes from a screen buffer by specifying the first cell and the number to read. These API treat the screen buffer as a string of consecutive character cells rather than a two-dimensional array, so if the number to read extends past the end of one row the data is read from the beginning of the next. If the number to read extends past the end of the screen buffer, the characters or attributes are read up to the end and the actual number read is returned. The following code fragment reads a string of 80 characters from row 20 of the screen buffer:

```
HANDLE hOutput;
CHAR CharString[80];
DWORD dwCharsRead;
BOOL bSuccess;
COORD Coord;

Coord.X = 0;
Coord.Y = 19;

bSuccess = ReadConsoleOutputCharacter(hOutput,
    CharString,
    80,
    Coord,
    &dwCharsRead
    );
```

Using **ReadConsoleOutput,** you can read blocks of character/attribute pairs. This works in much the same way as **WriteConsoleOutput** . A source rectangle in the screen buffer identifies the region from which to copy. The data read from this rectangle is copied into the destination array beginning at the specified coordinates. The destination buffer is treated as a two dimensional array whose elements contain both an ASCII or UNICODE character and a color attributes field. The size of the destination array is specified in terms of character rows and columns. The actual rectangle that is copied can be clipped if either the source rectangle extends outside the boundaries of the screen buffer, or the destination rectangle extends outside the boundaries of the destination buffer. An example of using **ReadConsoleOutput** is given in the section above on **WriteConsoleOutput**.

8.1.3.19   Scrolling the Screen Buffer

The current window origin or scroll position is defined as the cell of the screen buffer that is currently displayed at the top left corner of the window. Initially, the window origin is (0,0), i.e., the top left corner of the screen buffer is at the top left corner of the window. However, the origin of the screen buffer with respect to the window can change if the contents of the screen buffer are scrolled in the window. If the active screen buffer is larger than the console window, scroll bars are available for the user to scroll the contents. Scrolling the screen buffer in the window can happen automatically if you are using **WriteFile** in wrap at EOL mode and text is written past the last row of the window. Or the application can cause scrolling to occur by calling **SetConsoleWindowInfo**. Scrolling is not reported as an event in the input buffer.

You can call **GetConsoleScreenBufferInfo** to determine the current window origin (the *Left, Top* coordinates of the *srWindow* field of the CONSOLE_SCREEN_BUFFER_INFO struct.

You can cause the contents of the screen buffer to scroll in the window by calling **SetConsoleWindowInfo**. This can also be used to change the window size. The function takes a SMALL_RECT argument whose coordinates may specify the new topleft and bottomright corners of the window either as absolute screen buffer coordinates or as deltas from the current window coordinates. For example, the following code fragment modifies the absolute coordinates returned by **GetConsoleScreenBufferInfo** to scroll the view of the screen buffer up by one line:

```
HANDLE hOutput;
BOOL bResult;
CONSOLE_SCREEN_BUFFER_INFO Info;
SMALL_RECT srWindow;

bResult = GetConsoleScreenBufferInfo(hOutput, &Info);

srWindow = Info.srWindow;
srWindow.Top += 1;
srWindow.Bottom += 1;

bResult = SetConsoleWindowInfo(hOutput, TRUE, &srWindow);
```

The same scrolling could be done using deltas as follows:

```
HANDLE hOutput;
BOOL bResult;
SMALL_RECT srWindow;

srWindow.Top = 1;
srWindow.Bottom = 1;
srWindow.Left = 0; // no change
srWindow.Right = 0; // no change
```

```
bResult = SetConsoleWindowInfo(hOutput, FALSE, &srWindow);
```

These examples would fail if the last row of the screen buffer is currently displayed in the last row of the window, since scrolling the screen buffer up would leave the window extending beyond the edge of the screen buffer. To handle this situation, you could call **SetConsoleScreenBufferSize** to increase the number of rows in the screen buffer. This would make it possible to shift the window origin without exposing the bottom of the window. Alternatively, you could use **ScrollConsoleScreenBuffer** to scroll the contents of the screen buffer, discarding the top row of the screen buffer and leaving the window origin unchanged. The code fragment below shows a variation of this idea where the top five rows of the buffer contain static data and only the rows below that are scrolled:

```
HANDLE hOutput;
BOOL bResult;
CONSOLE_SCREEN_BUFFER_INFO Info;
SMALL_RECT srScrollRect, srClipRect;
CHAR_INFO Fill;

// first get the size of the screen buffer

bResult = GetConsoleScreenBufferInfo(hOutput, &Info);

// scroll rectangle is from row 5 to bottom of screen buffer

srScrollRect.Top = 5;
srScrollRect.Left = 0;
srScrollRect.Bottom = Info.dwSize.Y - 1;
srScrollRect.Right = Info.dwSize.X - 1;

// destination for top of scroll rectangle is row(4) */

dwDestinationOrigin.Y = 4;
dwDestinationOrigin.X = 0;

/* copying clipped to the original scroll rectangle */

/* so row 5 is discarded; row 4 is unchanged */

srClipRect = srScrollRect;

/* fill bottom row with green blanks */

Fill.Attributes = BACKGROUND_GREEN | FOREGROUND_RED;
Fill.Char.AsciiChar = ' ';

bResult = ScrollConsoleScreenBuffer(hOutput,
    &srScrollRect,
    &srClipRect,
    dwDestinationOrigin,
    &Fill
    );
```

The same code could be used to scroll the entire screen buffer by changing two lines:

```
// scroll from top of screen buffer instead of row 5

srScrollRect.Top = 0;

// scroll top row to row (-1), outside the screen buffer
```

```
dwDestinationOrigin.Y = -1;
```

Another use of this API is to implement delete line. The scroll rectangle would encompass all data below the deleted line and the destination origin would be the first character in the deleted line.

8.1.3.20   Control Handlers

SetConsoleCtrlHandler allows you to create and register one or more functions to handle Ctrl-C and Ctrl-break for the calling process. It may also be used to remove a handler from the list of handlers registered for a process. The handler functions will always be invoked if Ctrl-break is input; but Ctrl-C is only passed through if the console is in processed input mode.

The handler function takes a single argument that will identify which control character was input. The function returns a Boolean result. If TRUE, it indicates that the control character was handled and other handlers should not be invoked. If no handlers are registered for this application, a default handler that calls ExitProcess is called. If multiple handlers have been registered, they are called on a last registered, first called basis. If none of the handlers returns TRUE, the default handler is called.

```
// control handler that handles Ctrl-C, passes Ctrl-break

BOOL CtrlHandler(ULONG CtrlType) {
    switch (CtrlType) {
        CTRL_C_EVENT:
            // handle Ctrl-C

            return TRUE;

        CTRL_BREAK_EVENT:

        default:

            return FALSE;

    }

}

    .
    .
    .

BOOL bResult;

// add the handler to the list for this process

bResult = SetConsoleCtrlHandler(
    (PHANDLER_ROUTINE) &CtrlHandler, TRUE);
```

8.1.3.21   Summary

Mlist	Description
PeekConsoleInput	Read data from the input buffer without removing it.
ReadConsoleInput	Read at least one event from the input buffer.
WriteConsoleInput	Place events into the input buffer behind any existing events in the buffer.
ReadConsoleOutput	Read a block of characters and their attributes from a rectangular region of a screen buffer into a buffer.
WriteConsoleOutput	Write a block of characters and their attributes from a buffer into a rectangular region of a screen buffer.
ReadConsoleOutputCharacter	Read a string of consecutive characters from a specified location in a screen buffer.
ReadConsoleOutputAttribute	Read a string of consecutive character attributes from a specified location in a screen buffer.
WriteConsoleOutputCharacter	Write a string of consecutive characters to a specified location in a screen buffer.
WriteConsoleOutputAttribute	Write a string of consecutive character attributes to a specified location in a screen buffer.
FillConsoleOutputCharacter	Write a character to a specified number of consecutive character cells in a screen buffer.
FillConsoleOutputAttribute	Write a character attribute to a specified number of consecutive character cells in a screen buffer.
GetConsoleMode	Get a mask indicating the current mode of a console input buffer or an output screen buffer.
GetNumberOfConsoleInputEvents	Returns the number of pending events in the input buffer.
GetConsoleScreenBufferInfo	Returns information about a screen buffer, including its size in character rows and columns, cursor position, the location of its window, its default text display attribute.
GetLargestConsoleWindowSize	Returns the size in character rows and columns of the largest window that can fit on the display given the current font.

Mlist	Description
GetConsoleCursorInfo	Returns the size and visibility of the cursor for the specified screen buffer.
GetNumberOfConsoleMouseButtons	Returns the number of mouse buttons.
SetConsoleMode	Sets the mode for either an input or an output console handle.
SetConsoleActiveScreenBuffer	Specifies the screen buffer that will be displayed.
FlushConsoleInputBuffer	Empty the input buffer.
SetConsoleScreenBufferSize	Set the size in character rows and columns of a screen buffer.
SetConsoleCursorPosition	Set the cursor position for a screen buffer, which is the character cell to which **ReadFile** or **WriteFile** will write.
SetConsoleCursorInfo	Sets the size and visibility of the cursor for the specified screen buffer.
ScrollConsoleScreenBuffer	Move characters and attributes from a rectangular region of a screen buffer to a new location. Copying at the new location can be clipped to the dimensions of a clip rectangle.
SetConsoleWindowInfo	Set the location of a console window in terms of the coordinate system of its screen buffer using either absolute coordinates or deltas.
SetConsoleTextAttribute	Specify the attributes (color) for text subsequently written by **WriteFile** or **ReadFile**.
SetConsoleCtrlHandler	Add or remove a Ctrl-C and Ctrl-Break handler for the calling process.
AllocConsole	Create a console for the calling process if one does not exist.
FreeConsole	Free the console of the calling process.
GetConsoleTitle	Returns the title of a console window.
SetConsoleTitle	Sets the title of a console window.
CreateConsoleScreenBuffer	Creates a new screen buffer for console output.

Chapter 9 | Communications

9.1   Introduction 159

      9.1.1   About Communications 159

           9.1.1.1   Using the Comm API 159

           9.1.1.2   Getting a handle to a communications resource . . . 159

           9.1.1.3   Initializing a communications resource 160

           9.1.1.4   Configuring a communications resource 160

           9.1.1.5   Reading from a communications resource 162

           9.1.1.6   Writing to a communications resource 163

           9.1.1.7   Other communications functions 164

           9.1.1.8   Monitoring events 165

9.2   Summary 166

9.1 Introduction

The Comm API are used to access and control serial communications devices, including serial ports. Other devices, such as the keyboard, video display, and mouse, are accessed through their own API.

9.1.1 About Communications

The Communications API provide a single interface that may be used to work with a variety of communications resources. A communications resource is a physical or logical device that provides a single bidirectional asynchronous data stream, such as a serial port, parallel port, modem, FAX machine, etc. For each communications resource, there is a service provider with which the application will interface. A service provider consists of a library or driver that provides access to one or more resources.

The File IO API provide the basic interface for open, close, read, and write operations to communications resources. **CreateFile** is used to open a handle to a communications resource; and **CloseHandle** may be used to close the handle. The handle returned by **CreateFile** may be used in any of the Comm API to access the resource. It may also be inherited by child processes. **ReadFile** and **WriteFile** are used for read and write operations respectively.

The Communications API have a basic set of functions that provide an interface appropriate for serial communications. A set of extended functions are available for providers that have functionality not supported by the standard functions. This extended set allows you to configure a provider using parameters peculiar to that provider, as well as to invoke provider-specific functions.

9.1.1.1 Using the Comm API   Information to come

9.1.1.2 Getting a handle to a communications resource

An application uses **CreateFile** to open a handle to a communications resource. If the specified device is currently being used by another process, **CreateFile** will return 0xFFFFFFFF. The security attributes argument to **CreateFile** determines whether the handle can be inherited by child processes. Another option in this call is to open the handle for overlapped I/O by specifying the FILE_FLAG_OVERLAPPED flag. This allows the application to initiate an I/O operation (read, for example) and then proceed with other operations while the read executes in the background. Overlapped I/O is also necessary if you have more than one thread performing I/O operations, or if you want one thread to do an I/O operation while another thread is blocked calling **WaitCommEvent.**

The **CreateFile** call opens a handle to a communications resource that has been initialized and configured according to the values that were set up the last time the resource was opened. If the device has never been opened, it is configured using the system defaults. This allows settings specified by a MODE command to be retained when the device is reopened. The values inherited from the previous open include the configuration parameters of the Device Control Block (DCB) and the timeout values used in I/O operations.

9.1.1.3 Initializing a communications resource

To re-initialize a communications resource, you can call **SetupComm**. This reallocates the transmit and receive queues for a device, according to the sizes specified. Existing transmit and receive queues are purged and freed.

9.1.1.4 Configuring a communications resource

A communications resource is configured when it is opened by **CreateFile**. However, these settings may not conform to the requirements of your application. To determine the initial DCB configuration, call **GetCommState** . This fills in a serial port DCB with the current configuration parameters. Your application can then adjust the DCB values that are important to it, and reconfigure the device by specifying the modified DCB in a call to **SetCommState**.

SetCommState provides a basic interface that uses a serial port DCB to specify the desired configuration. Among the parameters specified by the DCB are baud rate, number of data bits, and number of stop bits. Some of the other DCB fields enable parity checking, flow control, and specify special characters. If you are only interested in setting a few fields of the DCB, it is a good idea to just modify a DCB that has been filled in by a call to **GetCommState** . This ensures that the other fields of the DCB have appropriate values. For example, a common error occurs when a device is configured with a DCB in which the XonChar is equal to the XoffChar. Note that some fields of the DCB structure have been changed from previous versions of Windows. In particular, the flags for controlling RTS and DTR flow control have been changed. Refer to the DCB reference page for more information.

Another way to fill in a DCB is with the **BuildCommDCB** call. **BuildCommDCB** uses a string with the same format as the DOS MODE command line to specify settings for baud rate, parity scheme, number of stopbits, and number of character bits. The remaining fields of the DCB are filled in according to the current settings for that device (or the defaults if the device has not been opened previously), except that Xon/Xoff and hardware flow control are always disabled.

GetCommProperties can be called to get information from a provider about the configuration settings that are supported by that provider. This information can then be used in the calls that set configuration.

The following code fragment opens a handle to "COM1" and fills in a DCB with the current configuration. The DCB is then modified and used to reconfigure the device:

```
HANDLE hCom;
DWORD dwError;
DCB dcb;
BOOL bSuccess;

hCom = CreateFile("COM1",
    GENERIC_READ | GENERIC_WRITE,
    0, // comm devices must be opened with exclusive access
    NULL, // no security attrs
    OPEN_EXISTING, // comm devices must use OPEN_EXISTING
    0, // not overlapped I/O
    NULL // hTemplate must be NULL for comm devices
    );

if (hCom == (HANDLE) 0xFFFFFFFF) {
    dwError= GetLastError();

    // handle error
}

// omit call to SetupComm to use default queue sizes

// get the current configuration

bSuccess = GetCommState(hCom, &dcb);

if (!bSuccess) {
    /* handle error *
}

// fill in DCB: baud=9600, 8 data bits, no parity, 1 stop bit

dcb.BaudRate = 9600;
dcb.ByteSize = 8;
dcb.Parity = NOPARITY;
dcb.StopBits = ONESTOPBIT;
bSuccess = SetCommState(hCom, &dcb);

if (!bSuccess) {
    /* handle error */
}
```

For those providers that have settable parameters not included in the serial port DCB, the **SetCommConfig** call can be used to specify a configuration by means of a Communications Configuration Structure (COMMCONFIG). This extended structure includes the basic serial port DCB as well as additional provider specific fields. For an application to use this call, it must be aware of the special configuration parameters for the provider being configured. This is necessary because the size and fields of the COMMCONFIG structure depend on the provider. The **GetCommConfig** call is used to determine the current configuration, returning a filled in COMMCONFIG structure.

Note that when using either **SetCommState** or **SetCommConfig** to reconfigure a device, the device's state is changed but the transmit and receive queues are not flushed and pending read and write operations are not aborted.

9.1.1.5 Reading from a communications resource

ReadFile is used to read from an open device, using a handle to a communications resource as returned from **CreateFile**. This can support several different read operations depending on the settings of the timeout values and the handle's overlapped flag. The timeout values are set when the device is opened according to the values set when the device was last opened. If the device has never been opened, all total and interval timeouts are set to 0. To determine the current timeout values, call **GetCommTimeouts**. The timeout values can be changed by calling **SetCommTimeouts**.

blocking	**ReadFile** does not return until the requested number of bytes have been read. This occurs if all total and interval timeout values are set to 0, and overlapped I/O is not enabled.
non-blocking	**ReadFile** returns immediately with whatever is available in the receive queue (even if it is empty), and indicates the actual number of bytes read. This is the same behavior as the ReadComm function in previous versions of Windows. Non-blocking reads occur if **SetCommTimeouts** has been called with an interval timeout of 0xFFFFFFFF and both total timeout parameters equal to zero.
interval timeout	An interval timeout occurs when the interval between the arrival of two characters exceeds a specified maximum. Timing does not begin until the first character has been received, which makes this type of timeout useful in implementing a wait-for-something read. If the interval value is zero, interval timing is not used. Interval timing is designed to force a read to return when there is a lull in the reception. An application using interval timeouts can set a fairly short timeout interval so that it can respond quickly to small, isolated bursts of one or a few characters, and yet still collect large buffers of characters with a single call when data is being received in a steady stream.
total timeout	A total timeout occurs when the total time for a read operation exceeds a calculated time period. Timing begins immediately. A constant and a multiplier specified in **SetCommTimeouts** are used together to calculate the total timeout period as follows: constant + (multiplier * bytes requested) This allows an application to set a total timeout that varies depending on the amount of data being requested. You may use just the constant by setting the multiplier to zero; or just the multiplier by setting the constant to zero. If both are zero, total timing is not used.

overlapped	Overlapped I/O can be enabled when **CreateFile** is called to open a device handle. If the specified number of characters can be read immediately, or if non-blocking reading has been enabled as described above, **ReadFile** will return TRUE. Otherwise, it will return FALSE and **GetLastError** will indicate ERROR_IO_PENDING, as the read completes in the background. The Event object in the OVERLAPPED structure (or the device handle if the Event object is NULL) will be signalled when the read is complete. Either of the wait functions, **WaitForMultipleObjects** or **WaitForSingleObject**, can be used to wait for the Event object or the file handle to be signalled. When this happens, call **GetOverlappedResult** to determine the number of bytes read. The timeout values are still used in conjunction with overlapped I/O to determine when the read is complete. Overlapped I/O allows an application to do more than one I/O operation at a time. For example, you could read from two or more devices simultaneously, read from one device while writing to another, or read and write from one device at the same time.

If a timeout occurs, **ReadFile** returns TRUE (a successful read) and indicates the number of characters read prior to the timeout. It is possible to use both interval and total timing, in which case, **ReadFile** will return when either one times out.

There are a few other circumstances where a **ReadFile** call can return with fewer than the requested number of characters, even though a timeout has not occurred. Some providers support the use of special characters (refer to documentation for the **ExtendedProviderFunction**) which when received, cause **ReadFile** to return immediately with characters read to that point. It is also possible to abort a read operation by calling the **PurgeComm** function which deletes the contents of the transmit or receive queue (or both), or can be made to abort pending read or write operations. If **PurgeComm**(PURGE_RXABORT) is called during a read operation, **ReadFile** will return FALSE and **GetLastError** will return ERROR_OPERATION_ABORTED.

If a communication error occurs during a read, all operations will abort. For example, if a break condition is detected, or a parity or framing error occurs, **ReadFile** will return FALSE and the contents of its buffer are not valid. Call **ClearCommError** to determine the specific error and the current status of the device. **ClearCommError** also clears the error flag to allow additional I/O operations to be made.

9.1.1.6 Writing to a communications resource

WriteFile is used to write to an open device, using a handle to a communications resource as returned from **CreateFile**. As with **ReadFile**, the behavior of **WriteFile** depends on the timeout values set by calling **SetCommTimeouts**, and the handle's overlapped flag which is set when the device is opened by **CreateFile**. The default behavior of **WriteFile** is to not use timeouts. If overlapped I/O is not enabled and timeouts are not used, **WriteFile** will block until the specified number of characters have been transmitted. A write can block if some kind of flow control is occurring or if **SetCommBreak** is called to suspend character transmission.

The two timeout values for **WriteFile**, *WriteTotalTimeoutMultiplier* and *WriteTotalTimeoutConstant*, are used to calculate a total timeout period in the same way as calculated for read operations. Interval timeouts are not provided for write operations. If a timeout occurs, **WriteFile** returns TRUE and the number of characters actually transmitted is returned.

TransmitCommChar sends a character to the head of transmit queue. This is useful in transmitting a high priority signal character to the receiving system. Transmission is still subject to flow control and write timeouts, and the operation is performed synchronously.

If **PurgeComm** is called to purge a transmit queue, the deleted characters will not be transmitted. To empty the transmit queue while ensuring that the contents are transmitted, call **FlushFileBuffers** (which is a synchronous operation). Note that **FlushFileBuffers** is subject to flow control but not to write timeouts, and it will not return until all pending writes have been transmitted.

If a communication error occurs while writing to a communications device, the write operation will abort. Call **ClearCommError** to determine the current status of the device and a code indicating the specific error. This call clears the error flag to allow additional read or write calls to be made.

9.1.1.7 Other communications functions

Other Comm functions may be invoked for a device by calling the **EscapeCommFunction**. This call directs the device to execute a function specified by a function code. For example, this can be used to suspend character transmission with the SETBREAK function and to resume character transmission with the CLRBREAK function. These particular functions may also be invoked by calling **SetCommBreak** and **ClearCommBreak**. **EscapeCommFunction** can also be used to implement manual modem control. For example, the CLRDTR and SETDTR functions can be used to implement manual DTR flow control. Note that an error occurs if this function is used to manipulate the DTR line when the device has been configured to enable DTR handshaking, or the RTS line if RTS handshaking is enabled.

For providers that have functionality not supported by the standard functions, the Comm API provides a set of extended functions. Two mentioned above are the **Get/SetCommConfig** functions that may be used to set provider specific configuration parameters. The **ExtendedProviderFunction** allows an application to invoke additional configuration functions that may not be supported by all providers, or to invoke specialized functions for a specific provider, if the application knows the function codes used by that provider. The extensibility of the **ExtendedProviderFunction** call allows applications to access functionality unique to a provider, without cluttering the standard API with specialized functions and without restricting providers to those functions defined in the standard API.

9.1.1.8 Monitoring events

An application can use **SetCommMask** to specify a set of events to be monitored for a particular communications resource. It can then use **WaitCommEvent** to wait for one of the specified events to occur. This could be used, for example, if you need to know when the CTS and DSR signals change state. The reference page for **SetCommMask** provides a complete list of the events in which an application can express interest. You must create an Event object which is then used as a parameter of **WaitCommEvent**. When one of the events specified in the event mask occurs, the Event object is signalled and **WaitCommEvent** returns with a filled in event mask indicating the event that satisfied the wait. **GetCommMask** can be used to determine the current set of events being monitored for a device. Calling **SetCommMask** for a device while a wait is pending on that device, will cause **WaitCommEvent** to return with an error indication.

Note that **WaitCommEvent** only detects events that occur after the wait was started. For example, the EV_RXCHAR event is specified to monitor when any character is received and placed in the receive queue. Existing characters in the receive queue when **WaitCommEvent** is called will not satisfy the wait. Also, many of the events occur when a signal (CTS, DSR, etc.) changes state. But this does not tell you what their current state is. The **GetCommModemStatus** call can be used to query the current state of the Clear-To-Send (CTS), Data-Set-Ready (DSR), Receive-Line-Signal-Detect (RLSD), and Ring indicator signals.

The following example code opens the serial port for overlapped I/O, sets the event mask to monitor CTS and DSR signals, and then waits for an event to occur. Overlapped I/O is typically used when a process is using **WaitCommEvent** because otherwise the other threads of the process would be unable to perform I/O operations during the wait.

```
HANDLE hCom, hEvent;
DWORD dwEvtMask;
BOOL bSuccess;

hCom = CreateFile("COM1",
    GENERIC_READ | GENERIC_WRITE,
    0, // exclusive access
    NULL, // no security attrs
    OPEN_EXISTING,
    FILE_FLAG_OVERLAPPED,
    NULL
    );
```

```
if (hCom == (HANDLE) 0xFFFFFFFF) {
    /* deal with error */
}

// set the event mask

bSuccess = SetCommMask(hCom, EV_CTS | EV_DSR);

if (!bSuccess) {
    /* deal with error */
}

/* create event object for use in WaitCommEvent */

hEvent = CreateEvent(NULL, // no security attributes
    FALSE, // auto reset event
    FALSE // not signalled
    NULL // no name
    );

assert(hEvent);

if (WaitCommEvent(hCom, &dwEvtMask, hEvent)) {
    if (dwEvtMask & EV_DSR) {
        /* . . . */
    }

    if (dwEvtMask & EV_CTS) {
        /* . . . */
    }

}
```

9.2 Summary

Mlist	Description
BuildCommDCB	Fills in a Device Control Block (DCB) with parameters specified in a string.
ClearCommBreak	Restores character transmission and clears break state.
ClearCommError	Returns info about error and clears error state
SetupComm	Allocates receive and transmit queues of specified sizes.
EnableCommNotification	Enables message posting for certain communications events.
EscapeCommFunction	Directs a device to carry out a function, e.g. clear the DTR signal.
ExtendedProviderFunction	Provides interface to access the extended functionality of non-standard devices.
GetCommConfig	Returns a COMMCONFIG structure indicating the current configuration of a device.

Mlist	Description
GetCommMask	Returns a mask indicating the set of events that would be monitored by a call to WaitCommEvent.
GetCommModemStatus	Returns the current state of the CTS, DSR, RLSD, and Ring indicator signals.
GetCommState	Returns a DCB indicating the current device configuration.
GetCommTimeouts	Returns the current values of the read and write timeouts.
PurgeComm	Abort pending read or write operations, or purge the receive or transmit queues.
SetCommBreak	Suspend character transmission.
SetCommConfig	Configure a device according to the parameters specified in a COMMCONFIG structure.
SetCommMask	Specify the set of events to be monitored when calling **WaitCommEvent**.
SetCommState	Configure a device according to the parameters in a DCB.
SetCommTimeouts	Set the timeout values used in read and write operations.
TransmitCommChar	Send a character to the head of the transmit queue.
WaitCommEvent	Wait for one of the events specified by SetCommMask to occur.

Chapter 10

Pipes Overview

Overview 171

10.1 Anonymous Pipes 171

10.2 Named Pipes 171

    10.2.1 Using Named Pipes 173

    10.2.2 Named Pipe Summary 174

Overview

This chapter describes the anonymous and named pipe functionality available in the Windows 32-bit API.

10.1 Anonymous Pipes

Pipes allow related processes to communicate with each other and transfer information. Most often, anonymous pipes are used for communication between a parent and child process, or between two children of the same process. Pipes are always local: they cannot be used across a network (named pipes should be used for communication over a network).

To create a pipe, a process calls CreatePipe, which returns two handles. The pipe is full duplex but normally one handle is used for writing to the pipe, and one for reading from the pipe. To read data from the pipe, a program calls ReadFile, with the handle that was returned for reading from the CreatePipe call. To write data to the pipe, a program calls WriteFile, with the handle that CreatePipe returned for writing.

With anonymous pipes, handle inheritance provides the only access to the pipe. As a result, only child processes of the process that created the pipe can access the pipe.

10.2 Named Pipes

Named Pipes allow two or more processes to communicate with each other. Unlike anonymous pipes, any process that knows the name of a named pipe can access it (subject to security checks); the processes accessing a pipe do not need to be related. To use a named pipe, one process must create the pipe by calling the CreateNamedPipe function, which returns a handle to the pipe. Although the process that creates the pipe is traditionally called the server, and the other process that accesses the pipe the client, the difference between clients and servers is greatly diminished in Win32 since any Win32 process can act as a server and as a client, allowing peer to peer communication. As used below, server refers to the process that creates the named pipe; client refers to the other process that connects to it. In addition to being used across a network, as remote pipes, named pipes can also be used locally, on a single machine.

There are two types of named pipes: byte-mode and message pipes. Byte-mode pipes allow transfer of a stream of bytes. Reads and Writes do not have to be of equal size. With message mode pipes, data is read as series of messages. If the the read buffer is larger than the incoming message size, only the number of bytes in the message is read.

Named pipes are usually opened for two-way communication, so that both the server and client can read from and write to the pipe. But the server can create the pipe to be used in only one direction. If the server opens the pipe as an inbound pipe (for reading), by specifying the PIPE_ACCESS_INBOUND flag, it can read data from the client but cannot write to the client. If the server opens the pipe as an outbound pipe (for writing), by specifying the PIPE_ACCESS_OUTBOUND flag, it can write data to the client, but cannot read data from the client. If a pipe is opened as duplex (for both reading and writing), by specifying PIPE_ACCESS_DUPLEX, that pipe can be read from and written to, using one handle.

Named pipes take the following form:

The server must always create the pipe locally, by specifying a period as the name of the server when calling CreateNamedPipe. For local communication, clients open the pipe by specifying a period as the server. Clients on a network must specify the name of the server.

For example, to create a named pipe, with duplex transmission, byte mode, with unlimited instances allowed, a server might do the following:

```
sprintf (szPipeName, "\\\\.\\PIPE\\test");
CreateNamedPipe (szPipeName,
        PIPE_ACCESS_DUPLEX
        FILE_FLAG_WRITE_THROUGH,
        PIPE_WAIT | PIPE_TYPE_BYTE,
        PIPE_UNLIMITED_INSTANCES,
        PIPE_OUTBUFFSIZE,
        PIPE_INBUFFSIZE,
        NULL,
        NULL);
```

The server may create multiple instances of the same named pipe by calling CreateNamedPipe for every instance of the name. Each instance can support one client connection.

A local client would then connect to the pipe by using \.PIPE est for the name of the pipe. Continuing the example, if the pipe was originally opened on the server TESTSERV, a remote client would open the pipe \TESTSERVPIPE est.

Note that two backslashes must be used before the name of the server.

When creating a named pipe, a process may also specify whether or not the pipe should be buffered. With buffering on, the transmission of data may be delayed to enhance performance. Buffering should be turned off for applications that need synchronized data transmission.

A pipe may be created with an overlapped flag (FILE_FLAG_OVERLAPPED), which causes read and write operations to signal an event when they are complete, allowing other functions to continue processing while the reading or writing is taking place. If the FILE_FLAG_OVERLAPPED flag is not specified, functions such as ReadFile and WriteFile will not return until they have finished processing. Overlapped support is important because it allows one thread to service multiple named pipes.

The server process can also specify whether it should wait for the client to connect to the pipe or should return an error code if the client has not already connected.

10.2.1 Using Named Pipes

A named pipe session might look something like the following:

```
Server Action                          Client Action
CreateNamedPipe
ConnectNamedPipe
                                       WaitNamedPipe (if necessary)
                                       CreateFile
ReadFile, WriteFile                    ReadFile, WriteFile
DisconnectNamedPipe
                                       CloseFile
ConnectNamedPipe
  ...
```

After the server process has created an instance of the named pipe by calling the CreateNamedPipe function, it waits for a client to connect to client by calling ConnectNamedPipe. If a client has not yet connected to the pipe by using CreateFile, the ConnectNamedPipe function will wait until a client does connect, if the pipe was created with blocking mode (PIPE_WAIT) specified, or it will return FALSE if non blocking mode (PIPE_NOWAIT) was specified. If a client calls CreateFile to open a pipe and is unsuccessful, it can call WaitNamedPipe to wait, up to a specified interval of time, until an instance of the pipe becomes available.

Once the client and server have connected, they can communicate using ReadFile and WriteFile.

A client can use TransactNamedPipe instead of using ReadFile and WriteFile if it is accessing a pipe that was opened in message mode. TransactNamedPipe writes data to and reads data from a named pipe. TransactNamedPipe is especially useful when a client and server are communication over a network; if a client writes data to a pipe, by calling WriteFile, to request information from the server, and then immediately calls ReadFile to read data from the pipe, TransactNamedPipe can improve performance, since it sends one request across the network instead of two.

A program can call PeekNamedPipe to view the data in a pipe without removing it from the pipe, allowing it to preview the information in the pipe. PeekNamedPipe also returns the number of bytes available to be read from the pipe. In addition, if the pipe was opened in message mode, PeekNamedPipe supplies the number of bytes remaining in the message (a partial message can be read). PeekNamedPipe differs from ReadFile in that it can return a partial message, it will never block, even if the pipe was created with the PIPE_WAIT flag, and it does not actually remove data from the pipe.

GetNamedPipeInfo returns information about a named piped, including the size of the output buffer, the size of the input buffer, and the maximum number of pipe instances of the specified pipe that can be created. GetNamedPipeHandleState also returns information about a pipe, including the number of pipe instances, the maximum time before a remote named pipe transfers data over a network, the maximum number of bytes that will be collected from the client before being transmitted over the network, and, if the server calls the function, the username of the client application. SetNamedPipeHandleState can be used for setting the maximum number of bytes collected from the client and the maximum time period that can elapse before data is transmitted over the network. The GetNamedPipeHandleState and SetNamedPipeHandleState functions are useful mainly for a client and server communication over a network.

In order to close the named pipe connection, the client should call CloseFile; the server should then call DisconnectNamedPipe. If the client does not call CloseFile, the server may still terminate the connection by calling DisconnectNamedPipe.

If a client only wants to make a single transaction, it may call the CallNamedPipe function, which is equivalent to calling CreateFile, WaitNamedPipe, if the pipe cannot be opened immediately, TransactNamedPipe, and CloseFile.

10.2.2 Named Pipe Summary

CallNamedPipe is called by a client; it creates the client end of a named pipe, writes to and reads from it, and closes it.

ConnectNamedPipe is called by the server; it waits for the client to connect to the pipe using **CreateFile**.

DisconnectNamedPipe is called by the server; it disconnects the named pipe (and, although it is not required, it should be called after the client has called **CloseFile**).

CreateNamedPipe is called by the server; it creates the named pipe.

PeekNamedPipe reads from a named pipe without removing data, and returns information about the remaining data.

GetNamedPipeHandleState obtains information about the state of a named pipe handle.

GetNamedPipeInfo obtains information about a named pipe.

SetNamedPipeHandleState sets the read and blocking modes of a named pipe.

TransactNamedPipe is called by the client for a message mode named pipe; it combines **WriteFile** and **ReadFile** into one transaction, which may increase performance over a network.

WaitNamedPipe is called by the client; it waits for an instance of a named pipe to become available.

Chapter 11 | Overview of Structured Exception Handling

11.1 Structured Exception Handling 179

    11.1.1   Goals 179

    11.1.2   Exception Architecture 180

        11.1.2.1 Frame-Based Exception Handlers 180

        11.1.2.2 Exception Dispatching 180

        11.1.2.3 Exception Handling and Unwind 181

    11.1.3   Exception Handling Syntax 182

        11.1.3.1 Terminology 182

        11.1.3.2 Goto Rule 182

        11.1.3.3 Exception Semantics 183

        11.1.3.4 Termination Semantics 184

        11.1.3.5 Examples 185

11.1 Structured Exception Handling

This section describes the exception handling capabilities of Win32. An exception is an event that occurs during the execution of a program which requires the execution of software outside the normal flow of control.

Exceptions can result from the execution of certain instruction sequences, in which case they are initiated by hardware. Other conditions may arise as the result of execution a software routine (e.g., an invalid parameter value), and are therefore initiated explicitly by software.

When an exception is initiated, a systematic search is performed in an attempt to find an exception handler that will dispose of (handle) the exception.

An exception handler is a function written to explicitly deal with the possibility that an exception may occur in a certain sequence of code.

Exception handlers are declared in a language-specific syntax and are associated with a specific scope of code. The scope may be a block, a set of nesed blocks, or an entire procedure or function.

Exception handling capabilities are an integral and pervasive part of the Win32 system. They enable a very robust implementation of the system software. It is envisioned that application developers will see the benefits of exception handling capabilities and also use them in a pervasive manner.

Structured exception handling is made available to application developers largely through compiler support. Although this chapter will use examples from the support available in Microsoft compilers provided with the initial Win32 development kit, Microsoft will work with other compiler vendors to ensure that they can provide this support as well.

11.1.1 Goals

The goals of the Win32 exception handling capabilities are the following:

■ Provide a single mechanism for exception handling that is usable across all languages.

■ Provide a single mechanism for the handling of hardware-generated, as well as software-generated exceptions.

■ Provide a single exception handling mechanism that can be used by privileged, as well as nonprivileged software.

■ Provide a single mechanism for the handling of exceptions and for the capabilities necessary to support sophisticated debuggers.

■ Provide an exception handling mechanism that is portable and which separates machine-dependent from machine-independent information.

11.1.2 Exception Architecture

The overall exception architecture of Win32 encompasses the process creation primitives, the Microsoft calling standards, and system routines that raise, dispatch, and unwind exceptions.

When an exception is initiated, an attempt is made to notify the process' debugger. If the process is not being debugged, or if the associated debugger does not handle the exception, then a search of the current thread's call frames is conducted in an attempt to locate an exception handler. If no frame-based handler can be found, or none of the frame-based handlers handle the exception, then another attempt is made to notify the process' debugger. If there is no debugger, or the associated debugger does not handle the exception then the system provides default handling based on the exception type.

Thus the search hierarchy is:

■ Debugger first chance

■ Frame-based handlers

■ Debugger second chance

11.1.2.1 Frame-Based Exception Handlers

An exception handler can be associated with each call frame in the procedure call hierarchy of a program. This requires that each procedure or function that either saves nonvolatile registers or establishes an associated exception handler, have a call frame.

Microsoft compilers for Win32 adhere to a standard calling convention for the construction of a call frame.

11.1.2.2 Exception Dispatching

When a hardware exception occurs, the Win32 trap handling software gets control and saves the hardware state of the current thread in a context record. The reason for the trap is determined, and an exception record is constructed which describes the exception and any pertinent parameters. Executive software is then called to dispatch the exception.

If the previous processor mode was kernel, then the exception dispatcher is called to search the kernel stack call frames in an attempt to locate an exception handler. If a frame-based handler cannot be located, or no frame-based handler handles the exception, then the system is shut down as in ExitWindows. Unhandled exceptions emanating from within privileged software are considered fatal bugs.

If the previous processor mode was user, then an attempt is made to notify the process' debugger. This notification includes the exception record and the identification of the thread. The debugger may handle the exception (e.g., breakpoint or single step) and modify the thread state as appropriate, or not handle the exception and defer to any frame-based exception handlers found on the user stack.

If the debugger indicates that it has handled the exception, then the machine state is restored and thread execution is continued. Otherwise, if the debugger indicates that it has not handled the exception, or there is no debugger, then the exception dispatcher is invoked to search for frame-based exception handlers.

If a frame-based handler handles the exception, then thread execution is continued. Otherwise, if no frame-based handler is found, or no frame-based handler handles the exception, then the debugger (if present) is given a second chance to handle the exception. If the exception remains unhandled, the system default action is taken. For most exceptions, the default exction is to call ExitProcess.

11.1.2.3 Exception Handling and Unwind

During the dispatching of an exception, each frame-based handler is called specifying the associated exception and context records as parameters. The exception handler can handle the exception and continue execution, not handle the exception and continue the search for an exception handler, or handle the exception and initiate an unwind operation.

Handling an exception may be as simple as noting an error and setting a flag that will be examined later, printing a warning or error message, or taking some other overt action. If execution can be continued, then it may be necessary to change the machine state by modifying the context record (e.g., advance the continuation instruction address).

If execution can be continued, then the exception handler returns to the exception dispatcher with a status code that specifies that execution should be continued. Continuing execution causes the exception dispatcher to stop its search for an exception handler. The machine state from the context record is restored and execution is continued accordingly.

If execution of the thread cannot be continued, then the exception handler usually initiates an unwind operation by calling a system supplied function specifying a target call frame and a continuation address. The unwind function walks the stack backwards searching for the target call frame. As it walks the stack, the unwind function calls each exception handler that is encountered to allow it to perform any cleanup actions that may be necessary (e.g., release a semaphore, etc.). When the target call frame is reached, the machine state is restored and execution is continued at the specified address.

11.1.3 Exception Handling Syntax

This section describes the syntax and usage of structured exception handling as it appears in Microsoft C.

The following keywords are interpreted by the Microsoft C compiler as part of the structured exception handling mechanism.

- try
- except
- finally
- GetExceptionCode
- GetExceptionInformation
- AbnormalTermination

Two sets of syntax are provided to handle exceptions.

For exception handling, The syntax is

```
try-except-statement ::= try compound-statement
    except (expression) compound-statement
```

For termination handlers it is

```
try-finally-statement ::=
    try compound-statement  finally compound-statement
```

Note that the compound statements require braces.

11.1.3.1 Terminology

The compound-statement after try is the body or guarded statement. The second compound statement is the exception handler or termination handler. The expression after except is the exception-filter.

11.1.3.2 Goto Rule

Jumping (via a goto) into the body of a try statement or into a handler is not allowed. This rule applies to both try-except and try-finally statements.

11.1.3.3 Exception Semantics

If an exception occurs in the body of a try-except, the exception-filter is evaluated. If the resulting value is EXCEPTION_EXECUTE_HANDLER, control is transferred to the exception handler. Note that the transfer of control to the exception handler is similar to a longjmp; stack frames are unwound back to (but not including) the frame of the try statement, and SP is reset (by code at the beginning of the exception handler). In addition, during the unwind all termination handlers are called.

If the value of the exception-filter is EXCEPTION_CONTINUE_SEARCH, the search for a handler continues (first for containing try-except statements, then for handlers in the dynamically preceding function activation, etc.).

If the value of the exception-filter is EXCEPTION_CONTINUE_EXECUTION, the exception is dismissed, i.e., control returns to the point where the exception occurred, provided this is allowed for in the case of the particular exception. (If not allowed, the underlying system convention for this case applies.)

This gives the C programmer a convenient hook to catch continuable exceptions, e.g., a CTRL-BREAK if the system raises that as an exception.

The exception-filter is evaluated in the context of the function activation executing the try-except (even though there may be dynamic descendents on the stack). Thus local variables may be accessed in the exception-filter.

Because the filter expression can invoke a function, the exception-filter logic can be as elaborate as one wants.

Two intrinsic functions may be used within the exception-filter to access information about the exception being filtered.

```
DWORD
GetExceptionCode(
    VOID
    )
```

Return Value   The value of the exception code from the exception record (.e.g EXCEPTION_ACCESS_VIOLATION) is returned by this instrinsic.

e.g.

```
try {
    .
    .
    .
}
except ( GetExceptionCode == EXCEPTION_ACCESS_VIOLATION ?
         EXCEPTION_EXECUTE_HANDLER :
```

```
                        EXCEPTION_CONTINUE_SEARCH ) {
                    .
                    .
                    .

        xxx

        LPEXCEPTION_INFORMATION
        GetExceptionInformation(
            VOID
            )
```

Return Value

This returns a pointer to a structure containing additional information about the exception. Through this pointer one can access the machine state that existed at the point of an exception and detailed information about the exception.

This function is useful for exception filters that need additional information about the exception. The format of the return value is:

```
Structure EXCEPTION_INFORMATION:

LPEXCEPTION_RECORD lpExceptionRecord -
    Supplies a pointer to the portable description
    of the exception.

LPCONTEXT lpContext -
    Supplies a pointer to the machine state at the time
    of the exception.  This structure is described
    with the Win32 debug APIs.
```

The **GetExceptionCode** function may also be used within the exception handler. However **GetExceptionInformation** can only be used within the exception-filter. The information it points to is generally on the stack and will be destroyed when control is transferred to the exception handler. Within the exception-filter, the programmer can copy the information to safe storage, e.g., by passing the value of **GetExceptionInformation** to an appropriate function.

The compiler detects out-of-context uses of these functions.

11.1.3.4 Termination Semantics

A termination handler is executed no matter how the body of the try-finally terminates. The termination handler itself can either terminate sequentially or by a transfer out of the handler. If the handler terminates sequentially, control continues according to how it reached the termination handler. The cases are:

■ If the body of the try-finally statement was aborted by an unwind (e.g. by a jump to an exception handler or a longjmp), control returns to the runtime, which will continue invoking termination handlers as required before jumping to the target of the unwind.

■ If the body of the try-finally terminated with normal control flow (sequentially, return, break, continue, or goto) that flow takes place. (If such a return, break, or goto exits a higher-level try-finally, it's termination handler will also be invoked.)

A termination handler may exit via a jump: goto, return (from the procedure containing the handler), break, longjmp, or jump to an exception handler. If so, the jump ends the termination/unwind handling that led to invocation of the termination handler. Of course, if this jump exits a containing try-finally, there will be another round of termination handling; but that would be an unusual case.

A termination handler is executed as an internal procedure with access to, or directly using, the frame of the function containing the try-finally. As in a exception-filter, local variables may be accessed in the termination handler, but such access may inhibit some optimization related to the local variables.

An intrinsic function **AbnormalTermination** is available within a termination handler. It returns FALSE if the body of the try-finally statement terminated sequentially (reached the closing "}"). In all other cases it returns TRUE.

11.1.3.5 Examples

The following example shows a version of strcpy that can handle a bad pointer and return NULL if it is encountered.

```
char *
SafeStrcpy(
    char *string1,
    char *string2
    )
{
    try {
        return strcpy(string1,string2);
        }
    except (EXCEPTION_EXECUTE_HANDLER) {
        return NULL;
        }
}
```

The following example shows how finally can be used to always free resources when leaving a block.

```
    LPSTR Buffer;

    try {
        Buffer = NULL;
        EnterCriticalSection(&CriticalSection);
        Buffer = LocalAlloc(LMEM_FIXED|LMEM_ZEROINIT,10);
        strcpy(Buffer,"Hello"); // <-- Possible access violation,
        printf("%s\n",Buffer);  //     if allocation fails.
        LocalFree(Buffer);
        }
    finally {
        // Whether or not the allocation succeeds, we'll leave
        // the critical section.
```

```
        LeaveCriticalSection(&CriticalSection);
        }
```

Chapter 12 Windows Debugging Support

12.1 Introduction to Win Debug Support 189

    12.1.1 Support in other Win32 APIs 189

        12.1.1.1 CreateProcess 189

        12.1.1.2 OpenProcess 190

        12.1.1.3 CreateThread 190

        12.1.1.4 Exception Handling 190

12.2 Debug APIs 191

    12.2.1 State Manipulation APIs 191

    12.2.2 Other Debug APIs 191

    12.2.3 State Change APIs 191

        12.2.3.1 Debug Event Details 192

12.1 Introduction to Win Debug Support

This specification describes the low level debug support found in Win32. This document does not address higher level debug functions like heap walk APIs or other features made available as part of the Windows 3.1 open tools initiative. Win32 provides a very simple event driven debug model. API support is very minimal including functions to:

- Wait for a debug event to occur

- Read and write the context of a thread

- Read and write the virtual memory of a process

- Continue a debug event

Note that higher level functions such as "set break point", and "single step" are not part of the Win32 debug support. It is expected that debuggers make use of the low level Win32 debug APIs in order to provide this level of functionality.

12.1.1 Support in other Win32 APIs

This section describes aspects of non-debugging APIs that have to do with implementing debuggers on top of Win32.

12.1.1.1 CreateProcess

The *dwCreationFlags* parameter to **CreateProcess** can be used to indicate debugging operations:

Value	Meaning
DEBUG_PROCESS	If this flag bit is set, then the creating process is treated as a debugger, and the process being created is created as a debugee. All debug events occuring in the debugee are reported to the debugger. If this bit is clear, but the calling process is a debugee, then the process becomes a debugee of the calling processes debugger. If this bit is clear and the calling processes is not a debugee then no debug related actions occur.
DEBUG_ONLY_THIS_PROCESS	If this flag is set, then the DEBUG_PROCESS flag bit must also be set. The calling process is is treated as a debugger, and the new process is created as its debuggee. If the new process creates additional processes, no debug related activities (with respect to the debugger) occur.

The purpose of this support is to provide a mechanism that a debugger can use to start a process and debug it.

- A debugger is given a chance to debug a process it creates and all decendents of that process. This is made possible by the debugger createing the process using the DEBUG_PROCESS flag bit. Assuming that the debugged process creates additional processes, if all these creations occur with the DEBUG_PROCESS flag cleared, then the debugger is allowed to debug all the additional processes as well.

- A debugger is given a chance to debug a debugger. This occurs when the debugger creates the debugger it is debugging using the DEBUG_PROCESS flag which in turn creates its debuggee using the DEBUG_PROCESS flag.

- A debugger is given a chance to debug a process and none of its decendents by creating its debuggee using both the DEBUG_PROCESS and DEBUG_ONLY_THIS_PROCESS flags.

12.1.1.2 OpenProcess

The **OpenProcess** API allows the PROCESS_VM_WRITE flag in the dwDesiredAccess parameter. This flag specifies the write access to the processes virtual memory is required.

12.1.1.3 CreateThread

The **CreateThread** API allows THREAD_GET_CONTEXT and THREAD_SET_CONTEXT access flags. These flags allow the reading and writing of a threads context.

The API is also supports THREAD_SUSPEND_RESUME access.

12.1.1.4 Exception Handling

When an exception occurs, the following takes place:

- If the process is being debugged, it's debugger is notified of the exception. This is known as first chance notification. All threads in the process freeze their execution. At some point the debugger continues the debug event.

- If the exception was not handled, the structured exception handling logic is invoked to locate an exception handler.

- If the exception is still pending, the debugger is notified a second time. This is known as last chance notification.

- If the exception is still pending (e.g. the debugger returned not handled), the process is terminated.

12.2 Debug APIs

The following sections describe the debug APIs as they appear in Win32. The APIs are divided into two sections. The state manipulation APIs are responsible for read and writing memory of a process, and reading and writing the registers of a thread. The debug event APIs are responsible for recognition and handling of debug events.

12.2.1 State Manipulation APIs

The state manipulation APIs are logically part of the Win32 tasking architecture. The APIs are object based APIs that operate on any process or thread object. The specified processes do not have to be debugged for these APIs to operate. The caller simply has to have a handle to the object with an appropriate access rights.

12.2.2 Other Debug APIs

The APIs described in this section allow an application to to interact with the debugger by changing it's code. This includes hard-coding breakppoints, and sending debug output strings to the debugger.

12.2.3 State Change APIs

The Win32 debug model is an event driven model. A debugger operates as follows:

- The debugger creates a process using CreateProcess and an appriate combination of the DEBUG_PROCESS and DEBUG_ONLY_THIS_PROCESS creation flag bits. Once this occurs, the debugger is notified of all debug events that occur within the process (and possibly within processes created by the process).

- The debugger enters its main loop. At the top of the loop the debugger calls WaitForDebugEvent. This call blocks the debugger until a debug event occurs.

- Upon receipt of a debug event, the debugger deals with the debug event. This may include interacting with the user, or manipulating the state of the debugee using ReadMemoryProcess, WriteMemoryProcess, GetContextThread, or SetContextThread.

- At the bottom of the loop, the debugger continues the debug event using ContinueDebugEvent.

Debug events are generated for a number of reasons. When a debug event is generated, all threads within the affected process are frozen. The threads will not continue until the debug event is continued. The following list describes the debug events that occur when a process is being debugged.

Event	Description
Exception	When a thread whose process is being debugged encounters an exception, a debug event is generated.
CreateThread	When a thread begins executing in a process being debugged, a debug event is generated before the thread gets a chance to execute in user mode.
CreateProcess	When the first thread in a process being debugged begins executing, a debug event is generated before the thread gets a chance to execute in user mode.
ExitThread	When a thread exits in a process being debugged, a debug event is generated. This occurs as soon as the system detects that the thread is exiting and has updated the exit code for the thread.
ExitProcess	When the last thread in a process being debugged exits, a debug event is generated. This occurs as soon as the the exit code of the process has been updated. This occurs after all DLL notification has occured. Note that when the last thread in a process exits, an exit thread debug event is not generated.
LoadDll	When a process being debugged loads a DLL either statically, or as a result of a call to LoadLibrary , a debug event is generated.
UnloadDll	When a process being debugged unloads a DLL as a result of a call to FreeLibrary, a debug event is generated. This debug event is not generated when a process terminates.
OutputString	When a process being debugged calls OutputDebugString, a debug event is generated.

12.2.3.1   Debug Event Details

The following sections describe the additional information available with each debug event.

12.2.3.1.1 EXCEPTION_DEBUG_EVENT

The debug event code EXCEPTION_DEBUG_EVENT is reported whenever a thread being debugged encounters an exception. Exceptions include attempting to access inaccessible memory, executing breakpoint instructions, single step traps, or any other set of exceptional conditions (noted in the structured exception handling section).

In addition to the normal exception conditions, two special software exceptions are used to signal the debugger. If a character-mode application uses the default C handling mechanism, an exception of type DBG_CONTROL_C is generated whenever the application encounters C. During process initialization, an exception of type DBG_DLLS_LOADED is generated after all DLLs are loaded, but before any of their init routines are called. This gives a debugger an opportunity to step through

DLL init routines or to set break points in DLLs before any DLL code has been executed.

The value of u.Exception contains the following information.

```
typedef struct _EXCEPTION_DEBUG_INFO {
    EXCEPTION_RECORD ExceptionRecord;
    ULONG FirstChance;
} EXCEPTION_DEBUG_INFO, *LPEXCEPTION_DEBUG_INFO;
```

Value	Meaning
ExceptionRecord	Contains information relevent to the exception. The structured exception handling section of this document contains additional information. In addition to other values, the ExceptionCode field of this structure may contain the common values of STATUS_ACCESS_VIOLATION, STATUS_BREAKPOINT, STATUS_SINGLE_STEP.
FirstChance	Supplies a non-zero value if this is the debuggers first chance at dealing with this exception. Debuggers will typically handle breakpoint and single step exceptions at this point. A value of zero specifies that this is the second time the debugger is being given a chance to handle this exception. This only occurs if during the search for structured exception handlers, either no handler is found, or the exception is continued.

There are no additional side effects of receiving this debug event.

12.2.3.1.2 CREATE_THREAD_DEBUG_EVENT

The debug event code of CREATE_THREAD_DEBUG_EVENT is reported whenever a new thread is created in a process being debugged. The major side effect of this event is that the debugger receiving this debug event is given a handle to the thread reporting the state change. The handle is granted THREAD_GET_CONTEXT, THREAD_SET_CONTEXT, and THREAD_SUSPEND_RESUME access to the thread. This allows the debugger to use GetContextThread and SetContextThread to read and write the thread's registers, and to suspend and resume a thread.

Upon receipt of this event, the debugger is expected to create a per-thread data structure. The thread handle can then be stored in the data structure. The debugger should use the dwProcessId/dwThreadId parameters to locate this structure. When the debugger receives an exit thread debug event for this thread, the debugger should deallocate its thread structure. The system will close the handle that the debugger has to the thread.

The value of u.CreateThread contains the following information.

```
typedef struct _CREATE_THREAD_DEBUG_INFO {
    HANDLE hThread;
    LPTHREAD_START_ROUTINE lpStartAddress;
```

```
} CREATE_THREAD_DEBUG_INFO, *LPCREATE_THREAD_DEBUG_INFO;
```

Value	Meaning
hThread	Supplies a handle to the thread identified by this debug event. A value of NULL indicates that the handle is not valid. The value of false is returned, and GetLastError returns DBG_UNABLE_TO_PROVIDE_HANDLE. Otherwise, the handle is valid in the context of the debugger, and has THREAD_GET_CONTEXT, THREAD_SET_CONTEXT, and THREAD_SUSPEND_RESUME access to the thread.
lpStartAddress	Supplies the starting address of the thread. Note that this is only a best approximation of the thread's starting address, since any application with an appropriate handle to the thread could change the threads context using SetContextThread.

12.2.3.1.3 CREATE_PROCESS_DEBUG_EVENT

The debug event code of CREATE_PROCESS_DEBUG_EVENT is reported whenever a new process being debugged by the caller is created. This debug event is generated before any other debug events for the process occur (even LOAD_DLL_DEBUG_EVENTs). The major side effects of this event are:

- A file handle to the processes image file is created and made valid in the debugger. The file handle is given GENERIC_READ access to the file. The file is opened for read sharing.

- A handle to the process is created and made valid in the debugger. The process handle is given PROCESS_VM_READ and PROCESS_VM_WRITE access to the process. This allows the debugger to read and write memory in the process using ReadMemoryProcess and WriteMemoryProcess.

- A handle to the initial thread in the process is created and made valid in the debugger. The thread handle is given THREAD_GET_CONTEXT, THREAD_SET_CONTEXT, and THREAD_SUSPEND_RESUME access to the thread. This allows the debugger to read and write the registers of the thread using GetContextThread and SetContextThread.

Upon receipt of this event, the debugger is expected to create a per-thread and per-process data structure. The thread handle can then be stored in the thread data structure and the process and file handle stored in the process structure. The debugger should use the *dwProcessId/dwThreadId* parameters to locate these structures. When the debugger receives an exit process debug event for this process, the debugger should deallocate its process structure, all remaining thread structures, and all symbol table structures associated with the process. The system will close the handle that the debugger has to the process and all threads within the process.

The value of u.CreateProcess contains the following information.

```
typedef struct _CREATE_PROCESS_DEBUG_INFO {
    HANDLE hFile;
    HANDLE hProcess;
    HANDLE hThread;
    LPVOID lpBaseOfImage;
    DWORD dwDebugInfoFileOffset;
    DWORD nDebugInfoSize;
    LPTHREAD_START_ROUTINE lpStartAddress;
} CREATE_PROCESS_DEBUG_INFO, *LPCREATE_PROCESS_DEBUG_INFO;
```

Value	Meaning
hFile	Supplies an open file handle valid in the context of the debugger. A value of NULL indicates that the handle is not valid. The value of false is returned, and GetLastError returns DBG_UNABLE_TO_PROVIDE_HANDLE. Otherwise, the file handle refers to executable image file that the process is being created to run within.
hProcess	Supplies an open process handle valid in the context of the debugger. A value of NULL indicates that the handle is not valid. The value of false is returned, and GetLastError returns DBG_UNABLE_TO_PROVIDE_HANDLE. Otherwise, the process handle has appropriate access to allow the debugger to read and write the memory of the process.
hThread	Supplies an open handle to the initial thread of the process. A value of NULL indicates that the handle is not valid. The value of false is returned, and GetLastError returns DBG_UNABLE_TO_PROVIDE_HANDLE. Otherwise, the thread handle has appropriate access to allow the debugger to read and write the registers of the thread.
lpBaseOfImage	Supplies the base address of the executable image that the process is running.
dwDebugInfoFileOffset	Supplies the file offset of the location of the debug information in the file. The format of the debug information is expected to be CodeView 4.0. Currently it is a derivitive of COFF.
nDebugInfoSize	Supplies the size of the debug information in the file. A value of zero specifies that there is no debug information.
lpStartAddress	Supplies the starting address of the thread. Note that this is only a best approximation of the thread's starting address, since any application with an appropriate handle to the thread could change the threads context using SetContextThread.

12.2.3.1.4 EXIT_THREAD_DEBUG_EVENT

The debug event code of EXIT_THREAD_DEBUG_EVENT is reported whenever a thread exits. Once this event occurs, the thread will no longer execute application or DLL code. The debugger is expected to deallocate any internal structures associated with the thread at this time.

The value of u.ExitThread contains the following information.

```
typedef struct _EXIT_THREAD_DEBUG_INFO {
    DWORD dwExitCode;
} EXIT_THREAD_DEBUG_INFO, *LPEXIT_THREAD_DEBUG_INFO;
```

Value	Meaning
dwExitCode	Supplies the exit code for the thread.

12.2.3.1.5 EXIT_PROCESS_DEBUG_EVENT

The debug event code of EXIT_PROCESS_DEBUG_EVENT is reported whenever a process exits. This actually happens when the last thread of a process exits. Once this event occurs, the thread will no longer execute application or DLL code. An EXIT_THREAD_DEBUG_EVENT does not occur when the last thread of a process exits. The debugger is expected to deallocate any internal structures associated with the process at this time.

The value of u.ExitProcess contains the following information.

```
typedef struct _EXIT_PROCESS_DEBUG_INFO {
    DWORD dwExitCode;
} EXIT_PROCESS_DEBUG_INFO, *LPEXIT_PROCESS_DEBUG_INFO;
```

Value	Meaning
dwExitCode	Supplies the exit code for the process.

12.2.3.1.6 LOAD_DLL_DEBUG_EVENT

The debug event code of LOAD_DLL_DEBUG_EVENT is reported whenever a process loads a DLL. This is either as a result of static links to a DLL being resolved by the system loader, or through an explicit call to LoadLibrary. The major side effect of this event is that it causes a file handle to be created which is valid in the debugger, and which refers to the DLL file. Note that this notification only occurs the first time a DLL is attached to the address space of a process. Multiple calls to LoadLibrary refering to the same DLL, or LoadLibrary calls on a DLL that is already attached to the process do not cause this event to be generated. If on the otherhand, a DLL is loaded into a process, and then unloaded from the process, and thread re-loaded, two load events are generated. This primary purpose of reporting this debug event is to allow a debugger an opportunity to load a symbol table associated with the DLL.

The value of u.LoadDll contains the following information.

```
typedef struct _LOAD_DLL_DEBUG_INFO {
    HANDLE hFile;
    LPVOID lpBaseOfDll;
    DWORD dwDebugInfoFileOffset;
    DWORD nDebugInfoSize;
} LOAD_DLL_DEBUG_INFO, *LPLOAD_DLL_DEBUG_INFO;
```

Value	Meaning
hFil	Supplies an open file handle valid in the context of the debugger. A value of NULL indicates that the handle is not valid. The value of false is returned, and GetLastError returns DBG_UNABLE_TO_PROVIDE_HANDLE. Otherwise, the file handle refers to the DLL being loaded. The file is opened with GENERIC_READ access to the file and for read sharing.
lpBaseOfDl	Supplies the base address of the DLL in the address space of the process loading the DLL.
dwDebugInfoFileOffse	Supplies the file offset of the location of the debug information in the file. The format of the debug information is expected to be CodeView 4.0. Currently it is a derivitive of COFF.
nDebugInfoSiz	Supplies the size of the debug information in the file. A value of zero specifies that there is no debug information.

12.2.3.1.7 UNLOAD_DLL_DEBUG_EVENT

The debug event code of UNLOAD_DLL_DEBUG_EVENT is reported whenever a process unloads a dll as a result of an explicit call to FreeLibrary. Note that this notification only occurs the last time a DLL is unloaded from the address space of a process. When a process exits, DLLs are logically unloaded from its address space, this does not cause this debug event to be propagated. The primary purpose of this event is to allow a debugger an opportunity to unload a symbol table associated with a DLL.

The value of u.UnloadDll contains the following information.

```
typedef struct _UNLOAD_DLL_DEBUG_INFO {
    LPVOID lpBaseOfDll;
} UNLOAD_DLL_DEBUG_INFO, *LPUNLOAD_DLL_DEBUG_INFO;
```

Value	Meaning
lpBaseOfDll	Supplies the base address of the DLL in the address space of the process un-loading the DLL.

12.2.3.1.8 OUTPUT_DEBUG_STRING_EVENT

The debug event code of OUTPUT_DEBUG_STRING is reported whenever a process being debugged calls OutputDebugString. If the process is not being debugged, but the kernel debugger is active, the string is sent to the debugger.

The value of u.OutputDebugString contains the following information.

```
typedef struct _OUTPUT_DEBUG_STRING_INFO {
    LPSTR lpDebugStringData;
    WORD fUnicode;
    WORD nDebugStringLength;
} OUTPUT_DEBUG_STRING_INFO, *LPOUTPUT_DEBUG_STRING_INFO;
```

Value	Meaning
lpDebugStringDat	Supplies the address of the debug string in the calling processes address space. The debugger is expected to use ReadVirtualMemory to fetch the value of the string.
fUnicod	Supplies a flag which is zero if the debug string data is 8-bit ASCII, and non-zero if the string is 16-bit Unicode.
nDebugStringLengt	Supplies the length (in bytes) of the debug string. The length includes the terminating NULL for the string.

Chapter 13

User Security

13.1   Goals 201

13.2   USER32 Securable Objects 201

    13.2.1   Object Access Types 202

13.3   Object Handles 204

    13.3.1   Desktop Creation 204

    13.3.2   Window Creation 205

    13.3.3   Menu Creation 206

    13.3.4   DDE Access Creation 206

    13.3.5   DDE Conversation Creation 207

13.4   Opening an Object 208

13.5   Object Access 208

13.6   Closing an Object 208

13.7   Window Classes 209

13.8   SM_SECURE System Metric 209

13.9   ES_PASSWORD Style Edit Controls 209

13.10 Window Enumeration 209

13.11 Accessing Screen Contents 209

13.12 Clipboard Access 210

13.13 DDE Security 210

    13.13.1   Registration 210

    13.13.2   Conversations 210

        13.13.2.1 WC –> WS 211

        13.13.2.2 AC –> WS 211

        13.13.2.3 WC –> AS 211

        13.13.2.4 AC –> AS 211

    13.13.3   Data Objects 211

13.14 Auditing 211

13.15 Server Initialization 212

13.16 Client Initialization 212

    13.16.1 Server Connection 212

    13.16.2 WindowStation Access 212

    13.16.3 Thread Initialization 212

13.17 Logon Processing 213

    13.17.1 Logon 213

    13.17.2 Logoff 213

    13.17.3 Windowstation Locking 214

13.18 System Shutdown 214

13.1 Goals

The Win32 security model has been designed to meet these goals:

- Minimize impact on Windows API semantics.

- Provide C2 level security.

- Be extensible to B level security without requiring modifications to the existing API.

- Be extensible to multi user systems.

- Be extensible to support new object types.

Apis are being added to implement security, but any existing APIs will not be modified to support security. Also, the use of any newly introduced APIs is optional – the system provides a default security behavior when these APIs are not used. For the C2 system, this default mirrors the Win3 object semantics.

13.2 USER32 Securable Objects

USER32 has six securable objects:

WindowStation Object	This object represents a screen/keyboard/mouse combination. This object serves to house or "contain" the other objects related to an individual user station. This object provides the front line of security for a user station and serves as a source for inheritable security for other objects.
Desktop Object	This object represents the new construct called a "desktop." This object resides within a WindowStation object, from which it inherits security. This object is also a container, containing Window and Menu objects.
Window Object	This object represents what is commonly known as a window. This object type resides within a Desktop object, from which it inherits security.
Menu Object	This object represents what is commonly known as a menu. This type resides within a Desktop object, from which it inherits security.
DDE Access Object	This object is used to control access to a DDE server. This type resides within a WindowStation object, but does not inherit security from its parent WindowStation.
DDE Conversation Object	This object represents a conversation connection between a DDE client and DDE server. This type resides within a DDE Access object, from which it inherits security.

Each object contains a common object header that specifies the object type, security descriptor and other security related information. This allows the same code to work for all current and future object types.

GDI32 has no shared objects, and therefore no security descriptors on any APIs. KERNEL32 has security on files, processes, threads, and synchronization objects.

13.2.1 Object Access Types

This is a list of the object type-specific access types defined for each of the USER32 objects:

WindowStation Object

WINSTA_ACCESSCLIPBOARD	(Implied by GenericWrite) This access type is needed to utilize the clipboard.
WINSTA_CREATEDESKTOP	(Implied by GenericWrite) This access type is needed to create new Desktop objects on the WindowStation.
WINSTA_ENUMDESKTOPS	(Implied by GenericRead) This access type is needed to enumerate existing desktop objects.
WINSTA_READATTRIBUTES	(Implied by GenericRead) This access type is needed to read the attributes of a WindowStation object. The attributes include: color settings and other global windowstation properties.
WINSTA_WRITEATTRIBUTES	(Implied by GenericWrite) This access type is needed to modify the attributes of a WindowStation object. The attributes include: color settings and other global windowstation properties.
WINSTA_ACCESSGLOBALATOMS	(Implied by GenericExecute) This access type is needed to create/read/write/destroy global atoms.
WINSTA_ENUMERATE	(Implied by GenericRead) This access type is needed for the windowstation to be enumerated.
WINSTA_READSCREEN	(Implied by GenericRead) This access type is needed to access screen contents.

WINSTA_EXITWINDOWS   (Implied by GenericExecute) This access
                              type is needed to successfully call
                              ExitWindows . Windowstations can be
                              shared between users and this access type
                              can be used to prevent other users of a
                              windowstation from logging off the
                              windowstation owner.

Desktop Object

DESKTOP_CREATEWINDOW   (Implied by GenericWrite) This access type
                              is needed to create a window associated with
                              the desktop.

DESKTOP_CREATEMENU   (Implied by GenericWrite) This access type
                              is needed to create a menu associated with
                              the desktop.

DESKTOP_ENUMWINDOWS   (Implied by GenericRead) This access type is
                              needed to enumerate window objects created
                              by other processes.

DESKTOP_HOOKCONTROL   (Implied by GenericWrite) This access type
                              is needed to establish any of the window
                              hooks on a queue belonging to another
                              thread or to establish a system-level hook.

DESKTOP_JOURNALRECORD   (Implied by GenericWrite) This access type
                              is needed to perform journal recording.

DESKTOP_JOURNALPLAYBACK   (Implied by GenericWrite) This access type
                              is needed to perform journal playback.

DESKTOP_ENUMERATE   (Implied by GenericRead) This access type is
                              needed for the desktop to be enumerated.

Window Object

WIN_ACCESSWINDOW   (Implied by GenericExecute) This access type is needed
                         to perform any window operation.

WIN_ENUMERATE   (Implied by GenericRead) This access type is needed
                         for the window to be enumerated by processes other
                         than the creating process.

Menu Object

MENU_ACCESSMENU   (Implied by GenericExecute) This access type is needed
                         to perform any menu operation.

DDE Access and Conversation Objects

DDE_ADVISE   (Implied by GenericRead) This access type is needed for a DDE
                    client to begin an advise loop.

DDE_EXECUTE	(Implied by GenericExecute) This access type is needed for a DDE client to execute a command on a DDE server.
DDE_POKE	(Implied by GenericWrite) This access type is needed for a DDE client to write data to a DDE server.
DDE_REQUEST	(Implied by GenericRead) This access type is needed for a DDE client to get data from a DDE server.

13.3 Object Handles

Under Win3, a handle to a window or menu object can be shared among applications and used by any application without having to "open" a reference to the object. To retain these semantics, a "handle" to any USER32 object is in reality an opaque pointer to the object body whose most-significant byte is set to a serial number. Such a handle can then be passed around to any application.

Under USER32, applications are not allowed to indiscriminately use an object, even if they have a handle to that object. For an application to use an object it must "open" a reference to it. The "open" is actually an access check to verify that the application is allowed to use object. If applicable, an object is opened to the application as part of object creation. For applications that get an object handle through other means (window enumeration, messages, dde, etc.), USER32 attempts to open that object the first time the application tries to use it. In this case, access may be denied, which could result in some strange behavior if the application is not prepared for this kind of error.

13.3.1 Desktop Creation

A new desktop inherits its SD from its parent windowstation. A desktop is not opened when it is created; it must be opened with **OpenDesktop**.

Generic mapping:

Value	Maps to
GENERIC_READ	DESKTOP_ENUMWINDOWS~| DESKTOP_ENUMERATE~| STANDARD_RIGHTS_READ
GENERIC_WRITE	DESKTOP_CREATEWINDOW~| DESKTOP_CREATEMENU~| DESKTOP_HOOKCONTROL~| DESKTOP_JOURNALRECORD~| JOURNALPLAYBACK~ | STANDARD_RIGHTS_WRITE
GENERIC_EXECUTE	STANDARD_RIGHTS_EXECUTE

Value	Maps to
GENERIC_ALL	DESKTOP_ENUMWINDOWS~|
	DESKTOP_ENUMERATE~|
	DESKTOP_CREATEWINDOW~|
	DESKTOP_CREATEMENU~|
	DESKTOP_HOOKCONTROL~ |
	DESKTOP_JOURNALRECORD~|
	JOURNALPLAYBACK~|
	STANDARD_RIGHTS_REQUIRED

The following discretionary ACEs are created:

ACE 0:

ACE Type = AccessAllowed
sid = LogonSid
AccessMask =
　　DESKTOP_CREATEWINDOW~\| DESKTOP_CREATEMENU~\|
　　DESKTOP_ENUMWINDOWS~\| DESKTOP_ENUMERATE~\|
　　DESKTOP_HOOKCONTROL~ \| DESKTOP_JOURNALRECORD~\|
　　JOURNALPLAYBACK~\| STANDARD_RIGHTS_REQUIRED
Not Inheritable

ACE 1:

ACE Type = AccessAllowed
sid = LogonSid
AccessMask =
　　GenericRead~\| GenericWrite~\|
　　GenericExecute~\| GenericAll
Inheritable Only
Inheritable by containers
Inheritable by non containers
Inheritance is to be propagated

13.3.2 Window Creation

A new window inherits its SD from its parent desktop and is implicitly opened during its creation.

Value	Mapping value
GENERIC_READ	WIN_ENUMERATE~| STANDARD_RIGHTS_READ
GENERIC_WRITE	STANDARD_RIGHTS_WRITE
GENERIC_EXECUTE	WIN_ACCESSWINDOW~|
	STANDARD_RIGHTS_EXECUTE

Value	Mapping value
GENERIC_ALL	WIN_ACCESSWINDOW~I WIN_ENUMERATE~I STANDARD_RIGHTS_REQUIRED

The following discretionary ACE is created:

ACE 0:

ACE Type = AccessAllowed
sid = LogonSid
AccessMask =
  WIN_ACCESSWINDOW~I WIN_ENUMERATE~I
  STANDARD_RIGHTS_REQUIRED
Not Inheritable

13.3.3 Menu Creation

A new menu inherits its SD from its parent desktop and is implicitly opened during its creation.

Value	Mapping value
GENERIC_READ	STANDARD_RIGHTS_READ
GENERIC_WRITE	STANDARD_RIGHTS_WRITE
GENERIC_EXECUTE	MENU_ACCESSMENU~I STANDARD_RIGHTS_EXECUTE
GENERIC_ALL	MENU_ACCESSMENU~I STANDARD_RIGHTS_REQUIRED

The following discretionary ACE is created:

ACE 0:

ACE Type = AccessAllowed
sid = LogonSid
AccessMask = MENU_ACCESSMENU~I
        STANDARD_RIGHTS_REQUIRED
Not Inheritable

13.3.4 DDE Access Creation

A new DDE conversation does not inherits its SD from its parent windowstation. The new object is gives read, write and execute permission to its owner and is implicitly opened during its creation. The DDE application must modify the object's security if other users are to be given access.

Value	Mapping value
GENERIC_READ	STANDARD_RIGHTS_READ
GENERIC_WRITE	STANDARD_RIGHTS_WRITE
GENERIC_EXECUTE	STANDARD_RIGHTS_EXECUTE
GENERIC_ALL	STANDARD_RIGHTS_REQUIRED

The following discretionary ACE is used:

ACE 0:

ACE Type = AccessAllowed
sid = LogonSid
AccessMask =
  GenericRead~| GenericWrite~| GenericExecute~| GenericAll~|
  STANDARD_RIGHTS_REQUIRED
Inheritable by non-containers

13.3.5 DDE Conversation Creation

A new DDE converation inherits its SD from its parent DDE access object and
implicitly opened during its creation.

Value	Mapping value
GENERIC_READ	DDE_ADVISE~| DDE_REQUEST~| STANDARD_RIGHTS_READ
GENERIC_WRITE	DDE_POKE~| STANDARD_RIGHTS_WRITE
GENERIC_EXECUTE	DDE_EXECUTE~| STANDARD_RIGHTS_EXECUTE
GENERIC_ALL	DDE_ADVISE~| DDE_REQUEST~| DDE_POKE~| DDE_EXECUTE~| STANDARD_RIGHTS_REQUIRED

The following discretionary ACE is created:

ACE 0:

ACE Type = AccessAllowed
sid = LogonSid
AccessMask =
  DDE_ADVISE~| DDE_REQUEST~| DDE_POKE~| DDE_EXECUTE ~|
  STANDARD_RIGHTS_REQUIRED
Not Inheritable

13.4 Opening an Object

Each object contains a list of processes for which it has been opened. Each time an object is accessed its process list is checked to find out if the object has been opened by the calling process. If not, the client is impersonated and an open access check is made by calling **AccessCheckAndAuditAlarm** with a "Maximum Allowed" access mask. If this call is successful, an entry is made into the object's process list. Each entry contains the process ID, granted access mask and GenerateOnClose value.

13.5 Object Access

When an object is to be accessed by an API, an open check is performed, and, if successful, **AreAllAccessesGranted** is used to verify that the object has been opened with the permissions required to perform the operation. No auditing of this check is performed.

13.6 Closing an Object

When an object is closed, the system audits the event. Depending on the object type other processing is performed:

WindowStation	Windowstations are only closed and destroyed by the USER32 windowstation control thread when commanded to do so by the System Manager.
Desktop	The desktop's open count is decremented. If it drops to zero, the desktop and all windows, menus and DDE conversations contained in the desktop are destroyed.
Window	The window is destroyed and by doing this the window handle is rendered invalid.
Menu	The menu is destroyed and by doing this the menu handle is rendered invalid.
DDE Access	All conversations are terminated and the access handle is rendered invalid.
DDE Conversation	The converation is terminated and the conversation handle is rendered invalid.

If the object is destroyed as a result of its being closed, the object's SD is dereferenced and retention checks are performed.

13.7 Window Classes

The concept of global window classes has been removed. The predefined window classes are the only ones that can be shared between processes. Additionally, the predefined window classes can no longer be subclassed. Applications are still allowed to subclass their individual windows by using **SetWindowLong**.

13.8 SM_SECURE System Metric

A new system metric, **SM_SECURE**, has been added. The return value of this metric is TRUE if the system is operating in secure mode, FALSE if not.

13.9 ES_PASSWORD Style Edit Controls

The contents of ES_PASSWORD style edit controls can no longer be copied to the clipboard. This style also can no longer be reset using **SetWindowLong**.

13.10 Window Enumeration

All APIs that return a window handle or pass a window handle to an enumeration function treat windows created by the calling process differently from those created by other processes. Windows created by the calling process are already opened and can be returned or passed to the enumeration function without restriction. If the prospective window to be returned or enumerated was not created by the calling process, the process must have DESKTOP_ENUMWINDOWS access permission in the window's desktop and the window itself must have WINDOW_ENUMWINDOW access permission. If both conditions are met the window is opened for the process and returned or passed to the enumeration function. If not, the window is ignored and the API proceeds to the next applicable window.

13.11 Accessing Screen Contents

When a windowstation is created, the engine is called with the windowstation handle and a list of display devices that are to be used in the windowstation. The engine initializes the devices and retains the windowstation handle so that when a DC is created for a display, it can be assigned to the proper windowstation. When a function that reads the screen contents is used, the engine calls the USER32 server with the DC's windowstation to determine the allowed access.

The access WINSTA_READSCREEN must be granted to a process in order to read the contents of a display screen with the following operations:

- GetPixel() when the DC is a display context.

- BitBlt() and StretchBlt when the source DC is a display context and the destination DC is used and is not a display context.

13.12 Clipboard Access

Any process reading from or writing to the clipboard must have WINSTA_ACCESSCLIPBOARD permission.

In a C2 level system, any process that has access rights to the clipboard can read or write to the clipboard.

In a B level system, objects that go into the clipboard will retain the security of their owner. Clipboard objects can move upwards through levels to higher securities but not downwards. For example if a top secret object is in the clipboard, the clipboard will appear empty to an unclassified process. If an unclassified object is in the clipboard, any top secret application will have access to that object.

13.13 DDE Security

The Win3 message-based DDE protocol is retained for NT. The DDEML library provides a high-level API interface that hides the protocol from the application. The DDEML is implemented as part of the USER32 server under NT.

13.13.1 Registration

The function **DdeInitialize** optionally fills a structure with information about the DDE conversations that can take place. Contained in this structure is a handle to the application's DDE access object. The application can use this handle to control access to its DDE server functions. The access object is not used for DDE client functions.

13.13.2 Conversations

An application that uses DDE will normally use either the DDE message protocol or use the DDE API set. For this discussion an application can act as a "window-based client" (WC), an "API-based client" (AC), a "window-based server" (WS), or an "API-based server" (AS). If the client and the server are owned by the same user, the connection is made as it is under Win3. To understand the effects of security on DDE conversations between applications owned by different users, the following scenarios must be examined:

- An WC connecting to an WS.

- An AC connecting to an WS.

- An WC connecting to an AS.

- An AC connecting to an AS.

13.13.2.1 WC –> WS

For this conversation to succeed, the WS must have access to the WC window and the WC must have access to the WS window. If the WS does not have access to the WC, the WS cannot acknowledge the WM_DDE_INITIATE. If the WC does not access to the WS, the WC cannot send any messages to the WS.

13.13.2.2 AC –> WS

A window is created by USER32 in behalf of the AC when it is registered. The existence of this window is hidden from the AC so that the AC cannot modify its security. Therefore, the WS will not be able to acknowledge the WM_DDE_INITIATE from the AC and the connection will fail.

13.13.2.3 WC –> AS

For this conversation to succeed, the AS must have access to the WC window. When the AS receives the initiate request, access to the WC window is checked and if access is granted, USER32 adds access rights for the WC to the AS window. If access to the WC window is not allowed to the server the initiate request is ignored. The AS performs an access check of the WC thread token against the access object. Connection is allowed or denied according to this check.

13.13.2.4 AC –> AS

For this type of conversation, all operations that access the windows that are used for the conversation transport are done on the server side. When a message is sent within the server, the application on whose behalf the message is being sent does not have to have access to that window. The security of these windows can be set up such that cannot be enumerated and thus be hidden from all applications. The AS performs the same AS access check on an AC as it does on a WC.

13.13.3 Data Objects

14.4 Client Impersonation

13.14 Auditing

Auditing and alarm generation will be performed on the following operations:

- Per system ACL-generated audits at:

- Object open.

- Object close.

- Privilege checks.

- System ACL access attempts.

- Windowstation creation and destruction.

13.15 Server Initialization

During server initialization:

- The windowstation control thread is started.

- STRINGs used for auditing purposes are initialized.

- Initial windowstation security descriptor is created.

13.16 Client Initialization

13.16.1 Server Connection

A connection is made to the USER32 server with a security quality of service that specifies that dynamic security context tracking and an impersonation level of SecurityImpersonation are used.

13.16.2 WindowStation Access

Part of the USER32 server connection routine performs an access check on the windowstation assigned to the new process. The name of the windowstation the new process is assigned to is retrieved from the new process' environment. An attempt is made to open this windowstation for maximum allowed access, and if successful, the process is allowed to execute. If the windowstation is opened and the application's default desktop does not exist, the desktop is created.

13.16.3 Thread Initialization

During creation of an application's server-side thread the desktop that the thread executes in is opened.

13.17 Logon Processing

The Windows logon is implemented as a DLL, which is loaded during USER32 server initialization. When a windowstation is created a call is made to the logon DLL to start a logon thread to handle logons on the new windowstation.

13.17.1 Logon

When a user is logged on the logon thread creates a unique SID to represent the logon. This is called the LogonSid. After the user has been logged on, the logon thread sets its windowstation's owner to be LogonSid and its discretionary ACL to some variation of:

ACE 0:

ACE Type = AccessAllowed
sid = LogonSid
AccessMask =
   WINSTA_ACCESSCLIPBOARD~| WINSTA_CREATEDESKTOP~|
   WINSTA_ENUMDESKTOPS~| WINSTA_ENUMERATE~|
   WINSTA_READATTRIBUTES~| WINSTA_WRITEATTRIBUTES~|
   WINSTA_ACCESSGLOBALATOMS~| WINSTA_EXITWINDOWS~|
   WINSTA_READSCREEN~| STANDARD_RIGHTS_REQUIRED
Not Inheritable

ACE 1:

ACE Type = AccessAllowed
sid = LogonSid
AccessMask =
   GenericRead~| GenericWrite~| GenericExecute~| GenericAll
Inheritable Only
Inheritable by containers
Inheritable by non-containers
Inheritance is to be propagated

The logon calls the NT Session Manager (SM) and passes it the windowstation name. The SM puts the windowstation name in the shell environment and then starts the Win32 shell or, if specified, a standard Windows program.

13.17.2 Logoff

The user is logged off when the user exits the shell or **ExitWindows** is called. The logoff results in the destruction of all desktops, windows and menus within the windowstation not owned by the logon process. The USER32 server then notifies the logon thread via event that the logoff has occurred.

A logoff also occurs if the windowstation is taken off line and destroyed. In this case, the windowstation's logon thread is also terminated.

13.17.3 Windowstation Locking

The windowstation can be locked by calling the function **LockWindowStation**. This function notifies the logon thread via event that the windowstation is locked. The logon thread causes the actual lock to occur by calling **LogonLockWindowStation**. The user then has to use the SAS to request that the windowstation be unlocked. The logon thread collects and verifies the user and password before the windowstation is unlocked.

13.18 System Shutdown

System shutdown is initiated by the system administrator via some yet-to-be-defined application. This application wakes up the System Manager, which, as part of its shutdown processing, tells the USER32 server to destroy the windowstations.

Chapter	Unicode Support
14	

14.1   Overview 217

14.2   Unicode Support in the Windows 32 API 217

14.3   Data Types 217

14.4   API Prototypes 218

14.5   Basic Steps 219

14.6   Window Classes 220

14.7   Messages 220

14.8   Resources 220

14.9   C Run Times 221

14.10 Filenames 222

14.11 Special Characters 222

14.12 Unicode Plain Text Format 225

14.13 Special Topics 226

14.14 Workarounds 227

14.1 Overview

Unicode™ can represent all the world's characters in modern computer use, including technical symbols and special characters needed in publishing. Each Unicode character is 16 bits wide. Often, the name "wide character" is used synonymously.

The Windows 32-bit API supports applications that use Unicode, in addition to applications that use the regular ANSI character set. Mixed use in the same application is also possible.

The Windows 32-bit API is designed to make porting from existing Windows applications straightforward. Unicode support is no exception. Adding Unicode support to your application is easy, and you can even maintain a single set of sources from which to compile a program that supports Unicode or the Windows ANSI character set.

14.2 Unicode Support in the Windows 32 API

Unicode is supported in the Windows 32-bit API by assigning Unicode strings an explicit data type and providing a separate set of entry points and messages to support this new data type. A series of macros and naming conventions is provided that make transparent migration to Unicode support, or even compiling a non-Unicode and Unicode version of an application from the same set of sources, a straightforward matter.

Implementing Unicode as a separate data type allows the compiler's type checking to assure that only functions expecting Unicode strings are called with Unicode parameters.

14.3 Data Types

Most string operations for Unicode can be coded using the same logic used for handling the Windows ANSI character set, except that the basic unit of operation is a 16-bit quantity instead of an 8-bit byte. The header files provide a number of type definitions that make it easy to create sources that can be compiled for Unicode or the ANSI character set.

The following example shows the method used in the Win32 header files to define three sets of types: a set of *generic type definitions,* which depend on the state of the **UNICODE** variable, and two sets of *explicit type definitions*. The first set of explicit type definitions provides a set of type definitions for use with the existing Windows (ANSI) character set, and the last is a set of type definitions for Unicode (or wide) characters.

```
/* Generic Types */

#ifdef UNICODE

 typedef wchar_t TCHAR;

#else

 typedef unsigned char TCHAR;

#endif

typedef TCHAR * LPTSTR, *LPTCH;

/* 8-bit character specific */

typedef unsigned char CHAR;

typedef CHAR *LPSTR, *LPCH;

/* Unicode specific (wide characters) */

typedef unsigned wchar_t WCHAR;

typedef WCHAR *LPWSTR, *LPWCH;
```

A rare example of a function that takes parameters using the explicit types is **MultiByteToWideChar**, which performs translation between ANSI (and other 8-bit character sets) and Unicode. Here the source parameter is **LPSTR** and the destination parameter is **LPWSTR**.

Applications are encouraged to use the generic data types, but the specific types exist for applications that require mixed type control.

14.4 API Prototypes

Function prototypes are also provided in three sets, as shown below. The generic function prototype consists of the standard API name implemented as a macro. It evaluates into one of the explicit function prototypes depending on whether the compile time variable UNICODE is defined. The letters A and W are added at the end of the API names in the explicit function prototypes. Note how the generic prototype uses the generic type **LPTSTR** for the text parameter, but the A&W prototypes use the 8-bit or wide character type **LPSTR** and **LPWSTR** instead.

```
APIENTRY SetWindowText(HANDLE hwnd, LPTSTR lpText);

APIENTRY SetWindowTextA(HANDLE hwnd, LPSTR lpText);

APIENTRY SetWindowTextW(HANDLE hwnd, LPWSTR lpText);
```

With this mechanism an application can either use the generic API to work transparently with Unicode dependent on the #define UNICODE variable, or, alteratively, it can make mixed calls by using the explicit function names with A and W.

This three-prototype approach applies to all functions with TEXT arguments. In every case, a function whose name ends in W expects wide- character arguments, etc. A generic function prototype should always be used with the generic string and character types.

Where the documentation shows a function prototype with only W/A arguments, this is a function that can only be used with the appropriate data type, independently from the state of the UNICODE variable at compile time.

> **NOTE** Wherever APIs take length parameters, these continue to be *byte* counts independent of the character type.

14.5 Basic Steps

To convert code that processes strings to use Unicode, follow these steps:

1. Change all character/string types used for text to **TCHAR** and **LPTSTR** or **LPTCH.**

2. Make sure that pointers to nontext data buffers or binary byte arrays are coded with the **LPBYTE** type and not mistakenly with the **LPTSTR** or **LPTCH** types. Declare pointers of indeterminate type explicitly as void pointers by using **LPVOID** as appropriate.

3. Make pointer arithmetic type-independent: subtracting TCHAR * values yields an answer in bytes if TCHAR evaluates to char, an answer in terms of 16-bit elements, when TCHAR evaluates to WCHAR. The following expression always calculates the number of elements of type TCHAR, whether they are compiled as Unicode or not.

```
cCount = *lpEnd-*lpStart;
```

Change the expression to:

```
cbSize = (*lpEnd-*lpStart)*sizeof(TCHAR);
```

to make the expression return the size in bytes in a type-independent manner. There is no need to change a statement like the following:

```
chNext = ++*lpText;
```

because the pointer increment points to the next character element.

4. Replace literal strings and manifest character constants with macros. Use the **TEXT** macro, which evaluates to **L'\\'** when the **UNICODE** variable is defined, and to **'\\'** otherwise, so that

```
while( *lpFileName++ != '\\\\' )...
```

becomes

```
while( *lpFilename++ != TEXT('\\\\') )...
```

Consider moving literal strings into resources, especially if they contain characters outside the ASCII range (that is, 0x00 to 0x7f).

5. Change the code to call the wide generic versions of the run-time library string functions (for example, use macros like **CharStrLen** defined below instead of **strlen**). This generic macro is evaluated to **wcslen** if the UNICODE variable is #defined, otherwise to **strlen**.

   NOTE   The count returned is in *number of characters* in either case.

6. Change any code that relies implicitly on 255 as the largest value for a character, for example, by using a character value as index into a table of size 256.

7. Compile your code. It should create the same binary as before. Next, set the #define UNICODE variable, and your program will be compiled as a Unicode program.

14.6 Window Classes

A window class is implemented by a window procedure. A window procedure can be registered with either the **RegisterWindowClassA** or **RegisterWindowClassW** function. By using the A version of the API, the program tells the system that the windows of the created class expect messages with text or character parameters to use the ANSI character set; by registering the window class with a call to the wide-character version of the API, the program can request that the system pass text parameters of messages as Unicode. An API **IsWindowUnicode** allows programs to query the nature of each window.

14.7 Messages

Messages between windows of different types are transparently translated by the system. It is expected that applications generally use the same type of window. Even though a window function is registered to receive messages in Unicode or ANSI format, the window procedure can still send messages of either type or call API functions of either type.

14.8 Resources

Windows 32-bit API resources in their binary form are stored in Unicode. When loading resources, applications can use the Unicode version of the resource APIs, for example **LoadStringW**, to obtain resources as Unicode data.

Using resources consistently instead of string constants will not only make your program easier to translate into other languages, but it will make it simple to create a Unicode and non-Unicode version of your program from the same sources.

14.9 C Run Times

The Unicode data type is compatible with the wide-character data type **wchar_t** in ANSI C, thus allowing access to the wide-character string functions. The C run-time libraries contain wide-character versions of the **strxxx** string functions. The wide-character version of the functions all start with **wcs**.

To compile for Unicode or ASCII from the same sources, define a simple set of macros that follow the same naming conventions as the rest of the Windows 32-bit API. A full set of macros will eventually be provided in the Windows 32-bit header files.

```
// generic string function macros
#ifdef UNICODE
#define CharStrCmp wcscmp
#define CharStrCpy wcscpy
#define CharStrLen wcslen
#else
#define CharStrCmp strcmp
#define CharStrCpy strcpy
#define CharStrLen strlen
#endif
// explicit string function macros
#define CharStrCmpA strcmp
#define CharStrCpyA strcpy
#define CharStrLenA strlen
#define CharStrCmpW wcscmp
#define CharStrCpyW wcscpy
#define CharStrLenW wcslen
```

The C run time also provides functions like **mbtowc** and **wctomb**, which can be used to translate the C character set to and from Unicode. A more general set of functions that can perform conversion between Unicode and any of a number of Windows character sets and MS-DOS code pages will be part of the Windows 32-bit API.

The **printf** function supports a **%ws** format parameter, which corresponds to a wide-character string parameter. Similarily, there is a **wcsprintf** function, where the format string itself is a Unicode string.

14.10 Filenames

In Windows, the character set used in the Window Manager and GDI (ANSI) is different from the character set used by the file system. The MS-DOS FAT file system uses one of the PC code pages as its character set, called the OEM character set in Windows.

The Windows 32-bit API can be hosted on top of a variety of file systems, some of which, for example NTFS, are capable of storing filenames in Unicode.

If you use Unicode versions of the file system functions, there is no need to perform translations to and from ANSI to OEM character sets around these APIs. An easy solution is to provide a NO-OP macro for AnsiToOEM and OEMtoAnsi functions whenever you compile for Unicode.

The special filename characters are the same in Unicode filenames: '\\,' '/,' '.,' '?,' '*.' All these characters are in the ASCII range of characters (0x00 to 0x7f) and their Unicode equivalents are simply zero extensions: 0x0000 to 0x007f.

14.11 Special Characters

There are a few special characters and characters with special semantics that are important when dealing with Unicode text strings.

14.11.0.0.1 UNICODE_NULL

The code 0x0000 is the Unicode string terminator for null-terminated strings. A single null byte is not sufficient for this, as many Unicode characters contain null bytes as either their high or low byte. An example is 'A,' which is 0x0041.

Rule 0: Always use (TCHAR) 0 when null-terminating strings.

14.11.0.0.2 Not a Character

The code points 0xFFFF and 0xFFFE are not characters and therefore do not have Unicode character names. They never form part of Unicode plain text. The use of 0xFFFF is reserved for program private use, for example, as sentinel code. It is illegal in plain text files or across the API. The special circumstance under which 0xFFFE might occur is explained in the next rule.

Rule 1: 0xFFFF won't be understood, except by yourself.

14.11.0.0.3 BYTE_ORDER_MARK

Since Unicode plain text is a sequence of 16-bit codes, it is sensitive to the byte-ordering that is used when writing the text. Intel and MIPS chips have the least significant byte first, while Motorola chips have the most significant byte first. Ideally, all Unicode would follow only one set of rules, but this would force one side to always swap the byte order on reading and writing plain text files, even when the file never leaves the system on which it was created.

Plain text files lack the file header, which would be the preferred place to specify byte order. To have a cheap way to indicate which byte order is used in a text, Unicode has defined a character 0xFEFF byte order mark (BOM) and a noncharacter 0xFFFE, which are the mirror byte-image of each other. The byte order mark is *not* a control character that selects the byte order of the text; rather, its function is to inform recipients that they are looking at a correctly byte-ordered file.

As a side benefit, since the sequence 0xFEFF is exceedingly rare at the outset of regular non-Unicode text files, it can serve as an *implicit* marker or *signature* to identify the file as Unicode. Programs that are written to read both Unicode and non-Unicode text files should use the presence of this sequence as a very strong hint that the file is in Unicode. Compare this to using Ctrl-Z to terminate text files.

Rule 2: Always prefix any Unicode plain text file with a BOM.

14.11.0.0.4 ASCII Control Characters

The first 32 sixteen-bit characters in Unicode are intended for encoding the 32 control characters. In this manner, existing use of control characters for formatting purposes can be supported. Unicode programs can treat these control codes in exactly the same way as they used to treat their equivalents in ASCII.

ASCII control characters, including arguments in escape sequences, are always converted to their Unicode wide-character equivalent.

When an ASCII plain text file is converted to Unicode, there is a chance that it will be converted back to ASCII later on, perhaps on the receiving end of a transmission. Converting escape sequences into Unicode on a character basis (ESC A turns into

0x001B escape, 0x0041 latin capital letter a) will allow the reverse conversion to be performed without the need to recognize and parse the escape sequence as such.

Rule 3: Translate escape sequences character by character into Unicode.

14.11.0.0.5 Line and Paragraph Separator

Unicode has two special characters, 0x2028 line separator and 0x2029 paragraph separator. A new line is begun after each line separator. A new paragraph is begun after each paragraph separator. Since these are *separator* codes, it is not necessary to either start the first line or paragraph or to end the last line or paragraph with them. Rather, doing so would indicate that there was an empty paragraph or line in that location.

The paragraph separator can be inserted between paragraphs of text. Its use allows plain text files to be created that can be laid out on a different line width at the receiving end. The line separator can be used to indicate an unconditional end of line. In fact, they work just like SHIFT+ENTER or ENTER work in Word. However, they do NOT correspond to CR and LF, or CR/LF. See the next rule.

Rule 4: Use the line and paragraph separator to divide plain text.

14.11.0.0.6 Interaction with CR/LF

The Unicode Standard does not prescribe a specific semantic to 0x000D carriage return and 0x000A line feed but leaves it up to your program to interpret these codes as well as to decide whether to require their use and whether CR/LF pairs or single codes are needed. This is really no change from the way these codes are used in ASCII.

Rule 5: Interpretation of ASCII control codes depends on the program.

14.11.0.0.7 Non-spacing Characters and Floating Accents

Many scripts contain characters which, on output, combine with other characters visually. A prominent example of this are the so-called floating accents. In Unicode, nonspacing characters follow their base character. The Windows 32-bit API will provide an extended ctype function, which lets an application determine whether a character is nonspacing. When breaking lines or otherwise separating text, make sure not to separate characters that belong together.

Rule 6: Keep nonspacing characters with their base character.

14.12 Unicode Plain Text Format

If at all possible, applications that read plain text files should set/read extended attributes to determine whether a file is Unicode or not. The Unicode standard provides a way to indicate the file type, and even the byte order inside the file, by use of a single wide character as the first character in the file:

```
0xFEFF = Byte order mark
```

```
0xFFFE = Illegal character (reverse of byte order mark)
```

Here is how these are used:

Table 14.1 Program Expects Unicode

FEFF	FFFE	neither
Treat FEFF as Unicode indicator. Skip it and process the rest of the file as Unicode.	Treat FFFE as byte-reversed Unicode indicator. Action: Flag wrong byte order as error. Optionally: Byte-swap file and process file as Unicode.	File is not marked. Action: Assume it is Unicode and process file as such. Optionally: Issue a warning that file may not be Unicode. Run a heuristic check.

Table 14.2 Program Does Not Expect Unicode

FEFF	FFFE	neither
Treat FEFF as possible Unicode indicator. Action: Flag as possible error, process as non-Unicode. Optionally: Map data to 8-bit before processing.	Treat FFFE as possible byte-reversed Unicode indicator. Action: Flag as possible error, process as non-Unicode. Optionally: Byte-swap file and map data to 8-bit before processing.	Don't expect file to be marked. Action: Assume it is non-Unicode data and process file as such. Optionally: Run a heuristic check.

Table 14.3 Program Will Take Either

FEFF	FFFE	neither
Treat FEFF as Unicode indicator. Skip it and process the rest of the file as Unicode.	Treat FFFE as byte-reversed Unicode indicator. Action: Flag wrong byte order as error. Optionally: Byte-swap file and process file as Unicode.	Non-Unicode files are normally unmarked. Action: Process as if non-Unicode. Optionally: Run a heuristic check.

If a byte order mark is found in the middle of a file, it is treated as ZERO WIDTH NO BREAK SPACE, that is, it does not print or word break.

The BYTE ORDER MARK character is not found in any code page, so it disappears if data is converted to ANSI. Unlike other Unicode characters, it is NOT replaced by a default character when converted.

The heuristic check for Unicode data could be as simple as a test whether the variation in the low order bytes is much higher than the variation in the high order bytes. For example, if ASCII is converted to Unicode, every second byte is 0. Also, detection 0x000a, and 0x000D for line feed and carriage return, and an even (vs. odd) file size are simple tests, that, taken together, will provide a strong indicator of the nature of the file.

"Treat as error" can mean any of the typical error handling actions for your application.

14.13 Special Topics

Suppose you decide to used mixed character types, and find that you have an ANSI string and need a Unicode string?

The Windows 32-bit API provides two handy functions: **WideCharacterToMultiByte** and **MultiByteToWideCharacter** which can handle the translation for you. ANSI C also defines a set of conversion functions **wctomb** and **mbtowc**, but they can only convert to and from the character set supported by the C run time.

The Window 32-bit API also provides the general function MultiByteToMultiByte which provides general code page conversion.

How does this interact with DBCS? DBCS is the "generalized" case of an 8-bit character set, since its smallest unit is a byte. It is, so to speak, the ANSI character set for the Japanese version. The Windows 32-bit API for the Japanese version will accept DBCS strings for the ANSI versions of the API. However, unlike Unicode, supporting DBCS character handling requires detailed changes in the character processing algorithms throughout an application program.

How do you get Unicode command line arguments? The function **GetCommandLine** can be called as Unicode API to return command line arguments in Unicode.

14.14 Workarounds

If your favorite function has not been exported in a Unicode version, you can often use a very simple workaround:

– Use an equivalent function that does have a Unicode version. For example, use **CreateFile** instead of **OpenFile**

– Map characters to/from 8-bits around the function call. For example, the number formatting functions atoi and itoa understand only the digits 0–9. Normally, mapping Unicode to 8-bit characters could cause loss of data; but in this case, you get the correct result by changing the following statements:

```
char str[4];

num = atoi(str);
```

to a type-independent:

```
TCHAR str[4];

CHAR strTmp[SIZE];

#ifdef UNICODE

 wctomb(strTmp, str, sizeof(strTmp));

 num = atoi(strTmp);

#else

 num = atoi(str);

#endif
```

where **wctomb** is the C runtime function to translate Unicode to ASCII. The atoi function stops at any character that is not a digit.

Programming Reference A-G

Windows Interfaces and Application Callbacks: A-G 229

■ _lclose

int _lclose(*hFile***)**
int *hFile*;   /* file to close */

The **_lclose** function closes the file specified by the *hFile* parameter. As a result, the file is no longer available for reading or writing.

Parameters   *hFile*   Specifies the handle of the file to be closed. The handle is returned by the function that created or last opened the file.

Return Value   The return value is zero if the function successfully closed the file. Otherwise, the return value is −1.

Example   This example copies a file to a temporary file, then closes both files:

```
int cbRead;
PBYTE pbBuf;

/* Allocate a buffer for file I/O. */

pbBuf = (PBYTE) LocalAlloc(LMEM_FIXED, 2048);

/* Copy the input file to the temporary file. */

do {
    cbRead = _lread(hfReadFile, (LPSTR) pbBuf, 2048);
    _lwrite(hfTempFile, (LPSTR) pbBuf, cbRead);
} while (cbRead != 0);

/* Free the buffer and close the files. */

LocalFree((HANDLE) pbBuf);

_lclose(hfReadFile);
_lclose(hfTempFile);
```

See Also   **_lopen, OpenFile**

■ _lcreat

int _lcreat(*lpszPathName, iAttribute***)**
LPSTR *lpszPathName*;   /* file to open   */
WORD *iAttribute*;   /* file attributes */

The **_lcreat** function creates or opens a specified file. If the file does not exist, the function creates a new file and opens it for writing. If the file does exist, the function truncates the file size to zero and opens it for reading and writing. When the function opens the file, the pointer is set to the beginning of the file.

Parameters   *lpszPathName*   Points to a null-terminated string that names the file to be opened. The string must consist of characters from the ANSI character set.

iAttribute   Specifies the file attributes. The parameter must be one of these values:

Value	Meaning
0	Normal; can be read or written without restriction.

Value	Meaning
1	Read-only; cannot be opened for write.
2	Hidden; not found by directory search.
3	System; not found by directory search.

Return Value

The return value is a file handle if the function was successful. Otherwise, the return value is −1.

Comments

This function should be used carefully. It is possible to open any file, even one that has already been opened by another function.

Example

This example uses the **_lcreat** function to open a temporary file:

```
int hfTempFile;
char szBuf[144];

/* Create a temporary file. */

GetTempFileName(0, "tst", 0, (LPSTR) szBuf);

hfTempFile = _lcreat((LPSTR) szBuf, 0);

if (hfTempFile == -1) {
    MessageBox(hwnd, "could not create temp file",
        "_lcreat", MB_ICONEXCLAMATION);
    break;
}
```

■ _llseek

LONG _llseek(hFile, lOffset, iOrigin**)**
int hFile;   /* file handle   */
int lOffset;   /* number of bytes to move */
int iOrigin;   /* position to move from   */

The **_llseek** function repositions the pointer in a previously opened file.

Parameters

hFile   Specifies the MS-DOS file handle of the file.

lOffset   Specifies the number of bytes the pointer is to be moved.

iOrigin   Specifies the starting position and direction of the pointer. The parameter must be one of the following values:

Value	Meaning
0	Move the file pointer *lOffset* bytes from the beginning of the file.
1	Move the file pointer *lOffset* bytes from its current position.
2	Move the file pointer *lOffset* bytes from the end of the file.

Return Value

The return value specifies the new offset of the pointer (in bytes) from the beginning of the file if the function was successful. Otherwise, the return value is −1.

Comments   When a file is initially opened, the file pointer is positioned at the beginning of the
file. The **_llseek** function permits random access to a file's contents by moving
the pointer an arbitrary amount without reading data.

Example   This example uses the **_llseek** function to move the file pointer to the end of an
existing file:

```
PBYTE pbBuf;
int hfAppendFile;

/* Open the write file. */

hfAppendFile = _lopen("append.txt", WRITE);

if (hfAppendFile == -1) {
    MessageBox(hwnd, "could not open append file",
        "_lopen", MB_ICONEXCLAMATION);
    break;
}

/* Move to the end of the file. */

if (_llseek(hfAppendFile, 0L, 2) == -1) {
    MessageBox(hwnd, "_llseek failed",
        "_llseek", MB_ICONEXCLAMATION);
    break;
}
```

See Also   **_lopen**

■ _lopen

int _lopen(*lpszPathName*, *iReadWrite***)**
LPSTR *lpszPathName*;   /* file name   */
int *iReadWrite*;   /* file access */

The **_lopen** function opens an existing file and sets the file pointer to the
beginning of the file.

Parameters   *lpszPathName*   Points to a null-terminated string that names the file to be
opened. The string must consist of characters from the ANSI character set.

iReadWrite   Specifies whether the function is to open the file with read access,
write access, or both. The parameter must be one of the following values:

Value	Meaning
OF_READ	Opens the file for reading only.
OF_READWRITE	Opens the file for reading and writing.
OF_SHARE_COMPAT	Opens the file with compatibility mode, allowing any process on a given machine to open the file any number of times. **_lopen** fails if the file has been opened with any of the other sharing modes.

Value	Meaning
OF_SHARE_DENY_NONE	Opens the file without denying other processes read or write access to the file. **_lopen** fails if the file has been opened in compatibility mode by any other process.
OF_SHARE_DENY_READ	Opens the file and denies other processes read access to the file. **_lopen** fails if the file has been opened in compatibility mode or for read access by any other process.
OF_SHARE_DENY_WRITE	Opens the file and denies other processes write access to the file. **_lopen** fails if the file has been opened in compatibility or for write access by any other process.
OF_WRITE	Opens the file for writing only.

Return Value   The return value is a file handle if the function opened the file. Otherwise, it is −1.

Example   This example uses the **_lopen** function to open an input file:

```
int hfReadFile;
/* Open the input file (read only). */

hfReadFile = _lopen("testfile", READ);

if (hfReadFile == -1) {
    MessageBox(hwnd, "could not open input file",
        "_lopen", MB_ICONEXCLAMATION);
    break;
}
```

See Also   **OpenFile**

■ _lread

```
DWORD _lread(hFile, lpBuffer, nBytes)
int hFile;
LPSTR lpBuffer;
int nBytes;
```

The **_lread** function reads data from the specified file.

Parameters   *hFile*   Specifies the handle of the file to be read.

lpBuffer   Points to a buffer that is to receive the data read from the file.

nBytes   Specifies the number of bytes to be read from the file.

Return Value   The return value indicates the number of bytes which the function actually read from the file. If the number of bytes read is less than *nBytes*, the function encountered the end of the file (EOF) before reading the specified number of bytes. The return value is −1 if the function failed.

Example

This example uses the **_lread** and **_lwrite** functions to copy data from one file to another:

```
int hfReadFile;
int cbRead;
PBYTE pbBuf;

/* Allocate a buffer for file I/O. */

pbBuf = (PBYTE) LocalAlloc(LMEM_FIXED, 2048);

/* Copy the input file to the temporary file. */

do {
    cbRead = _lread(hfReadFile, (LPSTR) pbBuf, 2048);
    _lwrite(hfTempFile, (LPSTR) pbBuf, cbRead);
} while (cbRead != 0);

/* Free the buffer and close the files. */

LocalFree((HANDLE) pbBuf);

_lclose(hfReadFile);
_lclose(hfTempFile);
```

See Also

_lwrite

■ _lwrite

DWORD _lwrite(*hFile*, *lpBuffer*, *nBytes***)**
int *hFile*;
LPSTR *lpBuffer*,
int *nBytes*;

The **_lwrite** function writes data into the specified file.

Parameters

hFile   Specifies the MS-DOS file handle of the file to be read.

lpBuffer   Points to a buffer that contains the data to be written to the file.

nBytes   Specifies the number of bytes to be written to the file.

Return Value

The return value indicates the number of bytes actually written to the file. The return value is −1 if the function failed.

Comments

The buffer specified by *lpBuffer* cannot extend past the end of a segment.

Example

This example uses the **_lread** and **_lwrite** functions to copy data from one file to another:

```
int cbRead;
PBYTE pbBuf;

/* Allocate a buffer for file I/O. */

pbBuf = (PBYTE) LocalAlloc(LMEM_FIXED, 2048);

/* Copy the input file to the temporary file. */

do {
```

```
                   cbRead = _lread(hfReadFile, (LPSTR) pbBuf, 2048);
                   _lwrite(hfTempFile, (LPSTR) pbBuf, cbRead);
              } while (cbRead != 0);

              /* Free the buffer and close the files. */

              LocalFree((HANDLE) pbBuf);

              _lclose(hfReadFile);
              _lclose(hfTempFile);
```

See Also   _lread

■ AbnormalTermination

BOOL AbnormalTermination(VOID)

This intrinsic function is available within a termination handler to determine whether the body of the try-finally statement terminated normally.

This function has no parameters.

Return Value   The return value is TRUE if the body of the try-finally statement was terminated by an exception. The return value is FALSE if the body of the try-finally terminated normally, executing all the way through the closing }.

See Also   **GetExceptionCode**

■ AbortDoc

int AbortDoc(*hDC*)
HDC *hDC*;   /* device-context handle */

The **AbortDoc** function terminates the current print job and erases everything drawn since the last call to the **StartDoc** function. This function replaces the ABORTDOC printer escape for Windows version 3.1 and later.

Parameters   *hDC*   Identifies the device context for the print job.

Return Value   The return value is positive if the function is successful. Otherwise, it is negative.

Comments   If Print Manager was used to start the print job, calling the **AbortDoc** function erases the entire spool job—the printer receives nothing. If Print Manager was not used to start the print job, the data may already have been sent to the printer with **AbortDoc** is called. In this case, the printer driver resets the printer (when possible) and closes the print job.

See Also   **Escape, SetAbortProc, StartDoc**

■ AbortSpooler

BOOL AbortSpooler(*hSpooler***)**
HANDLE *hSpooler*;

The **AbortSpooler** function deletes a spooler's spool file if the printer is configured for spooling. If the spooler is communicating directly with the printer, this function has no effect.

Parameters *hSpooler* Open handle to the spooler the function will abort.

Return Value If the function is successful, the return value is TRUE.

If the function fails, the return value is FALSE/NULL. Further information can be obtained by calling **GetLastError.**

See Also **OpenSpooler, CloseSpooler, ReadSpooler, WriteSpooler, StartDocSpooler, StartFrameSpooler, EndDocSpooler, EndFrameSpooler**

■ AbsoluteToSelfRelativeSD

BOOL AbsoluteToSelfRelativeSD(*AbsoluteSecurityDescriptor*, *SelfRelativeSecurityDescriptor*, *BufferLength***)**
PSECURITY_DESCRIPTOR *AbsoluteSecurityDescriptor*,
PSECURITY_DESCRIPTOR *SelfRelativeSecurityDescriptor*,
PULONG *BufferLength*;

The **AbsoluteToSelfRelativeSD** function creates a self-relative format version of an absolute format security descriptor.

Parameters *AbsoluteSecurityDescriptor* Pointer to an absolute format **SECURITY_DESCRIPTOR** data structure. The function will create a self-relative format version of this security descriptor. The function will not modify this security descriptor.

The **SECURITY_DESCRIPTOR** data structure is an opaque data structure defined as follows:

```
typedef  PVOID  PSECURITY_DESCRIPTOR;
```

SelfRelativeSecurityDescriptor Pointer to a buffer that the function will fill with a self-relative format security descriptor.

BufferLength Pointer to a variable that specifies the size of the buffer pointed to by *SelfRelativeSecurityDescriptor*. If the buffer is not large enough, the function fails, and sets the variable to the minimum buffer size required.

Return Value If the function is successful, the return value is TRUE.

If the function fails, the return value is FALSE. Call **GetLastError** for more detailed error information.

See Also **SelfRelativeToAbsoluteSD**

■ AccessCheck

BOOL AccessCheck (*SecurityDescriptor, ClientToken, DesiredAccess, GenericMapping,*
GrantedAccess, AccessStatus)
PSECURITY_DESCRIPTOR *SecurityDescriptor*;
HANDLE *ClientToken*;
ACCESS_MASK *DesiredAccess*;
PGENERIC_MAPPING *GenericMapping*;
PACCESS_MASK *GrantedAccess*;
PBOOL *AccessStatus*;

The **AccessCheck** function validates a client's desired access to an object against the access control associated with the object.

Parameters

SecurityDescriptor   Pointer to the security descriptor against which access is to be checked.

The **SECURITY_DESCRIPTOR** data structure has the following form:

```
typedef PVOID PSECURITY_DESCRIPTOR;
```

ClientToken   Handle to a token object representing a client attempting access.

This handle must be obtained from a communication session layer, such as from a named pipe, to prevent possible security policy violations.

DesiredAccess   The desired access mask. This mask must have been previously mapped to contain no generic accesses.

GenericMapping   Pointer to the generic mapping associated with the type of object being examined.

GrantedAccess   Pointer to a variable that the function will fill, if the function is successful, with an access mask indicating which accesses were actually granted

AccessStatus   Receives an indication of the success or failure of the access check.

If access is granted, STATUS_SUCCESS is returned. If access is denied, a value appropriate for return to the client is returned. This will be STATUS_ACCESS_DENIED or, when mandatory access controls are implemented, STATUS_OBJECT_NAME_NOT_FOUND.

Return Value

If the function is successful, the return value is TRUE.

If the function fails, the return value is FALSE. Call **GetLastError** for more detailed error information.

Comments

The function compares the input Security Descriptor against the input token and indicates by its return value if access is granted or denied. If access is granted then the desired access mask becomes the granted access mask for the object.

The semantics of the access check routine is described in the DSA Security Architecture workbook. Note that during an access check only the discretionary ACL is examined.

See Also   AccessCheckAndAuditAlarm, AreAllAccessesGranted,
AreAnyAccessesGranted, MapGenericMask, ObjectCloseAuditAlarm,
ObjectOpenAuditAlarm, ObjectPrivilegeAuditAlarm, PrivilegeCheck,
PrivilegedServiceAuditAlarm

■ AccessCheckAndAuditAlarm

BOOL AccessCheckAndAuditAlarm (*SubsystemName, HandleId, ObjectTypeName, ObjectName,
SecurityDescriptor, DesiredAccess, GenericMapping, Privileges, ObjectCreation,
GrantedAccess, AccessStatus, GenerateOnClose*)
PSTRING *SubsystemName*;
PVOID *HandleId*;
PSTRING *ObjectTypeName*;
PSTRING *ObjectName*;
PSECURITY_DESCRIPTOR *SecurityDescriptor*;
ACCESS_MASK *DesiredAccess*;
PGENERIC_MAPPING *GenericMapping*;
PPRIVILEGE_SET *Privileges*;
BOOL *ObjectCreation*;
PACCESS_MASK *GrantedAccess*;
PBOOL *AccessStatus*;
PBOOL *GenerateOnClose*;

The **AccessCheckAndAuditAlarm** function performs an access validation and generates the corresponding audit and alarm messages. It will also, optionally, determine whether necessary privileges are held by the subject.

This service may only be used by a server application that chooses to impersonate its client and thereby specifies the client security context implicitly.

Parameters   *SubsystemName*   Pointer to a string that is the name of the subsystem calling the function.

HandleId   A unique value representing the client's handle to the object. This value is ignored (and may be re-used) if the access is denied.

ObjectTypeName   Pointer to a string that is the name of the type of object being created or accessed.

ObjectName   Pointer to a string that is the name of the object being created or accessed.

SecurityDescriptor   Pointer to the security descriptor against which access is to be checked.

The **SECURITY_DESCRIPTOR** data structure has the following form:

```
typedef PVOID PSECURITY_DESCRIPTOR;
```

DesiredAccess   The desired access mask. This mask must have been previously mapped to contain no generic accesses.

GenericMapping   Pointer to the generic mapping associated with the type of object being examined.

Privileges   Optional pointer to a set of privileges the subject must have in order to successfully access the object. If the privileges are not held or are not active, the function will deny access, and set an appropriate access denial value into the variable pointed to by *AccessStatus*.

The **PRIVILEGE_SET** data structure has the following form:

```
typedef struct tagPRIVILEGE_SET {
    ULONG    PrivilegeCount;
    ULONG    Control;
    LUID_AND_ATTRIBUTES Privilege[];
} PRIVILEGE_SET;
```

ObjectCreation   Boolean flag that specifies, if TRUE, that the function will create a new object if access is granted. A value of FALSE specifies that the function will open an existing object if access is granted.

GrantedAccess   Pointer to a variable that the function will fill, if the function is successful, with an access mask indicating which accesses were actually granted.

AccessStatus   Pointer to a Boolean variable that the function sets to indicate the success or failure of the access check.

If access is granted, the function sets the variable to the value STATUS_SUCCESS. If access is denied, the function sets the variable to STATUS_ACCESS_DENIED or, when mandatory access controls are implemented, to STATUS_OBJECT_NOT_FOUND.

GenerateOnClose   Pointer to a Boolean variable that the audit generation routine sets. This Boolean must be passed to **ObjectCloseAuditAlarm** when the object handle is closed.

Return Value   If the function is successful, the return value is TRUE.

If the function fails, the return value is FALSE. Call **GetLastError** for more detailed error information.

Comments   This routine compares the input security descriptor against the caller's impersonation token and indicates if access is granted or denied. If access is granted, then the desired access mask becomes the granted access mask for the object. The semantics of the access check routine is described in the DSA Security Architecture workbook.

This routine will also generate any necessary audit messages as a result of the access attempt.

This function requires the caller to have SeSecurityPrivilege privilege. The test for this privilege is always against the primary token of the calling process, not the impersonation token of the thread.

See Also   **AccessCheck, AreAllAccessesGranted, AreAnyAccessesGranted, MapGenericMask, ObjectCloseAuditAlarm, ObjectOpenAuditAlarm, ObjectPrivilegeAuditAlarm, PrivilegeCheck, PrivilegedServiceAuditAlarm**

■ AccessResource

The **AccessResource** function has been deleted as calculated resources will not work in the Win32 application environment where all resources are contained in mapped image files.

■ AddAccessAllowedAce

BOOL AddAccessAllowedAce(*Acl, AceRevision, AccessMask, Sid*)
PACL *Acl;*
ULONG *AceRevision;*
ACCESS_MASK *AccessMask;*
PSID *Sid;*

The **AddAccessAllowedAce** function adds an ACCESS_ALLOWED ACE to an **ACL**. The access is granted to a specified **SID**. An **ACE** is an access control entry. An **ACL** is an access control list. An **SID** is a security identifier.

The **AddAccessAllowedAce** function places a very bland **ACE** header in the **ACE**. It provides no inheritance and no **ACE** flags.

This is expected to be the most common form of **ACL** modification.

Parameters

Acl   Pointer to an existing **ACL** data structure. The function will add an ACCESS_ALLOWED **ACE** to this **ACL**.

The **ACL** data structure has the following form:

```
typedef struct tagACL {
    UCHAR   AclRevision;
    UCHAR   Sbz1;
    USHORT  AclSize;
    USHORT  AceCount;
    USHORT  Sbz2;
    /* ordered list of ACEs */
} ACL;
```

AceRevision   Specifies the **ACL/ACE** revision level of the **ACE** being added.

AccessMask   Specifies the mask of accesses to be granted to the specified **SID**.

Sid   Pointer to the **SID** being granted access.

The **SID** data structure has the following form:

```
typedef PVOID * PSID;
```

Return Value

If the function is successful, the return value is TRUE.

If the function fails, the return value is FALSE. Call **GetLastError** for more detailed error information.

See Also

AddAce, DeleteAce, GetAce, GetAclInformation, InitializeAcl, IsValidAcl, SetAclInformation

■ AddAce

BOOL AddAce(*Acl, AceRevision, StartingAceIndex, AceList, AceListLength***)**
PACL *Acl;*
ULONG *AceRevision;*
ULONG *StartingAceIndex;*
PVOID *AceList;*
ULONG *AceListLength;*

The **AddAce** function adds one or more **ACE**s to an existing **ACL**. An **ACE** is an access control entry. An **ACL** is an access control list.

The caller specifies an **ACL** to modify, a list of **ACE**s to add, and a position within the **ACL** at which to add the **ACE**s.

Parameters   *Acl*   Pointer to an existing **ACL** data structure. The **ACE**s will be added to this **ACL**.

The **ACL** data structure has the following form:

```
typedef struct tagACL {
    UCHAR    AclRevision:
    UCHAR    Sbz1:
    USHORT   AclSize:
    USHORT   AceCount:
    USHORT   Sbz2:
    /* ordered list of ACEs */
} ACL;
```

AceRevision   Specifies the revision level of the **ACE**s being added to the **ACL**. This **ACE** revision level must match the **ACL**'s revision level.

StartingAceIndex   A zero-based index value that specifies a position within the **ACL**'s list of **ACE**s at which to add the new **ACE**s. A value of 0 inserts the **ACE**s at the beginning of the **ACL**'s list of **ACE**s. A value of MAXULONG appends the **ACE**s to the end of the **ACL**'s list of **ACE**s.

AceList   Pointer to a list of one or more **ACE**s stored contiguously.

AceListLength   The size in bytes of the input buffer pointed to by *AceList*.

Return Value   If the function is successful, the return value is TRUE.

If the function fails, the return value is FALSE. Call **GetLastError** for more detailed error information.

See Also   **AddAccessAllowedAce, DeleteAce, GetAce, GetAclInformation, InitializeAcl, IsValidAcl, SetAclInformation**

■ AddAtom

ATOM AddAtom(*lpString***)**
LPTSTR *lpString;*

The **AddAtom** function adds the character string pointed to by the *lpString* parameter to the atom table and creates a new atom that uniquely identifies the string. The atom can be used in a subsequent **GetAtomName** function to retrieve the string from the atom table.

The **AddAtom** function stores no more than one copy of a given string in the atom table. If the string is already in the table, the function returns the existing atom value and increases the string's reference count by one.

The **AddAtom** function may be used as either a wide-character function (where text arguments must use Unicode) or an ANSI function (where text arguments must use characters from the Windows 3.x character set installed).

Parameters
lpString   Points to the character string to be added to the table. The string must be a null-terminated string.

Return Value
The return value specifies the newly created atom if the function is successful. Otherwise, it is NULL.

Comments
The atom values returned by **AddAtom** range from 0xC000 to 0xFFFF. Atoms are case insensitive.

The atom values returned by **AddAtom** are within the range 0xC000 to 0xFFFF. Atoms are case insensitive. If AddAtom is passed a string of the form "#1234" then it will return the atom value that is the 16-bit representation of the decimal number specified in the string (e.g. 0x04D2 in this case). If the decimal value specified is 0x0000 or 0xC000 through 0xFFFF then this function will return NULL to indicate an error. If the pointer to the string is within the range 0x0001 through 0xBFFF then this function will return the low order portion of the pointer as the atom value.

See Also
GetAtomName, InitAtomTable

■ AddFontModule

int **AddFontModule**(*hmodFontResource*)
HMODULE *hmodFontResource*;

The **AddFontModule** function adds the font resource from the loaded font resource module identified by the *hmodFontResource* parameter to the Windows public font table. The font can subsequently be used by any application.

Parameters
hmodFontResource   Handle that identifies a loaded font resource module.

Return Value
The return value specifies the number of fonts added. The return value is zero if no fonts are loaded. −1 is returned on error.

Comments
Any application that adds or removes fonts from the Windows font table should notify other windows of the change by using the **SendMessage** function with the *hWnd* parameter set to −1 to send a WM_FONTCHANGE message to all top-level windows in the system.

An application must remove any font resource it has loaded once the application is through with the resource.

For a description of font resources, see the *Guide to Programming*.

See Also   **RemoveFontModule**

■ AddFontResource

int AddFontResource(*lpFilename***)**
LPTSTR *lpFilename*;

The **AddFontResource** function adds the font resource from the file named by the *lpFilename* parameter to the Windows font table. The font can subsequently be used by any application.

The **AddFontResource** function may be used as either a wide-character function (where text arguments must use Unicode) or an ANSI function (where text arguments must use characters from the Windows 3.x character set

Parameters   *lpFilename*   Points to a character string that names the font-resource file. The string must be a null-terminated filename.

Return Value   The return value specifies the number of fonts added. The return value is zero if no fonts are loaded or −1 on error.

Comments   Any application that adds or removes fonts from the Windows font table should notify other windows of the change by using the **SendMessage** function with the *hWnd* parameter set to −1 to send a WM_FONTCHANGE message to all top-level windows in the system.

An application must remove any font resource it has loaded once the application is through with the resource.

For a description of font resources, see the *Guide to Programming*.

See Also   **RemoveFontResource**

■ AddPrinter

BOOL AddPrinter(*lpPrinter***)**
LPPRINTER *lpPrinter*;

The **AddPrinter** function creates a printer on a printer server.

Parameters   *lpPrinter*   Pointer to a **PRINTER** data structure that specifies the the printer to add.

The **PRINTER** data structure has the following form:

```
typedef struct tagPRINTER {
    DWORD cVersion;
    LPPRINTERSERVER lpPrinterServer;
    LPTSTR lpPrinterName;
    LPTSTR lpPortName;
    LPTSTR lpDriverName;
    LPTSTR lpComment;
    LPTSTR lpLocation;
```

```
        LPDEVMODE lpDevMode;
        LPTSTR lpSepFile;
        LPTSTR lpPrintProcessor;
        LPTSTR lpDatatype;
        LPTSTR lpParameters;
        LPTSTR lpVendorData;
        DWORD Attributes;
        DWORD Priority;
        DWORD DefaultPriority;
        SYSTEMTIME StartTime;
        SYSTEMTIME UntilTime;
        DWORD Status;
        DWORD cJobs;
        DWORD AveragePPM;
    } PRINTER;
```

Return Value   If the function is successful, the return value is TRUE.

If the function fails, the return value FALSE/NULL. Further information can be obtained by calling **GetLastError**.

Comments   Once a printer has been created by calling **AddPrinter**, it is necessary to set the correct printer driver settings for it. This is done by calling the **PrinterProperties** function.

The **AddPrinter** function will fail if a printer of the same name already exists on the printer server, unless that printer is marked as pending deletion. In that case, the existing printer will be undeleted, and the **AddPrinter** creation parameters will be used to perform a **SetPrinter** operation on it.

See Also   **DeletePrinter, GetPrinter,**

■ AddPrinterDriver

BOOL AddPrinterDriver(lpPrinterServer, lpDriverInfo**)**
LPPRINTERSERVER lpPrinterServer,
LPDRIVERINFO lpDriverInfo;

The **AddPrinterDriver** function copies a specified printer driver to a printer server.

Parameters   lpPrinterServer   Pointer to a **PRINTERSERVER** data structure that specifies where the printer driver is to be copied to.

The **PRINTERSERVER** data structure has the following form:

```
typedef struct tagPRINTERSERVER {
    HANDLE    hProvidor;
    LPTSTR    lpName;
    LPTSTR    lpDescription;
    LPTSTR    lpLocation;
    LPVOID    lpVendorSpecificVariable;
} PRINTERSERVER;
```

lpDriverInfo   Pointer to a **DRIVERINFO** data structure that specifies the printer driver to be copied.

The **DRIVERINFO** data structure has the following form:

```
typedef struct tagDRIVERINFO {
    DWORD    cVersion;
    LPSTR    lpDriverName;
    LPSTR    lpEnvironment;
    LPSTR    lpDriverPath;
    LPSTR    lpDeviceName;
    LPSTR    lpDataFile;
    LPSTR    lpConfigFile;
} DRIVERINFO;
```

Return Value

If the function is successful, the return value is TRUE.

If the function fails, the return value is FALSE/NULL. Further information can be obtained by calling **GetLastError**.

See Also

GetPrinterDriver, EnumPrinterDrivers

■ AddPrintProcessor

BOOL AddPrintProcessor(*lpPrinterServer, lpEnvironment, lpPathName, lpName* **)**
LPPRINTERSERVER *lpPrinterServer;*
LPTSTR *lpEnvironment;*
LPTSTR *lpPathName;*
LPTSTR *lpName;*

The **AddPrintProcessor** function copies a specified print processor to a printer server, and adds it to the list of print processors available on that printer server.

The **AddPrintProcessor** function may be used as either a wide-character function (where text arguments must use Unicode) or an ANSI function (where text arguments must use characters from the Windows 3.x character set installed).

Parameters

lpPrinterServer   Pointer to a **PRINTERSERVER** data structure that specifies where the print processor is to be installed.

The **PRINTERSERVER** data structure has the following form:

```
typedef struct tagPRINTERSERVER {
    HANDLE    hProvidor;
    LPTSTR    lpName;
    LPTSTR    lpDescription;
    LPTSTR    lpLocation;
    LPVOID    lpVendorSpecificVariable;
} PRINTERSERVER;
```

lpEnvironment   Pointer to a string that specifies the machine and operating system environment. An example is the string "Win32.386".

lpPathName   Pointer to a string that specifies the fully-qualified path name of where the print processor currently resides.

lpName   Pointer to a string that specifies the name of the print processor to install.

Return Value   If the function is successful, the return value is TRUE.

If the function fails, the return value is FALSE/NULL. Further information can be obtained by calling **GetLastError**.

■ AdjustTokenGroups

BOOL AdjustTokenGroups(*TokenHandle, ResetToDefault, NewState, BufferLength, PreviousState, ReturnLength*)
HANDLE *TokenHandle*;
BOOLEAN *ResetToDefault*;
PTOKEN_GROUPS *NewState*;
ULONG *BufferLength*;
PTOKEN_GROUPS *PreviousState*;
PULONG *ReturnLength*;

The **AdjustTokenGroups** function enables and/or disables groups in the specified token. The function can optionally capture the previous state of changed groups. TOKEN_ADJUST_GROUPS access is required to enable or disable groups in a token.

The absence from the token of some of the groups listed to be changed doesn't affect the successful modification of the groups that are in the token.

Note that mandatory groups can not be disabled. An attempt to disable any mandatory groups will cause the call to fail, leaving the state of all groups unchanged.

Parameters   *TokenHandle*   Handle to the token whose groups the function will enable/disable.

ResetToDefault   Boolean value that, if TRUE, specifies that the function should set the groups to their default enabled/disabled states. If FALSE, the function will set the groups according to the *NewState* parameter.

NewState   Optional pointer to a **TOKEN_GROUPS** data structure that contains the groups whose states are to be enabled/disabled. If *ResetToDefault* is TRUE, the function ignores this parameter. If *ResetToDefault* is FALSE, **AdjustTokenGroups** sets each of the token's groups to the value of that group's **Enabled** flag within the **TOKEN_GROUPS** data structure pointed to by *NewState*.

The **TOKEN_GROUPS** data structure has the following form:

```
typedef struct tagTOKEN_GROUPS {
    ULONG              GroupCount;
    SID_AND_ATTRIBUTES Groups[];
} TOKEN_GROUPS ;
```

BufferLength   Optionally specifies the size in bytes of the buffer pointed to by *PreviousState*. A value is required if *PreviousState* is non-NULL.

PreviousState   Optional pointer to a buffer that the function will fill with a **TOKEN_GROUPS** data structure containing the pre-adjustment state of any groups the function modifies.

The **TOKEN_GROUPS** data structure is detailed in the discussion of the *NewState* parameter above.

Since the information is formatted as a **TOKEN_GROUPS** data structure, a pointer to the buffer can be passed as the *NewState* parameter in a subsequent call to this function, thus restoring the original state of the groups.

TOKEN_QUERY access is needed to use this parameter.

If this buffer does not contain enough space to receive the complete list of modified groups, then no group states are changed, and STATUS_BUFFER_TOO_SMALL is returned. In this case, the function sets the variable pointed to by the *ReturnLength* parameter to the actual number of bytes needed to hold the complete list of modified groups.

ReturnLength   Optional pointer to a variable that the function will set to the actual number of bytes needed to hold the previous group state information. This parameter is ignored if *PreviousState* is NULL.

Return Value

If the function is successful, the return value is TRUE.

If the function fails, the return value is FALSE. Call **GetLastError** for more detailed error information.

See Also

AdjustTokenPrivileges, GetTokenInformation, OpenProcessToken, OpenThreadToken, SetTokenInformation

■ AdjustTokenPrivileges

BOOL AdjustTokenPrivileges(*TokenHandle, DisableAllPrivileges, NewState, BufferLength, PreviousState, ReturnLength***)**
HANDLE *TokenHandle*;
BOOLEAN *DisableAllPrivileges*;
PTOKEN_PRIVILEGES *NewState*;
ULONG *BufferLength*;
PTOKEN_PRIVILEGES *PreviousState*;
PULONG *ReturnLength*;

The **AdjustTokenPrivileges** function enables and/or disables privileges in the specified token. It can optionally capture the previous state of changed privileges. TOKEN_ADJUST_PRIVILEGES access is required to enable or disable privileges in a token.

The absence of some of the privileges listed to be changed doesn't affect the successful modification of those privileges that are in the token.

Parameters

TokenHandle   Handle to the token whose privileges the function will enable/disable.

DisableAllPrivileges   Boolean value that, if TRUE, tells the function to disable all of the token's privileges. In that case, the function ignores the *NewState* parameter. If FALSE, the function enables/disables privileges using the *NewStateParameter.*

NewState   Optional pointer to a **TOKEN_PRIVILEGES** data structure that contains the privileges whose states are to be enabled/disabled. If present, and if *DisableAllPrivileges* is FALSE, the function sets each of the token's privileges to the value of that privilege's **Enabled** flag within this data structure.

The **TOKEN_PRIVILEGES** data structure has the following form:

```
typedef struct tagTOKEN_PRIVILEGES {
    ULONG                  PrivilegeCount;
    LUID_AND_ATTRIBUTES Privileges[];
} TOKEN_PRIVILEGES ;
```

BufferLength   Optionally specifies the size in bytes of the buffer pointed to by *PreviousState.* A value is required if *PreviousState* is non-NULL.

PreviousState   Optional pointer to a buffer that the function will fill with a **TOKEN_PRIVILEGES** data structure containing the pre-adjustment state of any privileges the function modifies.

The **TOKEN_PRIVILEGES** data structure is detailed in the discussion of the *NewState* parameter above.

Since the information is formatted as a **TOKEN_PRIVILEGES** data structure, a pointer to the buffer can be passed as the *NewState* parameter in a subsequent call to this function, thus restoring the original state of the privileges.

TOKEN_QUERY access is needed to use this parameter.

If the buffer is not large enough to receive the complete list of modified privileges, then no privilege states are changed, and STATUS_BUFFER_TOO_SMALL is returned. In this case, the function sets the variable pointed to by the *ReturnLength* parameter to the actual number of bytes needed to hold the complete list of modified privileges.

ReturnLength   Optional pointer to a variable that the function will set to the actual number of bytes needed to hold the previous privilege state information. This parameter is ignored if *PreviousState* is NULL.

Return Value   If the function is successful, the return value is TRUE.

If the function fails, the return value is FALSE. Call **GetLastError** for more detailed error information.

See Also   **AdjustTokenGroups, GetTokenInformation, OpenProcessToken, OpenThreadToken, SetTokenInformation**

■ AdjustWindowRect

BOOL AdjustWindowRect(*lpRect, lStyle, bMenu***)**
LPRECT *lpRect*;
LONG *lStyle*;
BOOL *bMenu*;

The **AdjustWindowRect** function computes the required size of the window rectangle based on the desired client-rectangle size. The window rectangle can then be passed to the **CreateWindow** function to create a window whose client area is the desired size. A client rectangle is the smallest rectangle that completely encloses a client area. A window rectangle is the smallest rectangle that completely encloses the window. The dimensions of the resulting window rectangle depend on the window styles and on whether the window has a menu.

Parameters   *lpRect*   Points to a RECT data structure that contains the coordinates of the client rectangle.

lStyle   Specifies the window styles of the window whose client rectangle is to be converted.

bMenu   Specifies whether the window has a menu.

Return Value   FALSE on error, TRUE on success

Comments   This function assumes a single menu row. If the menu bar wraps to two or more rows, the coordinates are incorrect.

See Also   **AdjustWindowRectEx**

■ AdjustWindowRectEx

BOOL AdjustWindowRectEx(*lpRect, lStyle, bMenu, dwExStyle***)**
LPRECT *lpRect*;
LONG *lStyle*;
BOOL *bMenu*;
DWORD *dwExStyle*;

This function computes the required size of the rectangle of a window with extended style based on the desired client-rectangle size. The window rectangle can then be passed to the **CreateWindowEx** function to create a window whose client area is the desired size.

A client rectangle is the smallest rectangle that completely encloses a client area. A window rectangle is the smallest rectangle that completely encloses the window. The dimensions of the resulting window rectangle depends on the window styles and on whether the window has a menu.

Parameters   *lpRect*   Points to a **RECT** structure that contains the coordinates of the client rectangle.

lStyle   Specifies the window styles of the window whose client rectangle is to be converted.

bMenu   Specifies whether the window has a menu.

dwExStyle   Specifies the extended style of the window being created.

Return Value   Return FALSE on failure, TRUE on success.

Comments   This function assumes a single menu row. If the menu bar wraps to two or more rows, the coordinates are incorrect.

See Also   **CreateWindowEx, AdjustWindowRect**

■ AllocConsole

BOOL AllocConsole(VOID)

A console may be allocated using **AllocConsole**.

This function has no parameters.

Return Value   The return value is TRUE if the function was successful, otherwise it is FALSE in which case extended error information can be retrieved by calling the **GetLastError** function.

The newly allocated console handle can be obtained by calling **GetStdHandle**.

This API creates a console for the current process. It also sets up standard input, output, and error handles. If the current process already has a console, the API will fail. If the current process creates a child process, the child will inherit the console.

This API may be called by detached processes.

Console applications (as identified by a flag in the .def file) are initialized with a console buffer. If one of these applications calls **AllocConsole**, the call will fail unless the initial console is first freed with **FreeConsole**.

This API is primarily for use by graphics applications which want to create a console window. Graphics applications are initialized without a console buffer.

See Also   **FreeConsole, GetStdHandle**

■ AllocDStoCSAlias

Th **AllocDStoCSAlias** function is deleted as it is x86 specific and has no corresponding semantics in the portable Win32 API. All read-write memory allocated via the Win32 API functions is executable.

■ AllocResource

The **AllocResource** function has been deleted as calculated resources will not work in the Win32 application environment where all resources are contained in mapped image files.

■ AllocSelector

The **AllocSelector** is deleted as it is x86 specific and has no corresponding semantics in the portable Win32 API.

■ AngleArc

BOOL AngleArc(*hDC, X, Y, nRadius, eStartAngle, eSweepAngle***)**
HDC *hDC*;
int *X*;
int *Y*;
DWORD *nRadius*;
FLOAT *eStartAngle*;
FLOAT *eSweepAngle*;

The **AngleArc** function draws an arc of a circle. It draws a portion of the circle centered at *(X, Y)* with radius *nRadius*. The start and end points of the arc are determined by the *eStartAngle* and *eSweepAngle* parameters. In addition, a straight line is drawn from the current position to the start point of the arc.

AngleArc moves the current position to the end point of the arc.

Parameters
hDC   Identifies the device context.

X   Specifies the logical *x*-coordinate of the center of the arc.

Y   Specifies the logical *y*-coordinate of the center of the arc.

nRadius   Specifies the radius of the circle in logical units. This is a positive value.

eStartAngle   Specifies the start angle in degrees relative to the *x*-axis. It is a floating point value.

eSweepAngle   Specifies the sweep angle in degrees relative to the starting angle. It is a floating point value.

Return Value
The return value specifies whether the arc was drawn. It is TRUE if the arc was drawn. Otherwise, it is FALSE.

Comments
The arc is drawn using logical coordinates and will be circular in logical space. An elliptical arc may be output dependent upon the current logical to device tranform.

The arc is drawn by constructing an imaginary circle around the specified center point with the specified radius. The starting point of the arc is determined by measuring counterclockwise from the *x*-axis of the circle by the number of degrees in the start angle. The end point is similarly located by measuring from the start point by the number of degrees in the sweep angle. A line is drawn from the current position to the starting point of the arc, and then the arc is drawn.

If the sweep angle is greater than 360 degrees the arc will be swept multiple times.

This function draws lines with the current pen. The figure is not filled.

ERROR_INVALID_PARAMETER

ERROR_NOT_ENOUGH_MEMORY

See Also   **Arc, MoveToEx**

■ AnimatePalette

BOOL AnimatePalette(*hPalette, iStartIndex, nNumEntries, lpPaletteColors***)**
HPALETTE *hPalette*;
UINT *iStartIndex*;
UINT *nNumEntries*;
LPPALETTEENTRY *lpPaletteColors*;

The **AnimatePalette** function replaces entries in the logical palette identified by the *hPalette* parameter. If the hPalette is realized in a foreground display DC, the colors displayed will change immediately.

Parameters   *hPalette*   Identifies the logical palette.

iStartIndex   Specifies the first entry in the palette to be animated.

nNumEntries   Specifies the number of entries in the palette to be animated.

lpPaletteColors   Points to the first member of an array of **PALETTEENTRY** structures to replace the palette entries identified by the *iStartIndex* and *nNumEntries* parameters.

Return Value   The return value specifies the outcome of the function. It is TRUE if the call is successful, Otherwise, it is FALSE.

Comments   The **AnimatePalette** function will only change entries with the PC_RESERVED flag set in the corresponding **palPaletteEntry** member of the **LOGPALETTE** structure that defines the current logical palette.

See Also   **CreatePalette**

■ AnsiLower

The **AnsiLower** function is obsolete. Under 32-bit Windows, it is implemented as a macro that calls the **CharLower** function.

■ AnsiLowerBuff

The **AnsiLowerBuff** function is obsolete. Under 32-bit Windows, it is implemented as a macro that calls the **CharLowerBuff** function.

■ AnsiNext

The **AnsiNext** function is obsolete. Under 32-bit Windows, it is implemented as a macro that calls the **CharNext** function.

■ AnsiPrev

The **AnsiPrev** function is obsolete. Under 32-bit Windows, it is implemented as a macro that calls the **CharPrev** function.

■ AnsiToOem

The **AnsiToOem** function is obsolete. Under 32-bit Windows, it is implemented as a macro that calls the **CharToOem** function.

■ AnsiToOemBuff

The **AnsiToOemBuff** function is obsolete. Under 32-bit Windows, it is implemented as a macro that calls the **CharToOemBuff** function.

■ AnsiUpper

The **AnsiUpper** function is obsolete. Under 32-bit Windows, it is implemented as a macro that calls the **CharUpper** function.

■ AnsiUpperBuff

The **AnsiUpperBuff** function is obsolete. Under 32-bit Windows, it is implemented as a macro that calls the **CharUpperBuff** function.

■ AnyPopup

BOOL AnyPopup(void)

This function indicates whether a pop-up window exists on the screen. It searches the entire Windows screen, not just the caller's client area. The **AnyPopup** function returns nonzero even if a pop-up window is completely covered by another window.

This function has no parameters.

Return Value   The return value is TRUE if a pop-up window exists. Otherwise, it is FALSE.

■ AppendMenu

BOOL AppendMenu(*hMenu, dwFlags, dwIDNewItem, lpNewItem*)
HMENU *hMenu*;
UINT *dwFlags*;
UINT *dwIDNewItem*;
MENUPOLY *lpNewItem*;

This function appends a new item to the end of a menu. The application can specify the state of the menu item by setting values in the *dwFlags* parameter.

The **AppendMenu** function may be used as either a wide-character function (where text arguments must use Unicode) or an ANSI function (where text arguments must use characters from the Windows 3.x character set installed).

Parameters   *hMenu*   Identifies the menu to be changed.

dwFlags   Specifies information about the state of the new menu item when it is added to the menu. It consists of one or more values listed in the following Comments section.

dwIDNewItem   Specifies either the command ID of the new menu item or, if *dwFlags* is set to MF_POPUP, the menu handle of the pop-up menu.

lpNewItem   Specifies the content of the new menu item. The interpretation of the *lpNewItem* parameter depends upon the setting of the *dwFlags* parameter.

dwFlags	lpNewItem
MF_STRING	Contains a pointer to a null-terminated character string.
MF_BITMAP	Contains a bitmap handle.
MF_OWNERDRAW	Contains an application-supplied 32-bit value which the application can use to maintain additional data associated with the menu item. This 32-bit value is available to the application in the **itemData** member of the structure pointed to by the *lParam* parameter of the WM_MEASUREITEM and WM_DRAWITEM messages sent when the menu item is initially displayed or is changed.

Return Value   The return value specifies the outcome of the function. It is TRUE if the function is successful. Otherwise, it is FALSE.

Comments   Whenever a menu changes (whether or not the menu resides in a window that is displayed), the application should call **DrawMenuBar**.

Each of the following groups list flags that are mutually exclusive and cannot be used together:

- MF_BYCOMMAND and MF_BYPOSITION
- MF_DISABLED, MF_ENABLED, and MF_GRAYED
- MF_BITMAP, MF_STRING, and MF_OWNERDRAW
- MF_MENUBARBREAK and MF_MENUBREAK
- MF_CHECKED and MF_UNCHECKED

The following list describes the flags which may be set in the *dwFlags* parameter:

Value	Meaning
MF_BITMAP	Uses a bitmap as the item. The lpNewItem parameter contains the handle of the bitmap.
MF_CHECKED	Places a checkmark next to the item. If the application has supplied checkmark bitmaps (see **SetMenuItemBitmaps**), setting this flag displays the checkmark on bitmap next to the menu item.
MF_DISABLED	Disables the menu item so that it cannot be selected, but does not gray it.
MF_ENABLED	Enables the menu item so that it can be selected and restores it from its grayed state.
MF_GRAYED	Disables the menu item so that it cannot be selected and grays it.
MF_MENUBARBREAK	Same as MF_MENUBREAK except that for pop-up menus, separates the new column from the old column with a vertical line.
MF_MENUBREAK	Places the item on a new line for static menu-bar items. For pop-up menus, places the item in a new column, with no dividing line between the columns.
MF_OWNERDRAW	Specifies that the item is an owner-draw item. The window that owns the menu receives a WM_MEASUREITEM message when the menu is displayed for the first time to retrieve the height and width of the menu item. The WM_DRAWITEM message is then sent whenever the owner must update the visual appearance of the menu item. This option is not valid for a top-level menu item.

Value	Meaning
MF_POPUP	Specifies that the menu item has a pop-up menu associated with it. The *dwIDNewItem* parameter specifies a handle to a pop-up menu to be associated with the item. This is used for adding either a top-level pop-up menu or adding a hierarchical pop-up menu to a pop-up menu item.
MF_SEPARATOR	Draws a horizontal dividing line. Can only be used in a pop-up menu. This line cannot be grayed, disabled, or highlighted. The *lpNewItem* and *dwIDNewItem* parameters are ignored.
MF_STRING	Specifies that the menu item is a character string; the *lpNewItem* parameter points to the string for the menu item.
MF_UNCHECKED	Does not place a checkmark next to the item (default). If the application has supplied checkmark bitmaps (see **SetMenuItemBitmaps**), setting this flag displays the checkmark off bitmap next to the menu item.

See Also **DrawMenuBar, SetMenuItemBitmaps, InsertMenu, ModifyMenu, RemoveMenu, DeleteMenu, CreateMenu, DestroyMenu**

■ Arc

BOOL Arc(*hDC, X1, Y1, X2, Y2, X3, Y3, X4, Y4***)**
HDC *hDC*;
int *X1*;
int *Y1*;
int *X2*;
int *Y2*;
int *X3*;
int *Y3*;
int *X4*;
int *Y4*;

The **Arc** function draws an elliptical arc.

The curve of the arc is defined by the ellipse formed by the given bounding rectangle. The bounding rectangle is specified by the points *(X1, Y1)* and *(X2, Y2)*. The arc extends counterclockwise from the point where it intersects the radial line from the center of the bounding rectangle to *(X3, Y3)*. The arc ends where it intersects the radial line from the center of the bounding rectangle to *(X4, Y4)*. If the start-point and end-point are the same, a complete ellipse is drawn.

The arc is drawn using the current pen. Since an arc does not define a closed area, it is not filled.

Parameters

X1   Specifies the logical *x*-coordinate of the upper-left corner of the bounding rectangle.

Y1   Specifies the logical *y*-coordinate of the upper-left corner of the bounding rectangle.

X2   Specifies the logical *x*-coordinate of the lower-right corner of the bounding rectangle.

Y2   Specifies the logical *y*-coordinate of the lower-right corner of the bounding rectangle.

X3   Specifies the logical *x*-coordinate of the end-point of the radial line defining the start-point of the arc.

Y3   Specifies the logical *y*-coordinate of the end-point of the radial line defining the start-point of the arc.

X4   Specifies the logical *x*-coordinate of the end-point of the radial line defining the end-point of the arc.

Y4   Specifies the logical *y*-coordinate of the end-point of the radial line defining the end-point of the arc.

Return Value   The return value is TRUE if the arc is drawn. Otherwise, it is FALSE.

Comments   The current position is neither used nor updated by this function.

See Also   **AngleArc, ArcTo, Chord, Ellipse, Pie**

■ **ArcTo**

BOOL ArcTo(*hDC, X1, Y1, X2, Y2, X3, Y3, X4, Y4***)**
HDC *hDC*;
int *X1*;
int *Y1*;
int *X2*;
int *Y2*;
int *X3*;
int *Y3*;
int *X4*;
int *Y4*;

The **ArcTo** function draws an elliptical arc.

The curve of the arc is defined by the ellipse formed from the given bounding rectangle. The bounding rectangle is specified by the points *(X1, Y1)* and *(X2, Y2)*. The arc extends counterclockwise from the point where it intersects the radial line from the center of the bounding rectangle to *(X3, Y3)*. The arc ends where it intersects the radial line from the center of the bounding rectangle to *(X4, Y4)*. If the start-point and end-point are the same, a complete ellipse is drawn.

A line is drawn from the current position to the start-point of the arc. If no error occurs, the current position is set to the end-point of the arc.

The arc is drawn using the current pen. Since an arc does not define a closed area, it is not filled.

Parameters

X1 Specifies the logical x-coordinate of the upper-left corner of the bounding rectangle.

Y1 Specifies the logical y-coordinate of the upper-left corner of the bounding rectangle.

X2 Specifies the logical x-coordinate of the lower-right corner of the bounding rectangle.

Y2 Specifies the logical y-coordinate of the lower-right corner of the bounding rectangle.

X3 Specifies the logical x-coordinate of the end-point of the radial line defining the start-point of the arc.

Y3 Specifies the logical y-coordinate of the end-point of the radial line defining the start-point of the arc.

X4 Specifies the logical x-coordinate of the end-point of the radial line defining the end-point of the arc.

Y4 Specifies the logical y-coordinate of the end-point of the radial line defining the end-point of the arc.

Return Value The return value is TRUE if the arc is drawn. Otherwise, it is FALSE.

Comments This function is similar to **Arc**, except that the current position is used.

See Also **Arc, AngleArc**

■ AreAllAccessesGranted

BOOL AreAllAccessesGranted(*GrantedAccess, DesiredAccess*)
ACCESS_MASK *GrantedAccess*;
ACCESS_MASK *DesiredAccess*;

The **AreAllAccessesGranted** function checks a desired access mask against a granted access mask. It is used by the Object Management component when dereferencing a handle.

Parameters *GrantedAccess* Specifies the granted access mask.

DesiredAccess Specifies the desired access mask.

Return Value If the *GrantedAccess* mask has all the bits set that the *DesiredAccess* mask has set, the function return value is TRUE. That is, the function returns TRUE if all of the desired accesses have been granted.

Otherwise, the function return value is FALSE.

See Also   **AreAnyAccessesGranted, MapGenericMask**

■ AreAnyAccessesGranted

BOOL AreAnyAccessesGranted(GrantedAccess, DesiredAccess**)**
ACCESS_MASK GrantedAccess;
ACCESS_MASK DesiredAccess;

The **AreAnyAccessesGranted** function tests whether any of a set of desired accesses are granted by a granted access mask. It is used by components other than the Object Management component for checking access mask subsets.

Parameters   *GrantedAccess*   Specifies the granted access mask.

                DesiredAccess   Specifies the desired access mask.

Return Value   If the *GrantedAccess* mask has any of the bits set that the *DesiredAccess* mask has set, the function return value is TRUE. That is, the function returns TRUE if all of the desired accesses have been granted.

                Otherwise the function return value is FALSE.

See Also   **AreAllAccessesGranted, MapGenericMask**

■ ArrangeIconicWindows

UINT ArrangeIconicWindows(hWnd**)**
HWND hWnd;

This function arranges all the minimized (iconic) child windows of the window specified by the *hWnd* parameter.

Parameters   *hWnd*   Identifies the window.

Return Value   The return value is the height of one row of icons, or zero if there were no icons.

Comments   Applications that maintain their own iconic child windows call this function to arrange icons in a client window. This function also arranges icons on the desktop window, which covers the entire screen. The **GetDesktopWindow** function retrieves the window handle of the desktop window.

                To arrange iconic MDI child windows in an MDI client window, an application sends the WM_MDIICONARRANGE message to the MDI client window.

See Also   **GetDesktopWindow**

■ Beep

BOOL Beep(*dwFreq, dwDuration***)**
DWORD *dwFreq*;
DWORD *dwDuration*;

The **Beep** function can be used to generate simple tones on the speaker.

Parameters: *dwFreq*   specifies the frequency of the sound in hertz (cycles per second). This parameter may range from 0x25 to 0x7FFF.

dwDuration   specifies the duration of the sound in milliseconds.

Return Value   The return value is TRUE if the function successfully generated the requested tone. It is FALSE if the function failed for any reason, either because of an invalid parameter or the speaker device is not available. Extended error status is available using the **GetLastError** function.

■ BeginDeferWindowPos

HWPI BeginDeferWindowPos(*nNumWindows***)**
int *nNumWindows*;

This function allocates memory to contain a multiple window-position data structure and returns a handle to the structure. The **DeferWindowPos** function fills this structure with information about the target position for a window that is about to be moved. The **EndDeferWindowPos** function accepts this structure and instantaneously repositions the windows using the information stored in the structure.

Parameters   *nNumWindows*   Specifies the initial number of windows for which position information is to be stored in the structure. The **DeferWindowPos** function increases the size of the structure if needed.

Return Value   The return value identifies the multiple window-position structure. The return value is NULL if system resources are not available to allocate the structure.

See Also   **DeferWindowPos, EndDeferWindowPos**

■ BeginPaint

HDC BeginPaint(*hWnd, lpPaint***)**
HWND *hWnd*;
LPPAINTSTRUCT *lpPaint*;

This function prepares the given window for painting and fills the paint structure pointed to by the *lpPaint* parameter with information about the painting.

The paint structure contains a handle to the device context for the window, a **RECT** structure that contains the smallest rectangle that completely encloses the update region, and a flag that specifies whether or not the background has been erased.

The **BeginPaint** function automatically sets the clipping region of the device context to exclude any area outside the update region. The update region is set by the **InvalidateRect** or **InvalidateRgn** functions and by the system after sizing, moving, creating, scrolling, or any other operation that affects the client area. If the update region is marked for erasing, **BeginPaint** sends a WM_ERASEBKGND message to the window.

An application should not call the **BeginPaint** function except in response to a WM_PAINT message. Each **BeginPaint** call must have a matching call to the **EndPaint** function.

Parameters	*hWnd* Identifies the window to be repainted.
	lpPaint Points to the **PAINTSTRUCT** structure that is to receive painting information, such as the device context for the window and the update rectangle.
Return Value	The return value identifies the device context for the specified window.
Comments	If the caret is in the area to be painted, the **BeginPaint** function automatically hides the caret to prevent it from being erased.
See Also	**EndPaint, InvalidateRect, InvalidateRgn**

■ BeginPath

BOOL BeginPath(*hDC***)**
HDC *hDC*;

The **BeginPath** function starts a path bracket; subsequent calls to drawing functions define the shape and size of a path. **BeginPath** initializes the path associated with the DC, discarding the previous path, if any. All subsequent drawing funtions called for that DC, up to the next call to **EndPath**, apply to the new path.

Parameters	*hDC* Identifies the device context.
Return Value	The return value is TRUE if the call succeeded, otherwise FALSE.
Comments	The following drawing functions will add to the path:

> **AngleArc**
>
> **Arc**
>
> **ArcTo**
>
> **Chord**
>
> **CloseFigure**
>
> **Ellipse**
>
> **ExtTextOut**
>
> **LineTo**
>
> **MoveToEx**

Pie

PolyBezier

PolyBezierTo

PolyDraw

Polygon

Polyline

PolylineTo

PolyPolygon

PolyPolyline

Rectangle

RoundRect

TextOut

See Also **EndPath, FillPath, PathToRegion, SelectClipPath, StrokeAndFillPath, StrokePath, WidenPath**

■ BeginWindowBuffer

BOOL BeginWindowBuffer(*hWnd***)**
HWND *,hWnd*;

Creates a bitmap buffer for hwnd. This api is used along with **EndWindowBuffer** for quick multi-primitive drawing operations. Using a buffer, these primitives all draw off-screen. When **EndWindowBuffer** is called, this buffer is drawn on screen. **FlushWindowBuffer** may be called to copy the buffer bits to the screen at any point before **EndWindowBuffer** is called.

Parameters *hWnd*   Window for which output is to be buffered.

Return Value TRUE for success, FALSE for failure.

See Also **EndWindowBuffer FlushWindowBuffer SetWindowBufferAttributes GetWindowBufferAttributes**

■ BitBlt

BOOL BitBlt(*hDCDest, X, Y, nWidth, nHeight, hDCSrc, XSrc, YSrc, Rop*)
HDC *hDCDest*;
int *X*;
int *Y*;
int *nWidth*;
int *nHeight*;
HDC *hDCSrc*;
int *XSrc*;
int *YSrc*;
DWORD *Rop*;

The **BitBlt** function moves or combines a block of pixels from the surface of hDCSrc to the surface of hDCDest. The *XSrc* and *YSrc* parameters specify the origin on the source surface of the block of pixels to be moved. The *X*, *Y*, *nWidth*, and *nHeight* parameters specify the origin, width, and height of the rectangle on the destination surface that is to be filled by the block of pixels. The *Rop* parameter (raster operation) defines how the pixels of the source and destination are combined.

Parameters

hDCDest   Identifies the device context to receive the pixels.

X   Specifies the logical *x*-coordinate of the upper-left corner of the destination rectangle.

Y   Specifies the logical *y*-coordinate of the upper-left corner of the destination rectangle.

nWidth   Specifies the width (in logical units) of the destination rectangle and source bitmap.

nHeight   Specifies the height (in logical units) of the destination rectangle and source bitmap.

hDCSrc   Identifies the device context from which the bitmap will be copied.

XSrc   Specifies the logical *x*-coordinate of the upper-left corner of the source bitmap.

YSrc   Specifies the logical *y*-coordinate of the upper-left corner of the source bitmap.

Rop   Specifies the raster operation to be performed. Raster-operation codes define how the the pixels are combined in output operations. For a list of raster-operation codes, see Table 1.1, Raster Operations. Use the constants in Windows.h to select the ROP.

Return Value

The return value specifies whether the call succeeded. The return value is TRUE if succesful, otherwise it is FALSE.

Comments

If there is a source for **BitBlt** then an error is returned if *hDCSrc* has a rotating or shearing transform. If the transforms in *hDCSrc* and *hDCDest* are not identical then the BitBlt call will be passed to StretchBlt or PgBlt as necessary, to stretch, compress, or rotate the source bitmat. If destination, source, and pattern bitmaps do not have the same color format, the **BitBlt** function converts the source and pattern bitmaps to match the destination. See chapter **To-Be-Written** for a complete description of color conversion.

Not all devices support the **BitBlt** function. For more information, see the RC_BITBLT raster capability in the **GetDeviceCaps** function.

Table 1.1 lists the various raster-operation codes for the *Rop* parameter:

Code	Description
BLACKNESS	Turns all output to physical color index 0. This is black for the default palettes.
DSTINVERT	Inverts the destination bitmap.
MERGECOPY	Combines the pattern and the source using the Boolean AND operator.
MERGEPAINT	Combines the inverted source with the destination bitmap using the Boolean OR operator.
NOTSRCCOPY	Copies the inverted source bitmap to the destination.
NOTSRCERASE	Inverts the result of combining the destination and source using the Boolean OR operator.
PATCOPY	Copies the pattern to the destination bitmap.
PATINVERT	Combines the destination with the pattern using the Boolean XOR operator.
PATPAINT	Combines the inverted source with the pattern using the Boolean OR operator. Combines the result of this operation with the destination using the Boolean OR operator.
SRCAND	Combines pixels of the destination and source using the Boolean AND operator.
SRCCOPY	Copies the source to the destination.
SRCERASE	Inverts the destination and combines the result with the source using the Boolean AND operator.
SRCINVERT	Combines pixels of the destination and source using the Boolean XOR operator.
SRCPAINT	Combines pixels of the destination and source using the Boolean OR operator.
WHITENESS	Turns all output to all binary 1s. This is white for the default palettes.

For a complete list of the raster-operation codes, see Chapter 11, Binary and Ternary Raster-Operation Codes, in *Reference, Volume 2*.

BitBlt returns an error if the source and destination device contexts represent different devices.

See Also   **GetDeviceCaps**

■ BringWindowToTop

BOOL BringWindowToTop(*hWnd*)
HWND *hWnd*;

This function brings a pop-up or child window to the top of a stack of overlapping windows. In addition, it activates pop-up and top-level windows. The **BringWindowToTop** function should be used to uncover any window that is partially or completely obscured by any overlapping windows.

Parameters   *hWnd*   Identifies the pop-up or child window that is to be brought to the top.

Return Value   This function does not return a value.

■ BuildCommDCB

BOOL BuildCommDCB(*lpDef*, *lpDCB*)
LPSTR *lpDef*;
LPDCB *lpDCB*;

The **BuildCommDCB** function translates the definition string specified by the *lpDef* parameter into appropriate device-control block codes and places these codes into the block pointed to by the *lpDCB* parameter.

The **BuildCommDCB** function may be used as either a wide-character function (where text arguments must use Unicode) or an ANSI function (where text arguments must use characters from the Windows 3.x character set installed).

Parameters   *lpDef*   Points to a null-terminated string that specifies the device-control information for a device. The string must have the same form as the DOS MODE command-line parameter.

lpDCB   Points to the **DCB** structure that is set by direction of the string given in the *lpDef* parameter.

The **DCB** structure has the following form:

```
typedef struct tagDCB {
    DWORD DCBlength;
    DWORD BaudRate;
    DWORD fBinary: 1;
    DWORD fParity: 1;
    DWORD fOutxCtsFlow: 1;
    DWORD fOutxDsrFlow: 1;
    DWORD fDtrControl: 2;
    DWORD fDummy: 2;
    DWORD fOutX: 1;
    DWORD fInX: 1;
    DWORD fPeChar: 1;
    DWORD fNull: 1;
    DWORD fRtsControl: 2;
    DWORD fDummy2: 2;
    WORD  TxDelay;
```

```
WORD   XonLim;
WORD   XoffLim;
BYTE   ByteSize;
BYTE   Parity;
BYTE   StopBits;
char   XonChar;
char   XoffChar;
char   PeChar;
char   EofChar;
char   EvtChar;
} DCB;
```

Return Value   TRUE – The operation was successful (the string was translated). FALSE – The operation failed. Extended error information is available using **GetLastError**.

Comments   The **BuildCommDCB** function only fills the buffer. An application should call **SetCommState** to apply these settings to the port. Also, by default, **BuildCommDCB** specifies Xon/Xoff and hardware flow control as disabled. An application should set the appropriate members in the **DCB** data structure to enable flow control.

The string pointed to by *lpDef* must have the same format as the MODE command line.

See Also   **SetCommState**

■ CallMsgFilter

BOOL CallMsgFilter(*lpMsg, nCode***)**
LPMSG *lpMsg*,
int *nCode*;

This function passes the given message and code to the current message filter function. The message filter function is an application-specified function that examines and modifies all messages. An application specifies the function by using the **SetWindowsHook** or **SetSystemHook** function.

Parameters   *lpMsg*   Points to an **MSG** structure that contains the message to be filtered.

nCode   Specifies a code used by the filter function to determine how to process the message.

Return Value   The return value specifies the state of message processing. It is FALSE if the message should be processed. It is TRUE if the message should not be processed further.

Comments   The **CallMsgFilter** function is usually called by Windows to let applications examine and control the flow of messages during internal processing in menus and scroll bars or when moving or sizing a window.

Values given for the *nCode* parameter must not conflict with any of the MSGF_ and HC_ values passed by Windows to the message filter function.

See Also   **SetWindowsHook**

■ CallNamedPipe

BOOL CallNamedPipe(*lpNamedPipeName, lpInBuffer, nInBufferSize, lpOutBuffer, nOutBufferSize,*
         *lpBytesRead, nTimeOut***)**
LPTSTR *lpNamedPipeName;*
LPVOID *lpInBuffer;*
DWORD *nInBufferSize;*
LPVOID *lpOutBuffer;*
DWORD *nOutBufferSize;*
LPDWORD *lpBytesRead;*
DWORD *nTimeOut;*

CallNamedPipe is equivalent to a series of calls to **CreateFile**, or
WaitNamedPipe (if **CreateFile** can't open the pipe immediately),
TransactNamedPipe, and **CloseFile**. **CreateFile** will be called with a desired
access flag of GENERIC_READ | GENERIC_WRITE, an inherit handle flag of
FALSE, and a share mode of zero (indicating no sharing of this pipe instance).

The **CallNamedPipe** function may be used as either a wide-character function
(where text arguments must use Unicode) or an ANSI function (where text
arguments must use characters from the Windows 3.x character set installed).

Parameters   *lpNamedPipeName*   Supplies the pipe name.

lpInBuffer   Supplies the buffer containing the data that is written to the pipe.

nInBufferSize   Supplies the size (in bytes) of the write buffer.

lpOutBuffer   Supplies the buffer that receives the data read from the pipe.

nOutBufferSize   Supplies the size (in bytes) of the read buffer.

lpBytesRead   Points to a DWORD that receives the number of bytes actually
read from the pipe.

nTimeOut   Gives the number of milliseconds to wait for the named pipe to be
available. Besides numeric values for nTimeOut, equates are available for special
values.

nTimeOut Special Values:

Value	Meaning
NMPWAIT_NO_WAIT	Do not wait for the named pipe. (If the named pipe is not available, the API returns an error.)
NMPWAIT_WAIT_FOREVER	No timeout.
NMPWAIT_USE_DEFAULT_WAIT	Use default timeout set in call to **CreateNamedPipe**.

Return Value	The return value is TRUE if the function is successful. Otherwise, it is FALSE in which case extended error information is available from the **GetLastError** function. occurs.
Comments	If a named pipe is being read in message mode and the next message is longer than nNumberOfBytesToRead, **CallNamedPipe** will return FALSE with an extended status set to ERROR_MORE_DATA. The remainder of the message may be read by a subsequent **ReadFile** or **PeekNamedPipe**.
See Also	**CreateNamedPipe, WaitNamedPipe, PeekNamedPipe**

■ CallNextHookProc

DWORD CallNextHookProc(*hhk, nCode, wParam, lParam***)**
HHOOK *hhk*;
int *nCode*;
DWORD *wParam*;
LONG *lParam*;

Hooks are installed in chains for particular hook types. This routine causes the next hook in the chain to be called. An application may call this routine as the last thing it does in its own hook procedure, or it may call next hook by calling **CallNextHookProc** and then do some operation after this routine returns, or it may choose not to call the next hook at all.

Parameters	*hhk* Identifies the current hook, as passed to this hook procedure.
	nCode Identifies the action code passed to this hook.
	wParam Part of the hook parameters passed to this hook.
	lParam Part of the hook parameters passed to this hook.
Return Value	The value returned from this call represents the value returned from the next hook called, and should be returned from the hook procedure. The return value is hook specific. See the individual hook descriptions for more information.
See Also	**SetWindowsHook, SetWindowsHookEx, UnhookWindowsHook, UnhookWindowsHookEx**

■ CallWindowProc

LONG CallWindowProc(*lpPrevWndFunc, hWnd, wMsg, dwParam, lParam***)**
WNDPROC *lpPrevWndFunc*;
HWND *hWnd*;
UINT *wMsg*;
DWORD *dwParam*;
LONG *lParam*;

This function passes message information to the function specified by the *lpPrevWndFunc* parameter. The **CallWindowProc** function is used for window subclassing. Normally, all windows with the same class share the same window function. A subclass is a window or set of windows belonging to the same window class whose messages are intercepted and processed by another function (or functions) before being passed to the window function of that class.

The **SetWindowLong** function creates the subclass by changing the window function associated with a particular window, causing Windows to call the new window function instead of the previous one. Any messages not processed by the new window function must be passed to the previous window function by calling **CallWindowProc**. This allows a chain of window functions to be created.

Only the process that creates a window will be allowed to subclass it. Processes cannot subclass windows created by other processes.

Parameters

lpPrevWndFunc   Is the procedure-instance address of the previous window function.

hWnd   Identifies the window that receives the message.

wMsg   Specifies the message number.

dwParam   Specifies additional message-dependent information.

lParam   Specifies additional message-dependent information.

Return Value

The return value specifies the result of the message processing. The possible return values depend on the message sent.

See Also

SetWindowLong

■ CallWndProc

```
void FAR PASCAL CallWndProc(nCode, wParam, lParam)
int nCode;          /* process-message flag              */
WORD wParam;        /* current-task flag                 */
DWORD lParam;       /* pointer to structure with message data */
```

The **CallWndProc** function is a library-defined callback function that the system calls whenever the **SendMessage** function is called. The system passes the message to the callback function before passing the message to the destination window procedure.

Parameters

nCode   Specifies whether the callback function should process the message or call the **DefHookProc** function. If the *nCode* parameter is less than zero, the callback function should pass the message to **DefHookProc** without further processing.

wParam   Specifies whether the message is sent by the current task. It is nonzero if the message is sent; otherwise, it is NULL.

lParam   Points to a structure that contains details about the message. The following shows the order, type, and description of each field of the structure:

Member	Description
llParam	Contains the low-order word of the *lParam* parameter of the message.
wParam	Contains the *wParam* parameter of the message.
wMsg	Specifies the message.
hwnd	Contains the window handle of the window that is to receive the message.

Return Value   None.

Comments   The **CallWndProc** callback function can examine or modify the message as desired. Once the function returns control to the system, the message, with any modifications, is passed on to the window function.

This callback function must reside in a dynamic-link library.

An application must install the callback function by specifying the WH_CALLWNDPROC filter type and the procedure-instance address of the callback function in a call to the **SetWindowsHook** function.

CallWndProc is a placeholder for the library-supplied function name. The actual name must be exported by including it in an **EXPORTS** statement in the library's module-definition file.

See Also   **DefHookProc, SendMessage, SetWindowsHook**

■ Catch

The **Catch** function is deleted as it is x86 specific and has no corresponding semantics in the portable Win32 API. Structured exception handling is built into the Win32 Application environment.

■ CBTProc

```
int FAR PASCAL CBTProc(nCode, wParam, lParam)
int nCode;            /* CBT hook code                      */
WORD wParam;          /* depends on the nCode parameter     */
DWORD lParam;         /* depends on the nCode parameter     */
```

The **CBTProc** function is a libaray-defined callback function that the system calls before performing any of the following operations:

■ Activating a window.

■ Creating or destroying a window.

■ Minimizing or maximizing a window.

- Moving or sizing a window.
- Completing a system command.
- Removing a mouse or keyboard event from the system message queue.
- Setting the input focus.
- Synchronizing with the system message queue.

The value returned by the callback function determines whether to allow or prevent the operation.

Parameters

nCode Specifies a CBT hook code that identifies the operation about to be carried out, or a value less than zero if the callback function should pass the *nCode*, *wParam*, and *lParam* parameters to the **DefHookProc** function. The following list describes the CBT hook codes:

Code	Meaning
HCBT_ACTIVATE	Indicates that the system is about to activate a window.
HCBT_CLICKSKIPPED	Indicates that the system has removed a mouse message from the system message queue. A CBT application that needs to install a journaling playback filter in response to the mouse message should do so when it receives this hook code.
HCBT_CREATEWND	Indicates that a window is about to be created. The system calls the callback function before sending the WM_CREATE message to the window. If the callback function returns TRUE, the system will destroy the window—the system will not send the WM_DESTROY message to the window.
HCBT_DESTROYWND	Indicates that a window is about to be destroyed.
HCBT_KEYSKIPPED	Indicates that the system has removed a keyboard message from the system message queue. A CBT application that needs to install a journaling playback filter in response to the keyboard message should do so when it receives this hook code.
HCBT_MINMAX	Indicates that a window is about to be minimized or maximized.
HCBT_MOVESIZE	Indicates that a window is about to be moved or sized.
HCBT_QS	Indicates that the system has retrieved a WM_QUEUESYNC message from the system message queue.
HCBT_SETFOCUS	Indicates that a window is about to receive the input focus.

Code	Meaning
HCBT_SYSCOMMAND	Indicates that a system command is about to be carried out. This allows a CBT application to prevent task switching by hot keys.

wParam   This parameter depends on the *nCode* parameter. See the following Comments section for details.

lParam   This parameter depends on the *nCode* parameter. See the following Comments section for details.

Return Value

For operations corresponding to the following CBT hook codes, the callback function should return zero to allow the operation, or 1 to prevent it:

- HCBT_ACTIVATE
- HCBT_CREATEWND
- HCBT_DESTROYWND
- HCBT_MINMAX
- HCBT_MOVESIZE
- HCBT_SYSCOMMAND

The return value is ignored for operations corresponding to the following CBT hook codes:

- HCBT_CLICKSKIPPED
- HCBT_KEYSKIPPED
- HCBT_QS

Comments

The callback function should not install a playback hook except in the situations described in the preceding list of hook codes.

This callback function must reside in a dynamic-link library.

An application must install the callback function by specifying the WH_CBT filter type and the procedure-instance address of the callback function in a call to the **SetWindowsHook** function.

CBTProc is a placeholder for the library-supplied function name. The actual name must be exported by including it in an **EXPORTS** statement in the library's module-definition file.

The following table describes the *wParam* and *lParam* parameters for each HCBT_ constant.

Constant	wParam	lParam
HCBT_ACTIVATE	Specifies the handle of the window about to be activated.	Specifies a long pointer to a **CBTACTIVATESTRUCT** structure that contains the handle of the currently active window and specifies whether the activation is changing because of a mouse click.
HCBT_CLICKSKIPPED	Identifies the mouse message removed from the system message queue.	Specifies a long pointer to a **MOUSEHOOKSTRUCT** structure that contains the hit-test code and the handle of the window for which the mouse message is intended. See the description of the WM_NCHITTEST message for a list of hit-test codes.
HCBT_CREATEWND	Specifies the handle of the new window.	Specifies a long pointer to a **CBT_CREATEWND** data structure that contains initialization parameters for the window.
HCBT_DESTROYWND	Specifies the handle of the window about to be destroyed.	This parameter is undefined; it should be set to 0L.
HCBT_KEYSKIPPED	Identifies the virtual key code.	Specifies the repeat count, scan code, key-transition code, previous key state, and context code. See the description of the WM_KEYUP or WM_KEYDOWN message for more information.
HCBT_MINMAX	Specifies the handle of the window being minimized or maximized.	The low-order word specifies a show-window value (SW_*) that specifies the operation. See the description of the **ShowWindow** function for a list of show-window values. The high-order word is undefined.
HCBT_MOVESIZE	Specifies the handle of the window to be moved or sized.	Specifies a long pointer to a **RECT** structure that contains the coordinates of the window.

Constant	wParam	IParam
HCBT_QS	This parameter is undefined; it should be set to 0.	This parameter is undefined; it should be set to 0L.
HCBT_SETFOCUS	Specifies the handle of the window gaining the input focus.	The low-order word specifies the handle of the window losing the input focus. The high-order word is undefined.
HCBT_SYSCOMMAND	Specifies a system-command value (SC_*) that specifies the system command. See the description of the WM_SYSCOMMAND message for more information about system command values.	If *wParam* is SC_HOTKEY, the low-order word contains the handle of the window that task switching will bring to the foreground; otherwise, *wParam* is undefined.

See Also   **DefHookProc, SetWindowsHook**

■ ChangeClipboardChain

BOOL ChangeClipboardChain(*hWnd***, ***hWndNext***)**
HWND *hWnd*;
HWND *hWndNext*;

This function removes the window specified by the *hWnd* parameter from the chain of clipboard viewers and makes the window specified by the *hWndNext* parameter the descendant of the *hWnd* parameter's ancestor in the chain.

Parameters   *hWnd*   Identifies the window that is to be removed from the chain. The handle must previously have been passed to the SetClipboardViewer function.

hWndNext   Identifies the window that follows *hWnd* in the clipboard-viewer chain (this is the handle returned by the **SetClipboardViewer** function, unless the sequence was changed in response to a WM_CHANGECBCHAIN message).

Return Value   The return value specifies the status of the *hWnd* window. It is TRUE if the window is found and removed. Otherwise, it is FALSE.

See Also   **SetClipboardViewer**

■ ChangeMenu

The Microsoft Windows version 3.0 SDK has replaced this function with five specialized functions. These new functions are:

Function	Description
AppendMenu	Appends a menu item to the end of a menu.
DeleteMenu	Deletes a menu item from a menu, destroying the menu item.
InsertMenu	Inserts a menu item into a menu.
ModifyMenu	Modifies a menu item in a menu.
RemoveMenu	Removes a menu item from a menu but does not destroy the menu item.

Applications written for versions of Windows previous to 3.0 may continue to call **ChangeMenu** as previously documented. Applications written for Windows 3.0 and later should call the new functions listed above.

Example

This example shows an example of a call to **ChangeMenu**, and how the call would be rewritten to call **AppendMenu**:

```
ChangeMenu(hMenu,                             /* handle of the menu */
    0,                                        /* not used           */
    "&White",                                 /* menu-item string   */
    IDM_PATTERN1,                             /* ID of menu item    */
    MF_APPEND | MF_STRING | MF_CHECKED);      /* flags              */

AppendMenu(hMenu,                             /* handle of the menu */
    MF_STRING | MF_CHECKED,                   /* flags              */
    IDM_PATTERN1,                             /* ID of menu item    */
    "&White");                                /* menu-item string   */
```

See Also

AppendMenu, DeleteMenu, InsertMenu, ModifyMenu, RemoveMenu

■ ChangeSelector

The **ChangeSelector** function is deleted since it was not actually shipped with Windows 3.0.

■ CharLower

LPTSTR CharLower(*lpString***)**
LPTSTR *lpString*;

The **CharLower** function converts the given character string to lowercase. The conversion is based on the language semantics of the language selected by the user at setup time or from the Control Panel.

The **CharLower** function may be used as either a wide-character function (where text arguments must use Unicode) or an ANSI function (where text arguments must use characters from the Windows 3.x character set installed).

Parameters

lpString Points to a null-terminated string or specifies single character. If lpString specifies single character, the high-order word is zero.

Return Value The return value points to a converted character string if the function parameter is a character string. Otherwise, it is a 32-bit value that contains the converted character.

■ CharLowerBuff

DWORD CharLowerBuff(lpString, nLength**)**
LPTSTR lpString;
DWORD nLength;

The **CharLowerBuff** function converts character string in a buffer to lowercase. The conversion is based on the language semantics of the language selected by the user at setup time or from the Control Panel.

The **CharLowerBuff** function may be used as either a wide-character function (where text arguments must use Unicode) or an ANSI function (where text arguments must use characters from the Windows 3.x character set installed).

Parameters *lpString* Points to a buffer containing one or more characters.

nLength Specifies the number of bytes to convert in the buffer identified by the *lpString* parameter.

Return Value The return value specifies the number of bytes converted.

See Also **CharLower, CharUpperBuff, CharUpper**

■ CharNext

LPTSTR CharNext(lpCurrentChar**)**
LPTSTR lpCurrentChar;

The **CharNext** function moves to the next character in a string.

The **CharNext** function may be used as either a wide-character function (where text arguments must use Unicode) or an ANSI function (where text arguments must use characters from the Windows 3.x character set installed).

Parameters *lpCurrentChar* Points to a character in a null-terminated string.

Return Value The return value points to the next character in the string, or, if there is no next character, to the null character at the end of the string.

Comments The **CharNext** function is used to move to the next character in a character string. If the string is extended ansi-ascii, it is used to move through one and two byte (or more) characters. If the string is unicode, it is used to move through 2 byte wide characters.

See Also **CharPrev**

■ CharPrev

LPTSTR CharPrev(*lpStart, lpCurrentChar*)
LPTSTR *lpStart*,
LPTSTR *lpCurrentChar*,

The **CharPrev** function moves to the previous character in a string.

The **CharPrev** function may be used as either a wide-character function (where text arguments must use Unicode) or an ANSI function (where text arguments must use characters from the Windows 3.x character set installed).

Parameters

lpStart   Points to the beginning of the string.

lpCurrentChar   Points to a character in a null-terminated string.

Return Value

The return value points to the previous character in the string, or to the first character in the string if the *lpCurrentChar* parameter is equal to the *lpStart* parameter.

Comments

The **CharPrev** function is used to move to the previous character in a character string. If the string is extended ansi-ascii, it is used to move through one and two byte (or more) characters. If the string is unicode, it is used to move through 2 byte wide characters.

See Also

CharNext

■ CharToOem

BOOL CharToOem(*lpAnsiStr, lpOemStr*)
LPTSTR *lpStr*,
LPTSTR *lpOemStr*,

The **CharToOem** function translates the string pointed to by the *lpStr* parameter into the OEM-defined character set.

The **CharToOem** function may be used as either a wide-character function (where text arguments must use Unicode) or an ANSI function (where text arguments must use characters from the Windows 3.x character set installed).

Parameters

lpStr   Points to a null-terminated string of characters.

lpOemStr   Points to the location where the translated string is to be copied. The *lpOemStr* parameter can be the same as *lpStr* to translate the string in place, only if the string buffer is big enough.

Return Value

TRUE is returned for success, FALSE for failure. If FALSE is returned, it is because either the parameters where invalid or there was not enough room in the target buffer for the translation.

See Also

CharToOemBuff, OemToChar, OemToCharBuff

■ CharToOemBuff

BOOL CharToOemBuff(*lpStr*, *lpOemStr*, *nLength***)**
LPTSTR *lpStr*;
LPSTR *lpOemStr*;
DWORD *nLength*;

The **CharToOemBuff** function translates the string in the buffer pointed to by the *lpStr* parameter into the OEM-defined character set.

The **CharToOemBuff** function may be used as either a wide-character function (where text arguments must use Unicode) or an ANSI function (where text arguments must use characters from the Windows 3.x character set installed).

Parameters   *lpStr*   Points to a buffer containing one or more characters.

lpOemStr   Points to the location where the translated string is to be copied. The *lpOemStr* parameter can be the same as *lpStr* to translate the string in place, only if the string buffer is big enough.

nLength   Specifies the number of bytes in the buffer identified by the *lpStr* parameter.

Return Value   TRUE is returned for success, FALSE for failure. If FALSE is returned, it is because either the parameters where invalid or there was not enough room in the target buffer for the translation.

See Also   **CharToOem, OemToCharBuff, OemToChar**

■ CharUpper

LPTSTR CharUpper(*lpString***)**
LPTSTR *lpString*;

The **CharUpper** function converts the given character string to uppercase. The conversion is based on the language semantics of the language selected by the user at setup time or from the Control Panel.

The **CharUpper** function may be used as either a wide-character function (where text arguments must use Unicode) or an ANSI function (where text arguments must use characters from the Windows 3.x character set installed).

lpString Points to a null-terminated string or specifies single character. If lpString specifies single character, the high-order word is zero.

Return Value   The return value points to a converted character string if the function parameter is a character string; otherwise, it is a 32-bit value that contains the converted character.

See Also   **CharLower**

■ CharUpperBuff

DWORD CharUpperBuff(*lpString, nLength***)**
LPTSTR *lpString*;
DWORD *nLength*;

The **CharUpperBuff** function converts a character string in a buffer to uppercase. The conversion is based on the language semantics of the language selected by the user at setup time or from the Control Panel.

The **CharUpperBuff** function may be used as either a wide-character function (where text arguments must use Unicode) or an ANSI function (where text arguments must use characters from the Windows 3.x character set installed).

Parameters   *lpString*   Points to a buffer containing one or more characters.

nLength   Specifies the number of bytes to convert in the buffer identified by the *lpString* parameter.

Return Value   The return value specifies the number of bytes converted.

See Also   **CharUpper, CharLowerBuff, CharLower**

■ CheckDlgButton

void CheckDlgButton(*hDlg, nIDButton, wCheck***)**
HWND *hDlg*;
int *nIDButton*;
UINT *wCheck*;

This function places a checkmark next to or removes a checkmark from a button control, or changes the state of a three-state button. The **CheckDlgButton** function sends a BM_SETCHECK message to the button control that has the specified ID in the given dialog box.

Parameters   *hDlg*   Identifies the dialog box that contains the button.

nIDButton   Specifies the button control to be modified.

wCheck   Specifies the action to take. If the *wCheck* parameter is nonzero, the **CheckDlgButton** function places a checkmark next to the button; if zero, the checkmark is removed. For three-state buttons, if *wCheck* is 2, the button is grayed; if *wCheck* is 1, it is checked; if *wCheck* is 0, the checkmark is removed.

Return Value   This function does not return a value.

See Also   **IsDlgButtonChecked, CheckRadioButton**

■ CheckMenuItem

DWORD CheckMenuItem(*hMenu, wIDCheckItem, dwCheck***)**
HMENU *hMenu*;
UINT *wIDCheckItem*;
UINT *dwCheck*;

This function places checkmarks next to or removes checkmarks from menu items in the pop-up menu specified by the *hMenu* parameter. The *wIDCheckItem* parameter specifies the item to be modified.

Parameters

hMenu   Identifies the menu.

wIDCheckItem   Specifies the menu item to be checked.

dwCheck   Specifies how to check the menu item and how to determine the item's

position in the menu. The *dwCheck* parameter can be a combination of the

MF_CHECKED or MF_UNCHECKED with MF_BYPOSITION or MF_BYCOMMAND flags. These flags can be combined by using the bitwise OR operator. They have the following meanings:

Value	Meaning
MF_BYCOMMAND	Specifies that the *wIDCheckItem* parameter gives the menu-item ID (MF_BYCOMMAND is the default).
MF_BYPOSITION	Specifies that the *wIDCheckItem* parameter gives the position of the menu item (the first item is at position zero).
MF_CHECKED	Adds checkmark.
MF_UNCHECKED	Removes checkmark.

Return Value

The return value specifies the previous state of the item. It is either MF_CHECKED or MF_UNCHECKED. The return value is -1 if the menu item does not exist.

Comments

The *wIDCheckItem* parameter may identify a pop-up menu item as well as a menu item. No special steps are required to check a pop-up menu item.

Top-level menu items cannot be checked.

A pop-up menu item should be checked by position since it does not have a menu-item identifier associated with it.

See Also

GetMenuCheckMarkDimensions, EnableMenuItem, SetMenuItemBitmaps, GetMenuItemID

■ CheckRadioButton

void CheckRadioButton(*hDlg, nIDFirstButton, nIDLastButton, nIDCheckButton*)
HWND *hDlg,*
int *nIDFirstButton;*
int *nIDLastButton;*
int *nIDCheckButton;*

This function checks the radio button specified by the *nIDCheckButton* parameter and removes the checkmark from all other radio buttons in the group of buttons specified by the *nIDFirstButton* and *nIDLastButton* parameters. The **CheckRadioButton** function sends a BM_SETCHECK message to the radio-button control that has the specified ID in the given dialog box.

Parameters   *hDlg*   Identifies the dialog box.

nIDFirstButton   Specifies the integer identifier of the first radio button in the group.

nIDLastButton   Specifies the integer identifier of the last radio button in the group.

nIDCheckButton   Specifies the integer identifier of the radio button to be checked.

Return Value   This function does not return a value.

See Also   **CheckDlgButton**

■ ChildWindowFromPoint

HWND ChildWindowFromPoint(*hWndParent, Point*)
HWND *hWndParent,*
POINT *Point,*

This function determines which, if any, of the child windows belonging to the given parent window contains the specified point.

Parameters   *hWndParent*   Identifies the parent window.

Point   Specifies the client coordinates of the point to be tested.

Return Value   The return value identifies the child window that contains the point. It is NULL if the given point lies outside the parent window. If the point is within the parent window but is not contained within any child window, the handle of the parent window is returned.

See Also   **WindowFromPoint**

■ ChooseColor

BOOL ChooseColor(*lpcc*)
LPCHOOSECOLOR *lpcc;*   /* pointer to structure with initialization data */

The **ChooseColor** function creates a system-defined dialog box that allows the user to choose a color.

Parameters

lpcc   Points to a **CHOOSECOLOR** structure that contains information used to initialize the dialog box. When the **ChooseColor** function returns, this structure contains information about the user's color selection.

The **CHOOSECOLOR** structure has the following form:

```
#include <commdlg.h>

typedef struct {    /* cc */
    DWORD   lStructSize;
    HWND    hwndOwner;
    HANDLE  hInstance;
    DWORD   rgbResult;
    LPDWORD lpCustColors;
    DWORD   Flags;
    DWORD   lCustData;
    WORD (FAR PASCAL *lpfnHook) (HWND, unsigned, WORD, LONG);
    LPSTR   lpTemplateName;
} CHOOSECOLOR;
```

For a full description, see TBD.

Return Value

The return value is TRUE if the user chooses a color. It is FALSE if the user cancels the dialog box, closes the dialog box, or an error occurs.

Comments

The dialog box does not support color palettes. The color choices offered by the dialog box are limited to the system colors and dithers among those colors.

Errors

Use the **CommDlgExtendedError** function to retrieve the error value, which may be one of the following:

    CDERR_FINDRESFAILURE
    CDERR_INITIALIZATION
    CDERR_LOCKRESFAILURE
    CDERR_LOADRESFAILURE
    CDERR_LOADSTRFAILURE
    CDERR_MEMALLOCFAILURE
    CDERR_MEMLOCKFAILURE
    CDERR_NOHINSTANCE
    CDERR_NOHOOK
    CDERR_NOTEMPLATE
    CDERR_STRUCTSIZE

Example

The following code fragment initializes a **CHOOSECOLOR** structure, then creates a color-selection dialog box:

```
/* Color Variables */

CHOOSECOLOR chsclr;
DWORD dwColor;
DWORD dwCustClrs[16];
BOOL  bSetColor = FALSE;
int i;

/* Set the custom-color controls to white. */
```

```
for (i = 0; i < 15; i++)
    dwCustClrs[i] = RGB(255, 255, 255);

/* Initialize dwColor to black. */

dwColor = RGB(0, 0, 0);

/* Initialize the necessary CHOOSECOLOR members */

chsclr.lStructSize = sizeof(CHOOSECOLOR);
chsclr.hwndOwner = hwnd;
chsclr.hInstance = NULL;
chsclr.rgbResult = dwColor;
chsclr.lpCustColors = (LPDWORD) dwCustClrs;
chsclr.Flags = CC_PREVENTFULLOPEN;
chsclr.lCustData = OL;
chsclr.lpfnHook = (FARPROC)NULL;
chsclr.lpTemplateName = (LPSTR)NULL;

if (bSetColor = ChooseColor(&chsclr))

    . /* Use chsclr.rgbResult to select the user-requested color. */
    .
```

■ ChooseFont

BOOL ChooseFont(*lpcf***)**
LPCHOOSEFONT *lpcf*;   /* pointer to structure with initialization data */

The **ChooseFont** function creates a system-defined dialog box that allows the user to choose a font by specifying a facename, point-size, color, and style (such as bold, italic, underline, or strikeout).

Parameters   *lpcf*   Points to an **CHOOSEFONT** structure that contains information used to initialize the dialog box. When the **ChooseFont** function returns, this structure contains information about the user's font selection.

The **CHOOSEFONT** structure has the following form:

```
typedef struct {      /* cf */
    DWORD     lStructSize;
    HWND      hwndOwner;
    HDC       hDC;
    LPLOGFONT lpLogFont;
    int       iPointSize;
    DWORD     Flags;
    DWORD     rgbColors;
    DWORD     lCustData;
    WORD (FAR PASCAL *lpfnHook)(HWND, unsigned, WORD, LONG);
    LPSTR     lpTemplateName;
    HANDLE    hInstance;
    LPSTR     lpszStyle;
    WORD      nFontType;
    int       nSizeMin;
    int       nSizeMax;
} CHOOSEFONT;
```

For a full description, see TBD.

Return Value   The return value is TRUE if the function is successful or FALSE if an error occurs.

Example   The following code fragment initializes a **CHOOSEFONT** structure, then creates a font-selection dialog box:

```
HDC hdc;
LOGFONT lf;
CHOOSEFONT chf;

hdc = GetDC(hwnd);
chf.hDC = CreateCompatibleDC(hdc);
ReleaseDC(hwnd, hdc);
chf.lStructSize = sizeof(CHOOSEFONT);
chf.hwndOwner = hwnd;
chf.lpLogFont = &lf;
chf.Flags = CF_SCREENFONTS | CF_EFFECTS;
chf.rgbColors = RGB(0, 255, 255);
chf.lCustData = 0L;
chf.lpfnHook = (FARPROC) NULL;
chf.lpTemplateName = (LPSTR) NULL;
chf.hInstance = (HANDLE) NULL;
chf.lpszStyle = (LPSTR) NULL;
chf.nFontType = SCREEN_FONTTYPE;
chf.nSizeMin = 0;
chf.nSizeMax = 0;
ChooseFont(&chf);
DeleteDC(hdc);
```

■ Chord

BOOL Chord(*hDC, X1, Y1, X2, Y2, X3, Y3, X4, Y4***)**
HDC *hDC*;
int *X1*;
int *Y1*;
int *X2*;
int *Y2*;
int *X3*;
int *Y3*;
int *X4*;
int *Y4*;

The **Chord** function draws an elliptical chord (a region bounded by the intersection of an ellipse and a line segment).

The curve of the chord is defined by the ellipse formed by the given bounding rectangle. The bounding rectangle is specified by the points *(X1, Y1)* and *(X2, Y2)*. The curve extends counterclockwise from the point where it intersects the radial line from the center of the bounding rectangle to *(X3, Y3)*. The curve ends where it intersects the radial line from the center of the bounding rectangle to *(X4, Y4)*. A line is drawn between the ends of the curve to create the chord. If the start-point and end-point of the curve are the same, a complete ellipse is drawn.

The chord is drawn using the current pen and filled with the current brush.

Parameters

hDC   Identifies the device context in which the chord will appear.

X1   Specifies the logical x-coordinate of the bounding rectangle's upper-left corner.

Y1   Specifies the logical y-coordinate of the bounding rectangle's upper-left corner.

X2   Specifies the logical x-coordinate of the bounding rectangle's lower-right corner.

Y2   Specifies the logical y-coordinate of the bounding rectangle's lower-right corner.

X3   Specifies the logical x-coordinate of the end-point of the radial line defining the start-point of the chord.

Y3   Specifies the logical y-coordinate of the end-point of the radial line defining the start-point of the chord.

X4   Specifies the logical x-coordinate of the end-point of the radial line defining the end-point of the chord.

Y4   Specifies the logical y-coordinate of the end-point of the radial line defining the end-point of the chord.

Return Value

The return value specifies whether or not the chord is drawn. It is TRUE if the chord is drawn. Otherwise, it is FALSE.

Comments

The current position is neither used nor updated by this function.

See Also

AngleArc, Arc, ArcTo, Pie

■ ClearCommBreak

BOOL ClearCommBreak(*hFile***)**
HANDLE *hFile*;

The **ClearCommBreak** function restores character transmission and places the transmission line in a nonbreak state.

Parameters

hFile   Specifies the communication device to be restored. The **CreateFile** function returns this value.

Return Value

The return value is TRUE if the function is successful or FALSE if an error occurs.

See Also

ClearCommError

■ ClearCommError

BOOL ClearCommError(*hFile*, *lpStat*, *lpErrors***)**
HANDLE *hFile*;
LPCOMSTAT *lpStat*;
LPDWORD *lpErrors*;

In case of a communications error, such as a buffer overrun or framing error, the communications software will abort all read and write operations on the communications port. No further read or write operations will be accepted until this function is called. A call to this function will enable the communications ports for further reads and writes.

This function fills the status buffer pointed to by the **lpStat** parameter with the current status of the communication device specified by the **hFile** parameter. **lpStat** is optional; if **lpStat** is NULL, no device status will be returned.

Parameters

hFile   Specifies the communication device to be cleared. The **CreateFile** function returns this value.

lpStat   Points to the **COMSTAT** structure that is to receive the device status. The structure contains information about a communication device. If NULL, no status is returned.

lpErrors   The memory pointed to will be filled with a mask containing the error values listed below.

Value	Meaning
CE_BREAK	The hardware detects a break condition.
CE_CTSTO	Clear-to-send timeout. CTS is low for the duration specified by CtsTimeout while trying to transmit a character.
CE_DSRTO	Data-set-ready timeout. DSR is low for the duration specified by DsrTimeout while trying to transmit a character.
CE_FRAME	The hardware detects a framing error.
CE_IOE	An I/O error occurs while trying to communicate with a device.
CE_MODE	Requested mode is not supported, or the **hFile** parameter is invalid. If set, this is the only valid error.
CE_OOP	The parallel device signals that it is out of paper.
CE_OVERRUN	A character is not read from the hardware before the next character arrives. The character is lost.
CE_RLSDTO	Receive-line-signal-detect timeout. RLSD is low for the duration specified by **RlsdTimeout** while trying to transmit a character.
CE_RXOVER	Receive queue overflow. There is either no room in the input queue or a character is received after the EOF character is received.
CE_RXPARITY	The hardware detects a parity error.

Value	Meaning
CE_TXFULL	The transmit queue is full while trying to queue a character.
CE_DNS	The parallel device is not selected.
CE_PTO	Timeout on a parallel device.

Return Value   The return value is TRUE if the function is successful or FALSE if an error occurs.

See Also   **ClearCommBreak, EscapeCommFunction**

■ ClearEventLog

BOOL ClearEventLog(*hEventLog, lpCurrentFile, lpBackupFile***)**
HANDLE *hEventLog;*
LPSTR *lpCurrentFile;*
LPSTR *lpBackupFile;*

The **ClearEventLog** function clears an event log, and optionally saves it in a backup file.

Parameters   *hEventLog*   Supplies the handle that was obtained from **OpenEventLog**.

lpCurrentFile   Supplies the name of the log file that is to be cleared/backed up. This parameter must be specified.

lpBackupFile   Supplies the name of a file in which to place the current copy of the log file for the module. A NULL pointer indicates that the file should not be backed up.

Return Value   If the function is successful, the return value is TRUE. The event log has been backed up and the current log for the module has been cleared.

If the function fails, the return value is FALSE. Call **GetLastError** for more detailed error information.

Comments   This API is used to optionally back up an existing log file of the module represented by *hEventLog* to another file and clear it. The caller must have write permission for the path specified, and must also have permission to move the current log file. If a file already exists with the same name as *lpBackupFile*, this operation will fail.

■ ClientToScreen

BOOL ClientToScreen(*hWnd, lpPoint***)**
HWND *hWnd;*
LPPOINT *lpPoint;*

The **ClientToScreen** function converts the client coordinates of a given point on the display to screen coordinates. The **ClientToScreen** function uses the client coordinates in the **POINT** structure, pointed to by the *lpPoint* parameter, to compute new screen coordinates; it then replaces the coordinates in the structure with the new coordinates. The new screen coordinates are relative to the upper-left corner of the system display.

Parameters	*hWnd* Identifies the window whose client area will be used for the conversion.
	lpPoint Points to a **POINT** structure that contains the client coordinates to be converted.
Return Value	Returns TRUE for success, FALSE for failure.
Comments	The **ClientToScreen** function assumes that the given point is in client coordinates and is relative to the given window.
See Also	**ScreenToClient**

■ ClipCursor

BOOL ClipCursor(*lpRect***)**
LPRECT *lpRect*;

This function confines the cursor to the rectangle on the display screen given by the *lpRect* parameter. If a subsequent cursor position, given with the **SetCursorPos** function or the mouse, lies outside the rectangle, Windows automatically adjusts the position to keep the cursor inside. If *lpRect* is NULL, the cursor is free to move anywhere on the display screen.

Parameters	*lpRect* Points to a **RECT** structure that contains the screen coordinates of the upper-left and lower-right corners of the confining rectangle.
Return Value	TRUE is returned for success, FALSE for failure.
Comments	The cursor is a shared resource. An application that has confined the cursor to a given rectangle must free it before relinquishing control to another application.
See Also	**SetCursorPos, ShowCursor, GetCursorPos, SetCursor**

■ CloseClipboard

BOOL CloseClipboard(void)

This function closes the clipboard. The **CloseClipboard** function should be called when a window has finished examining or changing the clipboard. It lets other applications access the clipboard.

Parameters	This function has no parameters.
	This function has no parameters.
Return Value	The return value specifies whether the clipboard is closed. It is nonzero if the clipboard is closed. Otherwise, it is zero.

See Also   OpenClipboard

■ CloseDesktop

BOOL CloseDesktop(*hDesk***)**
HANDLE *hDesk*;

This api closes a reference to a desktop. The usage count for the desktop referenced by this handle is decremented—the desktop is destroyed if the usage count drops to zero.

Parameters   *hDesk*   This is a reference to a desktop.

Return Value   The return value is TRUE if the function is successful or FALSE if an error occurs.

■ CloseEventLog

BOOL CloseEventLog(*hEventLog***)**
HANDLE *hEventLog*;

The **CloseEventLog** function closes the handle to an event log.

Parameters   *hEventLog*   Supplies the handle to be closed. This handle was obtained from **OpenEventLog**.

Return Value   If the function is successful, the return value is TRUE. The event log handle has been closed.

If the function fails, the return value is FALSE. Call **GetLastError** for more detailed error information.

■ CloseFigure

BOOL CloseFigure(*hDC***)**
HDC *hDC*;

The **CloseFigure** function closes an open figure in a path. It should only be called when there is an active path associated with the DC, started by a **BeginPath** call.

A figure in a path is open unless it is explicitly closed using **CloseFigure**. A figure can be open even if the current point and the starting point of the figure are the same.

This function closes the figure by drawing a line from the current position to the first point of the figure (usually, the point specified by the most recent **MoveTo** call), and connects the lines using the line join style. If a figure is closed using **LineTo** instead of **CloseFigure**, end caps will be used to create the corner instead of a join.

Any line or curve added to the path after **CloseFigure** starts a new figure.

Parameters	*hDC* Identifies the DC.
Return Value	The return value is TRUE if the call succeeded, otherwise FALSE.
Comment	**CloseFigure** can only be used in a path bracket, started by calling **BeginPath**.
Errors	Use the **GetLastError** function to retrieve the error value, which may be one of the following:

ERROR_INVALID_MODE

ERROR_INVALID_PARAMETER

See Also	**BeginPath, EndPath, ExtCreatePen**

■ CloseHandle

BOOL CloseHandle(*hObject***)**
HANDLE *hObject*;

An open handle to any object can be closed using **CloseHandle**.

Parameters	*hHandle* An open handle to an object.
Return Value	The return value is TRUE if the function is successful. Otherwise, it is FALSE in which case extended error information is available from the **GetLastError** function.
Comments	The following objects can be closed using **CloseHandle**.

- process
- thread
- event
- semaphore
- mutex
- file (including file mappings)
- console input or output

Closing an open handle to an object causes the handle to become invalid and the **HandleCount** of the associated object to be decremented and object retention checks to be performed. Once the last open handle to an object is closed, the object is removed from the system.

■ CloseMetaFileEx

HMF CloseMetaFileEx(*hDC***)**
HDC *hDC*;

The **CloseMetaFileEx** function closes the metafile device context and creates a metafile handle that can be used with other metafile calls.

Parameters   *hDC*   Identifies the metafile device context to be closed.

Return Value   The return value identifies the metafile if the function is successful. Otherwise, it is 0.

Comments   When the application no longer requires the metafile handle, it should free the handle by calling the **DeleteMetaFileEx** function.

See Also   **CopyMetaFileEx, CreateMetaFileEx, DeleteMetaFileEx, EnumMetaFileEx, GetMetaFileBitsEx, PlayMetaFileEx.**

■ CloseSpooler

BOOL CloseSpooler(*hSpooler***)**
HANDLE *hSpooler*;

The **CloseSpooler** function closes a spooler. If the spooler is writing to a spool file, **CloseSpooler** closes the spool file and schedules it for printing. If the spooler is writing directly to a printer, **CloseSpooler** discards any instance data created by the spooler as a result of the **OpenSpooler** call.

Parameters   *hSpooler*   Specifies an open handle to the spooler to be closed.

Return Value   If the function is successful, the return value is TRUE.

If the function fails, the return value is FALSE/NULL. Further information can be obtained by calling **GetLastError**.

See Also   **AbortSpooler, OpenSpooler, ReadSpooler, WriteSpooler**

■ CloseWindow

BOOL CloseWindow(*hWnd***)**
HWND *hWnd*;

This function minimizes the specified window. If the window is an overlapped window, it is minimized by removing the client area and caption of the open window from the display screen and moving the window's icon into the icon area of the screen.

Parameters   *hWnd*   Identifies the window to be minimized.

Return Value   TRUE is returned for success, FALSE for failure.

Comments   This function has no effect if the *hWnd* parameter is a handle to a pop-up or child window.

See Also **CreateWindow**

■ CloseWindowStation

BOOL CloseWindowStation(*hWindowStation***)**
HANDLE *hWindowStation*;

The **CloseWindowStation** function closes a reference to a windowstation. The reference must belong to the calling process. The windowstation must not be the windowstation that is associated with the calling process.

Parameters *hWindowStation*   Handle that specifies the windowstation whose reference the function will close.

Return Value If the function is successful, the return value is TRUE.

If the function fails, the return value is FALSE. Call **GetLastError** for more detailed error information.

See Also **OpenWindowStation, EnumWindowStations, GetProcessWindowStation, GetWindowStationAttrs, SetProcessWindowStation**

■ CombineRgn

int CombineRgn(*hDestRgn, hSrcRgn1, hSrcRgn2, nCombineMode***)**
HRGN *hDestRgn*;
HRGN *hSrcRgn1*;
HRGN *hSrcRgn2*;
int *nCombineMode*;

The **CombineRgn** function combines two existing regions. The method used to combine the regions is specified by the *nCombineMode* parameter.

Parameters *hDestRgn*   Identifies an existing region that will be replaced by the new region.

hSrcRgn1   Identifies an existing region.

hSrcRgn2   Identifies an existing region.

nCombineMode   Specifies the operation to be performed on the two existing regions. It can be any one of the following values:

RGN_AND	Uses overlapping areas of both regions (intersection).
RGN_COPY	Creates a copy of region 1 (identified by *hSrcRgn1*).
RGN_DIFF	Saves the areas of region 1 (identified by the *hSrcRgn1* parameter) that are not part of region 2 (identified by the *hSrcRgn2* parameter).
RGN_OR	Combines all of both regions (union).
RGN_XOR	Combines both regions but removes overlapping areas.

Return Value	The return value specifies the type of the resulting region. It can be any one of the following values:

NULLREGION	New region is empty.
SIMPLEREGION	New region is a single rectangle.
COMPLEXREGION	New region is more than a single rectangle.
ERROR	No new region created.

Comment	The three regions do not have to be distinct. For example *hSrcRgn1* can equal *hDestRgn*.

■ CommDlgExtendedError

DWORD CommDlgExtendedError(VOID);

The **CommDlgExtendedError** function indicates whether an error occured during the execution of one of the following common dialog functions:

- ChooseColor
- FindText
- GetOpenFileName
- GetSaveFileName
- PrintDlg
- ReplaceText

Return Value	If the prior call to a common dialog function was successful, the return value is 0; otherwise the return value is a non-zero integer that identifies an error condition.
Comments	The following list identifies the possible **CommDlgExtendedError** return values and their meaning:

Value	Meaning
CDERR_FINDRESFAILURE	Specifies that the common dialog function failed to find a specified resource.
CDERR_INITIALIZATION	Specifies that the common dialog function failed during initialization. This error often occurs when insufficient memory is available.
CDERR_LOCKRESFAILURE	Specifies that the common dialog function failed to lock a specified resource.
CDERR_LOADRESFAILURE	Specifies that the common dialog function failed to load a specified resource.
CDERR_LOADSTRFAILURE	Specifies that the common dialog function failed to load a specified string.

Value	Meaning
CDERR_MEMALLOCFAILURE	Specifies that the common dialog function was unable to allocate memory for internal data structures.
CDERR_MEMLOCKFAILURE	Specifies that the common dialog function was unable to lock the memory associated with a handle.
CDERR_NOHINSTANCE	Specifies that the ENABLETEMPLATE flag was set in the *Flags* member of a common-dialog data structure but the application failed to provide a corresponding instance handle.
CDERR_NOHOOK	Specifies that the ENABLEHOOK flag was set in the *Flags* member of a common-dialog data structure but the application failed to provide a pointer to a corresponding hook function.
CDERR_NOTEMPLATE	Specifies that the ENABLETEMPLATE flag was set in the *Flags* member of a common-dialog data structure but the application failed to provide a corresponding template.
CDERR_STRUCTSIZE	Specifies that the *lStructSize* member of the corresponding common-dialog data structure is invalid.
PDERR_CREATEICFAILURE	Specifies that the **PrintDlg** function failed when it attempted to create an information context.
PDERR_DNDMMISMATCH	Specifies that the data in the DEVMODE and DEVNAMES data structures describes two different printers.
PDERR_GETDEVMODEFAIL	Specifies that the printer device-driver failed to initialize a DEVMODE data structure. (This error constant only applies to printer drivers written for Windows 3.0 or later versions.)
PDERR_INITFAILURE	Specifies that the **PrintDlg** function failed during initialization.
PDERR_LOADDRVFAILURE	Specifies that the **PrintDlg** function failed to load the specified printer's device driver.
PDERR_NODEFAULTPRN	Specifies that a default printer does not exist.

Value	Meaning
PDERR_NODEVICES	Specifies that no printer device-drivers were found.
PDERR_PARSEFAILURE	Specifies that the common dialog function, , failed to parse the strings in the [devices] section of the file WIN.INI.
PDERR_RETDEFFAILURE	Specifies that the PD_RETURNDEFAULT flag was set in the *Flags* member of the PRINTDLG data structure but either the *hDevMode* or *hDevNames* field were nonzero.
PDERR_SETUPFAILURE	Specifies that the common dialog function, , failed to load the required resources.
CFERR_NOFONTS	Specifies that no fonts exist.

See Also **ChooseColor, FindText, GetFileTitle, GetOpenFileName, GetSaveFileName, PrintDlg, ReplaceText**

■ CompareFileTime

LONG APIENTRY CompareFileTime(*lpFileTime1*, *lpFileTime2***)**
LPFILETIME *lpFileTime1*;
LPFILETIME *lpFileTime2*;

This function compares two 64-bit file times.

Parameters   *lpFileTime1*   pointer to a 64-bit file time.

lpFileTime2   pointer to a 64-bit file time.

Return Value   The return value is one of the following values:

Value	Meaning
−1	$*lpFileTime1 < *lpFileTime2$
0	$*lpFileTime1 == *lpFileTime2$
+1	$*lpFileTime1 > *lpFileTime2$

See Also   **GetFileTime**

■ ConnectNamedPipe

BOOL ConnectNamedPipe(*hNamedPipe*, *lpOverlapped***)**
HANDLE *hNamedPipe*;
LPOVERLAPPED *lpOverlapped*;

The **ConnectNamedPipe** function is used by the server side of a named pipe to wait for a client to connect to the named pipe with a **CreateFile** request. The handle provided with the call to **ConnectNamedPipe** must have been previously returned by a successful call to **CreateNamedPipe**. The pipe must be in the disconnected, listening or connected states for **ConnectNamedPipe** to succeed.

The behavior of this call depends on the blocking/nonblocking mode selected with the PIPE_WAIT/PIPE_NOWAIT flags when the server end of the pipe was created with **CreateNamedPipe**.

If blocking mode is specified, **ConnectNamedPipe** will change the state from disconnected to listening and block. When a client connects with a **CreateFile**, the state will be changed from listening to connected and the **ConnectNamedPipe** returns TRUE. When the file handle is created with FILE_FLAG_OVERLAPPED on a blocking mode pipe, the **lpOverlapped** parameter can be specified. This allows the caller to continue processing while the **ConnectNamedPipe** API awaits a connection. When the pipe enters the signalled state the event is set to the signalled state.

When nonblocking is specified **ConnectNamedPipe** will not block. On the first call the state will change from disconnected to listening. When a client connects with an Open the state will be changed from listening to connected. The **ConnectNamedPipe** will return FALSE (with **GetLastError** returning ERROR_PIPE_LISTENING) until the state is changed to the connected state.

Parameters

hNamedPipe   Supplies a Handle to the server side of a named pipe.

lpOverlapped   Supplies an overlap structure to be used with the request. If NULL then the API will not return until the operation completes. When FILE_FLAG_OVERLAPPED is specified when the handle was created, **ConnectNamedPipe** may return ERROR_IO_PENDING to allow the caller to continue processing while the operation completes. The event (or File handle if hEvent=NULL) will be set to the not signalled state before ERROR_IO_PENDING is returned. The event will be set to the signalled state upon completion of the request. **GetOverlappedResult** is used to determine the error status.

The **OVERLAPPED** structure has the following form:

```
typedef struct _OVERLAPPED {
    DWORD   Internal;
    DWORD   InternalHigh;
    DWORD   Offset;
    DWORD   OffsetHigh;
    HANDLE  hEvent;
} OVERLAPPED;
typedef OVERLAPPED *LPOVERLAPPED;
```

Return Value

TRUE — The operation was successful, the pipe is in the connected state.

FALSE — The operation failed. Extended error status is available using **GetLastError**.

See Also   DisconnectNamedPipe, CreateNamedPipe, GetOverlappedResult

■ ContinueDebugEvent

BOOL ContinueDebugEvent(*dwProcessId, dwThreadId, dwContinueStatus*)
DWORD *dwProcessId*;
DWORD *dwThreadId*;
DWORD *dwContinueStatus*;

A debugger can continue a thread that previously reported a debug event using ContinueDebugEvent.

Parameters   *dwProcessId*   Supplies the process id of the process to continue. The combination of process id and thread id must identify a thread that has previously reported a debug event.

dwThreadId   Supplies the thread id of the thread to continue. The combination of process id and thread id must identify a thread that has previously reported a debug event.

dwContinueStatus   Supplies the continuation status for the thread reporting the debug event.

Value	Meaning
DBG_CONTINUE	If the thread being continued had previously reported an exception event, continuing with this value causes all exception processing to stop and the thread continues execution. For any other debug event, this continuation status simply allows the thread to continue execution.
DBG_EXCEPTION_NOT_HANDLE	If the thread being continued had previously reported an exception event, continuing with this value causes exception processing to continue. If this is a first chance exception event, then structured exception handler search/dispatch logic is invoked. Otherwise, the process is terminated. For any other debug event, this continuation status simply allows the thread to continue execution.
DBG_TERMINATE_THREAD	After all continue side effects are processed, this continuation status causes the thread to jump to a call to **ExitThread**. The exit code is the value DBG_TERMINATE_THREAD.

Value	Meaning
DBG_TERMINATE_PROCESS	After all continue side effects are processed, this continuation status causes the thread to jump to a call to **ExitProcess**. The exit code is the value DBG_TERMINATE_PROCESS.

Return Value
The return value is TRUE if the function is successful or FALSE if an error occurs.

Upon successful completion of this API, the specified thread is continued. Depending on the debug event previously reported by the thread certain side effects occur.

If the continued thread previously reported an exit thread debug event, the handle that the debugger has to the thread is closed.

If the continued thread previously reported an exit process debug event, the handles that the debugger has to the thread and to the process are closed.

■ CopyAcceleratorTable

int **CopyAcceleratorTable**(*hAccel*, *lpAccel*, *nCount*)
HACCEL *hAccel*;
LPACCEL *lpAccel*;
int *nCount*;

This function allows a copy of an accelerator table to be made.

Parameters
hAccel   This parameter identifies the accelerator table that will be copied.

lpAccel   This parameter points to an array of structures of type **ACCEL**. The accelerator table will be copied into this area. If this parameter is NULL, the number of accelerator table entries is returned.

nCount   This specifies how many structures of type **ACCEL** are pointed to by *lpAccel*

Return Value
This function returns the count of accelerator table entries (**ACCEL** structures) copied to *lpAccel*. If *lpAccel* is NULL, the number of accelerator table entries in *hAccel* is returned.

See Also
TranslateAccelerator CreateAcceleratorTable LoadAccelerators DestroyAcceleratorTable

■ CopyFile

BOOL **CopyFile**(*lpExistingFileName*, *lpNewFileName*, *bFailIfExists*)
LPTSTR *lpExistingFileName*;
LPTSTR *lpNewFileName*;
BOOL *bFailIfExists*;

A file, its security descriptor, and any other attributes can be copied using **CopyFile**.

The **CopyFile** function may be used as either a wide-character function (where text arguments must use Unicode) or an ANSI function (where text arguments must use characters from the Windows 3.x character set installed).

Parameters

lpExistingFileName   Supplies the name of an existing file that is to be copied.

lpNewFileName   Supplies the name where a copy of the existing files data and attributes are to be stored.

bFailIfExists   Supplies a flag that indicates how this operation is to proceed if the specified new file already exists. A value of TRUE specifies that this call is to fail. A value of FALSE causes the call to the function to succeed whether or not the specified new file exists.

Return Value

The return value is TRUE if the function is successful. Otherwise, it is FALSE, in which case extended error information is available from the **GetLastError** function.

Comments

CopyFile will not copy a file onto itself.

See Also

MoveFile

■ CopyLZFile

#include <lzexpand.h>

LONG CopyLZFile(hfSource, hfDest**)**
HANDLE hfSource;   /* handle identifying source file   */
HANDLE hfDest;   /* handle identifying destination file */

The **CopyLZFile** function copies a source file to a destination file. If the source file was compressed, this function creates a decompressed destination file. If the source file was not compressed, this function duplicates the original file.

Parameters

hfSource   Identifies the source file.

hfDest   Identifies the destination file.

Return Value

The return value specifies the size of the destination file in bytes if the function is successful; if an error occurs, the return value is less than zero. The following list identifies possible error return values and their meaning:

Value	Meaning
LZERROR_BADINHANDLE	The handle identifying the source file, *hfSource*, was not valid.
LZERROR_BADOUTHANDLE	The handle identifying the destination file, *hfDest*, was not valid.
LZERROR_READ	The source file format was not valid.
LZERROR_WRITE	There is insufficient space for the output file.

Value	Meaning
LZERROR_GLOBALLOC	There is insufficient memory for the required buffers.
LZERROR_UNKNOWNALG	The file was compressed with an unrecognized compression algorithm.

Comments

The **CopyLZFile** function is designed for copying and/or expanding multiple files. Applications should call **LZStart** prior to calling **CopyLZFile** in order to allocate required buffers and call **LZDone** after copying the files in order to free these buffers.

The file identified by *hfDest* is always uncompressed.

If the source or destination files are opened using a C-runtime function (rather than **_lopen** or **OpenFile**) they must be opened in binary mode.

Example

The following code fragment shows how the **CopyLZFile** function was used to create copies of four text files:

```
#include <windows.h>
#include <lzexpand.h>

char *szSrc[] = {"readme.txt", "data.txt", "update.txt", "list.txt"};
char *szDest[] = {"readme.bak", "data.bak", "update.bak", "list.bak"};
int nFileCount = 4;
OFSTRUCT ofStrSrc;
OFSTRUCT ofStrDest;
HANDLE hSrcFile, hDestFile;
int i;

/* Allocate internal buffers for the CopyLZFile function. */

LZStart();

/* Open, copy, and then close the files. */

for (i=0; i<nFileCount; i++){
    hSrcFile = LZOpenFile(szSrc[i], (LPOFSTRUCT) &ofStrSrc, OF_READ);
    hDestFile = LZOpenFile(szDest[i], (LPOFSTRUCT) &ofStrDest,
        OF_CREATE);
    CopyLZFile(hSrcFile, hDestFile);
    LZClose(hSrcFile);
    LZClose(hDestFile);
}

/* Free the internal buffers. */

LZDone();
```

See Also

_lopen, OpenFile, LZStart, LZDone, LZCopy

■ CopyMetaFileEx

HMF CopyMetaFileEx(*hSrcMetaFile, lpFilename***)**
HMF *hSrcMetaFile*;
LPTSTR *lpFilename*;

The **CopyMetaFileEx** function copies the source metafile and returns the metafile handle to the new metafile. If *lpFilename* points to a valid filename, the source is copied to a disk metafile. If *lpFilename* is NULL, the source is copied to a memory metafile.

The **CopyMetaFileEx** function may be used as either a wide-character function (where text arguments must use Unicode) or an ANSI function (where text arguments must use characters from the Windows 3.x character set.

Parameters   *hSrcMetaFile*   Identifies the source metafile.

lpFilename   Points to the filename of the file that is to receive the metafile. If the filename is valid, a disk metafile is created. If *lpFilename* is NULL, the source is copied to a memory metafile.

Return Value   The return value is the metafile handle which identifies the new metafile. Zero is returned if an error occurred.

Comments   When the application no longer requires the metafile handle, it should free the handle by calling the **DeleteMetaFileEx** function.

See Also   **DeleteMetaFileEx,**

■ CopyRect

BOOL CopyRect(*lpDestRect*, *lpSourceRect***)**
LPRECT *lpDestRect*;
LPRECT *lpSourceRect*;

This function copies the rectangle pointed to by the *lpSourceRect* parameter to the **RECT** structure pointed to by the *lpDestRect* parameter.

Parameters   *lpDestRect*   Points to a **RECT** structure.

lpSourceRect   Points to a **RECT** structure.

Return Value   FALSE on error, TRUE on success

■ CopySid

BOOL CopySid(*DestinationSidLength*, *DestinationSid*, *SourceSid***)**
ULONG *DestinationSidLength*;
PSID *DestinationSid*;
PSID *SourceSid*;

The **CopySid** function copies the value of a source **SID** security identifier to a destination **SID**.

Parameters   *DestinationSidLength*   Specifies the length, in bytes, of the destination **SID** buffer.

DestinationSid   Pointer to a buffer that the function will fill with a copy of the source **SID**.

SourceSid   Pointer to an **SID** data structure that the function will copy to the buffer pointed to by *DestinationSid.*

The **SID** data structure is an opaque data structure of variable length, defined as follows:

```
typedef PVOID * PSID;
```

Return Value   If the function is successful, the return value is TRUE.

If the function fails, the return value is FALSE. Call **GetLastError** for more detailed error information.

See Also   **EqualSid, GetLengthSid, InitializeSid, IsValidSid, GetSidIdentifierAuthority, GetSidLengthRequired, GetSidSubAuthority, GetSidSubAuthorityCount**

■ CountClipboardFormats

int CountClipboardFormats(void)

The **CountClipboardFormats** function retrieves a count of the number of formats the clipboard can render.

This function has no parameters.

Return Value   The return value specifies the number of data formats in the clipboard.

See Also   **RegisterClipboardFormat, EnumClipboardFormats**

■ CreateAcceleratorTable

HACCEL CreateAcceleratorTable(*lpAccel, nCount***)**
LPACCEL *lpAccel,*
int *nCount,*

This function creates an accelerator table.

Parameters   *lpAccel*   This points to the accelerator table description, which is an array of structures of type **ACCEL**.

nCount   This specifies how many structures of type **ACCEL** are pointed to by *lpAccel.*

Return Value   This function returns an accelerator table handle if successful. If not successful, this function returns NULL.

Comments   Accelerator table handles must be destroyed with a call to **DestroyAcceleratorTable**.

See Also   **TranslateAccelerator DestroyAcceleratorTable CopyAcceleratorTable LoadAccelerators**

■ CreateBitmap

HBITMAP CreateBitmap(*nWidth, nHeight, nPlanes, nBitCount, lpBits***)**
int *nWidth*;
int *nHeight*;
UINT *nPlanes*;
UINT *nBitCount*;
LPBYTE *lpBits*;

The **CreateBitmap** function creates bitmaps. The bitmap has the specified width, height, and at least as many bits per pixel as specified by *nPlanes* X *nBitCount*. The bitmap can subsequently be selected as the current bitmap for any memory device context using the **SelectObject** function.

Parameters

nWidth　Specifies the width (in pixels) of the bitmap.

nHeight　Specifies the height (in pixels) of the bitmap.

nPlanes　Used in determining the format of the bitmap.

nBitCount　Used in determining the format of the bitmap.

lpBits　If a bitmap is being initialized this points to a dword aligned array which specifies the initial bitmap. Each scanline must be 0-padded so the next scanline begins on a dword boundary. If it is NULL, the value of the bits in the new bitmap are undefined.

Return Value

The return value identifies a bitmap if the function is successful. Otherwise, it is 0.

Comments

The format of the bitmap is specified by *nPlanes* x *nBitCount*. A DIB bitmap managed by GDI will be created with at least this many bits per pixel.

If a monochrome bitmap is created the 0's will go to the foreground color and the 1's will go to the background color of the destination DC the bitmap is being BitBlt to. If the bitmap created is not monochrome the initial palette for the bitmap is undefined.

New applications should use **CreateDIBitmap** unless they want to create a monochrome bitmap with the special color mapping properties.

See Also

CreateDIBitmap

■ CreateBitmapIndirect

HBITMAP CreateBitmapIndirect(*lpBitmap***)**
LPBITMAP *lpBitmap*;

CreateBitmapIndirect creates bitmaps. The bitmap has the specified width, height, and at least as many bits per pixel as specfied by in the *lpBitmap* structure. The bitmap can subsequently be selected as the current bitmap for any memory device context using the **SelectObject** function.

If a monochrome bitmap (*nPlanes* = *nBitCount* = 1) is being created then lpBits may point to initialization data.

lBitmap Points to a **BITMAP** structure that contains information about the bitmap.

Return Value The return value identifies a bitmap if the function is successful. Otherwise, it is 0.

Comments This call is included only for compatiblity purposes. Applications are discouraged from using this call. An application should use **CreateDIBitmap**.

seealso

See Also **CreateDIBitmap BitBlt**

■ CreateBrushIndirect

HBRUSH CreateBrushIndirect(*lpLogBrush***)**
LPLOGBRUSH *lpLogBrush*;

The **CreateBrushIndirect** function creates a logical brush that has the style, color and pattern given in the structure pointed to by the *lpLogBrush* parameter. The brush can subsequently be selected as the current brush for any device context.

Parameters *lpLogBrush* Points to a LOGBRUSH structure that contains information about the brush.

Return Value The return value identifies a logical brush if the function is successful. Otherwise, it is 0.

Comments A brush created using a monochrome (one plane, one bit per pixel) bitmap is drawn using the current text and background colors. Pixels represented by a bit set to 0 will be drawn with the current text color, and pixels represented by a bit set to 1 will be drawn with the current background color.

■ CreateCaret

BOOL CreateCaret(*hWnd, hBitmap, nWidth, nHeight***)**
HWND *hWnd*;
HBITMAP *hBitmap*;
int *nWidth*;
int *nHeight*;

This function creates a new shape for the system caret and assigns ownership of the caret to the given window. The caret shape can be a line, block, or bitmap as defined by the *hBitmap* parameter. If *hBitmap* is a bitmap handle, the *nWidth* and *nHeight* parameters are ignored; the bitmap defines its own width and height. (The bitmap handle must have been previously created by using the **CreateBitmap**, **CreateDIBitmap**, or **LoadBitmap** function.)

If *nWidth* or *nHeight* is zero, the caret width or height is set to the system's window-border width or height. Using the window-border width or height guarantees that the caret will be visible on a high-resolution display.

The **CreateCaret** function automatically destroys the previous caret shape, if any, regardless of which window owns the caret. Once created, the caret is initially hidden. To show the caret, the **ShowCaret** function must be called.

Parameters

hWnd Identifies the window that owns the new caret.

hBitmap Identifies the bitmap that defines the caret shape. If *hBitmap* is NULL, the caret is solid; if *hBitmap* is 1, the caret is gray.

nWidth Specifies the width of the caret (in logical units).

nHeight Specifies the height of the caret (in logical units).

Return Value

Returns TRUE for success, FALSE for failure.

Comments

The system caret is a shared resource. A window should create a caret only when it has the input focus or is active. It should destroy the caret before losing the input focus or becoming inactive.

The system's window-border width or height can be retrieved by using the **GetSystemMetrics** function with the SM_CXBORDER and SM_CYBORDER indexes.

See Also

CreateBitmap, CreateDIBitmap, GetSystemMetrics, LoadBitmap, ShowCaret, HideCaret

■ CreateCaretEx

BOOL CreateCaretEx(*hWnd, hBitmap, lpPoints, nCount, crCaretOn, crCaretOff, flags***)**
HWND *hWnd*;
HBITMAP *hBitmap*;
LPPOINT *lpPoints*;
DWORD *nCount*;
COLORREF *crCaretOn*;
COLORREF *crCaretOff*;
DWORD *flags*;

This function creates a new shape for the system caret and assigns ownership of the caret to the given window. The caret shape can be a polygon or a bitmap as defined by the *hBitmap* parameter. (The **CreateCaret** call allows the creation of block and line carets). If *hBitmap* is a bitmap handle, the *lpPoints* and *nCount* parameters are ignored; the bitmap defines its own width and height. (The bitmap handle must have been previously created by using the **CreateBitmap**, **CreateDIBitmap**, or **LoadBitmap** function.)

Since this function allows carets to be polygons, carets can be slanted to fit within italic text, for example. Polygonal carets are useful for insertion points between any irregular shapes neither vertical or horizontal. (for horizontal and / or vertical carets, the **CreateCaret** function is easier to use).

The **CreateCaretEx** function automatically destroys the previous caret shape created by the calling thread. Once created, the caret is initially hidden. To show the caret, the **ShowCaret** function must be called.

Parameters
hWnd   Identifies the window that owns the new caret.

hBitmap   Identifies the bitmap that defines the caret shape. Can be NULL, in which case *lpPoints* defines the caret shape.

lpPoints   Identifies the polygon that defines the caret shape. Can be NULL, in which case *hBitmap* defines the caret shape. *lpPoints* points to an array of **POINT** structures that specifiy the vertices of the polygon.

nCount   Specifies the number of vertices given in the array, and must be at least 2.

crCaretOn   Only used when CARET_XOR flag is not set. Specifies the color used to draw the caret when it is on. If *hBitmap* is specified, that is used in place of *crCaretOn*.

crCaretOff   Only used when CARET_XOR flag is not set. Specifies the color used to draw the caret when it is off. If *hBitmap* is specified, this color fills in the caret area when the caret is off.

flags   Specifies the appearance of the caret. This parameter can be one of the following values:

CARET_FRAME *lpPoints* holds 2 points which are interpreted as the top left and bottom right cooridates for a frame. The frame's width is in SM_CXBORDER pixels and the frame's height is in SM_CYBORDER pixels (see **GetSystemMetrics)**

CARET_VERTLINE *lpPoints* holds 2 points which are the beginning point and ending point coordinates specifying a line. The line is interpreted as vertical because the line width will be enforced to SM_CXBORDER.

CARET_HORZLINE *lpPoints* holds 2 points which are the beginning point and ending point coordinates specifying a line. The line is interpreted as horizontal because the line height will be enforced to SM_CYBORDER.

CARET_HALFTONE The caret is halftoned.

CARET_SOLID The caret is drawn solid.

CARET_FLASH The caret flashes.

CARET_XOR The caret is XORed on the screen. If this is NOT set, the caret is drawn on the screen in colors *crCaretOn* (when the caret is on) and *crCaretOff* (when the caret is off). If this flag is not set and the caret is a bitmap, the bitmap will be copied to the screen in with the rop SRCCOPY (see **BitBlt**) when the caret is on, and the *crCaretOff* color will be drawn in place of the bitmap when the caret is off.

CARET_INVALWINDOW When this flag is set, the window manager will invalidate the area of the caret when the caret is either moved or destroyed. This will cause the window to receive a WM_PAINT message. This is useful for non-XOR cursors that may draw over screen bits that need to be regenerated.

Return Value	Returns TRUE for success, FALSE for failure.
Comments	Each thread has a caret it maintains. One thread creating a caret will not affect another thread loosing the caret. The caret is not a system resource, but a thread-specific resource.
	A window should create a caret when it has the input focus or is active. It should destroy the caret before losing the input focus or becoming inactive.
	The system's window-border width or height can be retrieved by using the **GetSystemMetrics** function with the SM_CXBORDER and SM_CYBORDER indexes.
See Also	**CreateCaret CreateBitmap, CreateDIBitmap, GetSystemMetrics, LoadBitmap, ShowCaret**

■ CreateCompatibleBitmap

HBITMAP CreateCompatibleBitmap(*hDC*, *nWidth*, *nHeight***)**
HDC *hDC*;
int *nWidth*;
int *nHeight*;

The **CreateCompatibleBitmap** function creates a bitmap that is compatible with the device specified by the *hDC* parameter. The bitmap has the same color format and the same color palette as the specified device. It can be selected as the current bitmap for any memory device context compatible with *hDC*.

Since a memory device context can have either color or monochrome bitmaps selected, the format of the bitmap returned by the **CreateCompatibleBitmap** function is not always the same; however, the format of a compatible bitmap for a nonmemory device context always has the same format and color palette of the device.

Parameters	*hDC* Identifies the device context.
	nWidth Specifies the width in pixels of the bitmap.
	nHeight Specifies the height in pixels of the bitmap.
Return Value	The return value identifies a bitmap if the function is successful. Otherwise, it is 0.

■ CreateCompatibleDC

HDC CreateCompatibleDC(*hDC***)**
HDC *hDC*;

The **CreateCompatibleDC** function creates a memory device context that is compatible with the device specified by the *hDC* parameter.

An application must select a bitmap into a memory DC to represent a device surface. The DC may then be used to prepare images in memory before copying them to the actual device surface of the compatible device.

Parameters
hDC   Identifies the device context. If *hDC* is 0, the function creates a memory device context that is compatible with the application's active display.

Return Value
The return value identifies the new memory device context if the function is successful. Otherwise, it is 0.

Comments
This function can only be used to create compatible device contexts for devices that support raster operations. For more information, see the RC_BITBLT raster capability in the **GetDeviceCaps** function, later in this chapter.

GDI output functions can be used with a memory device context only if a bitmap has been created and selected into that context.

When the application no longer requires the device context, it should free it by calling the **DeleteDC** function.

See Also
CreateCompatibleBitmap, DeleteDC, GetDeviceCaps

■ CreateConsoleScreenBuffer

HANDLE CreateConsoleScreenBuffer(*dwDesiredAccess, dwShareMode, lpSecurityAttributes, dwFlags, lpScreenBufferData***)**
DWORD *dwDesiredAccess*;
DWORD *dwShareMode*;
LPSECURITY_ATTRIBUTES *lpSecurityAttributes*;
DWORD *dwFlags*;
PVOID *Reserved*;

The **CreateConsoleScreenBuffer** function creates a console screen buffer and returns a handle to it.

Parameters
dwDesiredAccess   A set of Boolean bit flags that specify the caller's desired access to the console screen buffer.

The following flags are defined:

Flag	Meaning
GENERIC_READ	Read access to the console screen buffer is requested. This allows data to be read from the console screen buffer.
GENERIC_WRITE	Write access to the console screen buffer is requested. This allows data to be written to the console screen buffer.

dwShareMode   A set of Boolean bit flags that specify whether and how this console screen buffer can be shared.

A value of zero specifies that the console screen buffer can not be shared. That is, a value of zero specifies exclusive access.

The following flags are defined:

Flag	Meaning
FILE_SHARE_READ	Other open operations may be performed on the console screen buffer for read access.

Flag	Meaning
FILE_SHARE_WRITE	Other open operations may be performed on the console screen buffer for write access.

lpSecurityAttributes An optional parameter that, if present and supported on the target file system, is a pointer to a **SECURITY_DESCRIPTOR** for the new console screen buffer.

The **SECURITY_DESCRIPTOR** data structure has the following form:

```
typedef PVOID PSECURITY_DESCRIPTOR;
```

dwFlags Specifies the type of console screen buffer to create. The following value has meaning:

Value	Meaning
CONSOLE_TEXTMODE_BUFFER	Specifies the creation of a text console screen buffer.

Reserved Reserved for possible future use. Should be NULL.

Return Value

If the function succeeds, the return value is not −1 (0xFFFFFFFF). The return value is an open handle to the specified console screen buffer. Subsequent access to the file is controlled by the *dwDesiredAccess* parameter.

If the function fails, the return value is 0xFFFFFFFF (−1). Call **GetLastError** for more detailed error information.

Comments

Screen coordinates contained in events are in rows and columns. Screen buffers are created in CONSOLE_WINDOWED_MODE.

The screen buffer handle the function returns can be passed to console output routines.

■ CreateCursor

HCURSOR CreateCursor(*hModule, nXhotspot, nYhotspot, nWidth, nHeight, lpANDbitPlane,***
     lpXORbitPlane)
HANDLE *hModule*;
int *nXhotspot*;
int *nYhotspot*;
int *nWidth*;
int *nHeight*;
LPBYTE *lpANDbitPlane*;
LPBYTE *lpXORbitPlane*;

This function creates a cursor that has specified width, height, and bit patterns.

Parameters

hModule Identifies the module creating the cursor. **GetModuleHandle(NULL)** can be called to return the module handle of the current process.

nXhotspot Specifies the horizontal position of the cursor hotspot.

nYhotspot   Specifies the vertical position of the cursor hotspot.

nWidth   Specifies the width in pixels of the cursor.

nHeight   Specifies the height in pixels of the cursor.

lpANDbitPlane   Points to an array of bytes containing the bit values for the AND mask of the cursor. This can be the bits of a device-dependent monochrome bitmap.

lpXORbitPlane   Points to an array of bytes containing the bit values for the XOR mask of the cursor. This can be the bits of a device-dependent monochrome bitmap.

Return Value   The return value identifies the cursor if the function was successful. Otherwise, it is NULL.

See Also   **LoadCursor, DestroyCursor, GetModuleHandle**

■ CreateDC

HDC CreateDC(*lpDriverName, lpDeviceName, lpPort, lpInitData***)**
LPSTR *lpDriverName*;
LPSTR *lpDeviceName*;
LPSTR *lpPort*;
LPDEVMODE *lpInitData*;

The **CreateDC** function creates a device context for the specified device. The *lpDriverName, lpDeviceName,* and *lpPort* parameters specify the device driver, device name, and physical output medium (file or port), respectively.

Parameters   *lpDriverName*   Points to a null-terminated character string that specifies the name of the device driver (for example, "Epson").

lpDeviceName   Points to a null-terminated character string that specifies the name of the specific device to be supported (for example, "Epson FX-80"). The *lpDeviceName* parameter is used if the device driver supports more than one device.

lpPort   Points to a null-terminated character string that specifies the file or device name for the physical output medium (file or output port).

lpInitData   Points to a **DEVMODE** structure containing device-specific initialization data for the device driver. The **ExtDeviceModeEx** retrieves this structure filled in for a given device. The *lpInitData* parameter must be NULL if the device driver is to use the default initialization (if any) specified by the user through the Control Panel.

Return Value   The return value identifies a device context for the specified device if the function is successful. Otherwise, it is 0.

See Also   **ExtDeviceModeEx**

■ CreateDesktop

BOOL CreateDesktop(*lpDesktop, lpDevice, lpDeskAttrs***)**
LPSTR *lpDesktop*;
LPSTR *lpDevice*;
LPDESKATTRS *lpDeskAttrs*;

This api creates a desktop object with the name **lpDesktop**, with the physical characteristics defined by **lpDevice** and **lpDeskAttrs**. If successful, this will also create a desktop window owned by the process calling **CreateDesktop**. The security for this object will be inherited from the WindowStation object.

Parameters

lpDesktop   This is a NULL terminated string which will name the object to be created. References to this object may be created by calling the api **OpenDesktop**.

lpDevice   This is a NULL terminated string which points to a string naming the physical display device for which this desktop is being created. These device names can be enumerated through the **EnumDisplayDevices** api.

lpDeskAttrs   This is a pointer to a structure which describes the physical attributes of desktop to be created. These attributes have been queried from gdi previous and must match an existing display mode offered by gdi *exactly* or no desktop is created.

Return Value

The return value is TRUE if the function is successful or FALSE if an error occurs.

■ CreateDialog

HWND CreateDialog(*hInstance, lpTemplateName, hWndParent, lpDialogFunc***)**
HANDLE *hInstance*;
LPTSTR *lpTemplateName*;
HWND *hWndParent*;
WNDPROC *lpDialogFunc*;

This function creates a modeless dialog box that has the size, style, and controls defined by the dialog-box template given by the *lpTemplateName* parameter. The *hWndParent* parameter identifies the application window that owns the dialog box. The dialog function pointed to by the *lpDialogFunc* parameter processes any messages received by the dialog box.

The **CreateDialog** function sends a WM_INITDIALOG message to the dialog function before displaying the dialog box. This message allows the dialog function to initialize the dialog-box controls.

CreateDialog returns immediately after creating the dialog box. It does not wait for the dialog box to begin processing input.

The **CreateDialog** function may be used as either a wide-character function (where text arguments must use Unicode) or an ANSI function (where text arguments must use characters from the Windows 3.x character set installed).

Parameters	*hInstance* Identifies the module containing the dialog template resource. **GetModuleHandle(NULL)** can be called to return the module handle of the current process.
	lpTemplateName Points to a character string that names the dialog-box template. The string must be a null-terminated character string.
	hWndParent Identifies the window that owns the dialog box.
	lpDialogFunc Is the procedure-instance address for the dialog function. See the following Comments section for details.
Return Value	The return value is the window handle of the dialog box. It is NULL if the function cannot create the dialog box.
Comments	Use the WS_VISIBLE style for the dialog-box template if the dialog box should appear in the parent window upon creation.
	Use the **DestroyWindow** function to destroy a dialog box created by the **CreateDialog** function.

Callback Function

```
BOOL APIENTRY DialogFunc(hDlg, wMsg, wParam, lParam)
HWND hDlg;
WORD wMsg;
LONG wParam;
LONG lParam;
```

	DialogFunc is a placeholder for the application-supplied function name.
Parameters	*hDlg* Identifies the dialog box that receives the message.
	wMsg Specifies the message number.
	wParam Specifies additional message-dependent information.
	lParam Specifies additional message-dependent information.
Return Value	Except in response to the WM_INITDIALOG message, the dialog function should return nonzero if the function processes the message, and zero if it does not. In response to a WM_INITDIALOG message, the dialog function should return zero if it calls the **SetFocus** function to set the focus to one of the controls in the dialog box. Otherwise, it should return nonzero, in which case Windows will set the focus to the first control in the dialog box that can be given the focus.
Comments	The dialog function is used only if the dialog class is used for the dialog box. This is the default class and is used if no explicit class is given in the dialog-box template. Although the dialog function is similar to a window function, it must not call the **DefWindowProc** function to process unwanted messages. Unwanted messages are processed internally by the dialog-class window function.
See Also	**CreateDialogIndirect, CreateDialogIndirectParam, CreateDialogParam, DestroyWindow, DialogBoxIndirectParam, DialogBoxParam, SetFocus**

■ CreateDialogIndirect

HWND CreateDialogIndirect(*hInstance, lpDialogTemplate, hWndParent, lpDialogFunc*)
HANDLE *hInstance*;
LPDLGTEMPLATESTUB *lpDialogTemplate*;
HWND *hWndParent*;
WNDPROC *lpDialogFunc*;

This function creates a modeless dialog box that has the size, style, and controls defined by the dialog-box template given by the *lpDialogTemplate* parameter. The *hWndParent* parameter identifies the application window that owns the dialog box. The dialog function pointed to by the *lpDialogFunc* parameter processes any messages received by the dialog box.

The **CreateDialogIndirect** function sends a WM_INITDIALOG message to the dialog function before displaying the dialog box. This message allows the dialog function to initialize the dialog-box controls.

CreateDialogIndirect returns immediately after creating the dialog box. It does not wait for the dialog box to begin processing input.

The **CreateDialogIndirect** function may be used as either a wide-character function (where text arguments must use Unicode) or an ANSI function (where text arguments must use characters from the Windows 3.x character set installed).

Parameters
hInstance   Identifies the module creating the dialog. **GetModuleHandle(NULL)** can be called to return the module handle of the current process.

lpDialogTemplate   Points to a block of memory that contains a **DLGTEMPLATE** data structure.

hWndParent   Identifies the window that owns the dialog box.

lpDialogFunc   Is the procedure-instance address of the dialog function. See the following Comments section for details.

Return Value
The return value is the window handle of the dialog box. It is NULL if the function cannot create either the dialog box or any controls in the dialog box.

Comments
Use the WS_VISIBLE style in the dialog-box template if the dialog box should appear in the parent window upon creation.

Callback Function

BOOL APIENTRY *DialogFunc*(*hDlg, wMsg, wParam, lParam*)
HWND *hDlg*;
WORD *wMsg*;
LONG *wParam*;
LONG *lParam*;

DialogFunc is a placeholder for the application-supplied function name.

Parameters *hDlg* Identifies the dialog box that receives the message.

      wMsg Specifies the message number.

      wParam Specifies additional message-dependent information.

      lParam Specifies additional message-dependent information.

Return Value Except in response to the WM_INITDIALOG message, the dialog function should return nonzero if the function processes the message, and zero if it does not. In response to a WM_INITDIALOG message, the dialog function should return zero if it calls the **SetFocus** function to set the focus to one of the controls in the dialog box. Otherwise, it should return nonzero, in which case Windows will set the focus to the first control in the dialog box that can be given the focus.

Comments The dialog function is used only if the dialog class is used for the dialog box. This is the default class and is used if no explicit class is given in the dialog-box template. Although the dialog function is similar to a window function, it must not call the **DefWindowProc** function to process unwanted messages. Unwanted messages are processed internally by the dialog-class window function.

See Also **DefWindowProc, SetFocus, CreateDialog, CreateDialogParam, CreateDialogIndirectParam, DialogBoxParam, DialogBoxIndirectParam**

■ CreateDialogIndirectParam

HWND CreateDialogIndirectParam(*hInstance, lpDialogTemplate, hWndParent, lpDialogFunc, lInitParam***)**
HANDLE *hInstance*;
LPDLGTEMPLATESTUB *lpDialogTemplate*;
HWND *hWndParent*,
WNDPROC *lpDialogFunc*;
LONG *lInitParam*;

    This function creates a modeless dialog box, sends a WM_INITDIALOG message to the dialog function before displaying the dialog box, and passes *lInitParam* as the message *lParam*. This message allows the dialog function to initialize the dialog-box controls. Otherwise, this function is identical to the **CreateDialogIndirect** function.

    For more information on creating a modeless dialog box, see the description of the **CreateDialogIndirect** function.

    The **CreateDialogIndirectParam** function may be used as either a wide-character function (where text arguments must use Unicode) or an ANSI function (where text arguments must use characters from the Windows 3.x character set installed).

Parameters *hInstance* Identifies the module containing the dialog template resource. **GetModuleHandle(NULL)** can be called to return the module handle of the current process.

lpDialogTemplate   Points to a block of memory that contains a **DLGTEMPLATE** data structure.

hWndParent   Identifies the window that owns the dialog box.

lpDialogFunc   Is the procedure-instance address of the dialog function. For details, see the Comments section in the description of the **CreateDialogIndirect** function.

lInitParam   Is a value which **CreateDialogIndirectParam** passes as the *lParam* of a WM_INITDIALOG message to the dialog function when it creates the dialog box.

Return Value   The return value is the window handle of the dialog box. It is NULL if the function cannot create either the dialog box or any controls in the dialog box.

See Also   **CreateDialogIndirect CreateDialog, CreateDialogParam DialogBoxParam, DialogBoxIndirectParam,** WM_INITDIALOG

■ CreateDialogParam

HWND CreateDialogParam(*hInstance, lpTemplateName, hWndParent, lpDialogFunc, lInitParam***)**
HANDLE *hInstance*;
LPTSTR *lpTemplateName*;
HWND *hWndParent*;
WNDPROC *lpDialogFunc*;
LONG *lInitParam*;

This function creates a modeless dialog box, sends a WM_INITDIALOG message to the dialog function before displaying the dialog box, and passes *lInitParam* as the message *lParam*. This message allows the dialog function to initialize the dialog-box controls. Otherwise, this function is identical to the **CreateDialog** function.

For more information on creating a modeless dialog box, see the description of the **CreateDialog** function.

The **CreateDialogParam** function may be used as either a wide-character function (where text arguments must use Unicode) or an ANSI function (where text arguments must use characters from the Windows 3.x character set installed).

Parameters   *hInstance*   Identifies an instance of the module whose executable file contains the dialog-box template.

lpTemplateName   Points to a character string that names the dialog-box template. The string must be a null-terminated character string.

hWndParent   Identifies the window that owns the dialog box.

lpDialogFunc   Is the procedure-instance address for the dialog function. For details, see the Comments section of the **CreateDialog** function.

lInitParam   Is a value which **CreateDialogParam** passes as the *lParam* of a WM_INITDIALOG message to the dialog function when it creates the dialog box.

Return Value   The return value is the window handle of the dialog box. It is NULL if the function cannot create the dialog box.

See Also   **CreateDialog, CreateDialogIndirectParam, DialogBoxParam, DialogBoxIndirectParam,** WM_INITDIALOG

■ CreateDIBitmap

HBITMAP CreateDIBitmap(*hDC, lpInfoHeader, fInit, lpInitBits, lpInitInfo, iUsage***)**
HDC *hDC*;
LPBITMAPINFOHEADER *lpInfoHeader*;
DWORD *fInit*;
LPBYTE *lpInitBits*;
LPBITMAPINFO *lpInitInfo*;
DWORD *iUsage*;

The **CreateDIBitmap** function creates a bitmap from a device-independent bitmap (DIB) specification and optionally sets bits in the bitmap.

Parameters   *hDC*   If non-zero, identifies a device which will be asked to create and manage the bitmap.

lpInfoHeader   Points to a **BITMAPINFOHEADER** structure that describes the desired size and format of the bitmap being created.

fInit   If the CBM_INIT bit is set, **CreateDIBitmap** will initialize the bitmap with the bits specified by *lpInitBits* and *lpInitInfo*.

lpInitBits   Points to a byte array that contains the initial bitmap data. The format of the data depends on the **biBitCount** field of the **BITMAPINFO** structure identified by *lpInitInfo*. See the description of the **BITMAPINFO** structure in Chapter 7, Data Types and Structures in *Reference, Volume 2*, for more information.

lpInitInfo   Points to a **BITMAPINFO** structure that describes the dimensions and color format of *lpInitBits*.

iUsage   Specifies whether the **bmiColors[ ]** field of the *lpInitInfo* data structure was provided and if so, whether **bmiColors[ ]** contains explicit RGB values or indices. The *iUsage* parameter must be one of the following values:

DIB_PAL_COLORS	The color table is provided and consists of an array of 16-bit indices into the palette of the DC the bitmap will be selected into.
DIB_PAL_INDICES	There is no color table for the bitmap. The DIB bits are indices into the *hDC*'s surface palette.
DIB_RGB_COLORS	The color table is provided and contains literal RGB values.

Return Value   The return value identifies the bitmap if the function is successful. Otherwise, it is 0

■ CreateDIBPatternBrush

HBRUSH CreateDIBPatternBrush(*lpPackedDIB***,** *iUsage***)**
GLOBALHANDLE *lpPackedDIB*;
DWORD *iUsage*;

The **CreateDIBPatternBrush** function creates a logical brush that has the pattern specified by the device-independent bitmap (DIB) defined by the *lpPackedDIB* parameter. The brush can subsequently be selected for any device that supports raster operations.

Parameters   *lpPackedDIB*   Identifies a global memory object containing a packed device-independent bitmap. A packed DIB consists of a **BITMAPINFO** data structure immediately followed by the array of bytes which define the pixels of the bitmap.

iUsage   Specifies whether the **bmiColors[ ]** field of the **BITMAPINFO** data structure was provided and if so, whether **bmiColors[ ]** contains explicit RGB values or indices. The *iUsage* parameter must be one of the following values:

DIB_PAL_COLORS	The color table is provided and consists of an array of 16-bit indices into the palette of the DC the brush will be selected into.
DIB_RGB_COLORS	The color table is provided and contains literal RGB values.
DIB_PAL_INDICES	No color table is provided. The bitmap itself contains indices into the palette of the DC which the brush will be selected into.

Return Value   The return value identifies a logical brush if the function is successful. Otherwise, it is 0.

Comments   This call is included only for compatiblity purposes. Applications are discouraged from using this call. An application should use **CreateDIBPatternBrushPt**.

When an application selects a two-color DIB pattern brush into a monochrome device context, Windows ignores the colors specified in the DIB and instead displays the pattern brush using the current background and foreground colors of the device context. Pixels mapped to the first color (at offset 0 in the DIB color table) of the DIB are displayed using the foreground color, and pixels mapped to the second color (at offset 1 in the color table) are displayed using the background color.

See Also   **CreateDIBPatternBrushPt, SetTextColor, SetBkColor**

■ CreateDIBPatternBrushPt

HBRUSH CreateDIBPatternBrushPt(*lpPackedDIB, iUsage***)**
LPVOID *lpPackedDIB*;
DWORD *iUsage*;

The **CreateDIBPatternBrushPt** function creates a logical brush that has the pattern specified by the device-independent bitmap (DIB) defined by the *lpPackedDIB* parameter. The brush can subsequently be selected for any device that supports raster operations.

Parameters   *lpPackedDIB*   Pointer to a packed device-independent bitmap. A packed DIB consists of a **BITMAPINFO** data structure immediately followed by the array of bytes which define the pixels of the bitmap.

iUsage   Specifies whether the **bmiColors[ ]** field of the **BITMAPINFO** data structure was provided and if so, whether **bmiColors[ ]** contains explicit RGB values or indices. The *iUsage* parameter must be one of the following values:

DIB_PAL_COLORS	The color table is provided and consists of an array of 16-bit indices into the palette of the DC the brush will be selected into.
DIB_RGB_COLORS	The color table is provided and contains literal RGB values.
DIB_PAL_INDICES	No color table is provided. The bitmap itself contains indices into the palette of the DC which the brush will be selected into.

Return Value   The return value identifies a logical brush if the function is successful. Otherwise, it is 0.

■ CreateDIBSection

HBITMAP CreateDIBSection(*hDC, lpInfo, fInit, iUsage, lppBits***)**
IN HDC *hDC*;
IN LPBITMAPINFO *lpInfo*;
IN DWORD *fInit*;
IN DWORD *iUsage*;
OUT LPPBYTE *lppBits*;

The **CreateDIBSection** function creates a DIB bitmap from a device-independent bitmap (DIB) specification.

Parameters   *hDC*   If non-zero, identifies the DC that contains the logical palette to use for the DIB_PAL_COLORS initializer.

lpInfo   Points to a **BITMAPINFO** structure that describes the desired size and format of the bitmap being created and specifies the initial palette.

fInit   Specifies whether the bitmap's first scanline is the top scan or bottom scan.

BMF_TOPDOWN	The first scanline in the buffer *lppBits* is the top scanline.

BMF_DIB	The first scanline in the buffer *lppBits* is the bottom scanline.

iUsage Specifies whether the **bmiColors[ ]** field of *lpInfo* data structure contains explicit RGB values or indices into the currently realized logical palette.

DIB_PAL_COLORS	The color table is provided and consists of an array of 16-bit indices into the logical palette of the hDC.
DIB_RGB_COLORS	The color table is provided and contains literal RGB values.

lppBits Address of a pointer that GDI will fill in with the pointer to the memory allocated for the bits. The application can use this to access the bitmap bits directly. The bits will be stored in the format requested in *lpInfo*, scanlines are aligned on DWORD boundaries.

Return Value The return value identifies the bitmap if the function is successful. Otherwise, it is 0.

■ CreateDirectory

BOOL CreateDirectory(*lpPathName*, *lpSecurityAttributes***)**
LPTSTR *lpPathName*;
LPSECURITY_ATTRIBUTES *lpSecurityAttributes*;

A directory can be created using **CreateDirectory**.

The **CreateDirectory** function may be used as either a wide-character function (where text arguments must use Unicode) or an ANSI function (where text arguments must use characters from the Windows 3.x character set installed).

Parameters *lpPathName* Supplies the pathname of the directory to be created.

lpSecurityAttributes An optional parameter that, if present, and supported on the target file system supplies a security descriptor for the new directory.

Return Value The return value is TRUE if the function is successful. Otherwise, it is FALSE in which case extended error information is available from the **GetLastError** function.

This API causes a directory with the specified pathname to be created. If the underlying file system supports security on files and directories, then the **SecurityDescriptor** argument is applied to the new directory.

This call is similar to DOS (int 21h, function 39h) and OS/2's **DosCreateDir**.

See Also **RemoveDirectory**

■ CreateDiscardableBitmap

HBITMAP CreateDiscardableBitmap(*hDC, nWidth, nHeight***)**
HDC *hDC*;
int *nWidth*;
int *nHeight*;

The **CreateDiscardableBitmap** function creates a discardable bitmap that is compatible with the device identified by the *hDC* parameter. The bitmap has the same bits-per-pixel format and the same color palette as the specified device. An application can select this bitmap as the current bitmap for a memory device that is compatible with the one specified by the *hDC* parameter.

Parameters   *hDC*   Identifies a device context.

nWidth   Specifies the width (in bits) of the bitmap.

nHeight   Specifies the height (in bits) of the bitmap.

Return Value   The return value identifies a bitmap if the function is successful. Otherwise, it is NULL.

Comments   Under 32 bit Windows this function is the same as CreateCompatibleBitmap. The call is include only for compatibility purposes.

See Also   **CreateCompatibleBitmap**

■ CreateEllipticRgn

HRGN CreateEllipticRgn(*X1, Y1, X2, Y2***)**
int *X1*;
int *Y1*;
int *X2*;
int *Y2*;

The **CreateEllipticRgn** function creates an elliptical region.

Parameters   *X1*   Specifies the *x*-coordinate of the upper-left corner of the bounding rectangle of the ellipse.

Y1   Specifies the *y*-coordinate of the upper-left corner of the bounding rectangle of the ellipse.

X2   Specifies the *x*-coordinate of the lower-right corner of the bounding rectangle of the ellipse.

Y2   Specifies the *y*-coordinate of the lower-right corner of the bounding rectangle of the ellipse.

Return Value   The return value identifies a new region if the function is successful. Otherwise, it is 0.

■ CreateEllipticRgnIndirect

HRGN CreateEllipticRgnIndirect(*lpRect***)**
LPRECT *lpRect*;

The **CreateEllipticRgnIndirect** function creates an elliptical region.

Parameters   *lpRect*   Points to a RECT data structure that contains the coordinates of the upper-left and lower-right corners of the bounding rectangle of the ellipse.

Return Value   The return value identifies a new region if the function is successful. Otherwise, it is 0.

■ CreateEvent

HANDLE CreateEvent(*lpEventAttributes, bManualReset, bInitialState, lpName***)**
LPSECURITY_ATTRIBUTES *lpEventAttributes*;
BOOL *bManualReset*;
BOOL *bInitialState*;
LPTSTR *lpName*;

The **CreateEvent** function creates a named or unnamed event object and opens a handle to access it.

The **CreateEvent** function may be used as either a wide-character function (where text arguments must use Unicode) or an ANSI function (where text arguments must use characters from the Windows 3.x character set installed).

Parameters   *lpEventAttributes*   Pointer to a **SECURITY_ATTRIBUTES** data structure. This is an optional parameter that may be used to specify the security attributes of the new event.

The **SECURITY_ATTRIBUTES** data structure has the following form:

```
typedef struct tagSECURITY_ATTRIBUTES {
    DWORD   nLength;
    LPVOID  lpSecurityDescriptor;
    BOOL    bInheritHandle;
} SECURITY_ATTRIBUTES;
```

If the parameter is not specified, then the event is created without a security descriptor, and the resulting handle is not inherited on process creation.

bManualReset   Specifies whether the event must be manually reset. If the value is TRUE, it must be. If the value is FALSE, then after releasing a single waiter, the system automaticaly resets the event.

bInitialState   Specifies the initial state of the event object. If the value is TRUE, the event's current state value is set to one, the Signaled state. If the value is FALSE, it is set to zero, the Not-Signaled state.

lpName   Pointer to a string containing the name of the event. The creation will fail if this name matches the name of an existing named object.

The NULL-terminated name may contain any character except the pathname separator character "\".

If lpName is NULL, the event will be created without a name.

Return Value

If the function is successful, the return value is a handle to the new event.

If the function fails, the return value is NULL. Further information can be obtained by calling **GetLastError**.

Comments

The handle that **CreateEvent** returns has full access to the new event object. It may be used with any API function that requires a handle to an event object.

The **CreateEvent** function creates an event object with the specified initial state. If an event is in the Signaled state (TRUE), a wait operation on the event does not block. If the event is in the Not-Signaled state (FALSE), a wait operation on the event blocks until the specified event attains a state of Signaled, or the timeout value is exceeded.

In addition to the STANDARD_RIGHTS_REQUIRED access flags, the following object type specific access flags are valid for event objects:

Type	Meaning
EVENT_MODIFY_STATE	Modify state access (set and reset) to the event is desired.
SYNCHRONIZE	Synchronization access (wait) to the event is desired.
EVENT_ALL_ACCESS	This set of access flags specifies all of the possible access flags for an event object.

These object specific access flags are used when duplicating the event handle via **DuplicateHandle**.

In addition to the standard object sharing mechanisms available in Windows32 — inheritance and calls to **DuplicateHandle** — named events may be opened by any thread with appropriate access using **OpenEvent**. This allows the event object to be shared by any application that knows the name of the event.

See Also

CreateEvent, OpenEvent

■ CreateFile

```
HANDLE CreateFile(lpFileName, dwDesiredAccess, dwShareMode, lpSecurityAttributes,
        dwCreationDisposition, dwFlagsAndAttributes, hTemplateFile)
LPTSTR lpFileName;
DWORD dwDesiredAccess;
DWORD dwShareMode;
LPSECURITY_ATTRIBUTES lpSecurityAttributes;
DWORD dwCreationDisposition;
DWORD dwFlagsAndAttributes;
HANDLE hTemplateFile;
```

The **CreateFile** function creates, opens, or truncates a file, returning a handle that can be used to access the file. The handle allows reading data, writing data, and moving the file pointer.

The **CreateFile** function may be used as either a wide-character function (where text arguments must use Unicode) or an ANSI function (where text arguments must use characters from the Windows 3.x character set installed).

Parameters

lpFileName   Supplies the file name of the file to open. Depending on the value of the *dwCreationDisposition* parameter, this name may or may not already exist. This is a null-terminated string.

dwDesiredAccess   Supplies the caller's desired access to the file. It may be one of the following values:

Value	Meaning
GENERIC_READ	Read access to the file is requested. This allows data to be read from the file and the file pointer to be modified.
GENERIC_WRITE	Write access to the file is requested. This allows data to be written to the file and the file pointer to be modified.

dwShareMode   Supplies a set of flags that indicates how this file is to be shared with other openers of the file. A value of zero for this parameter indicates no sharing of the file, or exclusive access to the file is to occur.

Value	Meaning
FILE_SHARE_READ	Other open operations may be performed on the file for read access.
FILE_SHARE_WRITE	Other open operations may be performed on the file for write access.

lpSecurityAttributes   An optional parameter that, if present, and supported on the target file system supplies a security descriptor for the new file.

dwCreationDisposition   Supplies a creation disposition that specifies how this call is to operate. This parameter must be one of the following values:

Value	Meaning
CREATE_NEW	Create a new file. If the specified file already exists, then fail. The attributes for the new file are what is specified in the *dwFlagsAndAttributes* parameter or'd with FILE_ATTRIBUTE_ARCHIVE. If the *hTemplateFile* is specified, then the file's security descriptor is assigned using the value of the template file. Otherwise, the security descriptor comes from the security descriptor attribute.

Value	Meaning
CREATE_ALWAYS	Always create the file. If the file already exists, then it is overwritten. The attributes for the new file are what is specified in the *dwFlagsAndAttributes* parameter or'd with FILE_ATTRIBUTE_ARCHIVE. If the *hTemplateFile* is specified, then the file's security descriptor is assigned using the value of the template file. Otherwise, the security descriptor comes from the security descriptor attribute.
OPEN_EXISTING	Open the file, but if it does not exist, then fail the call. The attributes and security descriptor of the file are not modified.
OPEN_ALWAYS	Open the file if it exists. If it does not exist, then create the file using the same rules as if the disposition were CREATE_NEW.
TRUNCATE_EXISTING	Open the file, but if it does not exist, then fail the call. Once opened, the file is truncated such that its size is zero bytes. The attributes and security descriptor of the file are not modified. This disposition requires that the caller open the file with at least GENERIC_WRITE access.

dwFlagsAndAttributes Specifies the file attributes for the file. Any combination of flags is acceptable except that all other flags override the normal file attribute, FILE_ATTRIBUTE_NORMAL.

Flag	Meaning
FILE_ATTRIBUTE_NORMAL	A normal file should be created.
FILE_ATTRIBUTE_READONLY	A read-only file should be created.
FILE_ATTRIBUTE_HIDDEN	A hidden file should be created.
FILE_ATTRIBUTE_SYSTEM	A system file should be created.
FILE_FLAG_WRITE_THROUGH	Indicates that the system should always write through any intermediate cache and go directly to the file. The system may still cache writes, but may not lazily flush the writes.

Flag	Meaning
FILE_FLAG_OVERLAPPED	Indicates that the system should initialize the file so that **ReadFile, WriteFile, ConnectNamedPipe** and **TransactNamedPipe** operations that take a significant time to process will return ERROR_IO_PENDING. An event will be set to the signalled state when the operation completes. When FILE_FLAG_OVERLAPPED is specified the system will not maintain the file pointer. The position to Read/Write from is passed to the system as part of the Overlapped structure argument to **ReadFile** and **WriteFile**. Specifying FILE_FLAG_OVERLAPPED also enables more than one operation to be simultaneously performed with the handle (a simultaneous ReadFile and WriteFile, for example).
FILE_FLAG_NO_BUFFERING	Indicates that the file is to be opened with no intermediate buffering or caching done by the system. Reads and writes to the file must be done on sector boundaries. Buffer addresses for reads and writes must be aligned on at least disk sector boundaries in memory. The call will fail if these boundary conditions are not met. You can determine sector size by calling the **GetDiskFreeSpace** API function.
FILE_FLAG_RANDOM_ACCESS	Specifies a flag which tells the system that the opened file will be accessed randomly. This flag may be used as a hint by the system to influence its cacheing of the file.
FILE_FLAG_SEQUENTIAL_SCAN	Specifies a flag which tells the system that the file will be accessed sequentially from beginning to end with no backing up or modifying the file pointer. This may be used as a hint by the file system caching logic. The programmer may in fact set the file pointer or randomly access the bit. If this occurs, optimum caching may not occur.

hTemplateFile   An optional parameter, then if specified, supplies a handle with GENERIC_READ access to a template file. The template file is used to supply attributes for the file being created. These attributes include the security descriptor, file attributes, extended attributes. When the new file is created, the relevant attributes from the template file are used in creating the new file. These attributes override any attributes supplied as explicit parameters (e.g. *lpSecurityAttributes*, *dwFlagsAndAttributes*).

Return Value

If the return value is not equal to –1 (0xFFFFFFFF), it is an open handle to the specified file.

If the return value is equal to –1 (0xFFFFFFFF), the function has failed. Call the **GetLastError** function for further information.

Comments

Subsequent access to the file is controlled by the *DesiredAccess* parameter.

If a file is created as a result of calling the **CreateFile** function, the following action will be taken:

- The attributes of the file are determined by the value of the *dwFlagsAndAttributes* parameter or'd with the FILE_ATTRIBUTE_ARCHIVE bit.

- The length of the file will be set to zero.

- If the *hTemplateFile* parameter is specified, the security descriptor and any extended attributes associated with the file are assigned to the new file. Otherwise, the security attributes assigned to the new file come from the *lpSecurityAttributes* parameter (or from the containing directory).

If an existing file is opened as a result of calling the **CreateFile** function, the *dwFlagsAndAttributes*, *hTemplateFile*, and *lpSecurityAttributes* parameters are ignored.

If the name given to **CreateFile** is a named pipe name then **CreateFile** opens the client end of the named pipe. **CreateFile** will use any instance of the named pipe that is in the listening state. Once opened by **CreateFile** the named pipe instance cannot be opened by another client; however, the opening process can duplicate the handle as many times as required. The desired access given when a pipe is opened must be consistent with the OpenMode given to **CreateNamedPipe**. Pipes are always opened with the pipe-specific states set to block read and write operations and read as a byte stream. The pipe specific states may be modified with **SetNamedPipeHandleState**.

For DOS based systems running share.exe the file sharing semantics work as described above. Without share.exe no share level protection exists.

This call is logically equivalent to DOS (int 21h, function 5Bh), or DOS (int 21h, function 3Ch) depending on the value of the *FailIfExists* parameter.

Example

This example returns a handle to the current console input buffer:

```
hReadWriteInput = CreateFile("CONIN$",
   GENERIC_READ | GENERIC_WRITE,
   0, /* exclusive access */
```

```
            NULL,
            OPEN_EXISTING,
            0,
            NULL
            );
```

See Also   **OpenFile, GetDiskFreeSpace**

■ CreateFileMapping

HANDLE CreateFileMapping(*hFile, lpFileMappingAttributes, flProtect, dwMaximumSizeHigh,*
  *dwMaximumSizeLow, lpName***)**
HANDLE *hFile*;
LPSECURITY_ATTRIBUTES *lpFileMappingAttributes*;
DWORD *flProtect*;
DWORD *dwMaximumSizeHigh*;
DWORD *dwMaximumSizeLow*;
LPTSTR *lpName*;

The **CreateFileMapping** function creates a named or unnamed file mapping object for a specified file.

The **CreateFileMapping** function may be used as either a wide-character function (where text arguments must use Unicode) or an ANSI function (where text arguments must use characters from the Windows 3.x character set installed).

Parameters   *hFile* Supplies an open handle to the file the function will create a mapping object for. The file must be opened with an access mode that is compatible with the protection flags specified by *flProtect*.

A caller can specify (HANDLE)0xFFFFFFFF as the value for *hFile* When this is done, the caller must also specify a mapping object size via the *dwMaximumSizeHigh* and *dwMaximumSizeLow* parameters. The function will create a file mapping object of the specified size that is backed by the system paging file rather than by a named file in the file system. The file mapping object so created can be shared through duplication, inheritance, or by name.

This feature — backing to the system paging file — provides a simple means to create named, shared memory in situations where there is no need for the persistence of a file. The system takes care of reclaiming the page file space when the mapping object is no longer in use. The programmer need not manage, nor worry about the disposal of, a temporary file.

lpFileMappingAttributes Pointer to a **SECURITY_ATTRIBUTES** data structure. This is an optional parameter that may be used to specify the security attributes of the new file mapping object.

The **SECURITY_ATTRIBUTES** data structure has the following form:

```
typedef struct tagSECURITY_ATTRIBUTES {
    DWORD   nLength;
    LPVOID  lpSecurityDescriptor;
    BOOL    bInheritHandle;
} SECURITY_ATTRIBUTES;
```

If the parameter is not specified, then the file mapping object is created without a security descriptor, and the resulting handle is not inherited on process creation.

flProtect   Specifies the protection desired for the mapping object when the file is mapped.

Value	Meaning
PAGE_READONLY	Read access to the committed region of pages is allowed. An attempt to write or execute the committed region results in an access violation. The file specified by *hFile* must have been created with GENERIC_READ access.
PAGE_READWRITE	Read and write access to the committed region of pages is allowed. The file specified by *hFile* must have been created with GENERIC_READ and GENERIC_WRITE access.

dwMaximumSizeHigh   Specifies the high order 32-bits of the maximum size of the file mapping object.

dwMaximumSizeLow   Supplies the low order 32-bits of the maximum size of the file mapping object. A value of zero along with a value of zero in *dwMaximumSizeHigh* indicates that the maximum size of the file mapping object is equal to the current size of the file specified by *hFile*.

lpName   Pointer to a string containing the name of the file mapping object.

The NULL-terminated name may contain any character except the pathname seperator character "\".

If lpName is NULL, the file mapping object will be created without a name.

Return Value

If the function is successful, the return value is a handle to the new file mapping object.

If the function fails, the return value is NULL. Further information can be obtained by calling **GetLastError**.

Comments

The handle that **CreateFileMapping** returns has full access to the new file mapping object. It may be used with any API function that requires a handle to a file mapping object.

Creating a file mapping object creates the potential for mapping a view of the file into an address space. File mapping objects may be shared either through process creation, handle duplication, or by name. Having a handle to a file mapping object allows for mapping of the file. It does not mean that the file is actually mapped.

A file mapping object has a maximum size. This is used to size the file. A file may not grow beyond the size specified in the mapping object.

It is recommended, though not required, that files you intend to map be opened for exclusive access. Win32 does not require that a mapped file and a file accessed via the input/output primitive functions (**ReadFile/WriteFile**) are coherent. Win32 does guarantee that all views of a single mapping object are coherent. This means that if multiple processes have a handle to a given file mapping object, they will see a coherent view of the data when they map a view of the object. Using named file mapping objects in conjunction with opening a named file mapping object is very similar to using named shared memory.

In addition to the STANDARD_RIGHTS_REQUIRED access flags, the following object type specific access flags are valid for file mapping objects:

Value	Meaning
FILE_MAP_WRITE	Write map access to the file mapping object is desired. This allows a writable view of the file to be mapped. Note that if *flProtect* does not include PAGE_READWRITE, this access type does not allow writing the mapped file.
FILE_MAP_READ	Read map access to the file mapping object is desired. This allows a readablee view of the file to be mapped.
FILE_MAP_ALL_ACCESS	This set of access flags specifies all of the possible access flags for a file mapping object.

These object specific access flags are used when duplicating the file mapping handle via **DuplicateHandle**.

See Also   **CreateFileMapping, OpenFileMapping**

■ CreateFont

HFONT CreateFont(*nHeight*, *nWidth*, *nEscapement*, *nOrientation*, *nWeight*, *cItalic*, *cUnderline*, *cStrikeOut*, *iCharSet*, *iOutputPrecision*, *iClipPrecision*, *iQuality*, *iPitchAndFamily*, *lpFacename***)**
int *nHeight*;
int *nWidth*;
int *nEscapement*;
int *nOrientation*;
int *nWeight*;
DWORD *cItalic*;
DWORD *cUnderline*;
DWORD *cStrikeOut*;
DWORD *iCharSet*;
DWORD *iOutputPrecision*;
DWORD *iClipPrecision*;
DWORD *iQuality*;
DWORD *iPitchAndFamily*;
LPTSTR *lpFacename*;

The **CreateFont** function creates a logical font that has the specified characteristics. The logical font can subsequently be selected as the font for any device.

The **CreateFont** function may be used as either a wide-character function (where text arguments must use Unicode) or an ANSI function (where text arguments must use characters from the Windows 3.x character set

Parameters

nHeight   Specifies the desired height (in logical units) of the font. The font height can be specified in three ways: If *nHeight* is greater than zero, it is transformed into device units and matched against the cell height of the available fonts. If it is zero, a reasonable default size is used. If it is less than zero, it is transformed into device units and the absolute value is matched against the character height of the available fonts. For all height comparisons, the font mapper looks for the largest font that does not exceed the requested size, and, if there is no such font, looks for the smallest font available. This mapping will occur when the font is actually used for the first time.

nWidth   Specifies the average width (in logical units) of characters in the font. If *nWidth* is zero, the aspect ratio of the device will be matched against the digitization aspect ratio of the available fonts to find the closest match, determined by the absolute value of the difference.

nEscapement   Specifies the angle (in tenths of degrees) of each line of text written in the font (relative to the bottom of the page).

nOrientation   Specifies the angle (in tenths of degrees) of each character's baseline (relative to the bottom of the page).

nWeight   Specifies the desired weight of the font in the range 0 to 1000 (for example, 400 is normal, 700 is bold). If *nWeight* is zero, a default weight is used.

cItalic   **TRUE** if the desired font is Italic.

cUnderline   **TRUE** if text drawn with this font will be underlined.

cStrikeOut   **TRUE** if text drawn with this font will be struck out.

iCharSet   Specifies the desired character set. The following values are predefined:

ANSI_CHARSET
OEM_CHARSET
SYMBOL_CHARSET
UNICODE_CHARSET

Fonts with other character sets may exist in the system. If an application uses a font with an unknown character set, it should not attempt to translate or interpret strings that are to be rendered with that font.

iOutputPrecision   Specifies the desired output precision. The output precision defines how closely the output must match the requested font's height, width, character orientation, escapement, and pitch. It can be any one of the following values:

OUT_CHARACTER_PRECIS
OUT_DEFAULT_PRECIS
OUT_STRING_PRECIS
OUT_STROKE_PRECIS

iClipPrecision   Specifies the desired clipping precision. The clipping precision defines how to clip characters that are partially outside the clipping region. It can be any one of the following values:

CLIP_CHARACTER_PRECIS
CLIP_DEFAULT_PRECIS
CLIP_STROKE_PRECIS

iQuality   Specifies the desired output quality. The output quality defines how carefully GDI must attempt to match the logical-font attributes to those of an actual physical font. It can be any one of the following values:

DEFAULT_QUALITY
DRAFT_QUALITY
PROOF_QUALITY

iPitchAndFamily   Specifies the pitch and family of the font. The two low-order bits specify the pitch of the font and can be any one of the following values:

DEFAULT_PITCH
FIXED_PITCH
VARIABLE_PITCH

Bits 4 through 7 of the field specify the font family and can be any one of the following values:

FF_DECORATIVE
FF_DONTCARE
FF_MODERN
FF_ROMAN
FF_SCRIPT
FF_SWISS

lpFacename   Points to a null-terminated character string that specifies the typeface name of the font. The length of this string must not exceed 32 characters. The **EnumFonts** function can be used to enumerate the typeface names of all currently available fonts.

Return Value   The return value identifies a logical font if the function is successful. Otherwise, it is NULL.

■ CreateFontIndirect

HFONT CreateFontIndirect(*lpLogFont***)**
LPLOGFONT *lpLogFont*;

The **CreateFontIndirect** function creates a logical font that has the characteristics given in the structure pointed to by the *lpLogFont* parameter. The font can subsequently be selected as the current font for any device context.

Parameters   *lpLogFont*   Points to a **LOGFONT** structure that defines the characteristics of the logical font.

Return Value

The return value identifies a logical font if the function is successful. Otherwise, it is 0.

Comments

The **CreateFontIndirect** function creates a logical font that has all the specified characteristics. When the font is selected by using the **SelectObject** function, GDI's font mapper attempts to match the logical font with an existing physical font. If it fails to find an exact match, it provides an alternate whose characteristics match as many of the requested characteristics as possible. For a description of the font mapper, see Chapter 2, Graphics Device Interface Functions.

■ CreateHatchBrush

HBRUSH CreateHatchBrush(*nIndex, crColor***)**
int *nIndex*;
COLORREF *crColor*;

The **CreateHatchBrush** function creates a logical brush that has the specified hatched pattern and color. The brush can subsequently be selected as the current brush for any device context.

Parameters

nIndex Specifies the hatch style of the brush. It can be any one of the following values:

Value	Meaning
HS_BDIAGONAL	45-degree downward hatch (left to right)
HS_CROSS	Horizontal and vertical crosshatch
HS_DIAGCROSS	45-degree crosshatch
HS_FDIAGONAL	45-degree downward hatch (left to right)
HS_HORIZONTAL	Horizontal hatch
HS_VERTICAL	Vertical hatch

crColor Specifies the foreground color of the brush (the color of the hatches).

Return Value

The return value identifies a logical brush if the function is successful. Otherwise, it is 0.

■ CreateIC

HDC CreateIC(*lpDriverName, lpDeviceName, lpPort, lpInitData***)**
LPSTR *lpDriverName*;
LPSTR *lpDeviceName*;
LPSTR *lpPort*;
LPSTR *lpInitData*;

The **CreateIC** function creates an information context for the specified device. The information context provides a fast way to get information about the device without creating a device context.

Parameters

lpDriverName   Points to a null-terminated character string that specifies the name of the device driver (for example, "Epson").

lpDeviceName   Points to a null-terminated character string that specifies the name of the specific device to be supported (for example, "Epson FX-80"). The *lpDeviceName* parameter is used if the device driver supports more than one device.

lpPort   Points to a null-terminated character string that specifies the file or device name for the physical output medium (file or output port).

lpInitData   Points to a **DEVMODE** structure containing device-specific initialization data for the device driver. The **ExtDeviceModeEx** retrieves this structure filled in for a given device. The *lpInitData* parameter must be NULL if the device driver is to use the default initialization (if any) specified by the user through the Control Panel.

Return Value

The return value identifies an information context for the specified device if the function is successful. Otherwise, it is 0.

Comments

GDI output functions will not produce any output when used with an information context.

■ CreateIcon

HICON CreateIcon(*hModule*, *nWidth*, *nHeight*, *nPlanes*, *nBitsPixel*, *lpANDbits*, *lpXORbits*)
HANDLE *hModule*;
int *nWidth*;
int *nHeight*;
BYTE *nPlanes*;
BYTE *nBitsPixel*;
LPBYTE *lpANDbits*;
LPBYTE *lpXORbits*;

This function creates an icon that has specified width, height, colors, and bit patterns.

Parameters

hModule   Identifies the module creating the icon. **GetModuleHandle(NULL)** can be called to return the module handle of the current process.

nWidth   Specifies the width in pixels of the icon.

nHeight   Specifies the height in pixels of the icon.

nPlanes   Specifies the number of planes in the XOR mask of the icon.

nBitsPixel   Specifies the number of bits per pixel in the XOR mask of the icon.

lpANDbits   Points to an array of bytes that contains the bit values for the AND mask of the icon. This array must specify a monochrome mask.

lpXORbits   Points to an array of bytes that contains the bit values for the XOR mask of the icon. This can be the bits of a monochrome or device-dependent color bitmap.

Return Value   The return value identifies an icon if the function is successful. Otherwise, it is
                            NULL.

See Also   **DestroyIcon, LoadIcon**

■ CreateIconFromResource

HICON CreateIconFromResource(*presbits, dwResSize, fIcon, dwVer*)
PBYTE *presbits*;
DWORD *dwResSize*;
BOOL *fIcon*;
DWORD *dwVer*;

The **CreateIconFromResource** function creates an icon or cursor from resource
bits describing the icon.

Parameters   *presbits*   A pointer to the icon or cursor resource bits.

                            dwResSize   Specifies the size in bytes of the set of bits pointed to by *presbits*.

                            fIcon   Specifies whether an icon or a cursor is to be created. A value of TRUE
                            specifies an icon, FALSE specifies a cursor. An icon has a predefined hot spot,
                            while a cursor has a hotspot at its center.

                            dwVer   Specifies an icon/cursor format version number for the resource bits
                            pointed to by *presbits*. If those bits are in the Windows 2.X format, then *dwVer*
                            should be 0x00020000. If the resource bits are in the Windows 3.x format, then
                            dwVer should be 0x00030000. All applications marked as Windows 3.X
                            applications or as Windows 32 applications use the Windows 3.x format for icons
                            and cursors.

Return Value   If the function is successful, the return value is a handle to the icon or cursor.

                            If the function is unsuccessful, the return value is NULL. More detailed
                            information can be obtained by calling the **GetLastError** function.

Comments   The resource bits pointed to by *presbits* are typically loaded by calls to
                            LookupIconIdFromDirectory and **LoadResource**. Here is some typical code; in
                            order to save space, we haven't included function result error checking, but your
                            code should :

```
/*
 * Step 1: Lookup the icon id from the directory.
 */

/* locate an icon directory named FLOPPY */
h = FindResource(ghInstance, "FLOPPY", RT_GROUP_ICON);

/* load and lock that icon directory */
h = LoadResource(ghInstance, h);
p = LockResource(h);

/* search the icon directory to get
   a resource id for the icon that best
   fits the current display device */
id = LookupIconIdFromDirectory(p, TRUE);
```

```
/* unlock and free the icon directory */
UnlockResource(h);
FreeResource(h);

/*
 * Step 2: Load the bits and create an icon from them.
 */

/* locate that best fit icon's resource bits */
h = FindResource(ghInstance,
    MAKEINTRESOURCE(id), MAKEINTRESOURCE(RT_ICON));

/* determine the size of the icon resource bits */
cb = SizeofResource(ghInstance, h);

/* load and lock the icon resource bits */
h = LoadResource(ghInstance, h);
p = LockResource(h);

/* create an icon from the icon resource bits */
ghIcon = CreateIconFromResource(p, cb, TRUE, 0x00030000);

/* unlock and free the icon resource bits */
UnlockResource(h);
FreeResource(h);
```

These icon API functions — **LookupIconIdFromDirectory**, **CreateIconFromResource**, **GetIconInfo**, **CreateIconIndirect** — exist so that shell applications and icon browsers can look through resources efficiently, load / play / store resource bits, and perform similar operations.

See Also   **CreateIconIndirect, GetIconInfo, LookupIconIdFromDirectory**

■ CreateIconIndirect

HICON CreateIconIndirect(*piconinfo***)**
PICONINFO *piconinfo*;

The **CreateIconIndirect** function creates an icon or cursor from an **ICONINFO** data structure.

Parameters   *piconinfo*   A pointer to an **ICONINFO** structure. The function will use the information in this structure's fields to create the icon or cursor. The **ICONINFO** structure is defined as follows:

```
typedef struct _ICONINFO {
    BOOL    fIcon;
    DWORD   xHotspot;
    DWORD   yHotspot;
    HBITMAP hbmMask;
    HBITMAP hbmColor;
} ICONINFO ;
```

For detailed information on the fields of this structure, see **ICONINFO**.

The system will make a COPY of the hbmMask and hbmColor bitmaps in order to create the icon or cursor.

Return Value

If the function is successful, the return value is a handle to the icon or cursor that is created.

If the function fails, the return value is NULL. More detailed information can be obtained by calling the **GetLastError** function.

Comments

The **ICONINFO** structure contains a flag indicating whether the structure describes an icon or a cursor, x and y coordinates for the icon's hotspot, and two bitmaps to be used for the icon or cursor . Icons or cursors are drawn with an AND mask, and an XOR mask. For color icons, the XOR mask is in color. The AND mask removes bits from the destination, and the XOR mask puts bits into the destination.

Since the system makes copies of the bitmaps passed in via hbmMask and hbmColor, it is up to the application to manage the original bitmaps even after calling the CreateIconIndirect function. The application must delete these bitmaps when they are no longer needed.

See Also

CreateIcon, CreateIconFromResource, DestroyIcon, DrawIcon, GetIconInfo, LoadIcon, LookupIconIdFromDirectory,

■ CreateMailslot

HANDLE CreateMailslot(_lpName, nMaxMessageSize, nMailslotSize, lReadTimeout,_
   lpSecurityAttributes**)**
LPTSTR _lpName_;
DWORD _nMaxMessageSize_;
DWORD _nMailslotSize_;
DWORD _lReadTimeout_;
LPSECURITY_ATTRIBUTES _lpSecurityAttributes_;

The **CreateMailslot** function creates a local mailslot with a given name (it is an error if a mailslot with that name already exists) and returns a handle for serving-side operations on that mailslot.

The **CreateMailslot** function may be used as either a wide-character function (where text arguments must use Unicode) or an ANSI function (where text arguments must use characters from the Windows 3.x character set installed).

Parameters

lpName   A pointer to the name of the mailslot. This must be a local mailslot name, of the form:

    \\.\MAILSLOT\name

where "name" is a standard file name (and may include multiple levels of pseudo-directories separated by backslashes).

nMaxMessageSize   Maximum size of a single message that can be written to the mailslot, in bytes. This may be ignored by an implementation.

nMailslotSize   Size of the mailslot buffer, in bytes. This can be a numeric value or a special equate. This may also be ignored by an implementation.

Value	Meaning
MAILSLOT_SIZE_AUTO	Set value based on *nMaxMessageSize*. (The relationship is implementation-dependent.) This equate has a value of 0, for compatibility with the LanMan 2.0 **DosMakeMailslot** API.

lReadTimeout   The amount of time, in milliseconds, to wait for a message to be written to the mailslot before timing out a read operation.

Value	Meaning
0	Return immediately if no message is present. (This is not treated as an error.)
MAILSLOT_WAIT_FOREVER	Wait forever for a message. (This equate must have a value of −1, for compatibility with LanMan 2.0 applications.)

lpSecurityAttributes   An optional parameter that, if present and supported on the target system, supplies a security descriptor for the mailslot. This parameter includes the bInheritHandle flag, which defaults to FALSE if this parameter isn't present. (See the Win32 Base APIs document section on CreateProcess for more info.)

Return Value   If the function fails, the return value is 0xFFFFFFFF. More detailed information can be obtained by calling the **GetLastError** function.

If the function succeeds, the return value is a server side handle to the mailslot, for use in subsequent mailslot operations.

Comments   The mailslot exists until:

1. the last (possibly inherited or duplicated) handle to it is closed via CloseHandle

OR

2. the process owning the last (possibly inherited or duplicated) handle exits, whichever comes first.

This last item is important, as it is a documented way to do things with the DosXxxMailslot APIs.

See Also   **GetMailslotInfo, SetMailslotInfo**

■ CreateMenu

HMENU CreateMenu(void)

This function creates a menu. The menu is initially empty, but can be filled with menu items by using the **AppendMenu** or **InsertMenu** function.

This function has no parameters.

Return Value   The return value identifies the newly created menu. It is NULL if the menu cannot be created.

See Also   **AppendMenu, InsertMenu, DestroyMenu, CreatePopupMenu**

■ CreateMetaFileEx

HDC CreateMetaFileEx(_hDCRef, lpFilename, lpRect, lpDescription_**)**
HDC _hDCRef_;
LPTSTR _lpFilename_;
LPRECT _lpRect_;
LPTSTR _lpDescription_;

The **CreateMetaFileEx** function creates a metafile device context.

The **CreateMetaFileEx** function may be used as either a wide-character function (where text arguments must use Unicode) or an ANSI function (where text arguments must use characters from the Windows 3.x character set.

Parameters   _hDCRef_   Identifies the reference device for the metafile. It is used by this function only to identify a device and units. The metafile code will not refer to the _hDCRef_ after this function completes. Therefore, there is no restriction on what is done with _hDCRef_ after this call. If NULL, the default display device will be the reference device for the metafile.

lpFilename   Points to the filename for the metafile. If NULL, the metafile will be memory based and its contents will be lost when the metafile is deleted in **DeleteMetaFileEx**.

lpRect   Points to the RECT structure that contains the picture frame of the metafile in 0.01 millimeter units. The rectangle must be well-ordered and enclose the entire picture. The left edge is to the left of the right edge and the bottom edge is below the top edge. Positive _x_ is to the right, positive _y_ is down. Points on the edge are included in the rectangle. If NULL, the tightest bounding rectangle around the picture will define the picture frame.

lpDescription   Points to a description string that contains the creator name followed by the title name. The creator name is null-terminated and the title name is ended with two null characters (for example, "XYZ Graphics Editor\0Bald Eagle\0\0" where '\0' represents the null character). If _lpDescription_ is NULL, there is no creator name or title name.

Return Value   The return value identifies a metafile device context if the function is successful. Otherwise, it is zero.

Comments   A metafile device context is used to create and store a graphics picture in a metafile. It can be used in place of the _hDC_ parameter in any GDI function to render a recording of a picture. In general, an application can use the same rendering code for any output device to create a metafile.

Once created, a metafile picture can be played to any output devices. The picture frame gives the physical size and location of the picture which can be scaled or rotated when displayed.

The reference device provides a scale for the metafile picture. When played to a different device, the metafile code attempts to reproduce the picture that would have been drawn on the reference device.

The metafile device context returned by this function contains the same default attributes as those of a newly created device context.

The disk-based metafiles created cannot be exported to the Windows 3.x systems directly. To export Windows 3.x metafiles, use the **GetMetaFileBitsEx** function.

It is recommended that the filename for the metafile have a .NMF extension.

See Also   **CloseMetaFileEx, DeleteMetaFileEx, GetMetaFileBitsEx, GetMetaFileDescriptionEx, GetMetaFileHeaderEx**.

■ CreateMutex

HANDLE CreateMutex(*lpMutexAttributes*, *bInitialOwner*, *lpName***)**
LPSECURITY_ATTRIBUTES *lpMutexAttributes*;
BOOL *bInitialOwner*;
LPTSTR *lpName*;

The **CreateMutex** function creates a named or unnamed mutex object and opens a handle to access it.

The **CreateMutex** function may be used as either a wide-character function (where text arguments must use Unicode) or an ANSI function (where text arguments must use characters from the Windows 3.x character set installed).

Parameters   *lpMutexAttributes*   Pointer to a **SECURITY_ATTRIBUTES** data structure. This is an optional parameter that may be used to specify the security attributes of the new mutex.

The **SECURITY_ATTRIBUTES** data structure has the following form:

```
typedef struct tagSECURITY_ATTRIBUTES {
    DWORD   nLength;
    LPVOID  lpSecurityDescriptor;
    BOOL    bInheritHandle;
} SECURITY_ATTRIBUTES;
```

If the parameter is not specified, then the mutex is created without a security descriptor, and the resulting handle is not inherited on process creation.

bInitialOwner   A boolean value that determines whether the creator of the object desires immediate ownership of the mutex object.

lpName   Pointer to a string containing the name of the mutex. The creation will fail if this name matches the name of an existing named object. The NULL terminated name may contain any character except the pathname separator character "\". If lpName is NULL, the mutex will be created without a name.

Return Value   If the function is successful, the return value is a handle to the new mutex.

If the function fails, the return value is NULL. Further information can be obtained by calling **GetLastError**.

Comments

The handle that **CreateMutex** returns has full access to the new mutex object. It may be used with any API function that requires a handle to a mutex object.

CreateMutex creates a new mutex object, and opens a handle to the object, with ownership as determined by the *bInitialOwner* parameter. The status of the newly created mutex object is set to not abandoned.

In addition to the STANDARD_RIGHTS_REQUIRED access flags, the following object type specific access flags are valid for mutex objects:

Value	Meaning
SYNCHRONIZE	Synchronization access (wait or release) to the mutex object is desired.
MUTEX_ALL_ACCESS	All possible types of access to the mutex object are desired.

These object specific access flags are used when duplicating the mutex handle via **DuplicateHandle**.

In addition to the standard object sharing mechanisms available in Windows32 — inheritance and calls to **DuplicateHandle** — named mutexes may be opened by any thread with appropriate access using **OpenMutex**. This allows the mutex object to be shared by any application that knows the name of the mutex.

See Also

OpenMutex

■ CreateNamedPipe

HANDLE CreateNamedPipe(*lpName, dwOpenMode, dwPipeMode, nMaxInstances, nOutBufferSize, nInBufferSize, nDefaultTimeOut, lpSecurityAttributes***)**
LPTSTR *lpName*;
DWORD *dwOpenMode*;
DWORD *dwPipeMode*;
DWORD *nMaxInstances*;
DWORD *nOutBufferSize*;
DWORD *nInBufferSize*;
DWORD *nDefaultTimeOut*;
LPSECURITY_ATTRIBUTES *lpSecurityAttributes*;

This service either creates the first instance of a specific named pipe and establishes its basic attributes or creates a new instance of an existing named pipe which inherits the attributes of the first instance of the named pipe. To create an instance of a named pipe the user must have FILE_CREATE_PIPE_INSTANCE access to the named pipe object. If a new named pipe is being created, then the Access Control List (ACL) from the security attributes parameter defines the discretionary access control for the named pipe.

If a new named pipe is created, then the configuration of the named pipe is determined from the PIPE_ACCESS_INBOUND, PIPE_ACCESS_OUTBOUND and PIPE_ACCESS_DUPLEX flags of the open mode parameter. If duplex is specified, then all instances of the named pipe are full duplex and can be read and written by clients. If either PIPE_ACCESS_INBOUND or PIPE_ACCESS_OUTBOUND is specified, but not both, then the named pipe is a simplex pipe and can only be read (outbound) or written (inbound) by clients. If neither one is specified, then ERROR_INVALID_PARAMETER is returned. Specifying both PIPE_ACCESS_INBOUND and PIPE_ACCESS_OUTBOUND is equivalent to specifying PIPE_ACCESS_DUPLEX. All instances of a named pipe must use the same pipe access value. If a different value is used then ERROR_ACCESS_DENIED is returned.

The type of the named pipe, the maximum instances, and the default timeout value are processed specially depending upon whether this is the first or subsequent instance of a name pipe being created. On the first instance these parameters are processed and used for subsequent instances of the pipe until all instances are closed.

The in and out buffer sizes are advisory. The actual buffer sizes that is reserved for each side of the named pipe is either the system default, the system minimum, the system maximum, or the specified size rounded up to the next allocation boundary. In addition, if a user writes more data than the buffer size, the full data will be written/read.

An instance of a named pipe is always deleted when the last handle to the instance of the named pipe is closed.

The **CreateNamedPipe** function may be used as either a wide-character function (where text arguments must use Unicode) or an ANSI function (where text arguments must use characters from the Windows 3.x character set installed).

Parameters

lpName   Supplies the pipe name Documented in "Pipe Names" section earlier. This must be a local name.

dwOpenMode   Supplies the set of flags that define the mode which the pipe is to be opened with. The open mode consists of access flags (one of three values) logically ORed with a write through flag (one of two values) and an overlapped flag (one of two values), as described below.

dwOpenMode Flags:

Value	Meaning
PIPE_ACCESS_DUPLEX	Pipe is bidirectional. (This is semantically equivalent to calling **CreateFile** with access flags of GENERIC_READ | GENERIC_WRITE.)
PIPE_ACCESS_INBOUND	Data goes from client to server only. (This is semantically equivalent to calling **CreateFile** with access flags of GENERIC_READ.)

Value	Meaning
PIPE_ACCESS_OUTBOUND	Data goes from server to client only. (This is semantically equivalent to calling **CreateFile** with access flags of GENERIC_WRITE.)
FILE_FLAG_WRITE_THROUGH	The redirector is not permitted to delay the transmission of data to the named pipe buffer on the remote server. This disables a performance enhancement for applications that need synchronization with every write operation.
FILE_FLAG_OVERLAPPED	Indicates that the system should initialize the file so that **ReadFile**, **WriteFile** and other operations that may take a significant time to process will return ERROR_IO_PENDING. An event will be set to the signalled state when the operation completes. Specifying FILE_FLAG_OVERLAPPED also enables more than one operation to be simultaneously performed with the handle (a simultaneous ReadFile and WriteFile, for example).

dwPipeMode   Supplies the pipe-specific modes (as flags) of the pipe. This parameter is a combination of a read-mode flag, a type flag, and a wait flag. (See the "Blocking vs. Nonblocking Modes" section earlier for a description of the wait flag.)

dwPipeMode Flags:

Value	Meaning
PIPE_WAIT	Blocking mode is to be used for this handle.
PIPE_NOWAIT	Nonblocking mode is to be used for this handle.
PIPE_READMODE_BYTE	Read pipe as a byte stream.
PIPE_READMODE_MESSAGE	Read pipe as a message stream. Note that this is not allowed with PIPE_TYPE_BYTE.
PIPE_TYPE_BYTE	Pipe is a byte-stream pipe. Note that this is not allowed with PIPE_READMODE_MESSAGE.
PIPE_TYPE_MESSAGE	Pipe is a message-stream pipe.

nMaxInstances   Gives the maximum number of instances for this pipe. Acceptable values are 1 to PIPE_UNLIMITED_INSTANCES-1 and PIPE_UNLIMITED_INSTANCES.

nMaxInstances Special Values:

Value	Meaning
PIPE_UNLIMITED_INSTANCES	Unlimited instances of this pipe can be created.

nOutBufferSize   Specifies an advisory on the number of bytes to reserve for the outgoing buffer.

nInBufferSize   Specifies an advisory on the number of bytes to reserve for the incoming buffer.

nDefaultTimeOut   An optional parameter to a timeout value in milliseconds that is to be used if a timeout value is not specified when waiting for an instance of a named pipe. This parameter is only meaningful when the first instance of a named pipe is created. If neither **CreateNamedPipe** or **WaitNamedPipe** specify a timeout 50 milliseconds will be used. To use the default *nDefaultTimeOut* must be set to zero.

lpSecurityAttributes   An optional parameter that, if present and supported on the target system, supplies a security descriptor for the named pipe. This parameter includes an inheritance flag for the handle. If this parameter is not present, the handle is not inherited by child processes.

Return Value   Returns one of the following: 0xFFFFFFFF — An error occurred. Call **GetLastError** for more information.

Anything else — Returns a handle for use in the server side of subsequent named pipe operations.

See Also   **CallNamedPipe, WaitNamedPipe, ConnectNamedPipe, DisconnectNamedPipe, GetNamedPipeInfo, PeekNamedPipe, TransactNamedPipe**

■ CreatePalette

HPALETTE CreatePalette(*lpLogPalette***)**
LPLOGPALETTE *lpLogPalette*;

The **CreatePalette** function creates a logical color palette.

Parameters   *lpLogPalette*   Points to a LOGPALETTE data structure that contains information about the colors in the logical palette.

Return Value   The return value identifies a logical palette if the function was successful. Otherwise, it is 0.

■ CreatePatternBrush

HBRUSH CreatePatternBrush(*hBitmap***)**
HBITMAP *hBitmap*;

The **CreatePatternBrush** function creates a logical brush that has the pattern specified by the *hBitmap* parameter. The brush can subsequently be selected for any device that supports raster operations.

Parameters	*hBitmap* Identifies the bitmap.
Return Value	The return value identifies a logical brush if the function is successful. Otherwise, it is 0.
Comments	A pattern brush can be deleted without affecting the associated bitmap by using the **DeleteObject** function. This means the bitmap can be used to create any number of pattern brushes.

A brush created using a monochrome (one bit per pixel) bitmap is drawn using the text and background colors of the device context it is drawn to. Pixels represented by a 0 bit will be drawn with the current text color, and pixels represented by a 1 bit will be drawn with the current background color.

See Also **CreateBitmap, CreateBitmapIndirect, LoadBitmap, CreateCompatibleBitmap**

■ CreatePen

HPEN CreatePen(*iPenStyle, nWidth, crColor***)**
int *iPenStyle*;
int *nWidth*;
COLORREF *crColor*,

The **CreatePen** function creates a logical pen having the specified style, width, and color. The pen can be subsequently selected as the current pen for any device context.

Parameters *nPenStyle* Specifies the pen style. It can be any one of the following values:

PS_SOLID	0
PS_DASH	1
PS_DOT	2
PS_DASHDOT	3
PS_DASHDOTDOT	4
PS_NULL	5
PS_INSIDEFRAME	6

If the width of the pen is greater than 1 and the pen style is PS_INSIDEFRAME, the line is drawn inside the frame of all primitives except polygons and polylines; the pen is drawn with a logical (dithered) color if the pen color does not match an available RGB value. The PS_INSIDEFRAME style is identical to PS_SOLID if the pen width is less than or equal to 1.

nWidth   Specifies the width of the pen (in logical units).

crColor   Specifies a color reference for the pen color.

Return Value   The return value identifies a logical pen if the function is successful. Otherwise, it is 0.

■ CreatePenIndirect

HPEN CreatePenIndirect(*lpLogPen***)**
LPLOGPEN *lpLogPen*;

The **CreatePenIndirect** function creates a logical pen that has the style, width and color given in the structure pointed to by the *lpLogPen* parameter.

Parameters   *lpLogPen*   Points to the LOGPEN data structure that contains information about the logical pen.

Return Value   The return value identifies a logical pen object if the function is successful. Otherwise, it is 0.

See Also   **CreatePen**

■ CreatePipe

BOOL APIENTRY CreatePipe(*hReadPipe, hWritePipe, lpPipeAttributes, nSize***)**
OUT PHANDLE *hReadPipe*;
OUT PHANDLE *hWritePipe*;
IN LPSECURITY_ATTRIBUTES *lpPipeAttributes*;
IN DWORD *nSize*;

The **CreatePipe** function is used to create an anonymous pipe I/O device. Two handles to the device are created. One handle is opened for reading and the other is opened for writing. These handles may be used in subsequent calls to **ReadFile** and **WriteFile** to transmit data through the pipe.

Parameters   *lpReadPipe*   Returns a handle to the read side of the pipe. Data may be read from the pipe by specifying this handle value in a subsequent call to ReadFile.

lpWritePipe   Returns a handle to the write side of the pipe. Data may be written to the pipe by specifying this handle value in a subsequent call to WriteFile.

lpPipeAttributes   An optional parameter that may be used to specify the attributes of the new pipe. If the parameter is not specified, then the pipe is created without a security descriptor, and the resulting handles are not inherited on process creation. Otherwise, the optional security attributes are used on the pipe, and the inherit handles flag affects both resulting pipe handles.

nSize   Supplies the requested buffer size for the pipe. This is only a suggestion and is used by the operating system to calculate an appropriate buffering mechanism. A value of zero indicates that the system is to choose the default buffering scheme.

The return value is TRUE if the pipe was created, or FALSE if an error occurred.

See Also　　　**CreateNamedPipe**

■ CreatePolygonRgn

HRGN CreatePolygonRgn(_lpPoints_, _nCount_, _iPolyFillMode_**)**
LPPOINT _lpPoints_;
int _nCount_;
int _iPolyFillMode_;

The **CreatePolygonRgn** function creates a polygonal region.

Parameters　　　_lpPoints_　Points to an array of **POINT** data structures that define the vertices of the polygon. The polygon is assumed closed. Specify each vertex only once.

nCount　Specifies the number of points in the array.

iPolyFillMode　Specifies the filling mode used to determine which pixels are in the region. The _iPolyFillMode_ parameter may be either of the following values:

Value	Meaning
ALTERNATE	Selects alternate mode.
WINDING	Selects winding number mode.

See **SetPolyFillMode** function for an explanation of these modes.

Return Value　　　The return value identifies a new region if the function is successful. Otherwise, it is 0.

See Also　　　**SetPolyFillMode**

■ CreatePolyPolygonRgn

HRGN CreatePolyPolygonRgn(_lpPoints_, _lpPolyCounts_, _nCount_, _iPolyFillMode_**)**
LPPOINT _lpPoints_;
LPINT _lpPolyCounts_;
int _nCount_;
int _iPolyFillMode_;

The **CreatePolyPolygonRgn** function creates a region consisting of a series of polygons. The polygons may overlap.

Parameters　　　_lpPoints_　Points to an array of **POINT** data structures that define the vertices of the polygons. The polygons are specified consecutively. Each polygon is assumed closed. Specify each vertex only once.

lpPolyCounts　Points to an array of integers, each of which specifies the number of points in one of the polygons in the _lpPoints_ array.

nCount　Specifies the total number of integers in the _lpPolyCounts_ array.

iPolyFillMode   Specifies the filling mode used to determine which pixels are in the region. The *iPolyFillMode* parameter may be either of the following values:

Value	Meaning
ALTERNATE	Selects alternate mode.
WINDING	Selects winding number mode.

Return Value   The return value identifies the region if the function was successfull. Otherwise, it is 0.

See Also   **SetPolyFillMode**

■ CreatePopupMenu

HMENU CreatePopupMenu(void)

This function creates and returns a handle to an empty pop-up menu.

An application adds items to the pop-up menu by calling **InsertMenu** and **AppendMenu**. The application can add the pop-up menu to an existing menu or pop-up menu, or it may display and track selections on the pop-up menu by calling **TrackPopupMenu**.

This function has no parameters.

Return Value   The return value identifies the newly created menu. It is NULL if the menu cannot be created.

See Also   **AppendMenu, InsertMenu, TrackPopupMenu, CreateMenu**

■ CreateProcess

BOOL CreateProcess(*lpApplicationName, lpCommandLine, lpProcessAttributes, lpThreadAttributes, bInheritHandles, dwCreationFlags, lpEnvironment, lpCurrentDirectory, lpStartupInfo, lpProcessInformation***)**
LPTSTR *lpApplicationName;*
LPTSTR *lpCommandLine;*
LPSECURITY_ATTRIBUTES *lpProcessAttributes;*
LPSECURITY_ATTRIBUTES *lpThreadAttributes;*
BOOL *bInheritHandles;*
DWORD *dwCreationFlags;*
LPVOID *lpEnvironment;*
LPTSTR *lpCurrentDirectory;*
LPSTARTUPINFO *lpStartupInfo;*
LPPROCESS_INFORMATION *lpProcessInformation;*

A process and thread object are created and a handle opened to each object using CreateProcess. Note that **WinExec** and **LoadModule** are still supported, but are implemented as a call to **CreateProcess**.

The **CreateProcess** function may be used as either a wide-character function (where text arguments must use Unicode) or an ANSI function (where text arguments must use characters from the Windows 3.x character set installed).

Parameters

lpApplicationName   Supplies an optional pointer to a null terminated character string that contains the name of the image file to execute. This is a fully qualified DOS path name. If not specified, then the image file name is the first whitespace delimited token on the command line. If arguments are to be passed to the new process, this argument should be NULL, and lpCommandLine should be used instead.

lpCommandLine   Supplies a null terminated character string that contains the command line for the application to be executed. The entire command line is made available to the new process using GetCommandLine. If the lpApplicationName parameter was not specified, then the first token of the command line specifies file name of the application (note that this token begins at the beginning of the command line and ends at the first "white space" character) . If the file name does not contain an extension (the presence of a "."), then .EXE is assumed. If the file name does not contain a directory path, Windows will search for the executable file in:

- The current directory
- The windows directory
- The windows system directory
- The directories listed in the path environment variable

lpProcessAttributes   A pointer to a **SECURITY_ATTRIBUTES** data structure. This is an optional parameter that may be used to specify the attributes of the new process. If the parameter is not specified, then the process is created without a security descriptor, and the resulting handle is not inherited on process creation.

The **SECURITY_ATTRIBUTES** data structure has the following form:

```
typedef struct tagSECURITY_ATTRIBUTES {
    DWORD    nLength;
    LPVOID   lpSecurityDescriptor;
    BOOL     bInheritHandle;
} SECURITY_ATTRIBUTES;
```

lpThreadAttributes   An optional parameter that may be used to specify the attributes of the new thread. If the parameter is not specified, then the thread is created without a security descriptor, and the resulting handle is not inherited on process creation.

dwCreationFlags   Supplies additional flags that control the creation of the process.

dwCreationFlags Flags:

Value	Meaning
DEBUG_PROCESS	If this flag bit is set, then the creating process is treated as a debugger, and the process being created is created as a debugee. All debug events occuring in the debugee are reported to the debugger. If this bit is clear, but the calling process is a debugee, then the process becomes a debugee of the calling processes debugger. If this bit is clear and the calling processes is not a debugee then no debug related actions occur.
DEBUG_ONLY_THIS_PROCESS	If this flag is set, then the DEBUG_PROCESS flag bit must also be set. The calling process is is treated as a debugger, and the new process is created as its debuggee. If the new process creates additional processes, no debug related activities (with respect to the debugger) occur.
CREATE_SUSPENDED	The process is created, but the initial thread of the process remains suspended. The creator can resume this thread using ResumeThread. Until this is done, code in the process will not execute.
CREATE_NEW_CONSOLE	The created process will have a new console, instead of inheriting the parent's console.
	If both CREATE_NEW_CONSOLE and DETACHED_PROCESS are set, an error will be returned.
	Debuggers may find this flag useful.
DETACHED_PROCESS	The created process will have no console. Calling a console function from a function with no console results in an error.
	The process can call **AllocateConsole** if it later wants to have a console.
	If both CREATE_NEW_CONSOLE and DETACHED_PROCESS are set, an error will be returned.

bInheritHandles   Supplies a flag that specifies whether or not the new process is to inherit handles to objects visible to the calling process. A value of TRUE causes handles to be inherited by the new process. If TRUE was specified, then for each handle visible to the calling process, if the handle was created with the inherit handle option, the handle is inherited to the new process. The handle has the same granted access in the new process as it has in the calling process, and the value of the handle is the same.

lpEnvironment   An optional parameter, that if specified, supplies a pointer to an environment block. If the parameter is not specified, the environment block of the current process is used. This environment block is made available to the new process using GetEnvironmentStrings.

lpCurrentDirectory   An optional parameter, that if specified, supplies a string representing the current drive and directory for the new process. The string must be a fully qualified pathname that includes a drive letter. If the parameter is not specified, then the new process is created with the same current drive and directory as the calling process. This option is provided primarily for shells that want to start an application and specify its initial drive and working directory.

lpStartupInfo   Points to a **STARTUPINFO** structure that specifies how the applications window is to be shown.

The **STARTUPINFO** structure has the following form:

```
typedef struct _STARTUPINFO {
    DWORD   cb;
    LPSTR   lpReserved;
    LPSTR   lpDesktop;
    LPSTR   lpTitle;
    DWORD   dwX;
    DWORD   dwY;
    DWORD   dwXSize;
    DWORD   dwYSize;
    DWORD   dwFlags;
    WORD    wShowWindow;
    WORD    cbReserved2;
    LPBYTE  lpReserved2;
} STARTUPINFO;
typedef STARTUPINFO *LPSTARTUPINFO;
```

lpProcessInformation   Points to a **PROCESS_INFORMATION** structure that receives identification information about the new process.

The **PROCESS_INFORMATION** structure has the following form:

```
typedef struct _PROCESS_INFORMATION {
    HANDLE hProcess;
    HANDLE hThread;
    DWORD dwProcessId;
    DWORD dwThreadId;
} PROCESS_INFORMATION;
typedef PROCESS_INFORMATION *PPROCESS_INFORMATION;
typedef PROCESS_INFORMATION *LPPROCESS_INFORMATION;
```

Return Value   The return value is TRUE if the function is successful. Otherwise, it is FALSE in which case extended error information is available from the **GetLastError** function.

Comments   Creating a process causes the specified application to begin execution. The *lpStartupInfo* parameter specifies the initial state of the applications initial window when it is created. If the process was created with the *bInheritHandles* flag set, then the new process has access to all objects that the calling process has access to and that were created with the **InheritHandle** attribute set; otherwise, the new process does not have access to any of the calling processes objects.

The process remains in the system until all threads within the process have terminated and all handles to the process and any of its threads have been closed through calls to **CloseHandle**. The handles for both the process and the main thread must be closed through calls to **CloaseHandle**. If these handles are not needed, it is best to close them immediately after process creation.

Note that **CreateProcess** may succeed even if the DLLs used by the process are unavailable or references to those DLLs can not be resolved.

When the last thread in a process terminates, all objects opened by the process are implicitly closed. The process's termination status changes from its initial value of STATUS_PENDING to the termination status of the last thread to terminate. The process object then attains a state of signaled satisfying all waits on the object.

In addition to creating a process, **CreateProcess** also creates a thread object. The thread is created with an initial stack whose size is described in the image header of the specified application executable file. The thread begins execution at the images entrypoint.

The process is assigned a 32-bit process identifier. The ID is valid until the process terminates. It may be used to identify the process, or open a handle to the process to perform some action on the process. The initial thread in the process is also assigned a 32-bit thread identifier. The ID is valid until the thread terminates and by be used to uniquely identify the thread within the system.

The preferred way to shut down a process is by using the **ExitProcess** command. That's because it notifies all DLLs attached to the process of the approaching termination. Other means of shutting down a process do not notify the attached DLLs.

The code that creates a process should make sure the process handle gets closed, as shown in the examples below.

ExitProcess, **ExitThread**, **CreateThread**, and a process that is starting (as the result of a **CreateProcess** call) are serialized between each other within a process. Only one of these events can happen in an address space at a time. This means that:

- During process startup and DLL initialization routines, new threads may be created, but they will not begin execution until DLL initialization is done for the process.

- Only one thread in a process may be in a DLL initialization or detach routine at a time.

- **ExitProcess** will block until no threads are in their DLL initialization or detach routines.

Example

This example shows how to create a process, wait for it to exit, pick up its exit status, and close the thread and process handles:

```
/* try to create a process */
b - CreateProcess(...) ;

/* if we were successful... */
if ( b ) {
        hProcess - ProcessInformation.hProcess;
        hThread - ProcessInformation.hThread;

        /* wait for the process to complete */
        dw - WaitForSincleObject(hProcess, NULL) ;

        /* if we saw success ... */
        if (dw -- STATUS_SUCCESS) {

                /* pick up an exit code for the process */
                b - GetExitCodeProcess(hProcess, &dwExitCode) ;
                }

        /* close the process and thread object handles */
        CloseHandle(hThread) ;
        CloseHandle(hProcess) ;
        }
```

This next example shows how to create a detached process, where you don't care about its exit status or when it completes. After creating the process, you immediately close your handles to the thread and process:

```
/* try to create a process */
b - CreateProcess(...) ;

/* if we were successful... */
if ( b ) {
        /* close the thread and process object handles */
        CloseHandle(ProcessInformation.hThread) ;
        CloseHandle(ProcessInformation.hProcess) ;
        }
```

See Also   **OpenProcess, ExitProcess, TerminateProcess, CloseHandle**
SECURITY_ATTRIBUTES PROCESS_INFORMATION STARTUPINFO

■ CreateRectRgn

HRGN CreateRectRgn(*X1, Y1, X2, Y2*)
int *X1*;
int *Y1*;
int *X2*;
int *Y2*;

The **CreateRectRgn** function creates a rectangular region.

Parameters   *X1*   Specifies the *x*-coordinate of the upper-left corner of the region.

Y1   Specifies the *y*-coordinate of the upper-left corner of the region.

X2   Specifies the *x*-coordinate of the lower-right corner of the region.

Y2   Specifies the *y*-coordinate of the lower-right corner of the region.

Return Value   The return value identifies a new region if the function is successful. Otherwise, it is 0.

Comments   The region will be exclusive of the bottom and right edges.

■ CreateRectRgnIndirect

HRGN CreateRectRgnIndirect(*lpRect***)**
LPRECT *lpRect*;

The **CreateRectRgnIndirect** function creates a rectangular region.

Parameters   *lpRect*   Points to a **RECT** structure that contains the coordinates of the upper-left and lower-right corners of the region.

Return Value   The return value identifies a new region if the function is successful. Otherwise, it is 0.

Comments   The region will be exclusive of the bottom and right edges.

■ CreateRoundRectRgn

HRGN CreateRoundRectRgn(*X1, Y1, X2, Y2, X3, Y3***)**
int *X1*;
int *Y1*;
int *X2*;
int *Y2*;
int *X3*;
int *Y3*;

The **CreateRoundRectRgn** function creates a rectangular region with rounded corners.

Parameters   *X1*   Specifies the *x*-coordinate of the upper-left corner of the region.

Y1   Specifies the *y*-coordinate of the upper-left corner of the region.

X2   Specifies the *x*-coordinate of the lower-right corner of the region.

Y2   Specifies the *y*-coordinate of the lower-right corner of the region.

X3   Specifies the width of the ellipse used to create the rounded corners.

Y3   Specifies the height of the ellipse used to create the rounded corners.

Return Value   The return value identifies a new region if the function was successful. Otherwise, it is 0.

■ CreateScalableFontResource

BOOL CreateScalableFontResource(_hdc, lpszResourceFile, lpszFontFile, lpszCurrentPath_**)**
HDC _hdc_;   /* device-context handle */
LPSTR _lpszResourceFile_; /* filename for font resource */
LPSTR _lpszFontFile_; /* filename for scalable font */
LPSTR _lpszCurrentPath_; /* path to font file   */

The **CreateScalableFontResource** function creates a font resource file containing the font directory information and the font module name for a specified scalable font file.

Parameters

 hdc Identifies the device context.

 lpszResourceFile Points to a null-terminated string specifying the name of the font resource file that this function creates.

 lpszFontFile Points to a null-terminated string specifying the name of the scalable font file this function uses to create the resource font file.

 lpszCurrentPath Points to a null-terminated string specifying the path to the scalable font file.

Return Value

The return value is TRUE if the function is successful. Otherwise, it is FALSE.

Comments

The **CreateScalableFontResource** function is used by applications that install TrueType fonts. An application uses the **CreateScalableFontResource** function to create a font resource file (typically with a .FOT filename extension) and then the **AddFontResource** function to install the font. The TrueType font file (typically with a .TTF filename extension) must be in the SYSTEM subdirectory of the WINDOWS directory to be used by the **AddFontResource** function.

The **CreateScalableFontResource** function currently supports only TrueType technology scalable fonts.

See Also

AddFontResource

■ CreateSemaphore

HANDLE CreateSemaphore(_lpSemaphoreAttributes, lInitialCount, lMaximumCount, lpName_**)**
LPSECURITY_ATTRIBUTES _lpSemaphoreAttributes_;
LONG _lInitialCount_;
LONG _lMaximumCount_;
LPTSTR _lpName_;

The **CreateSemaphore** function creates a named or unnamed semaphore object and opens a handle to access it.

The **CreateSemaphore** function may be used as either a wide-character function (where text arguments must use Unicode) or an ANSI function (where text arguments must use characters from the Windows 3.x character set installed).

Parameters
lpSemaphoreAttributes   Pointer to a **SECURITY_ATTRIBUTES** data structure. This is an optional parameter that may be used to specify the security attributes of the new semaphore.

The **SECURITY_ATTRIBUTES** data structure has the following form:

```
typedef struct tagSECURITY_ATTRIBUTES {
    DWORD   nLength;
    LPVOID  lpSecurityDescriptor:
    BOOL    bInheritHandle;
} SECURITY_ATTRIBUTES;
```

If the parameter is not specified, then the semaphore is created without a security descriptor, and the resulting handle is not inherited on process creation.

lInitialCount   Specifies an initial count for the semaphore. This value must be positive and less than or equal to the maximum count.

lMaximumCount   Specifies the maximum count for the semaphore. This value must be greater than zero.

lpName   Pointer to a string containing the name of the semaphore. The creation will fail if this name matches the name of an existing named object.

The NULL-terminated name may contain any character except the pathname separator character "\".

If lpName is NULL, the semaphore will be created without a name.

Return Value
If the function is successful, the return value is a handle to the new semaphore.

If the function fails, the return value is NULL. Further information can be obtained by calling **GetLastError**.

Comments
The handle that **CreateSemaphore** returns has full access to the new semaphore object. It may be used with any API function that requires a handle to a semaphore object.

The **CreateSemaphore** function creates a semaphore object with the specified initial and maximum counts.

In addition to the STANDARD_RIGHTS_REQUIRED access flags, the following object type specific access flags are valid for semaphore objects:

Value	Meaning
SEMAPHORE_MODIFY_STATE	Modify state access (release) to the semaphore is desired.
SYNCHRONIZE	Synchronization access (wait) to the semaphore is desired.
SEMAPHORE_ALL_ACCESS	This set of access flags specifies all of the possible access flags for a semaphore object.

These object specific access flags are used when duplicating the semaphore handle via **DuplicateHandle**.

In addition to the standard object sharing mechanisms available in Windows32 — inheritance and calls to **DuplicateHandle** — named semaphores may be opened by any thread with appropriate access using **OpenSemaphore**. This allows the semaphore object to be shared by any application that knows the name of the semaphore.

See Also	**CreateSemaphore, OpenSemaphore**

CreateSolidBrush

HBRUSH CreateSolidBrush(*crColor***)**
COLORREF *crColor,*

The **CreateSolidBrush** function creates a logical brush that has the specified solid color. The brush can subsequently be selected as the current brush for any device context.

Parameters   *crColor*   Specifies the color of the brush.

Return Value   The return value identifies a logical brush if the function is successful. Otherwise the return value is 0.

CreateThread

HANDLE CreateThread(*lpThreadAttributes, dwStackSize, lpStartAddress, lpParameter,*
     *dwCreationFlags, lpThreadId***)**
LPSECURITY_ATTRIBUTES *lpThreadAttributes;*
DWORD *dwStackSize;*
LPTHREAD_START_ROUTINE *lpStartAddress;*
LPVOID *lpParameter,*
DWORD *dwCreationFlags;*
LPDWORD *lpThreadId;*

A thread object can be created to execute within the address space of the calling process using **CreateThread**.

Parameters   *lpThreadAttributes*   An optional parameter that may be used to specify the attributes of the new thread. If the parameter is not specified, then the thread is created without a security descriptor, and the resulting handle is not inherited on process creation.

dwStackSize   Supplies the size in bytes of the stack for the new thread. A value of zero specifies that the thread's stack size should be the same size as the stack size of the first thread in the process. This size is specified in the application's executable file.

lpStartAddress   Supplies the starting address of the new thread. The address is a procedure that returns a DWORD exit code, and that accepts a single 32-bit pointer argument.

lpParameter   Supplies a single parameter value passed to the thread.

dwCreationFlags   Supplies additional flags that control the creation of the thread. The default is NULL.

dwCreationFlags Flags:

Value	Meaning
CREATE_SUSPENDED	The thread is created in a suspended state. The creator can resume this thread using ResumeThread. Until this is done, the thread will not begin execution.

lpThreadId   Returns the thread identifier of the thread. The thread ID is valid until the thread terminates.

Return Value

The return value is a handle to the new thread if the function is successful. Otherwise, is is NULL, in which case extended error information is available from the **GetLastError** function.

Comments

Creating a thread causes a new thread of execution to begin in the address space of the current process. The thread has access to all objects opened by the process.

The thread begins executing at the address specified by the *StartAddress* parameter. If the thread returns from this procedure, then the DWORD return value is used to terminate the thread using **ExitThread**.

The **CreateThread** call may succeed even if *lpStartAddress* points to data, code, or is not accessible. When the thread executes, if the start address is bad, an exception will occur, and the thread will terminate. This behavior is similar to the asynchronous nature of **CreateProcess**, where the process is created even if it refers to bad or missing DLLs. This case — termination due to a bad start address — is handled as an error exit for the new process.

The thread remains in the system until it has terminated and all handles to the thread have been closed through a call to **CloseHandle**.

When a thread terminates, it attains a state of signaled satisfying all waits on the object.

If a security descriptor is not provided, the returned handle has full access to the new thread, and may be used in any API that requires a handle to a thread object.

If a security decriptor is provided, the handle will have access based on an access check against the caller's context. If the access check denies access, the handle will not have access to the thread. In addition to the STANDARD_RIGHTS_REQUIRED access flags, the following object type specific access flags are valid for thread objects:

Value	Meaning
THREAD_QUERY_INFORMATION	This access is required to read certain information from the thread object.
THREAD_SET_INFORMATION	This access is required to set certain information in the thread object.

Value	Meaning
SYNCHRONIZE	This access is required to wait on a thread object.
THREAD_GET_CONTEXT	This access is required to read the context of a thread using GetThreadContext.
THREAD_SET_CONTEXT	This access is required to write the context of a thread using SetThreadContext.
THREAD_SUSPEND_RESUME	This access is required to suspend or resume a thread using SuspendThread or ResumeThread.
THREAD_ALL_ACCESS	This set of access flags specifies all of the possible access flags for a thread object. This includes CREATE_SUSPENDED; the thread will be created suspended.

These object specific access flags are used when duplicating the thread handle via **DuplicateHandle**.

ExitProcess, ExitThread, CreateThread, and a process that is starting (as the result of a **CreateProcess** call) are serialized between each other within a process. Only one of these events can happen in an address space at a time. This means that:

- During process startup and DLL initialization routines, new threads may be created, but they will not begin execution until DLL initialization is done for the process.

- Only one thread in a process may be in a DLL initialization or detach routine at a time.

- **ExitProcess** will block until no threads are in their DLL initialization or detach routines.

See Also   · **CloseHandle, CreateProcess, CreateThread, ExitProcess, ExitThread, ExitThread**

■ CreateUserObjectSecurity

BOOL CreateUserObjectSecurity (*ParentDescriptor, CreatorDescriptor, NewDescriptor,*
      *IsDirectoryObject, Token, GenericMapping***)**
PSECURITY_DESCRIPTOR *ParentDescriptor,*
PSECURITY_DESCRIPTOR *CreatorDescriptor,*
PSECURITY_DESCRIPTOR * *NewDescriptor,*
BOOL *IsDirectoryObject,*
HANDLE *Token;*
PGENERIC_MAPPING *GenericMapping,*

The **CreateUserObjectSecurity** function allocates and initializes a self-relative security descriptor for a new server application's object. It is called when a new server application object is being created. It is called only from user mode.

The generated security descriptor will be in self-relative form. **CreateUserObjectSecurity** allocates memory for the security descriptor's components using **VirtualAlloc.**

Parameters

ParentDescriptor   Optional pointer to a **SECURITY_DESCRIPTOR** data structure for the parent directory under which the new object is being created. A NULL value indicates there is no parent directory.

The **SECURITY_DESCRIPTOR** data structure has the following form:

```
typedef PVOID PSECURITY_DESCRIPTOR;
```

CreatorDescriptor   Optional pointer to a **SECURITY_DESCRIPTOR** data structure presented by the creator of the object. A NULL value indicates that the creator of the object did not explicitly pass security information for the new object.

NewDescriptor   Pointer to a pointer to a **SECURITY_DESCRIPTOR** data structure. The function will set the pointed-to pointer to the address of the newly-allocated self-relative security descriptor.

IsDirectoryObject   Boolean value that, if TRUE, specifies that the new object is going to be a directory object. A directory object is a container of other objects.

Token   Optional handle to the token of the client on whose behalf the object is being created. A value of NULL indicates that the caller is impersonating a client, in which case the impersonation token is used. A client token retrieves default security information for the new object, such as default owner, primary group, and discretionary access control. The token must be open for TOKEN_QUERY access.

GenericMapping   Pointer to a **GENERIC_MAPPING** data structure that maps each generic right to specific rights.

The **GENERIC_MAPPING** data structure has the following form:

```
typedef PVOID PSECURITY_DESCRIPTOR;
```

Return Value   If the function is successful, the return value is TRUE.

                          If the function fails, the return value is FALSE. Call **GetLastError** for more
                          detailed error information.

See Also   **AbsoluteToSelfRelativeSD, DestroyUserObjectSecurity,
                          GetUserObjectSecurity, SelfRelativeToAbsoluteSD, SetUserObjectSecurity**

■ CreateWindow

HWND CreateWindow(*lpClassName, lpWindowName, dwStyle, X, Y, nWidth, nHeight, hWndParent,*
    *hMenu, hInstance, lpParam***)**
LPTSTR *lpClassName*;
LPTSTR *lpWindowName*;
DWORD *dwStyle*;
int *X*;
int *Y*;
int *nWidth*;
int *nHeight*;
HWND *hWndParent*;
HMENU *hMenu*;
HANDLE *hInstance*;
LPVOID *lpParam*;

This function creates an overlapped, pop-up, or child window. The
CreateWindow function specifies the window class, window title, window style,
and (optionally) initial position and size of the window. The **CreateWindow**
function also specifies the window's parent (if any) and menu.

For overlapped, pop-up, and child windows, the **CreateWindow** function sends
WM_CREATE, WM_GETMINMAXINFO, and WM_NCCREATE messages to
the window. The *lParam* parameter of the WM_CREATE message contains a
pointer to a **CREATESTRUCT** structure. If WS_VISIBLE style is given,
CreateWindow sends the window all the messages required to activate and show
the window.

If the window style specifies a title bar, the window title pointed to by the
lpWindowName parameter is displayed in the title bar. When using
CreateWindow to create controls such as buttons, check boxes, and text controls,
the *lpWindowName* parameter specifies the text of the control.

The **CreateWindow** function may be used as either a wide-character function
(where text arguments must use Unicode) or an ANSI function (where text
arguments must use characters from the Windows 3.x character set installed).

Parameters   *lpClassName*   Points to a null-terminated character string that names the
                          window class. The class name can be any name registered with the RegisterClass
                          function or any of the predefined control-class names specified in Table T.2,
                          "Control Classes."

lpWindowName   Points to a null-terminated character string that represents the window name.

dwStyle   Specifies the style of window being created. It can be any combination of the styles given in Table *** $R[C#] ***.3, Window Styles the control styles given in Table 4.4, Control Styles, or a combination of styles created by using the bitwise OR operator. ,

X   Specifies the initial *x*-position of the window. For an overlapped or pop-up window, the *X* parameter is the initial *x*-coordinate of the window's upper-left corner (in screen coordinates). If this value is CW_USEDEFAULT, Windows selects the default position for the window's upper-left corner. For a child window, *X* is the *x*-coordinate of the upper-left corner of the window in the client area of its parent window.

Y   Specifies the initial *y*-position of the window. For an overlapped window, the *Y* parameter is the initial *y*-coordinate of the window's upper-left corner. For a pop-up window, *Y* is the *y*-coordinate (in screen coordinates) of the upper-left corner of the pop-up window. For list-box controls, *Y* is the *y*-coordinate of the upper-left corner of the control's client area. For a child window, *Y* is the *y*-coordinate of the upper-left corner of the child window. All of these coordinates are for the window, not the window's client area.

nWidth   Specifies the width (in device units) of the window. For overlapped windows, the *nWidth* parameter is either the window's width (in screen coordinates) or CW_USEDEFAULT. If *nWidth* is CW_USEDEFAULT, Windows selects a default width and height for the window (the default width extends from the initial *x*-position to the right edge of the screen, and the default height extends from the initial *y*-position to the top of the icon area).

nHeight   Specifies the height (in device units) of the window. For overlapped windows, the *nHeight* parameter is the window's height in screen coordinates. If the *nWidth* parameter is CW_USEDEFAULT, Windows ignores *nHeight*.

hWndParent   Identifies the parent or owner window of the window being created. A valid window handle must be supplied when creating a child window or an owned window. An owned window is an overlapped window that is destroyed when its owner window is destroyed, hidden when its owner is made iconic, and which is always displayed on top of its owner window. For pop-up windows, a handle can be supplied, but is not required. If the window does not have a parent or is not owned by another window, the *hWndParent* parameter must be set to NULL.

hMenu   Identifies a menu or a child-window identifier. The meaning depends on the window style. For overlapped or pop-up windows, the *hMenu* parameter identifies the menu to be used with the window. It can be NULL, if the class menu is to be used. For child windows, *hMenu* specifies the child-window identifier, an integer value that is used by a dialog-box control to notify its parent of events (such as the EN_HSCROLL message). The child-window identifier is determined by the application and should be unique for all child windows with the same parent window.

hInstance   Identifies the instance creating the window.
GetModuleHandle(NULL) can be called to return the module handle of the current process.

lpParam   Points to a value that is passed to the window through the **CREATESTRUCT** structure referenced by the *lParam* parameter of the WM_CREATE message. If an application is calling **CreateWindow** to create a multiple document interface (MDI) client window, *lpParam* must point to a **CLIENTCREATESTRUCT** structure.

Return Value   The return value identifies the new window. It is NULL if the window is not created.

Comments   For overlapped windows where the *X* parameter is CW_USEDEFAULT, the *Y* parameter can be one of the show-style parameters described with the **ShowWindow** function. For the first overlapped window to be created by the application it should be SW_SHOWDEFAULT, which tells Windows to show the window in the default manner specified through the STARTUPINFO structure as part of CreateProcess.

Class	Meaning
BUTTON	Designates a small rectangular child window that represents a button the user can turn on or off by clicking it. Button controls can be used alone or in groups, and can either be labeled or appear without text. Button controls typically change appearance when the user clicks them.
COMBOBOX	Designates a control consisting of a selection field similar to an edit control plus a list box. The list box may be displayed at all times or may be dropped down when the user selects a pop box next to the selection field.
	Depending on the style of the combo box, the user can or cannot edit the contents of the selection field. If the list box is visible, typing characters into the selection box will cause the first list box entry that matches the characters typed to be highlighted. Conversely, selecting an item in the list box displays the selected text in the selection field.
EDIT	Designates a rectangular child window in which the user can enter text from the keyboard. The user selects the control, and gives it the input focus by clicking it or moving to it by using the TAB key. The user can enter text when the control displays a flashing caret. The mouse can be used to move the cursor and select characters to be replaced, or to position the cursor for inserting characters. The BACKSPACE key can be used to delete characters.

Class	Meaning
	Edit controls use the variable-pitch system font and display ANSI characters. Applications compiled to run with previous versions of Windows display text with a fixed-pitch system font unless they have been marked by the Windows 3.0 **MARK** utility with the **MEMORY FONT** option. An application can also send the WM_SETFONT message to the edit control to change the default font.
	Edit controls expand tab characters into as many space characters as are required to move the cursor to the next tab stop. Tab stops are assumed to be at every eighth character position.
LISTBOX	Designates a list of character strings. This control is used whenever an application needs to present a list of names, such as filenames, that the user can view and select. The user can select a string by pointing to it and clicking. When a string is selected, it is highlighted and a notification message is passed to the parent window. A vertical or horizontal scroll bar can be used with a list-box control to scroll lists that are too long for the control window. The list box automatically hides or shows the scroll bar as needed.
MDICLIENT	Designates an MDI client window. The MDI client window receives messages which control the MDI application's child windows. The recommended style bits are WS_CLIPCHILDREN and WS_CHILD. To create a scrollable MDI client window which allows the user to scroll MDI child windows into view, an application can also use the WS_HSCROLL and WS_VSCROLL styles.
SCROLLBAR	Designates a rectangle that contains a thumb and has direction arrows at both ends. The scroll bar sends a notification message to its parent window whenever the user clicks the control. The parent window is responsible for updating the thumb position, if necessary. Scroll-bar controls have the same appearance and function as scroll bars used in ordinary windows. Unlike scroll bars, scroll-bar controls can be positioned anywhere in a window and used whenever needed to provide scrolling input for a window.
	The scroll-bar class also includes size-box controls. A size-box control is a small rectangle that the user can expand to change the size of the window.
STATIC	Designates a simple text field, box, or rectangle that can be used to label, box, or separate other controls. Static controls take no input and provide no output.

Style	Meaning
DS_MODALFRAME	Creates a dialog box with a modal dialog-box frame that can be combined with a title bar and System menu by specifying the WS_CAPTION and WS_SYSMENU styles.
DS_NOIDLEMSG	Suppresses WM_ENTERIDLE messages that Windows would otherwise send to the owner of the dialog box while the dialog box is displayed.
DS_SYSMODAL	Creates a system-modal dialog box.
DS_SHADOW	Creates a dialog box with an automatic shadow.
DS_SHOWSMOOTH	Specifies that the dialog is shown by first having it update in a bitmap, and then copying those bits directly to the screen. In many cases this will improve the perceived speed because copying from an off-screen bitmap to the screen is very fast, making the window "snap" onto the screen. See the SW_SHOWSMOOTH flag to **ShowWindow**.
WS_BORDER	Creates a window that has a border.
WS_CAPTION	Creates a window that has a title bar (implies the WS_BORDER style). This style cannot be used with the WS_DLGFRAME style.
WS_CHILD	Creates a child window. Cannot be used with the WS_POPUP style.
WS_CHILDWINDOW	Creates a child window that has the WS_CHILD style.
WS_CLIPCHILDREN	Excludes the area occupied by child windows when drawing within the parent window. Used when creating the parent window.
WS_CLIPSIBLINGS	Clips child windows relative to each other; that is, when a particular child window receives a paint message, the WS_CLIPSIBLINGS style clips all other overlapped child windows out of the region of the child window to be updated. (If WS_CLIPSIBLINGS is not given and child windows overlap, it is possible, when drawing within the client area of a child window, to draw within the client area of a neighboring child window.) For use with the WS_CHILD style only.

Style	Meaning
WS_DISABLED	Creates a window that is initially disabled.
WS_DLGFRAME	Creates a window with a double border but no title.
WS_GROUP	Specifies the first control of a group of controls in which the user can move from one control to the next by using the DIRECTION keys. All controls defined with the WS_GROUP style after the first control belong to the same group. The next control with the WS_GROUP style ends the style group and starts the next group (that is, one group ends where the next begins). Only dialog boxes use this style.
WS_HSCROLL	Creates a window that has a horizontal scroll bar.
WS_ICONIC	Creates a window that is initially iconic. For use with the WS_OVERLAPPED style only.
WS_MAXIMIZE	Creates a window of maximum size.
WS_MAXIMIZEBOX	Creates a window that has a maximize box.
WS_MINIMIZE	Creates a window of minimum size.
WS_MINIMIZEBOX	Creates a window that has a minimize box.
WS_OVERLAPPED	Creates an overlapped window. An overlapped window has a caption and a border.
WS_OVERLAPPEDWINDOW	Creates an overlapped window having the WS_OVERLAPPED, WS_CAPTION, WS_SYSMENU, WS_THICKFRAME, WS_MINIMIZEBOX, and WS_MAXIMIZEBOX styles.
WS_POPUP	Creates a pop-up window. Cannot be used with the WS_CHILD style.
WS_POPUPWINDOW	Creates a pop-up window that has the WS_BORDER, WS_POPUP, and WS_SYSMENU styles. The WS_CAPTION style must be combined with the WS_POPUPWINDOW style to make the system menu visible.
WS_SYSMENU	Creates a window that has a System-menu box in its title bar. Used only for windows with title bars.

Style	Meaning
WS_TABSTOP	Specifies one of any number of controls through which the user can move by using the TAB key. The TAB key moves the user to the next control specified by the WS_TABSTOP style. Only dialog boxes use this style.
WS_THICKFRAME	Creates a window with a thick frame that can be used to size the window.
WS_VISIBLE	Creates a window that is initially visible. This applies to overlapped and pop-up windows. For overlapped windows, the Y parameter is used as a **Show Window** function parameter if the X parameter is CW_USEDEFAULT.
WS_VSCROLL	Creates a window that has a vertical scroll bar.

BUTTON Class

Style	Meaning
BS_AUTOCHECKBOX	Identical to BS_CHECKBOX, except that the button automatically toggles its state whenever the user clicks it.
BS_AUTORADIOBUTTON	Identical to BS_RADIOBUTTON, except that the button is checked, the application is notified by BN_CLICKED, and the checkmarks are removed from all other radio buttons in the group.
BS_AUTO3STATE	Identical to BS_3STATE, except that the button automatically toggles its state when the user clicks it.
BS_AUTOSIZE	When specified, this style will cause a button to automatically size itself to the tightest fit around the button. This is especially useful for image buttons, where the bitmap is device dependent.
BS_CHECKBOX	Designates a small rectangular button that may be checked; its border is bold when the user clicks the button. Any text appears to the right of the button.
BS_DEFPUSHBUTTON	Designates a button with a bold border. This button represents the default user response. Any text is displayed within the button. Windows sends a message to the parent window when the user clicks the button.

Style	Meaning
BS_GROUPBOX	Designates a rectangle into which other buttons are grouped. Any text is displayed in the rectangle's upper-left corner.
BS_LEFTTEXT	Causes text to appear on the left side of the radio button or check-box button. Use this style with the BS_CHECKBOX, BS_RADIOBUTTON, or BS_3STATE styles.
BS_OWNERDRAW	Designates an owner-draw button. The parent window is notified when the button is clicked. Notification includes a request to paint, invert, and disable the button.
BS_PUSHBUTTON	Designates a button that contains the given text. The control sends a message to its parent window whenever the user clicks the button.
BS_RADIOBUTTON	Designates a small circular button that can be checked; its border is bold when the user clicks the button. Any text appears to the right of the button. Typically, two or more radio buttons are grouped together to represent mutually exclusive choices, so no more than one button in the group is checked at any time.
BS_3STATE	Identical to BS_CHECKBOX, except that a button can be grayed as well as checked. The grayed state typically is used to show that a check box has been disabled.

COMBOBOX Class

Style	Meaning
CBS_AUTOHSCROLL	Automatically scrolls the text in the edit control to the right when the user types a character at the end of the line. If this style is not set, only text which fits within the rectangular boundary is allowed.
CBS_DISABLENOSCROLL	The list box shows a disabled vertical scroll bar when the list box does not contain enough items to scroll. Without this style, the scroll bar is hidden when the list box does not contain enough items.
CBS_DROPDOWN	Similar to CBS_SIMPLE, except that the list box is not displayed unless the user selects an icon next to the selection field.

Style	Meaning
CBS_DROPDOWNLIST	Similar to CBS_DROPDOWN, except that the edit control is replaced by a static text item which displays the current selection in the list box.
CBS_HASSTRINGS	An owner-draw combo box contains items consisting of strings. The combo box maintains the memory and pointers for the strings so the application can use the LB_GETTEXT message to retrieve the text for a particular item.
CBS_OEMCONVERT	Text entered in the combo box edit control is converted from the ANSI character set to the OEM character set and then back to ANSI. This ensures proper character conversion when the application calls the **AnsiToOem** function to convert an ANSI string in the combo box to OEM characters. This style is most useful for combo boxes that contain filenames and applies only to combo boxes created with the CBS_SIMPLE or CBS_DROPDOWN styles.
CBS_OWNERDRAWFIXED	The owner of the list box is responsible for drawing its contents; the items in the list box are all the same height.
CBS_OWNERDRAWVARIABLE	The owner of the list box is responsible for drawing its contents; the items in the list box are variable in height.
CBS_SIMPLE	The list box is displayed at all times. The current selection in the list box is displayed in the edit control.
CBS_SORT	Automatically sorts strings entered into the list box.

EDIT Class

Style	Meaning
ES_AUTOHSCROLL	Automatically scrolls text to the right by 10 characters when the user types a character at the end of the line. When the user presses the ENTER key, the control scrolls all text back to position zero.
ES_AUTOVSCROLL	Automatically scrolls text up one page when the user presses ENTER on the last line.
ES_CENTER	Centers text in a multiline edit control.

Style	Meaning
ES_LEFT	Aligns text flush-left.
ES_LOWERCASE	Converts all characters to lowercase as they are typed into the edit control.
ES_MULTILINE	Designates multiple-line edit control. (The default is single-line.) If the ES_AUTOVSCROLL style is specified, the edit control shows as many lines as possible and scrolls vertically when the user presses the ENTER key. If ES_AUTOVSCROLL is not given, the edit control shows as many lines as possible and beeps if ENTER is pressed when no more lines can be displayed.
	If the ES_AUTOHSCROLL style is specified, the multiple-line edit control automatically scrolls horizontally when the caret goes past the right edge of the control. To start a new line, the user must press ENTER. If ES_AUTOHSCROLL is not given, the control automatically wraps words to the beginning of the next line when necessary; a new line is also started if ENTER is pressed. The position of the wordwrap is determined by the window size. If the window size changes, the wordwrap position changes, and the text is redisplayed.
	Multiple-line edit controls can have scroll bars. An edit control with scroll bars processes its own scroll-bar messages. Edit controls without scroll bars scroll as described above, and process any scroll messages sent by the parent window.
ES_NOHIDESEL	Normally, an edit control hides the selection when the control loses the input focus, and inverts the selection when the control receives the input focus. Specifying ES_NOHIDESEL deletes this default action.
ES_OEMCONVERT	Text entered in the edit control is converted from the ANSI character set to the OEM character set and then back to ANSI. This ensures proper character conversion when the application calls the **AnsiToOem** function to convert an ANSI string in the edit control to OEM characters. This style is most useful for edit controls that contain filenames.
ES_PASSWORD	Displays all characters as an asterisk (*) as they are typed into the edit control. An application can use the EM_SETPASSWORDCHAR message to change the character that is displayed.

Style	Meaning
ES_READONLY	Prevents the user from entering or editing text in the entry field.
ES_RIGHT	Aligns text flush-right in a multiline edit control.
ES_UPPERCASE	Converts all characters to uppercase as they are typed into the edit control.

LISTBOX Class

Style	Meaning
LBS_DISABLENOSCROLL	The list box shows a disabled vertical scroll bar when the list box does not contain enough items to scroll. Without this style, the scroll bar is hidden when the list box does not contain enough items.
LBS_EXTENDEDSEL	The user can select multiple items using the SHIFT key and the mouse or special key combinations.
LBS_HASSTRINGS	Specifies an owner-draw list box which contains items consisting of strings. The list box maintains the memory and pointers for the strings so the application can use the LB_GETTEXT message to retrieve the text for a particular item.
LBS_MULTICOLUMN	Specifies a multicolumn list box that is scrolled horizontally. The LB_SETCOLUMNWIDTH message sets the width of the columns.
LBS_MULTIPLESEL	String selection is toggled each time the user clicks or double-clicks the string. Any number of strings can be selected.
LBS_NOINTEGRALHEIGHT	The size of the list box is exactly the size specified by the application when it created the list box. Normally, Windows sizes a list box so that the list box does not display partial items.
LBS_NOREDRAW	List-box display is not updated when changes are made. This style can be changed at any time by sending a WM_SETREDRAW message.
LBS_NOTIFY	Parent window receives an input message whenever the user clicks or double-clicks a string.

Style	Meaning
LBS_OWNERDRAWFIXED	The owner of the list box is responsible for drawing its contents; the items in the list box are the same height.
LBS_OWNERDRAWVARIABLE	The owner of the list box is responsible for drawing its contents; the items in the list box are variable in height.
LBS_SORT	Strings in the list box are sorted alphabetically.
LBS_STANDARD	Strings in the list box are sorted alphabetically and the parent window receives an input message whenever the user clicks or double-clicks a string. The list box contains borders on all sides.
LBS_USETABSTOPS	Allows a list box to recognize and expand tab characters when drawing its strings. The default tab positions are 32 dialog units. (A dialog unit is a horizontal or vertical distance. One horizontal dialog unit is equal to *** $E1/4 *** of the current dialog base width unit. The dialog base units are computed based on the height and width of the current system font. The **GetDialogBaseUnits** function returns the current dialog base units in pixels.)
LBS_WANTKEYBOARDINPUT	The owner of the list box receives WM_VKEYTOITEM or WM_CHARTOITEM messages whenever the user presses a key when the list box has input focus. This allows an application to perform special processing on the keyboard input.

SCROLLBAR Class

Style	Meaning
SBS_BOTTOMALIGN	Used with the SBS_HORZ style. The bottom edge of the scroll bar is aligned with the bottom edge of the rectangle specified by the *X*, *Y*, *nWidth*, and *nHeight* parameters given in the **CreateWindow** function. The scroll bar has the default height for system scroll bars.

Style	Meaning
SBS_HORZ	Designates a horizontal scroll bar. If neither the SBS_BOTTOMALIGN nor SBS_TOPALIGN style is specified, the scroll bar has the height, width, and position given in the **CreateWindow** function.
SBS_LEFTALIGN	Used with the SBS_VERT style. The left edge of the scroll bar is aligned with the left edge of the rectangle specified by the X, Y, $nWidth$, and $nHeight$ parameters given in the **CreateWindow** function. The scroll bar has the default width for system scroll bars.
SBS_RIGHTALIGN	Used with the SBS_VERT style. The right edge of the scroll bar is aligned with the right edge of the rectangle specified by the X, Y, $nWidth$, and $nHeight$ parameters given in the **CreateWindow** function. The scroll bar has the default width for system scroll bars.
SBS_SIZEBOX	Designates a size box. If neither the SBS_SIZEBOXBOTTOMRIGHTALIGN nor SBS_SIZEBOXTOPLEFTALIGN style is specified, the size box has the height, width, and position given in the **CreateWindow** function.
SBS_SIZEBOXBOTTOMRIGHTALIGN	Used with the SBS_SIZEBOX style. The lower-right corner of the size box is aligned with the lower-right corner of the rectangle specified by the X, Y, $nWidth$, and $nHeight$ parameters given in the **CreateWindow** function. The size box has the default size for system size boxes.
SBS_SIZEBOXTOPLEFTALIGN	Used with the SBS_SIZEBOX style. The upper-left corner of the size box is aligned with the upper-left corner of the rectangle specified by the X, Y, $nWidth$, and $nHeight$ parameters given in the **CreateWindow** function. The size box has the default size for system size boxes.

Style	Meaning
SBS_TOPALIGN	Used with the SBS_HORZ style. The top edge of the scroll bar is aligned with the top edge of the rectangle specified by the *X*, *Y*, *nWidth*, and *nHeight* parameters given in the **CreateWindow** function. The scroll bar has the default height for system scroll bars.
SBS_VERT	Designates a vertical scroll bar. If neither the SBS_RIGHTALIGN nor SBS_LEFTALIGN style is specified, the scroll bar has the height, width, and position given in the **CreateWindow** function.

STATIC Class

Style	Meaning
SS_BLACKFRAME	Specifies a box with a frame drawn with the same color as window frames. This color is black in the default Windows color scheme.
SS_BLACKRECT	Specifies a rectangle filled with the color used to draw window frames. This color is black in the default Windows color scheme.
SS_CENTER	Designates a simple rectangle and displays the given text centered in the rectangle. The text is formatted before it is displayed. Words that would extend past the end of a line are automatically wrapped to the beginning of the next centered line.
SS_GRAYFRAME	Specifies a box with a frame drawn with the same color as the screen background (desktop). This color is gray in the default Windows color scheme.
SS_GRAYRECT	Specifies a rectangle filled with the color used to fill the screen background. This color is gray in the default Windows color scheme.
SS_ICON	Designates an icon displayed in the dialog box. The given text is the name of an icon (not a filename) defined elsewhere in the resource file. The *nWidth* and *nHeight* parameters are ignored; the icon automatically sizes itself.

Style	Meaning
SS_LEFT	Designates a simple rectangle and displays the given text flush-left in the rectangle. The text is formatted before it is displayed. Words that would extend past the end of a line are automatically wrapped to the beginning of the next flush-left line.
SS_LEFTNOWORDWRAP	Designates a simple rectangle and displays the given text flush-left in the rectangle. Tabs are expanded, but words are not wrapped. Text that extends past the end of a line is clipped.
SS_NOPREFIX	Unless this style is specified, windows will interpret any & characters in the control's text to be accelerator prefix characters. In this case, the & is removed and the next character in the string is underlined. If a static control is to contain text where this feature is not wanted, SS_NOPREFIX may be added. This static-control style may be included with any of the defined static controls. You can combine SS_NOPREFIX with other styles by using the bitwise OR operator. This is most often used when filenames or other strings that may contain an & need to be displayed in a static control in a dialog box.
SS_RIGHT	Designates a simple rectangle and displays the given text flush-right in the rectangle. The text is formatted before it is displayed. Words that would extend past the end of a line are automatically wrapped to the beginning of the next flush-right line.
SS_SIMPLE	Designates a simple rectangle and displays a single line of text flush-left in the rectangle. The line of text cannot be shortened or altered in any way. (The control's parent window or dialog box must not process the WM_CTLCOLOR message.)
SS_USERITEM	Specifies a user-defined item.
SS_WHITEFRAME	Specifies a box with a frame drawn with the same color as window backgrounds. This color is white in the default Windows color scheme.
SS_WHITERECT	Specifies a rectangle filled with the color used to fill window backgrounds. This color is white in the default Windows color scheme.

See Also   **AnsiToOem, GetDialogBaseUnits, ShowWindow, CreateWindowEx**

■ CreateWindowEx

HWND CreateWindowEx(*dwExStyle, lpClassName, lpWindowName, dwStyle, X, Y, nWidth, nHeight,
    hWndParent, hMenu, hInstance, lpParam***)**
DWORD *dwExStyle*;
LPTSTR *lpClassName*;
LPTSTR *lpWindowName*;
DWORD *dwStyle*;
int *X*;
int *Y*;
int *nWidth*;
int *nHeight*;
HWND *hWndParent*;
HMENU *hMenu*;
HINSTANCE *hInstance*;
LPVOID *lpParam*;

This function creates an overlapped, pop-up, or child window with an extended style specified in the *dwExStyle* parameter. Otherwise, this function is identical to the **CreateWindow** function. See the description of the **CreateWindow** function for more information on creating a window and for a full descriptions of the other parameters of **CreateWindowEx**.

The **CreateWindowEx** function may be used as either a wide-character function (where text arguments must use Unicode) or an ANSI function (where text arguments must use characters from the Windows 3.x character set installed).

Parameters   *dwExStyle*   Specifies the extended style of the window being created. It may be one of the following values:

Style	Meaning
WS_EX_DLGMODALFRAME	Designates a window with a double border that may optionally be created with a title bar by specifying the WS_CAPTION style flag in the *dwStyle* parameter.
WS_EX_NOPARENTNOTIFY	Specifies that a child window created with this style will not send the WM_PARENTNOTIFY message to its parent window when the child window is created or destroyed.
WS_EX_TOPMOST	Specifies that a window created with this style should be placed above all non-topmost windows and stay above them even when the window is deactivated. An application can use the **SetWindowPos** function to add or remove this attribute.

Style	Meaning
WS_EX_SHADOW	Specifies that this window should have an automatic shadow. If specifies, use this window's window clipping region to manage this shadow. The shadow depth can be queried through system metrics SM_CXSHADOWDEPTH and SM_CYSHADOWDEPTH. The shadow color can be queried through the system color COLOR_SHADOW.

lpClassName   Points to a null-terminated character string that names the window class.

lpWindowName   Points to a null-terminated character string that represents the window name.

dwStyle   Specifies the style of window being created.

X   Specifies the initial *x*-position of the window.

Y   Specifies the initial *y*-position of the window.

nWidth   Specifies the width (in device units) of the window.

nHeight   Specifies the height (in device units) of the window.

hWndParent   Identifies the parent or owner window of the window being created.

hMenu   Identifies a menu or a child-window identifier. The meaning depends on the window style.

hInstance   Identifies the instance creating the window. **GetModuleHandle(NULL)** can be called to return the module handle of the current process.

lpParam   Points to a value that is passed to the window through the **CREATESTRUCT** structure referenced by the *lParam* parameter of the WM_CREATE message.

Return Value   The return value identifies the new window. It is NULL if the window is not created.

Comments   Table T.2, "Control Classes," lists the window control classes. Table T.3, "Window Styles," lists the window styles. Table T.4, "Control Styles," lists the control styles. See the description of the **CreateWindow** function for these tables.

See Also   **CreateWindow**

■ DdeAbandonTransaction

BOOL DdeAbandonTransaction(_hConv_, _idTransaction_**)**
HCONV _hConv_;
DWORD _idTransaction_;

The **DdeAbandonTransaction** function abandons the asynchronous transaction identified by the *idTransaction* parameter and releases all resources associated with the transaction. Only a DDE client application should call the **DdeAbandonTransaction** function. If the server application responds to the transaction after the client has called **DdeAbandonTransaction**, the system discards the transaction results. This function has no effect on synchronous transactions.

Parameters
hConv Identifies the conversation in which the transaction was initiated. If this parameter is NULL, all transactions are abandoned (the *idTransaction* parameter is ignored.)

idTransaction Identifies the transaction to terminate. If this parameter is NULL, all active transactions in the specified conversation are abandoned.

Return Value
The return value is TRUE if the function is successful or FALSE if an error occurs.

Errors
Use the **DdeGetLastError** function to retrieve the error value, which may be one of the following:

> DMLERR_INVALIDPARAMETER
> DMLERR_NO_ERROR
> DMLERR_UNFOUND_QUEUE_ID

See Also
DdeClientTransaction, DdeGetLastError, DdeQueryConvInfo

■ DdeAccessData

LPBYTE DdeAccessData(*hData, pcbDataLen*)
HDDEDATA *hData*;
LPDWORD *pcbDataLen*;

The **DdeAccessData** function provides read-only access to the data in the global memory object identified by the *hData* parameter. An application must call the **DdeUnaccessData** function when it is finished accessing the data in the object.

Parameters
hData Identifies the global memory object to access.

pcbDataLen Points to a variable that receives the length (in bytes) of the data in the global memory object identified by the *hData* parameter. If this parameter is NULL, no length information is returned.

Return Value
The return value points to the first byte of data in the global memory object associated with the *hData* parameter. If there is an error, the return value is NULL.

Errors
Use the **DdeGetLastError** function to retrieve the error value, which may be one of the following:

> DMLERR_INVALIDPARAMETER
> DMLERR_NO_ERROR

See Also   **DdeAddData, DdeCreateDataHandle, DdeFreeDataHandle,
DdeGetLastError, DdeUnaccessData**

■ DdeAddData

HDDEDATA DdeAddData(*hData*, *pSrcBuf*, *cbAddData*, *offObj*)
HDDEDATA *hData*;
LPBYTE *pSrcBuf*;
DWORD *cbAddData*;
DWORD *offObj*;

The **DdeAddData** function adds data to the global memory object identified by the *hData* parameter. An application may add data beginning at any offset from the beginning of the object. If new data overlaps data already in the object, the new data overwrites the old data in the bytes where the overlap occurs. The contents of locations in the object that have not been written to are undefined.

Parameters   *hData*   Identifies the global memory object that receives additional data.

pSrcBuf   Points to a buffer containing the data to add to the global memory object.

cbAddData   Specifies the length (in bytes) of the data to be added to the global memory object.

offObj   Specifies an offset (in bytes) from the beginning of the global memory object. The additional data is copied to the object beginning at this offset.

Return Value   The return value is a new handle to the global memory object. The new handle should be used in all references to the object.

Errors   Use the **DdeGetLastError** function to retrieve the error value, which may be one of the following:

DMLERR_INVALIDPARAMETER
DMLERR_MEMORY_ERROR
DMLERR_NO_ERROR

See Also   **DdeAccessData, DdeCreateDataHandle, DdeGetLastError,
DdeUnaccessData**

■ DdeCallback

```
HDDEDATA EXPENTRY DdeCallback(wType, wFmt, hConv, hsz1, hsz2, hData, dwData1, dwData2)
WORD wType;            /* transaction type                    */
WORD wFmt;             /* clipboard data format               */
HCONV hConv;           /* handle of the conversation          */
HSZ hsz1;              /* handle of a string                  */
HSZ hsz2;              /* handle of a string                  */
HDDEDATA hData;        /* handle of a global memory object    */
DWORD dwData1;         /* transaction-specific data           */
DWORD dwData2;         /* transaction-specific data           */
```

The **DdeCallback** function is an application-defined callback function that processes DDE transactions sent to the function as a result of DDEML calls by other applications.

Parameters

wType   Specifies the type of the current transaction. This parameter consists of a combination of transaction-class flags and transaction-type flags. The following list describes each of the transaction classes and provides a list of the transaction types in each class. For information about a specific transaction type, see the individual description of that type.

Value	Meaning
XCLASS_BOOL	A DDE callback function should return TRUE or FALSE when it finishes processing a transaction that belongs to this class. The XCLASS_BOOL transaction types consist of the following:
	■ XTYP_ADVSTART
	■ XTYP_CONNECT
XCLASS_DATA	A DDE callback function should return a DDE data handle, CBR_BLOCK, or NULL when it finishes processing a transaction that belongs to this class. The XCLASS_DATA transaction types consist of the following:
	■ XTYP_ADVREQ
	■ XTYP_REQUEST
	■ XTYP_WILDCONNECT
XCLASS_FLAGS	A DDE callback function should return DDE_FACK, DDE_FBUSY, or DDE_FNOTPROCESSED when it finishes processing a transaction that belongs to this class. The XCLASS_FLAGS transaction types consist of the following:
	■ XTYP_ADVDATA
	■ XTYP_EXECUTE
	■ XTYP_POKE

Value	Meaning
XCLASS_NOTIFICATION	The transaction types that belong to this class are for notification purposes only. The return value from the callback function is ignored. The XCLASS_NOTIFICATION transaction types consist of the following:

- XTYP_ADVSTOP
- XTYP_CONNECT_CONFIRM
- XTYP_DISCONNECT
- XTYP_ERROR
- XTYP_MONITOR
- XTYP_REGISTER
- XTYP_XACT_COMPLETE
- XTYP_UNREGISTER

wFmt   Specifies the format in which data is sent or received.

hConv   Identifies the conversation associated with the current transaction.

hsz1   Identifies a string. The meaning of this parameter depends on the type of the current transaction. See the description of the transaction type for the meaning of this parameter.

hsz2   Identifies a string. The meaning of this parameter depends on the type of the current transaction. See the description of the transaction type for the meaning of this parameter.

hData   Identifies DDE data. The meaning of this parameter depends on the type of the current transaction. See the description of the transaction type for the meaning of this parameter.

dwData1   Specifies transaction-specific data. See the description of the transaction type for the meaning of this parameter.

dwData2   Specifies transaction-specific data. See the description of the transaction type for the meaning of this parameter.

Return Value   The return value depends on the transaction class. See the descriptions of the individual transaction types for the return values.

Comments   The callback function is called asynchronously for transactions that do not involve creating or terminating conversations. An application that does not frequently accept incoming messages will have reduced DDE performance because the DDEML uses messages to initiate transactions.

An application must register the callback function by specifing a pointer to the function in a call to the **DdeInitialize** function.

DdeCallback is a placeholder for the application- or library-supplied function name. The actual name must be exported by including it in an **EXPORTS** statement in the application's module-definition file.

See Also   DdeEnableCallback, DdeInitialize

■ DdeClientTransaction

HDDEDATA DdeClientTransaction(*lpbData, cbDataLen, hConv, hszItem, wFmt, wType, dwTimeout,*
    lpdwResult)
LPBYTE *lpbData*;
DWORD *cbDataLen*;
HCONV *hConv*;
HSZ *hszItem*;
UINT *wFmt*;
UINT *wType*;
DWORD *dwTimeout*;
LPDWORD *lpdwResult*;

The **DdeClientTransaction** function begins a data transaction between a client and a server application. Only a DDE client application can call this function, and only after establishing a conversation with the server.

Parameters

lpbData   Points to the beginning of the data that the client needs to pass to the server. Optionally, an application can specify the handle of the data to pass to the server, in which case the *cbDataLen* parameter should be set to 0. This parameter is required only if the *wType* parameter is XTYP_EXECUTE or XTYP_POKE. Otherwise, it should be NULL.

cbDataLen   Specifies the length (in bytes) of the data pointed to by the *lpbData* parameter. A value of 0 indicates that *lpbData* is a data handle that identifies the data being sent or that no data is being sent.

hConv   Identifies the conversation.

hszItem   Identifies the data item for which data is being exchanged during the transaction. This handle must have been created by a previous call to the **DdeCreateStringHandle** function. This parameter is ignored (and should be set to NULL) if the *wType* parameter is XTYP_EXECUTE.

wFmt   Specifies the standard clipboard format in which the data item is being submitted or requested.

wType   Specifies the transaction type. It can be one of the following values:

Value	Meaning
XTYP_ADVSTART	Begins an advise loop. Any number of distinct advise loops can exist within a conversation. An application can alter the advise loop type by combining the XTYP_ADVSTART transaction type with one or more of the following flags:

Value	Meaning
XTYPF_NODATA	Instructs the server to notify the client of any data changes without actually sending the data. This flag gives the client the option of ignoring the notification or requesting the changed data from the server.
XTYPF_ACKREQ	Instructs the server to wait until the client acknowledges that it received the previous data item before sending the next data item. This flag prevents a fast server from sending data faster than the client can process it.

XTYP_ADVSTOP	Ends an advise loop.
XTYP_EXECUTE	Begins an execute transaction.
XTYP_POKE	Begins a poke transaction.
XTYP_REQUEST	Begins a request transaction.

dwTimeout Specifies the maximum length of time (in milliseconds) that the client will wait for a response from the server application in a synchronous transaction. This parameter should be set to TIMEOUT_ASYNC for asynchronous transactions.

lpdwResult Points to a variable that receives the result of the transaction. An application that does not check the result can set this value to NULL. For synchronous transactions, the lower 16 bits of this variable will contain any applicable DDE_ flags resulting from the transaction. This provides support for applications dependent on DDE_APPSTATUS bits. (It is recommended that applications no longer use these bits because they may not be supported in future versions of the DDE Management Library.) For asynchronous transactions, this variable is filled with a unique transaction identifier for use with the **DdeAbandonTransaction** function and XTYP_XACT_COMPLETE callbacks.

Return Value

For successful synchronous transactions in which the client expects data from the server, the return value is a data handle that identifies the data. For successful synchronous transactions in which the client does not expect data, the return value is TRUE. For successful asynchronous transactions, the return value is TRUE. The return value is FALSE for all unsuccessful transactions.

Errors

Use the **DdeGetLastError** function to retrieve the error value, which may be one of the following:

DMLERR_INVALIDPARAMETER
DMLERR_NO_CONV_ESTABLISHED
DMLERR_NO_ERROR

Comments   Transactions can be synchronous or asynchronous. During a synchronous transaction, the **DdeClientTransaction** function does not return until the transaction completes successfully or fails. Synchronous transactions cause the client to enter a modal loop while waiting for various asynchronous events. Because of this, the client application is still be able to respond to user input even while waiting on synchronous transactions. However, the client cannot begin a second synchronous transaction because of the activity associated with the first transaction. Therefore, the **DdeClientTransaction** function fails if a synchronous transaction is already in progress. During an asynchronous transaction, the **DdeClientTransaction** function returns immediately with a transaction identifier for reference. When the server provides the results of an asynchronous transaction, a callback is generated with all of the results and data provided in the callback. A client application may choose to abandon an asynchronous transaction by calling the **DdeAbandonTransaction** function.

See Also   **DdeAbandonTransaction, DdeAccessData, DdeConnect, DdeConnectList, DdeCreateStringHandle**

■ DdeCmpStringHandles

UINT DdeCmpStringHandles(*hsz1, hsz2***)**
HSZ *hsz1*;
HSZ *hsz2*;

The **DdeCmpStringHandles** function compares the values of two string handles.

Parameters   *hsz1*   Specifies the first string handle.

    hsz2   Specifies the second string handle.

Return Value   The return value can be one of the following:

    −1   The value of *hsz1* is either 0 or is less than the value of *hsz2*.

    0   The values of *hsz1* and *hsz2* are equal (both may be 0).

    1   The value of *hsz2* is either 0 or is less than the value of *hsz1*.

See Also   **DdeAccessData, DdeCreateStringHandle, DdeFreeStringHandle**

■ DdeConnect

HCONV DdeConnect(*hszAppName, hszTopic, lpvCC***)**
HSZ *hszAppName*;
HSZ *hszTopic*;
LPVOID *lpvCC*;

The **DdeConnect** function establishes a conversation with a server application that supports the specified application name and topic name. If more than one such server exists, only one is selected. The client application should not make assumptions regarding which server will be selected. If an instance-specific name is specified in the *hszAppName* parameter, a conversation will be established only with the specified instance. (Instance-specific application names are passed to an application's DDE callback function during the XTYP_REGISTER and XTYP_UNREGISTER transactions.)

Parameters

hszAppName Identifies the string that specifies the name of the server application with which a conversation is to be established. This handle must have been created by a previous call to the **DdeCreateStringHandle** function. If this parameter is NULL, a conversation with any available server will be established.

hszTopic Identifies the string that specifies the name of the topic on which a conversation is to be established. This handle must have been created by a previous call to the **DdeCreateStringHandle** function. If this parameter is NULL, a conversation on any topic supported by the selected server will be established.

lpvCC Points to a **CONVCONTEXT** structure that provides conversaton information needed for international support. All CF_TEXT strings within any conversation established by a call to the **DdeConnect** function should use the information in this structure. An application can use the system default values by setting this parameter to NULL.

Return Value

The return value is the handle of the established conversation, or NULL if an error occurs.

Errors

Use the **DdeGetLastError** function to retrieve the error value, which may be one of the following:

DMLERR_INVALIDPARAMETER
DMLERR_NO_CONV_ESTABLISHED
DMLERR_NO_ERROR

See Also

DdeConnectList, DdeCreateStringHandle, DdeDisconnect, DdeDisconnectList

■ DdeConnectList

HCONVLIST DdeConnectList(hszAppName, hszTopic, hConvList, lpvCC**)**
HSZ *hszAppName*;
HSZ *hszTopic*;
HCONV *hConvList*;
LPVOID *lpvCC*;

The **DdeConnectList** function establishes a conversation with all server applications that support the specified application name and topic name. An application can also use this function to enumerate a list of conversation handles. Enumeration removes the handles of any terminated conversations from the list and attempts to establish conversations for each remaining handle that does not already have a conversation established. The resulting list contains the handles of all conversations that can currently be established given the specified appication name, topic name, and language criteria.

Parameters

hszAppName   Identifies the string that specifies the name of the server application with which a conversation is to be established. If this parameter is NULL, conversations with all available servers that support the specified topic name will be established.

hszTopic   Identifies the string that specifies the name of the topic on which a conversation is to be established. This handle must have been created by a previous call to the **DdeCreateStringHandle** function. If this parameter is NULL, conversations on all topics supported by the selected server (or servers) will be established.

hConvList   Identifies the conversation list to be enumerated, or NULL if a new conversation is to be established.

lpvCC   Points to a **CONVCONTEXT** structure that provides language information needed for international support. All CF_TEXT strings within any conversation established by a call to the **DdeConnect** function should use the information in this structure. An application can specify the system default values by setting this parameter is NULL.

Return Value

The return value is the handle of a new conversation list, or NULL if an error occurs. The handle of the old conversation list is no longer valid.

Errors

Use the **DdeGetLastError** function to retrieve the error value, which may be one of the following:

DMLERR_NO_CONV_ESTABLISHED
DMLERR_NO_ERROR
DMLERR_SYS_ERROR

See Also

DdeConnect, DdeCreateStringHandle, DdeDisconnect, DdeDisconnectList, DdeQueryNextServer

■ DdeCreateDataHandle

HDDEDATA DdeCreateDataHandle(*lpbSrcBuf, cbInitData, offSrcBuf, hszItem, wFmt, afCmd***)**
LPBYTE *lpbSrcBuf*;
DWORD *cbInitData*;
DWORD *offSrcBuf*;
HSZ *hszItem*;
UINT *wFmt*;
UINT *afCmd*;

The **DdeCreateDataHandle** function creates a global memory object and fills the object with the data pointed to by the *lpbSrcBuf* parameter. A DDE server application uses this function during transactions that involve passing data to a client.

Parameters   *lpbSrcBuf*   Points to a buffer that contains data to be copied to the global memory object. If this parameter is NULL, no data is copied to the object.

cbInitData   Specifies the amount (in bytes) of memory to allocate for the global memory object. If this parameter is 0, the *lpbSrcBuf* parameter is ignored.

offSrcBuf   Specifies an offset (in bytes) from the beginning of the buffer pointed to by the *lpbSrcBuf* parameter. The data beginning at this offset is copied from the buffer to the global memory object.

hszItem   Identifies the string that specifies the data item corresponding to the global memory object. This handle must have been created by a previous call to the **DdeCreateStringHandle** function.

wFmt   Specifies the standard clipboard format of the data.

afCmd   Specifies the creation flags. It can be one of the following values:

Value	Meaning
HDATA_APPOWNED	Specifies that the server application that calls the **DdeCreateDataHandle** function will own the data handle that this function creates. This allows the server to share the data handle with multiple clients instead of creating a separate handle for each request. If this flag is set, the server must eventually free the shared memory object associated with this handle by using the **DdeFreeDataHandle** function. If this flag is not set, the data handle becomes invalid in the application that creates the handle once the handle is returned by the server's callback function or used as a parameter in another DDE Management Library function.

Return Value   The return value is a data handle if the function is successful. Otherwise, the return value is NULL.

Comments   Any locations in the global memory object that are not filled are undefined. Data handles that are returned by the server's callback function or used as a parameter in another DDE Management Library function become read-only.

If the application will be adding data to the global memory object (using the **DdeAddData** function) so that the object exceeds 64K bytes in length, then the application should specify a total length (*cbInitData* + *offSrcData*) that is equal to the anticipated maximum length of the object. This avoids unnecessary data copying and memory reallocation by the system.

Errors   Use the **DdeGetLastError** function to retrieve the error value, which may be one of the following:

DMLERR_INVALIDPARAMETER
DMLERR_MEMORY_ERROR
DMLERR_NO_ERROR

See Also   **DdeAccessData, DdeFreeDataHandle, DdeGetData**

■ DdeCreateStringHandle

HSZ DdeCreateStringHandle(*lpszString*, *idLang***)**
LPSTR *lpszString*;
DWORD *idLang*;

The **DdeCreateStringHandle** function creates a handle that identifies the string pointed to by the *lpszString* parameter. A DDE client or server application can pass the string handle as a parameter to other DDE Management Library functions.

Two identical case-sensitive strings always correspond to the same string handle. String handles are unique across all processes that use the DDE Management Library. That is, when an application creates a handle for a string, and another application creates a handle for an identical string, the string handles returned to both applications are identical. All applications that have either created a string handle or have received one in the callback routine and kept it via the **DdeKeepStringHandle** function must free that string handle when it is no longer needed.

Parameters   *lpszString*   Points to a buffer that contains the null-terminated string for which a handle is to be created. This string may be any length.

idLang   Specifies the language code for the string. If this parameter is NULL, the system will use the default language code.

Return Value   The return value is a string handle if the function is successful. Otherwise, the return value is NULL.

Errors   Use the **DdeGetLastError** function to retrieve the error value, which may be one of the following:

    DMLERR_INVALIDPARAMETER
    DMLERR_NO_ERROR
    DMLERR_SYS_ERROR

See Also   **DdeAccessData, DdeCmpStringHandles, DdeFreeStringHandle, DdeKeepStringHandle, DdeQueryString**

■ DdeDisconnect

BOOL DdeDisconnect(*hConv***)**
HCONV *hConv*;

The **Disconnect** function terminates a conversation started by either the **DdeConnect** or **DdeConnectList** function and invalidates the conversation handle specified by the *hConv* parameter. Any incomplete transactions started before calling **DdeDisconnect** are immediately abandoned. The XTYP_DISCONNECT transaction type is sent to the callback function of the partner in the conversation. Generally, only client applications need to disconnect conversations.

Parameters   *hConv*   Identifies the active conversation to be terminated.

Return Value   The return value is TRUE if the function is successful or FALSE if an error occurs.

Errors   Use the **DdeGetLastError** function to retrieve the error value, which may be one of the following:

DMLERR_NO_CONV_ESTABLISHED
DMLERR_NO_ERROR

See Also   **DdeConnect, DdeConnectList, DdeDisconnectList**

■ DdeDisconnectList

BOOL DdeDisconnectList(*hConvList***)**
HCONVLIST *hConvList*;

The **DdeDisconnectList** function destroys the conversation list identified by the *hConvList* parameter and terminates all conversations associated with the list.

Parameters   *hConvList*   Identifies the conversation list. This handle must have been created by a previous call to the **DdeConnectList** function.

Return Value   The return value is TRUE if the function is successful or FALSE if an error occurs.

Errors   Use the **DdeGetLastError** function to retrieve the error value, which may be one of the following:

DMLERR_INVALIDPARAMETER
DMLERR_NO_ERROR

See Also   **DdeConnect, DdeConnectList, DdeDisconnect**

■ DdeEnableCallback

BOOL DdeEnableCallback(*hConv, wCmd***)**
HCONV *hConv*;
UINT *wCmd*;

The **DdeEnableCallback** function enables or disables a specific conversation or all conversations that the calling application currently has established.

After disabling a conversation, the system places all transactions for the conversation in a transaction queue associated with the application. The application should re-enable the conversation as soon as possible to avoid losing queued transactions.

Parameters	*hConv* Identifies the conversation to enable or disable. If this parameter is NULL, the function affects all conversations.

wCmd   Specifies the command code. It can be one of the following values:

Value	Meaning
EC_ENABLEALL	Enables all conversations.
EC_ENABLEONE	Enables the conversation specified by the *hConv* parameter.
EC_DISABLE	Disables the specified conversation. If the *hConv* parameter is NULL, all conversations are disabled.

Return Value

The return value is TRUE if the function is successful or FALSE if an error occurs.

Errors

Use the **DdeGetLastError** function to retrieve the error value, which may be one of the following:

DMLERR_NO_ERROR
DMLERR_INVALIDPARAMETER

Comments

An application can disable a specific conversation by returning CBR_BLOCK from its callback function. When the conversation is re-enabled by using the **DdeEnableCallback** function, the system generates the same transaction as was in process when the conversation was disabled.

See Also

DdeConnect, DdeConnectList, DdeDisconnect, DdeInitialize

■ DdeFreeDataHandle

BOOL DdeFreeDataHandle(*hData***)**
HDDEDATA *hData*;

The **DdeFreeDataHandle** function frees a global memory object created by the **DdeCreateDataHandle** function and destroys the data handle associated with the object. When an application finishes using a global memory object that it owns, it must call this function to free the object. An unowned object is automatically released when its handle is returned by a DDE callback function or used as a parameter in a DDE Management Library function.

Parameters

hData   Identifies the global memory object to be freed. This handle must have been created by a previous call to the **DdeCreateDataHandle** function.

Return Value

The return value is TRUE if the function is successful or FALSE if an error occurs.

Errors

Use the **DdeGetLastError** function to retrieve the error value, which may be one of the following:

DMLERR_INVALIDPARAMETER
DMLERR_NO_ERROR

See Also   DdeAccessData, DdeCreateDataHandle

■ DdeFreeStringHandle

BOOL DdeFreeStringHandle(*hsz***)**
HSZ *hsz*;

The **DdeFreeStringHandle** frees a string handle in the calling application.

Parameters   *hsz*   Identifies the string handle to be freed. This handle must have been created by a previous call to the **DdeCreateStringHandle** function.

Return Value   The return value is TRUE if the function is successful or FALSE if an error occurs.

See Also   DdeCmpStringHandles, DdeCreateStringHandle, DdeKeepStringHandle

■ DdeGetData

DWORD DdeGetData(*hData*, *pDest*, *cbMax*, *offSrc***)**
HDDEDATA *hData*;
LPBYTE *pDest*;
DWORD *cbMax*;
DWORD *offSrc*;

The **DdeGetData** function copies data from the global memory object identified by the *hData* parameter to the local buffer pointed to by the *pDest* parameter.

Parameters   *hData*   Identifies the global memory object that contains the data to copy.

pDest   Points to the buffer that receives the data. If this parameter is NULL, the **DdeGetData** function returns the amount (in bytes) of data that would be copied to the buffer.

cbMax   Specifies the maximum amount (in bytes) of data to copy to the buffer pointed to by the *pDest* parameter. Typically, this parameter specifies the length of the buffer pointed to by the *pDest* parameter.

offSrc   Specifies an offset within the global memory object. Data is copied from the object beginning at this offset.

Return Value   The return value is the amount of data copied to the destination buffer or, if NULL was specified in the *pDest* parameter, the amount of data that would be copied to the destination buffer.

Errors   Use the **DdeGetLastError** function to retrieve the error value, which may be one of the following:

DMLERR_INVALID_HDDEDATA
DMLERR_INVALIDPARAMETER
DMLERR_NO_ERROR

See Also   **DdeAccessData, DdeFreeDataHandle, DdeCreateDataHandle**

■ DdeGetLastError

UINT DdeGetLastError(VOID)

The **DdeGetLastError** function returns the most recent error value set by the failure of a DDE Management Library function and sets the error code to DMLERR_NO_ERROR.

This function has no parameters.

Return Value   The return value is the last error code.

■ DdeImpersonateClient

BOOL DdeImpersonateClient(*hConv***)**
HANDLE *hConv*;

The **DdeImpersonateClient** function impersonates a DDE client application in a DDE client conversation.

Parameters   *hConv*   Handle to the DDE client conversation.

Return Value   If the function is successful, the return value is TRUE.

If the function fails, the return value is FALSE. Call **GetLastError** for more detailed error information.

See Also   **DdeRevertToSelf, ImpersonateNamedPipeClient, NamedPipeRevertToSelf**

■ DdeInitialize

UINT DdeInitialize(*pfnCallback, afCmd, dwRes***)**
PFNCALLBACK *pfnCallback*;
DWORD *afCmd*;
DWORD *dwRes*;

The **DdeInitialize** function initializes an application for making DDE Management Library (DDEML) function calls. An application must call this function before calling any other DDEML function.

Parameters   *pfnCallback*   Points to the application-defined DDE callback function. This function processes DDE transactions sent by the system. See the following "Comments" section for details.

afCmd   Specifies an array of APPCMD_ and CBF_ flags. The APPCMD_ flags provide special instructions to the **DdeInitialize** function. The CBF_ flags set filters that prevent specific types of transactions from reaching the callback function. Using these flags enhances the performance of a DDE application by eliminating unnecessary calls to the callback function.

This parameter can be any combination of the following flags:

Flag	Meaning

APPCMD_CLIENTONLY

Prevents the application from becoming a server in a DDE conversation. The application will only be a client. This flag reduces resource consumption by the DDEML. This flag includes the functionality of the CBF_FAIL_ALLSVRXACTIONS flag.

CBF_FAIL_CONNECTIONS

Prevents the callback function from receiving XTYP_CONNECT and XTYP_WILDCONNECT transactions.

CBF_FAIL_SELFCONNECTIONS

Prevents the callback function from receiving XTYP_CONNECT transactions from its own application instance. This prevents an application from establishing a DDE conversation with its own instance. An application should use this flag if it needs to communicate with other instances of itself but not with itself.

CBF_FAIL_ADVISES

Prevents the callback function from receiving XTYP_ADVSTART and XTYP_ADVSTOP transactions. The system will return the DDE_FNOTPROCESSED result code to each client that sends an XTYP_ADVSTART or XTYP_ADVSTOP transaction to this application.

CBF_FAIL_EXECUTES

Prevents the callback function from receiving XTYP_EXECUTE transactions. The system will return the DDE_FNOTPROCESSED result code to each client that sends an XTYP_EXECUTE transaction to this application.

CBF_FAIL_POKES

Prevents the callback function from receiving XTYP_POKE transactions. The system will return the DDE_FNOTPROCESSED result code to each client that sends an XTYP_POKE transaction to this application.

CBF_FAIL_REQUESTS

Prevents the callback function from receiving XTYP_REQUEST transactions. The system will return the DDE_FNOTPROCESSED result code to each client that sends an XTYP_REQUEST transaction to this application.

CBF_FAIL_ALLSVRXACTIONS

Prevents the callback function from receiving any server transactions. The system will return the DDE_FNOTPROCESSED result code to each client that sends a transaction to this application. This flag is equivalent to combining all CBF_FAIL_ flags.

CBF_SKIP_CONNECT_CONFIRMS

Prevents the callback function from receiving XTYP_CONNECT_CONFIRM notifications.

CBF_SKIP_REGISTRATIONS

Prevents the callback function from receiving XTYP_REGISTER notifications.

Flag	Meaning

CBF_SKIP_UNREGISTRATIONS
Prevents the callback function from receiving XTYP_UNREGISTER notifications.

CBF_SKIP_DISCONNECTS
Prevents the callback function from receiving XTYP_DISCONNECT notifications.

CBF_SKIP_ALLNOTIFICATIONS
Prevents the callback function from receiving any notifications. This flag is equivalent combining all CBF_SKIP_ flags.

dwRes   This parameter reserved; it must be set to 0L.

Return Value   The return value is one of the following:

DMLERR_DLL_USAGE
DMLERR_INVALIDPARAMETER
DMLERR_NO_ERROR
DMLERR_SYS_ERROR

Comments   The callback function has the following form:

HDDEDATA EXPENTRY *DDECallback(wType, wFmt, hConv, hsz1, hsz2, hData, dwData1, dwData2)*
WORD *wType*;
WORD *wFmt*;
CONV *hConv*;
HSZ *hsz1*;
HSZ *hsz2*;
HDDEDATA *hData*;
DWORD *dwData1*;
DWORD *dwData2*;

A DDE callback function processes DDE transactions sent by the system as a result of DDEML calls by other applications.

DDECallback is a placeholder for the application-supplied function name. The actual name must be exported by including it in an **EXPORTS** statement in the application's module-definition file.

Parameters   *wType*   Specifies the type of the current transaction. This parameter consists of a combination of XCLASS_, XTYP_, and XTYPF_ flags.

Value	Meaning

XCLASS_BOOL
A DDE callback function should return TRUE or FALSE when it finishes processing a transaction type that belongs to this class. The XCLASS_BOOL transaction types consist of the following:

Value	Meaning

XTYP_ADVSTART

A server receives this transaction type from a client requesting an advise loop with the server, unless the server has specified the CBF_FAIL_ADVISES flag in the **DdeInitialize** function. The *hsz1* parameter identifies the topic name. The *hsz2* parameter identifies the item name. The server should return TRUE to allow the advise loop, or FALSE to refuse it. If the server returns TRUE, subsequent calls by the server to the **DdePostAdvise** function cause the system to send XTYP_ADVREQ transactions to the server.

XTYP_CONNECT

A server receives this transaction type when a client attempts to establish a conversation with the server, unless the server has specified the CBF_FAIL_CONNECTIONS flag in the **DdeInitialize** function. The *hsz1* parameter identifies the topic name. The *hsz2* parameter identifies the application name of the server. The *hDdata* parameter identifies a **CONVCONTEXT** data structure, or NULL if the default system context is to be used. The server cannot block this transaction type; the CBR_BLOCK return code is ignored. The server should return TRUE to allow the conversation, or FALSE to refuse it. If the server returns TRUE and a conversation is established, the system sends the XTYP_CONNECT_CONFIRM transaction to server unless the server specified the CBF_SKIP_CONNECT_CONFIRMS flag in the **DdeInitialize** function.

XCLASS_DATA

A DDE callback function should return a DDE data handle, CBR_BLOCK, or NULL when it finishes processing a transaction type that belongs to this class. The XCLASS_DATA transaction types consist of the following:

Value	Meaning

XTYP_ADVREQ

The system sends this transaction type to a server to inform the server that an advise transaction is outstanding on the specified topic/item pair and that data corresponding to the topic/item has changed (as indicated by a call to the **DdePostAdvise** function by this server). The *hsz1* parameter identifies the topic name. The *hsz2* parameter identifies the item name. The server should call the **DdeCreateDataHandle** function to create a data handle that identifies the changed data, then return the handle. The server should return NULL if it is unable to complete the transaction.

Value	Meaning

XTYP_REQUEST

> A server receives this transaction type when a client requests data from the server. The *hsz1* parameter identifies the topic name. The *hsz2* parameter identifies the item name. The server should call the **DdeCreateDataHandle** function to create a data handle that identifies the requested data, then return the handle. The server should return NULL if it is unable to complete the transaction. This causes the client to receive a DDE_FNOTPROCESSED flag.

XTYP_WILDCONNECT

> A server receives this transaction type when a client attempts to establish multiple conversations with the server. The *hsz1* parameter identifies the topic name. If this parameter is NULL, the client is requesting a conversation on all topics names that the server supports. The *hsz2* parameter identifies the application. If this parameter is NULL, the client is requesting a conversation on all application names that the server supports. The *hData* parameter identifies a **CONVCONTEXT** data structure, or NULL if the default system context is to be used.

> The server should return a data handle that identifies an array of **HSZPAIR** structures. The array should contain one structure for each application/topic that matches the application/topic pair requested by the client. The array must be terminated by a NULL string handle. The system sends the XTYP_CONNECT_CONFIRM transaction to server to confirm each conversation and to pass the conversation handles to the server. The server will not receive these confirmations if it specified the CBF_SKIP_CONNECT_CONFIRMS flag in the **DdeInitialize** function.

> The server should return NULL to refuse the XTYP_WILDCONNECT transaction.

XCLASS_FLAGS

A DDE callback function should return one of the following values when it finishes processing a transaction type that belongs to this class:

Value	Meaning

DDE_FACK_

> The transaction was accepted and is being processed.

DDE_FBUSY

> The server is busy and cannot respond to the transaction. The client should repeat the transaction later.

DDE_FNOTPROCESSED

> The server has rejected the transaction.

The XCLASS_FLAGS transaction types consist of the following:

Value	Meaning

XTYP_ADVDATA

A client receives this transaction type after establishing an advise loop with a server. The *hsz1* parameter identifies the topic name. The *hsz2* parameter identifies the item name. The *hData* parameter identifies the data associated with the topic/item pair. This parameter is NULL if the client specified the XTYPF_NODATA flag when it requested the advise loop.

XTYP_EXECUTE

A server receives this transaction type from a client that is requesting the server to execute a command. The *hsz1* parameter identifies the topic name. The *hData* parameter identifies the execute string. The server does not receive this transaction type if it specified the CBF_FAIL_EXECUTES flag in the **DdeInitialize** function.

XTYP_POKE

A server receives this transaction type from a client that is sending unsolicited data to the server. a call to the *hsz1* parameter identifies the topic name. The *hsz2* parameter identifies the item name. The *hData* parameter identifies the unsolicited data from the client. The server does not receive this transaction type if it specified the CBF_FAIL_POKES flag in the **DdeInitialize** function.

XCLASS_NOTIFICATION

The transaction types that belong to this class are for notification purposes. The return value from the callback function is ignored. The XCLASS_NOTIFICATION transaction types consist of the following:

Value	Meaning

XTYP_ADVSTOP

A server receives this transaction type from a client that is terminating an advise loop. The *hsz1* parameter identifies the topic name. The *hsz2* parameter identifies the item name. The server does not receive this transaction type if it specified the CBF_FAIL_ADVISES flag in the **DdeInitialize** function.

XTYP_CONNECT_CONFIRM

A server receives this transaction type to confirm that a conversation has been established with a client, unless the server specified the CBF_FAIL_CONFIRMS flag in the **DdeInitialize** function. The server cannot block this transaction type; the CBR_BLOCK return code is ignored.

Value	Meaning

XTYP_REGISTER

A DDE callback function receives this transaction type whenever a DDEML server uses the **DdeNameService** function to register an application name, or whenever a non-DDEML server starts that supports the System topic. The *hsz1* parameter identifies the base application name being registered. The *hsz2* parameter identifies the instance-specific application name being registered. An application should use the *hsz1* parameter to include the name of the server in the list of servers available to the user. An application should use the *hsz2* parameter in a call to the **DdeConnect** function to establish a conversation with the server. The application cannot block this transaction type; the CBR_BLOCK return code is ignored. The application does not receive this transaction type if it specified the CBF_SKIP_REGISTRATIONS flag in the **DdeInitialize** function.

XTYP_TERM

A server receives this transaction type when a client terminates a conversation, unless the server specified the CBF_SKIP_DISCONNECTS flag in the **DdeInitialize** function. The *hConv* parameter identifies the conversation that has terminated.

XTYP_UNREGISTER

A DDE callback function receives this transaction type whenever a DDEML server uses the **DdeNameService** function to unregister an application name. The *hsz1* parameter identifies the base application name being unregistered. The *hsz2* parameter identifies the instance-specific application name being unregistered. An application should use the *hsz1* parameter to remove the name of the server from the list of servers available to the user. An application should use the *hsz2* parameter to identify which application instance has terminated. The application cannot block this transaction type; the CBR_BLOCK return code is ignored. The application does not receive this transaction type if it specified the CBF_SKIP_UNREGISTRATIONS flag in the **DdeInitialize** function.

Value	Meaning

XTYPE_XACT_COMPLETE

A client receives this transaction type to confirm that an asynchronous transaction, initiated by a call to the **DdeClientTransaction** function, has completed. The *hsz1* parameter identifies the topic name. The *hsz2* parameter identifies the item name. The *hData* parameter identifies the data sent from the server. This parameter is TRUE if the completed transaction was successful but involved no transfer of data. It is NULL if the transaction failed. The *dwData1* parameter specifies the transaction identifier of the completed transaction. The low word of the *dwData2* parameter specifies and applicable DDE_ flags. This supports applications dependant on DDE_APPSTATUS bits.

wFmt   Specifies the format in which data is sent or received.

hConv   Identifies the conversation associated with the current transaction.

hsz1   Identifies a string. The meaning of this parameter depends on the type of the current transaction.

hsz2   Identifies a string. The meaning of this parameter depends on the type of the current transaction.

hData   Identifies DDE data. The meaning of this parameter depends on the type of the current transaction.

dwData1   Specifies transaction-specific data.

dwData2   Specifies transaction-specific data.

Comments   The callback function may receive a transaction that requires a significant amount of processing. In this case, the callback function should return the CBR_BLOCK constant, then process the transaction asynchronously. The CBR_BLOCK constant blocks future transactions on the same conversation. When the callback function finishes processing the transaction, it should call the **DdeEnableCallback** function to unblock other transactions. Because **DdeEnableCallback** causes the system to repeat the last transaction, the callback function should store the result of the transaction before calling **DdeEnableCallback** to avoid reprocessing the transaction.

See Also   **DdeClientTransaction, DdeConnect, DdeCreateDataHandle, DdeEnableCallback, DdeNameService, DdePostAdvise, DdeUninitialize**

■ DdeKeepStringHandle

BOOL DdeKeepStringHandle(*hsz***)**
HSZ *hsz*;

The **DdeKeepStringHandle** function increments the use count associated with the handle specified by the *hsz* parameter. This function allows an application to save a string handle that was passed to the application's DDE callback function. Otherwise, a string handle passed to the callback function is destroyed when the callback function returns.

Parameters
hsz   Identifies the string handle to be saved.

Return Value
The return value is TRUE if the function is successful or FALSE if an error occurs.

See Also
DdeCreateStringHandle, DdeFreeStringHandle, DdeQueryString

■ DdeNameService

```
HDDEDATA DdeNameService(hsz1, hszRes, afCmd)
HSZ hsz1;
HSZ hszRes;
UINT afCmd;
```

The **DdeNameService** function registers or unregisters the application name of a DDE server. This function causes the system to send XTYP_REGISTER or XTYP_UNREGISTER transactions to other running DDE Management Library (DDEML) client applications.

A server application should call this function to register each application name that it supports, and to unregister names that it previously registered but no longer supports. A server should also call this function to unregister its application names just before terminating.

Parameters
hsz1   Identifies the string that specifies the application name that the server is registering or unregistering. An application that is unregistering all of its application names should set this parameter to NULL.

hszRes   This parameter is reserved for future use. An application should set it to NULL.

afCmd   Specifies the name service flags. This parameter may be one of the following values:

Value	Meaning
DNS_REGISTER	Registers the given application name.
DNS_UNREGISTER	Unregisters the given application name. If the *hsz1* parameter is NULL, all application names registered by the server will be unregistered.
DNS_FILTERON	Turns on application-name initiation filtering. This filter prevents a server from receiving XTYP_CONNECT transactions for application names that it has not registered. This is the default setting for this filter.

Value	Meaning
DNS_FILTEROFF	Turns off application-name initiation filtering. If this flag is set, the server will receive an XTYP_CONNECT transaction for any DDE initiate it receives, regardless of the application name.

Return Value   The return value is TRUE if the function is succesful or FALSE if an error occurs.

Errors   Use the **DdeGetLastError** function to retrieve the error value, which may be one of the following:

DMLERR_DLL_USAGE
DMLERR_INVALIDPARAMETER
DMLERR_NO_ERROR

Comments   The application name identified by the *hsz1* parameter should be a base name (that is, the name should contain no instance-specific information). The system generates an instance-specific name and sends it along with the base name during the XTYP_REGISTER and XTYP_UNREGISTER transactions. The receiving applications can then connect to the specific application instance.

See Also   **DdeConnect, DdeConnectList**

■ DdePostAdvise

BOOL DdePostAdvise(*hszTopic, hszItem***)**
HSZ *hszTopic*;
HSZ *hszItem*;

The **DdePostAdvise** function causes the system to send an XTYP_ADVREQ transaction to the calling (server) application's callback function for each client that has an advise loop active on the specified topic/item pair. A server application should call this function whenever the data associated with the topic/item pair changes. No further action is required on the part of the server to advise the client(s) of changes to the data.

Servers that have non-enumerable topics or items should set the *hszTopic* and *hszItem* parameters to NULL so that the system generates transactions for all active advise loops. The server's callback function returns NULL for any advise loops that do not need to be updated.

Parameters   *hszTopic*   Identifies a string that specifies the topic name. An application can set this parameter to NULL to send notifications for all topics with active advise loops.

hszItem   Identifies a string that specifies the item name. An application can set this parameter to NULL to send notifications for all items with active advise loops.

Return Value   The return value is TRUE if the function is successful or FALSE if an error occurs.

Errors   Use the **DdeGetLastError** function to retrieve the error value, which may be one of the following:

DMLERR_DLL_USAGE
DMLERR_NO_ERROR

See Also   **DdeInitialize**

■ DdeQueryConvInfo

BOOL DdeQueryConvInfo(hConv, idTransaction, pConvInfo**)**
HCONV hConv;
DWORD idTransaction;
PCONVINFO pConvInfo;

The **DdeQueryConvInfo** function retrieves information about a DDE transaction and about the conversation in which the transaction takes place.

Parameters   *hConv*   Identifies the conversation.

idTransaction   Identifies the transaction. For asynchronous transactions, this parameter should be a transaction identifier returned by the **DdeClientTransaction** function. For synchronous transactions, this parameter should be QID_SYNC.

pConvInfo   Points to the **CONVINFO** structure that will recieve information about the transaction and conversation. The *cb* member of the **CONVINFO** structure must specify the length of the buffer allocated for the structure.

Return Value   The return value is TRUE if the function is successful or FALSE if an error occurs.

Errors   Use the **DdeGetLastError** function to retrieve the error value, which may be one of the following:

DMLERR_NO_CONV_ESTABLISHED
DMLERR_NO_ERROR
DMLERR_UNFOUND_QUEUE_ID

See Also   **DdeConnect, DdeConnectList**

■ DdeQueryNextServer

HCONV DdeQueryNextServer(hConvList, hConvPrev**)**
HCONVLIST hConvList;
HCONV hConvPrev;

The **DdeQueryNextServer** function obtains the next conversation handle in the specified conversation list.

Parameters

hConvList Identifies the conversation list. This handle must have been created by a previous call to the **DdeConnectList** function.

hConvPrev Identifies the conversation handle previously returned by this function. If this parameter is NULL, this function returns the first conversation handle in the list.

Return Value

The return value is the next conversation handle in the list. If the list contains no more conversation handles, the return value is NULL.

See Also

DdeConnectList, DdeDisconnectList

■ DdeQueryString

```
UINT DdeQueryString(hsz, lpsz, cchMax)
HSZ hsz;
LPSTR lpsz;
DWORD cchMax;
```

The **DdeQueryString** function copies text associated with a string handle into a buffer.

The string returned in the buffer is always be null-terminated. If the string text is longer than ($cchMax - 1$), only the first ($cchMax - 1$) characters of string text are copied.

If the *lpsz* parameter is NULL, this function obtains the length of the string associated with the string handle. The length does not include the null terminator.

Parameters

hsz Identifies the string to copy. This handle must have been created by a previous call to the **DdeCreateStringHandle** function.

lpsz Points to a buffer that receives the string text, or NULL to obtain the length of the string.

cchMax Specifies the length of the buffer pointed to by the *lpsz* parameter. If the text is longer than ($cchMax - 1$), it will be truncated. This parameter is ignored if the *lpsz* parameter is set to NULL.

Return Value

The return value is the length of the returned text (not including the null terminator) if the *lpsz* parameter specified a valid pointer. The return value is the length of the text associated with the *hsz* parameter (not including the null terminator) if the *lpsz* parameter specified a NULL pointer. The return value is NULL if an error occurs.

See Also

DdeCmpStringHandles, DdeCreateStringHandle, DdeFreeStringHandle

■ DdeRevertToSelf

BOOL DdeRevertToSelf(*hConv***)**
HANDLE *hConv*;

The **DdeRevertToSelf** function terminates impersonation of a DDE client application in a DDE client conversation.

Parameters   *hConv*   Handle to the DDE client conversation.

Return Value   If the function is successful, the return value is TRUE.

If the function fails, the return value is FALSE. Call **GetLastError** for more detailed error information.

See Also   **DdeImpersonateClient, ImpersonateNamedPipeClient, NamedPipeRevertToSelf**

■ DdeSetUserHandle

BOOL DdeSetUserHandle(*hConv, dwUser***)**
HCONV *hConv*;
DWORD *dwUser*;

The **DdeSetUserHandle** function associates an application-supplied 32-bit value with a conversation handle. This is useful for simplifying the processing of asynchronous transactions. An application can use the **DdeQueryConvInfo** function to retrieve this value.

Parameters   *hConv*   Identifies the conversation.

dwUser   Specifies the value to associate with the conversation handle.

Return Value   The return value is TRUE if the function is successful or FALSE if an error occurs.

Errors   Use the **DdeGetLastError** function to retrieve the error value, which may be one of the following:

DMLERR_INVALIDPARAMETER
DMLERR_NO_ERROR

See Also   **DdeQueryConvInfo**

■ DdeUnaccessData

BOOL DdeUnaccessData(*lpbData***)**
LPBYTE *lpbData*;

The **DdeUnaccessData** function invalidates a pointer to a global memory object. An application must call this function when it is finished using a pointer obtained by using the **DdeAccessData** function.

Parameters	*lpbData* Specifies the pointer to be invalidated. This pointer must have been obtained by a previous call to the **DdeAccessData** function.
Return Value	The return value is TRUE if the function is successful or FALSE if an error occurs.
Errors	Use the **DdeGetLastError** function to retrieve the error value, which may be one of the following: DMLERR_INVALIDPARAMETER DMLERR_NO_ERROR
See Also	**DdeAccessData, DdeAddData, DdeCreateDataHandle, DdeFreeDataHandle**

■ DdeUninitialize

BOOL Uninitialize(*VOID* **)**

The **DdeUninitialize** function frees all DDE Management Library resources aassociated with the calling application.

This function has no parameters.

Return Value	The return value is TRUE if the function is successful or FALSE if an error occurs.
See Also	**DdeInitialize**

■ DebugActiveProcess

BOOL DebugActiveProcess(DWORD dwProcessId)

This API allows a debugger to attach to an active process and debug the process. The debugger specifies the process that it wants to debug through the process id of the target process. The debugger gets debug access to the process as if it had created the process with the DEBUG_ONLY_THIS_PROCESS creation flag.

Parameters	*dwProcessId* Supplies the process id of a process the caller wants to debug.
Return Value	TRUE – The operation was successful. FALSE/NULL – The operation failed. Extended error status is available using GetLastError.
Comments	The debugger must have appropriate access to the calling process such that it can open the process for PROCESS_ALL_ACCESS. For Dos/Win32 this never fails (the process id just has to be a valid process id). For NT/Win32 this check can fail if the target process was created with a security descriptor that denies the debugger appropriate access. Once the process id check has been made and the system determines that a valid debug attachment is being made, this call returns

success to the debugger. The debugger is then expected to wait for debug events. The system will suspend all threads in the process and feed the debugger debug events representing the current state of the process.

The system will feed the debugger a single create process debug event representing the process specified by dwProcessId. The lpStartAddress field of the create process debug event is NULL. For each thread currently part of the process, the system will send a create thread debug event. The lpStartAddress field of the create thread debug event is NULL. For each DLL currently loaded into the address space of the target process, the system will send a LoadDll debug event. The system will arrange for the first thread in the process to execute a breakpoint instruction after it is resumed. Continuing this thread causes the thread to return to whatever it was doing prior to the debug attach.

After all of this has been done, the system resumes all threads

within the process. When the first thread in the process resumes, it will execute a breakpoint instruction causing an exception debug event to be sent to the debugger.

All future debug events are sent to the debugger using the normal mechanism and rules.

■ DebugBreak

VOID DebugBreak(VOID)

The **DebugBreak** function causes a breakpoint exception to occur in the caller. This allows the calling thread to signal the debugger forcing it to take some action. If the process is not being debugged, the standard exception search logic is invoked. In most cases, this will cause the calling process to terminate (due to an unhandled breakpoint exception).

This function has no parameters.

Return Value　　　This function does not return a value.

■ DefDlgProc

LONG DefDlgProc(hDlg, wMsg, wParam, lParam)
HWND hDlg,
UINT wMsg,
DWORD wParam,
LONG lParam;

The **DefDlgProc** function is the window procedure for the DIALOG window class. This function *is not* meant to be called as the default handler for messages within a dialog procedure. Doing this will result in recursive execution. This function is used by applications that want to create new window classes that inherit dialog functionality.

Parameters	*hDlg* Identifies the dialog box.
	wMsg Specifies the message number.
	wParam Specifies additional message-dependent information.
	lParam Specifies additional message-dependent information.
Return Value	The return value specifies the result of the message processing and depends on the actual message sent.
Comments	The source code for the **DefDlgProc** function is provided on the SDK disks.

An application creates a dialog box by calling one of the following functions:

Function	Description
CreateDialog	Creates a modeless dialog box.
CreateDialogIndirect	Creates a modeless dialog box.
CreateDialogIndirectParam	Creates a modeless dialog box and passes data to it when it is created.
CreateDialogParam	Creates a modeless dialog box and passes data to it when it is created.
DialogBox	Creates a modal dialog box.
DialogBoxIndirect	Creates a modal dialog box.
DialogBoxIndirectParam	Creates a modal dialog box and passes data to it when it is created.
DialogBoxParam	Creates a modal dialog box and passes data to it when it is created.

To create a new window class that inherits dialog functionality, query the default dialog class information and create a clone of this class with your own application attributes:

```
GetClassInfo(hModule, (LPSTR)DIALOGCLASS, lpWndClass);
lpWndClass.lpszClassName = "mydialogclass";
RegisterClass(lpWndClass);
```

Or, you can create your own class directly, as long as you reserve the proper number of window extra bytes that dialog windows require:

```
wndclass.style = 0L;
...
...
wndclass.cbWndExtra = DLGWINDOWEXTRA;
wndclass.lpfnWndProc = DefDlgProc;
wndclass.lpszClassName = "mydialogclass";
RegisterClass(&wndclass);
```

If your application wants to use window words in windows of this class, they must be located past DLGWINDOWEXTRA, which is a byte count.

See Also   **DefWindowProc**

■ DeferWindowPos

HWPI DeferWindowPos(hWinPosInfo, hWnd, hWndInsertAfter, x, y, cx, cy, dwFlags**)**
HWPI hWinPosInfo;
HWND hWnd;
HWND hWndInsertAfter;
int x;
int y;
int cx;
int cy;
UINT dwFlags;

This function updates the multiple window-position structure identified by the hWinPosInfo parameter for the window identified by hWnd parameter and returns the handle of the updated structure. The **EndDeferWindowPos** function uses the information in this structure to change the position and size of a number of windows simultaneously. The **BeginDeferWindowPos** function creates the multiple window-position structure used by this function.

The x and y parameters specify the new position of the window, and the cx and cy parameters specify the new size of the window.

Parameters   hWinPosInfo   Identifies a multiple window-position structure that contains size and position information for one or more windows. This structure is returned by the BeginDeferWindowPos function or the most recent call to the DeferWindowPos function.

hWnd   Identifies the window for which update information is to be stored in the structure.

hWndInsertAfter   Identifies the window following which the window identified by the hWnd parameter is to be updated.

x   Specifies the x-coordinate of the window's upper-left corner.

y   Specifies the y-coordinate of the window's upper-left corner.

cx   Specifies the window's new width.

cy   Specifies the window's new height.

dwFlags   Specifies one of eight possible values that affect the size and position of the window. It can be a combination of the following values:

Value	Meaning
SWP_DRAWFRAME	Draws a frame (defined in the window's class description) around the window.
SWP_HIDEWINDOW	Hides the window.
SWP_NOACTIVATE	Does not activate the window.

Value	Meaning
SWP_NOMOVE	Retains current position (ignores the *x* and *y* parameters).
SWP_NOREDRAW	Does not redraw changes.
SWP_NOSIZE	Retains current size (ignores the *cx* and *cy* parameters).
SWP_NOZORDER	Retains current ordering (ignores the *hWndInsertAfter* parameter).
SWP_SHOWWINDOW	Displays the window.

Return Value   The return value identifies the updated multiple window-position data structure. The handle returned by this function may differ from the handle passed to the function as the *hWinPosInfo* parameter. The new handle returned by this function should be passed to the next call to **DeferWindowPos** or the **EndDeferWindowPos** function.

The return value is NULL if insufficient system resources are available for the function to complete successfully.

Comments   If the SWP_NOZORDER flag is not specified, Windows places the window identified by the *hWnd* parameter in the position following the window identified by the *hWndInsertAfter* parameter. If *hWndInsertAfter* is NULL, Windows places the window identified by *hWnd* at the top of the list. If *hWndInsertAfter* is set to 1, Windows places the window identified by *hWnd* at the bottom of the list.

If the SWP_SHOWWINDOW or the SWP_HIDEWINDOW flags are set, scrolling and moving cannot be done simultaneously.

All coordinates for child windows are relative to the upper-left corner of the parent window's client area.

See Also   **BeginDeferWindowPos, EndDeferWindowPos**

■ DefFrameProc

LONG DefFrameProc(*hWnd, hWndMDIClient, wMsg, dwParam, lParam***)**
HWND *hWnd*;
HWND *hWndMDIClient*;
UINT *wMsg*;
DWORD *dwParam*;
LONG *lParam*;

This function provides default processing for any Windows messages that the window function of a multiple document interface (MDI) frame window does not process. All window messages that are not explicitly processed by the window function must be passed to the **DefFrameProc** function, not the **DefWindowProc** function.

Parameters   *hWnd*   Identifies the MDI frame window.

hWndMDIClient   Identifies the MDI client window.

wMsg   Specifies the message number.

dwParam   Specifies additional message-dependent information.

lParam   Specifies additional message-dependent information.

Return Value   The return value specifies the result of the message processing and depends on the actual message sent. If the *hWndMDIClient* parameter is NULL, the return value is the same as for the **DefWindowProc** function.

Comments   Normally, when an application's window procedure does not handle a message, it passes the message to the **DefWindowProc** function, which processes the message. MDI applications use the **DefFrameProc** and **DefMDIChildProc** functions instead of **DefWindowProc** to provide default message processing. All messages that an application would normally pass to **DefWindowProc** (such as nonclient messages and WM_SETTEXT) should be passed to **DefFrameProc** instead. In addition to these, **DefFrameProc** also handles the following messages:

Message	Default Processing by DefFrameProc
WM_COMMAND	The frame window of an MDI application receives the WM_COMMAND message to activate a particular MDI child window. The window ID accompanying this message will be the ID of the MDI child window assigned by Windows, starting with the first ID specified by the application when it created the MDI client window. This value of the first ID must not conflict with menu-item IDs.
WM_MENUCHAR	When the ALTHYPHEN key is pressed, the control menu of the active MDI child window will be selected.
WM_SETFOCUS	**DefFrameProc** passes focus on to the MDI client, which in turn passes the focus on to the active MDI child window.
WM_SIZE	If the frame window procedure passes this message to **DefFrameProc**, the MDI client window will be resized to fit in the new client area. If the frame window procedure sizes the MDI client to a different size, it should not pass the message to **DefWindowProc**.

See Also   **DefMDIChildProc, DefWindowProc, DefHookProc**

■ DefHookProc

DWORD DefHookProc(*code, wParam, lParam, lplpfnNextHook*)
int *code*;
DWORD *wParam*;
LONG *lParam*;
FARPROC * *lplpfnNextHook*;

This function calls the next function in a chain of hook functions. A hook function is a function that processes events before they are sent to an application's message-processing loop in the WinMain function. When an application defines more than one hook function by using the **SetWindowsHook** function, Windows forms a linked list or hook chain. Windows places functions of the same type in a chain.

Parameters   *code*   Specifies a code used by the Windows hook function (also called the message filter function) to determine how to process the message.

wParam   Specifies the first long parameter of the message that the hook function is processing.

lParam   Specifies the second long parameter of the message that the hook function is processing.

lplpfnNextHook   Points to the variable that contains the procedure-instance address of the previously installed hook function returned by the **SetWindowsHook** function. Windows changes the value at this location after an application calls the **UnhookWindowsHook** function.

This parameter is UNUSED in Win32.

Return Value   The return value specifies a value that is directly related to the *code* parameter.

See Also   **SetWindowsHook, UnhookWindowsHook**

■ DefineHandleTable

The **DefineHandleTable** function is implemented by a macro that does nothing. Its parameter is ignored.

■ DefMDIChildProc

LONG DefMDIChildProc(*hWnd, wMsg, dwParam, lParam*)
HWND *hWnd*;
UINT *wMsg*;
DWORD *dwParam*;
LONG *lParam*;

This function provides default processing for any Windows messages that the window function of a multiple document interface (MDI) child window does not process. All window messages that are not explicitly processed by the window function must be passed to the **DefMDIChildProc** function, not the **DefWindowProc** function.

Parameters

hWnd   Identifies the MDI child window.

wMsg   Specifies the message number.

dwParam   Specifies additional message-dependent information.

lParam   Specifies additional message-dependent information.

Return Value

The return value specifies the result of the message processing and depends on the actual message sent.

Comments

This function assumes that the parent of the window identified by the *hWnd* parameter was created with the MDICLIENT class.

Normally, when an application's window procedure does not handle a message, it passes the message to the **DefWindowProc** function, which processes the message. MDI applications use the **DefFrameProc** and **DefMDIChildProc** functions instead of **DefWindowProc** to provide default message processing. All messages that an application would normally pass to **DefWindowProc** (such as nonclient messages and WM_SETTEXT) should be passed to **DefMDIChildProc** instead. In addition to these, **DefMDIChildProc** also handles the following messages:

Message	Default Processing by DefMDIChildProc
WM_CHILDACTIVATE	Performs activation processing when child windows are sized, moved, or shown. This message must be passed.
WM_GETMINMAXINFO	Calculates the size of a maximized MDI child window based on the current size of the MDI client window.
WM_MENUCHAR	Sends the key to the frame window.
WM_MOVE	Recalculates MDI client scroll bars, if they are present.
WM_SETFOCUS	Activates the child window if it is not the active MDI child.
WM_SIZE	Performs necessary operations when changing the size of a window, especially when maximizing or restoring an MDI child window. Failing to pass this message to **DefMDIChildProc** will produce highly undesirable results.
WM_SYSCOMMAND	Also handles the next window command.

See Also

DefFrameProc, DefWindowProc, DefHookProc

■ DefWindowProc

LONG DefWindowProc(*hWnd, wMsg, dwParam, lParam***)**
HWND *hWnd*;
UINT *wMsg*,
DWORD *dwParam*,
LONG *lParam*;

This function provides default processing for any Windows messages that a given application does not process. All window messages that are not explicitly processed by the class window function must be passed to the **DefWindowProc** function.

Parameters
hWnd   Identifies the window that passes the message.

wMsg   Specifies the message number.

dwParam   Specifies additional message-dependent information.

lParam   Specifies additional message-dependent information.

Return Value
The return value specifies the result of the message processing and depends on the actual message sent.

Comments
The source code for the **DefWindowProc** function is provided on the SDK disks.

■ DeleteAce

BOOL DeleteAce(*Acl, AceIndex***)**
PACL *Acl*,
ULONG *AceIndex*,

The **DeleteAce** function deletes an **ACE** from an existing **ACL**. An **ACE** is an access control entry. An **ACL** is an access control list.

The caller specifies an **ACL** to modify and an index value that indicates the **ACE** to delete.

Parameters
Acl   Pointer to an existing **ACL** data structure. The **ACE** will be removed from this **ACL**.

The **ACL** data structure has the following form:

```
typedef struct tagACL {
    UCHAR   AclRevision;
    UCHAR   Sbz1;
    USHORT  AclSize;
    USHORT  AceCount;
    USHORT  Sbz2;
    /* ordered list of ACEs */
} ACL;
```

AceIndex   An zero-based index that specifies the **ACE** to delete. An **ACL** maintains a list of **ACE**s. A value of 0 corresponds to the **ACL**'s first **ACE**, 1 to its second **ACE**, and so on.

Return Value	If the function is successful, the return value is TRUE.
	If the function fails, the return value is FALSE. Call **GetLastError** for more detailed error information.
See Also	**AddAccessAllowedAce, AddAce, GetAce, GetAclInformation, InitializeAcl, IsValidAcl, SetAclInformation**

■ DeleteAtom

ATOM DeleteAtom(*nAtom*)
ATOM *nAtom*;

The **DeleteAtom** function deletes an atom and, if the atom's reference count is zero, removes the associated string from the atom table.

An atom's reference count specifies the number of times the atom has been added to the atom table. The **AddAtom** function increases the count on each call; the **DeleteAtom** function decreases the count on each call. **DeleteAtom** removes the string only if the atom's reference count is zero.

Parameters	*nAtom* Identifies the atom and character string to be deleted.
Return Value	The return value specifies the outcome of the function. It is NULL if the function is successful. It is equal to the *nAtom* parameter if the function failed and the atom has not been deleted.
See Also	**AddAtom**

■ DeleteCriticalSection

VOID DeleteCriticalSection(*lpCriticalSection*)
LPCRITICAL_SECTION *lpCriticalSection*;

An application thread may delete an un-owned critical section using **DeleteCriticalSection**.

Parameters	*lpCriticalSection* Supplies the address of a critical section object to delete.
Comments	Deleting a critical section deallocates all system resources stored in the critical section. Once deleted, the critical section may not be used in **EnterCriticalSection** or **LeaveCriticalSection**. The critical section object itself is not deallocated by this call. It is the user's responsibility to either free this object or reinitialize it using InitializeCriticalSection.
	In order to delete a critical section, the critical section must not be owned.
See Also	**InitializeCriticalSection, EnterCriticalSection, DeleteCriticalSection**

■ DeleteDC

BOOL DeleteDC(*hDC***)**
HDC *hDC*;

The **DeleteDC** function deletes the specified device context.

Parameters   *hDC*   Identifies the device context.

Return Value   The return value is TRUE if the device context was successfully deleted, otherwise it is FALSE.

Comments   An application must not delete a device context whose handle was obtained by calling the **GetDC** function. Instead, it must call the **ReleaseDC** function to free the device context.

See Also   **GetDC, ReleaseDC CreateDC**

■ DeleteFile

BOOL DeleteFile(*lpFileName***)**
LPTSTR *lpFileName*;

An existing file can be deleted using **DeleteFile**.

The **DeleteFile** function may be used as either a wide-character function (where text arguments must use Unicode) or an ANSI function (where text arguments must use characters from the Windows 3.x character set installed).

Parameters   *lpFileName*   Supplies the file name of the file to be deleted.

Return Value   The return value is TRUE if the function is successful. Otherwise, it is FALSE in which case extended error information is available from the **GetLastError** function.

This API provides the same functionality as DOS (int 21h, function 41H) and OS/2's **DosDelete**.

See Also   **CreateFile**

■ DeleteMenu

BOOL DeleteMenu(*hMenu, wPosition, dwFlags***)**
HMENU *hMenu*;
UINT *wPosition*;
UINT *dwFlags*;

This function deletes an item from the menu identified by the *hMenu* parameter; if the menu item has an associated pop-up menu, **DeleteMenu** destroys the handle by the pop-up menu and frees the memory used by the pop-up menu.

Parameters	*hMenu* Identifies the menu to be changed.
	wPosition Specifies the menu item which is to be deleted, as determined by the *dwFlags* parameter:

dwFlags	wPosition
MF_BYPOSITION	Specifies the position of the menu item; the first item in the menu is at position 0.
MF_BYCOMMAND	Specifies the command ID of the existing menu item.

dwFlags   Specifies how the *wPosition* parameter is interpreted. It may be set to either MF_BYCOMMAND or MF_BYPOSITION.

Return Value	The return value specifies the outcome of the function. It is TRUE if the function is successful. Otherwise, it is FALSE.
Comments	Whenever a menu changes (whether or not the menu resides in a window that is displayed), the application should call **DrawMenuBar**.
See Also	**DrawMenuBar, RemoveMenu**

■ DeleteMetaFileEx

BOOL DeleteMetaFileEx(*hMF*)
HMF *hMF*;

The **DeleteMetaFileEx** function invalidates the given metafile handle. If *hMF* referred to a memory metafile, the metafile contents are lost. If *hMF* referred to a disk-based metafile, the metafile contents are retained and access to the metafile can be reestablished by retrieving a new handle using the **GetMetaFileEx** function.

Parameters	*hMF* Identifies the metafile.
Return Value	The return value is TRUE if the handle has been invalidated. Otherwise, it is FALSE.
See Also	**GetMetaFileEx, CreateMetaFileEx, CopyMetaFileEx.**

■ DeleteObject

BOOL DeleteObject(*hObject*)
HANDLE *hObject*;

The **DeleteObject** function deletes a logical pen, brush, font, bitmap, region or palette, freeing all system resources associated with the object. After the object is deleted, the *hObject* handle is no longer valid.

Parameters	*hObject* Identifies a logical pen, brush, font, bitmap, region or palette.

Return Value

The return value specifies whether the specified object is deleted. It is TRUE if the object is deleted. It is FALSE if the *hObject* parameter is not a valid handle or is currently selected into a device context.

Comments

The object to be deleted must not be currently selected into a device context.

When a pattern brush is deleted, the bitmap associated with the brush is not deleted. The bitmap must be deleted independently.

■ DeletePrinter

BOOL DeletePrinter(*lpPrinter***)**
LPPRINTER *lpPrinter*;

The **DeletePrinter** function deletes a printer.

Parameters

lpPrinter   Pointer to a **PRINTER** data structure that specifies the printer to delete.

The **PRINTER** data structure has the following form:

```
typedef struct tagPRINTER {
    DWORD cVersion;
    LPPRINTERSERVER lpPrinterServer;
    LPTSTR lpPrinterName;
    LPTSTR lpPortName;
    LPTSTR lpDriverName;
    LPTSTR lpComment;
    LPTSTR lpLocation;
    LPDEVMODE lpDevMode;
    LPTSTR lpSepFile;
    LPTSTR lpPrintProcessor;
    LPTSTR lpDatatype;
    LPTSTR lpParameters;
    LPTSTR lpVendorData;
    DWORD Attributes;
    DWORD Priority;
    DWORD DefaultPriority;
    SYSTEMTIME StartTime;
    SYSTEMTIME UntilTime;
    DWORD Status;
    DWORD cJobs;
    DWORD AveragePPM;
} PRINTER;
```

Return Value

If the function is successful, the return value is TRUE.

If the function fails, the return value is FALSE/NULL. Further information can be obtained by calling **GetLastError**.

Comments

If there are print jobs remaining to be processed for the specified printer, **DeletePrinter** marks the printer as pending deletion, then deletes it when all the print jobs have been printed. No print jobs can be added to a printer which is marked as pending deletion. A printer marked as pending deletion cannot be held, but its print jobs can be held, resumed, and restarted. If the printer is held and there are jobs for the printer, **DeletePrinter** will fail with an InvalidState error.

See Also **AddPrinter, PRINTER**

■ DestroyAcceleratorTable

BOOL DestroyAcceleratorTable(*hAccel***)**
HANDLE *hAccel*;

This function destroys an accelerator table. Accelerator tables are created with calls to **CreateAcceleratorTable** or **LoadAccelerators**.

Parameters *hAccel* This parameter specifies the accelerator table to be destroyed.

Return Value This function returns TRUE if the specified accelerator table is successfully destroyed, otherwise it returns FALSE.

See Also **TranslateAccelerator CreateAcceleratorTable LoadAccelerators CopyAcceleratorTable**

■ DestroyCaret

BOOL DestroyCaret(void)

This function destroys the current caret shape, frees the caret from the window that currently owns it, and removes the caret from the screen if it is visible. The **DestroyCaret** function checks the ownership of the caret and destroys the caret only if a window in the current task owns it.

If the caret shape was previously a bitmap, **DestroyCaret** does not free the bitmap.

Parameters This function has no parameters.

This function has no parameters.

Return Value This function returns TRUE for success, FALSE for failure.

Comments The caret is a shared resource. If a window has created a caret shape, it destroys that shape before it loses the input focus or becomes inactive.

See Also **CreateCaret, HideCaret, ShowCaret**

■ DestroyCursor

BOOL DestroyCursor(*hCursor***)**
HCURSOR *hCursor*;

This function destroys a cursor that was previously created by the **CreateCursor** function and frees any memory that the cursor occupied. It should not be used to destroy any cursor that was not created with the **CreateCursor** function.

Parameters	*hCursor* Identifies the cursor to be destroyed. The cursor must not be in current use.
Return Value	The return value is nonzero if the function was successful. It is zero if the function failed.
See Also	**CreateCursor, LoadCursor**

■ DestroyIcon

BOOL DestroyIcon(*hIcon***)**
HICON *hIcon*;

This function destroys an icon that was previously created by the **CreateIcon** function and frees any memory that the icon occupied. It should not be used to destroy any icon that was not created with the **CreateIcon** function.

Parameters	*hIcon* Identifies the icon to be destroyed. The icon must not be in current use.
Return Value	The return value is TRUE if the function was successful. It is FALSE if the function failed.
See Also	**CreateIcon, LoadIcon**

■ DestroyMenu

BOOL DestroyMenu(*hMenu***)**
HMENU *hMenu*;

This function destroys the menu specified by the *hMenu* parameter and frees any memory that the menu occupied.

Parameters	*hMenu* Identifies the menu to be destroyed.
Return Value	The return value specifies whether or not the specified menu is destroyed. It is nonzero if the menu is destroyed. Otherwise, it is zero.
See Also	**CreateMenu, DeleteMenu, RemoveMenu, ModifyMenu**

■ DestroyUserObjectSecurity

BOOL DestroyUserObjectSecurity (*ObjectDescriptor***)**
PSECURITY_DESCRIPTOR * *ObjectDescriptor*;

The **DestroyUserObjectSecurity** function deletes a security descriptor associated with a server application's object. A server apppication will normally call this function during object deletion. The function expects the descriptor referenced by the parameter *ObjectDescriptor* to be one created via a call to **CreateUserObjectSecurity**. This function can be called only from user mode.

Parameters	*ObjectDescriptor* Pointer to a pointer to a **SECURITY_DESCRIPTOR** data structure. The function will delete this security descriptor.
	The **SECURITY_DESCRIPTOR** data structure has the following form:

```
typedef PVOID PSECURITY_DESCRIPTOR;
```

Return Value	If the function is successful, the return value is TRUE.
	If the function fails, the return value is FALSE. Call **GetLastError** for more detailed error information.
See Also	**AbsoluteToSelfRelativeSD**, **CreateUserObjectSecurity**, **GetUserObjectSecurity**, **SelfRelativeToAbsoluteSD**, **SetUserObjectSecurity**

■ DestroyWindow

BOOL DestroyWindow(*hWnd***)**
HWND *hWnd*;

This function destroys the specified window. The **DestroyWindow** function hides or permanently closes the window, sending the appropriate messages to the window to deactivate it and remove the input focus. It also destroys the window menu, flushes the application queue, destroys outstanding timers, removes clipboard ownership, and breaks the clipboard-viewer chain, if the window is at the top of the viewer chain. It sends WM_DESTROY and WM_NCDESTROY messages to the window.

If the given window is the parent of any windows, these child windows are automatically destroyed when the parent window is destroyed. **DestroyWindow** destroys child windows first, and then the window itself.

DestroyWindow also destroys modeless dialog boxes created by the **CreateDialog** function.

Parameters	*hWnd* Identifies the window to be destroyed.
Return Value	The return value specifies whether or not the specified window is destroyed. It is nonzero if the window is destroyed. Otherwise, it is zero.
Comments	If a thread creates a window, only that thread is allowed to destroy it by calling **DestroyWindow**. Other threads in the process will not be permitted to do so. This can happen inside a window procedure or outside the message loop. This is not a general policy regarding threads and objects they create; currently it only applies to window objects.
See Also	**CreateDialog**, **CreateWindow**

■ DeviceCapabilitiesEx

int DeviceCapabilitiesEx(*lpDriverName, lpDeviceName, lpPort, iIndex, lpOutput, lpDevMode***)**
LPSTR *lpDriverName*;
LPSTR *lpDeviceName*;
LPSTR *lpPort*;
int *iIndex*;
LPSTR *lpOutput*;
LPDEVMODE *lpDevMode*;

The **DeviceCapabilitiesEx** function retrieves capabilities of the device driver.

Parameters

lpDriverName   Points to a null-terminated character string that specifies the name of the device driver (for example, "Epson").

lpDeviceName   Points to a null-terminated character string that specifies the name of the specific device to be supported (for example, "Epson FX-80"). The *lpDeviceName* parameter is used if the device driver supports more than one device.

lpPort   Points to a null-terminated character string that specifies the file or device name for the physical output medium (file or output port such as "LPT1").

iIndex   Specifies the capabilities to query. It can be any one of the following values:

Value	Meaning

DC_BINNAMES
Copies a structure identical to that returned by the ENUMPAPERBINS escape. A printer driver does not need to support this index if it has only bins corresponding to predefined indexes, in which case no data is copied and the return value is 0. If the index is supported, the return value is the number of bins copied. If pOutput is NULL, the return value is the number of bin entries required.

DC_BINS
Retrieves a list of available bins. The function copies the list to *lpOutput* as a **WORD** array. If *lpOutput* is NULL, the function returns the number of supported bins to allow the application the opportunity to allocate a buffer with the correct size. See the description of the **dmDefaultSource** field of the **DEVMODE** structure for information on these values. An application can determine the name of device-specific bins by using the **ENUMPAPERBINS** escape.

DC_DRIVER
Returns the printer driver version number.

DC_DUPLEX
Returns the level of duplex support. The function returns 1 if the printer is capable of duplex printing. Otherwise, the return value is zero.

Value	Meaning

DC_ENUMRESOLUTIONS

Returns a list of available resolutions. If *lpOutput* is NULL, the function returns the number of available resolution configurations. Resolutions are represented by pairs of **LONG** integers representing the horizontal and vertical resolutions.

DC_EXTRA

Returns the number of bytes required for the device-specific portion of the **DEVMODE** structure for the printer driver.

DC_FIELDS

Returns the **dmFields** field of the printer driver's **DEVMODE** data structure. The **dmFields** bitfield indicates which fields in the device-independent portion of the structure are supported by the printer driver.

DC_FILEDEPENDENCIES

Returns a list of files which also need to be loaded when a driver is installed. If *lpOutput* is NULL, the function returns the number of files. If *lpOutput* is not NULL, it is a pointer to an array of filenames in the form char[chFileName, 64]. This information is used by the PostScript driver to return the WPD filename if the printer model is an external printer. Mini-drivers return the generic library and external color brute library if color is present.

DC_MAXEXTENT

Returns a **POINT** structure containing the maximum paper size that the **dmPaperLength** and **dmPaperWidth** fields of the printer driver's **DEVMODE** structure can specify.

DC_MINEXTENT

Returns a **POINT** structure containing the minimum paper size that the **dmPaperLength** and **dmPaperWidth** fields of the printer driver's **DEVMODE** structure can specify.

DC_PAPERS

Retrieves a list of supported paper sizes. The function copies the list to pOutput as a WORD array and returns the number of entries in the array. If pOutput is NULL, the function returns the number of supported paper sizes to allow the application the opportunity to allocate a buffer with the correct size. See the description of the dmPaperSize field of the DEVMODE data structure for information on these values.

DC_PAPERSIZE

Copies the dimensions of supported paper sizes in tenths of a millimeter to an array of **POINT** structures in *lpOutput*. This allows an application to obtain information about nonstandard paper sizes.

DC_SIZE

Returns the **dmSize** field of the printer driver's **DEVMODE** data structure.

DC_VERSION

Returns the specification version to which the printer driver conforms.

lpOutput　Points to an array of bytes. The actual format of the array depends on the setting of *iIndex*. If set to zero, **DeviceCapabilitiesEx** returns the number of bytes required for the output data.

lpDevMode　Points to a **DEVMODE** structure. If *lpDevMode* is NULL, this function retrieves the current default initialization values for the specified printer driver. Otherwise, the function retrieves the values contained in the structure to which *lpDevMode* points.

Return Value　The return value depends on the setting of the *iIndex* parameter; see the description of that parameter for details. However, −1 will be return in the case of an error.

■ DeviceModeEx

```
BOOL DeviceModeEx(hWnd, lpDriverName, lpDeviceName, lpPort)
HWND hWnd;
LPSTR lpDriverName;
LPSTR lpDeviceName;
LPSTR lpPort;
```

The **DeviceModeEx** function sets the current printing modes for the device by prompting for those modes using a dialog box. An application calls the **DeviceModeEx** function to allow the user to change the printing modes of the device. The function copies the mode information to the environment block associated with the device and maintained by GDI.

Parameters　*hWnd*　Identifies the window that will own the dialog box.

lpDriverName　Points to a null-terminated character string that specifies the name of the device driver, for example: "Epson".

lpDeviceName　Points to a null-terminated character string that specifies the name of the specific device to be supported, for example: "Epson FX-80". The device name is the same as the name passed to the **CreateDC** function.

lpPort　Points to a null-terminated character string that specifies the file or device name for the physical output medium (file or output port). The output name is the same as the name passed to the **CreateDC** function.

Return Value　This function returns TRUE if it is successful, FALSE otherwise.

See Also　**CreateDC**

■ DialogBox

```
int DialogBox(hInstance, lpTemplateName, hWndParent, lpDialogFunc)
HANDLE hInstance;
LPTSTR lpTemplateName;
HWND hWndParent;
WNDPROC lpDialogFunc;
```

This function creates a modal dialog box that has the size, style, and controls specified by the dialog-box template given by the *lpTemplateName* parameter. The *hWndParent* parameter identifies the application window that owns the dialog box. The callback function pointed to by the *lpDialogFunc* parameter processes any messages received by the dialog box.

The **DialogBox** function does not return control until the callback function terminates the modal dialog box by calling the **EndDialog** function.

The **DialogBox** function may be used as either a wide-character function (where text arguments must use Unicode) or an ANSI function (where text arguments must use characters from the Windows 3.x character set installed).

Parameters

hInstance   Identifies the module that contains the dialog template resource. **GetModuleHandle(NULL)** can be called to return the module handle of the current process.

lpTemplateName   Points to a character string that names the dialog-box template. The string must be a null-terminated character string.

hWndParent   Identifies the window that owns the dialog box.

lpDialogFunc   Is the procedure-instance address of the dialog function. See the following Comments section for details.

Return Value

The return value specifies the value of the *nResult* parameter in the **EndDialog** function that is used to terminate the dialog box. Values returned by the application's dialog box are processed by Windows and are not returned to the application. The return value is −1 if the function could not create the dialog box.

Comments

The **DialogBox** function calls the **GetDC** function in order to obtain a display-context. Problems will result if all the display contexts in the Windows display-context cache have been retrieved by **GetDC** and **DialogBox** attempts to access another display context.

Callback Function

```
int APIENTRY DialogFunc(hDlg, wMsg, wParam, lParam)
HWND hDlg;
WORD wMsg;
LONG wParam;
LONG lParam;
```

DialogFunc is a placeholder for the application-supplied function name.

Parameters

hDlg   Identifies the dialog box that receives the message.

wMsg   Specifies the message number.

wParam   Specifies additional message-dependent information.

lParam   Specifies additional message-dependent information.

Return Value

The callback function should return nonzero if the function processes the message and zero if it does not.

Comments	Although the callback function is similar to a window function, it must not call the **DefWindowProc** function to process unwanted messages. Unwanted messages are processed internally by the dialog-class window function.
See Also	**DefWindowProc, EndDialog, GetDC, CreateDialog, CreateDialogIndirect, CreateDialogParam, CreateDialogIndirectParam, DialogBoxParam, DialogBoxIndirectParam**

■ DialogBoxIndirect

int DialogBoxIndirect(*hInstance*, *hDialogTemplate*, *hWndParent*, *lpDialogFunc***)**
HANDLE *hInstance*;
LPDLGTEMPLATESTUB *hDialogTemplate*;
HWND *hWndParent*,
WNDPROC *lpDialogFunc*;

This function creates an application's modal dialog box that has the size, style, and controls specified by the dialog-box template associated with the *hDialogTemplate* parameter. The *hWndParent* parameter identifies the application window that owns the dialog box. The callback function pointed to by *lpDialogFunc* processes any messages received by the dialog box.

The **DialogBoxIndirect** function does not return control until the callback function terminates the modal dialog box by calling the **EndDialog** function.

Parameters	*hInstance* Identifies the module that contains the dialog template resource. **CurrentProcessModule** can be called to return the module handle of the current process.
	hDialogTemplate Identifies a block of global memory that contains a **DLGTEMPLATE** structure.
	hWndParent Identifies the window that owns the dialog box.
	lpDialogFunc Is the procedure-instance address of the dialog function. See the following Comments section for details.
Return Value	The return value specifies the value of the *wResult* parameter specified in the **EndDialog** function that is used to terminate the dialog box. Values returned by the application's dialog box are processed by Windows and are not returned to the application. The return value is −1 if the function could not create the dialog box.

Callback Function

BOOL APIENTRY *DialogFunc*(*hDlg, wMsg, wParam, lParam*)
HWND *hDlg*,
WORD *wMsg*;
LONG *wParam*,
LONG *lParam*;

DialogFunc is a placeholder for the application-supplied function name.

Parameters	*hDlg* Identifies the dialog box that receives the message.
	wMsg Specifies the message number.
	wParam Specifies additional message-dependent information.
	lParam Specifies additional message-dependent information.
Return Value	The callback function should return TRUE if the function processes the message and FALSE if it does not.
Comments	Although the callback function is similar to a window function, it must not call the **DefWindowProc** function to process unwanted messages. Unwanted messages are processed internally by the dialog-class window function.
See Also	**EndDialog, CreateDialog, CreateDialogIndirect, CreateDialogParam, CreateDialogIndirectParam, DialogBoxParam, DialogBoxIndirectParam**

■ DialogBoxIndirectParam

int DialogBoxIndirectParam(*hInstance, hDialogTemplate, hWndParent, lpDialogFunc, lInitParam***)**
HANDLE *hInstance*;
LPDLGTEMPLATESTUB *hDialogTemplate*;
HWND *hWndParent*;
WNDPROC *lpDialogFunc*;
LONG *lInitParam*;

This function creates an application's modal dialog box, sends a WM_INITDIALOG message to the dialog function before displaying the dialog box and passes *lInitParam* as the message *lParam*. This message allows the dialog function to initialize the dialog-box controls.

For more information on creating an application modal dialog box, see the description of the **DialogBoxIndirect** function.

Parameters	*hInstance* Identifies the module that is creating the dialog window. **GetModuleHandle(NULL)** can be called to return the module handle of the current process.
	hDialogTemplate Identifies a block of global memory that contains a **DLGTEMPLATE** structure.
	hWndParent Identifies the window that owns the dialog box.
	lpDialogFunc Is the procedure-instance address of the dialog function. For details, see the Comments section in the description of the **DialogBoxIndirect** function.
	lInitParam Is a value which **DialogBoxIndirectParam** passes as the *lParam* of a WM_INITDIALOG message to the dialog function when it creates the dialog box.

Return Value

The return value specifies the value of the *nResult* parameter specified in the **EndDialog** function that is used to terminate the dialog box. Values returned by the application's dialog box are processed by Windows and are not returned to the application. The return value is −1 if the function could not create the dialog box.

See Also

DialogBoxIndirect, EndDialog, CreateDialog, CreateDialogIndirect, CreateDialogParam, CreateDialogIndirectParam, DialogBoxParam, WM_INITDIALOG

■ DialogBoxParam

int DialogBoxParam(hInstance, lpTemplateName, hWndParent, lpDialogFunc, lInitParam**)**
HANDLE hInstance;
LPTSTR lpTemplateName;
HWND hWndParent;
WNDPROC lpDialogFunc;
LONG lInitParam;

This function creates a modal dialog box, sends a WM_INITDIALOG message to the dialog function before displaying the dialog box, and passes *lInitParam* as the message *lParam*. This message allows the dialog function to initialize the dialog-box controls.

For more information on creating a modal dialog box, see the description of the **DialogBox** function.

Parameters

hInstance   Identifies the module that is creating the dialog window. **GetModuleHandle(NULL)** can be called to return the module handle of the current process.

lpTemplateName   Points to a character string that names the dialog-box template. The string must be a null-terminated character string.

hWndParent   Identifies the window that owns the dialog box.

lpDialogFunc   Is the procedure-instance address of the dialog function. For details, see the Comments section of the description of the **DialogBox** function.

lInitParam   Is a value which **DialogBoxParam** passes as the *lParam* of a WM_INITDIALOG message to the dialog function when it creates the dialog box.

Return Value

The return value specifies the value of the *nResult* parameter in the **EndDialog** function that is used to terminate the dialog box. Values returned by the application's dialog box are processed by Windows and are not returned to the application. The return value is −1 if the function could not create the dialog box.

See Also

DialogBox, EndDialog WM_INITDIALOG

■ DialogProc

BOOL FAR PASCAL DialogProc(*hDlg, wMsg, wParam, lParam*)
HWND *hDlg,*   /* handle of the dialog box   */
WORD *wMsg;*   /* message   */
WORD *wParam,*   /* first message parameter   */
DWORD *lParam,*   /* second message parameter   */

The **DialogProc** function is an application-defined callback function that processes messages sent to a modeless dialog box.

Parameters

hDlg   Identifies the dialog box.

wMsg   Specifies the message.

wParam   Specifies additional message information. The contents of this parameter depend on the message being sent.

lParam   Specifies additional message information. The contents of this parameter depend on the message being sent.

Return Value

Except in response to the WM_INITDIALOG message, the dialog procedure should return nonzero if it processes the message, and zero if it does not. In response to a WM_INITDIALOG message, the dialog procedure should return zero if it calls the **SetFocus** function to set the focus to one of the controls in the dialog box. Otherwise, it should return nonzero, in which case the system will set the focus to the first control in the dialog box that can be given the focus.

Comments

The dialog procedure is used only if the dialog class is used for the dialog box. This is the default class and is used if no explicit class is given in the dialog-box template. Although the dialog procedure is similar to a window procedure, it must not call the **DefWindowProc** function to process unwanted messages. Unwanted messages are processed internally by the dialog-class window procedure.

DialogProc is a placeholder for the application-supplied function name. The actual name must be exported by including it in an **EXPORTS** statement in the application's module-definition file.

See Also

CreateDialog, CreateDialogIndirect, CreateDialogIndirectParam, CreateDialogParam, DefWindowProc, SetFocus

■ DisconnectNamedPipe

BOOL DisconnectNamedPipe(*hNamedPipe*)
HANDLE *hNamedPipe;*

The **DisconnectNamedPipe** function can be used by the server side of a named pipe to force the client side to close the client side's handle. (Note that the client side must still call CloseFile to do this.) The client will receive an error the next time it attempts to access the pipe. Disconnecting the pipe may cause data to be lost before the client reads it. (If the application wants to make sure that data is not lost, the serving side should call **FlushFileBuffers** before calling **DisconnectNamedPipe**.)

Parameters   *hNamedPipe*   Supplies a handle for the server side of a named pipe.

Return Value   The return value is TRUE if the function is successful. Otherwise, it is FALSE in which case extended error information is available from the **GetLastError** function.

See Also   **ConnectNamedPipe, FlushFileBuffers**

■ DispatchMessage

LONG DispatchMessage(*lpMsg***)**
CONST MSG FAR* *lpMsg*;

This function passes the message in the **MSG** structure pointed to by the *lpMsg* parameter to the window function of the specified window.

Parameters   *lpMsg*   Points to an **MSG** structure that contains message information from the Windows application queue.

The structure must contain valid message values. If *lpMsg* points to a WM_TIMER message and the *lParam* parameter of the WM_TIMER message is not NULL, then the *lParam* parameter is the address of a function that is called instead of the window function.

Return Value   The return value specifies the value returned by the window function. Its meaning depends on the message being dispatched, but generally the return value is ignored.

■ DlgDirList

int DlgDirList(*hDlg, lpPathSpec, nIDListBox, nIDStaticPath, wFiletype***)**
HWND *hDlg*;
LPTSTR *lpPathSpec*;
int *nIDListBox*;
int *nIDStaticPath*;
UINT *wFiletype*;

This function fills a list-box control with a file or directory listing. It fills the list box specified by the *nIDListBox* parameter with the names of all files matching the pathname given by the *lpPathSpec* parameter.

The **DlgDirList** function shows subdirectories enclosed in square brackets ([ ]), and shows drives in the form [-*x*-], where *x* is the drive letter.

The *lpPathSpec* parameter has the following form:

```
[drive:] [ [\u]directory[\idirectory]...\u] [filename]
```

In this example, *drive* is a drive letter, *directory* is a valid directory name, and *filename* is a valid filename that must contain at least one wildcard character. The wildcard characters are a question mark (?), meaning match any character, and an asterisk (*), meaning match any number of characters.

If the *lpPathSpec* parameter includes a drive and/or directory name, the current drive and directory are changed to the designated drive and directory before the list box is filled. The text control identified by the *nIDStaticPath* parameter is also updated with the new drive and/or directory name.

After the list box is filled, *lpPathSpec* is updated by removing the drive and/or directory portion of the pathname.

DlgDirList sends LB_RESETCONTENT and LB_DIR messages to the list box.

The **DlgDirList** function may be used as either a wide-character function (where text arguments must use Unicode) or an ANSI function (where text arguments must use characters from the Windows 3.x character set installed).

Parameters

hDlg   Identifies the dialog box that contains the list box.

lpPathSpec   Points to a pathname string. The string must be a null-terminated character string.

nIDListBox   Specifies the identifier of a list-box control. If *nIDListBox* is zero, **DlgDirList** assumes that no list box exists and does not attempt to fill it.

nIDStaticPath   Specifies the identifier of the static-text control used for displaying the current drive and directory. If *nIDStaticPath* is zero, **DlgDirList** assumes that no such text control is present.

wFiletype   Specifies DOS file attributes of the files to be displayed. It can be any combination of the following values:

Value	Meaning
0x0000	Read/write data files with no additional attributes
0x0001	Read-only files
0x0002	Hidden files
0x0004	System files
0x0010	Subdirectories
0x0020	Archives
0x2000	LB_DIR flag. If the LB_DIR flag is set, Windows places the messages generated by **DlgDirList** in the application's queue; otherwise they are sent directly to the dialog function.
0x4000	Drives
0x8000	Exclusive bit. If the exclusive bit is set, only files of the specified type are listed. Otherwise, files of the specified type are listed in addition to normal files.

Return Value

The return value specifies the outcome of the function. It is nonzero if a listing was made, even an empty listing. A zero return value implies that the input string did not contain a valid search path.

See Also   **DlgDirSelectEx, DlgDirListComboBox, DlgDirSelectComboBoxEx**

■ DlgDirListComboBox

int DlgDirListComboBox(*hDlg, lpPathSpec, nIDComboBox, nIDStaticPath, wFiletype***)**
HWND *hDlg*;
LPTSTR *lpPathSpec*;
int *nIDComboBox*;
int *nIDStaticPath*;
UINT *wFiletype*;

This function fills the list box of a combo-box control with a file or directory listing. It fills the list box of the combo box specified by the *nIDComboBox* parameter with the names of all files matching the pathname given by the *lpPathSpec* parameter.

The **DlgDirListComboBox** function shows subdirectories enclosed in square brackets ([ ]), and shows drives in the form [-*x*-], where *x* is the drive letter.

The *lpPathSpec* parameter has the following form:

```
[drive:] [ [\u]directory[\idirectory]...\u] [filename]
```

In this example, *drive* is a drive letter, *directory* is a valid directory name, and *filename* is a valid filename that must contain at least one wildcard character. The wildcard characters are a question mark (?), meaning match any character, and an asterisk (*), meaning match any number of characters.

If the *lpPathSpec* parameter includes a drive and/or directory name, the current drive and directory are changed to the designated drive and directory before the list box is filled. The text control identified by the *nIDStaticPath* parameter is also updated with the new drive and/or directory name.

After the combo-box list box is filled, *lpPathSpec* is updated by removing the drive and/or directory portion of the pathname.

DlgDirListComboBox sends CB_RESETCONTENT and CB_DIR messages to the combo box.

The **DlgDirListComboBox** function may be used as either a wide-character function (where text arguments must use Unicode) or an ANSI function (where text arguments must use characters from the Windows 3.x character set installed).

Parameters   *hDlg*   Identifies the dialog box that contains the combo box.

lpPathSpec   Points to a pathname string. The string must be a null-terminated character string.

nIDComboBox   Specifies the identifier of a combo-box control in a dialog box. If *nIDComboBox* is zero, **DlgDirListComboBox** assumes that no combo box exists and does not attempt to fill it.

nIDStaticPath   Specifies the identifier of the static-text control used for displaying the current drive and directory. If *nIDStaticPath* is zero, **DlgDirListComboBox** assumes that no such text control is present.

wFiletype Specifies DOS file attributes of the files to be displayed. It can be any combination of the following values:

Value	Meaning
0x0000	Read/write data files with no additional attributes
0x0001	Read-only files
0x0002	Hidden files
0x0004	System files
0x0010	Subdirectories
0x0020	Archives
0x2000	LB_DIR flag. If the LB_DIR flag is set, Windows places the messages generated by **DlgDirList** in the application's queue; otherwise they are sent directly to the dialog function.
0x4000	Drives
0x8000	Exclusive bit. If the exclusive bit is set, only files of the specified type are listed. Otherwise, files of the specified type are listed in addition to normal files.

Return Value
The return value specifies the outcome of the function. It is nonzero if a listing was made, even an empty listing. A zero return value implies that the input string did not contain a valid search path.

See Also
DlgDirList, DlgDirSelectEx, DlgDirSelectComboBoxEx

■ DlgDirSelectComboBoxEx

BOOL DlgDirSelectComboBoxEx(*hDlg, lpString, nCount, nIDComboBox***)**
HWND *hDlg;*
LPTSTR *lpString;*
int *nCount;*
int *nIDComboBox;*

This function retrieves the current selection from the list box of a combo box created with the CBS_SIMPLE style. It cannot be used with combo boxes created with either the CBS_DROPDOWN or CBS_DROPDOWNLIST style. It assumes that the list box has been filled by the **DlgDirListComboBox** function and that the selection is a drive letter, a file, or a directory name.

The **DlgDirSelectComboBoxEx** function copies the selection to the buffer given by the *lpString* parameter. If the current selection is a directory name or drive letter, **DlgDirSelectComboBoxEx** removes the enclosing square brackets (and hyphens, for drive letters) so that the name or letter is ready to be inserted into a new pathname. If there is no selection, *lpString* does not change.

DlgDirSelectComboBoxEx sends CB_GETCURSEL and CB_GETLBTEXT messages to the combo box.

The **DlgDirSelectComboBoxEx** function may be used as either a wide-character function (where text arguments must use Unicode) or an ANSI function (where text arguments must use characters from the Windows 3.x character set installed).

Parameters

hDlg Identifies the dialog box that contains the combo box.

lpString Points to a buffer that is to receive the selected pathname.

nCount Specifies the length of the string pointed to by lpString.

nIDComboBox Specifies the integer ID of the combo-box control in the dialog box.

Return Value

The return value specifies the status of the current combo-box selection. It is nonzero if the current selection is a directory name. Otherwise, it is zero.

Comments

The **DlgDirSelectComboBox** function does not allow more than one filename to be returned from a combo box.

See Also

DlgDirSelectEx, DlgDirListComboBox

■ DlgDirSelectEx

BOOL DlgDirSelectEx(*hDlg, lpString, nCount, nIDListBox***)**
HWND *hDlg;*
LPTSTR *lpString;*
int *nCount;*
int *nIDListBox;*

This function retrieves the current selection from a list box. It assumes that the list box has been filled by the **DlgDirList** function and that the selection is a drive letter, a file, or a directory name.

The **DlgDirSelectEx** function copies the selection to the buffer given by the *lpString* parameter. If the current selection is a directory name or drive letter, **DlgDirSelectEx** removes the enclosing square brackets (and hyphens, for drive letters) so that the name or letter is ready to be inserted into a new pathname. If there is no selection, *lpString* does not change.

DlgDirSelectEx sends LB_GETCURSEL and LB_GETTEXT messages to the list box.

The **DlgDirSelectEx** function may be used as either a wide-character function (where text arguments must use Unicode) or an ANSI function (where text arguments must use characters from the Windows 3.x character set installed).

Parameters

hDlg Identifies the dialog box that contains the list box.

lpString Points to a buffer that is to receive the selected pathname.

nCount Specifies the length of the buffer pointed to by lpString.

nIDListBox Specifies the integer ID of a list-box control in the dialog box.

Return Value	The return value specifies the status of the current list-box selection. It is nonzero if the current selection is a directory name. Otherwise, it is zero.
Comments	The **DlgDirSelectEx** function does not allow more than one filename to be returned from a list box.
	The list box must not be a multiple-selection list box. If it is, this function will not return a zero value and *lpString* will remain unchanged.
See Also	**DlgDirList, DlgDirSelectComboBoxEx, DlgDirListComboBox**

■ DllEntryPoint

BOOL *DllEntryPoint(hDll, dwReason, lpReserved)*
HANDLE *hDll;*
DWORD *dwReason;*
LPVOID *lpReserved;*

DllEntryPoint is an optional entry into a DLL which, if provided, will be called when processes and threads are initialized and terminated, or upon calls to **LoadLibrary** and **FreeLibrary**.

Parameters

hDll Supplies the DLL with a handle to the DLL. This handle may be used in subsequent calls to GetModuleFileName and other module API calls.

dwReason Supplies a flag word that indicates why the DLL entry routine is being called.

Reason	Values
DLL_PROCESS_ATTACH	Indicates that the DLL is attching to the address space of the current process. This is either as a result of the process starting up, or after a call to LoadLibrary. DLLs should use this as a hook to initialize any instance data or to allocate a TLS index.
	During initial process startup, or after a call to LoadLibrary, the list of loaded DLLs for the process is scanned. For each DLL that has not already been called with a DLL_PROCESS_ATTACH flag, the DLL is called. It is important to note that this call is made in the context of the thread that caused the process address space to change.
DLL_THREAD_ATTACH	Indicates that a new thread is being created in the current process. All DLLs attached to the process at the time the thread starts will be called. DLLs may use this hook to initialize a TLS slot for the thread. The thread that calls the DLL with the DLL_PROCESS_ATTACH flag will not call the DLL with the DLL_THREAD_ATTACH flag.

Reason	Values
	It is important to note that after a DLL is loaded with LoadLibrary, only threads created after the DLL is loaded will be called with this flag value. Win32 does not cause pre-existing threads to call the newly loaded DLL.
DLL_THREAD_DETACH	Indicates that a thread is exiting cleanly and that if the DLL has stored any TLS data, it should use this hook to free the data. The exiting thread will call all currently loaded DLLs with this flag value. It is important to note that there are cases where a thread will call with this flag value even if it never called the DLL with the DLL_THREAD_ATTACH flag. This can happen in two situations:
	The thread was the initial thread in the process in which case it called the DLL with the DLL_PROCESS_ATTACH message.
	The thread was already running when a LoadLibrary call was made. Since the thread was "pre-existing", it never called the DLL as a result of the successful LoadLibrary.
DLL_PROCESS_DETACH	Indicates that the calling process is detaching the DLL from its address space. This is eather due to a clean process exit, or from a FreeLibrary call. The DLL should use this opportunity to return any TLS indexes allocated with TlsAlloc and to free any thread local data. When a DLL is detached from a process (as a result of process termination, or FreeLibrary), individual threads do not call the DLL_THREAD_DETACH flag. The only notification given to the DLL is the DLL_PROCESS_DETACH notification. DLLs should use this opportunity to clean up all per-thread resources for all threads attached and known to the DLL.

Return Value   The return value is used only when a dll is called with a flag value of DLL_PROCESS_ATTACH. All other calls to **DllEntryPoint** will ignore the return value.

Return Value	Meaning
TRUE	A value of TRUE should be returned if **DllEntryPoint** was successful.

Return Value	Meaning
FALSE	FALSE should be returned if initialization failed. If **DllEntryPoint** was called as part of a call to **LoadLibrary**, **LoadLibary** will fail. If **DllEntryPoint** was called during process initialization, the process will terminate with an error.

See Also   **TlsAlloc**

■ DOS3Call

The **DOS3Call** function is deleted as it is x86 specific and has no corresponding semantics in the portable Win32 API. The Win32 API functions defined for File I/O eliminate the need for calling DOS directly from a Win32 application.

■ DosDateTimeToFileTime

BOOL APIENTRY DosDateTimeToFileTime(*wFatDate*, *wFatTime*, *lpFileTime***)**
WORD *wFatDate*;
WORD *wFatTime*;
LPFILETIME *lpFileTime*;

This function converts a DOS date and time value, which is represented as two 16-bit unsigned integers, into a 64-bit file time.

Parameters *wFatDate* Supplies the 16-bit DOS representation of date.

       wFatTime Supplies the 16-bit DOS representation of time.

       lpFileTime Returns the 64-bit file time converted from the DOS date and time format.

Return Value The return value is TRUE if the date and time were successfully converted; otherwise, it returns FALSE, in which case extended error information is available from the **GetLastError** function.

See Also   **FileTimeToDosDateTime, FileTimeToSystemTime, SystemTimeToFileTime**

■ DPtoLP

BOOL DPtoLP(*hDC*, *lpPoints*, *nCount***)**
HDC *hDC*;
LPPOINT *lpPoints*;
int *nCount*;

The **DPtoLP** function converts device coordinates into logical coordinates. The conversion depends on the DC's mapping mode, the settings of the origins and extents for the window and viewport, and the world transform.

Parameters	*hDC* Identifies the device context.
	lpPoints Points to an array of **POINT** structures. Each point will be transformed.
	nCount Specifies the number of points in the array.
Return Value	The return value is TRUE if all the points have been converted, otherwise it is FALSE.
Comments	This function will fail if the coordinates of any input point exceed 27 bits, or if the coordinates of any output point exceed 32 bits. In the case of such an overflow, the results for all the points are undefined.

■ DragAcceptFiles

BOOL DragAcceptFiles(*hWnd, fAccept*)
HWND *hWnd*;   /* handle of the registering window   */
BOOL *fAccept*;   /* flag for whether dropped files are accepted */

The **DragAcceptFiles** function registers whether a window accepts dropped files.

Parameters	*hWnd* Identifies the window that registers whether it accepts dropped files.
	fAccept Specifies whether the window specified by the *hWnd* parameter accepts dropped files. This value is TRUE to accept dropped files or FALSE to discontinue accepting dropped files.
Return Value	The return value is TRUE if the function is successful. Otherwise, it is FALSE.
Comments	An application that calls **DragAcceptFiles** with *fAccept* set to TRUE has identified itself as able to process the **WM_DROPFILES** message from File Manager.

■ DragFinish

VOID DragFinish(*hDrop*)
HANDLE *hDrop*;   /* handle of memory to free */

The **DragFinish** function releases memory that Windows allocated for use in transferring filenames to the application.

Parameters	*hDrop* Identifies the internal data structure describing dropped files. This handle was retrieved from the *wParam* parameter of the **WM_DROPFILES** message.
Return Value	This function does not return a value.

■ DragQueryFile

WORD DragQueryFile(*hDrop, iFile, lpFile, cb***)**
HANDLE *hDrop*;   /* identifies structure for dropped files */
WORD *iFile*;   /* index of file to query   */
LPSTR *lpFile*;   /* buffer for returned filename   */
WORD *cb*;   /* size of buffer for filename   */

The **DragQueryFile** function retrieves filenames for dropped files.

Parameters

hDrop   Identifies the internal data structure containing filenames for the dropped files.

iFile   Specifies the index of the file to query. If the value of the *iFile* parameter is –1, **DragQueryFile** returns the number of files dropped. If the value of the *iFile* parameter is between 0 and the total number of files dropped, **DragQueryFile** copies the filename corresponding to that value to the buffer pointed to by the *lpFile* parameter.

lpFile   Points to a null-terminated string that contains the filename of a dropped file when the function returns. If this parameter is NULL, **DragQueryFile** returns the required size of the buffer (in bytes).

cb   Specifies the size (in bytes) of the *lpFile* buffer.

Return Value

When the function copies a filename to the *lpFile* buffer, the return value is the number of bytes copied. If the *iFile* parameter is 0xFFFF, the return value is the number of dropped files. If the *iFile* parameter is between 0 and the total number of dropped files and the *lpFile* parameter is NULL, the return value is the required size of the *lpFile* buffer.

See Also

DragQueryPoint

■ DragQueryPoint

BOOL DragQueryPoint(*hDrop, lppt***)**
HANDLE *hDrop*;   /* handle of structure for dropped file   */
LPPOINT *lppt*;   /* pointer to structure for mouse coordinates */

The **DragQueryPoint** function retrieves the position of the mouse pointer when a file is dropped.

Parameters

hDrop   Identifies the internal data structure describing the dropped file.

lppt   Points to a **POINT** structure the function fills with the coordinates of the mouse pointer when the file was dropped.

Return Value

The return value is TRUE if the drop occurs in the client area of the window, or FALSE if the drop occurs outside the client area.

Comment

The **DragQueryPoint** function fills the **POINT** structure with the coordinates of the mouse pointer when the user released the left mouse button. The window for which coordinates are returned is the window that received the **WM_DROPFILES** message.

See Also   **DragQueryFile**

■ DrawFocusRect

BOOL DrawFocusRect(*hDC, lpRect*)
HDC *hDC*;
LPRECT *lpRect*;

This function draws a rectangle in the style used to indicate focus.

Parameters   *hDC*   Identifies the device context.

lpRect   Points to a **RECT** structure that specifies the coordinates of the rectangle to be drawn.

Return Value   FALSE on error, TRUE on success

Comments   Since this is an XOR function, calling this function a second time with the same rectangle removes the rectangle from the display.

The rectangle drawn by this function cannot be scrolled. To scroll an area containing a rectangle drawn by this function, call **DrawFocusRect** to remove the rectangle from the display, scroll the area, and then call **DrawFocusRect** to draw the rectangle in the new position.

■ DrawIcon

BOOL DrawIcon(*hDC, X, Y, hIcon*)
HDC *hDC*;
int *X*;
int *Y*;
HICON *hIcon*;

This function draws an icon on the specified device. The **DrawIcon** function places the icon's upper-left corner at the location specified by the *X* and *Y* parameters. The location is subject to the current mapping mode of the device context.

Parameters   *hDC*   Identifies the device context for a window.

X   Specifies the logical *x*-coordinate of the upper-left corner of the icon.

Y   Specifies the logical *y*-coordinate of the upper-left corner of the icon.

hIcon   Identifies the icon to be drawn.

Return Value   The return value specifies the outcome of the function. It is TRUE if the function is successful. Otherwise, it is FALSE.

Comments   The icon resource must have been previously loaded by using the **LoadIcon** function.

See Also   **LoadIcon, OpenIcon, CreateIcon**

■ DrawMenuBar

BOOL DrawMenuBar(*hWnd***)**
HWND *hWnd*;

This function redraws the menu bar. If a menu bar is changed *after* Windows has created the window, this function should be called to draw the changed menu bar.

Parameters   *hWnd*   Identifies the window whose menu needs redrawing.

Return Value   This function returns TRUE for success, FALSE for failure.

■ DrawText

int DrawText(*hDC, lpString, nCount, lpRect, wFormat***)**
HDC *hDC*;
LPTSTR *lpString*;
int *nCount*;
LPRECT *lpRect*;
UINT *wFormat*;

This function draws formatted text in the rectangle specified by the *lpRect* parameter. It formats text by expanding tabs into appropriate spaces, justifying text to the left, right, or center of the given rectangle, and breaking text into lines that fit within the given rectangle. The type of formatting is specified by the *wFormat* parameter.

The **DrawText** function uses the device context's selected font, text color, and background color to draw the text. Unless the DT_NOCLIP format is used, **DrawText** clips the text so that the text does not appear outside the given rectangle. All formatting is assumed to have multiple lines unless the DT_SINGLELINE format is given.

The **DrawText** function may be used as either a wide-character function (where text arguments must use Unicode) or an ANSI function (where text arguments must use characters from the Windows 3.x character set installed).

Parameters   *hDC*   Identifies the device context.

lpString   Points to the string to be drawn. If the *nCount* parameter is –1, the string must be null-terminated.

nCount   Specifies the number of bytes in the string. If *nCount* is –1, then *lpString* is assumed to be a pointer to a null-terminated string and **DrawText** computes the character count automatically.

lpRect   Points to a **RECT** structure that contains the rectangle (in logical coordinates) in which the text is to be formatted.

wFormat   Specifies the method of formatting the text. It can be any combination of the following values:

Value	Meaning
DT_BOTTOM	Specifies bottom-justified text. This value must be combined with DT_SINGLELINE.
DT_CALCRECT	Determines the width and height of the rectangle. If there are multiple lines of text, **DrawText** will use the width of the rectangle pointed to by the *lpRect* parameter and extend the base of the rectangle to bound the last line of text. If there is only one line of text, **DrawText** will modify the right side of the rectangle so that it bounds the last character in the line. In either case, **DrawText** returns the height of the formatted text but does not draw the text.
DT_CENTER	Centers text horizontally.
DT_EXPANDTABS	Expands tab characters. The default number of characters per tab is eight.
DT_EXTERNALLEADING	Includes the font external leading in line height. Normally, external leading is not included in the height of a line of text.
DT_LEFT	Aligns text flush-left.
DT_NOCLIP	Draws without clipping. **DrawText** is somewhat faster when DT_NOCLIP is used.
DT_NOPREFIX	Turns off processing of prefix characters. Normally, **DrawText** interprets the mnemonic-prefix character & as a directive to underscore the character that follows, and the mnemonic-prefix characters && as a directive to print a single &. By specifying DT_NOPREFIX, this processing is turned off.
DT_RIGHT	Aligns text flush-right.
DT_SINGLELINE	Specifies single line only. Carriage returns and linefeeds do not break the line.
DT_TABSTOP	Sets tab stops. Bits 15–8 (high-order byte of the low-order word) of the *wFormat* parameter is the number of characters for each tab. The default number of characters per tab is eight.
DT_TOP	Specifies top-justified text (single line only).
DT_VCENTER	Specifies vertically centered text (single line only).

Value	Meaning
DT_WORDBREAK	Specifies word breaking. Lines are automatically broken between words if a word would extend past the edge of the rectangle specified by the *lpRect* parameter. A carriage return/line sequence will also break the line.

Note that the DT_CALCRECT, DT_EXTERNALLEADING, DT_INTERNAL, DT_NOCLIP, and DT_NOPREFIX values cannot be used with the DT_TABSTOP value:

Return Value   The return value specifies the height of the text.

Comments   If the selected font is too large for the specified rectangle, the **DrawText** function does not attempt to substitute a smaller font.

See Also   **GrayString, TextOut, TabbedTextOut**

■ DuplicateHandle

```
BOOL DuplicateHandle(hSourceProcessHandle, hSourceHandle, hTargetProcessHandle,
        lpTargetHandle, dwDesiredAccess, bInheritHandle, dwOptions)
HANDLE hSourceProcessHandle;
HANDLE hSourceHandle;
HANDLE hTargetProcessHandle;
LPHANDLE lpTargetHandle;
DWORD dwDesiredAccess;
BOOL bInheritHandle;
DWORD dwOptions;
```

A duplicate handle can be created with the **DuplicateHandle** function.

Parameters   *hSourceProcessHandle*   An open handle to the process that contains the handle to be duplicated. The handle must have been created with PROCESS_DUP_HANDLE access to the process.

hSourceHandle   An open handle to any object that is valid in the context of the source process.

hTargetProcessHandle   An open handle to the process that is to receive the duplicated handle. The handle must have been created with PROCESS_DUP_HANDLE access to the process.

lpTargetHandle   A pointer to a variable which receives the new handle that points to the same object as **SourceHandle** does. This handle value will be valid in the context of the target process.

dwDesiredAccess   The access requested for the new handle. This parameter is ignored if the DUPLICATE_SAME_ACCESS option is specified.

bInheritHandle   Supplies a flag that if TRUE, marks the target handle as inheritable. If this is the case, then the target handle will be inherited to new processes each time the target process creates a new process using **CreateProcess**.

dwOptions   Specifies optional behaviors for the caller.

Value	Meaning
DUPLICATE_CLOSE_SOURCE	The **SourceHandle** will be closed by this service prior to returning to the caller. This occurs regardless of any error status returned.
DUPLICATE_SAME_ACCESS	The *DesiredAccess* parameter is ignored and instead the **GrantedAccess** associated with **SourceHandle** is used as the **DesiredAccess** when creating the **TargetHandle**.

Return Value   The return value is TRUE if the function is successful. Otherwise, it is FALSE in which case extended error information is available from the **GetLastError** function.

Comments   The following objects can be duplicated using **DuplicateHandle**.

- process
- thread
- event
- semaphore
- mutex
- file (including file mappings)
- console input or output

This function requires PROCESS_DUP_ACCESS to both the **SourceProcessHandle** and the **TargetProcessHandle**. This function is used to pass an object handle from one process to another. Once this call is complete, the target process needs to be informed of the value of the target handle. The target process can then operate on the object using this handle value.

Console handles cannot be duplicated to another process; they can only be duplicated within the same process.

■ Ellipse

BOOL Ellipse(*hDC, X1, Y1, X2, Y2***)**
HDC *hDC*;
int *X1*;
int *Y1*;
int *X2*;
int *Y2*;

The **Ellipse** function draws an ellipse. The center of the ellipse is the center of the bounding rectangle specified by the *X1*, *Y1*, *X2*, and *Y2* parameters. The ellipse border is drawn with the current pen, and the interior is filled with the current brush.

If the bounding rectangle is empty, nothing is drawn. If the bounding rectangle is a square, a circle is drawn.

Parameters

hDC   Identifies the device context.

X1   Specifies the logical *x*-coordinate of the upper-left corner of the bounding rectangle.

Y1   Specifies the logical *y*-coordinate of the upper-left corner of the bounding rectangle.

X2   Specifies the logical *x*-coordinate of the lower-right corner of the bounding rectangle.

Y2   Specifies the logical *y*-coordinate of the lower-right corner of the bounding rectangle.

Return Value

The return value is TRUE if the ellipse is drawn, otherwise it is FALSE.

Comments

The current position is neither used nor updated by this function.

■ EmptyClipboard

BOOL EmptyClipboard(void)

This function empties the clipboard and frees handles to data in the clipboard. It then assigns ownership of the clipboard to the window that currently has the clipboard open.

This function has no parameters.

Return Value

The return value specifies the status of the clipboard. It is nonzero if the clipboard is emptied. It is zero if an error occurs.

Comments

The clipboard must be open when the **EmptyClipboard** function is called.

See Also

OpenClipboard, SetClipboardData

■ EnableCommNotification

BOOL EnableCommNotification(*hFile, hWnd, dwInTrigger, dwOutTrigger***)**
HANDLE *hFile*;
HANDLE *hWnd*;
DWORD *dwInTrigger*;
DWORD *dwOutTrigger*;

This API is used to enable message posting for certain communications events.

Parameters   *hFile*   Specifies the communication device to enable. The CreateFile() function returns this value.

hWnd   Specifies the window to receive the messages.

dwInTrigger   Specifies the trigger value for the receive queue (in bytes).

dwOutTrigger   Specifies the trigger value for the transmit queue (in bytes).

Return Value   TRUE – The operation was successful. FALSE – The operation failed. Extended error information is available using GetLastError().

Comments   When message posting is enabled, WM_COMMNOTIFY messages will be posted to the specified window with the following information:

> msg = WM_COMMNOTIFY
> dwParam = handle of comm device
> lParam = notification status

Notification status is one or more of the following: ReceiveTrigger occurs when at least dwInTrigger bytes are in the input queue. TransmitTrigger occurs when fewer than dwOutTrigger bytes still remain in the transmit queue. Call will fail if an invalid handle is specified, or the function is not supported by the communications provider, or when a Windows 3.0 version of COMM.DRV is installed.

■ EnableMenuItem

DWORD EnableMenuItem(*hMenu, wIDEnableItem, dwEnable***)**
HMENU *hMenu*;
UINT *wIDEnableItem*;
UINT *dwEnable*;

This function enables, disables, or grays a menu item.

Parameters   *hMenu*   Specifies the menu.

wIDEnableItem   Specifies the menu item to be enabled. The *wIDEnableItem* parameter can specify pop-up menu items as well as menu items.

dwEnable   Specifies the action to take. It can be a combination of MF_DISABLED, MF_ENABLED, or MF_GRAYED, with MF_BYCOMMAND or MF_BYPOSITION. These values can be combined by using the bitwise OR operator. These values have the following meanings:

Value	Meaning
MF_BYCOMMAND	Specifies that the *wIDEnableItem* parameter gives the menu item ID.
MF_BYPOSITION	Specifies that the *wIDEnableItem* parameter gives the position of the menu item (the first item is at position zero).
MF_DISABLED	Menu item is disabled.

Value	Meaning
MF_ENABLED	Menu item is enabled.
MF_GRAYED	Menu item is grayed.

Return Value The return value specifies the previous state of the menu item. The return value is −1 if the menu item does not exist.

Comments To disable or enable input to a menu bar, see the WM_SYSCOMMAND message.

See Also **GetMenuItemID**

■ EnableScrollBar

BOOL EnableScrollBar(*hwnd, fwSBFlags, fwArrowFlags***)**
HWND *hwnd*;   /* handle of the window or scroll bar */
WORD *fwSBFlags*;   /* scroll-bar type flag   */
WORD *fwArrowFlags*; /* scroll-bar arrow flag   */

The **EnableScrollBar** function enables or disables one or both arrows of a scroll bar.

Parameters *hwnd* Identifies a window or a scroll-bar control, depending on the value of the *fwSBFlags* parameter.

fwSBFlags Specifies the scroll-bar type. It can be one of the following values:

Value	Meaning
SB_BOTH	Enables or disables the arrows of the horizontal and vertical scroll bars associated with the given window. The *hwnd* parameter identifies the window.
SB_CTL	Identifies the scroll bar as a scroll-bar control. The *hwnd* parameter must identify a scroll-bar control.
SB_HORZ	Enables or disables the arrows of the horizontal scroll bar associated with the given window. The *hwnd* parameter identifies the window.
SB_VERT	Enables or disables the arrows of the vertical scroll bar associated with the given window. The *hwnd* parameter identifies the window.

fwArrowFlags Specifies whether the scroll-bar arrows are enabled or disabled, and which arrows are enabled/disabled. It can be one of the following values:

Value	Meaning
ESB_ENABLE_BOTH	Enables both arrows of a scroll bar.
ESB_DISABLE_LTUP	Disables the left arrow of a horizontal scroll bar, or the up arrow of a vertical scroll bar.
ESB_DISABLE_RTDN	Disables the right arrow of a horizontal scroll bar, or the down arrow of a vertical scroll bar.
ESB_DISABLE_BOTH	Disables both arrows of a scroll bar.

Return Value	The return value is TRUE if the arrows are enabled or disabled as specified. It is FALSE if the arrows are already in the requested state or an error occurs.
Example	This example enables an edit control's vertical scroll bar when the control receives the input focus, and disables the scroll bar when the control loses the focus:
See Also	**ShowScrollBar**

■ EnableWindow

BOOL EnableWindow(*hWnd*, *bEnable***)**
HWND *hWnd*;
BOOL *bEnable*;

This function enables or disables mouse and keyboard input to the specified window or control. When input is disabled, input such as mouse clicks and key presses are ignored by the window. When input is enabled, all input is processed.

The **EnableWindow** function enables mouse and keyboard input to a window if the *bEnable* parameter is nonzero, and disables it if *bEnable* is zero.

Parameters	*hWnd* Identifies the window to be enabled or disabled.
	bEnable Specifies whether the given window is to be enabled or disabled.
Return Value	The return value specifies the previous enable state of the window. It is nonzero if the window was initially disabled. It is zero if the window was initially enabled or if an error occurs.
Comments	A window must be enabled before it can be activated. For example, if an application is displaying a modeless dialog box and has disabled its main window, the main window must be enabled before the dialog box is destroyed. Otherwise, another window will get the input focus and be activated. If a child window is disabled, it is ignored when Windows tries to determine which window should get mouse messages.
	Initially, all windows are enabled by default. **EnableWindow** must be used to disable a window explicitly.
See Also	**IsWindowEnabled**

■ EndDeferWindowPos

BOOL EndDeferWindowPos(*hWinPosInfo***)**
HWPI *hWinPosInfo*;

This function simultaneously updates the position and size of one or more windows in a single screen-refresh cycle. The *hWinPosInfo* parameter identifies a multiple window-position structure that contains the update information for the windows. The **DeferWindowPos** function stores the update information in the structure; the **BeginDeferWindowPos** function creates the initial structure used by these functions.

Parameters   *hWinPosInfo*   Identifies a multiple window-position structure that contains size and position information for one or more windows. This structure is returned by the **BeginDeferWindowPos** function or the most recent call to the **DeferWindowPos** function.

Return Value   Returns TRUE for success, FALSE for failure.

See Also   **BeginDeferWindowPos, DeferWindowPos**

■ EndDialog

BOOL EndDialog(*hDlg, nResult***)**
HWND *hDlg,*
int *nResult*;

This function terminates a modal dialog box and returns the given result to the **DialogBox** function that created the dialog box. The **EndDialog** function is required to complete processing whenever the **DialogBox** function is used to create a modal dialog box. The function must be used in the dialog function of the modal dialog box and should not be used for any other purpose.

The dialog function can call **EndDialog** at any time, even during the processing of the WM_INITDIALOG message. If called during the WM_INITDIALOG message, the dialog box is terminated before it is shown or before the input focus is set.

EndDialog does not terminate the dialog box immediately. Instead, it sets a flag that directs the dialog box to terminate as soon as the dialog function ends. The **EndDialog** function returns to the dialog function, so the dialog function must return control to Windows.

Parameters   *hDlg*   Identifies the dialog box to be destroyed.

nResult   Specifies the value to be returned from the dialog box to the **DialogBox** function that created it.

Return Value   Returns TRUE for success, FALSE for failure.

See Also   **DialogBox**

■ EndDoc

int EndDoc(*hDC***)**
HDC *hDC*;   /* device-context handle */

The **EndDoc** function ends a print job. This function replaces the ENDDOC printer escape for Windows version 3.1 and later.

Parameters	*hDC* Identifies the device context for the print job.
Return Value	The return value is positive if the function is successful. Otherwise, it is negative.
Comments	Applications should call the **EndDoc** function immediately after finishing a print job.
See Also	**StartDoc**

■ EndPage

int EndPage(*hDC***)**
HDC *hDC*;   /* device-context handle */

The **EndPage** function informs the device that the application has finished writing to a page. This function is typically used to direct the device driver to advance to a new page.

This function replaces the NEWFRAME printer escape for Windows version 3.1 and later.

Parameters	*hDC* Identifies the device context for the print job.
Return Value	The return value is positive if the function is successful. Otherwise, it is an error value, which can be one of the following:

Value	Meaning
SP_ERROR	General error.
SP_APPABORT	Job was terminated because the application's abort function returned zero.
SP_USERABORT	User terminated the job through Print Manager.
SP_OUTOFDISK	Not enough disk space is currently available for spooling, and no more space will become available.
SP_OUTOFMEMORY	Not enough memory is available for spooling.

Comments	The **ResetDC** function can be used to change the device mode, if necessary, after calling the **EndPage** function.
See Also	**StartPage**

■ EndPaint

BOOL EndPaint(*hWnd, lpPaint***)**
HWND *hWnd*;
LPPAINTSTRUCT *lpPaint*;

This function marks the end of painting in the given window. The **EndPaint** function is required for each call to the **BeginPaint** function, but only after painting is complete.

Parameters *hWnd*   Identifies the window that is repainted.

lpPaint   Points to a **PAINTSTRUCT** structure that contains the painting information retrieved by the **BeginPaint** function.

Return Value Returns TRUE for success, FALSE for failure.

Comments If the caret was hidden by the **BeginPaint** function, **EndPaint** restores the caret to the screen.

See Also **BeginPaint**

■ EndPath

BOOL EndPath(*hDC***)**
HDC *hDC*;

The **EndPath** function ends a path bracket; that is, it ends the sequence of functions defining the size and shape of the path started by **BeginPath**.

Parameters *hDC*   Identifies the DC.

Return Value The return value is TRUE if the call succeeded, otherwise FALSE.

Errors Use the **GetLastError** function to retrieve the error value, which may be one of the following:

ERROR_INVALID_MODE

ERROR_INVALID_PARAMETER

See Also **BeginPath**

■ EndWindowBuffer

BOOL EndWindowBuffer(*hWnd***)**
HWND *hWnd*;

Ends buffering for *hWnd*, copies buffer to the screen. This function is used along with **BeginWindowBuffer** for quick multi-primitive drawing operations. Using a buffer, these primitives all draw off-screen. When **EndWindowBuffer** is called, this buffer is drawn on screen.

Parameters *hWnd*   Window for which output is to be buffered.

Return Value TRUE for success, FALSE for failure.

See Also **BeginWindowBuffer FlushWindowBuffer SetWindowBufferAttributes GetWindowBufferAttributes**

■ EnterCriticalSection

VOID EnterCriticalSection(_lpCriticalSection_**)**
LPCRITICAL_SECTION _lpCriticalSection_;

An application thread may enter a critical section gaining exclusive access to a resource using **EnterCriticalSection**.

Parameters   _lpCriticalSection_   Supplies the address of a critical section object to enter.

Entering a critical section causes the calling thread to block until the critical section attains a signaled state. Once this occurs, the thread is granted ownership of the critical section object, and the object becomes not signaled. A thread is allowed to recursively enter a critical section. Unlike OS/2's **DosEnterCritSec**, calling this function has no effect on the other threads in a process.

See Also   **LeaveCriticalSection, InitializeCriticalSection, DeleteCriticalSection**

■ EnumChildProc

BOOL FAR PASCAL EnumChildProc(_hwnd_, _lParam_**)**
HWND _hwnd_;   /* handle of a child window   */
DWORD _lParam_;   /* application-defined value */

The **EnumChildProc** function is an application-defined callback function that receives child window handles as a result of a call to the **EnumChildWindows** function.

Parameters   _hwnd_   Identifies a child window of the parent window specified in the **EnumChildWindows** function.

lParam   Specifies the application-defined value specified in the **EnumChildWindows** function.

Return Value   The callback function should return TRUE to continue enumeration or FALSE to stop enumeration.

Comments   The callback function can carry out any desired task.

EnumChildProc is a placeholder for the application-supplied function name. The actual name must be exported by including it in an **EXPORTS** statement in the application's module-definition file.

See Also   **EnumChildWindows**

■ EnumChildWindows

BOOL EnumChildWindows(_hWndParent_, _lpEnumFunc_, _lParam_**)**
HWND _hWndParent_;
FARPROC _lpEnumFunc_;
LONG _lParam_;

This function enumerates the child windows that belong to the specified parent window by passing the handle of each child window, in turn, to the application-supplied callback function pointed to by the *lpEnumFunc* parameter.

The **EnumChildWindows** function continues to enumerate windows until the called function returns zero or until the last child window has been enumerated.

Parameters

hWndParent   Identifies the parent window whose child windows are to be enumerated.

lpEnumFunc   Is the procedure-instance address of the callback function.

lParam   Specifies the value to be passed to the callback function for the application's use.

Return Value

The return value specifies nonzero if all child windows have been enumerated. Otherwise, it is zero.

Comments

This function does not enumerate pop-up windows that belong to the *hWndParent* parameter.

Callback Function

BOOL APIENTRY *EnumFunc(hWnd, lParam)*
HWND *hWnd*;
LONG *lParam*;

EnumFunc is a placeholder for the application-supplied function name.

Parameters

hWnd   Identifies the window handle.

lParam   Specifies the long parameter argument of the **EnumChildWindows** function.

Return Value

The callback function should return a nonzero value to continue enumeration; it should return zero to stop enumeration.

See Also

EnumWindows

■ EnumClipboardFormats

WORD EnumClipboardFormats(*wFormat*)
WORD *wFormat*;

This function enumerates the formats found in a list of available formats that belong to the clipboard. On each call to this function, the *wFormat* parameter specifies a known available format, and the function returns the format that appears next in the list. The first format in the list can be retrieved by setting *wFormat* to zero.

Parameters

wFormat   Specifies a known format.

Return Value   The return value specifies the next known clipboard data format. It is zero if *wFormat* specifies the last format in the list of available formats. It is zero if the clipboard is not open.

Comments   Before it enumerates the formats by using the **EnumClipboardFormats** function, an application must open the clipboard by using the **OpenClipboard** function.

The order that an application uses for putting alternative formats for the same data into the clipboard is the same order that the enumerator uses when returning them to the pasting application. The pasting application should use the first format enumerated that it can handle. This gives the donor a chance to recommend formats that involve the least loss of data.

See Also   **OpenClipboard, CountClipboardFormats, RegisterClipboardFormat**

■ EnumDesktops

BOOL EnumDesktops(*lpEnumFunc, lParam***)**
FARPROC *lpEnumFunc*;
LONG *lParam*;

This function enumerates all the desktop objects associated with the current WindowStation. The function enumerates by calling the callback function pointed to by **lpEnumFunc**. This function continues to enumerate desktops until the called function returns zero or until the last desktop has been enumerated.

Parameters   *lpEnumFunc*   Pointer to the enumeration function (see below).

lParam   An application defined parameter passed into the enumeration function.

Return Value   Returns TRUE if all desktops have been enumerated, otherwise returns FALSE.

Callback function

BOOL **EnumDesktopFunc**(*lpDesktop, lpDeskAttrs, lParam*)
LPSTR *lpDesktop*;
LPDESKATTRS *lpDeskAttrs*;
LONG *lParam*;

This function is the **EnumDesktops** callback function format used to enumerate through the desktop objects.

Parameters   *lpDesktop*   This is a pointer to a string buffer which will hold the desktop name.

lpDeskAttrs   This is pointer to a **DESKATTRS** structure that will contain physical attribute information about the desktop information being returned.

lParam   The application supplied **lParam** value passed into EnumDesktops.

Return Value   TRUE is returned if enumeration is to continue. FALSE is returned if enumerate is to stop.

■ EnumDisplayDevices

BOOL EnumDisplayDevices(*lpEnumFunc, lParam***)**
FARPROC *lpEnumFunc*;
LONG *lParam*;

This function is used to enumerate the names of the available display devices. This function calls the function pointed to be **lpEnumFunc** in turn with each new device name.

Parameters

lpEnumFunc   Pointer to the enumeration function (see below).

lParam   An application defined parameter passed into the enumeration function.

Return Value

Returns TRUE if all desktops have been enumerated, otherwise returns FALSE.

Callback function

BOOL **EnumDisplayDevicesFunc(***lpDevice, lParam***)**
LPSTR *lpDevice*;
LONG *lParam*;

This function is the **EnumDisplayDevices** callback function format used to enumerate through the available display devices. More information about each device can be queried through the **GetDesktopTypes** api.

Parameters

lpDevice   This is a pointer to a string buffer which will hold the device name.

lParam   The application supplied lParam value passed into **EnumDisplayDevices.**

Return Value

TRUE is returned if enumeration is to continue. FALSE is returned if enumerate is to stop.

■ EnumFontFamilies

int EnumFontFamilies(*hdc, lpszFamily, lpFontFunc, lpData***)**
HDC *hdc*;   /* device-context handle   */
LPSTR *lpszFamily*;   /* string for family name   */
FARPROC *lpFontFunc*; /* pointer to callback function   */
LPSTR *lpData*;   /* pointer to application-supplied data */

The **EnumFontFamilies** function enumerates the fonts in a specified font family that are available on a given device.

Parameters

hdc   Identifies the device context.

lpszFamily   Points to a null-terminated string that specifies the family name of the desired fonts. If *lpszFamily* is NULL, **EnumFontFamilies** randomly selects and enumerates one font of each available type family.

lpFontFunc   Specifies the procedure-instance address of the application-defined callback function. See the description of the **EnumFontFamProc** function.

lpData   Points to application-supplied data. The data is passed to the callback function along with the font information.

Return Value

The return value specifies the last value returned by the callback function. Its meaning is implementation specific.

Comments

The **EnumFontFamilies** function differs from the **EnumFonts** function in that it retrieves the style names associated with a TrueType font. With **EnumFontFamilies**, information can be retrieved about unusual font styles (for example, "Outline") that could not be enumerated by using the **EnumFonts** function. Applications should use **EnumFontFamilies** instead of **EnumFonts**.

For each font having the typeface name specified by the *lpszFamily* parameter, the **EnumFontFamilies** function retrieves information about that font and passes it to the function pointed to by the *lpFontFunc* parameter. The application-supplied callback function can process the font information as desired. Enumeration continues until there are no more fonts or the callback function returns zero.

The address passed as the *lpFontFunc* parameter must be created by using the **MakeProcInstance** function.

The callback function must use the Pascal calling convention and must be declared **FAR**.

See Also

EnumFonts EnumFontFamProc

■ EnumFonts

int EnumFonts(*hDC, lpFaceName, lpFontFunc, lpData***)**
HDC *hDC*;
LPTSTR *lpFaceName*;
PROC *lpFontFunc*;
LPVOID *lpData*;

The **EnumFonts** function enumerates the fonts available on a given device. For each font having the typeface name specified by the *lpFaceName* parameter, the **EnumFonts** function retrieves information about that font and passes it to the function pointed to by the *lpFontFunc* parameter. The application-supplied callback function can process the font information as desired. Enumeration continues until there are no more fonts or the callback function returns zero.

The **EnumFonts** function may be used as either a wide-character function (where text arguments must use Unicode) or an ANSI function (where text arguments must use characters from the Windows 3.x character set

Parameters

hDC   Identifies the device context.

lpFaceName   Points to a null-terminated character string that specifies the typeface name of the desired fonts. If *lpFaceName* is NULL, **EnumFonts** randomly selects and enumerates one font of each available typeface.

lpFontFunc   Is the address of the callback function. See the following Comments section for details.

lpData   Points to the application-supplied data. The data is passed to the callback function along with the font information.

Return Value   The return value specifies the last value returned by the callback function. Its meaning is user defined.

Comments   The callback function must be declared as an APIENTRY, so that the correct calling conventions will be used.

Callback Function

int APIENTRY FontFunc(*lpLogFont*, *lpTextMetric*, *fFontType*, *lpData***)**
LPLOGFONT *lpLogFont*;
LPTEXTMETRIC *lpTextMetric*;
DWORD *fFontType*;
LPVOID *lpData*;

This function may have any name, *FontFunc* is just an example.

Parameters   *lpLogFont*   Points to a **LOGFONT** structure that contains information about the logical attributes of the font.

lpTextMetric   Points to a **TEXTMETRIC** structure that contains information about the physical attributes of the font.

fFontType   Bit flags specifying the type of the font.

lpData   Points to the application-supplied data passed by **EnumFonts**.

Return Value   The return value can be any integer. If zero is returned, the enumeration will be terminated.

Comments   The AND (&) operator can be used with the RASTER_FONTTYPE and DEVICE_FONTTYPE constants to determine the font type. The RASTER_FONTTYPE bit of the *FontType* parameter specifies whether the font is a raster or vector font. If the bit is one, the font is a raster font; if zero, it is a vector font. The DEVICE_FONTTYPE bit of *FontType* specifies whether the font is a device- or GDI-based font. If the bit is one, the font is a device-based font; if zero, it is a GDI-based font.

If the device is capable of text transformations (scaling, italicizing, and so on) only the base font will be enumerated. The user must inquire into the device's text-transformation abilities to determine which additional fonts are available directly from the device.

EnumFonts only enumerates fonts from the GDI internal table. This does not include fonts that are generated by a device, such as fonts that are transformations of fonts from the internal table. The **GetDeviceCaps** function can be used to determine which transformations a device can perform. This information is available by using the TEXTCAPS index.

See Also   **GetDeviceCaps**

■ EnumFontsProc

int FAR PASCAL EnumFontsProc(*lpLogFont*, *lpTextMetric*, *nFontType*, *lpData*)
LPLOGFONT *lpLogFont*;
LPTEXTMETRIC *lpTextMetric*;
short *nFontType*;
LPSTR *lpData*;

The **EnumFontsProc** function is an application defined callback function that processes font data from the **EnumFonts** function.

Parameters   *lpLogFont*   Points to a **LOGFONT** structure that contains information about the logical attributes of the font.

The **LOGFONT** structure has the following form:

```
typedef struct tagLOGFONT {
    LONG lfHeight;
    LONG lfWidth;
    LONG lfEscapement;
    LONG lfOrientation;
    LONG lfWeight;
    BYTE  lfItalic;
    BYTE  lfUnderline;
    BYTE  lfStrikeOut;
    BYTE  lfCharSet;
    BYTE  lfOutPrecision;
    BYTE  lfClipPrecision;
    BYTE  lfQuality;
    BYTE  lfPitchAndFamily;
    BYTE  lfFaceName[LF_FACESIZE];
} LOGFONT;
```

lpTextMetric   Points to a **TEXTMETRIC** structure that contains information about the physical attributes of the font.

The **TEXTMETRIC** structure has the following form:

```
typedef struct tagTEXTMETRIC {
    DWORD      tmHeight;
    DWORD      tmAscent;
    DWORD      tmDescent;
    DWORD      tmInternalLeading;
    DWORD      tmExternalLeading;
    DWORD      tmAveCharWidth;
    DWORD      tmMaxCharWidth;
    DWORD      tmWeight;
    DWORD      tmOverhang;
    DWORD      tmDigitizedAspectX;
    DWORD      tmDigitizedAspectY;
    BYTE       tmItalic;
    BYTE       tmUnderlined;
    BYTE       tmStruckOut;
    BYTE       tmFirstChar;
    BYTE       tmLastChar;
    BYTE       tmDefaultChar;
    BYTE       tmBreakChar;
    BYTE       tmPitchAndFamily;
```

```
        BYTE      tmCharSet;
    } TEXTMETRIC;
```

nFontType   Specifies the type of the font.

lpData   Points to the application-supplied data passed by **EnumFonts**.

Return Value   This function must return a nonzero value to continue enumeration; to stop enumeration, it must return zero.

Comments   An application must register the **EnumFontsProc** function by passing its address to the **EnumFonts** function.

EnumFontsProc is a placeholder for the application-supplied function name. The actual name must be exported by including it in an **EXPORTS** statement in the application's module-definition file.

■ EnumJobs

BOOL EnumJobs(*lpPrinter*, *FirstJob*, *NoJobs*, *lpJob*, *cbBuf*, *lpcbNeeded*, *lpcReturned***)**
LPPRINTER *lpPrinter*;
DWORD *FirstJob*;
DWORD *NoJobs*;
LPJOB *lpJob*;
DWORD *cbBuf*;
LPDWORD *lpcbNeeded*;
LPDWORD *lpcReturned*;

The **EnumJobs** function retrieves information about a specified set of print jobs for a specified printer.

Parameters   *lpPrinter*   Pointer to a **PRINTER** data structure that specifies the printer containing the print jobs to enumerate.

The **PRINTER** data structure has the following form:

```
typedef struct tagPRINTER {
    DWORD cVersion;
    LPPRINTERSERVER lpPrinterServer;
    LPTSTR lpPrinterName;
    LPTSTR lpPortName;
    LPTSTR lpDriverName;
    LPTSTR lpComment;
    LPTSTR lpLocation;
    LPDEVMODE lpDevMode;
    LPTSTR lpSepFile;
    LPTSTR lpPrintProcessor;
    LPTSTR lpDatatype;
    LPTSTR lpParameters;
    LPTSTR lpVendorData;
    DWORD Attributes;
    DWORD Priority;
    DWORD DefaultPriority;
    SYSTEMTIME StartTime;
    SYSTEMTIME UntilTime;
    DWORD Status;
    DWORD cJobs;
    DWORD AveragePPM;
```

```
} PRINTER:
```

FirstJob   Specifies the position of the first print job to enumerate. For example, a value of 10 indicates that the enumeration should begin at the printer's tenth print job.

NoJobs   Specifies the number of print jobs to enumerate.

lpJob   Pointer to a buffer that the function will fill with an array of *NoJobs* **JOB** data structures.

The **JOB** data structure has the following form:

```
typedef struct tagJOB {
    DWORD cVersion;
    DWORD JobId;
    LPPRINTERSERVER lpPrinterServer;
    LPTSTR lpPrinterName;
    LPTSTR lpUserName;
    LPTSTR lpDocument;
    LPTSTR lpNotifyName;
    LPTSTR lpDatatype;
    LPTSTR lpPrintProcessor;
    LPTSTR lpParameters;
    LPTSTR lpDriverName;
    LPDEVMODE lpDevMode;
    LPTSTR lpStatus;
    DWORD Status;
    DWORD Priority;
    DWORD Position;
    SYSTEMTIME StartTime;
    SYSTEMTIME UntilTime;
    DWORD TotalPages;
    DWORD PagesPrinted;
    DWORD Size;
    SYSTEMTIME Submitted;
    SYSTEMTIME Time;
} JOB;
```

cBuf   The size in bytes of the buffer pointed to by *lpJob*.

lpcbNeeded   Pointer to a DWORD that the function will set to the size in bytes of a buffer large enough to store *NoJobs* **JOB** data structures. This will be set to zero if *cBuf* was large enough.

lpcReturned   Pointer to a DWORD that the function will set to the number of **JOB** data structures written to the buffer pointed to by *lpJob*.

Return Value

If the function is successful, the return value is TRUE.

If the function fails, the return value is FALSE/NULL. Further information can be obtained by calling **GetLastError**.

See Also

GetJob, SetJob, PRINTER, JOB

■ EnumMetaFileEx

BOOL EnumMetaFileEx(*hDC, hMF, lpMetaFunc, lpData***)**
HDC *hDC*;
HMF *hMF*;
PROC *lpMetaFunc*;
LPVOID *lpData*;

The **EnumMetaFileEx** function enumerates the GDI calls within the metafile identified by the *hMF* parameter. The **EnumMetaFileEx** function retrieves each GDI call within the metafile and passes it to the function pointed to by the *lpMetaFunc* parameter. This callback function, an application-supplied function, can process each GDI call as desired. Enumeration continues until there are no more GDI calls or the callback function returns FALSE.

Parameters

hDC   Identifies the device context to be passed to MetaFunc. This may be NULL.

hMF   Identifies the metafile.

lpMetaFunc   Is the address of the callback function. See the following Comments section for details.

lpData   Points to the callback-function data.

Return Value

The return value is TRUE if the callback function enumerates all the GDI calls in a metafile. Otherwise, it returns FALSE.

Comments

This function will perform the same setup on the given *hDC* that the **PlayMetaFileEx** function would. Therefore, if the callback function calls **PlayMetaFileRecordEx**, it should use *only* this given *hDC*. If the given *hDC* is NULL, **PlayMetaFileRecordEx** should not be called.

The callback function must be declared as an APIENTRY, so that the correct calling conventions will be used.

Callback Function

BOOL APIENTRY MetaFunc(*hDC, lpHTable, lpMetaRecordEx, nObj, lpData***)**
HDC *hDC*;
LPHANDLETABLE *lpHTable*;
LPMETARECORDEX *lpMetaRecordEx*;
LONG *nObj*;
LPVOID *lpData*;

This function may have any name, *MetaFunc* is just an example.

Parameters

hDC   Identifies the device context that was passed to EnumMetaFileEx.

lpHTable   Points to a table of handles associated with the objects (pens, brushes, and so on) in the metafile.

lpMetaRecordEx   Points to a metafile record contained in the metafile. The metafile record should not be modified. If modification is needed, it should be made on a copy of this metafile record.

nObj   Specifies the number of handles in the handle table.

lpData   Points to the application-supplied data.

Return Value   The function can carry out any desired task. It must return TRUE to continue enumeration, or FALSE to stop it.

See Also   **PlayMetaFileEx, PlayMetaFileRecordEx.**

■ EnumMetaFileProc

int FAR PASCAL EnumMetaFileProc(*hDC*, *lpHTable*, *lpMFR*, *nObj*, *lpClientData***)**
HDC *hDC*;
LPHANDLETABLE *lpHTable*;
LPMETARECORD *lpMFR*;
int *nObj*;
BYTE FAR * *lpClientData*;

The **EnumMetaFileProc** function is an application defined callback function that processes metafile data from the **EnumMetaFile** function.

Parameters   *hDC*   Identifies the special device context that contains the metafile.

lpHTable   Points to a table of handles associated with the objects (pens, brushes, and so on) in the metafile.

lpMFR   Points to a metafile record contained in the metafile.

nObj   Specifies the number of objects with associated handles in the handle table.

lpClientData   Points to the application-supplied data.

Return Value   This function must return a nonzero value to continue enumeration; to stop enumeration, it must return zero.

Comments   An application must register the function by passing its address to the **EnumMetaFile** function.

EnumMetaFileProc is a placeholder for the application-supplied function name. The actual name must be exported by including it in an **EXPORTS** statement in the application's module-definition file.

■ EnumObjects

int EnumObjects(*hDC*, *iObjectType*, *lpObjectFunc*, *lpData***)**
HDC *hDC*;
int *iObjectType*;
PROC *lpObjectFunc*;
LPVOID *lpData*;

The **EnumObjects** function enumerates the pens and brushes available for a device context. For each object of the given type, the callback function is called with the information for that object. The callback function is called until there are no more objects or the callback function returns zero.

Parameters   *hDC*   Identifies the device context.

nObjectType   Specifies the object type. It can be one of the following values:

OBJ_BRUSH
OBJ_PEN

lpObjectFunc   The address of the application supplied callback function. See the following Comments section for details.

lpData   Points to the application-supplied data. The data is passed to the callback function along with the object information.

Return Value   The return value specifies the last value returned by the callback function. Its meaning is user-defined. ERROR will be returned if an error occured.

Comments   The callback function must be declared as an APIENTRY, so that the correct calling conventions will be used.

Callback Function

int APIENTRY *ObjectFunc*(*lpLogObject*, *lpData*)
LPVOID *lpLogObject*;
LPVOID *lpData*;

This function may have any name, *ObjectFunc* is just an example.

Parameters   *lpLogObject*   Points to a **LOGPEN** or **LOGBRUSH** structure that contains information about the logical attributes of the object.

lpData   Points to the application-supplied data passed to the **EnumObjects** function.

Return Value   The return value can be any integer. If zero is returned, the enumeration will be terminated. ERROR should not be returned from this function.

■ EnumObjectsProc

int FAR PASCAL EnumObjectsProc(_lpLogObject_**,** _lpData_**)**
LPSTR *lpLogObject*;
LPSTR *lpData*;

The **EnumObjectsProc** function is an application defined callback function that processes objects data from the **EnumObjects** function.

Parameters   *lpLogObject*   Points to a **LOGPEN** or **LOGBRUSH** structure that contains information about the attributes of the object.

The **LOGPEN** structure has the following form:

```
typedef struct tagLOGPEN {
    DWORD     lopnStyle;
    POINT     lopnWidth;
    COLORREF  lopnColor;
} LOGPEN;
```

The **LOGBRUSH** structure has the following form:

```
typedef struct tagLOGBRUSH {
    DWORD     lbStyle;
    COLORREF  lbColor;
    LONG      lbHatch;
} LOGBRUSH;
```

lpData   Points to the application-supplied data passed by the **EnumObjects** function.

Return Value

This function must return a nonzero value to continue enumeration; to stop enumeration, it must return zero.

Comments

An application must register this function by passing its address to the **EnumObjects** function. **EnumObjectsProc** is a placeholder for the application-supplied function name. The actual name must be exported by including it in an **EXPORTS** statement in the application's module-definition file.

Example

The following code fragment retrieves the number of horizontally hatched brushes and fills **LOGBRUSH** structures with information about each of them:

```
#define MAXBRUSHES 50

    HDC hdc;
    FARPROC lpProcCallback;
    HANDLE hmem;
    LPBYTE pbCountBrush;

    lpProcCallback = MakeProcInstance(Callback, hInst);

    hmem = GlobalAlloc(GMEM_FIXED, sizeof(LOGBRUSH)
            * MAXBRUSHES);
    pbCountBrush = (LPBYTE) GlobalLock(hmem);
    *pbCountBrush = 0;
    EnumObjects(hdc, OBJ_BRUSH, lpProcCallback,
            pbCountBrush);

    FreeProcInstance(lpProcCallback);


int FAR PASCAL Callback(LPLOGBRUSH lpLogBrush, LPBYTE pbData)
{
    /*
     * pbData contains the number of horizontally hatched brushes.
     * lpDest is set to follow the byte reserved for pbData and the
     * LOGBRUSH structures that have already been filled with brush
     * information.
     */

    LPLOGBRUSH lpDest =
        (LPLOGBRUSH) (pbData + 1 + (*pbData * sizeof(LOGBRUSH)));

    if (lpLogBrush->lbStyle == BS_HATCHED && /* if horiz hatch */
```

```
        lpLogBrush->lbHatch == HS_HORIZONTAL) {
    *lpDest++ = *lpLogBrush; /* fill structure with brush info */
    (*pbData) ++;              /* increment brush count        */
    if (*pbData >= MAXBRUSHES)
        return 0;
}

return 1;
}
```

See Also   **FreeProcInstance, GlobalAlloc, GlobalLock, MakeProcInstance**

■ EnumPrinterDrivers

BOOL EnumPrinterDrivers(*lpPrinterServer, lpEnvironment, lpDriverInfo, cbBuf, pcbNeeded, lpcReturned***)**
LPPRINTERSERVER *lpPrinterServer*;
LPSTR *lpEnvironment*;
LPDRIVERINFO *lpDriverInfo*;
DWORD *cbBuf*;
LPDWORD *pcbNeeded*;
LPDWORD *lpcReturned*;

The **EnumPrinterDrivers** function enumerates all the printer drivers installed on a specified printer server.

Parameters   *lpPrinterServer*   Pointer to a **PRINTERSERVER** data structure that specifies the printer server whose printer drivers will be enumerated.

The **PRINTERSERVER** data structure has the following form:

```
typedef struct tagPRINTERSERVER {
    HANDLE   hProvidor;
    LPTSTR   lpName;
    LPTSTR   lpDescription;
    LPTSTR   lpLocation;
    LPVOID   lpVendorSpecificVariable;
} PRINTERSERVER;
```

lpEnvironment   Pointer to a string that specifies the machine and operating system environment. An example is the string "Win32.486".

lpDriverInfo   Pointer to a buffer that the function will fill with **DRIVERINFO** data structures for the enumerated printer drivers.

The **DRIVERINFO** data structure has the following form:

```
typedef struct tagDRIVERINFO {
    DWORD   cVersion;
    LPSTR   lpDriverName;
    LPSTR   lpEnvironment;
    LPSTR   lpDriverPath;
    LPSTR   lpDeviceName;
    LPSTR   lpDataFile;
    LPSTR   lpConfigFile;
} DRIVERINFO;
```

cbBuf   Specifies the size in bytes of the buffer pointed to by *lpDriverInfo*.

pcbNeeded   Pointer to a DWORD that the function will set to the number of bytes required to store all the **DRIVERINFO** data structures the function will return. The function sets this to zero if *cbBuf* was large enough.

lpcReturned   Pointer to a DWORD that the function will set to the number of printer drivers enumerated.

Return Value   If the function is successful, the return value is TRUE.

If the function fails, the return value is FALSE/NULL. Further information can be obtained by calling **GetLastError**.

See Also   **AddPrinterDriver, GetPrinterDriver**

■ EnumPrinters

BOOL EnumPrinters(*Type, lpPrinter, cbBuf, pcbNeeded, lpcReturned***)**
DWORD *Type*;
LPPRINTER *lpPrinter*;
DWORD *cbBuf*;
LPDWORD *pcbNeeded*;
LPDWORD *lpcReturned*;

The **EnumPrinters** function enumerates printers in various ways.

Parameters   *Type*   Specifies whether the enumeration should include local printers, desktop printers and/or network printers. *Type* is defined as a set of bit flags. This allows an application to specify any combination of these types of printers to be enumerated.

A local printer is one that is physically attached to the user's computer. A desktop is one that the user has indicated is frequently used. A network printer is one that the network vendor defines as such. For example, Lan Manager may define all printers in the user's network domain as network printers.

The following values have meaning:

Value	Meaning
PRINTER_LOCAL	Return local printers.
PRINTER_DESKTOP	Return desktop printers.
PRINTER_NETWORK	Return network printers.

lpPrinter   Pointer to memory that will contain all the **PRINTER** data structures the function will return.

cbBuf   The size in bytes of the buffer pointed to by *lpPrinter*.

pcbNeeded   Pointer to a DWORD that the function will set to the number of bytes required to store all the **PRINTER** data structures the function will return. This DWORD will be set to zero if *cbBuf* was large enough.

lpcReturned   Pointer to a DWORD that the function will set to the number of printers enumerated.

Return Value

If the function is successful, the return value is TRUE.

If the function fails, the return value is FALSE. Further information can be obtained by calling **GetLastError**.

See Also

AddPrinter, DeletePrinter, GetPrinter, SetPrinter

■ EnumPropProc

```
int FAR PASCAL EnumPropProc(hwnd, lpString, hData)
HWND hwnd;        /* handle of window with property  */
LPSTR lpString;   /* property string or atom         */
HANDLE hData;     /* data handle                     */
```

The **EnumPropFixedProc** function is an application-defined callback function that receives a window's property data as a result of a call to the **EnumProps** function.

Parameters

hwnd   Identifies the handle of the window that contains the property list.

lpString   Points to the null-terminated string associated with the data handle identified by the *hData* parameter. The application specified the string and data handle in a previous call to the **SetProp** function. If the application passed an atom instead of a string to the **SetProp** function, the *lpString* parameter contains the atom in the low-order word, and zero in the high-order word.

hData   Identifies the data handle.

Return Value

The callback function should return a nonzero value to continue enumeration; it should return zero to stop enumeration.

Comments

The following restrictions apply to the callback function:

■ The callback function must not yield control or do anything that might yield control to other tasks.

■ The callback function can call the **RemoveProp** function. However, the **RemoveProp** function can remove only the property passed to the callback function through the callback function's parameters.

■ The callback function should not attempt to add properties.

EnumPropProc is a placeholder for the application-supplied function name. The actual name must be exported by including it in an **EXPORTS** statement in the application's module-definition file.

See Also

EnumProps, RemoveProp, SetProp

■ EnumProps

int EnumProps(*hWnd, lpEnumFunc***)**
HWND *hWnd*;
FARPROC *lpEnumFunc*;

This function enumerates all entries in the property list of the specified window. It enumerates the entries by passing them, one by one, to the callback function specified by *lpEnumFunc*. **EnumProps** continues until the last entry is enumerated or the callback function returns zero.

Parameters
hWnd   Identifies the window whose property list is to be enumerated.

lpEnumFunc   Specifies the procedure-instance address of the callback function. See the following Comments section for details.

Return Value
The return value specifies the last value returned by the callback function. It is −1 if the function did not find a property for enumeration.

Comments
An application can remove only those properties which it has added. It should not remove properties added by other applications or by Windows itself.

The following restrictions apply to the callback function:

1. The callback function must not yield control or do anything that might yield control to other tasks.

2. The callback function can call the **RemoveProp** function. However, the **RemoveProp** function can remove only the property passed to the callback function through the callback function's parameters.

3. A callback function should not attempt to add properties.

Callback Function

The callback function must have the form shown below.

int APIENTRY *EnumFunc(***hWnd, lpString, hData***)*
HWND *hWnd*;
LPSTR *lpString*;
HANDLE *hData*;

EnumFunc is a placeholder for the application-supplied function name. The

Parameters
hWnd   Identifies a handle to the window that contains the property list.

lpString   Points to the null-terminated character string associated with the data handle when the application called the **SetProp** function to set the property. If the application passed an atom instead of a string to the **SetProp** function, the *lpString* parameter contains the atom in its low-order word, and the high-order word is zero.

hData   Identifies the data handle.

Return Value
The callback function can carry out any desired task. It must return a nonzero value to continue enumeration, or a zero value to stop it.

See Also   RemoveProp, SetProp, GetProp

■ EnumPropsEx

int EnumPropsEx(hWnd, lpEnumFunc, lParam**)**
HWND hWnd;
FARPROC lpEnumFunc;
DWORD lParam;

This function enumerates all entries in the property list of the specified window. It enumerates the entries by passing them, one by one, to the callback function specified by *lpEnumFunc*. **EnumPropsEx** continues until the last entry is enumerated or the callback function returns zero.

Parameters   *hWnd*   Identifies the window whose property list is to be enumerated.

lpEnumFunc   Specifies the procedure-instance address of the callback function. See the following Comments section for details.

lParam   User-specified data to be passed to the callback function.

Return Value   The return value specifies the last value returned by the callback function. It is –1 if the function did not find a property for enumeration.

Comments   An application can remove only those properties which it has added. It should not remove properties added by other applications or by Windows itself.

The following restrictions apply to the callback function:

1. The callback function must not yield control or do anything that might yield control to other tasks.
2. The callback function can call the **RemoveProp** function. However, the **RemoveProp** function can remove only the property passed to the callback function through the callback function's parameters.
3. A callback function should not attempt to add properties.

Callback Function

The callback function must have the form shown below.

int APIENTRY EnumFunc(hWnd, lpString, hData, lParam**)**
HWND hWnd;
LPSTR lpString;
HANDLE hData;
DWORD lParam;

EnumFunc is a placeholder for the application-supplied function name.

Parameters   *hWnd*   Identifies a handle to the window that contains the property list.

lpString   Points to the null-terminated character string associated with the data handle when the application called the **SetProp** function to set the property. If the application passed an atom instead of a string to the **SetProp** function, the *lpString* parameter contains the atom in its low-order word, and the high-order word is zero.

hData   Identifies the data handle.

lParam   User-specified data.

Return Value   The callback function can carry out any desired task. It must return a nonzero value to continue enumeration, or a zero value to stop it.

See Also   **EnumProps, GetProp, RemoveProp, SetProp**

■ EnumQueueMessages

BOOL EnumQueueMessages(*wMsgFilterMin, wMsgFilterMax, lpMsgMatch, wMatch, lpEnumProc, lParam***)**
WORD *wMsgFilterMin*;
WORD *wMsgFilterMax*;
LPMSG *lpMsgMatch*;
WORD *wMatch*;
FARPROC *lpEnumProc*;
LONG *lParam*;

This function allows an application to enumerate through all the messages in a given thread's message queue. It also allows fine filtering, allowing an application to enumerate specific kinds of window messages or all window messages.

Parameters   *wMsgFilterMin*   Specifies the value of the lowest message id to be searched for.

wMsgFilterMax   Specifies the value of the highest message id to be searched for.

lpMsgMatch   Specifies a structure of type **MSG** which allows search keys to be based on **MSG** structure contents, such as wParam and lParam.

wMatch   Specifies which parts of the **MSG** structure pointed to by *lpMsgMatch* are to be considered search keys.

Value	Meaning
MATCHF_HWND	Match all messages whose message field **hwnd** matches equivalent content in *lpMsgMatch*.
MATCHF_MESSAGE	Match all messages whose message field **message** matches equivalent content in *lpMsgMatch*.
MATCHF_WPARAM	Match all messages whose message field **wParam** matches equivalent content in *lpMsgMatch*.
MATCHF_LPARAM	Match all messages whose message field **lParam** matches equivalent content in *lpMsgMatch*.
MATCHF_WPARAMBITS	Match all messages whose message field **wParam** has the same bits set as those found in the **wParam** in *lpMsgMatch*.

Value	Meaning
MATCHF_LPARAMBITS	Match all messages whose message field **lParam** has the same bits set as those found in the **lParam** in *lpMsgMatch*.

lpEnumProc   This is the procedure address of the application-supplied callback function. See the following "Comments" section for details.

lParam   Specifies the value to be passed to the callback function for the application's use.

Return Value

Returns TRUE if all the specified messages have been enumerated successfully, otherwise it returns FALSE. This function may also return FALSE if invalid parameters are passed.

Comments

This is what the **EnumQueueMessages** callback function looks like:

BOOL APIENTRY *EnumProc(id, lpMsg, lParam)*
DWORD *id*;
LPMSG *lpMsg*;
LONG *lParam*;

EnumProc is a placeholder for the application-supplied function name.

Parameters

id   Identifies a particular message in the message queue. This *id* can be passed to functions such as **PeekMessageEx**, **SetQueueMessage**, and **InsertQueueMessage**.

lpMsg   Identifies the window message contents.

lParam   Specifies the application-supplied *lParam* argument passed in to the **EnumQueueMessages** function.

Return Value

This function must return a non-zero value to continue enumeration, or zero to stop enumeration.

■ EnumTaskWindows

The **EnumTaskWindows** function is now obsolete. It has been replaced by the **EnumThreadWindows** function.

EnumTaskWindows is macroed onto the **EnumThreadWindows** function to maintain compatibility for older applications. They may continue to call **EnumTaskWindows** as previously documented. New Windows32 applications should use **EnumThreadWindows**.

Comments

EnumTaskWindows used a task handle as its first parameter. **EnumThreadWindows** uses a thread id as its first parameter.

This is how **EnumTaskWindows** is macroed onto **EnumThreadWindows**:

```
#define EnumTaskWindows(dwThreadId, lpfn, lParam)\
        EnumThreadWindows(dwThreadId, lpfn, lParam)
```

See Also   EnumThreadWindows

■ EnumTaskWndProc

BOOL FAR PASCAL EnumTaskWndProc(*hwnd, lParam***)**
HWND *hwnd*;   /* handle of a window   */
DWORD *lParam*;   /* application-defined value */

The **EnumTaskWndProc** function is an application-defined callback function that receives the window handles associated with a task as a result of a call to the **EnumTaskWindows** function.

Parameters   *hwnd*   Identifies a window associated with the task specified in the **EnumTaskWindows** function.

lParam   Specifies the application-defined value specified in the **EnumTaskWindows** function.

Return Value   The callback function should return TRUE to continue enumeration or FALSE to stop enumeration.

Comments   The callback function can carry out any desired task.

EnumTaskWndProc is a placeholder for the application-supplied function name. The actual name must be exported by including it in an **EXPORTS** statement in the application's module-definition file.

See Also   EnumTaskWindows

■ EnumThreadWindows

BOOL EnumThreadWindows(*dwThreadId, lpfn, lParam***)**
DWORD *dwThreadId*;
FARPROC *lpfn*;
DWORD *lParam*;

The **EnumThreadWindows** function enumerates all windows associated with a thread. It enumerates the windows by passing the window handles, one by one, to the callback function pointed to by *lpfn*.

EnumThreadWindows continues until the last window is enumerated or the callback function pointed to by *lpfn* returns FALSE.

Parameters   *dwThreadId*   Identifies the thread whose windows are to be enumerated.

lpfn   Points to a callback function that **EnumThreadWindows** will pass window handles and *lParam* to. For more information, see the description in the Comments section below.

lParam   Specifies an application-defined value that the system passes to the callback function along with each window handle.

Return Value	If all windows associated with the specified thread are enumerated, this function returns TRUE.
	If all windows associated with the specified thread are not enumerated, this function returns FALSE.
Comments	The callback function pointed to by *lpfn* must have the following form:

BOOL APIENTRY *EnumFunc(hWnd, lParam)*
HWND *hWnd;*
LONG *lParam;*

EnumFunc is a placeholder for the application-supplied function name.

Parameters	*hWnd* Identifies the window handle.
	lParam Specifies the *lParam* argument of **EnumThreadWindows** function.
Return Value	The function must return TRUE to continue enumeration, or FALSE to stop enumeration.
See Also	**EnumChildWindows, EnumWindows**

■ EnumWindows

BOOL EnumWindows(*lpEnumFunc, lParam***)**
FARPROC *lpEnumFunc;*
LONG *lParam;*

This function enumerates all parent windows on the screen by passing the handle of each window, in turn, to the callback function pointed to by the *lpEnumFunc* parameter. Child windows are not enumerated.

The **EnumWindows** function continues to enumerate windows until the called function returns zero or until the last window has been enumerated.

Parameters	*lpEnumFunc* Is the procedure-instance address of the callback function. See the following "Comments" section for details.
	lParam Specifies the value to be passed to the callback function for the application's use.
Return Value	The return value is TRUE if all windows have been enumerated. Otherwise, it is FALSE.
Comments	The callback function must have the following form:

Callback Function

BOOL APIENTRY *EnumFunc(hWnd, lParam)*
HWND *hWnd;*
LONG *lParam;*

EnumFunc is a placeholder for the application-supplied function name.

Parameters	*hWnd* Identifies the window handle.
	lParam Specifies the *lParam* argument of the **EnumWindows** function.
Return Value	The function must return a nonzero value to continue enumeration, or zero to stop it.
See Also	**EnumChildWindows**

■ EnumWindowsProc

BOOL FAR PASCAL EnumWindowsProc(*hwnd, lParam*)
HWND *hwnd*;   /* handle of a parent window */
DWORD *lParam*,   /* application-defined value   */

The **EnumWindowsProc** function is an application-defined callback function that receives parent window handles as a result of a call to the **EnumWindows** function.

Parameters	*hwnd* Identifies a parent window currently.
	lParam Specifies the application-defined value specified in the **EnumWindows** function.
Return Value	The callback function should return TRUE to continue enumeration or FALSE to stop enumeration.
Comments	The callback function can carry out any desired task.
	EnumWindowsProc is a placeholder for the application-supplied function name. The actual name must be exported by including it in an **EXPORTS** statement in the application's module-definition file.
See Also	**EnumWindows**

■ EnumWindowStationFunc

BOOL EnumWindowStationFunc(*lpWindowStation, lpWinStaAttrs, lParam*)
LPTSTR *lpWindowStation*;
LPWINSTAATTRS *lpWinStaAttrs*;
LONG *lParam*;

The **EnumWindowStationFunc** is an application-defined callback function that **EnumWindowStations** calls while enumerating windowstations.

Parameters	*lpWindowStation* Pointer to a buffer that contains the windowstation name.
	lpWinStaAttrs Pointer to a **WINSTAATTRS** structure that contains information about the windowstation being enumerated.

The **WINSTAATTRS** data structure has the following form:

```
typedef struct tagWINSTAATTRS {
    DWORD   cb;
    DWORD   cPhysicalDisplays;
```

```
    DWORD    dwReserved:
} WINSTAATTRS ;
```

lParam   An application-defined parameter passed to **EnumWindowStations**, which then passes it on to this function.

Return Value

If enumeration is to continue, the return value is TRUE.

If enumeration is to stop, the return value is FALSE.

Comments

An application must register the **EnumWindowStationFunc** function by passing its address to the **EnumWindowStations** function.

EnumWindowStationFunc is a placeholder for the application-supplied function name. The actual name must be exported by including it in an **EXPORTS** statement in the application's module-definition file.

See Also

EnumWindowStations, GetWindowStationAttrs, OpenWindowStation, CloseWindowStation, GetProcessWindowStation, SetProcessWindowStation

■ EnumWindowStations

BOOL EnumWindowStations(*lpEnumFunc*, *lParam***)**
FARPROC lpEnumFunc;
LONG lParam;

The **EnumWindowStations** function enumerates all windowstations available in the system.

The **EnumWindowStations** function repeatedly calls the enumeration callback function pointed to by *lpEnumFunc* until that callback function returns zero or the last windowstation has been enumerated.

Parameters

lpEnumFunc   Pointer to the enumeration callback function. See **EnumWindowStationFunc** for further details.

lParam   An application-defined parameter that **EnumWindowStations** will pass to the enumeration callback function.

Return Value

If the function succesfully enumerates all windowstations, the return value is TRUE.

If the function fails to enumerate all windowstations, the return value is FALSE. Call **GetLastError** for more detailed error information.

See Also

EnumWindowStationFunc, OpenWindowStation, CloseWindowStation, GetProcessWindowStation, SetProcessWindowStation, GetWindowStationAttrs

■ EqualRect

BOOL EqualRect(*lpRect1*, *lpRect2*)
LPRECT *lpRect1*;
LPRECT *lpRect2*;

This function determines whether two rectangles are equal by comparing the coordinates of their upper-left and lower-right corners. If the values of these coordinates are equal, **EqualRect** returns a nonzero value; otherwise, it returns zero.

Parameters   *lpRect1*   Points to a **RECT** structure that contains the upper-left and lower-right corner coordinates of the first rectangle.

lpRect2   Points to a **RECT** structure that contains the upper-left and lower-right corner coordinates of the second rectangle.

Return Value   The return value specifies whether the specified rectangles are equal. It is nonzero if the two rectangles are identical. Otherwise, it is zero.

■ EqualRgn

BOOL EqualRgn(*hSrcRgn1*, *hSrcRgn2*)
HRGN *hSrcRgn1*;
HRGN *hSrcRgn2*;

The **EqualRgn** function checks the two given regions to determine whether they are identical.

Parameters   *hSrcRgn1*   Identifies a region.

hSrcRgn2   Identifies a region.

Return Value   The return value is TRUE if the two regions are equal. Otherwise, it is FALSE. A return value of ERROR means at least one of the region handles was invalid.

■ EqualSid

BOOL EqualSid(*Sid1*, *Sid2*)
PSID *Sid1*;
PSID *Sid2*;

The **EqualSid** function tests two **SID** security identifier values for equality. Two **SID**s must match exactly to be considered equally.

Parameters   *Sid1*   Pointer to an **SID** data structure to compare. The **SID** structure is assumed to be valid.

The **SID** data structure is an opaque data structure of variable length, defined as follows:

```
typedef PVOID * PSID;
```

Sid2   Pointer to a **SID** data structure to compare. The **SID** structure is assumed to be valid.

Return Value   If the value of *Sid1* is equal to *Sid2*, the function return value is TRUE.

If the **SID**s are not equal, the function return value is FALSE. Call **GetLastError** for more detailed error information.

If either **SID** is invalid, the function return value is undefined.

See Also   **CopySid, GetLengthSid, InitializeSid, IsValidSid, GetSidIdentifierAuthority, GetSidLengthRequired, GetSidSubAuthority, GetSidSubAuthorityCount**

■ EscapeCommFunction

BOOL EscapeCommFunction(*hFile, dwFunc***)**
HANDLE *hFile*;
DWORD *dwFunc*;

This function directs the communication device specified by the **hFile** parameter to carry out the extended function specified by the **nFunc** parameter.

Parameters   *hFile*   Specifies the communication device to carry out the extended function. The **CreateFile** function returns this value.

nFunc   Specifies the function code of the extended function.

Function	Meaning
CLRDTR	Clears the data-terminal-ready (DTR) signal.
CLRRTS	Clears the request-to-send (RTS) signal.
RESETDEV	Resets the device if possible.
SETDTR	Sends the data-terminal-ready (DTR) signal.
SETRTS	Sends the request-to-send (RTS) signal.
SETXOFF	Causes transmission to act as if an XOFF character has been received.
SETXON	Causes transmission to act as if an XON character has been received.
SETBREAK	Suspends character transmission and places the transmission line in a break state until a CLRBREAK or **ClearCommBreak** function is called. This function is identical to **SetCommBreak**. Note that no flush of data is implied by this function.
CLRBREAK	Restores character transmission and places the transmission line in a nonbreak state. This is identical to **ClearCommBreak**.

Return Value   The return value is TRUE if the function is successful or FALSE if an error occurs.

See Also   **SetCommBreak, ClearCommBreak**

■ ExcludeClipRect

int ExcludeClipRect(*hDC, X1, Y1, X2, Y2***)**
HDC *hDC*;
int *X1*;
int *Y1*;
int *X2*;
int *Y2*;

The **ExcludeClipRect** function creates a new clipping region that consists of the existing clipping region minus the specified rectangle.

Parameters   *hDC*   Identifies the device context.

X1   Specifies the logical *x*-coordinate of the upper-left corner of the rectangle.

Y1   Specifies the logical *y*-coordinate of the upper-left corner of the rectangle.

X2   Specifies the logical *x*-coordinate of the lower-right corner of the rectangle.

Y2   Specifies the logical *y*-coordinate of the lower-right corner of the rectangle.

Return Value   The return value specifies the new clipping region's complexity. It can be any one of the following values:

Value	Meaning
NULLREGION	New region is empty.
SIMPLEREGION	New region is a single rectangle.
COMPLEXREGION	New region is more than a single rectangle.
ERROR	The clip region is not modified.

Comments   The lower and right edges of the given rectangle are not excluded from the clip region.

■ ExcludeUpdateRgn

int ExcludeUpdateRgn(*hDC, hWnd***)**
HDC *hDC*;
HWND *hWnd*;

This function prevents drawing within invalid areas of a window by excluding an updated region in the window from a clipping region.

Parameters   *hDC*   Identifies the device context associated with the clipping region.

hWnd   Identifies the window being updated.

Return Value   The return value is the type of excluded region. It can be any one of the following values:

Value	Meaning
COMPLEXREGION	The region has overlapping borders.
ERROR	No region was created.
NULLREGION	The region is empty.
SIMPLEREGION	The region has no overlapping borders.

See Also   **ValidateRgn**

■ ExitProcess

VOID ExitProcess(dwExitCode**)**
DWORD dwExitCode;

The current process can exit using **ExitProcess**.

Parameters   dwExitCode   Supplies the termination status for each thread in the process.

Comments   **ExitProcess** is the prefered method of exiting an application. This API provides a clean application shutdown. This includes calling all attached DLLs at their instance termination entrypoint. If an application terminates by any other method, the DLLs that the process is attached to will not be notified of the process termination.

After notifying all DLLs of the process termination, this API terminates the current process.

ExitProcess, **ExitThread**, **CreateThread**, and a process that is starting (as the result of a **CreateProcess** call) are serialized between each other within a process. Only one of these events can happen in an address space at a time. This means that:

■ During process startup and DLL initialization routines, new threads may be created, but they will not begin execution until DLL initialization is done for the process.

■ Only one thread in a process may be in a DLL initialization or detach routine at a time.

■ **ExitProcess** will block until no threads are in their DLL initialization or detach routines.

See Also   **CreateProcess, CreateThread, ExitProcess, ExitThread, OpenProcess TerminateProcess**

■ ExitThread

VOID ExitThread(*dwExitCode***)**
DWORD *dwExitCode*;

The current thread can exit using **ExitThread**.

Parameters   *dwExitCode*   Supplies the termination status for the thread.

Comments   **ExitThread** is the preferred method of exiting a thread. When this API is called (either explicitly or by returning from a thread procedure), The current thread's stack is deallocated and the thread terminates. If the thread is the last thread in the process when this API is called, the behavior of this API does not change (except that the threads process enters the signaled state and its termination status is updated). DLLs are not notified as a result of a call to **ExitThread**.

ExitProcess, **ExitThread**, **CreateThread**, and a process that is starting (as the result of a **CreateProcess** call) are serialized between each other within a process. Only one of these events can happen in an address space at a time. This means that:

- During process startup and DLL initialization routines, new threads may be created, but they will not begin execution until DLL initialization is done for the process.

- Only one thread in a process may be in a DLL initialization or detach routine at a time.

- **ExitProcess** will block until no threads are in their DLL initialization or detach routines.

See Also   **CreateProcess, CreateThread, ExitProcess, ExitThread, TerminateThread**

■ ExitWindows

BOOL ExitWindows(*dwReserved, wReturnCode***)**
DWORD *dwReserved*;
WORD *wReturnCode*;

The **ExitWindows** function initiates the standard Windows shutdown procedure. If all applications agree to terminate, the Windows session is terminated. Under DOS, termination simply exits Windows and returns to DOS. Under NT, termination means the file system is shut down and a dialog box comes up informing the user to either reboot or turn the machine off.

Parameters   *dwReserved*   Reserved for future use. [this needs to be merged with win3.1 changes]

wReturnCode   For DOS/Win32 only, this is the return value returned from Windows to DOS when Windows exits.

Return Value   This function returns FALSE if one or more applications refuse to terminate. If all applications agree to terminate, this function never returns.

Comments   The **ExitWindows** function asks applications if they want to terminate by sending the WM_QUERYENDSESSION message. This message is sent to the main window of an application. This allows applications to query the user for typically one of three choices: save a file and exit, don't save a file and exit, or cancel exiting. One application cancelling a shutdown will cause no applications to shutdown. The applications of all desktops are enumerated. If all applications agree to shutdown, they are sent the WM_ENDSESSION message, which informs them the system is shutting down. The default handling of the WM_ENDSESSION message is to call **ExitProcess** with **dwExitCode** set to 1.

'Shutdown mode' is a system-wide mode. No new applications will be allowed to start up in this mode. The user will not be allowed to interact with applications in this mode (except for the user queries for file saving).

System shutdown should not be confused with application shutdown, where the user double clicks on the system menu or selects the 'close' menuitem from the system menu. This sends a WM_CLOSE message to the main window, which causes that window to be destroyed. This sends a WM_DESTROY message to the main window—applications process this message by calling **PostQuitMessage**, which causes a WM_QUIT to be returned from **GetMessage** inside the application's main loop, which causes the main loop to exit from main, which ends up calling **ExitProcess** with **dwExitCode** set to the return value of main. Before the WM_QUERYENDSESSION message is sent to an application, the system determines if it is in a hung state. If it is, the 'end task' dialog will appear informing the user of the situation. The user will either choose to terminate the application or try to continue.

■ ExtCreatePen

HPEN ExtCreatePen(*iPenStyle, lpStyle, nWidth, hBrush***)**
DWORD *iPenStyle*;
LPDWORD *lpStyle*;
DWORD *nWidth*;
HBRUSH *hBrush*;

The **ExtCreatePen** function creates a logical pen having the specified style, width, and brush. If the style is PS_COSMETIC USER or PS_GEOMETRIC_USER, lpStyle specifies the actual line style pattern as an array of dash lengths and space lengths. The pen can be subsequently selected as the current pen for any device context.

Parameters   *iPenStyle*   Specifies a combination of pen style, end caps, and joins. The values from each category should be OR'd together.

The pen style can be any one of the following values:

    PS_SOLID   0x00000000

PS_DASH	0x00000001
PS_DOT	0x00000002
PS_DASHDOT	0x00000003
PS_DASHDOTDOT	0x00000004
PS_NULL	0x00000005
PS_INSIDEFRAME	0x00000006
PS_COSMETIC_SOLID	0x00000007
PS_GEOMETRIC_SOLID	0x00000008
PS_COSMETIC_USER	0x00000009
PS_GEOMETRIC_USER	0x0000000A

The end cap can be any one of the following values:

PS_ENDCAP_DEFAULT	0x00000000
PS_ENDCAP_ROUND	0x00000100
PS_ENDCAP_SQUARE	0x00000200
PS_ENDCAP_FLAT	0x00000300

The line join can be any one of the following values:

PS_JOIN_DEFAULT	0x00000000
PS_JOIN_BEVEL	0x00010000
PS_JOIN_MITER	0x00020000
PS_JOIN_ROUND	0x00030000

If the width of the pen is greater than 1 and the pen style is PS_INSIDEFRAME, the line is drawn inside the frame of all primitives except polygons and polylines. The PS_INSIDEFRAME style is identical to PS_SOLID if the pen width is less than or equal to 1. The end cap and join are only used if the width is greater than 1.

lpStyle   Is option and points to an array of DWORDS, the first specifying the count of lengths, followed by a list of lengths specifying the length of the dashes followed by the length of the spaces. *lpStyle* is only used if *iPenStyle* is PS_GEOMETRIC_USER or PS_COSMETIC_USER. If *iPenStyle* specifies cosmetic lines, the lengths are in device units. Otherwise lengths are in logical units.

nWidth   Specifies the width of the pen. If *iPenStyle* specifies cosmetic lines, the width is in device units. Otherwise the width is in logical units.

hBrush   Specifies a brush for the pen. This can be any arbitrary brush.

Return Value   The return value identifies a logical pen if the function is successful. Otherwise, it is 0.

■ ExtDeviceModeEx

LONG ExtDeviceModeEx(*hWnd, lpDriverName, lpDevModeOutput, lpDeviceName, lpPort,*
  *lpDevModeInput, lpProfile, fMode***)**
HWND *hWnd;*
LPSTR *lpDriverName;*
LPDEVMODE *lpDevModeOutput;*
LPSTR *lpDeviceName;*
LPSTR *lpPort;*
LPDEVMODE *lpDevModeInput;*
LPSTR *lpProfile;*
DWORD *fMode;*

The **ExtDeviceModeEx** function retrieves or modifies device initialization
information for a given printer driver, or displays a driver-supplied dialog box for
configuring the printer driver. Printer drivers that support device initialization by
applications export this **ExtDeviceModeEx** so that applications can call it.

Parameters

hWnd   Identifies a window. If the application calls ExtDeviceModeEx to display
a dialog box, the specified window is the parent of the dialog box.

lpDriverName   Points to a null-terminated character string that specifies the
name of the device driver, for example: "Epson".

lpDevModeOutput   Points to a **DEVMODE** structure. The driver writes the
initialization information supplied in the *lpDevModeInput* parameter to this
structure.

lpDeviceName   Points to a null-terminated character string that specifies the
name of the specific device to be supported, for example: "Epson FX-80". The
device name is the same as the name passed to the **CreateDC** function.

lpPort   Points to a null-terminated character string that specifies the file or
device name for the physical output medium (file or output port). The output
name is the same as the name passed to the **CreateDC** function.

lpDevModeInput   Points to a **DEVMODE** structure that supplies initialization
information to the printer driver.

lpProfile   Points to a null-terminated string that contains the name of the
initialization file which initialization information is recorded in and read from. If
this parameter is NULL, WIN.INI is the default.

fMode   A set of bit flags which determine the types of operations the function
will perform. If *fMode* is zero, **ExtDeviceModeEx** returns the number of bytes
required by the printer device driver's **DEVMODE** structure. Otherwise, *fMode*
must have one or more of the following bits set:

Value	Meaning
DM_COPY	Writes the printer driver's current print settings to the **DEVMODE** structure identified by the *lpDevModeOutput* parameter. The calling application must allocate a buffer sufficiently large to contain the information. If this bit is clear, *lpDevModeOutput* can be NULL.

Value	Meaning
DM_MODIFY	Changes the printer driver's current print settings to match the partial initialization data in the **DEVMODE** structure identified by *lpDevModeInput* before prompting, copying, or updating.
DM_PROMPT	Presents the printer driver's Print Setup dialog box and then changes the current print settings to those the user specifies.
DM_UPDATE	Writes the printer driver's current print settings to the printer environment and the WIN.INI initialization file.

Return Value If the *fMode* parameter is zero, the return value is the size of the **DEVMODE** structure required to contain the printer driver initialization data. If the function displays the initialization dialog box, the return value is either IDOK or IDCANCEL, depending on which button the user selected. If the function does not display the dialog box and was successful, the return value is IDOK. The return value is less than zero if the function failed.

Comments An application can set the *fMode* parameter to DM_COPY to obtain a **DEVMODE** structure filled in with the printer driver's initialization data. The application can then pass this structure to the **CreateDC** function to set a private environment for the printer device context.

See Also **CreateDC**

■ ExtendedProviderFunction

BOOL ExtendedProviderFunction(*hFile, wCategory, wFunction, lpParams, lpData, dwParamLength, lpDataLength***)**
HANDLE *hFile*;
WORD *wCategory*;
WORD *wFunction*;
LPVOID *lpParams*;
LPVOID *lpData*;
DWORD *dwParamLength*;
LPDWORD *lpDataLength*;

The ExtendedProviderFunction() API is provided so that extended provider functionality may be easily and consistently accessed. For example, under certain bridging software such as LAT, a call is needed in order to enable and disable the external interface.

Parameters *hFile* Specifies the device to receive the extended function. The CreateFile() function returns this value. If this parameter is NULL, then the lpParam parameter must point to a fully-qualified path (TFQP) string which properly identifies the provider.

wCategory Specifies the function category (seebelow).

wFunction   Specifies the function to be performed within the function category. The low order bit indicates whether the data buffer is input or output. If set, the data buffer is input, otherwise it is output.

lpParam   Pointer to a list of command-specificarguments.

lpData   Pointer to a data buffer. The buffer should be large enough to accommodate any expected response data.

dwParamLength   The length of the parameter buffer inbytes.

lpDataLength   On entry, this must point to a DWORD containing the size of the data buffer pointed to by lpData. On exit (for operations which return data), this DWORD is replaced with the resulting buffer size (in bytes).

Return Value

TRUE – The operation was successful. FALSE – The operation failed. Extended error information is available using GetLastError().

Comments

The category codes for communications providers are defined as follows:

Category	Description
0000h	Base Provider Functions
0001h	Reserved (optional OS/2 serial device control compatibility)
0002h	Extended Configuration Functions
0003h	Device Driver Interface for SPI
0004h – 007Fh	Reserved for future use.
0080h – 00FFh	OEM-defined.
0100h – FFFFh	Reserved.

Function codes 0000h through 007Fh within all reserved and predefined categories are reserved for future expansion. All providers must support category 0000h. OEMs and ISVs may add new categories and function codes outside the reserved ranges. The range 0080h through 00FFh is recommended. The range 0100h through FFFFh is reserved and may not be used at all.

The data buffer may be used for either input or output operations or both or not at all. Note that the two low order bits(0 and 1) of the function code are used to denote the direction(s) of the data buffer as follows:

Bits 1 and 0	Meaning
00	NEITHER: The data buffer is not used
01	INPUT: The contents of the data buffer are passed to the provider.
10	OUTPUT: The contents of the data buffer are filled in by the provider.
11	BOTH: The buffer is used for both input and output.

This convention allows calls to be optimized in a network environment. The contents of the parameter buffer is always passed to the provider. The provider may not return anything in the parameter buffer. To summarize, the last digit of the function code indicates the direction of the data buffer as follows:

NEITHER	0	4	8	C
INPUT	1	5	9	D
OUTPUT	2	6	A	E
BOTH	3	7	B	F

OEMs and ISVs developing providers must adhere to this standard. Network software may make use of this information to minimize the amount of data transferred to and from server systems.

Category 0000h Identify 0000h

This is used to obtain a provider's identification. Returned data includes descriptive text, version information, etc.

Input Parameter Packet Format:

```
+-----------------------------------+
| DWORD    Set to zero.             |
+-----------------------------------+
```

Output Data Packet Format:

```
+-----------------------------------+
| PROVIDERID    Provider ID struct  |
+-----------------------------------+
```

Category 0002h GetSpecialChars 0041h

This function is used to obtain the list of special characters as set with the SetSpecialChars subfunction.

Input Parameter Packet Format:

```
+-----------------------------------+
| DWORD    Set to zero.             |
+-----------------------------------+
```

Output Data Packet Format:

```
+-----------------------------------+
| WORD      Count of Special        |
|           Characters              |
+-----------------------------------+
| CHAR      First Special Char      |
+-----------------------------------+
| CHAR      ...                     |
+-----------------------------------+
| CHAR      Last Special Char       |
+-----------------------------------+
```

A count of zero indicates that no special characters are set. Special character support is optional.

SetSpecialChars 0042h This function is used to set the list of special characters.

Any 7- or 8-bit ASCII character may be designated as a special character. If any of these special characters are received, the buffered data (including the special character) is returned immediately through the next Read call. There can be up to 256 special characters specified.

Input Parameter Packet Format:

```
+-----------------------------------+
| DWORD   Set to zero.              |
+-----------------------------------+
```

Input Data Packet Format:

```
+-----------------------------------+
| WORD     Count of Special         |
|          Characters               |
+-----------------------------------+
| CHAR     First Special Char       |
+-----------------------------------+
| CHAR     ...                      |
+-----------------------------------+
| CHAR     Last Special Char        |
+-----------------------------------+
```

Each call to SetSpecialChars sets a new special character list. Any previously set special character list is lost. Setting the count to zero clears any currently stored special characters. Providers may support special character mode as an option.

Get16BitMode 0045h

This function is used to determine if 16-bit mode is in effect. See Set16BitMode for more information.

Input Parameter Packet Format:

```
+-----------------------------------+
| DWORD   Set to zero.              |
+-----------------------------------+
```

Output Data Packet Format:

```
+-----------------------------------+
| DWORD   Current Enable Mask       |
+-----------------------------------+
```

The Current Enable Mask is a bit mask indicating the current 16-bit mode support as follows:

Bit	Meaning
0	If set, enable 16-bit mode on incoming data.
1	If set, enable 16-bit mode on outgoing data.

Set16BitMode 0046h

This function is used to set or clear 16-bit mode. This

special mode captures or sets the control lines for each character received or transmitted, respectively. For every character received, a 16-bit value is placed into the receiver's buffer. The low order byte is the character; the upper byte is a mask of the control lines as follows:

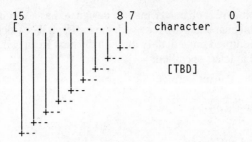

For every character transmitted, the low order byte is the character and the high order byte is the control line mask as follows:

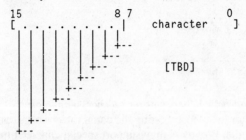

Input Parameter Packet Format:

```
+--------------------------------+
| WORD    Enable Mask            |
+--------------------------------+
```

The Enable Mask is a bit mask indicating the desired 16- bit mode support. A value of zero indicates that 16-bit mode is to be disabled.

Bit	Meaning
0	If set, enable 16-bit mode on .endmonoincoming data.
1	If set, enable 16-bit mode on outgoing data.
others	Must be zero.

Providers may support 16-bit mode as an option.

OEM-Defined Functions 0080h-00FFh

This function range is available for provider defined function calls. Applications should examine the provider identity to ensure compatibility before making any extended provider calls.

■ ExtFloodFill

BOOL ExtFloodFill(*hDC, X, Y, crColor, iFillType***)**
HDC *hDC*;
int *X*;
int *Y*;
COLORREF *crColor*,
UINT *iFillType*;

The **ExtFloodFill** function fills an area of the display surface with the current brush.

If *iFillType* is set to FLOODFILLBORDER, the area to be filled with current brush is determined as the area completely bounded by the border of the color specified by the *crColor* parameter. The **ExtFloodFill** function begins at the point specified by the *X* and *Y* parameters and fills in all directions to the boundary whose color is given by *crColor*.

If *iFillType* is set to FLOODFILLSURFACE, the **ExtFloodFill** function begins at the point specified by *X* and *Y* and continues in all directions, filling all adjacent areas containing the color specified by *crColor*.

Parameters

hDC Identifies the device context.

X Specifies the logical *x*-coordinate of the point where filling begins.

Y Specifies the logical *y*-coordinate of the point where filling begins.

crColor Specifies the color that determines the area to be filled. The interpretation of *crColor* depends on the value of the *iFillType* parameter.

iFillType Specifies the type of flood fill to be performed. It must be one of the following values:

Value	Meaning
FLOODFILLBORDER	The fill area is bounded by the the border of color specified by crColor. This style is identical to the filling performed by the FloodFill function.
FLOODFILLSURFACE	The fill area is defined by the color specified by *crColor*. Filling continues outward in all directions as long as the color is encountered. This style is useful for filling areas with multicolored boundaries.

Return Value

The return value is TRUE if the function is successful. It is FALSE if:

- The filling could not be completed.
- The given point has the boundary color specified by *crColor* (if FLOODFILLBORDER was requested).
- The given point does not have the color specified by *crColor* (if FLOODFILLSURFACE was requested).
- The point is outside the clipping region, i.e. it is not visible on the device.

Comments	Only memory device contexts and devices that support raster-display technology support the **ExtFloodFill** function. For more information, see the RC_BITBLT raster capability in the **GetDeviceCaps** function, later in this chapter.
See Also	**GetDeviceCaps**

■ ExtractIcon

HICON ExtractIcon(*hInst, lpszExeName, nIconIndex***)**
HANDLE *hInst*;
LPSTR *lpszExeName*;
WORD *nIconIndex*;

The **ExtractIcon** function retrieves the handle of an icon from a specified executable file, dynamic-link library, or icon file.

Parameters	*hInst* Identifies the instance of the application calling the function.
	lpszExeName Points to a null-terminated string specifying the name of an executable file, dynamic-link library, or icon file.
	nIconIndex Specifies the index of the icon to retrieve. If this value is zero, the function returns the handle of the first icon in the specified file. If this value is –1, the function returns the total number of icons in the specified file.
Return Value	The return value is the handle of an icon if function is successful. If the return value is 1, the file specified in the *lpszExeName* parameter was not an executable file, dynamic-link library, or icon file. If the return value is NULL, no icons were found in the file.

■ ExtTextOut

BOOL ExtTextOut(*hDC, X, Y, fOptions, lpRect, lpString, nCount, lpDx***)**
HDC *hDC*;
int *X*;
int *Y*;
UINT *fOptions*;
LPRECT *lpRect*;
LPTSTR *lpString*;
int *nCount*;
LPINT *lpDx*;

The **ExtTextOut** function writes a character string using the currently selected font. A rectangle may be provided, to be used for clipping, opaquing, or both.

The **ExtTextOut** function may be used as either a wide-character function (where text arguments must use Unicode) or an ANSI function (where text arguments must use characters from the Windows 3.x character set

Parameters

hDC   Identifies the device context.

X   Specifies the logical *x*-coordinate of the reference point.

Y   Specifies the logical *y*-coordinate of the reference point. How the text is positioned relative to this reference point depends on the mode set with SetTextAlign. The default mode places the upper left corner of the first character cell at the reference point.

fOptions   Specifies how to use the rectangle. Any combination of the following bits may be set:

Value	Meaning
ETO_CLIPPED	Specifies that the text will be clipped to the rectangle.
ETO_OPAQUE	Specifies that the current background color fills the rectangle.

lpRect   Points to a **RECT** structure. The *lpRect* parameter may be NULL.

lpString   Points to the specified character string.

nCount   Specifies the number of bytes in the string.

lpDx   Points to an array of values that indicate the distance between origins of adjacent character cells. For example, *lpDx*[*i*] logical units will separate the origins of character cell *i* and character cell *i* + 1.

Return Value

The return value is TRUE if the string is drawn. Otherwise, it is FALSE.

Comments

If *lpDx* is NULL, the function uses the default spacing between characters.

The character-cell origins and the contents of the array pointed to by the *lpDx* parameter are given in logical units. A character-cell origin is defined as the upper-left corner of the character cell.

By default, the current position is not used or updated by this function. However, an application can call the **SetTextAlign** function with the *fMode* parameter set to TA_UPDATECP to permit Windows to use and update the current position each time the application calls **ExtTextOut** for a given device context. When this flag is set, Windows ignores the *X* and *Y* parameters on subsequent **ExtTextOut** calls.

See Also

SetTextAlign

■ FatalAppExit

VOID FatalAppExit(*dwAction*, *lpMessageText*)
WORD *wAction*;
LPTSTR *lpMessageText*;

The **FatalAppExit** function displays a message containing the text specified by the *lpMessageText* parameter and terminates the application when the message box is closed. When called under the debugging version of Windows, the message box gives the user the opportunity to terminate the application or to return to the caller.

The **FatalAppExit** function may be used as either a wide-character function (where text arguments must use Unicode) or an ANSI function (where text arguments must use characters from the Windows 3.x character set installed).

Parameters

dwAction   This parameter is reserved and must be set to 0.

lpMessageText   Points to a null-terminated string that is displayed in the message box. The message is displayed on a single line. To accommodate low-resolution displays, the string should be no more than 35 characters in length.

Return Value

This function does not return a value.

Comments

An application that encounters an unexpected error should terminate by freeing all its memory and then returning from its main message loop. It should call **FatalAppExit** only when it is not capable of terminating any other way. **FatalAppExit** may not always free an application's memory or close its files, and it may cause a general failure of Windows.

See Also

FatalExit

■ FatalExit

VOID FatalExit(*dwExitCode***)**
DWORD *dwExitCode*;

The **FatalExit** function hands control over to the debugger. The behavior thereafter is specific to the debugger being used.

An application should call this function only for debugging purposes; it should not call the function in a retail version of the application. Calling this function in the retail version will terminate the application.

Parameters

Code   Specifies the error code associated with this exit.

Return Value

This function does not return a value.

Comments

The **FatalExit** function is for debugging only.

An application should call this function whenever the application detects a fatal error.

■ FileTimeToDosDateTime

BOOL APIENTRY FileTimeToDosDateTime(*lpFileTime***,** *lpFatDate***,** *lpFatTime***)**
LPFILETIME *lpFileTime*;
LPWORD *lpFatDate*;
LPWORD *lpFatTime*;

This function converts a 64-bit file time into DOS date and time value which is represented as two 16-bit unsigned integers.

Since the DOS date format can only represent dates between 1/1/80 and 12/31/2099, this conversion can fail if the input file time is outside of this range.

Parameters   *lpFileTime*   Supplies the 64-bit file time to convert to DOS date and time format.

lpFatDate   Returns the 16-bit DOS representation of date.

lpFatTime   Returns the 16-bit DOS representation of time.

Return Value   The return value is TRUE if the function is successful or FALSE if an error occurs. Extended error status is available using **GetLastError.**

See Also   **DosDateTimeToFileTime, SystemTimeToFileTime, FileTimeToSystemTime**

■ FileTimeToSystemTime

BOOL APIENTRY FileTimeToSystemTime(*lpFileTime, lpSystemTime***)**
LPFILETIME *lpFileTime;*
LPSYSTEMTIME *lpSystemTime;*

This functions converts a 64-bit file time value to a time in system time format.

Parameters   *lpFileTime*   Supplies the 64-bit file time to convert to system date and time format.

lpSystemTime   Returns the converted value of the 64-bit file time.

Return Value   The return value is TRUE if the function is successful or FALSE if an error occurs. Extended error status is available using **GetLastError.**

See Also   **SystemTimeToFileTime, FileTimeToDosDateTime, DosDateTimeToFileTime**

■ FillConsoleOutputAttribute

BOOL FillConsoleOutputAttribute(*hConsoleOutput, wAttribute, nLength, dwWriteCoord,*
        *lpNumberOfAttrsWritten***)**
HANDLE *hConsoleOutput;*
WORD *wAttribute;*
DWORD *nLength;*
COORD *dwWriteCoord;*
LPDWORD *lpNumberOfAttrsWritten;*

An attribute may be written to the screen buffer a specified number of times using **FillConsoleOutputAttribute.**

Parameters   *hConsoleOutput*   Supplies an open handle to the screen buffer (CONOUT$) that is to be written. The handle must have been created with GENERIC_WRITE access.

wAttribute   The attribute to write to the screen buffer.

nLength   Number of times to write the character to the screen..

dwWriteCoord   Screen buffer coordinates to write the attribute to.

lpNumberOfAttrsWritten   Points to a DWORD that the function will set on exit to the number of attributes written to the screen buffer.

Return Value   If the function is successful, the return value is TRUE.

If the function fails, or the end of the file is reached, the return value is FALSE. Extended error information can be obtained by calling the **GetLastError** function.

Comments   This API writes an attribute to the screen buffer a specified number of times, beginning with the position specified by dwWriteCoord. If the number of attributes to write extends beyond the end of the specified row in the screen buffer, attributes are written to the next row. If the number of attributes to write extends beyond the end of the screen buffer, the attributes up to the end of the screen buffer are written.

The character values at the positions written are left unchanged.

See Also   FillConsoleOutputCharacter

■ FillConsoleOutputCharacter

BOOL FillConsoleOutputCharacter(*hConsoleOutput, cCharacter, nLength, dwWriteCoord,*
        *lpNumberOfCharsWritten***)**
HANDLE *hConsoleOutput*;
CHAR *cCharacter*;
DWORD *nLength*;
COORD *dwWriteCoord*;
LPDWORD *lpNumberOfCharsWritten*;

A character may be written to the screen buffer a specified number of times using **FillConsoleOutputCharacter**.

The **FillConsoleOutputCharacter** function may be used as either a wide-character function (where text arguments must use Unicode) or an ANSI function (where text arguments must use characters from the Windows 3.x character set installed).

Parameters   *hConsoleOutput*   Supplies an open handle to the screen buffer (CONOUT$) that is to be written. The handle must have been created with GENERIC_WRITE access.

cCharacter   The character to write to the screen buffer.

nLength   Number of times to write the character to the screen.

dwWriteCoord   Screen buffer coordinates to write the character to.

lpNumberOfCharsWritten   Points to a DWORD that the function will set on exit to the number of elements written to the screen buffer.

Return Value   If the function is successful, the return value is TRUE.

If the function fails, or the end of the file is reached, the return value is FALSE. Extended error information can be obtained by calling the **GetLastError** function.

Comments   The **FillConsoleOutputCharacter** function writes a character to the screen buffer a specified number of times, beginning with the position specified by dwWriteCoord. If the number of characters to write extends beyond the end of the specified row in the screen buffer, characters are written to the next row. If the number of characters to write extends beyond the end of the screen buffer, the characters up to the end of the screen buffer are written.

The attribute values at the positions written are left unchanged.

See Also   **FillConsoleOutputAttribute**

■ FillPath

BOOL FillPath(*hDC***)**
HDC *hDC*;

The **FillPath** function closes any open figures in the current path and fills the result using the current brush and polygon filling mode. See **SetPolyFillMode** for a description of the filling modes.

Parameters   *hDC*   Identifies the device context.

Return Value   The return value is TRUE if the call succeeded, otherwise FALSE.

Comments   The DC must have an inactive path bracket, started by calling **BeginPath** and ended by calling **EndPath**. **FillPath** discards the path.

Errors   Use the **GetLastError** function to retrieve the error value, which may be one of the following:

ERROR_INVALID_MODE

ERROR_INVALID_PARAMETER

ERROR_NOT_ENOUGH_MEMORY

See Also   **BeginPath, StrokeAndFillPath, StrokePath, SetPolyFillMode**

■ FillRect

BOOL FillRect(*hDC, lpRect, hBrush***)**
HDC *hDC*;
LPRECT *lpRect*;
HBRUSH *hBrush*;

This function fills a given rectangle by using the specified brush. The **FillRect** function fills the complete rectangle, including the left and top borders, but does not fill the right and bottom borders.

Parameters

hDC   Identifies the device context.

lpRect   Points to a **RECT** structure that contains the logical coordinates of the rectangle to be filled.

hBrush   Identifies the brush used to fill the rectangle.

Return Value

FALSE on error, TRUE on success

Comments

The brush must have been created previously by using either the **CreateHatchBrush**, **CreatePatternBrush**, or **CreateSolidBrush** function, or retrieved using the **GetStockObject** function.

When filling the specified rectangle, the **FillRect** function does not include the rectangle's right and bottom sides. GDI fills a rectangle up to, but does not include, the right column and bottom row, regardless of the current mapping mode.

FillRect compares the values of the **top**, **bottom**, **left**, and **right** members of the specified rectangle. If **bottom** is less than or equal to **top**, or if **right** is less than or equal to **left**, the rectangle is not drawn.

See Also

CreateHatchBrush, CreatePatternBrush, CreateSolidBrush, GetStockObject

■ FillRgn

BOOL FillRgn(*hDC, hRgn, hBrush***)**
HDC *hDC*;
HRGN *hRgn*;
HBRUSH *hBrush*;

The **FillRgn** function fills the region specified by the *hRgn* parameter with the brush specified by the *hBrush* parameter.

Parameters

hDC   Identifies the device context.

hRgn   Identifies the region to be filled. The coordinates in the region are assumed to be in logical units.

hBrush   Identifies the brush to be used to fill the region.

Return Value

The return value is TRUE if the function is successful or FALSE if an error occurs.

■ FindAtom

ATOM FindAtom(*lpString***)**
LPTSTR *lpString*;

The **FindAtom** function searches the atom table for the character string pointed to by the *lpString* parameter and retrieves the atom associated with that string.

The **FindAtom** function may be used as either a wide-character function (where text arguments must use Unicode) or an ANSI function (where text arguments must use characters from the Windows 3.x character set installed).

Parameters
lpString Points to the character string to be searched for. The string must be null-terminated.

Return Value
The return value identifies the atom associated with the given string. It is NULL if the string is not in the table.

See Also
AddAtom, DeleteAtom, GetAtomName, GlobalAddAtom, GlobalDeleteAtom, GlobalFindAtom, GlobalGetAtomName, InitAtomTable

■ FindClose

BOOL FindClose(hFindFile**)**
HANDLE hFindFile;

A find file context created by **FindFirstFile** can be closed using **FindClose**.

Parameters
hFindFile Supplies a find file handle returned in a previous call to **FindFirstFile** that is no longer needed.

Return Value
The return value is TRUE if the function is successful. Otherwise, it is FALSE in which case extended error information is available from the **GetLastError** function.

This API is used to inform the system that a find file handle created by **FindFirstFile** is no longer needed. On systems that maintain internal state for each find file context, this API informs the system that this state no longer needs to be maintained.

Once this call has been made, the *hFindFile* may not be used in a subsequent call to either **FindNextFile** or **FindClose**.

This API has no DOS counterpart, but is similar to OS/2's **DosFindClose**.

See Also
FindFirstFile

■ FindExecutable

HANDLE FindExecutable(lpszFile, lpszDir, lpszResult**)**
LPSTR lpszFile;   /* pointer to string for filename   */
LPSTR lpszDir;   /* pointer to string for default directory   */
LPSTR lpszResult;   /* pointer to string for executable file on return */

The **FindExecutable** function retrieves the name and handle of the executable file that is associated with a specified filename.

Parameters	*lpszFile* Points to a null-terminated string specifying a filename. This can be a document or executable file.
	lpszDir Points to a null-terminated string specifying the default directory.
	lpszResult Points to a buffer that receives a filename when the function returns. This filename is a null-terminated string specifying the executable file that is started when an "open" association is run on the file specified in the *lpszFile* parameter.
Return Value	The return value is the instance handle of the executable file that is associated with the specified filename if function is successful. (This handle could also be the handle of a DDE server application.) If the return value is less than or equal to 32, it specifies an error code. The possible error values are listed in the following "Comments" section.
Comments	When **FindExecutable** returns, the *lpszResult* parameter may contain the path to the DDE server that is started if no server responds to a request to initiate a DDE conversation.
See Also	**ShellExecute**

■ FindFirstFile

HANDLE FindFirstFile(*lpFileName*, *lpFindFileData***)**
LPTSTR *lpFileName*;
LPWIN32_FIND_DATA *lpFindFileData*;

A directory can be searched for the first entry whose name and attributes match the specified name using **FindFirstFile**.

The **FindFirstFile** function may be used as either a wide-character function (where text arguments must use Unicode) or an ANSI function (where text arguments must use characters from the Windows 3.x character set installed).

Parameters   *lpFileName*   Supplies the file name of the file to find. The file name may contain the DOS wild card characters '*' and '?'.

lpFindFileData   On a successful find, this parameter returns information about the located file:

WIN32_FIND_DATA Structure:

Member	Description
DWORD *dwFileAttributes*	Returns the file attributes of the found file.
FILETIME *ftCreationTime*	Returns the time that the file was created. A value of 0,0 specifies that the file system containing the file does not support this time field.

Member	Description
FILETIME *ftLastAccessTime*	Returns the time that the file was last accessed. A value of 0,0 specifies that the file system containing the file does not support this time field.
FILETIME *ftLastWriteTime*	Returns the time that the file was last written. All file systems support this time field.
DWORD *nFileSizeHigh*	Returns the high order 32 bits of the file's size.
DWORD *nFileSizeLow*	Returns the low order 32-bits of the file's size in bytes.
UCHAR *cFileName*[MAX_PATH]	Returns the null terminated name of the file.

Return Value

The return value, if the function is successful, is a find first handle that can be used in a subsequent call to **FindNextFile** or **FindClose**. Otherwise it is −1 (0xFFFFFFFF) in which case extended error information is available from the **GetLastError** function.

Comments

This API is provided to open a find file handle and return information about the first file whose name match the specified pattern. Once established, the find file handle can be used to search for other files that match the same pattern. When the find file handle is no longer needed, it should be closed.

Note that while this interface only returns information for a single file, an implementation is free to buffer several matching files that can be used to satisfy subsequent calls to **FindNextFile**. Also note that matches are done by name only. This API does not do attribute based matching.

This API is similar to DOS (int 21h, function 4Eh), and OS/2's **DosFindFirst**. For portability reasons, its data structures and parameter passing is somewhat different.

The constant FILE_ATRRIBUTE_NORMAL is returned in the *dwFileAttributes* field of the structure pointed to by *lpFindFileData* when a file has no attribute bits set. By returning this constant, the same data structure can then be used to set normal file attributes for a file.

See Also

FindNextFile, GetFileAttributes, SetFileAttributes

■ FindNextFile

```
BOOL FindNextFile(hFindFile, lpFindFileData)
HANDLE hFindFile;
LPWIN32_FIND_DATA lpFindFileData;
```

Once a successful call has been made to **FindFirstFile**, subsequent matching files can be located using **FindNextFile**.

The **FindNextFile** function may be used as either a wide-character function (where text arguments must use Unicode) or an ANSI function (where text arguments must use characters from the Windows 3.x character set installed).

Parameters

hFindFile   Supplies a find file handle returned in a previous call to **FindFirstFile**.

lpFindFileData   On a successful find, this parameter returns information about the located file:

WIN32_FIND_DATA Structure:

Member	Description
DWORD *dwFileAttributes*	Returns the file attributes of the found file.
FILETIME *ftCreationTime*	Returns the time that the file was created. A value of 0,0 specifies that the file system containing the file does not support this time field.
FILETIME *ftLastAccessTime*	Returns the time that the file was last accessed. A value of 0,0 specifies that the file system containing the file does not support this time field.
FILETIME *ftLastWriteTime*	Returns the time that the file was last written. All file systems support this time field.
DWORD *nFileSizeHigh*	Returns the high order 32 bits of the file's size.
DWORD *nFileSizeLow*	Returns the low order 32-bits of the file's size in bytes.
UCHAR *cFileName*[MAX_PATH]	Returns the null terminated name of the file.

Return Value

The return value is TRUE if the function is successful. Otherwise, it is FALSE in which case extended error information is available from the **GetLastError** function.

Comments

This API is used to continue a file search from a previous call to **FindFirstFile**. This API returns successfully with the next file that matches the search pattern established in the original **FindFirstFile** call. If no file match can be found NO_MORE_FILES is returned.

Note that while this interface only returns information for a single file, an implementation is free to buffer several matching files that can be used to satisfy subsequent calls to **FindNextFile**. Also not that matches are done by name only. This API does not do attribute based matching.

This API is similar to DOS (int 21h, function 4Fh), and OS/2's **DosFindNext**. For portability reasons, its data structures and parameter passing is somewhat different.

The constant FILE_ATRRIBUTE_NORMAL is returned in the *dwFileAttributes* field of the structure pointed to by *lpFindFileData* when a file has no attribute bits set. By returning this constant, the same data structure can then be used to set normal file attributes for a file.

See Also   **FindFirstFile, GetFileAttributes, SetFileAttributes**

■ FindResource

HANDLE FindResource(hModule, lpName, lpType**)**
HANDLE hModule;
LPTSTR lpName;
LPTSTR lpType;

The **FindResource** function determines the location of a resource in the specified resource file. The *lpName* and *lpType* parameters define the resource name and type, respectively.

The **FindResource** function may be used as either a wide-character function (where text arguments must use Unicode) or an ANSI function (where text arguments must use characters from the Windows 3.x character set installed).

Parameters   *hModule*   Identifies the module whose executable file contains the resource.

lpName   Points to a null-terminated string that represents the name of the resource.

lpType   Points to a null-terminated string that represents the type name of the resource. For predefined resource types, the *lpType* parameter should be one of the following values:

Value	Meaning
RT_ACCELERATOR	Accelerator table
RT_BITMAP	Bitmap resource
RT_DIALOG	Dialog box
RT_FONT	Font resource
RT_FONTDIR	Font directory resource
RT_MENU	Menu resource
RT_RCDATA	User-defined resource (raw data)

Return Value   The return value identifies the named resource. It is NULL if the requested resource cannot be found. On NT/Windows the return value will be the offset of the resource data entry within the resource section object of the image file identified by *hModule*.

Comments	An application must not call **FindResource** and the **LoadResource** function to load cursor, icon, and string resources. Instead, it must load these resources by calling the following functions:

- **LoadCursor**
- **LoadIcon**
- **LoadString**

An application can call **FindResource** and **LoadResource** to load other predefined resource types. However, it is recommended that the application load the corresponding resources by calling the following functions:

- **LoadAccelerators**
- **LoadBitmap**
- **LoadMenu**

If the high-order word of the *lpName* or *lpType* parameter is zero, the low-order word specifies the integer ID of the name or type of the given resource. Otherwise, the parameters are long pointers to null-terminated strings. If the first character of the string is a pound sign (#), the remaining characters represent a decimal number that specifies the integer ID of the resource's name or type. For example, the string #258 represents the integer ID 258.

To reduce the amount of memory required for the resources used by an application, the application should refer to the resources by integer ID instead of by name.

See Also **LoadAccelerators, LoadBitmap, LoadCursor, LoadIcon, LoadMenu, LoadResource, LoadString, FreeResource, LockResource, SizeofResource, UnlockResource**

■ FindText

HWND FindText(*lpfr***)**
LPFINDREPLACE *lpfr*; /* pointer to structure with initialization data */

The **FindText** function creates a system-defined modeless dialog box that allows the user to find text within a document. The application must perform the actual search operation.

Parameters *lpfr* Points to a **FINDREPLACE** structure that contains information used to initialize the dialog box. When the user makes a selection in the dialog box, the system fills this structure with information about the user's selection, then sends a message to the application. This message contains a pointer to the **FINDREPLACE** data structure.

The **FINDREPLACE** structure has the following form:

```
typedef struct {      /* fr */
    DWORD   lStructSize;
    HWND    hwndOwner;
```

```
        HANDLE  hInstance;
        DWORD   Flags;
        LPSTR   lpstrFindWhat;
        LPSTR   lpstrReplaceWith;
        WORD    wFindWhatLen;
        WORD    wReplaceWithLen;
        DWORD   lCustData;
        WORD (FAR PASCAL *lpfnHook)(HWND, unsigned, WORD, LONG);
        LPSTR   lpTemplateName;
} FINDREPLACE;
```

For a full description, see TBD.

Return Value

The return value is the window handle of the dialog box, or NULL if an error occurs. An application can use this handle to communicate with, or terminate, the dialog box.

Comments

The dialog procedure for the **FindText** function passes user requests to the application through special messages. The *lParam* parameter of these messages contains a pointer to a **FINDREPLACE** structure. The procedure sends the messages to the window identified by the *hwndOwner* member of the **FINDREPLACE** data structure. An application can register the identifier for these messages by specifying the "commdlg_FindReplace" string in a call to the **RegisterWindowMessage** function.

Errors

Use the **CommDlgExtendedError** function to retrieve the error value, which may be one of the following:

> CDERR_FINDRESFAILURE
> CDERR_INITIALIZATION
> CDERR_LOCKRESFAILURE
> CDERR_LOADRESFAILURE
> CDERR_LOADSTRFAILURE
> CDERR_MEMALLOCFAILURE
> CDERR_MEMLOCKFAILURE
> CDERR_NOHINSTANCE
> CDERR_NOHOOK
> CDERR_NOTEMPLATE
> CDERR_STRUCTSIZE

Example

The following code fragment initializes a **FINDREPLACE** structure and calls the **FindText** function to display the common dialog:

```
case IDM_FINDTXT:

    fr.lStructSize = sizeof(FINDREPLACE);
    fr.hwndOwner = hwnd;
    fr.hInstance = NULL;
    fr.Flags = 0L;
    fr.lpstrFindWhat = szFindWhat;
    fr.lpstrReplaceWith = (LPSTR)NULL;
    fr.wFindWhatLen = sizeof(szFindWhat);
    fr.wReplaceWithLen = 0;
    fr.lCustData = 0L;
    fr.lpfnHook = (FARPROC)NULL;
    fr.lpTemplateName = (LPSTR)NULL;
```

```
     hDlg = FindText(&fr);

     break;
```

In addition to initializing the fields in the **FINDREPLACE** data structure and calling the **FindText** function, an application must register the special **FINDMSGSTRING** message and process messages from the dialog window.

The following code shows how an application registered the message with the **RegisterWindowMesage** function:

```
/* Register the FindReplace message */

FindReplaceMsg = RegisterWindowMessage((LPSTR) FINDMSGSTRING);
```

Once the application registers the message it can process messages using the **RegisterWindowMessage** return value. The following sample code shows how an application processed messages for the find dialog window and then called its own **SearchFile** function to locate the string of text:

```
long FAR PASCAL _loadds MainWndProc(hwnd, msg, wParam, lParam)
HWND hwnd;
WORD msg;                  /* type of message        */
WORD wParam;               /* additional information */
LONG lParam;               /* additional information */
{

  switch (msg) {
    case WM_COMMAND: /* message: command from application menu */
        switch (wParam) {


          .
          . /* Process messages */
          .
          }

default:
    /*
     * Handle the special findreplace message (FindReplaceMsg) which
     * was registered at initialization time.
     */

    if (msg == FindReplaceMsg){
        lpFR = (LPFINDREPLACE) lParam;
        fReverse = (lpFR->Flags & FR_DOWN ? FALSE : TRUE);
        fCase = (lpFR->Flags & FR_MATCHCASE ? TRUE : FALSE);
        SearchFile(fReverse, fCase);
        return (NULL);
    }
    return (DefWindowProc(hwnd, msg, wParam, lParam));

}
```

See Also   **ReplaceText**

■ FindWindow

HWND FindWindow(*lpClassName***, ***lpWindowName***)**
LPTSTR *lpClassName*;
LPTSTR *lpWindowName*;

> This function returns the handle of the window whose class is given by the *lpClassName* parameter and whose window name, or caption, is given by the *lpWindowName* parameter. This function does not search child windows.
>
> The **FindWindow** function may be used as either a wide-character function (where text arguments must use Unicode) or an ANSI function (where text arguments must use characters from the Windows 3.x character set installed).

Parameters
> *lpClassName*　Points to a null-terminated character string that specifies the window's class name. If lpClassName is NULL, all class names match.
>
> *lpWindowName*　Points to a null-terminated character string that specifies the window name (the window's text caption). If *lpWindowName* is NULL, all window names match.

Return Value
> The return value identifies the window that has the specified class name and window name. It is NULL if no such window is found.

See Also
> **EnumWindows, GetClassName**

■ FlashWindow

BOOL FlashWindow(*hWnd***, ***bInvert***)**
HWND *hWnd*;
BOOL *bInvert*;

> This function flashes the given window once. Flashing a window means changing the appearance of its caption bar as if the window were changing from inactive to active status, or vice versa. (An inactive caption bar changes to an active caption bar; an active caption bar changes to an inactive caption bar.)
>
> Typically, a window is flashed to inform the user that the window requires attention, but that it does not currently have the input focus.

Parameters
> *hWnd*　Identifies the window to be flashed. The window can be either open or iconic.
>
> *bInvert*　Specifies whether the window is to be flashed or returned to its original state. The window is flashed from one state to the other if the *bInvert* parameter is nonzero. If the *bInvert* parameter is zero, the window is returned to its original state (either active or inactive).

Return Value
> The return value specifies the window's state before call to the **FlashWindow** function. It is nonzero if the window was active before the call. Otherwise, it is zero.

Comments   The **FlashWindow** function flashes the window only once; for successive flashing, the application should create a system timer.

The *bInvert* parameter should be zero only when the window is getting the input focus and will no longer be flashing; it should be nonzero on successive calls while waiting to get the input focus.

This function always returns a nonzero value for iconic windows. If the window is iconic, **FlashWindow** will simply flash the icon; *bInvert* is ignored for iconic windows.

■ FlattenPath

BOOL FlattenPath(*hDC***)**
HDC *hDC*;

The **FlattenPath** function transforms the specified path, turning all portions of the path which consist of curves into sequences of lines.

Parameters   *hDC*   Identifies the device context of the path.

Return Value   The return value is TRUE if the call succeeded, otherwise FALSE.

Errors   Use the **GetLastError** function to retrieve the error value, which may be one of the following:

Comments   The DC must have an inactive path bracket, started by calling **BeginPath** and ended by calling **EndPath**.

ERROR_INVALID_MODE

ERROR_INVALID_PARAMETER

ERROR_NOT_ENOUGH_MEMORY

See Also   **SetFlatness**

■ FloodFill

BOOL FloodFill(*hDC, X, Y, crColor***)**
HDC *hDC*;
int *X*;
int *Y*;
COLORREF *crColor*;

The **FloodFill** function fills an area of the display surface with the current brush. The area is assumed to be bounded as specified by the crColor parameter. The **FloodFill** function begins at the point specified by the *X* and *Y* paramteres and continues in all directions to the color boundry.

This call is included only for compatiblity purposes. Applications are discouraged from using this call. An application should use **ExtFloodFill** with **FLOODFILLBORDER** specified.

See Also   **ExtFloodFill**

FlushConsoleInputBuffer

BOOL FlushConsoleInputBuffer(*hConsoleInput***)**
HANDLE *hConsoleInput*;

This API may be used to flush the input buffer.

Parameters   *hConsoleInput*   Supplies an open handle to console input.

Return Value   The return value is TRUE if the function was successful, otherwise it is FALSE in which case extended error information can be retrieved by calling the **GetLastError** function.

FlushFileBuffers

BOOL FlushFileBuffers(*hFile***)**
HANDLE *hFile*;

Buffered data may be flushed out to the file using the **FlushFileBuffers** service:

Parameters   *hFile*   Supplies an open handle to a file whose buffers are to be flushed. The file handle must have been created with GENERIC_WRITE access to the file.

Return Value   The return value is TRUE if the function is successful. Otherwise, it is FALSE in which case extended error information is available from the **GetLastError** function.

The **FlushFileBuffers** service causes all buffered data to be written to the specified file.

Note that for comm devices only the transmit buffer is flushed when this API is used.

FlushViewOfFile

BOOL FlushViewOfFile(*lpBaseAddress, dwNumberOfBytesToFlush***)**
LPVOID *lpBaseAddress*;
DWORD *dwNumberOfBytesToFlush*;

A byte range within a mapped view of a file can be flushed to disk using FlushViewOfFile.

Parameters   *lpBaseAddress*   Supplies the base address of a set of bytes that are to be flushed to the on disk representation of the mapped file.

dwNumberOfBytesToFlush   Supplies the number of bytes to flush.

Return Value   The return value is TRUE if the function is successful or FALSE if an error occurs. All dirty pages within the specified range are stored in the on-disk representation of the mapped file.

Comments   Flushing a range of a mapped view causes any dirty pages within that range to be written to disk. This operation automatically happens whenever a view is unmapped (either explicitly or as a result of process termination).

See Also   **MapViewOfFile, UnmapViewOfFile**

■ FlushWindowbuffer

BOOL FlushWindowBuffer(*hWnd***)**
HWND *hWnd*;

This functions draws any changed bits from the bitmap buffer to the screen. If no drawing has occured since the last flush, this call is very fast.

Parameters   *hWnd*   Specifies the window that is bitmap-buffered.

Return Value   TRUE is returned for success, FALSE for failure.

See Also   **SetWindowBufferAttributes GetWindowBufferAttributes**

■ FrameRect

BOOL FrameRect(*hDC, lpRect, hBrush***)**
HDC *hDC*;
LPRECT *lpRect*;
HBRUSH *hBrush*;

This function draws a border around the rectangle specified by the *lpRect* parameter. The **FrameRect** function uses the given brush to draw the border. The width and height of the border is always one logical unit.

Parameters   *hDC*   Identifies the device context of the window.

lpRect   Points to a **RECT** structure that contains the logical coordinates of the upper-left and lower-right corners of the rectangle.

hBrush   Identifies the brush to be used for framing the rectangle.

Return Value   FALSE on error, TRUE on success

Comments   The brush identified by the *hBrush* parameter must have been created previously by using the **CreateHatchBrush**, **CreatePatternBrush**, or **CreateSolidBrush** function.

If the **bottom** member is less than or equal to the **top** member, or if the **right** member is less than or equal to the **left** member, the rectangle is not drawn.

See Also   **CreateHatchBrush, CreatePatternBrush, CreateSolidBrush**

■ FrameRgn

BOOL FrameRgn(hDC, hRgn, hBrush, nWidth, nHeight**)**
HDC hDC;
HRGN hRgn;
HBRUSH hBrush;
int nWidth;
int nHeight;

The **FrameRgn** function draws a border around the region specified by the hRgn parameter, using the brush specified by the hBrush parameter. The nWidth parameter specifies the width of the border in vertical brush strokes; the nHeight parameter specifies the height in horizontal brush strokes.

Parameters   hDC   Identifies the device context.

hRgn   Identifies the region to be enclosed in a border. The coordinates in the region are assumed to be in logical units.

hBrush   Identifies the brush to be used to draw the border.

nWidth   Specifies the width in vertical brush strokes in logical units.

nHeight   Specifies the height in horizontal brush strokes in logical units.

Return Value   The return value is TRUE if the function is successful. Otherwise, it is FALSE.

■ FreeConsole

BOOL FreeConsole(VOID)

A console may be freed using **FreeConsole**.

This function has no parameters.

Return Value   The return value is TRUE if the function was successful, otherwise it is FALSE in which case extended error information can be retrieved by calling the **GetLastError** function.

That API frees the current process's console. If other processes share the console, the console is not destroyed but the current process may not reference it.

See Also   **AllocConsole**

■ FreeDDElParam

BOOL FreeDDElParam(msg, lParam**)**
UINT msg;
LONG lParam;

The **FreeDDElParam** function is used by an application receiving a posted DDE message to properly dispose of the **lParam** value . The receiving application should call **FreeDDElParam** after it has unpacked the **lParam** value.

This function only needs to be called for **posted** DDE messages.

This function does NOT free the contents of the **lParam**. It does free the memory the data was stored in.

Parameters *msg* The posted DDE message.

lParam The **lParam** the function will dispose of.

Return Value If the function is successful, the return value is TRUE.

If the function fails, the return value is FALSE.

See Also **PackDDElParam, UnpackDDElParam**

■ FreeLibrary

```
BOOL FreeLibrary(hLibModule)
HANDLE hLibModule;
```

The **FreeLibrary** function decreases the reference count of the loaded library module by one. When the reference count reaches zero, the memory occupied by the module is freed.

Parameters *hLibModule* Identifies the loaded library module.

Return Value The return value is TRUE if the function is successful; otherwise it is FALSE in which case extended error status is available by calling the **GetLastError** function.

Comments When the reference count for the specified library module is decremented to zero, the library module's DLL Instance Termination entry point is called. This will allow a library module a chance to cleanup resources that we allocated on behalf of the current process. Finally, after the termination entry point returns, the library module is removed from the address space of the current process.

If more than one process has loaded a library module, then the library module will remain in use until all process's that loaded the module have called **FreeLibrary** to unload the library.

■ FreeModule

The **FreeModule** function is implemented by a macro that calls **FreeLibrary**. This works because **FreeModule** is defined to only work with library modules.

■ FreeProcInstance

The **FreeProcInstance** function is implemented by a macro that does nothing. Its parameter is ignored.

FreeResource

BOOL FreeResource(*hResData***)**
HANDLE *hResData*;

The **FreeResource** function removes a loaded resource from memory by freeing the allocated memory occupied by that resource.

The **FreeResource** function does not actually free the resource until the reference count is zero (that is, the number of calls to the function equals the number of times the application called the **LoadResource** function for this resource). This ensures that the data remains available while an application is actually using it.

Parameters   *hResData*   Identifies the data associated with the resource. The handle is assumed to have been created by using the **LoadResource** function.

Return Value   The return value specifies the outcome of the function. The return value is TRUE if the function has failed and the resource has not been freed. The return value is FALSE if the function is successful.

Comments   On NT/Windows this function will be a macro that always returns TRUE.

See Also   **LoadResource, LockResource**

FreeSelector

The **FreeSelector** function is deleted as it is x86 specific and has no corresponding semantics in the portable Win32 API.

GetAce

BOOL GetAce(*Acl, AceIndex, Ace***)**
PACL *Acl*;
ULONG *AceIndex*;
PVOID *Ace*;

The **GetAce** function obtains a pointer to an **ACE** stored in an **ACL**. An **ACE** is an access control entry. An **ACL** is an access control list.

The caller specifies the **ACL** and an index value that indicates the desired **ACE**.

Parameters   *Acl*   Pointer to an existing **ACL** data structure that contains the **ACE** of interest.

The **ACL** data structure has the following form:

```
typedef struct tagACL {
    UCHAR   AclRevision;
    UCHAR   Sbz1;
    USHORT  AclSize;
```

```
        USHORT  AceCount;
        USHORT  Sbz2;
        /* ordered list of ACEs */
} ACL;
```

AceIndex An zero-based index that specifies the **ACE** of interest. An **ACL** maintains a list of **ACE**s. A value of 0 corresponds to the **ACL**'s first **ACE**, 1 to its second **ACE**, and so on.

Ace Pointer to a variable that the function will set to the address of the **ACE**.

Return Value If the function is successful, the return value is TRUE.

If the function fails, the return value is FALSE. Call **GetLastError** for more detailed error information.

See Also **AddAccessAllowedAce, AddAce, DeleteAce, GetAclInformation, InitializeAcl, IsValidAcl, SetAclInformation**

■ GetAclInformation

BOOL GetAclInformation(*Acl, AclInformation, AclInformationLength, AclInformationClass***)**
PACL *Acl*;
PVOID *AclInformation*;
ULONG *AclInformationLength*;
ACL_INFORMATION_CLASS *AclInformationClass*;

The **GetAclInformation** function retrieves information about an **ACL**. An **ACL** is a security access control list.

Parameters *Acl* Pointer to an existing **ACL** data structure. The function will retrieve information about this **ACL**.

The **ACL** data structure has the following form:

```
typedef struct tagACL {
    UCHAR   AclRevision;
    UCHAR   Sbz1;
    USHORT  AclSize;
    USHORT  AceCount;
    USHORT  Sbz2;
    /* ordered list of ACEs */
} ACL;
```

AclInformation Pointer to a buffer that the function will fill with the information requested by the caller. The buffer must be aligned on at least a longword boundary. The actual structures put into the buffer depend on the information class requested. See the discussion of the *AclInformationClass* parameter below.

AclInformationLength Specifies the size, in bytes, of the buffer pointed to by *AclInformation*.

AclInformationClass Specifies the class of information requested. The following values have meaning:

Value	Meaning
AclRevisionInformation	The function will fill the buffer pointed to by *AclInformation* with an **ACL_REVISION_INFORMATION** data structure.
	The **ACL_REVISION_INFORMATION** data structure has the following form:

```
typedef struct tagACL_REVISION_INFORMATION {
    ULONG   AclRevision;
} ACL_REVISION_INFORMATION ;
```

AclSizeInformation	The function will fill the buffer pointed to by *AclInformation* with an **ACL_SIZE_INFORMATION** data structure.
	The **ACL_SIZE_INFORMATION** data structure has the following form:

```
typedef struct tagACL_SIZE_INFORMATION {
    ULONG   AceCount;
    ULONG   AclBytesInUse;
    ULONG   AclBytesFree;
} ACL_SIZE_INFORMATION ;
```

Return Value If the function is successful, the return value is TRUE.

If the function fails, the return value is FALSE. Call **GetLastError** for more detailed error information.

See Also **AddAccessAllowedAce, AddAce, DeleteAce, GetAce, InitializeAcl, IsValidAcl, SetAclInformation**

■ GetActiveWindow

HWND GetActiveWindow(void)

This function retrieves the window handle of the active window associated with the calling thread.

Return Value The return value is the window handle of the active window associated with the calling thread. The function returns NULL if the calling thread does not have an active window.

Comments Normally, Windows takes care of window activation. A window may be explicitly activated using the **SetActiveWindow** API function.

See Also **SetActiveWindow**

■ GetAspectRatioFilterEx

BOOL GetAspectRatioFilterEx(*hDC, lpAspectRatio***)**
HDC *hDC;*
LPSIZE *lpAspectRatio;*

This function retrieves the setting for the current aspect-ratio filter. The aspect ratio is the ratio formed by a device's pixel width and height. Information about a device's aspect ratio is used in the creation, selection, and displaying of fonts. Windows provides a special filter, the aspect-ratio filter, to select fonts designed for a particular aspect ratio from all of the available fonts. The filter uses the aspect ratio specified by the **SetMapperFlags** function.

Parameters   *hDC*   Identifies the device context that contains the specfied aspect ratio.

lpAspectRatio   Pointer to a *SIZE* structure where the current aspect ratio filter will be returned.

Return Value   Returns TRUE if successful, FALSE otherwise.

See Also   **SetMapperFlags**

■ GetAsyncKeyState

SHORT GetAsyncKeyState(*vKey***)**
int *vKey;*

This function determines whether a key is up or down at the time the function is called, and whether the key was pressed after a previous call to the **GetAsyncKeyState** function. If the most significant bit of the return value is set, the key is currently down; if the least significant bit is set, the key was pressed after a previous call to the function.

GetAsyncKeyState will only work for a particular thread while input is directed to that thread. If another thread or process is currently has the input focus, calls to **GetAsyncKeyState** will return 0.

Parameters   *vKey*   Specifies one of 256 possible virtual-key code values.

Return Value   The return value specifies whether the key was pressed since the last call to **GetAsyncKeyState** and whether the key is currently up or down. If the most significant bit is set, the key is down, and if the least significant bit is set, the key was pressed after a preceding **GetAsyncKeyState** call.

Comments   See Appendix A for a list of virtual key code constants.

An application can use the virtual key code constants VK_SHIFT, VK_CONTROL and VK_MENU as values for the *vKey* parameter. This gives the state of the Shift, Control, or Alt keys without distinguishing between left and right. An application can also use the following virtual key code constants as values for *vKey* in order to distinguish between the left and right instances of those keys:

VK_LSHIFT	VK_RSHIFT
VK_LCONTROL	VK_RCONTROL
VK_LMENU	VK_RMENU

These left- and right-distinguishing constants are only exposed and available to an application when using the **GetKeyboardState, SetKeyboardState, GetAsyncKeyState, GetKeyState,** and **MapVirtualKey** functions.

See Also   **GetKeyState, GetKeyboardState, SetKeyboardState, MapVirtualKey**

■ GetAtomHandle

The **GetAtomHandle** function is not supported for 32-bit applications.

■ GetAtomName

DWORD GetAtomName(*nAtom, lpBuffer, dwSize***)**
ATOM *nAtom*;
LPTSTR *lpBuffer*,
DWORD *dwSize*;

The **GetAtomName** function retrieves a copy of the character string associated with the *nAtom* parameter and places it in the buffer pointed to by the *lpBuffer* parameter. The *dwSize* parameter specifies the maximum size of the buffer.

The **GetAtomName** function may be used as either a wide-character function (where text arguments must use Unicode) or an ANSI function (where text arguments must use characters from the Windows 3.x character set installed).

Parameters   *nAtom*   Identifies the character string to be retrieved.

lpBuffer   Points to the buffer that is to receive the character string.

dwSize   Specifies the maximum size (in bytes) of the buffer.

Return Value   The return value specifies the actual number of bytes copied to the buffer. It is zero if the specified atom is not valid.

■ GetBitmapBehind

HBITMAP GetBitmapBehind(*hWnd***)**
HWND *hWnd*;

If this window was created with the CS_SAVEBITS class style, then this window may or may not be managing the bits of the windows behind it. If conditions are right and this window is managing the bits of the windows behind it, this function will return a copy of the bitmap that holds these bits. These bits are not necessarily a completely accurate picture of what the windows beneath *hWnd* look like.

Parameters *hWnd* Specifies the window for which to return the bitmap of the windows behind.

Return Value Returns NULL if there are no bits or on error. Otherwise returns a real bitmap handle of the bits behind *hWnd*. The application is responsible for ultimately destroying this bitmap.

■ GetBitmapBits

DWORD GetBitmapBits(*hBitmap*, *dwCount*, *lpBits***)**
HBITMAP *hBitmap*;
DWORD *dwCount*;
LPBYTE *lpBits*;

The **GetBitmapBits** function copies the bits of the specified bitmap into the buffer that is pointed to by the *lpBits* parameter. The *dwCount* parameter specifies the number of bytes to be copied to the buffer. Call **GetBitmapBits** with *lpBits* equal to NULL to determine the correct *dwCount* value for the given bitmap.

Parameters *hBitmap* Identifies the bitmap.

dwCount Specifies the number of bytes to be copied.

lpBits Points to the buffer that is to receive the bitmap. The bitmap is an array of bytes.

Return Value The return value specifies the actual number of bytes in the bitmap. It is zero if there is an error.

Comment This call is included only for compatiblity purposes. Applications are discouraged from using this call. An application should use **GetDIBits**.

seealso

See Also **GetObject SetBitmapBits**

■ GetBitmapDimensionEx

BOOL GetBitmapDimensionEx(*hBitmap*, *lpDimension***)**
HBITMAP *hBitmap*;
LPSIZE *lpDimension*;

The **GetBitmapDimensionEx** function returns the dimensions of the bitmap previously set by the **SetBitmapDimensionEx** function. If no dimensions have been set, a default of 0,0 will be returned.

Parameters *hBitmap* Identifies the bitmap.

lpDimension Points to a **SIZE** structure. The dimensions are returned here.

Return Value   The return value is TRUE if the function was successful. Otherwise it is FALSE.

See Also   **SetBitmapDimensionEx**

■ GetBkColor

COLORREF GetBkColor(*hDC***)**
HDC *hDC*;

The **GetBkColor** function returns the current background color of the specified device.

Parameters   *hDC*   Identifies the device context.

Return Value   The return value specifies a COLORREF value for the current background color. It is CLR_INVALID if an error occured.

See Also   **SetBkColor**

■ GetBkMode

int GetBkMode(*hDC***)**
HDC *hDC*;

The **GetBkMode** function returns the background mix mode of the specified device context. The background mix mode is used with text, hatched brushes, and pen styles that are not solid lines.

Parameters   *hDC*   Identifies the device context.

Return Value   The return value specifies the current background mix mode. It is 0 if an error occured.

See Also   **SetBkMode**

■ GetBoundsRect

UINT GetBoundsRect(*hdc, lprcBounds, flags***)**
HDC *hdc*;   /* DC to return bounds rectangle for   */
RECT FAR* *lprcBounds*;   /* points to buffer for bounds rectangle */
UINT *flags*;   /* specifies information to return   */

The **GetBoundsRect** function returns the current accumulated bounding rectangle for the specified device context.

Windows maintains two accumulated bounding rectangles — one for the application and one reserved for use by Windows. An application can query and set its own rectangle, but can only query the Windows rectangle.

Parameters   *hDC*   Identifies the device context to retrun the bounding rectangle for.

lprcBounds   Points to a buffer that will receive the current bounding rectangle. The application's rectangle is returned in logical coordinates and the Windows rectangle is returned in screen coordinates.

flags   Specifies the type of information to return. This parameter may be some combination of the following values:

Value	Meaning
DCB_RESET	Force the bounding rectangle to be cleared after it is returned.
DCB_WINDOWMGR	Query the Windows bounding rectangle instead of the application's.

Return Value   The return value specifies the current bounds rectangle state. It may be some combination of the following values:

Value	Meaning
DCB_ACCUMULATE	Bounds rectangle accumulation is occurring.
DCB_RESET	The bounds rectangle is empty.
DCB_SET	The bounds rectangle is not empty.
DCB_ENABLE	Bounds accumulation is on.
DCB_DISABLE	Bounds accumulation is off.

Comment   To be sure the bounds rectangle is empty, you must check both the DCB_RESET bit and the DCB_ACCUMULATE flag in the return value. If the DCB_RESET flag is on and the DCB_ACCUMULATE flag is OFF, the bounds rectane is empty.

See Also   **SetBoundsRect**

■ GetBrushOrgEx

BOOL GetBrushOrgEx(*hDC*, *lpPoint***)**
HDC *hDC*;
LPPOINT *lpPoint*;

The **GetBrushOrgEx** function retrieves the current brush origin for the given device context.

Parameters   *hDC*   Identifies the device context.

lpPoint   Pointer to a *POINT* structure where the brush origin is to be returned in device coordinates.

Return Value   Returns TRUE is successful, otherwise FALSE.

Comments	The initial brush origin is at the coordinate (0,0).
See Also	**SetBrushOrg**

■ GetCapture

HWND GetCapture(void)

This function retrieves a handle that identifies the window that has the mouse capture. Only one window has the mouse capture at any given time; this window receives mouse input whether or not the cursor is within its borders.

This function returns the mouse capture window associated with the current thread. If there is none, it returns NULL.

A NULL return value does not mean no other thread or process in the system has the mouse captured; it just means the current thread does not have the mouse captured.

This function has no parameters.

Return Value   Returns the mouse capture window associated with the current thread. If there is none, it returns NULL.

Comments   A window receives the mouse capture when its handle is passed as the *hWnd* parameter of the **SetCapture** function.

See Also   **SetCapture, ReleaseCapture**

■ GetCaretBlinkTime

UINT GetCaretBlinkTime(void)

This function retrieves the caret blink rate. The blink rate is the elapsed time in milliseconds between flashes of the caret.

This function has no parameters.

Return Value   The return value specifies the blink rate (in milliseconds).

See Also   **SetCaretBlinkTime**

■ GetCaretPos

BOOL GetCaretPos(*lpPoint***)**
LPPOINT *lpPoint*;

This function retrieves the caret's current position (in client coordinates), and copies them to the **POINT** structure pointed to by the *lpPoint* parameter.

Parameters   *lpPoint*   Points to the POINT structure that is to receive the client coordinates of the caret.

Return Value   Returns TRUE for success, FALSE for failure.

Comments   The caret position is always given in the client coordinates of the window that contains the caret.

See Also   **SetCaretPos**

■ GetCharABCWidths

```
BOOL GetCharABCWidths(hdc, wFirstChar, wLastChar, lpABC)
HDC hdc;              /* device-context handle           */
WORD wFirstChar;      /* first character in range to query  */
WORD wLastChar;       /* last character in range to query   */
LPABC lpABC;          /* pointer to ABC structure for widths */
```

The **GetCharABCWidths** function retrieves the widths of consecutive characters in a specified range from the current font. The widths are returned in the units of the target device.

Parameters   *hdc*   Identifies the device context.

wFirstChar   Specifies the first character in the range of characters from the current font for which character widths are returned.

wLastChar   Specifies the last character in the range of characters from the current font for which character widths are returned.

lpABC   Points to an **ABC** structure that receives the character widths when the function returns.

Return Value   The return value is TRUE if the function is successful. Otherwise, it is FALSE.

Comments   The TrueType rasterizer provides ABC character spacing after a specific point size has been selected. "A" spacing is the distance that is added to the current position before placing the glyph. "B" spacing is the width of the black part of the glyph. "C" spacing is added to the current position to account for the white space to the right of the glyph. The total advanced width is given by A+B+C.

When the **GetCharABCWidths** function retrieves negative "A" or "C" widths for a character, that character includes underhangs or overhangs.

To convert the ABC widths to font design units, an application should use the value stored in the **otmEMSquare** member of the **OUTLINETEXTMETRIC** structure. This value can be retrieved by calling the **GetOutlineTextMetrics** function.

The ABC widths of the default character are used for characters that are outside the range of the currently selected font.

See Also   **GetCharWidth, GetOutlineTextMetrics**

■ GetCharWidth

BOOL GetCharWidth(*hDC*, *iFirstChar*, *iLastChar*, *lpBuffer*)
HDC *hDC*;
UINT *wchFirstChar*,
UINT *wchLastChar*,
LPINT *lpBuffer*,

The **GetCharWidth** function retrieves the widths of individual characters, in logical coordinates, for a consecutive group of characters in the current font. For example, if *iFirstChar* identifies the letter *a* and *iLastChar* identifies the letter *z*, **GetCharWidth** retrieves the widths of all lowercase characters. The function stores the values in the buffer pointed to by *lpBuffer*.

Parameters   *hDC*   Identifies the device context.

iFirstChar   Specifies the first character.

iLastChar   Specifies the last character, which must not precede *iFirstChar*. This range is inclusive.

lpBuffer   Points to a buffer that will receive the widths.

Return Value   The return value is TRUE if the function is successful. Otherwise, it is FALSE.

Comments   If a character does not exist in the current font, it will be assigned the width of the default character.

■ GetClassInfo

BOOL GetClassInfo(*hInstance*, *lpClassName*, *lpWndClass*)
HANDLE *hInstance*;
LPTSTR *lpClassName*;
LPWNDCLASS *lpWndClass*;

This function retrieves information about a window class. The *hInstance* parameter identifies the instance of the application that created the class, and the *lpClassName* parameter identifies the window class. If the function locates the specified window class, it copies the **WNDCLASS** data used to register the window class to the **WNDCLASS** structure pointed to by the *lpWndClass* parameter.

The **GetClassInfo** function may be used as either a wide-character function (where text arguments must use Unicode) or an ANSI function (where text arguments must use characters from the Windows 3.x character set installed).

Parameters   *hInstance*   Identifies the instance of the application that created the class. To retrieve information on classes defined by Windows (such as buttons or list boxes), set hInstance to NULL.

lpClassName   Points to a null-terminated string that contains the name of the class to find. If the high-order word of this parameter is NULL, the low-order word is assumed to be a value returned by the **MAKEINTRESOURCE** macro used when the class was created.

lpWndClass   Points to the **WNDCLASS** structure that will receive the class information.

Return Value   The return value is TRUE if the function found a matching class and successfully copied the data; the return value is FALSE if the function did not find a matching class.

■ GetClassLong

LONG GetClassLong(*hWnd, nIndex***)**
HWND *hWnd*;
int *nIndex*;

This function retrieves the long value specified by the *nIndex* parameter from the **WNDCLASS** structure of the window specified by the *hWnd* parameter.

Parameters   *hWnd*   Identifies the window.

nIndex   Specifies the byte offset of the value to be retrieved. It can also be the following value:

Value	Meaning
GCL_HBRBACKGROUND	Retrieves a handle to the background brush.
GCL_HCURSOR	Retrieves a handle to the cursor.
GCL_HICON	Retrieves a handle to the icon.
GCL_HMODULE	Retrieves a handle to the module.
GCL_MENUNAME	Retrieves a pointer to the menu-name string.
GCL_WNDPROC	Retrieves a pointer to the window function.

Return Value   The return value specifies the value retrieved from the **WNDCLASS** structure.

Comments   To access any extra four-byte values allocated when the window-class structure was created, use a positive byte offset as the index specified by the *nIndex* parameter. The first four-byte value in the extra space is at offset zero, the next four-byte value is at offset 4, and so on.

See Also   **SetClassLong, GetClassWord, SetClassWord**

■ GetClassName

int GetClassName(*hWnd, lpClassName, nMaxCount***)**
HWND *hWnd*;
LPTSTR *lpClassName*;
int *nMaxCount*;

This function retrieves the class name of the window specified by the *hWnd* parameter.

The **GetClassName** function may be used as either a wide-character function (where text arguments must use Unicode) or an ANSI function (where text arguments must use characters from the Windows 3.x character set installed).

Parameters   *hWnd*   Identifies the window whose class name is to be retrieved.

lpClassName   Points to the buffer that is to receive the class name.

nMaxCount   Specifies the maximum number of bytes to be stored in the *lpClassName* parameter. If the actual name is longer, a truncated name is copied to the buffer.

Return Value   The return value specifies the number of bytes actually copied to *lpClassName*. The return value is zero if the specified class name is not valid.

See Also   **GetClassInfo, GetClassWord, GetClassLong, FindWindow**

■ GetClassWord

DWORD GetClassWord(*hWnd, nIndex***)**
HWND *hWnd*;
int *nIndex*;

This function retrieves the value specified by the *nIndex* parameter from the **WNDCLASS** structure of the window specified by the *hWnd* parameter.

Parameters   *hWnd*   Identifies the window.

nIndex   Specifies the byte offset of the value to be retrieved. It can also be one of the following values:

Value	Meaning
GCW_CBCLSEXTRA	Tells how many bytes of additional class information you have. For information on how to access this memory, see the following "Comments" section.
GCW_CBWNDEXTRA	Tells how many bytes of additional window information you have. For information on how to access this memory, see the following "Comments" section.
GCW_STYLE	Retrieves the window-class style bits.

Return Value   The return value specifies the value retrieved from the **WNDCLASS** structure.

Comments   To access any extra two-byte values allocated when the window-class structure was created, use a positive byte offset as the index specified by the *nIndex* parameter, starting at zero for the first two-byte value in the extra space, 2 for the next two-byte value and so on. The return value will contain the retrieved two-byte value in its low-order word, with zero in its high-order word.

The following values for *nIndex* are supported for backwards compatibility. The preferred way to obtain the corresponding handles is with the **GetClassLong** function.

Value	Meaning
GCW_HBRBACKGROUND	Retrieves a handle to the background brush.
GCW_HCURSOR	Retrieves a handle to the cursor.
GCW_HICON	Retrieves a handle to the icon.
GCW_HMODULE	Retrieves a handle to the module.

GetClassWord stores and retrieves LONGs only when supporting the backward compatibility cases documented above. GetClassWord stores and retrieves WORDs in all other cases. For this reason, applications that store their own handles into private class word indexes should beware: this won't work.

See Also   **SetClassWord, GetClassLong, SetClassLong**

■ GetClientRect

BOOL GetClientRect(*hWnd, lpRect***)**
HWND *hWnd*;
LPRECT *lpRect*;

This function copies the client coordinates of a window's client area into the structure pointed to by the *lpRect* parameter. The client coordinates specify the upper-left and lower-right corners of the client area. Since client coordinates are relative to the upper-left corners of a window's client area, the coordinates of the upper-left corner are always (0,0).

Parameters   *hWnd*   Identifies the window associated with the client area.

lpRect   Points to a **RECT** structure.

Return Value   This function returns TRUE for success, FALSE for failure.

See Also   **GetWindowRect**

■ GetClipboardData

HANDLE GetClipboardData(*wFormat***)**
UINT *wFormat*;

This function retrieves data from the clipboard in the format given by the *wFormat* parameter. The clipboard must have been opened previously.

Parameters   *wFormat*   Specifies a data format. For a description of the data formats, see the SetClipboardData function, later in this chapter.

Return Value   The return value identifies the memory block that contains the data from the clipboard. The handle type depends on the type of data specified by the *wFormat* parameter. It is NULL if there is an error.

Comments   The available formats can be enumerated in advance by using the **EnumClipboardFormats** function.

The data handle returned by **GetClipboardData** is controlled by the clipboard, not by the application. The application should copy the data immediately, instead of relying on the data handle for long-term use. The application should not free the data handle or leave it locked.

Windows supports three formats for text, CF_UNICODETEXT, CF_TEXT and CF_OEMTEXT. CF_TEXT is specified for ansi text. CF_UNICODETEXT is specified for unicode text, and CF_OEMTEXT is specified for oem text. If an application calls **GetClipboardData** to retrieve data in one text format and one of the other text formats is the only available text format, Windows automatically converts the text to the requested format before supplying it to your application.

If the clipboard contains data in the CF_PALETTE (logical color palette) format, the application should assume that any other data in the clipboard is realized against that logical palette.

See Also   **EnumClipboardFormats, SetClipboardData**

GetClipboardFormatName — return value specifies the actual length of the string (in bytes)...

■ GetClipboardFormatName

int GetClipboardFormatName(*wFormat, lpFormatName, nMaxCount***)**
UINT *wFormat*;
LPTSTR *lpFormatName*;
int *nMaxCount*;

This function retrieves from the clipboard the name of the registered format specified by the *wFormat* parameter. The name is copied to the buffer pointed to by the *lpFormatName* parameter.

The **GetClipboardFormatName** function may be used as either a wide-character function (where text arguments must use Unicode) or an ANSI function (where text arguments must use characters from the Windows 3.x character set installed).

Parameters   *wFormat*   Specifies the type of format to be retrieved. It must not specify any of the predefined clipboard formats.

lpFormatName   Points to the buffer that is to receive the format name.

nMaxCount   Specifies the maximum length (in bytes) of the string to be copied to the buffer. If the actual name is longer, it is truncated.

Return Value	The return value specifies the actual length of the string (in bytes) copied to the buffer. It is zero if the requested format does not exist or is a predefined format.
See Also	**RegisterClipboardFormat, EnumClipboardFormats**

■ GetClipboardOwner

HWND GetClipboardOwner(void)

This function retrieves the window handle of the current owner of the clipboard.

This function has no parameters.

Return Value	The return value identifies the window that owns the clipboard. It is NULL if the clipboard is not owned.
Comments	The clipboard can still contain data even if the clipboard is not currently owned.
See Also	**GetClipboardViewer**

■ GetClipboardViewer

HWND GetClipboardViewer(void)

This function retrieves the window handle of the first window in the clipboard-viewer chain.

This function has no parameters.

Return Value	The return value identifies the window currently responsible for displaying the clipboard. It is NULL if there is no viewer.
See Also	**GetClipboardOwner, SetClipboardViewer**

■ GetClipBox

int GetClipBox(hDC, lpRect)
HDC hDC;
LPRECT lpRect;

The **GetClipBox** function retrieves the dimensions of the tightest bounding rectangle around the current visible area on the device. The visible region is reduced by the clip region and clip path, as well as overlapping windows.

Parameters	hDC Identifies the device context.
	lpRect Points to the **RECT** structure that is to receive the rectangle dimensions.
Return Value	The return value specifies the clipping region's complexity. It can be any one of the following values:

Value	Meaning
NULLREGION	Region is empty.
SIMPLEREGION	Region is a single rectangle.
COMPLEXREGION	Region is more than a single rectangle.
ERROR	

■ GetClipCursor

void GetClipCursor(*lprc***)**
LPRECT *lprc*;   /* address of structure for rectangle */

The **GetClipCursor** function retrieves the screen coordinates of the rectangle to which the cursor has been confined by a previous call to the **ClipCursor** function.

Parameters

lprc   Points to a **RECT** data structure that receives the screen coordinates of the confining rectangle. The structure receives the dimensions of the screen if the cursor is not confined to a rectangle. The **RECT** structure has the following form:

```
typedef struct tagRECT {
    LONG left;
    LONG top;
    LONG right;
    LONG bottom;
} RECT;
```

Return Value

This function does not return a value.

See Also

ClipCursor, GetCursorPos

■ GetClipRgn

BOOL GetClipRgn(*hDC, hRgn***)**
HDC *hDC*;
HRGN *hRgn*;

The **GetClipRgn** function retrieves the current clipping region for the specified device context.

Parameters

hDC   Identifies the device context.

hRgn   Identifies an existing region that will be replaced by the clip region.

Return Value

The return value is *TRUE* if the function succeeded, otherwise it is *FALSE*.

Comment

The region represented by hRgn will be a copy of the clip region. Changes to this region will not affect the current clipping.

■ GetCodeHandle

The **GetCodeHandle** has been deleted. This function defines semantics that do not make sense in an environment where image files are mapped and there for do not have handles associated with their code addresses.

■ GetCodeInfo

The **GetCodeInfo** function is deleted as it is x86 specific and has no corresponding semantics in the portable Win32 API.

■ GetCommandLine

LPTSTR GetCommandLine(VOID)

The **GetCommandLine** function obtains the current process' command line.

The **GetCommandLine** function may be used as either a wide-character function (where text arguments must use Unicode) or an ANSI function (where text arguments must use characters from the Windows 3.x character set installed).

Return Value   The return value is the address of the current process' command line.

See Also   **CreateProcess GetEnvironmentVariable, GetStartupInfo, SetEnvironmentVariable**

■ GetCommConfig

BOOL GetCommConfig(*hFile***,** *lpCommConfig***,** *dwSize***)**
HANDLE *hFile*;
LPVOID *lpCommConfig*;
DWORD *dwSize*;

This is used to obtain the current configuration state. The data returned may be saved and used in a subsequent **SetCommConfig** call.

Parameters   *hFile*   Specifies the communication device to get the configuration information from. The CreateFile() function returns this value.

lpCommConfig   Points to a buffer that is to receive the configuration information.

dwSize   Specifies the size of the buffer pointed to by lpCommConfig.

Return Value   TRUE – The operation was successful. FALSE – The operation failed. Extended error information is available using GetLastError().

Comments   The SetCommConfig() API is used to set configuration state.

■ GetCommMask

BOOL GetCommMask(HANDLE hFile, LPDWORD lpEvtMask)

This function retrieves the value of the event mask for the specified device.

Parameters *hFile*   Specifies the communications device whose event mask is to be retrieved.

lpEvtMask   Points to an event mask to be filled in with mask of events which are currently enabled.

Return Value The return value is TRUE if the function is successful or FALSE if an error occurs.

Comments See **SetCommMask** for bit mask definitions.

■ GetCommModemStatus

BOOL GetCommModemStatus(*hFile*, *lpModemStatus***)**
HANDLE *hFile*;
LPDWORD *lpModemStatus*;

GetCommModemStatus obtains the non-delta values of the modem control register.

Parameters *hFile*   Created via a call the CreateFile.

lpModemStatus   Contains the non-delta values of the modem control register.

In can be set to the following values:

Value	Meaning
MS_CTS_ON	Clear to send signal is on.
MS_RING_ON	Ring Indicator signal is on.
MS_RLSD_ON	Receive Line signal Detect signal is on.
MS_DSR_ON	Data Set Ready signal is on.

Return Value This function returns TRUE if the operation was successful, or FALSE if an error occurred. Extended error information is available by calling the **GetLastError** function.

Comments If the underlying hardware does not support the above values then **GetCommModemStatus** will return FALSE.

■ GetCommProperties

BOOL GetCommProperties(*hFile*, *lpCommProp***)**
HANDLE *hFile*;
LPCOMMPROP *lpCommProp*;

This function fills the buffer pointed to by lpCommProp with the communications properties associated with the communications device specified by hFile.

Parameters

hFile Specifies the device to be examined. The CreateFile() function returns this value.

lpCommProp Points to the **COMMPROP** data structure that is to receive the communications properties structure.

The **DCB** structure has the following form:

```
typedef struct _COMMPROP {
    WORD    wPacketLength;
    WORD    wPacketVersion;
    DWORD   dwServiceMask;
    DWORD   dwMaxConfigData;
    DWORD   dwMaxTxQueue;
    DWORD   dwMaxRxQueue;
    DWORD   dwMaxBaud;
    DWORD   dwDefTxQueue;
    DWORD   dwDefRxQueue;
    DWORD   dwDefBaud;
    DWORD   dwProvSubType;
    DWORD   dwProvCapabilities;
    DWORD   dwSettableParams;
    DWORD   dwSettableBaud;
    DWORD   dwSettableData;
    DWORD   dwSettableStopParity;
    DWORD   dwCurrentTxQueue;
    DWORD   dwCurrentRxQueue;
    DWORD   dwProvSpec1;
    DWORD   dwProvSpec2;
    WCHAR   ProvChar[1];
} COMMPROP;
typedef COMMPROP *LPCOMMPROP;
```

Return Value

TRUE – The operation was successful. FALSE – The operation failed. Extended error information is available using GetLastError().

■ GetCommState

BOOL GetCommState(*hFile*, *lpDCB***)**
HANDLE *hFile*;
LPDCB *lpDCB*;

The **GetCommState** function fills the buffer pointed to by the *lpDCB* parameter with the device control block of the communication device specified by the *hFile* parameter.

Parameters

hFile Specifies the device to be examined. The **CreateFile** function returns this value.

lpDCB Points to the **DCB** structure that is to receive the current device control block. The structure defines the control setting for the device.

The **DCB** structure has the following form:

```
typedef struct tagDCB {
    DWORD DCBlength;
    DWORD BaudRate;
    DWORD fBinary: 1;
    DWORD fParity: 1;
```

```
                DWORD fOutxCtsFlow: 1;
                DWORD fOutxDsrFlow: 1;
                DWORD fDtrControl: 2;
                DWORD fDummy: 2;
                DWORD fOutX: 1;
                DWORD fInX: 1;
                DWORD fPeChar: 1;
                DWORD fNull: 1;
                DWORD fRtsControl: 2;
                DWORD fDummy2: 2;
                WORD  TxDelay;
                WORD  XonLim;
                WORD  XoffLim;
                BYTE  ByteSize;
                BYTE  Parity;
                BYTE  StopBits;
                char  XonChar;
                char  XoffChar;
                char  PeChar;
                char  EofChar;
                char  EvtChar;
              } DCB;
```

Return Value   The return value is TRUE if the function is successful or FALSE if an error occurs.

See Also   **SetCommState**

■ GetCommTimeouts

BOOL GetCommTimeouts(_hFile, lpCommTimeouts_**)**
HANDLE _hFile_;
LPCOMMTIMEOUTS _lpCommTimeouts_;

This function returns the timeout characteristics for all read and write operations on the handle specified by hFile.

Parameters   _hFile_   Specifies the communication device from which timeouts should be read. The CreateFile() function returns this value.

lpCommTimeouts   Points to a structure which is to receive the current communications timeouts.

Return Value   TRUE – The operation was successful. FALSE – The operation failed. Extended error status is available using GetLastError().

Comments   See the description under **SetCommTimeouts** for details.

See Also   **SetCommTimeouts**

■ GetConsoleCursorInfo

BOOL GetConsoleCursorInfo(_hConsoleOutput, lpConsoleCursorInfo_**)**
HANDLE _hConsoleOutput_;
PCONSOLE_CURSOR_INFO _lpConsoleCursorInfo_;

This API may be used to query the cursor size and visibility.

Parameters   *hConsoleOutput*   Supplies an open handle to console output.

lpConsoleCursorInfo   A pointer to a buffer to receive the requested information.

Return Value   The return value is TRUE if the function was successful, otherwise it is FALSE in which case extended error information can be retrieved by calling the **GetLastError** function.

The buffer specified by the *lpConsoleCursorInfo* parameter has the following type definition:

```
typedef struct _CONSOLE_CURSOR_INFO {
    DWORD dwSize;
    BOOL  bVisible;
} CONSOLE_CURSOR_INFO, *PCONSOLE_CURSOR_INFO;
```

Member	Description
dwSize	Percentage of character cell filled. Percentage is indicated with a number between 1–100.
bVisible	TRUE if cursor is visible.

■ GetConsoleMode

BOOL GetConsoleMode(*hConsoleHandle*, *lpMode***)**
HANDLE *hConsoleHandle*;
LPDWORD *lpMode*;

The console input or output mode may be queried using **GetConsoleMode**.

Parameters   *hConsoleHandle*   Supplies a console input or output handle.

lpMode   Supplies a pointer to a dword in which to store the mode.

Input Mode Flags:

Value	Meaning
ENABLE_LINE_INPUT	Characters will not be returned to callers of **ReadFile** until a carriage return is input.
ENABLE_ECHO_INPUT	Characters will be written to the screen as they are read.
ENABLE_WINDOW_INPUT	The caller is windows-aware
ENABLE_PROCESSED_INPUT	Ctrl-c, backspace, tab, carriage return, linefeed and ctrl-z will be processed in the input buffer.

Output Mode Flags:

Value	Meaning
ENABLE_PROCESSED_OUTPUT	When set, backspace, tab, bell, carriage return & linefeed are processed.

Value	Meaning
ENABLE_WRAP_AT_EOL_OUTPUT	The cursor will move to the beginning of the next line when the end of the row is reached.

Return Value

The return value is TRUE if the function was successful, otherwise it is FALSE in which case extended error information can be retrieved by calling the **GetLastError** function.

Comments

A console consists of a keyboard, a mouse input buffer, and one or more screen buffers.

A console has several input and output modes. An input or output mode determines how the console behaves during input or output operations. For example, for input operations a console can be in character or line mode. Line mode lets the user use a variety of line editing features, sending a line's characters on only when the user presses the Enter key. Character mode sends each character as the user types it.

Modes are two-state entities, so they can be represented using bit flags. The flag constants noted above in the parameters section let you deal with the input/output mode bit flags in a high-level manner. When you call **GetConsoleMode**, it fills up a double word with bit flags that represent a console's input and output mode settings. You can then use the flag constants and Boolean operators to analyze the information.

This function's companion API function is **SetConsoleMode**. That function lets you set a console's input and output modes.

Examples

In this example we take different actions based on whether a console is set up for line or character mode:

```
/* if a call to GetConsoleMode succeeds... */
if (GetConsoleMode(hSomeConsole, &dwModeFlags) {
    /* if we're in line mode ... */
    if (dwModeFlags && ENABLE_LINE_INPUT) {
        /* do line mode stuff */
        }
    else {
        /* we're in character mode */
        /* do character mode stuff */
        }
    }
else {
    /* deal with failure of GetConsoleMode call */
    }
```

See Also

SetConsoleMode

■ GetConsoleScreenBufferInfo

BOOL GetConsoleScreenBufferInfo(*hConsoleOutput, lpConsoleScreenBufferInfo***)**
HANDLE *hConsoleOutput*;
PCONSOLE_SCREEN_BUFFER_INFO *lpConsoleScreenBufferInfo*;

This API may be used to query information about the screen buffer.

Parameters *hConsoleOutput*   Supplies an open handle to console output.

lpConsoleScreenBufferInfo   A pointer to a **CONSOLE_SCREEN_BUFFER_INFO** structure which will receive the information.

The **CONSOLE_SCREEN_BUFFER_INFO** data structure has the following form:

```
typedef struct tagCONSOLE_SCREEN_BUFFER_INFO {
    COORD       dwSize;
    COORD       dwCursorPosition;
    WORD        wAttributes;
    SMALL_RECT  srWindow;
    COORD       dwMaximumWindowSize;
} CONSOLE_SCREEN_BUFFER_INFO ;
```

Return Value   The return value is TRUE if the function was successful, otherwise it is FALSE, in which case extended error information can be retrieved by calling the **GetLastError** function.

See Also   **CONSOLE_SCREEN_BUFFER_INFO**

■ GetConsoleTitle

DWORD GetConsoleTitle(*lpConsoleTitle*, *nSize***)**
LPTSTR *lpConsoleTitle*;
DWORD *nSize*;

The **GetConsoleTitle** function retrieves the string that appears as the title of a console window. Each console has its own window title.

The **GetConsoleTitle** function may be used as either a wide-character function (where text arguments must use Unicode) or an ANSI function (where text arguments must use characters from the Windows 3.x character set installed).

Parameters   *lpConsoleTitle*   Pointer to a buffer the function will fill with the string that appears as the title of a console window.

nSize   Specifies the size in bytes of the buffer pointed to by *lpConsoleTitle*.

Return Value   If the function is successful, the return value is the actual length in bytes of the string copied to the buffer.

If the function fails, the return value is zero. Further information can be obtained by calling **GetLastError**.

See Also   **SetConsoleTitle**

■ GetCurrentDirectory

DWORD GetCurrentDirectory(*nBufferLength*, *lpBuffer***)**
DWORD *nBufferLength*;
LPTSTR *lpBuffer*;

The **GetCurrentDirectory** function is used to retrieve the current directory for a process.

The **GetCurrentDirectory** function may be used as either a wide-character function (where text arguments must use Unicode) or an ANSI function (where text arguments must use characters from the Windows 3.x character set installed).

Parameters

nBufferLength   Supplies the length in bytes of the buffer that is to receive the current directory string. This length should include room for a terminating null character. Note that UNICODE characters, including terminating null characters, use two bytes each.

lpBuffer   Returns the current directory string for the current process. The string is a null terminated string and specifies the absolute path to the current directory.

Return Value

If the buffer pointed to by *lpBuffer* is large enough and the function succeeds, the return value is less than or equal to *nBufferLength* minus the size in bytes of a terminating null character, and signifies the number of bytes written to the buffer, NOT including the bytes used for a terminating null character.

If the buffer pointed to by *lpBuffer* is NOT large enough, the return value is greater than *nBufferLength* minus the size in bytes of a terminating null character, and signifies the size in bytes of the buffer required to hold the pathname. Again, this size does NOT include room for a terminating null character.

The return value is zero if the function failed.

Comments

Be careful with numbers when you're using **GetCurrentDirectory**. The size of the buffer you supply is specified in bytes. The buffer must include enough room for a terminating null character. The function return value is in bytes. As mentioned above, it does not include the size of a terminating null character. If you're using the UNICODE flavor of the function, you need to remember that each UNICODE character, including a terminating null character, uses up two bytes.

Example

This example shows how you might go about printing the current directory:

```
/* ASCII version */
/* variables */
char    szCurrentDir[MAX_PATH];
DWORD   dwResult ;

/* try to get current directory */
dwResult = GetCurrentDirectory(sizeof(szCurrentDir), szCurrentDir) ;

/* if buffer not large enough ... */
if (dwResult > sizeof(szCurrentDir) - 1) {
        /* take appropriate action */
        }
/* else if there's been another kind of error ... */
else if (! dwResult) {
        /* take appropriate action */
```

```
                    }
/* else we're okay */
else {
      /* take appropriate action */
      printf("The Current Directory Is: %s", szCurrentDir) ;
      }
```

See Also   **SetCurrentDirectory, GetSystemDirectory, GetWindowsDirectory, CreateDirectory, RemoveDirectory**

■ GetCurrentObject

HANDLE GetCurrentObject(hDC, iObjectType**)**
HDC hDC;
UINT iObjectType;

The **GetCurrentObject** function returns the currently selected object of the specified type.

Parameters   hDC   Identifies the device context.

iObjectType   Specifies the object type to be queried.

Value	Meaning
OBJ_PEN	Returns the current selected pen
OBJ_BRUSH	Returns the current selected brush
OBJ_PAL	Returns the current selected pal
OBJ_FONT	Returns the current selected font
OBJ_BITMAP	Returns the current selected bitmap if hDC is a memory DC

Return Value   The function returns the handle of the current selected object of the specified type. It is zero if an error occurs.

Comments   GetCurrentObject can be used to query the current state of a DC when combined with GetObject.

See Also   **SelectObject GetObject**

■ GetCurrentPDB

The **GetCurrentPDB** function is deleted as it is x86 specific and has no corresponding semantics in the portable Win32 API. Two new functions, **GetCommandLine** and **GetEnvironmentStrings** can be used to access the equivalent information in the Win32 application environment.

See Also   **GetCommandLine, GetEnvironmentStrings**

■ GetCurrentPositionEx

BOOL GetCurrentPositionEx(*hDC, lpPoint***)**
HDC *hDC*;
LPPOINT *lpPoint*;

This function retrieves the current position in logical coordinates.

Parameters   *hDC*   Identifies the device context to get the current position from.

lpPoint   Points to a *POINT* structure that gets filled with the current position.

Return Value   The return value is TRUE if the function is successful, FALSE if there is an error.

■ GetCurrentProcess

HANDLE GetCurrentProcess(VOID)

A pseudo handle to the current process may be retrieved using **GetCurrentProcess**.

Return Value   The return value is the pseudo handle of the current process.

A special constant is exported by Win32 that is interpreted as a handle to the current process. This handle may be used to specify the current process whenever a process handle is required. On Win32, this handle has PROCESS_ALL_ACCESS to the current process. On NT/Win32, this handle has the maximum access allowed by any security descriptor placed on the current process.

See Also   **GetCurrentProcessId**

■ GetCurrentProcessId

DWORD GetCurrentProcessId(VOID)

The process ID of the current process may be retrieved using **GetCurrentProcessId**.

Return Value   The return value is a unique value representing the process ID of the currently executing process. The return value may be used to open a handle to a process.

See Also   **GetCurrentProcess**

■ GetCurrentTask

HANDLE GetCurrentTask(void)

The **GetCurrentTask** function returns the handle of the current (running) task.

Parameters	This function has no parameters.
Return Value	The return value identifies the current task if the function is successful. Otherwise, it is NULL.

■ GetCurrentThread

HANDLE GetCurrentThread(VOID)

A pseudo handle to the current thread may be retrieved using **GetCurrentThread**.

Return Value	The return value is the pseudo handle of the current thread.
	A special constant is exported by Win32 that is interpreted as a handle to the current thread. This handle may be used to specify the current thread whenever a thread handle is required. On Win32, this handle has THREAD_ALL_ACCESS to the current thread. On NT/Win32, this handle has the maximum access allowed by any security descriptor placed on the current thread.
See Also	**GetCurrentThreadId**

■ GetCurrentThreadId

DWORD GetCurrentThreadId(VOID)

The thread ID of the current thread may be retrieved using **GetCurrentThreadId**.

Return Value	The return value is a unique value representing the thread ID of the currently executing thread. The return value may be used to identify a thread in the system.
See Also	**GetCurrentThread**

■ GetCurrentTime

DWORD GetCurrentTime(void)

This function retrieves the current Windows time. Windows time is the number of milliseconds that have elapsed since the system was booted.

This function has no parameters.

Return Value	The return value specifies the current time (in milliseconds).
Comments	The **GetCurrentTime** and **GetMessageTime** functions return different times. **GetMessageTime** returns the Windows time when the given message was created, not the current Windows time.
	The system timer eventually overflows and resets to zero.

See Also GetMessageTime, GetSystemTime, SetSystemTime

■ GetCursor

HCURSOR GetCursor(VOID)

The **GetCursor** function retrieves the handle of the current cursor.

Parameters This function has no parameters.

Return Value The return value is the handle of the current cursor, or NULL if there is no cursor.

See Also **SetCursor**

■ GetCursorPos

BOOL GetCursorPos(*lpPoint***)**
LPPOINT *lpPoint*;

This function retrieves the cursor's current position (in client coordinates), that copies them to the **POINT** structure pointed to by the *lpPoint* parameter.

Parameters *lpPoint* Points to the POINT structure that is to receive the client coordinates of the cursor.

Return Value Returns TRUE for success, FALSE for failure.

Comments The cursor position is always given in client coordinates and is not affected by the mapping mode of the window that contains the cursor.

See Also **SetCursorPos, ShowCursor, SetCursor, ClipCursor**

■ GetDC

HDC GetDC(*hWnd***)**
HWND *hWnd*;

This function retrieves a handle to a display context for the client area of the given window. The display context can be used in subsequent GDI functions to draw in the client area.

The **GetDC** function retrieves a common, class, or private display context depending on the class style specified for the given window. For common display contexts, **GetDC** assigns default attributes to the context each time it is retrieved. For class and private contexts, **GetDC** leaves the previously assigned attributes unchanged.

Parameters *hWnd* Identifies the window whose display context is to be retrieved.

Return Value	The return value identifies the display context for the given window's client area if the function is successful. Otherwise, it is NULL.
Comments	After painting with a common display context, the **ReleaseDC** function must be called to release the context. Class and private display contexts do not have to be released. The number of display contexts is only limited by available memory.
See Also	**ReleaseDC, GetWindowDC**

■ GetDCEx

```
HDC GetDCEx(hwnd, hrgnClip, flags);
HWND hwnd;        /* window where drawing will occur  */
HRGN hrgnClip;    /* clip region that may be combined */
DWORD flags;      /* specifies how DC is created      */
```

The **GetDCEx** function retrieves the handle of a display context for the specified window. The display context can be used in subsequent GDI functions to draw in the client area.

This function is an extension to the **GetDC** function that gives an application more control over how and whether a DC for a window is clipped.

Parameters

hwnd   Identifies the window where drawing will occur.

hrgnClip   Secifies a clip region that may be combined with the visible region of the clienty window.

flags   Specifies how the DC is created. This parameter may be some combination of the following values:

Value	Meaning
DCX_WINDOW	Returns a DC corresponding to the window rectangle rather than the client rectangle.
DCX_CACHE	Returns a DC from the cache, rather than the OWNDC or CLASSDC window. Essentially overrides CS_OWNDC and CS_CLASSDC.
DCX_DEFAULTCLIP	Returns a DC using the default clipping flags specified by WS_CLIPCHILDREN, WS_CLIPSIBLINGS, and WS_PARENTDC.
DCX_PARENTCLIP	Use the visible region of the parent window. The parent's WS_CLIPCHILDREN and WS_PARENTDC style bits are ignored. The DC origin is set to the top left corner of the the window specified by the *hwnd* parameter.
DCX_CLIPSIBLINGS	Exclude the visible regions of all sibling windows above the window specified by the *hwnd* parameter.

Value	Meaning
DCX_CLIPCHILDREN	Exclude the visible regions of all child windows below the window specified by the *hwnd* parameter.
DCX_NORESETATTRS	Do not reset the attributes of this DC to the default attributes when this DC is released.
DCX_NORECOMPUTE	If an exact match in the cache is not found, return NULL rather than creating a new DC. When used with DCX_NORESETATTRS, this gives applications a way to determine whether they need to reselect any special attributes.
DCX_LOCKWINDOWUPDATE	Allow drawing even if there is a LockWindowUpdate() call in effect that would otherwise exclude this window. Used for drawing during tracking.
DCX_EXCLUDERGN	The clip region specified by the *hrgnClip* is excluded from the visible region of the returned DC.
DCX_INTERSECTRGN	The clip region specified by the *hrgnClip* parameter is intersected with the visible region of the returned DC.
DCX_EXCLUDEUPDATE	The returned DC excludes any update region of the window.
DCX_INTERSECTUPDATE	The returned DC is intersected with any update region of the window. (The DC is prepared the same way that the **BeginPaint** function prepares the DC, but the window is not validated.)
DCX_VALIDATE	When specified with DCX INTERSECTUPDATE, this flag causes the DC to be completely validated. Using this function with both DCX_INTERSECTUPDATE and DCX_VALIDATE is identical to using the **BeginPaint** function.

Return Value   The return value identifies the display context for the specified window if the function is successful. The return value is NULL if the *hwnd* parameter is invalid.

Comments   Unless the display context belongs to a window class, the **ReleaseDC** function must be called to release the context after painting. Since only five common display contexts are available at any given time, failure to release a display context can prevent other applications from accessing a display context.

A display context belonging to the window's class is returned by the **GetDC** function if CS_CLASSDC, CS_OWNDC or CS_PARENTDC was specified as a style in the **WNDCLASS** structure when the class was registered.

See Also **BeginPaint, GetDC, GetWindowDC, ReleaseDC**

■ GetDesktopAttrs

UINT **GetDesktopAttrs**(*hDesk, lpDesktop, cbDesktop, lpDeskAttrs*)
HANDLE *hDesk*;
LPSTR *lpDesktop*;
UINT *cbDesktop*;
LPDESKATTRS *lpDeskAttrs*;

This function is used to return desktop information about the desktop object referenced by **hDesk**.

Parameters *hDesk* This is a handle referencing a desktop object.

lpDesktop This is a pointer to a string buffer which will hold the desktop name.

cbDesktop This is a count specifying the exact size of the buffer pointed to by **lpDesktop.**

lpDeskAttrs This is an optional pointer to a **DESKATTRS** structure that will contain physical attribute information about the desktop information being returned. The **cb** field of the **DESKATTRS** structure must be set to the size of this structure before this routine is called.

Return Value This is a count of the bytes copied into **lpDesktop**. If this count is 0, this function is returning error. If this count is equal to **cbDesktop**, it is possible the string buffer was too short to contain the entire desktop name.

■ GetDesktopTypes

UINT **GetDesktopTypes**(*lpDevice, lpDeskAttrs, cDeskAttrs*)
LPSTR *lpDevice*;
LPDESKATTRS *lpDeskAttrs*;
UINT *cDeskAttrs*;

This routine will return a list of possible desktop types for a given device.

Parameters *lpDevice* This points to the device name for which the desktop types are being queried.

lpDeskAttrs This points to an array of **DESKATTR** structures to be filled in with desktop information for this device. The **cb** field of the **DESKATTRS** structure must be set to the size of this structure before this routine is called.

cDeskAttrs this specifies how many **DESKATTR** structures **lpDeskAttrs** points to.

Return Value   If **lpDeskAttrs** is NULL, this function returns the number of available desktop types for this device. Otherwise, this function returns the number of **DESKATTR** structures filled in with desktop information. 0 is returned for error.

■ GetDesktopWindow

HWND GetDesktopWindow(void)

This function returns the window handle to the Windows desktop window. The desktop window covers the entire screen and is the area on top of which all icons and other windows are painted.

This function has no parameters.

Return Value   The return value identifies the Windows desktop window.

See Also   **GetWindow**

■ GetDeviceCaps

int GetDeviceCaps(*hDC, nIndex***)**
HDC *hDC*;
int *nIndex*;

This function retrieves device-specific information about a given display device. The *nIndex* parameter specifies the type of information desired.

Parameters   *hDC*   Identifies the device context.

nIndex   Specifies the item to return. It can be any one of the following values:

Index	Meaning
TECHNOLOGY	Device technology. It can be any one of the following values:

Value	Meaning
DT_PLOTTER	Vector plotter
DT_RASDISPLAY	Raster display
DT_RASPRINTER	Raster printer
DT_RASCAMERA	Raster camera
DT_CHARSTREAM	Character stream
DT_METAFILE	Metafile
DT_DISPFILE	Display file

Index	Meaning
HORZSIZE	Width of the physical display (in millimeters).
VERTSIZE	Height of the physical display (in millimeters).
HORZRES	Width of the display (in pixels).
VERTRES	Height of the display (in raster lines).

Index	Meaning
LOGPIXELSX	Number of pixels per logical inch along the display width.
LOGPIXELSY	Number of pixels per logical inch along the display height.
BITSPIXEL	Number of adjacent color bits for each pixel.
PLANES	Number of color planes.
NUMBRUSHES	Number of device-specific brushes.
NUMPENS	Number of device-specific pens.
NUMFONTS	Number of device-specific fonts.
NUMCOLORS	Number of entries in the device's color table.
ASPECTX	Relative width of a device pixel as used for line drawing.
ASPECTY	Relative height of a device pixel as used for line drawing.
ASPECTXY	Diagonal width of the device pixel as used for line drawing.
PDEVICESIZE	Size of the **PDEVICE** internal data structure.
CLIPCAPS	Flag that indicates the clipping capabilities of the device. It is 1 if the device can clip to a rectangle, 0 if it cannot.
SIZEPALETTE	Number of entries in the system palette. This index is valid only if the device driver sets the RC_PALETTE bit in the RASTERCAPS index and is available only if the driver version is 3.0 or higher.
NUMRESERVED	Number of reserved entries in the system palette. This index is valid only if the device driver sets the RC_PALETTE bit in the RASTERCAPS index and is available only if the driver version is 3.0 or higher.
COLORRES	Actual color resolution of the device in bits per pixel. This index is valid only if the device driver sets the RC_PALETTE bit in the RASTERCAPS index and is available only if the driver version is 3.0 or higher.
RASTERCAPS	Value that indicates the raster capabilities of the device, as shown in the following list:

Capability	Meaning
RC_BANDING	Requires banding support.
RC_BITBLT	Capable of transferring bitmaps.
RC_BITMAP64	Capable of supporting bitmaps larger than 64K.

Capability	Meaning
RC_DI_BITMAP	Capable of supporting **SetDIBits** and **GetDIBits**
RC_DIBTODEV	Capable of supporting the **SetDI-BitsToDevice** function.
RC_FLOODFILL	Capable of performing flood fills.
RC_GDI20_OUTPUT	Capable of supporting Windows version 2.0 features.
RC_PALETTE	Palette-based device.
RC_SCALING	Capable of scaling.
RC_STRETCHBLT	Capable of performing the **StretchBlt** function.
RC_STRETCHDIB	Capable of performing the **StretchDIBits** function.

CURVECAPS

A bitmask that indicates the curve capabilities of the device. The bits have the following meanings:

Bit	Meaning
0	Device can do circles.
1	Device can do pie wedges.
2	Device can do chord arcs.
3	Device can do ellipses.
4	Device can do wide borders.
5	Device can do styled borders.
6	Device can do borders that are wide and styled.
7	Device can do interiors.

The higher bytes are 0.

LINECAPS

A bitmask that indicates the line capabilities of the device. The bits have the following meanings:

Bit	Meaning
0	Reserved.
1	Device can do polyline.
2	Reserved.
3	Reserved.

Bit	Meaning
4	Device can do wide lines.
5	Device can do styled lines.
6	Device can do lines that are wide and styled.
7	Device can do interiors.

The higher bytes are 0.

POLYGONALCAPS A bitmask that indicates the polygonal capabilities of the device. The bits have the following meanings:

Bit	Meaning
0	Device can do alternate fill polygon.
1	Device can do rectangle.
2	Device can do winding number fill polygon.
3	Device can do scanline.
4	Device can do wide borders.
5	Device can do styled borders.
6	Device can do borders that are wide and styled.
7	Device can do interiors.

The higher bytes are 0.

TEXTCAPS A bitmask that indicates the text capabilities of the device. The bits have the following meanings:

Bit	Meaning
0	Device can do character output precision.
1	Device can do stroke output precision.
2	Device can do stroke clip precision.
3	Device can do 90-degree character rotation.
4	Device can do any character rotation.
5	Device can do scaling independent of X and Y.
6	Device can do doubled character for scaling.
7	Device can do integer multiples for scaling.
8	Device can do any multiples for exact scaling.
9	Device can do double-weight characters.
10	Device can do italicizing.
11	Device can do underlining.
12	Device can do strikeouts.

Bit	Meaning
13	Device can do raster fonts.
14	Device can do vector fonts.
15	Reserved. Must be returned zero.

The higher bytes are 0.

Return Value   The return value specifies the value of the desired item.

■ GetDialogBaseUnits

LONG GetDialogBaseUnits(void)

This function returns the dialog base units used by Windows when creating dialog boxes. An application should use these values to calculate the average width of characters in the system font.

This function has no parameters.

Return Value   The return value specifies the dialog base units. The high-order word contains the height in pixels of the current dialog base height unit derived from the height of the system font, and the low-order word contains the width in pixels of the current dialog base width unit derived from the width of the system font.

Comments   The values returned represent dialog base units before being scaled to actual dialog units. The actual dialog unit in the x direction is 1/4th of the width returned by **GetDialogBaseUnits**. The actual dialog unit in the y direction is 1/8th of the height returned by the function.

To determine the actual height and width in pixels of a control, given the height (x) and width (y) in dialog units and the return value (lDlgBaseUnits) from calling **GetDialogBaseUnits**, use the following formula:

```
(x * LOWORD(lDlgBaseUnits))/4
(y * HIWORD(lDlgBaseUnits))/8
```

To avoid rounding problems, perform the multiplication before the division in case the dialog base units are not evenly divisible by four.

■ GetDIBits

int GetDIBits(hDC, hBitmap, iStartScan, nNumScans, lpBits, lpBitsInfo, iUsage**)**
HDC hDC;
HBITMAP hBitmap;
UINT iStartScan;
UINT nNumScans;
LPBYTE lpBits;
LPBITMAPINFO lpBitsInfo;
UINT iUsage;

The **GetDIBits** function retrieves the bits of the specified bitmap and copies them, in a device-independent format, into the buffer pointed to by *lpBits*. The *lpBitsInfo* parameter specifies the format for the returned bitmap data.

Parameters

hDC   Identifies the device context.

hBitmap   Identifies the bitmap.

iStartScan   Specifies the first scan line to retrieve.

nNumScans   Specifies the number of scan lines to be retrieved.

lpBits   Points to a buffer that will receive the bitmap data. If this parameter is NULL, then the dimensions and format of the bitmap will be written into the *BITMAPINFO* structure pointed to by *lpBitsInfo*.

lpBitsInfo   Points to a **BITMAPINFO** structure that specifies the desired format for the device-independent bitmap data. If data is being retrieved (i.e. *lpBits* is non-null), the bitmap's color table will be appended to this structure. The first 6 fields of the **BITMAPINFOHEADER** must be filled in to specify the size and format of the device-independant bitmap. If the requested format for the DIB matches it's internal format, the RGB values for the bitmap will be copied out. If the DIB format requested doesn't match the internal format a color table will be synthesized. The following describes the color table synthesized for each format:

1_BPP	The color table will consist of a black and white entry.
4_BPP	The color table will consist of a mix of colors which is identical to the standard VGA palette.
8_BPP	The color table will consist of a general mix of colors.
24_BPP	No color table is returned.

iUsage   Specifies the format of the **bmiColors[ ]** field of the *lpBits* parameter whenever this field is to be returned. It must be one of the following values:

DIB_PAL_COLORS	The color table should consist of an array of 16-bit indices into the currently realized logical palette.
DIB_RGB_COLORS	The color table should consist of literal RGB values.
DIB_PAL_INDICES	No color table is returned. Just the **BITMAPINFOHEADER** portion of the **BITMAPINFO** will be filled in.

Return Value

The return value specifies the number of scan lines copied from the bitmap. It is zero if there was an error.

Comments

If the *lpBits* parameter is NULL, **GetDIBits** fills in the **BITMAPINFO** structure to which the *lpBitsInfo* parameter points, but does not retrieve bits from the bitmap.

The bitmap identified by the *hBitmap* parameter must not be selected into a device context when the application calls this function.

The origin for the device-independent bitmap is the bottom-left corner of the bitmap, not the top-left corner.

■ GetDiskFreeSpace

BOOL GetDiskFreeSpace(lpRootPathName, lpSectorsPerCluster, lpBytesPerSector,
        lpNumberOfFreeClusters, lpTotalNumberOfClusters**)**
LPTSTR lpRootPathName;
LPDWORD lpSectorsPerCluster;
LPDWORD lpBytesPerSector;
LPDWORD lpNumberOfFreeClusters;
LPDWORD lpTotalNumberOfClusters;

The **GetDiskFreeSpace** function is used to retrieve the amount of free space on a disk and other information about the disk.

The **GetDiskFreeSpace** function may be used as either a wide-character function (where text arguments must use Unicode) or an ANSI function (where text arguments must use characters from the Windows 3.x character set installed).

Parameters

lpRootPathName   An optional parameter, that if specified, supplies the root directory of the disk whose free space is to be returned for. If this parameter is not specified, then the root of the current directory is used.

lpSectorsPerCluster   Returns the number of sectors per cluster where a cluster is the allocation granularity on the disk.

lpBytesPerSector   Returns the number of bytes per sector.

lpNumberOfFreeClusters   Returns the total number of free clusters on the disk.

lpTotalNumberOfClusters   Returns the total number of clusters on the disk.

Return Value

The return value is TRUE if the function was successful, otherwise it is FALSE, in which case extended error status is available by calling the **GetLastError** function.

See Also

GetDriveType

■ GetDlgCtrlID

int GetDlgCtrlID(hWnd**)**
HWND hWnd;

This function returns the ID value of the child window identified by the *hWnd* parameter.

Parameters

hWnd   Identifies the child window.

Return Value	The return value is the numeric identifier of the child window if the function is successful. If the function fails, or if *hWnd* is not a valid window handle, the return value is NULL.
Comments	Since top-level windows do not have an ID value, the return value of this function is invalid if the *hWnd* parameter identifies a top-level window.

■ GetDlgItem

HWND GetDlgItem(*hDlg, nIDDlgItem***)**
HWND *hDlg,*
int *nIDDlgItem,*

This function retrieves the handle of a control contained in the dialog box specified by the *hDlg* parameter.

Parameters	*hDlg* Identifies the dialog box that contains the control.
	nIDDlgItem Specifies the integer ID of the item to be retrieved.
Return Value	The return value identifies the given control. It is NULL if no control with the integer ID given by the *nIDDlgItem* parameter exists.
Comments	The **GetDlgItem** function can be used with any parent-child window pair, not just dialog boxes. As long as the *hDlg* parameter specifies a parent window and the child window has a unique ID (as specified by the *hMenu* parameter in the **CreateWindow** function that created the child window), **GetDlgItem** returns a valid handle to the child window.
See Also	**CreateWindow, GetDlgItemInt, GetDlgItemText**

■ GetDlgItemInt

int GetDlgItemInt(*hDlg, nIDDlgItem, lpTranslated, bSigned***)**
HWND *hDlg,*
int *nIDDlgItem,*
BOOL * *lpTranslated;*
BOOL *bSigned,*

This function translates the text of a control in the given dialog box into an integer value. The **GetDlgItemInt** function retrieves the text of the control identified by the *nIDDlgItem* parameter. It translates the text by stripping any extra spaces at the beginning of the text and converting decimal digits, stopping the translation when it reaches the end of the text or encounters any nonnumeric character. If the *bSigned* parameter is nonzero, **GetDlgItemInt** checks for a minus sign (-) at the beginning of the text and translates the text into a signed number. Otherwise, it creates an unsigned value.

GetDlgItemInt returns zero if the translated number is greater than INT_MAX (for signed numbers) or UINT_MAX (for unsigned). When errors occur, such as encountering nonnumeric characters and exceeding the given maximum,

GetDlgItemInt copies zero to the location pointed to by the *lpTranslated* parameter. If there are no errors, *lpTranslated* receives a nonzero value. If *lpTranslated* is NULL, **GetDlgItemInt** does not warn about errors. **GetDlgItemInt** sends a WM_GETTEXT message to the control.

Parameters

hDlg   Identifies the dialog box.

nIDDlgItem   Specifies the integer identifier of the dialog-box item to be translated.

lpTranslated   Points to the Boolean variable that is to receive the translated flag.

bSigned   Specifies whether the value to be retrieved is signed.

Return Value

The return value specifies the translated value of the dialog-box item text. Since zero is a valid return value, the *lpTranslated* parameter must be used to detect errors. If a signed return value is desired, it should be cast as an **int** type.

See Also

SetDlgItemInt, GetDlgItemText

■ GetDlgItemText

```
int GetDlgItemText(hDlg, nIDDlgItem, lpString, nMaxCount)
HWND hDlg;
int nIDDlgItem;
LPTSTR lpString;
int nMaxCount;
```

This function retrieves the caption or text associated with a control in a dialog box. The **GetDlgItemText** function copies the text to the location pointed to by the *lpString* parameter and returns a count of the number of bytes it copies.

GetDlgItemText sends a WM_GETTEXT message to the control.

The **GetDlgItemText** function may be used as either a wide-character function (where text arguments must use Unicode) or an ANSI function (where text arguments must use characters from the Windows 3.x character set installed).

Parameters

hDlg   Identifies the dialog box that contains the control.

nIDDlgItem   Specifies the integer identifier of the dialog-box item whose caption or text is to be retrieved.

lpString   Points to the buffer to receive the text.

nMaxCount   Specifies the maximum length (in bytes) of the string to be copied to *lpString*. If the string is longer than *nMaxCount*, it is truncated.

Return Value

The return value specifies the actual number of bytes copied to the buffer. It is zero if no text is copied.

See Also

SetDlgItemText, GetDlgItemInt, SetDlgItemInt

■ GetDOSEnvironment

The **GetDOSEnvironment** function is deleted as it is x86 specific and has no corresponding semantics in the portable Win32 API. A new function, GetEnvironmentStrings, can be used to access the equivalent information in the Win32 application environment.

■ GetDoubleClickTime

UINT GetDoubleClickTime(void)

This function retrieves the current double-click time for the mouse. A double-click is a series of two clicks of the mouse button, the second occurring within a specified time after the first. The double-click time is the maximum number of milliseconds that may occur between the first and second click of a double-click.

This function has no parameters.

Return Value   The return value specifies the current double-click time (in milliseconds).

See Also   **SetDoubleClickTime**

■ GetDriveType

DWORD GetDriveType(lpRootPathName)
LPTSTR lpRootPathName;

The **GetDriveType** function determines whether a disk drive is removable, fixed, CD ROM, RAM disk, or a network drive.

The **GetDriveType** function may be used as either a wide-character function (where text arguments must use Unicode) or an ANSI function (where text arguments must use characters from the Windows 3.x character set installed).

Parameters   lpRootPathName   An optional parameter, that if specified, supplies the root directory of the disk whose drive type is to be determined. If this parameter is not specified, then the root of the current directory is used.

Return Value   The return value specifies the type of drive. It can be one of the following values:

Value	Meaning
0	The drive type can not be determined.
1	The root directory does not exist.
DRIVE_REMOVEABLE	Disk can be removed from the drive.
DRIVE_FIXED	Disk cannot be removed from the drive.
DRIVE_REMOTE	Drive is a remote (network) drive.
DRIVE_CDROM	Drive is a CD rom drive.
DRIVE_RAMDISK	Drive is a RAM disk.

See Also   **GetDiskFreeSpace**

■ GetEnvironmentStrings

LPVOID GetEnvironmentStrings(VOID)

Return Value   The address of the current processes environment block is returned. The block is
                  opaque and must only be interpreted via the environment variable access
                  functions.

Comments   The return value is opaque. Applications msut only access the environment
                  variables within this block using the environment variable access functions
                  GetEnvironmentVariable and **SetEnvironmentVariable**.

See Also   **GetEnvironmentVariable SetEnvironmentVariable**

■ GetEnvironmentVariable

DWORD APIENTRY GetEnvironmentVariable(_lpName_, _lpBuffer_, _nSize_**)**
LPTSTR _lpName_,;
LPTSTR _lpBuffer_;
DWORD _nSize_;

                  The **GetEnvironmentVariable** function retrieves an environment variable of the
                  current process.

                  The **GetEnvironmentVariable** function may be used as either a wide-character
                  function (where text arguments must use Unicode) or an ANSI function (where
                  text arguments must use characters from the Windows 3.x character set installed).

Parameters   _lpName_   Pointer to a null terminate string that is the name of the environment
                  variable whose value is being requested.

                  lpBuffer   Pointer to a buffer that is to contain the value of the specified variable
                  name.

                  nSize   Specifies the maximum number of bytes that can be stored in the buffer
                  pointed to by lpBuffer, including the null terminator.

Return Value   The return value is the actual number of bytes stored in the memory pointed to by
                  the _lpBuffer_ parameter, not including the trailing null-terminating character. The
                  return value is zero if the environment variable name was not found in the current
                  process's environment.

See Also   **SetEnvironmentVariable**

■ GetExceptionCode

DWORD GetExceptionCode(VOID)

GetExceptionCode is used by exception filters and handlers to determine the type of exception encountered.

This function has no parameters.

Return Value   EXCEPTION_ACCESS_VIOLATION

See Also   **GetExceptionInformation**

■ GetExceptionInformation

LPEXCEPTION_INFORMATION GetExceptionInformation(VOID)

GetExceptionInformation is used by exception filters to retrieve details of the exception, including the machine state at the time of the exception.

This function has no parameters.

Return Value   The return value is a pointer to an **EXCEPTION_INFORMATION** structure.

The **EXCEPTION_INFORMATION** structure has the following form:

```
typedef struct tagEXCEPTION_INFORMATION {
    LPEXCEPTION_RECORD lpExceptionRecord;
    LPCONTEXT          lpContext;
} EXCEPTION_INFORMATION ;
```

Comments   This function is not available to the exception handler. The exception filter can copy some or all of this information to safe storage which the handler can later access.

See Also   **GetExceptionCode, EXCEPTION_INFORMATION**

■ GetExitCodeProcess

BOOL GetExitCodeProcess(*hProcess*, *lpExitCode*)
HANDLE *hProcess*;
LPDWORD *lpExitCode*;

The termination status of a process can be read using **GetExitCodeProcess**.

Parameters   *hProcess*   Supplies a handle to the process whose termination status is to be read. The handle must have been created with PROCESS_QUERY_INFORMATION access.

lpExitCode   Returns the current termination status of the process.

Return Value   The return value is TRUE if the function is successful. Otherwise, it is FALSE in which case extended error information is available from the **GetLastError** function.

If a process is in the signaled state, calling this function returns the termination status of the last thread in the process to terminate. If the process is not yet signaled, the termination status returned is STILL_ACTIVE.

See Also   **ExitProcess, TerminateProcess**

■ GetExitCodeThread

BOOL GetExitCodeThread(hThread, lpExitCode**)**
HANDLE hThread;
LPDWORD lpExitCode;

The termination status of a thread can be read using **GetExitCodeThread**.

Parameters   hThread   Supplies a handle to the thread whose termination status is to be read.
The handle must have been created with THREAD_QUERY_INFORMATION
access.

lpExitCode   Returns the current termination status of the thread.

Return Value   The return value is TRUE if the function is successful. Otherwise, it is FALSE in
which case extended error information is available from the **GetLastError**
function.

If a Thread is in the signaled state, calling this function returns the termination
status of the thread. If the thread is not yet signaled, the termination status
returned is STILL_ACTIVE.

See Also   **ExitThread, TerminateThread**

■ GetExpandedName

#include <lzexpand.h>

int GetExpandedName(lpszSource, lpszBuffer**)**
LPTSTR lpSource;   /* specifies name of compressed file   */
LPTSTR lpBuffer;   /* points to buffer receiving the original filename */

The **GetExpandedName** function retrieves the original name of a compressed file
if the files was compressed with the COMPRESS.EXE utility and the **-r** option
was specified.

Parameters   lpSource   Points to a string that specifies the name of a compressed file.

lpBuffer   Points to a buffer that receives the name of the compressed file.

Return Value   The return value is TRUE if the function is successful; if an error occurs, the
return value is less than zero. The following list identifies possible error return
values and their meaning:

Value	Meaning
LZERROR_BADINHANDLE	The handle identifying the source file, *hfSource*, was not valid.

Example

The following code fragment shows how the **GetExpandedName** function was used to obtain the original filename of a compressed file:

```
#include <windows.h>
#include <lzexpand.h>

LPSTR lpszSrc = {"readme.cmp"};
LPSTR pszFileName;
OFSTRUCT ofStrSrc;
OFSTRUCT ofStrDest;
HANDLE hSrcFile, hDestFile, hCompFile;
int cBufLngth;
char cBuf1[256];

/* Open the compressed source file. */

hSrcFile = OpenFile(lpszSrc, (LPOFSTRUCT) &ofStrSrc, OF_READ);

/* Initialize internal data structures
 * for the decompression operation.
 */

hCompFile = LZInit(hSrcFile);

/* Retrieve the original name for the compressed file. */

GetExpandedName(lpszSrc, pszFileName);

/* Create the destination file using the original name. */

hDestFile = LZOpenFile(pszFileName,
        (LPOFSTRUCT) &ofStrDest, OF_CREATE);

/* Copy the compressed source file to the destination file. */

cBufLngth = LZRead(hCompFile, cBuf1, 256);
 while (cBufLngth == 256) {
    _lwrite(hDestFile, cBuf1, cBufLngth);
     cBufLngth = LZRead(hCompFile, cBuf1, 256);
 }
_lwrite(hDestFile, cBuf1, cBufLngth);

/* Close the files. */

LZClose(hSrcFile);
LZClose(hDestFile);
```

Comments

This function retrieves the original filename from the header of the compressed file. If the source file is not compressed, this function copies the filename at which *lpszSource* points to the buffer at which *lpszBuffer* points.

If **-r** option was not set when the file was compressed, the string in the buffer at which *lpszBuffer* points is invalid.

■ GetFileAttributes

GetDriveType

DWORD GetFileAttributes(_lpFileName_**)**
LPTSTR _lpFileName_;

You can obtain a file's attributes using **GetFileAttributes**.

The **GetFileAttributes** function may be used as either a wide-character function (where text arguments must use Unicode) or an ANSI function (where text arguments must use characters from the Windows 3.x character set installed).

Parameters

lpFileName Supplies the file name of the file whose attributes are to be retrieved.

Return Value

The return value, if the function is successful, is the attributes of the specified file. The attributes may be a combination of the following values, unless it is equal to FILE_ATTRIBUTE_NORMAL:

Attribute	Description
FILE_ATTRIBUTE_NORMAL	The file has no attribute bits set. By returning this constant, the file attributes can then be used to set normal file attributes for a file.
FILE_ATTRIBUTE_READONLY	The file is marked read-only.
FILE_ATTRIBUTE_HIDDEN	The file is marked as hidden.
FILE_ATTRIBUTE_SYSTEM	The file is marked as a system file.
FILE_ATTRIBUTE_ARCHIVE	The file is marked for archive.
FILE_ATTRIBUTE_DIRECTORY	The file is marked as a directory.

If the function failed, the return value is -1 (0xFFFFFFFF) in which case extended error information is available from the **GetLastError** function.

Comments

This API provides the same functionality as DOS (int 21h, function 43H with AL=0), and provides a subset of OS/2's **DosQueryFileInfo**.

See Also

SetFileAttributes, FindFirstFile, FindNextFile

■ GetFileResource

BOOL GetFileResource(_lpstrFilename, lpstrResType, lpstrResID, dwFileOffset, dwResLen, lpData_**)**
LPSTR _lpstrFilename_;
LPSTR _lpstrResType_;
LPSTR _lpstrResID_;
DWORD _dwFileOffset_;
DWORD _dwResLen_;
LPSTR _lpData_;

The **GetFileResource** function copies the specified resource from the file specified by _lpstrFilename_ into the buffer pointed to by _lpData_. To obtain the appropriate _dwResLen_, the application must call **GetFileResourceSize** before **GetFileResource**.

Parameters *lpstrFilename*   Points to the buffer that contains the name of the file that contains the resource.

lpstrResType   Points to the buffer that contains the name of the resource type. This value may also be the result of MAKEINTRESOURCE of the numbered resource type.

lpstrResID   Points to the buffer that contains the name of the resource ID to locate. This value may also be the result of MAKEINTRESOURCE of the numbered resource ID. Named resources should only be used for file-specific information that must be accessed by multiple applications.

dwFileOffset   Points to the offset of the resource within the file. This pointer can be NULL.

dwResLen   Specifies the size of the resource, in bytes. The **GetFileResourceSize** function returns this value. If the buffer is not large enough, the resource data is truncated to the size of the buffer.

lpData   Points to the buffer that will receive a copy of the resource.

Return Value If **GetFileResource** copied the specified resource to *lpData*, the return value is TRUE. The function failed, the return value is FALSE. Failure could indicate that the function could not find the file, could not find the specified resource, or produced a DOS error code. However, **GetFileResource** does not provide information about the type of error that occurred.

See Also **GetFileResourceSize**

■ GetFileResourceSize

```
DWORD GetFileResourceSize(lpstrFilename, lpstrResType, lpstrResID, lpdwFileOffset)
LPSTR lpstrFilename;
LPSTR lpstrResType;
LPSTR lpstrResID;
DWORD FAR *lpdwFileOffset;
```

The **GetFileResourceSize** function searches the file specified by *lpstrFilename* for the resource of the type and ID specified by *lpstrResType* and *lpstrResID*.

Parameters *lpstrFilename*   Points to the buffer that contains the name of the file in which to search for the resource.

lpstrResType   Points to the buffer that contains the name of the resource type to locate. This value may also be the result of MAKEINTRESOURCE of the numbered resource type.

lpstrResID   Points to the buffer that contains the name of the resource ID to locate. This value may also be the result of MAKEINTRESOURCE of the numbered resource ID. Named resources should only be used for file-specific information that must be accessed by multiple applications.

lpdwFileOffset   Points to the offset of the resource within the file. This pointer can be NULL.

Return Value   The return value is the size of the resource, in bytes. The return value is NULL, if the function failed. Failure could indicate that the function could not find the file, the file does not have any resources attached, or the function produced a DOS error code. However, **GetFileResourceSize** does not provide information about the type of error that occurred.

See Also   **GetFileResource**

■ GetFileSecurity

BOOL GetFileSecurity(*lpFileName, pRequestedInformation, pSecurityDescriptor, nLength,*
   *lpnLengthNeeded***)**
LPTSTR *lpFileName*;
PSECURITY_INFORMATION *pRequestedInformation*;
PSECURITY_DESCRIPTOR *pSecurityDescriptor*;
DWORD *nLength*;
LPDWORD *lpnLengthNeeded*;

The **GetFileSecurity** function obtains specified information about the security of a file or directory. The information obtained is constrained by the caller's access rights and privileges.

The **GetFileSecurity** function fills the buffer pointed to by *pSecurityDescriptor* with a copy of the file or directory's security descriptor containing the requested security descriptor fields, based on the caller's access rights and privileges. In order to read the file or directory's security descriptor, the caller must have READ_CONTROL access or be the owner of the file or directory. Additionally, the caller must have SeSecurityPrivilege privilege to read the system ACL.

The **GetFileSecurity** function may be used as either a wide-character function (where text arguments must use Unicode) or an ANSI function (where text arguments must use characters from the Windows 3.x character set installed).

Parameters   *lpFileName*   Pointer to a zero-terminated string that names the file or directory whose security this function will obtain.

pRequestedInformation   A pointer to a **SECURITY_INFORMATION** data structure that specifies the security information being requested.

The **SECURITY_INFORMATION** data structure has the following form:

```
typedef ULONG SECURITY_INFORMATION;
```

pSecurityDescriptor   A pointer to a buffer that the function will fill with a copy of the security descriptor of the object specified by *lpFileName*. As noted above, the caller must have the right to view the specified aspects of the object's security status. The **SECURITY_DESCRIPTOR** data structure is returned in self-relative format.

The **SECURITY_DESCRIPTOR** data structure has the following form:

```
typedef PVOID PSECURITY_DESCRIPTOR;
```

nLength Specifies the size in bytes of the buffer pointed to by *pSecurityDescriptor*.

lpnLengthNeeded Pointer to a variable that the function will set to the number of bytes needed to store the complete security descriptor. If the value set is less than or equal to *nLength*, then the entire security descriptor is returned in the buffer pointed to by *pSecurityDescriptor*. Otherwise none of the descriptor is returned.

Return Value   If the function is successful, the return value is TRUE.

If the function fails, the return value is FALSE. The function will fail if access is denied or if the buffer pointed to by *pSecurityDescriptor* is too small to hold the security descriptor. Call **GetLastError** for more detailed error information.

See Also   **SetFileSecurity, GetObjectSecurity, SetObjectSecurity, CreateUserObjectSecurity, DestroyUserObjectSecurity, GetUserObjectSecurity, SetUserObjectSecurity**

■ GetFileSize

DWORD GetFileSize(HANDLE hFile, LPDWORD lpFileSizeHigh)

This function returns the size of the file specified by hFile. It is capable of returning 64-bits worth of file size.

The return value contains the low order 32-bits of the file's size. The optional lpFileSizeHigh returns the high order 32-bits of the file's size.

Parameters   *hFile* Supplies an open handle to a file whose size is to be returned. The handle must have been created with either GENERIC_READ or GENERIC_WRITE access to the file.

lpFileSizeHigh An optional parameter, that if specified, returns the high order 64-bits of the file's size.

Return Value   0xffffffff – If the value of size of the file cannot be determined, or an invalid handle or handle with inappropriate access, or a handle to a non-file is specified, this error is returned. If the file's size (low 32-bits) is −1, then this value is returned, and GetLastError() will return 0. Extended error status is available using GetLastError.

Otherwise, returns the low order 32-bits of the specified file's size.

■ GetFileTime

BOOL GetFileTime(hFile, lpCreationTime, lpLastAccessTime, lpLastWriteTime**)**
HANDLE hFile;
LPFILETIME lpCreationTime;
LPFILETIME lpLastAccessTime;
LPFILETIME lpLastWriteTime;

The date and time that a file was created, last accessed or last modified can be read using **GetFileTime**. File time stamps are returned as 64-bit values, that represent the number of 100 nanoseconds since January 1st, 1601. This date was chosen because it is the start of a new quadricentury. At 100ns resolution 32 bits is good for about 429 seconds (or 7 minutes) and a 63-bit integer is good for about 29,247 years, or around 10,682,247 days.

This API provides the same functionality as DOS (int 21h, function 47H with AL=0), and provides a subset of OS/2's **DosQueryFileInfo**.

Parameters

hFile   Supplies an open handle to a file whose modification date and times are to be read. The file handle must have been created with GENERIC_READ access to the file.

lpCreationTime   An optional parameter that if specified points to the location to return the date and time the file was created. A returned time of all zero indicates that the file system containing the file does not support this time value.

lpLastAccessTime   An optional parameter that if specified points to the location to return the date and time the file was last accessed. A returned time of all zero indicates that the file system containing the file does not support this time value.

lpLastWriteTime   An optional parameter that if specified points to the location to return the date and time the file was last written. All file systems must support this time and thus a valid value will always be returned for this time value.

Return Value

The return value is TRUE if the function is successful or FALSE if an error occurs. Extended error status is available using **GetLastError**.

See Also

SetFileTime, GetFileType, GetFileSize

■ GetFileTitle

int GetFileTitle(lpszFile, lpszTitle, wBufSize**)**
LPSTR lpszFile;   /* pointer to a DOS file name (including path) */
LPSTR lpszTitle;   /* pointer to buffer that receives file name   */
WORD wBufSize;   /* length of buffer at which lpszTitle points   */

The **GetFileTitle** function returns the title of the file identified by *lpszFile*.

Parameters

lpszFile   Points to a DOS filename (including the path).

lpszTitle   Points to a buffer into which the function will copy the filename.

wBufSize   Specifies the length of the buffer at which *lpszTitle* points.

Return Value   If the function is successful, the return value is 0; if the filename is invalid, the return value is a negative number; if the buffer at which *lpszTitle* points is too small, the return value is a positive integer that specifies the required buffer size.

Comments   If the filename at which *lpszFile* points is an empty string, a string with the wildcard (*) or bracket characters, a string that ends with a colon (:), slash (/), or backslash (\), or a string which contains a filename that is longer than the buffer at which *lpszTitle* points, the function will return an error.

■ GetFileType

DWORD APIENTRY GetFileType(*hFile***)**
HANDLE *hFile*;

The **GetFileType** function is used to determine the file type of the specified file.

Parameters   *hFile*   Supplies an open handle to a file whose type is to be determined

Return Value   The return value is one of the following values:

Value	Meaning
FILE_TYPE_UNKNOWN	The type of the specified file is unknown.
FILE_TYPE_DISK	The specified file is a disk file.
FILE_TYPE_CHAR	The specified file is a character file (LPT, console...)
FILE_TYPE_PIPE	The specified file is a pipe (either a named pipe or a pipe created by **CreatePipe**).

See Also   **GetFileSize, GetFileTime**

■ GetFileVersionInfo

BOOL GetFileVersionInfo(*lpstrFilename, dwHandle, dwLen, lpData***)**
LPSTR *lpstrFilename*;
DWORD *dwHandle*;
DWORD *dwLen*;
LPSTR *lpData*;

The **GetFileVersionInfo** function returns version information about the file specified by *lpstrFilename*. To obtain the appropriate *dwHandle* and *dwLen*, the **GetFileVersionInfoSize** function must be called before **GetFileVersionInfo**.

The file's version information is organized in a **VS_VERSION_INFO** block.

Parameters   *lpstrFilename*   Points to the buffer that contains the name of the file.

      dwHandle   Identifies the file version information. The **GetFileVersionInfoSize** function returns this handle.

      dwLen   Specifies the size of the buffer identified by *lpData*. The **GetFileVersionInfoSize** function returns the buffer size required to hold the file version information. If the buffer is not large enough, the file version information is truncated to the size of the buffer.

      lpData   Points to the buffer that contains the file version information.

Return Value   If the specified file exists and version information is available, this function returns TRUE. The function returns FALSE if the specified file doesn't exist or if *dwHandle* is invalid. **GetFileVersionInfo** does not provide information about the type of error that occurred.

See Also   **GetFileVersionInfoSize, VerQueryValue, VS_VERSION_INFO**

■ GetFileVersionInfoSize

DWORD GetFileVersionInfoSize(*lpstrFilename, lpdwHandle***)**
LPSTR *lpstrFilename*;
DWORD FAR **lpdwHandle*;

      The **GetFileVersionInfoSize** function determines whether it can obtain version information from the file specified by *lpstrFilename*. If version information is available, **GetFileVersionInfoSize** returns the size of the buffer required to hold the version information. This function also returns a handle in *lpdwHandle* that is required by a subsequent call to **GetFileVersionInfo**.

      The file's version information is organized in a **VS_VERSION_INFO** block.

Parameters   *lpstrFilename*   Points to the buffer that contains the name of the file.

      lpdwHandle   Address of a DWORD value in which **GetFileVersionInfoSize** returns file version information. This handle is required by the **GetFileVersionInfo** function.

Return Value   The return value is the buffer size, in bytes, required to hold the version information. The return value is NULL, if the function failed. Failure could indicate that the function could not find the file, could not find the file's version information, or produced a DOS error code. However, **GetFileVersionInfoSize** does not provide information about the type of error that occurred.

See Also   **GetFileVersionInfo, VS_VERSION_INFO**

■ GetFocus

HWND GetFocus(VOID)

      This routine returns the focus window associated with the current thread. If the current thread does not have the keyboard focus, NULL is returned. If NULL is returned this does not mean that any other thread does not have the focus; each thread has its own local focus state.

This function has no parameters.

Return Value   Window handle of the current thread that has the keyboard focus, NULL if there isn't one.

■ GetFontData

DWORD GetFontData(*hdc, dwTable, dwOffset, lpBuffer, cbData***)**
HDC *hdc*;   /* device-context handle   */
DWORD *dwTable*;   /* metric table to query   */
DWORD *dwOffset*;   /* offset into table being queried */
LPSTR *lpBuffer*,   /* buffer for returned data   */
DWORD *cbData*;   /* length of data to query   */

The **GetFontData** function retrieves font metric data from a scalable font file. The data to retrieve is identified by specifying an offset into the font file and the length of the data to return.

Parameters   *hdc*   Identifies the device context.

dwTable   Specifies the name of the metric table to be returned.

dwOffset   Specifies the offset into the table at which to begin retrieving data. A value of zero indicates that data is retrieved starting at the beginning of the font file.

lpBuffer   Points to a buffer that receives the font metric data.

cbData   Specifies the length of the data to retrieve. Specifying $-1L$ for this parameter indicates that the function should retrieve data from the specified offset to the end of the file.

Return Value   The return value specifies the number of bytes returned in the buffer pointed to by the *lpBuffer* parameter, or -1 if the function does not succeed.

Comments   If an application attempts to use this function to retrieve data for a non-scalable font, **GetFontData** returns -1.

See Also   **GetTextMetrics**

■ GetFreeSpace

The **GetFreeSpace** function is implemented by a macro that returns 0x100000L.

■ GetFreeSystemResources

WORD GetFreeSystemResources(fwSysResource)
WORD fwSysResource;   /* type of resource to check */

The **GetFreeSystemResources** function returns the percentage of free system resource space.

<table>
<tr><td>Parameter</td><td>*fwSysResource*   Specifies the type of resource to check. This parameter may have one of the following values:</td></tr>
</table>

Value	Meaning
0	Return percentage of free system resource space.
1	Return percentage of free GDI resource space. GDI resources include device-context handles, brushes, pens, regions, fonts and bitmaps.
2	Return percentage of free USER resource space. User resources inlcude window and menu handles.

Return Value   The return value specifies the percentage of free resource space.

Comments   The return value from this function does not guarantee that an application will be able to create a new object. Applications should not use this function to determine if it will be possible to create an object.

See Also   **GetFreeSpace**

■ GetFullPathName

DWORD GetFullPathName(*lpFileName*, *nBufferLength*, *lpBuffer*, *lpFilePart***)**
LPTSTR *lpFileName*;
DWORD *nBufferLength*;
LPTSTR *lpBuffer*,
LPTSTR * *lpFilePart*;

This function is used to return the fully qualified path name corresponding to the specified file name.

The **GetFullPathName** function may be used as either a wide-character function (where text arguments must use Unicode) or an ANSI function (where text arguments must use characters from the Windows 3.x character set installed).

Parameters   *lpFileName*   Supplies the file name of the file whose fully qualified pathname is to be returned.

nBufferLength   Supplies the length in bytes of the buffer that is to receive the fully qualified path.

lpBuffer   Returns the fully qualified pathname corresponding to the specified file.

lpFilePart   Returns the address of the last component of the fully qualified pathname.

Return Value   The return value is the length in bytes of the string copied to *lpBuffer*, not including the terminating null character. If the return value is greater than *nBufferLength*, the return value is the size of the buffer required to hold the pathname. The return value is zero if the function failed, in which case extended error information is available from the **GetLastError** function.

This function is used to return a fully qualified pathname corresponding to the specified filename. It does this by merging the current drive and directory together with the specified file name. In addition to this, it calculates the address of the file name portion of the fully qualified pathname. This function does not verify that the resulting pathname refers to an existing file or is otherwise a valid filename on the associated volume.

See Also   **SearchPath, GetTempPath**

■ GetGlyphOutline

DWORD GetGlyphOutline(_hdc, wChar, wFormat, lpMetrics, cbBuffer, lpBuffer, lpMatrix_**)**
HDC _hdc_;   /* device-context handle   */
WORD _wChar_,   /* character to query   */
WORD _wFormat_,   /* format of data to return   */
LPGLYPHMETRICS _lpMetrics_;   /* pointer to structure for metrics */
DWORD _cbBuffer_;   /* size of buffer for data   */
LPSTR _lpBuffer_,   /* pointer to buffer for data   */
LPMAT2 _lpMatrix_;   /* pointer to MAT2 structure   */

The **GetGlyphOutline** function retrieves the outline curve or bitmap for an outline character in the current font.

Parameters   _hdc_   Identifies the device context.

wChar   Specifies the character for which data is returned.

wFormat   Specifies the format in which the function returns the data. It can be one of the following values:

Value	Meaning
1	Return the glyph bitmap. See the following "Comments" section for information about memory allocation.
2	Return the curve data points in the rasterizer's native format and use the font's design units. When this value is specified, any transformation specified in the _lpMatrix_ parameter is ignored.

lpMetrics   Points to the **GLYPHMETRICS** structure describing the placement of the glyph in the character cell.

cbBuffer   Specifies the size of the buffer into which the function copies information about the outline character. If this value is zero, the function returns the required size of the buffer.

lpBuffer   Points to the buffer into which the function copies information about the outline character. If this value is NULL, the function returns the required size of the buffer.

lpMatrix Points to a **MAT2** structure specifying a transformation matrix for the character.

Return Value

The return value is the size of the buffer required for the retrieved information if either the *cbBuffer* or *lpBuffer* parameter is zero. Otherwise, it is a positive value if the function is successful, or 0xFFFFFFFF (–1) if there is an error.

Comments

The glyph outline returned by the **GetGlyphOutline** function is for a grid-fitted glyph. (A grid-fitted glyph has been modified so that its bitmapped image conforms as closely as possible to the original design of the glyph.) If an application needs an unmodified glyph outline, it should request the glyph outline for a character in a font whose size is equal to the font's EM units. The value for a font's EM units is stored in the **otmEMSquare** member of the **OUTLINETEXTMETRIC** structure.

An application can rotate characters retrieved in bitmap format by specifying a 2 by 2 transformation matrix in the *lpMatrix* parameter.

See Also

GetOutlineTextMetrics,

■ GetIconInfo

BOOL GetIconInfo(*hIcon, piconinfo***)**
HICON *hIcon*;
PICONINFO *piconinfo*;

The **GetIconInfo** function obtains information about an icon or cursor.

Parameters

hIcon A handle to the icon or cursor of interest.

piconinfo A pointer to an **ICONINFO** structure. The function will fill in the structure's fields. This structure is defined as follows:

```
typedef struct _ICONINFO {
    BOOL    fIcon;
    DWORD   xHotspot;
    DWORD   yHotspot;
    HBITMAP hbmMask;
    HBITMAP hbmColor;
} ICONINFO ;
```

For detailed information on the fields of this structure, see **ICONINFO**.

Return Value

If the function is successful, the return value is TRUE. Additionally, the function will fill in the fields of the **ICONINFO** structure pointed to by *piconinfo*. The function will create bitmaps for the *hbmMask* and *hbmColor* fields of this structure; it is the caller's responsibility to manage these bitmaps and delete them when they are no longer needed.

If the function fails, the return value is FALSE. Additional information may be obtained by calling **GetLastError**.

See Also   **CreateIcon, CreateIconFromResource, CreateIconIndirect, DestroyIcon, DrawIcon, LoadIcon, LookupIconIdFromDirectory**

■ GetInputDesktop

HANDLE GetInputDesktop(VOID)

The **GetInputDesktop** function returns an open handle to the desktop currently receiving input.

The calling process must have DESKTOP_ENUMERATE permission for the input desktop.

This function takes no parameters.

Return Value   If the function is successful, the return value is a handle to the input desktop.

If the function fails, the return value is NULL. Call **GetLastError** for more detailed error information.

■ GetInputState

BOOL GetInputState(void)

This function determines whether there are mouse, keyboard, or timer events in the current thread's message queue that require processing. An event is a record that describes hardware-level input. Mouse events occur when a user moves the mouse or clicks a mouse button. Keyboard events occur when a user presses one or more keys.

This function has no parameters.

Return Value   The return value specifies whether mouse or keyboard input occured. It is nonzero if input is detected. Otherwise, it is zero.

See Also   **GetQueueStatus**

■ GetInstanceData

The **GetInstanceData** function has been deleted. This function defines semantics that do not make sense in an environment where each application runs in its own address space.

■ GetJob

BOOL GetJob(*lpPrinter, JobId, lpJob, cbBuf, pcbNeeded***)**
LPPRINTER *lpPrinter;*
DWORD *JobId;*
LPJOB *lpJob;*
DWORD *cbBuf;*
LPDWORD *pcbNeeded;*

The **GetJob** function retrieves information about a print job on a specified printer.

Parameters

lpPrinter Pointer to a **PRINTER** data structure that specifies the printer where the print job resides.

The **PRINTER** data structure has the following form:

```
typedef struct tagPRINTER {
    DWORD cVersion;
    LPPRINTERSERVER lpPrinterServer;
    LPTSTR lpPrinterName;
    LPTSTR lpPortName;
    LPTSTR lpDriverName;
    LPTSTR lpComment;
    LPTSTR lpLocation;
    LPDEVMODE lpDevMode;
    LPTSTR lpSepFile;
    LPTSTR lpPrintProcessor;
    LPTSTR lpDatatype;
    LPTSTR lpParameters;
    LPTSTR lpVendorData;
    DWORD Attributes;
    DWORD Priority;
    DWORD DefaultPriority;
    SYSTEMTIME StartTime;
    SYSTEMTIME UntilTime;
    DWORD Status;
    DWORD cJobs;
    DWORD AveragePPM;
} PRINTER;
```

JobId A job identifier that specifies the print job of interest.

lpJob Pointer to a **JOB** structure whose fields the function will fill.

The **JOB** data structure has the following form:

```
typedef struct tagJOB {
    DWORD cVersion;
    DWORD JobId;
    LPPRINTERSERVER lpPrinterServer;
    LPTSTR lpPrinterName;
    LPTSTR lpUserName;
    LPTSTR lpDocument;
    LPTSTR lpNotifyName;
    LPTSTR lpDatatype;
    LPTSTR lpPrintProcessor;
    LPTSTR lpParameters;
    LPTSTR lpDriverName;
    LPDEVMODE lpDevMode;
    LPTSTR lpStatus;
    DWORD Status;
    DWORD Priority;
    DWORD Position;
```

```
      SYSTEMTIME StartTime;
      SYSTEMTIME UntilTime;
      DWORD TotalPages;
      DWORD PagesPrinted;
      DWORD Size;
      SYSTEMTIME Submitted;
      SYSTEMTIME Time;
} JOB;
```

cbBuf   The size in bytes of the buffer pointed to by *lpJob*.

pcbNeeded   Pointer to the amount of data required to store the **JOB** data structure. This will be set to zero if *cbBuf* is large enough.

Return Value   If the function is successful, the return value is TRUE.

If the function fails, the return value is FALSE/NULL. Extended error information can be obtained by calling **GetLastError**.

See Also   **SetJob, EnumJobs, GetJobFromHandle, JOB, PRINTER**

■ GetJobFromHandle

BOOL GetJobFromHandle(*hfile, lpJob, cbBuf, pcbNeeded***)**
HANDLE *hFile*;
LPJOB *lpJob*;
DWORD *cbBuf*;
LPDWORD *pcbNeeded*;

The **GetJobFromHandle** function retrieves information about a printer's spool job. The printer is specified using a file handle.

Parameters   *hFile*   A file handle that specifies the printer. This handle is created by opening a printer. Here are some examples:

```
      hFile = OpenFile("LPT1:");
      hFile = OpenFile("\dev\My Favorite Printer");
      hFile = OpenFile("\\server\printer");
```

lpJob   A pointer to a buffer in which the function will return a **JOB** data structure.

The **JOB** data structure has the following form:

cbBuf   Specifies the size in bytes of the buffer pointed to by *lpJob*.

pcbNeeded   Pointer to a DWORD which the function will set to the number of bytes required to store the **JOB** data structure returned in the buffer pointed to by *lpJob*. The DWORD will be set to zero if *cbBuf* was large enough.

Return Value   If the function is successful, the return value is TRUE.

If the function fails, the return value is FALSE. Further information can be obtained by calling **GetLastError**.

See Also   GetJob, SetJob, EnumJobs

■ GetKeyboardState

BOOL GetKeyboardState(_lpKeyState_**)**
LPKEYSTATE _lpKeyState_;

This function copies the status of the 256 virtual-keyboard keys to the buffer specified by the _lpKeyState_ parameter. The high bit of each byte is set to 1 if the key is down, or it is set to 0 if it is up. The low bit is set to 1 if the key was pressed an odd number of times since startup. Otherwise, it is set to 0.

Parameters   _lpKeyState_   Points to the 256-byte buffer of virtual-key codes.

Return Value   TRUE is returned for success, FALSE for failure.

Comments   An application can call this routine to get the current state of all the virtual keys on the keyboard. This state table is changed as a thread reads input messages out of its message queue. This table is not changed as input goes into the message queue.

To obtain state information for an individual key call **GetKeyState**.

See Appendix A for a list of virtual key code constants.

An application can use the virtual key code constants VK_SHIFT, VK_CONTROL and VK_MENU as indices into the buffer pointed to by _lpKeyState_. This gives the state of the Shift, Control, or Alt keys without distinguishing between left and right. An application can also use the following virtual key code constants as indices in order to distinguish between the left and right instances of those keys:

VK_LSHIFT	VK_RSHIFT
VK_LCONTROL	VK_RCONTROL
VK_LMENU	VK_RMENU

These left- and right-distinguishing constants are only exposed and available to an application when using the **GetKeyboardState**, **SetKeyboardState**, **GetAsyncKeyState**, **GetKeyState**, and **MapVirtualKey** functions.

See Also   **GetAsyncKeyState**, **GetKeyState**, **SetKeyboardState**, **MapVirtualKey**

■ GetKeyNameText

int GetKeyNameText(_lParam_, _lpString_, _nSize_**)**
LONG _lParam_;
LPTSTR _lpString_;
int _nSize_;

The **GetKeyNameText** function retrieves a string which contains the name of a key.

The keyboard driver maintains a list of names in the form of character strings for keys with names longer than a single character. The key name is translated according to the layout of the currently installed keyboard. The translation is performed for the principal language supported by the keyboard driver.

The **GetKeyNameText** function may be used as either a wide-character function (where text arguments must use Unicode) or an ANSI function (where text arguments must use characters from the Windows 3.x character set installed).

Parameters

lParam Specifies the 32-bit parameter of the keyboard message (such as WM_KEYDOWN) which the function is processing. Byte 3 (bits 16–23) of the long parameter is a scan code. Bit 24 is the extended bit that distinguishes some keys on an enhanced keyboard. Bit 25 is a don't care bit; the application calling this function sets this bit to indicate that the function should not distinguish between left and right control and shift keys, for example.

lpString Specifies a buffer to receive the key name.

nSize Specifies the maximum length in bytes of the key name, not including the terminating NULL character.

Return Value

The return value is the actual length in bytes of the string copied to *lpString*.

■ GetKeyState

SHORT GetKeyState(*nVirtKey***)**
int *nVirtKey*;

This function retrieves the state of the virtual key specified by the *nVirtKey* parameter. The state specifies whether the key is up, down, or toggled.

Parameters

nVirtKey Specifies a virtual key. If the desired virtual key is a letter or digit (A through Z, a through z,, or 0 through 9), nVirtKey must be set to the ASCII value of that character. For other keys, it must be one of the values listed in Appendix A, "Virtual-Key Codes" in Reference, Volume 2.

Return Value

The return value specifies the state of the given virtual key. If the high-order bit is 1, the key is down. Otherwise, it is up. If the low-order bit is 1, the key is toggled. A toggle key, such as the CAPSLOCK key, is toggled if it has been pressed an odd number of times since the system was started. The key is untoggled if the low bit is 0.

The key state returned from this function changes as a given thread reads key messages from its message queue. The state does not reflect the interrupt level state associated with the physical hardware. Use **GetAsyncKeyState** for that information.

Comments   An application calls the **GetKeyState** function in response to a keyboard-input message. This function retrieves the state of the key when the input message was generated.

To obtain state information for all the virtual keys call **GetKeyboardState**.

See Appendix A for a list of virtual key code constants.

An application can use the virtual key code constants VK_SHIFT, VK_CONTROL and VK_MENU as values for the *nVirtKey* parameter. This gives the state of the Shift, Control, or Alt keys without distinguishing between left and right. An application can also use the following virtual key code constants as values for *nVirtKey* in order to distinguish between the left and right instances of those keys:

VK_LSHIFT	VK_RSHIFT
VK_LCONTROL	VK_RCONTROL
VK_LMENU	VK_RMENU

These left- and right-distinguishing constants are only exposed and available to an application when using the **GetKeyboardState**, **SetKeyboardState**, **GetAsyncKeyState**, **GetKeyState**, and **MapVirtualKey** functions.

See Also   **GetAsyncKeyState, GetKeyboardState, SetKeyboardState, MapVirtualKey**

■ GetLargestConsoleWindowSize

COORD GetLargestConsoleWindowSize(*hConsoleOutput***)**
HANDLE *hConsoleOutput*;

The largest window possible, given the current font. The return value does not take the screen buffer size into account.

Parameters   *hConsoleOutput*   Supplies a console output handle.

Return Value   The return value is the maximum window size in rows and columns. A size of zero will be returned if an error occurs. Extended error information can be retrieved by calling the GetLastError function.

■ GetLastActivePopup

HWND GetLastActivePopup(*hWnd***)**
HWND *hWnd*;

This function determines which pop-up window owned by the window identified by the *hWnd* parameter was most recently active.

Parameters   *hWnd*   Identifies the owner window.

Return Value   The return value identifies the most-recently active pop-up window. The return value will be *hWnd* if any of the following conditions are met:

- The window identified by *hWnd* itself was most recently active.
- The window identified by *hWnd* does not own any pop-up windows.
- The window identified by *hWnd* is not a top-level window or is owned by another window.

See Also   **ShowOwnedPopups, AnyPopup**

■ GetLastError

DWORD GetLastError(VOID)

This function returns the most recent error code set by a Win32 API call. Applications should call this function immediately after a Win32 API call returns a failure indications (e.g. FALSE, NULL or –1) to determine the cause of the failure.

Return Value   The return value is the most recent error code for the current thread as set by a Win32 API call.

The last error code value is a per thread field, so that multiple threads do not overwrite each other's last error code value.

See Also   **SetLastError**

■ GetLengthSid

ULONG GetLengthSid(*Sid*)
PSID *Sid*;

The **GetLengthSid** function returns the length, in bytes, of a structurally valid **SID** security identifier.

Parameters   *Sid*   Pointer to the **SID** data structure whose length is to be returned. The **SID**'s structure is assumed to be valid. If the **SID** is invalid, the function return value is undefined.

The **SID** data structure is an opaque data structure of variable length, defined as follows:

```
typedef PVOID * PSID;
```

Return Value   If the function is successful, the return value is the length, in bytes, of the **SID**.

If the function fails, due to an invalid **SID**, the return value is undefined.

See Also   **CopySid, EqualSid, InitializeSid, IsValidSid, GetSidIdentifierAuthority, GetSidLengthRequired, GetSidSubAuthority, GetSidSubAuthorityCount**

■ GetLogicalDrives

DWORD GetLogicalDrives(void)

The **GetLogicalDrives** function returns a bitmask representing the current system's currently-available drives.

This function takes no parameters.

Return Value   The return value is a bitmask representing the current available drives on the system. Bit position 0 is drive A, bit position 1 is drive B, bit position 2 is drive C, and so on.

See Also   **GetLogicalDriveStrings**

■ GetLogicalDriveStrings

DWORD GetLogicalDriveStrings(*lpBuffer, dwSize*)
LPTSTR *lpBuffer*,
DWORD *dwSize*;

The **GetLogicalDriveStrings** function fills a buffer with valid drive strings for the system. Each string in the buffer may be used wherever a root directory of a drive is required, as with the **GetDriveType** and **GetDiskFreeSpace** functions.

The **GetLogicalDriveStrings** function may be used as either a wide-character function (where text arguments must use Unicode) or an ANSI function (where text arguments must use characters from the Windows 3.x character set installed).

Parameters   *lpBuffer*   Pointer to a buffer that the function will fill with a series of null-terminated strings, one for each valid drive in the system. The last string is null. Here's a sample of what the function might put into this buffer, with NULL standing for a null string terminator

        c:\NULLd:\NULL\\server\shareNULLNULL

dwSize   Specifies the maximum size (in bytes) of the buffer pointed to by *lpBuffer*. This size does not include the trailing NULL character.

Return Value   If the function succeeds, the return value is the length in bytes of the strings copied to the buffer pointed to by *lpBuffer*, not including the terminating null character. Note that an ANSI-ASCII null character uses one byte, a Unicode null character uses two bytes.

If the buffer is not large enough, the return value will be greater than *dwSize*. It is the size of the buffer required to hold the drive strings.

If the function fails, the return value is 0. Additional error information can be obtained by calling **GetLastError**.

See Also   **GetLogicalDrives**

■ GetMailslotInfo

BOOL GetMailslotInfo(*hMailslot, lpMaxMessageSize, lpMailslotSize, lpNextSize, lpMessageCount, lpReadTimout***)**
HANDLE *hMailslot*;
LPDWORD *lpMaxMessageSize*;   /* Optional */
LPDWORD *lpMailslotSize*;   /* Optional */
LPDWORD *lpNextSize*;   /* Optional */
LPDWORD *lpMessageCount*;   /* Optional */
LPDWORD *lpReadTimeout*;   /* Optional */

The **GetMailslotInfo** function gets information about a given mailslot. It also returns the first message, if any, that the mailslot contains.

Parameters

hMailslot   A server side mailslot handle.

lpMaxMessageSize   Maximum message size allowed for this mailslot, in bytes. This may be the same number as was passed to **CreateMailslot**, or larger.

lpMailslotSize   Mailslot size, in bytes. This may be the same number as was passed to **CreateMailslot**, or larger. If **CreateMailslot** is called with MAILSLOT_SIZE_AUTO for the mailslot size, **GetMailslotInfo** will return the calculated size in this parameter.

lpNextSize   Size of next message in bytes. It may be the following special value:

Value	Meaning
MAILSLOT_NO_MESSAGE	There is no next message.

lpMessageCount   Total number of messages waiting to be read.

lpReadTimeout   The amount of time, in milliseconds, a read operation can wait for a message to be written to the mailslot, before timing out.

Return Value

If the function is successful, the return value is TRUE. Additionally, the variables pointed to by the parameters are filled with the appropriate values.

If the function fails, the return value is FALSE. More detailed information can be obtained by calling the **GetLastError** function.

It is not an error if all of the pointers passed to **GetMailslotInfo** are NULL. However, this would have no effect on anything.

See Also   **SetMailslotInfo**, **CreateMailslot**

■ GetMapMode

int GetMapMode(*hDC***)**
HDC *hDC*;

The **GetMapMode** function retrieves the current mapping mode. See the **SetMapMode** function for a description of the mapping modes.

Parameters	*hDC* Identifies the device context.
Return Value	The return value specifies the mapping mode. Zero is returned if there is an error.
See Also	**SetMapMode**

■ GetMenu

HMENU GetMenu(*hWnd***)**
HWND *hWnd*;

This function retrieves a handle to the menu of the specified window.

Parameters	*hWnd* Identifies the window whose menu is to be examined.
Return Value	The return value identifies the menu. It is NULL if the given window has no menu. The return value is undefined if the window is a child window.
See Also	**SetMenu**

■ GetMenuCheckMarkDimensions

LONG GetMenuCheckMarkDimensions(void)

This function returns the dimensions of the default checkmark bitmap. Windows displays this bitmap next to checked menu items. Before calling the **SetMenuItemBitmaps** function to replace the default checkmark, an application should call the **GetMenuCheckMarkDimensions** function to determine the correct size for the bitmaps.

This function has no parameters.

Return Value	The return value specifies the height and width of the default checkmark bitmap. The high-order word contains the height in pixels and the low-order word contains the width.
See Also	**SetMenuItemBitmaps**

■ GetMenuItemCount

UINT GetMenuItemCount(*hMenu***)**
HMENU *hMenu*;

This function determines the number of items in the menu identified by the *hMenu* parameter. This may be either a pop-up or a top-level menu.

Parameters	*hMenu* Identifies the handle to the menu to be examined.
Return Value	The return value specifies the number of items in the menu specified by the *hMenu* parameter if the function is successful. Otherwise, it is −1.

See Also   **GetMenuItemID**

■ GetMenuItemID

UINT GetMenuItemID(*hMenu, nPos*)
HMENU *hMenu*;
int *nPos*;

This function obtains the menu-item identifier for a menu item located at the position defined by the *nPos* parameter.

Parameters   *hMenu*   Identifies a handle to the pop-up menu that contains the item whose ID is being retrieved.

nPos   Specifies the position (zero-based) of the menu item whose ID is being retrieved.

Return Value   The return value specifies the item ID for the specified item in a pop-up menu if the function is successful; if *hMenu* is NULL or if the specified item is a pop-up menu (as opposed to an item within the pop-up menu), the return value is −1.

See Also   **GetMenuItemCount**

■ GetMenuState

DWORD GetMenuState(*hMenu, wId, dwFlags*)
HMENU *hMenu*;
UINT *wId*;
UINT *dwFlags*;

This function obtains the number of items in the pop-up menu associated with the menu item specified by the *wId* parameter if the *hMenu* parameter identifies a menu with an associated pop-up menu. If *hMenu* identifies a pop-up menu, this function obtains the status of the menu item associated with *wId*.

Parameters   *hMenu*   Identifies the menu.

wId   Specifies the menu-item ID.

dwFlags   Specifies the nature of the *wId* parameter. If the *dwFlags* parameter contains MF_BYPOSITION, *wId* specifies a (zero-based) relative position; if *dwFlags* contains MF_BYCOMMAND, *wId* specifies the item ID.

Return Value   The return value specifies the outcome of the function. It is −1 if the specified item does not exist. If the menu itself does not exist, a fatal exit occurs. If *wId* identifies a pop-up menu, the return value contains the number of items in the pop-up menu in bits 15–8, and the menu flags associated with the pop-up menu in bits 7–0 (the low-order byte); otherwise, it is a mask (Boolean OR) of the values from the following list (this mask describes the status of the menu item that *wId* identifies):

Value	Meaning
MF_CHECKED	Checkmark is placed next to item (pop-up menus only).
MF_DISABLED	Item is disabled.
MF_ENABLED	Item is enabled.
MF_GRAYED	Item is disabled and grayed.
MF_MENUBARBREAK	Same as MF_MENUBREAK, except for pop-up menus where the new column is separated from the old column by a vertical dividing line.
MF_MENUBREAK	Item is placed on a new line (static menus) or in a new column (pop-up menus) without separating columns.
MF_SEPARATOR	Horizontal dividing line is drawn (pop-up menus only). This line cannot be enabled, checked, grayed, or highlighted. The *lpNewItem* and *wIDNewItem* parameters are ignored.
MF_UNCHECKED	Checkmark is not placed next to item (default).

See Also **GetMenuString, GetMenu, GetMenuItemCount, GetMenuItemID**

■ GetMenuString

int GetMenuString(*hMenu, wIDItem, lpString, nMaxCount, dwFlag***)**
HMENU *hMenu*;
UINT *wIDItem*;
LPTSTR *lpString*;
int *nMaxCount*;
DWORD *dwFlag*;

This function copies the label of the specified menu item into the *lpString* parameter.

The **GetMenuString** function may be used as either a wide-character function (where text arguments must use Unicode) or an ANSI function (where text arguments must use characters from the Windows 3.x character set installed).

Parameters *hMenu* Identifies the menu.

wIDItem Specifies the identifier of the menu item (from the resource file) or the offset of the menu item in the menu, depending on

the value of the *dwFlag* parameter.

lpString   Points to the buffer that is to receive the label.

nMaxCount   Specifies the maximum length in bytes of the label to be copied. If the label is longer than the maximum specified in *nMaxCount*, the extra characters are truncated.

dwFlag   Specifies the nature of the *wID* parameter. If *dwFlag* contains MF_BYPOSITION, *wId* specifies a (zero-based) relative position; if the *dwFlag* parameter contains MF_BYCOMMAND, *wId* specifies the item ID.

Return Value   The return value specifies the actual number of bytes copied to the buffer.

Comments   The *nMaxCount* parameter should be the size of a NULL character (one for ANSI-ASCII, two for Unicode) larger than the number of bytes in the label to accommodate the null character that terminates a string.

■ GetMessage

BOOL GetMessage(*lpMsg, hWnd, wMsgFilterMin, wMsgFilterMax***)**
LPMSG *lpMsg*;
HWND *hWnd*;
UINT *wMsgFilterMin*;
UINT *wMsgFilterMax*;

This function retrieves a message from the thread queue and places the message in the structure pointed to by the *lpMsg* parameter.

GetMessage retrieves only messages associated with the window specified by the *hWnd* parameter and within the range of message values given by the *wMsgFilterMin* and *wMsgFilterMax* parameters. If *hWnd* is NULL, **GetMessage** retrieves messages for any window that belongs to the application making the call. (The **GetMessage** function does not retrieve messages for windows that belong to other threads.) If *wMsgFilterMin* and *wMsgFilterMax* are both zero, **GetMessage** returns all available messages (no filtering is performed).

The constants WM_KEYFIRST and WM_KEYLAST can be used as filter values to retrieve all messages related to keyboard input; the constants WM_MOUSEFIRST and WM_MOUSELAST can be used to retrieve all mouse-related messages.

Parameters   *lpMsg*   Points to an **MSG** structure that contains message information from the Windows application queue.

hWnd   Identifies the window whose messages are to be examined. If *hWnd* is NULL, **GetMessage** retrieves messages for any window that belongs to the application making the call.

wMsgFilterMin   Specifies the integer value of the lowest message value to be retrieved.

wMsgFilterMax   Specifies the integer value of the highest message value to be retrieved.

Return Value   The return value is TRUE if a message other than WM_QUIT is retrieved. It is FALSE if the WM_QUIT message is retrieved.

The return value is usually used to decide whether to terminate the application's main loop and exit the program.

See Also   **PeekMessage, WaitMessage**

■ GetMessageExtraInfo

LONG GetMessageExtraInfo(VOID)

The **GetMessageExtraInfo** function retrieves the extra information associated with the last message retrieved by the **GetMessage** function.

Parameters   This function has no parameters.

This function does not have any parameters.

Return Value   The return value specifies the extra information.

See Also   **GetMessage**

■ GetMessagePos

DWORD GetMessagePos(void)

The **GetMessagePos** function what the position of the cursor was when the last message obtained by the **GetMessage** function was sent. The position is in screen coordinates.

This function has no parameters.

Return Value   The return value specifies the *x*- and *y*-coordinates of the cursor position. The *x*-coordinate is in the low-order word of the DWORD return value, and the *y*-coordinate is in the high-order word. You can use the **LOWORD** and **HIWORD** macros to extract these coordinates.

Comments   To obtain the current position of the cursor instead of the position when the last message occurred, use the **GetCursorPos** function.

See Also   **GetCursorPos, GetMessage**

■ GetMessageTime

LONG GetMessageTime(void)

This function returns the message time for the last message retrieved by the **GetMessage** function. The time is a long integer that specifies the elapsed time (in milliseconds) from the time the system was booted to the time the message was created (placed in the application queue).

This function has no parameters.

Return Value

The return value specifies the message time.

Comments

Do not assume that the return value is always increasing. The return value will wrap around to zero if the timer count exceeds the maximum value for long integers.

To calculate time delays between messages, subtract the time of the second message from the time of the first message.

■ GetMetaFileEx

HMF GetMetaFileEx(*lpFilename***)**
LPTSTR *lpFilename*;

The **GetMetaFileEx** function creates a handle for the metafile named by the *lpFilename* parameter.

The **GetMetaFileEx** function may be used as either a wide-character function (where text arguments must use Unicode) or an ANSI function (where text arguments must use characters from the Windows 3.x character set.

Parameters

lpFilename   Points to the null-terminated character filename that specifies the metafile. The metafile must already exist.

Return Value

The return value identifies a metafile if the function is successful. Otherwise, it is 0.

Comments

When the application no longer requires the metafile handle, it should free the handle by calling the **DeleteMetaFileEx** function.

The **GetMetaFileEx** function does not accept the Windows 3.x metafiles. To import Windows 3.x metafiles, use the **SetMetaFileBitsEx** function.

See Also

SetMetaFileBitsEx.

■ GetMetaFileBitsEx

DWORD GetMetaFileBitsEx(*hMF, nSize, lpData, iFormat, hDCRef***)**
HMF *hMF*;
DWORD *nSize*;
LPBYTE *lpData*;
UINT *iFormat*;
HDC *hDCRef*;

The **GetMetaFileBitsEx** function retrieves the contents of the specified metafile and copies them into the buffer pointed to by the *lpData* parameter.

Parameters

hMF   Identifies the metafile.

nSize   Specifies the size, in bytes, of the buffer reserved for the data.

lpData   Points to the buffer to receive the metafile data. The buffer must be sufficiently large to contain the data. If this pointer is NULL, the function returns the size necessary to hold the data.

iFormat   Specifies the format the metafile data should be returned in. It must be one of the following values:

Value	Meaning
META_FORMAT_10000	Windows NT metafile format with version number 0x10000. This is the default format.
META_FORMAT_300	Windows 3.0 metafile format with version number 0x300.

hDCRef   Identifies the reference device if *iFormat* is META_FORMAT_300. Otherwise it is not used. The reference device context defines the mapping mode and units of the metafile contents to be retrieved.

Return Value

The return value is the size of the metafile data in bytes. If an error occurs, 0 is returned.

Comments

The **GetMetaFileBitsEx** function does not invalidate the metafile handle *hMF*.

An application may use this function to export metafiles to the Windows 3.x systems. It should be aware that although metafiles are generally scalable in Windows NT, it is not always the case in the Windows 3.x systems. Some GDI functions such as **SelectClipRgn** use device units and are not scalable in Windows 3.x. There is also a potential loss of information and precision due to the conversion and complexity of some GDI calls.

The Windows 3.0 metafile retrieved from this function does not contain any **SetViewportOrg** and **SetViewportExt** calls. It has a **SetMapMode** record with a mapping mode identical to that of the reference device context. The upper left corner of the metafile picture will start at the origin of the reference device.

To retrieve a scalable Windows 3.0 metafile, the reference device context must have the MM_ANISOTROPIC mapping mode. In this case, the window extents are set to the extents of the metafile picture in the device units of the reference device and recorded in a **SetWindowExt** call. The metafile picture will be scaled correctly on a Windows 3.x system because Windows 3.x applications define the viewport origin and viewport extents before playing such a metafile.

See Also

SetMetaFileBitsEx

■ GetModuleFileName

DWORD GetModuleFileName(hModule, lpFilename, dwSize**)**
HANDLE hModule;
LPTSTR lpFilename;
DWORD dwSize;

The **GetModuleFileName** function retrieves the full pathname of the executable file from which the specified module was loaded. The function copies the null-terminated filename into the buffer pointed to by the lpFilename parameter.

The **GetModuleFileName** function may be used as either a wide-character function (where text arguments must use Unicode) or an ANSI function (where text arguments must use characters from the Windows 3.x character set installed).

Parameters
hModule   Identifies the module whose executable file name is being requested. A value of NULL references the module handle associated with the .EXE file that was used to create the current process.

lpFilename   Points to the buffer that is to receive the filename.

dwSize   Specifies the maximum number of bytes to copy. If the filename is longer than the maximum number of bytes specified by the dwSize parameter, it is truncated.

Return Value
The return value specifies the actual length in bytes of the string copied to the buffer.

A return value of zero indicates an error and extended error status is available using the **GetLastError** function.

■ GetModuleHandle

HANDLE GetModuleHandle(lpModuleName**)**
LPTSTR lpModuleName;

The **GetModuleHandle** function retrieves the handle of a module that is currently loaded in the context of the calling process.

The module handle this function returns should be used carefully in a multi-thread environment. See the comments below.

The **GetModuleHandle** function may be used as either a wide-character function (where text arguments must use Unicode) or an ANSI function (where text arguments must use characters from the Windows 3.x character set installed).

Parameters
lpModuleName   Points to a string that names the library file. The string must be null-terminated. If this parameter is NULL, then the handle for the current application's .EXE file is returned. This handle is useful for finding resources in the .EXE file.

Return Value
The return value is a module handle if the function is successful. A return value of NULL indicates either that the module has not been loaded into the context of the

current process or an error occured. The exact reason is available using the **GetLastError** function.

Comments

In a multi-threaded program, this function must be used with care. Between receiving the module handle from this call, and using that handle in a subsequent call, another thread (in the same process) could preempt the currently running thread and free the module, thus rendering the module handle invalid. Or, worse, another module could have been loaded and received the same module handle, causing the caller's handle to refer to a different module than the one intended.

See Also

LoadModule, FreeModule, GetModuleFileName, GetProcAddress

■ GetModuleUsage

The **GetModuleUsage** function has been deleted. This function defines semantics that do not make sense in an environment where each application runs in its own address space.

■ GetMsgProc

void FAR PASCAL GetMsgProc(nCode, wParam, lParam**)**
int nCode;   /* process-message flag   */
WORD wParam,   /* undefined   */
DWORD lParam,   /* pointer to MSG structure */

The **GetMsgProc** function is a library-defined callback function that the system calls whenever the **GetMessage** function has retrieved a message from an application queue. The system passes the retrieved message to the callback function before passing the message to the destination window procedure.

Parameters

nCode   Specifies whether the callback function should process the message or call the **DefHookProc** function. If the nCode parameter is less than zero, the callback function should pass the message to **DefHookProc** without further processing.

wParam   Specifies a NULL value.

lParam   Points to an **MSG** structure that contains information about the message. The **MSG** structure has the following form:

```
typedef struct tagMSG {        /* msg */
    HWND    hwnd;
    WORD    message;
    WORD    wParam;
    LONG    lParam;
    DWORD   time;
    POINT   pt;
} MSG;
```

Comments

The **GetMsgProc** callback function can examine or modify the message as desired. Once the callback function returns control to the system, the **GetMessage** function returns the message, with any modifications, to the application that originally called it. The callback function does not require a return value.

This callback function must reside in a dynamic-link library.

An application must install the callback function by specifying the WH_GETMESSAGE filter type and the procedure-instance address of the callback function in a call to the **SetWindowsHook** function.

GetMsgProc is a placeholder for the library-supplied function name. The actual name must be exported by including it in an **EXPORTS** statement in the library's module-definition file.

See Also   **DefHookProc, GetMessage, SetWindowsHook**

■ GetNamedPipeHandleState

BOOL GetNamedPipeHandleState(*hNamedPipe, lpState, lpCurInstances, lpMaxCollectionCount,*
         *lpCollectDataTimeout, lpUserName, nMaxUserNameSize***)**
HANDLE *hNamedPipe;*
LPDWORD *lpState;*
LPDWORD *lpCurInstances;*
LPDWORD *lpMaxCollectionCount;*
LPDWORD *lpCollectDataTimeout;*
LPTSTR *lpUserName;*
DWORD *nMaxUserNameSize;*

The **GetNamedPipeHandleState** function retrieves information about a given named pipe handle. The information returned by this function can vary during the lifetime of an instance of a named pipe. The handle must be created with the GENERIC_READ access rights.

The **GetNamedPipeHandleState** function may be used as either a wide-character function (where text arguments must use Unicode) or an ANSI function (where text arguments must use characters from the Windows 3.x character set installed).

Parameters   *hNamedPipe*   Supplies the handle of an opened named pipe.

lpState   An optional parameter that if non-null, points to a DWORD which will be set with flags indicating the current state of the handle. The following flags may be specified:

Value	Meaning
PIPE_NOWAIT	Nonblocking mode is to be used for this handle.
PIPE_READMODE_MESSAGE	Read the pipe as a message stream. If this flag is not set, the pipe is read as a byte stream.

lpCurInstances   An optional parameter that if non-null, points to a DWORD which will be set with the number of current pipe instances.

lpMaxCollectionCount   If non-null, this points to a DWORD which will be set to the maximum number of bytes that will be collected on the client's machine before transmission to the server. This parameter must be NULL on a handle to the server end of a named pipe or when client and server applications are on the same machine.

lpCollectDataTimeout   If non-null, this points to a DWORD which will be set to the maximum time (in milliseconds) that can pass before a remote named pipe transfers information over the network. This parameter must be NULL if the handle is for the server end of a named pipe or when client and server applications are on the same machine.

lpUserName   An optional parameter on the server end of a named pipe. Points to an area which will be filled-in with the null-terminated string containing the name of the username of the client application. This parameter is invalid if not NULL on a handle to a client end of a named pipe.

nMaxUserNameSize   Size in bytes of the memory allocated at **lpUserName**. Ignored if **lpUserName** is NULL.

Return Value   The return value is TRUE if the function is successful. Otherwise, it is FALSE in which case extended error information is available from the **GetLastError** function.

Comments   It is not an error if all of the pointers passed to this function are null.

See Also   **SetNamedPipeHandleState**

■ GetNamedPipeInfo

BOOL GetNamedPipeInfo(*hNamedPipe, lpFlags, lpOutBufferSize, lpInBufferSize, lpMaxInstances***)**
HANDLE *hNamedPipe*;
LPDWORD *lpFlags*;
LPDWORD *lpOutBufferSize*;
LPDWORD *lpInBufferSize*;
LPDWORD *lpMaxInstances*;

The **GetNamedPipeInfo** function retrieves information about a named pipe. The information returned by this API is preserved the lifetime of an instance of a named pipe. The handle must be created with the GENERIC_READ access rights.

Parameters   *hNamedPipe*   Supplies a handle to a named pipe.

lpFlags   An optional parameter that if non-null, points to a DWORD which will be set with flags indicating the type of named pipe and handle.

lpFlags:

Value	Meaning
PIPE_END_SERVER	The handle is the server end of a named pipe.
PIPE_TYPE_MESSAGE	The pipe is a message-stream pipe. If this flag is not set, the pipe is a byte-stream pipe.

lpOutBufferSize   An optional parameter that if non-null, points to a DWORD which will be set with the size (in bytes) of the buffer for outgoing data. A return value of zero indicates the buffer is allocated as needed.

lpInBufferSize   An optional parameter that if non-null, points to a DWORD which will be set with the size (in bytes) of the buffer for incoming data. A return value of zero indicates the buffer is allocated as needed.

lpMaxInstances   An optional parameter that if non-null, points to a DWORD which will be set with the maximum number of pipe instances that can be created. Besides various numeric values, a special value may be returned for this.

lpMaxInstances Special Values:

Value	Meaning
PIPE_UNLIMITED_INSTANCES	Unlimited instances of the pipe can be created. This is an indicator that the maximum is requested; the value of the equate may be higher or lower than the actual implementation's limit, which may vary over time.

Return Value   The return value is TRUE if the function is successful. Otherwise, it is FALSE in which case extended error information is available from the **GetLastError** function.

Comments   It is not an error if all of the pointers passed to this function are null. However, there is no reason for calling it this way.

■ GetNearestColor

COLORREF GetNearestColor(*hDC, crColor***)**
HDC *hDC*;
COLORREF *crColor*,

The **GetNearestColor** function returns the RGB color that will be displayed when the given color reference is used.

Parameters   *hDC*   The device context.

crColor   Color to be matched.

Return Value   The return value is the nearest RGB color is successful, otherwise it is CLR_INVALID.

■ GetNearestPaletteIndex

UINT GetNearestPaletteIndex(*hPalette, crColor***)**
HPALETTE *hPalette*;
COLORREF *crColor*,

The function returns the index of the entry in a logical palette which most closely matches a color value. If this call is made on palettes with any PC_EXPLICIT entries the return value in undefined.

Parameters   *hPalette*   Identifies the logical palette.

crColor   Specifies the color to be matched.

Return Value   The return value is the index of an entry in a logical palette. The entry contains the color which most nearly matches the specified color. CLR_INVALID is returned if an error occurs.

■ GetNextDlgGroupItem

HWND GetNextDlgGroupItem(*hDlg, hCtl, bPrevious***)**
HWND *hDlg,*
HWND *hCtl,*
BOOL *bPrevious;*

This function searches for the next (or previous) control within a group of controls in the dialog box identified by the *hDlg* parameter. A group of controls consists of one or more controls with WS_GROUP style.

Parameters   *hDlg*   Identifies the dialog box being searched.

hCtl   Identifies the control in the dialog box where the search starts.

bPrevious   Specifies how the function is to search the group of controls in the dialog box. If the *bPrevious* parameter is nonzero, the function searches for the previous control in the group. If *bPrevious* is zero, the function searches for the next control in the group.

Return Value   The return value identifies the next or previous control in the group.

Comments   If the current item is the last item in the group and *bPrevious* is zero, the **GetNextDlgGroupItem** function returns the window handle of the first item in the group. If the current item is the first item in the group and *bPrevious* is nonzero, **GetNextDlgGroupItem** returns the window handle of the last item in the group.

See Also   **GetNextDlgTabItem**

■ GetNextDlgTabItem

HWND GetNextDlgTabItem(*hDlg, hCtl, bPrevious***)**
HWND *hDlg,*
HWND *hCtl,*
BOOL *bPrevious;*

This function obtains the handle of the first control that has the WS_TABSTOP style that precedes (or follows) the control identified by the *hCtl* parameter.

Parameters	*hDlg* Identifies the dialog box being searched.
	hCtl Identifies the control to be used as a starting point for the search.
	bPrevious Specifies how the function is to search the dialog box. If the *bPrevious* parameter is nonzero, the function searches for the previous control in the dialog box. If *bPrevious* is zero, the function searches for the next control in the dialog box. Identifies the control to be used as a starting point for the search.
Return Value	The return value identifies the previous (or next) control that has the WS_TABSTOP style set.
See Also	**GetNextDlgGroupItem**

■ GetNextWindow

HWND GetNextWindow(*hWnd, wCmd***)**
HWND *hWnd*;
WORD *wCmd*;

This function searches for a handle that identifies the next (or previous) window in the window-manager's list. The window-manager's list contains entries for all top-level windows, their associated child windows, and the child windows of any child windows. If the *hWnd* parameter is a handle to a top-level window, the function searches for the next (or previous) handle to a top-level window; if *hWnd* is a handle to a child window, the function searches for a handle to the next (or previous) child window.

Parameters   *hWnd*   Identifies the current window.

wCmd   Specifies whether the function returns a handle to the next window or to the previous window. It can be either of the following values:

Value	Meaning
GW_HWNDNEXT	The function returns a handle to the next window.
GW_HWNDPREV	The function returns a handle to the previous window.

Return Value   The return value identifies the next (or the previous) window in the window-manager's list.

See Also   **GetWindow, GetTopWindow**

■ GetNumberOfConsoleInputEvents

BOOL GetNumberOfConsoleInputEvents(*hConsoleInput, lpNumberOfEvents***)**
HANDLE *hConsoleInput*;
LPDWORD *lpNumberOfEvents*;

This API may be used to query the number of events in the input queue.

Parameters
hConsoleInput Supplies an open handle to console input.

lpNumberOfEvents Points to a DWORD that the function will set on exit to the number of events in the input queue.

Return Value
If the function is successful, the return value is TRUE.

If the function fails, or the end of the file is reached, the return value is FALSE. Extended error information can be obtained by calling the **GetLastError** function.

■ GetNumberOfConsoleMouseButtons

BOOL GetNumberOfConsoleMouseButtons(*lpNumberOfMouseButtons*)
LPDWORD *lpNumberOfMouseButtons*;

The **GetNumberOfConsoleMouseButtons** function determines the number of buttons the console's mouse has.

Parameters
lpNumberOfMouseButtons A pointer to a DWORD which the function will set to the number of buttons.

Return Value
If the function is successful, the return value is TRUE. Additionally, the function will place the number of mouse buttons into the DWORD pointed to by *lpNumberOfMouseButtons*.

If the function is unsuccessful, the return value is FALSE. Extended error information can be obtained by calling **GetLastError**.

■ GetNumTasks

WORD GetNumTasks(void)

The **GetNumTasks** function returns the number of currently running tasks.

Parameters
This function has no parameters.

Return Value
The return value specifies the number of current tasks.

■ GetObject

int GetObject(*hObject, nCount, lpObject*)
HANDLE *hObject*;
int *nCount*;
LPVOID *lpObject*;

The **GetObject** function fills a buffer with the data that defines the logical object specified by the *hObject* parameter. The **GetObject** function copies *nCount* bytes of data to the buffer pointed to by *lpObject*. The function retrieves data structures of the **LOGPEN, LOGBRUSH, LOGFONT,** or **BITMAP** type, or an integer, depending on the logical object. The buffer must be sufficiently large to receive the data.

If *hObject* specifies a bitmap, the function returns only the width, height, and color format information of the bitmap. The actual bits must be retrieved by using the **GetDIBits** function.

If *hObject* specifies a logical palette, it retrieves a two-byte value that specifies the number of entries in the palette; it does not retrieve the entire **LOGPALETTE** structure that defines the palette. To get information on palette entries, an application must call the **GetPaletteEntries** function.

Parameters   *hObject*   Identifies a logical pen, brush, font, bitmap, or palette.

nCount   Specifies the number of bytes to be copied to the buffer.

lpObject   Points to the buffer that is to receive the information. If NULL, then the return value contains the number of bytes needed for the logical object.

Return Value   The return value specifies the actual number of bytes retrieved, or the number of bytes needed to hold the object if *lpObject* was NULL. It is zero if an error occurs.

See Also   **GetDIBits, GetPaletteEntries**

■ GetObjectSecurity

BOOL GetObjectSecurity(*handle, pRequestedInformation, pSecurityDescriptor, nLength,*
     *lpnLengthNeeded***)**
HANDLE *handle*;
PSECURITY_INFORMATION *pRequestedInformation*;
PSECURITY_DESCRIPTOR *pSecurityDescriptor*;
DWORD *nLength*;
LPDWORD *lpnLengthNeeded*;

The **GetObjectSecurity** function obtains specified information about the security status of an object. The information obtained is constrained by the caller's access rights and privileges.

The **GetObjectSecurity** function fills the buffer pointed to by *pSecurityDescriptor* with a copy of the object's security descriptor containing the requested security descriptor fields, based on the caller's access rights and privileges. In order to read the object's security descriptor, the caller must have READ_CONTROL access or be the owner of the object. Additionally, the caller must have SeSecurityPrivilege privilege to read the system ACL.

Parameters   *handle*   Object handle of a windowstation, desktop, window, menu, DDE access, DDE conversation, or base object whose security status this function will obtain.

pRequestedInformation   A pointer to a **SECURITY_INFORMATION** data structure that specifies the security information being requested.

The **SECURITY_INFORMATION** data structure has the following form:

```
typedef ULONG SECURITY_INFORMATION;
```

pSecurityDescriptor   A pointer to a buffer that the function will fill with a copy of the security descriptor of the object specified by *handle*. As noted above, the caller must have the right to view the specified aspects of the object's security status. The **SECURITY_DESCRIPTOR** data structure is returned in self-relative format.

The **SECURITY_DESCRIPTOR** data structure has the following form:

```
typedef PVOID PSECURITY_DESCRIPTOR;
```

nLength   Specifies the size in bytes of the buffer pointed to by *pSecurityDescriptor*.

lpnLengthNeeded   Pointer to a variable that the function will set to the number of bytes needed to store the complete security descriptor. If the value set is less than or equal to *nLength*, then the entire security descriptor is returned in the buffer pointed to by *pSecurityDescriptor*. Otherwise none of the descriptor is returned.

Return Value   If the function is successful, the return value is TRUE.

If the function fails, the return value is FALSE. The function will fail if access is denied or if the buffer pointed to by *pSecurityDescriptor* is too small to hold the security descriptor. Call **GetLastError** for more detailed error information.

See Also   **SetObjectSecurity, GetFileSecurity, SetFileSecurity, CreateUserObjectSecurity, DestroyUserObjectSecurity, GetUserObjectSecurity, SetUserObjectSecurity**

■ GetOpenClipboardWindow

HWND GetOpenClipboardWindow(VOID)

The **GetOpenClipboardWindow** function retrieves the handle of the window that currently has the clipboard open.

Parameters   This function has no parameters.

This function has no parameters.

Return Value   The return value is the handle of the window that has the clipboard open. If the clipboard is not open, the return value is NULL.

See Also   **GetClipboardOwner, GetClipboardViewer, OpenClipboard**

■ GetOpenFileName

BOOL GetOpenFileName(*lpofn*)
LPOPENFILENAME *lpofn*;   /* pointer to structure with initialization data */

The **GetOpenFileName** function creates a system-defined dialog box that allows the user to specify the name of a file to open.

Parameters

lpofn   Points to an **OPENFILENAME** structure that contains information used to initialize the dialog box. When the **GetOpenFileName** function returns, this structure contains information about the user's file selection.

The **OPENFILENAME** structure has the following form:

```
typedef struct tagOFN { /* ofn */
    DWORD    lStructSize;
    HWND     hwndOwner;
    HANDLE   hInstance;
    LPSTR    lpstrFilter;
    LPSTR    lpstrCustomFilter;
    DWORD    nMaxCustFilter;
    DWORD    nFilterIndex;
    LPSTR    lpstrFile;
    DWORD    nMaxFile;
    LPSTR    lpstrFileTitle;
    DWORD    nMaxFileTitle;
    LPSTR    lpstrInitialDir;
    LPSTR    lpstrTitle;
    DWORD    Flags;
    WORD     nFileOffset;
    WORD     nFileExtension;
    LPSTR    lpstrDefExt;
    DWORD    lCustData;
    WORD (FAR PASCAL *lpfnHook)(HWND, unsigned, WORD, LONG);
    LPSTR    lpTemplateName;
} OPENFILENAME;
```

For a full description, see TBD.

Return Value

The return value is TRUE if the user if the user specifies the name of a file to open. It is FALSE if the user cancels or closes the dialog box, or if the buffer identified by the **lpstrFile** member of the **OPENFILENAME** structure is too small to contain the selected filename string.

Errors

Use the **CommDlgExtendedError** function to retrieve the error value, which may be one of the following:

CDERR_FINDRESFAILURE
CDERR_INITIALIZATION
CDERR_LOCKRESFAILURE
CDERR_LOADRESFAILURE
CDERR_LOADSTRFAILURE
CDERR_MEMALLOCFAILURE
CDERR_MEMLOCKFAILURE
CDERR_NOHINSTANCE
CDERR_NOHOOK
CDERR_NOTEMPLATE
CDERR_STRUCTSIZE

See Also

GetSaveFileName

■ GetOutlineTextMetrics

DWORD GetOutlineTextMetrics(*hdc, cbData, lpOTM***)**
HDC *hdc*;   /* device-context handle   */
WORD *cbData*;   /* size of data to return   */
LPOUTLINETEXTMETRIC *lpOTM*;   /* pointer to structure for metrics */

The **GetOutlineTextMetrics** function retrieves metric data for TrueType fonts.

Parameters

hdc   Identifies the device context.

cbData   Specifies the size (in bytes) of the data to be returned by this function.

lpOTM   Points to an **OUTLINETEXTMETRIC** data structure. If this parameter is NULL, the function returns the size of the buffer required for the retrieved metric data.

Return Value

The return value is TRUE or the size of the buffer required for the metric data if the function is successful. Otherwise, it is FALSE.

Comments

The **OUTLINETEXTMETRIC** structure contains most of the font metric information provided with the TrueType format, including a **TEXTMETRIC** structure. The sizes returned in these structures are in logical units; they depend on the current mapping mode.

NOTE   The order of the structure elements may change for the final release of TrueType.

See Also   **GetTextMetrics**

■ GetOverlappedResult

BOOL GetOverlappedResult(*hFile, lpOverlapped, lpNumberOfBytesTransferred, bWait***)**
HANDLE *hFile*;
LPOVERLAPPED *lpOverlapped*;
LPDWORD *lpNumberOfBytesTransferred*;
BOOLEAN *bWait*;

The **GetOverlappedResult** function returns the result of the last operation that used *lpOverlapped* and returned ERROR_IO_PENDING.

Parameters

hFile   Supplies the open handle to the file that the overlapped structure *lpOverlapped* was supplied to *ReadFile*, *WriteFile*, *ConnectNamedPipe* or *TransactNamedPipe*.

lpOverlapped   Points to an **OVERLAPPED** structure previously supplied to *ReadFile*, *WriteFile*, *ConnectNamedPipe* or *TransactNamedPipe*.

The **OVERLAPPED** structure has the following form:

```
typedef struct _OVERLAPPED {
    DWORD    Internal;
    DWORD    InternalHigh;
    DWORD    Offset;
```

```
        DWORD   OffsetHigh;
        HANDLE  hEvent:
} OVERLAPPED:
typedef OVERLAPPED *LPOVERLAPPED:
```

lpNumberOfBytesTransferred Returns the number of bytes transferred by the operation.

bWait A boolean value that affects the behavior when the operation is still in progress. If TRUE and the operation is still in progress, **GetOverlappedResult** will wait for the operation to complete before returning. If FALSE and the operation is incomplete, **GetOverlappedResult** will return FALSE. In this case the extended error information available from the **GetLastError** function will be set to ERROR_IO_INCOMPLETE.

Return Value The return value is TRUE if the function is successful. Otherwise, it is FALSE in which case extended error information is available from the **GetLastError** function.

Comments **GetOverlappedResult** waits on the event specified by the *hEvent* member of the **OVERLAPPED** structure. If *hEvent* is null, **GetOverlappedResult** waits on *hFile*.

If *hEvent* refers to an auto-reset event, the caller must not wait on the event after initiating the transfer until **GetOverlappedResult** is called. Otherwise the caller's wait would reset the event to the not-signalled state, causing **GetOverlappedResult** to block indefinitely.

See Also **GetLastError, CreateEvent, OVERLAPPED**

■ GetPaletteEntries

UINT GetPaletteEntries(*hPalette, iStartIndex, nNumEntries, lpPaletteEntries***)**
HPALETTE *hPalette*;
UINT *iStartIndex*;
UINT *nNumEntries*;
LPPALETTEENTRY *lpPaletteEntries*;

The **GetPaletteEntries** function retrieves a range of palette entries in a logical palette.

Parameters *hPalette* Identifies the logical palette.

iStartIndex Specifies the first entry in the logical palette to be retrieved.

nNumEntries Specifies the number of entries in the logical palette to be retrieved.

lpPaletteEntries Points to an array of **PALETTEENTRY** structures to receive the palette entries. The array must contain at least as many data structures as specified by the *ulNumEntries* parameter. If this parameter is NULL, then the number of entries in the palette will be returned.

Return Value	The return value is the number of entries retrieved from the logical palette if querying entries, or the number of entries in the palette if lpPaletteEntries was NULL. It is zero if the function failed.
Comment	If nNumEntries specifies more entries than exist in the palette, the remaining fields of lpPaletteEntries will not be altered.

■ GetParent

HWND GetParent(*hWnd***)**
HWND *hWnd*;

	This function retrieves the window handle of the specified window's parent window (if any).
Parameters	*hWnd* Identifies the window whose parent window handle is to be retrieved.
Return Value	The return value identifies the parent window. It is NULL if the window has no parent window.
See Also	**SetParent**

■ GetPixel

DWORD GetPixel(*hDC, X, Y***)**
HDC *hDC*;
int *X*;
int *Y*;

	The **GetPixel** function retrieves the RGB color value of the pixel at the point specified by the *X* and *Y* parameters. The point must be in the clipping region.
Parameters	*hDC* Identifies the device context.
	X Specifies the logical *x*-coordinate of the point to be examined.
	Y Specifies the logical *y*-coordinate of the point to be examined.
Return Value	The return value specifies an RGB color value for the color of the given point. It is CLR_INVALID if the coordinates do not specify a point in the clipping region or an error occurs.
Comments	Not all devices support the **GetPixel** function. For more information, see the RC_BITBLT raster capability in the **GetDeviceCaps** function, earlier in this chapter.
See Also	**GetDeviceCaps**

■ GetPolyFillMode

int GetPolyFillMode(*hDC***)**
HDC *hDC*;

The **GetPolyFillMode** function retrieves the current polygon filling mode.

Parameters   *hDC*   Identifies the device context.

Return Value   The return value specifies the polygon filling mode. It can be either of the
following values:

Value	Meaning
ALTERNATE	Alternate mode.
WINDING	Winding-number mode.

For a description of these modes, see the **SetPolyFillMode** function.

If an error occured, the return value is 0.

See Also   **SetPolyFillMode**

■ GetPrinter

BOOL GetPrinter(*lpPrinterServer, lpName, lpPrinter, cbBuf, pcbNeeded***)**
LPPRINTERSERVER *lpPrinterServer*;
LPTSTR *lpName*;
LPPRINTER *lpPrinter*;
DWORD *cbBuf*;
LPDWORD *pcbNeeded*;

The **GetPrinter** function retrieves information about a printer. The printer is
specified by its name and its printer server.

The **GetPrinter** function may be used as either a wide-character function (where
text arguments must use Unicode) or an ANSI function (where text arguments
must use characters from the Windows 3.x character set installed).

Parameters   *lpPrinterServer*   Pointer to a **PRINTERSERVER** data structure describing
where the printer resides. If this value is NULL, the printer resides locally.

The **PRINTERSERVER** data structure has the following form:

```
typedef struct tagPRINTERSERVER {
    HANDLE   hProvidor;
    LPTSTR   lpName;
    LPTSTR   lpDescription;
    LPTSTR   lpLocation;
    LPVOID   lpVendorSpecificVariable;
} PRINTERSERVER;
```

lpName   Pointer to a string that is the name of the printer whose information
will be retrieved.

lpPrinter   Pointer to a **PRINTER** data structure whose fields the function will fill with information about the specified printer.

The **PRINTER** data structure has the following form:

```
typedef struct tagPRINTER {
    DWORD cVersion;
    LPPRINTERSERVER lpPrinterServer;
    LPTSTR lpPrinterName;
    LPTSTR lpPortName;
    LPTSTR lpDriverName;
    LPTSTR lpComment;
    LPTSTR lpLocation;
    LPDEVMODE lpDevMode;
    LPTSTR lpSepFile;
    LPTSTR lpPrintProcessor;
    LPTSTR lpDatatype;
    LPTSTR lpParameters;
    LPTSTR lpVendorData;
    DWORD Attributes;
    DWORD Priority;
    DWORD DefaultPriority;
    SYSTEMTIME StartTime;
    SYSTEMTIME UntilTime;
    DWORD Status;
    DWORD cJobs;
    DWORD AveragePPM;
} PRINTER;
```

cBuf   Specifies the size in bytes of the buffer pointed to by *lpPrinter*.

pcbNeeded   Pointer to the amount of data required to store the **PRINTER** data structure. This will be set to zero if *cBuf* was large enough.

Return Value

If the function is successful, the return value is TRUE.

If the function fails, the return value is FALSE/NULL. Further information can be obtained by calling **GetLastError**.

See Also

SetPrinter, AddPrinter PRINTER, PRINTERSERVER

■ GetPrinterDriver

BOOL GetPrinterDriver(*lpPrinter,* *lpEnvironment,* *lpDriverInfo,* *cbBuf,* *lpcbNeeded***)**
LPPRINTER *lpPrinter;*
LPSTR *lpEnvironment;*
LPDRIVERINFO *lpDriverInfo;*
DWORD *cbBuf;*
LPDWORD *lpcbNeeded;*

The **GetPrinterDriver** function retrieves information about a specified printer driver.

Parameters

lpPrinter   Pointer to a PRINTER data structure that specifies the printer of the printer driver that is to be retrieved.

The **PRINTER** data structure has the following form:

```
typedef struct tagPRINTER {
    DWORD cVersion;
    LPPRINTERSERVER lpPrinterServer;
    LPTSTR lpPrinterName;
    LPTSTR lpPortName;
    LPTSTR lpDriverName;
    LPTSTR lpComment;
    LPTSTR lpLocation;
    LPDEVMODE lpDevMode;
    LPTSTR lpSepFile;
    LPTSTR lpPrintProcessor;
    LPTSTR lpDatatype;
    LPTSTR lpParameters;
    LPTSTR lpVendorData;
    DWORD Attributes;
    DWORD Priority;
    DWORD DefaultPriority;
    SYSTEMTIME StartTime;
    SYSTEMTIME UntilTime;
    DWORD Status;
    DWORD cJobs;
    DWORD AveragePPM;
} PRINTER;
```

lpEnvironment   Pointer to a string that specifies the machine and operating system environment. An example is the string "Win32.386".

lpDriverInfo   A pointer to a buffer that the function will fill with a **DRIVERINFO** data structure that describes the printer driver.

The **DRIVERINFO** data structure has the following form:

```
typedef struct tagDRIVERINFO {
    DWORD   cVersion;
    LPSTR   lpDriverName;
    LPSTR   lpEnvironment;
    LPSTR   lpDriverPath;
    LPSTR   lpDeviceName;
    LPSTR   lpDataFile;
    LPSTR   lpConfigFile;
} DRIVERINFO;
```

cbBuf   Specifies the size in bytes of the buffer pointed to by *lpDriverInfo*.

pcbNeeded   Pointer to a DWORD that the function will fill with the number of bytes required to store the driver's **DRIVERINFO** data structure. The function will set this to zero if *cbBuf* was large enough.

Return Value   If the function is successful, the return value is TRUE.

If the function fails, the return value is FALSE/NULL. Further information can be obtained by calling **GetLastError**.

Comments   One piece of information included in a **DRIVERINFO** data structure is the fully-qualified pathname of the printer driver. An application can then load the driver by calling **LoadLibrary**. Windows32 does this itself when it needs to know the printer driver to load when executing the **CreateDC** function.

See Also   **AddPrinterDriver, EnumPrinterDrivers**

■ GetPriorityClipboardFormat

int GetPriorityClipboardFormat(*lpPriorityList*, *nCount*)
LPWORD *lpPriorityList*;
int *nCount*;

This function returns the first clipboard format in a list for which data exist in the clipboard.

Parameters   *lpPriorityList*   Points to an integer array that contains a list of clipboard formats in priority order. For a description of the data formats, see the SetClipboardData function later in this chapter.

nCount   Specifies the number of entries in *lpPriorityList*. This value must not be greater than the actual number of entries in the list.

Return Value   The return value is the highest priority clipboard format in the list for which data exist. If no data exist in the clipboard, this function returns NULL. If data exist in the clipboard which did not match any format in the list, the return value is –1.

See Also   **EnumClipboardFormats**

■ GetPrivateProfileInt

DWORD GetPrivateProfileInt(*lpAppName*, *lpKeyName*, *dwDefault*, *lpFileName*)
LPTSTR *lpAppName*;
LPTSTR *lpKeyName*;
DWORD *dwDefault*;
LPTSTR *lpFileName*;

The **GetPrivateProfileInt** function retrieves the value of an integer key from the specified initialization file.

The **GetPrivateProfileInt** function may be used as either a wide-character function (where text arguments must use Unicode) or an ANSI function (where text arguments must use characters from the Windows 3.x character set installed).

The function searches the file for a key that matches the name specified by the *lpKeyName* parameter under the application heading specified by the *lpAppName* parameter. An integer entry in the initialization file must have the following form:

```
[application name]
keyname - value
        .
        .
```

Parameters   *lpAppName*   Points to the null-terminated string name of a Windows application that appears in the initialization file.

lpKeyName   Points to a null-terminated string key name that appears in the initialization file.

dwDefault   Specifies the default value for the given key if the key cannot be found in the initialization file.

lpFileName   Points to a null-terminated string that names the initialization file. If *lpFileName* does not contain a path to the file, Windows searches for the file in the Windows directory.

Return Value   The return value specifies the result of the function. The return value is zero if the value that corresponds to the specified key name is not an integer or if the integer is negative. If the value that corresponds to the key name consists of digits followed by nonnumeric characters, the function returns the value of the digits. For example, if the entry *KeyName=102abc* is accessed, the function returns 102. If the key is not found, this function returns the default value, *dwDefault*.

Comments   The **GetPrivateProfileInt** function is not case dependent, so the strings in *lpAppName* and *lpKeyName* may be in any combination of uppercase and lowercase letters.

See Also   **GetPrivateProfileString, GetProfileInt, GetProfileString**

■ GetPrivateProfileSection

DWORD GetPrivateProfileSection(*lpAppName, lpReturnedString, nSize, lpFileName***)**
LPTSTR *lpAppName*;
LPTSTR *lpReturnedString*;
DWORD *nSize*;
LPTSTR *lpFileName*;

This function copies all of the key name and value pairs for a particular application section from the specified initialization file, into the buffer pointed to by the *lpReturnedString* parameter. The function searches the specified initialization file for an application secton that matches the name specified by the *lpAppName* parameter. If the application name is found, the corresponding key name, value pairs are copied to the buffer pointed to by *lpReturnedString*. If the application name is not found this function returns 0.

The **GetPrivateProfileSection** function may be used as either a wide-character function (where text arguments must use Unicode) or an ANSI function (where text arguments must use characters from the Windows 3.x character set installed).

Parameters: *lpAppName*   Points to a null-terminated character string that names the application.

lpReturnedString   Points to the buffer that receives the key name and value pairs associated with the named application section.

nSize   Specifies the maximum number of bytes (including the last null character) that can be copied to the buffer.

lpFileName Points to a string that names the initialization file. If *lpFileName* does not contain a path to the file, Windows searches for the file in the Windows directory.

Return Value

The return value specifies the number of bytes copied to the buffer identified by the *lpReturnedString* parameter, not including the terminating null character. If the buffer is not large enough to contain all the key name, value pairs associated with the named application section, the return value is equal to the length specified by the *nSize* parameter minus 2.

The format of the returned key name, value pairs is one or more null terminated strings, terminated by the final null character. Each string has the following format:

KeyName=Value

GetPrivateProfileSection is not case-dependent, so the strings in *lpAppName* may be in any combination of uppercase and lowercase letters.

This operation is atomic, in that no updates to the specified initialization file are allowed while the key name, value pairs for the application section are being copied to the *lpReturnedString* buffer.

See Also

GetPrivateProfileInt, GetPrivateProfileString, GetProfileSection, GetProfileInt, GetProfileString, WritePrivateProfileString, WritePrivateProfileSection, WriteProfileString, WriteProfileSection

■ GetPrivateProfileString

DWORD GetPrivateProfileString(*lpAppName, lpKeyName, lpDefault, lpReturnedString, dwSize, lpFileName***)**
LPTSTR *lpAppName*;
LPTSTR *lpKeyName*;
LPTSTR *lpDefault*;
LPTSTR *lpReturnedString*;
DWORD *dwSize*;
LPTSTR *lpFileName*;

The **GetPrivateProfileString** function copies a character string from the specified initialization file into the buffer pointed to by the *lpReturnedString* parameter.

The **GetPrivateProfileString** function may be used as either a wide-character function (where text arguments must use Unicode) or an ANSI function (where text arguments must use characters from the Windows 3.x character set installed).

The function searches the file for a key that matches the name specified by the *lpKeyName* parameter under the application heading specified by the *lpAppName* parameter. If the key is found, the corresponding string is copied to the buffer. If the key does not exist, the default character string specified by the *lpDefault* parameter is copied. A string entry in the initialization file must have the following form:

```
[application name]
keyname = string
        .
        .
        .
```

If *lpKeyName* is NULL, the **GetPrivateProfileString** function enumerates all key names associated with *lpAppName* by filling the location pointed to by *lpReturnedString* with a list of key names (not values). Each key name in the list is terminated with a null character.

Parameters   *lpAppName*   Points to the null-terminated string name of a Windows application that appears in the initialization file.

lpKeyName   Points to a null-terminated string key name that appears in the initialization file.

lpDefault   Specifies the default value for the given key if the key cannot be found in the initialization file. This should be a null-terminated string.

lpReturnedString   Points to the buffer that receives the character string.

dwSize   Specifies the maximum number of bytes (including the last null character) to be copied to the buffer pointed to by *lpReturnedString*.

lpFileName   Points to a null-terminated string that names the initialization file. If *lpFileName* does not contain a path to the file, Windows searches for the file in the Windows directory.

Return Value   The return value specifies the number of bytes copied to the buffer identified by the *lpReturnedString* parameter, not including the terminating null character. Note that an ANSI-ASCII null character is 1 byte, a Unicode null character is 2 bytes. If the buffer is not large enough to contain the entire string and *lpKeyName* is not NULL, the return value is equal to the length specified by the *dwSize* parameter. If the buffer is not large enough to contain the entire string and *lpKeyName* is NULL, the return value is equal to the length specified by the *dwSize* parameter minus 2.

Comments   **GetPrivateProfileString** is not case dependent, so the strings in *lpAppName* and *lpKeyName* may be in any combination of uppercase and lowercase letters.

See Also   **GetPrivateProfileInt, GetProfileString, GetProfileInt**

■ GetProcAddress

FARPROC GetProcAddress(*hModule, lpProcName***)**
HANDLE *hModule*;
LPSTR *lpProcName*;

The **GetProcAddress** function retrieves the memory address of the function whose name is pointed to by the *lpProcName* parameter. The **GetProcAddress** function searches for the function in the module specified by the *hModule* parameter, or in the current module if *hModule* is NULL. The function must be an exported function; the module's definition file must contain an appropriate **EXPORTS** line for the function.

Parameters   *hModule*   Identifies the library module that contains the function.

lpProcName   Points to the function name, or contains the ordinal value of the function. If it is an ordinal value, the value must be in the low-order word and zero must be in the high-order word. The string must be a null-terminated string.

Return Value   The return value points to the function's entry point if the function is successful. Otherwise, it is NULL, in which case an extended error status is available using the **GetLastError** function.

If the *lpProcName* parameter is an ordinal value and a function with the specified ordinal does not exist in the module, **GetProcAddress** can still return a non-NULL value. In cases where the function may not exist, specify the function by name rather than ordinal value.

Comments   Only use **GetProcAddress** to retrieve addresses of exported functions that belong to library modules. The **MakeProcInstance** function can be used to access functions within different instances of the current module.

The spelling of the function name (pointed to by *lpProcName*) must be identical to the spelling as it appears in the source library's definition (.DEF) file. The function can be renamed in the definition file. Case sensitive matching is used.

See Also   **MakeProcInstance**

■ GetProcessWindowStation

HANDLE GetProcessWindowStation(VOID)

The **GetProcessWindowStation** function returns a handle to the windowstation associated with the calling process.

GetProcessWindowStation has no parameters.

Return Value   If the function is successful, the return value is a handle to the windowstation associated with the calling process.

If the function fails, the return value is NULL. This can occur if the process is not a Windows32 application. Call **GetLastError** for more detailed error information.

See Also   **SetProcessWindowStation, GetWindowStationAttrs, OpenWindowStation, CloseWindowStation, EnumWindowStations**

■ GetProfileInt

DWORD GetProfileInt(*lpAppName*, *lpKeyName*, *dwDefault*)
LPTSTR *lpAppName*;   /* points to the section name   */
LPTSTR *lpKeyName*;   /* points to the keyname   */
DWORD *dwDefault*;   /* value to return if keyname not found */

The **GetProfileInt** function retrieves the value of an integer from a specified keyname within a specified section of the WIN.INI initialization file.

The **GetProfileInt** function may be used as either a wide-character function (where text arguments must use Unicode) or an ANSI function (where text arguments must use characters from the Windows 3.x character set installed).

Parameters

lpAppName   Points to the null-terminated string containing the name of the section in the WIN.INI initialization file. The name of the section is case-independent; the string may be any combination of uppercase and lowercase letters.

lpKeyName   Points to the null-terminated string containing the keyname whose value is to be retrieved.

dwDefault   Specifies the default value to return if the keyname cannot be found.

Return Value

The return value is the value of the keyname. The return value is zero if the keyname value is not an integer or if the integer is negative. If the keyname is not found, the return value is the integer specified in the *dwDefault* parameter.

Comments

The **GetProfileInt** function cannot be used to retrieve a negative integer. If you need to retrieve a negative value, you should call the **GetProfileString** function, and convert the returned string into the negative value.

See Also

GetPrivateProfileInt, GetProfileString, GetPrivateProfileString

■ GetProfileSection

DWORD GetProfileSection(*lpAppName*, *lpReturnedString*, *nSize*)
LPTSTR *lpAppName*;
LPTSTR *lpReturnedString*;
DWORD *nSize*;

This function copies the all key name and value pairs for a particular application section from the Windows initialization file, WIN.INI, into the buffer pointed to by the *lpReturnedString* parameter. The function searches WIN.INI for an application section that matches the name specified by the *lpAppName* parameter. If the application name is found, the corresponding key name, value pairs are copied to the buffer pointed to by *lpReturnedString*. If the application name is not found this function returns 0.

The **GetProfileSection** function may be used as either a wide-character function (where text arguments must use Unicode) or an ANSI function (where text arguments must use characters from the Windows 3.x character set installed).

Parameters   *lpAppName*   Points to a null-terminated character string that names the application.

lpReturnedString   Points to the buffer that receives the key name and value pairs associated with the named application section.

nSize   Specifies the maximum number of bytes (including the last null character) that can be copied to the buffer.

Return Value   The return value specifies the number of bytes copied to the buffer identified by the *lpReturnedString* parameter, not including the terminating null character. If the buffer is not large enough to contain all the key name, value pairs associated with the named application section, the return value is equal to the length specified by the nSize parameter minus 2.

The format of the returned key name, value pairs is one or more null terminated strings, terminated by the final null character. Each string has the following format:

KeyName=Value

GetProfileSection is not case-dependent, so the strings in *lpAppName* may be in any combination of uppercase and lowercase letters.

This operation is atomic, in that no updates to the Windows initialization file are allowed while the key name, value pairs for the application section are being copied to the *lpReturnedString* buffer.

See Also   **GetProfileInt, GetProfileString, GetPrivateProfileInt, GetPrivateProfileString, GetPrivateProfileSection, WritePrivateProfileString, WritePrivateProfileSection, WriteProfileString, WriteProfileSection**

■ GetProfileString

```
DWORD GetProfileString(lpAppName, lpKeyName, lpDefault, lpReturnedString, nSize)
LPTSTR lpAppName;          /* points to the section name     */
LPTSTR lpKeyName;          /* points to the keyname          */
LPTSTR lpDefault;          /* points to the default string   */
LPTSTR lpReturnedString;   /* points to the destination buffer */
DWORD nSize;               /* size of the destination buffer */
```

The **GetProfileString** function retrieves the string associated with the specified keyname within the specified section in the WIN.INI initialization file.

The **GetProfileString** function may be used as either a wide-character function (where text arguments must use Unicode) or an ANSI function (where text arguments must use characters from the Windows 3.x character set installed).

Parameters   *lpAppName*   Points to a null-terminated string that specifies the section containing the key name. The name of the section is case-independent; the string may be any combination of uppercase and lowercase letters.

lpKeyName Points to the null-terminated string containing the keyname whose associated string is to be retrieved. If this value is NULL, all keynames in the section specified by the *lpAppName* parameter are copied to the buffer specified by the *lpReturnedString* parameter. For more information, see the "Comments" section.

lpDefault Specifies the default value for the given key if the key cannot be found in the initialization file.

lpReturnedString Points to the buffer that receives the character string.

nSize Specifies the size (in bytes) of the buffer pointed to by the *lpReturnedString* parameter.

Return Value   The return value is the number of bytes copied to the buffer, not including the terminating null character.

Comments   If the *lpKeyName* parameter is set to NULL, the **GetProfileString** function will copy all keynames to the supplied buffer. Each string will be null-terminated, with the final string ending with two null-termination characters. If the supplied destination buffer is too small to hold all the strings, the last string will be truncated and followed with two null-termination characters.

Sections in the WIN.INI initialization file have the following form:

```
[section name]
keyname = value
.
.
.
```

See Also   **GetPrivateProfileString, WriteProfileString, GetProfileInt, GetPrivateProfileInt, GetProfileSection**

■ GetProp

HANDLE GetProp(*hWnd, lpString*)
HWND *hWnd*;
LPTSTR *lpString*;

This function retrieves a data handle from the property list of the specified window. The character string pointed to by the *lpString* parameter identifies the handle to be retrieved. The string and handle are assumed to have been added to the property list by using the **SetProp** function.

The **GetProp** function may be used as either a wide-character function (where text arguments must use Unicode) or an ANSI function (where text arguments must use characters from the Windows 3.x character set installed).

Parameters   *hWnd* Identifies the window whose property list is to be searched.

lpString Points to a null-terminated character string or an atom that identifies a string. If an atom is given, it must have been created previously by using the

AddAtom function. The atom, a 16-bit value, must be placed in the low-order word of the *lpString* parameter; the high-order word must be set to zero.

Return Value	The return value identifies the associated data handle if the property list contains the given string. Otherwise, it is NULL.
Comments	The value retrieved by the **GetProp** function can be any 16-bit value useful to the application.
See Also	**AddAtom, SetProp, RemoveProp, EnumProps**

■ GetQueueStatus

DWORD GetQueueStatus(*flags***)**
UINT *flags*;

GetQueueStatus returns hint bits that are used to determine whether there is interesting input in the message queue and should be retrieved with a **Get/PeekMessage** call.

The **GetQueueStatus** api can be used to very quickly check for the existence of certain kinds of messages in the message queue. Generally it is intended for use inside of speed-critical loops to determine whether or not there are any interesting messages that should be handled with **PeekMessage** or **GetMessage**. **GetQueueStatus** returns two sets of information: whether or not any new messages have been added to the queue since **GetQueueStatus** (or **GetMessage** or **PeekMessage**) was called last, and what kinds of events are currently in the queue.

Parameters   *flags*   Specifies the queue-status flags to retrieve. This parameter can be a combination of the following values:

Value	Description
QS_KEY	A WM_CHAR message is in the queue.
QS_MOUSE	A WM_MOUSEMOVE or WM_*BUTTON* message is in the queue.
QS_MOUSEMOVE	A WM_MOUSEMOVE message is in the queue.
QS_MOUSEBUTTON	A WM_*BUTTON* message is in the queue.
QS_PAINT	A WM_PAINT message is in the queue.
QS_POSTMESSAGE	A posted message other than those listed above is in the queue.
QS_SENDMESSAGE	A message sent by another application is in the queue.
QS_TIMER	A WM_TIMER message is in the queue.
QS_HOTKEY	A hotkey is in the queue.
QS_SETFOREGROUND	A SetForeGround message is in the queue.
QS_INPUT	An input message is in the queue.

Value	Description
QS_ALLEVENTS	Any message is in the queue.

Return Value

The LOWORD of the return value containts a combination of QS_* flags that indicate what kind of events have geen added to the queue since the last call to **GetQueueStatus, GetMessage,** or **PeekMessage.**

The HIWORD of the return value contains QS_* flags that indicate what kind of events are presently in the queue.

The existence of a QS_* flag in the return value does not GUARANTEE that a call to **PeekMessage** or **GetMessage** will actually return a message.

Get/PeekMessage perform some internal filtering computation that may cause the message to be processed internally.

For this reason, **GetQueueStatus** (and **GetInputState**, for that matter) should only be considered hints as to whether **Get/PeekMessage** should be called.

The QS_* bits are:

Value	Meaning
QS_KEY	A key event is in the message queue.
QS_MOUSEMOVE	A mouse move event is in the message queue.
QS_MOUSEBUTTON	A mouse button event is in the message queue.
QS_POSTMSG	An application or part of the system added a message to the current queue by calling PostMessage.
QS_TIMER	A timer event is ready for processing.
QS_PAINT	A paint event is ready for processing.
QS_SENDMSG	A message sent from another thread or application is ready for processing.
QS_HOTKEY	A hot key event has been generated and is ready for processing.

See Also   **GetInputState, GetMessage, PeekMessage**

■ GetRasterizerCaps

BOOL GetRasterizerCaps(*lpStatus*, *cb***)**
LPRASTERIZER_STATUS *lpStatus*;   /* pointer to structure for status   */
int *cb*;   /* number of bytes in structure   */

The **GetRasterizerCaps** function returns flags indicating whether TrueType fonts are installed in the system.

Parameters

lpStatus   Points to a **RASTERIZER_STATUS** structure that receives information about the rasterizer.

cb   Specifies the number of bytes that will be copied into the structure pointed to by the *lpStatus* parameter.

Return Value   The return value is TRUE if the function is successful. Otherwise, it is FALSE.

Comments   The **GetRasterizerCaps** function enables applications and printer drivers to determine whether TrueType is installed.

If the TT_AVAILABLE flag is set in the *wFlags* member of the **RASTERIZER_STATUS** structure, at least one TrueType font is installed. If the TT_ENABLED flag is set, TrueType is enabled for the system.

See Also   **GetOutlineTextMetrics**

GetRgnBox

int GetRgnBox(*hRgn***,** *lpRect***)**
HRGN *hRgn*;
LPRECT *lpRect*;

The **GetRgnBox** function retrieves the bounding rectangle of the region specified by *hRgn*.

Parameters   *hRgn*   Identifies the region.

lpRect   Points to a **RECT** structure to receive the bounding rectangle.

Return Value   The return value specifies the region's complexity. It can be any of the following values.

Value	Meaning
NULLREGION	New region is empty.
SIMPLEREGION	New region is a single rectangle.
COMPLEXREGION	New region is more than a single rectangle.

The return value is 0 if the *hRgn* parameter does not specify a valid region.

GetROP2

int GetROP2(*hDC***)**
HDC *hDC*;

The **GetROP2** function retrieves the foreground mix mode. The mix mode specifies how the pen or interior color and the color already on the surface are combined to yield a new color.

Parameters   *hDC*   Identifies the device context.

Return Value   The return value specifies the foreground mix mode. The return value is 0 if an error occured.

Comments	For more information about the drawing modes, see Chapter 11, Binary and Ternary Raster-Operation Codes, in *Reference, Volume 2*.
See Also	**SetROP2**

■ GetSaveFileName

BOOL GetSaveFileName(*lpofn***)**
LPOPENFILENAME *lpofn*;   /* pointer to structure with initialization data */

The **GetSaveFileName** function creates a system-defined dialog box that allows the user to specify the name of a file to save.

Parameters   *lpofn*   Points to an **OPENFILENAME** structure that contains information used to initialize the dialog box. When the **GetSaveFileName** function returns, this structure contains information about the user's file selection.

The **OPENFILENAME** structure has the following form:

```
typedef struct tagOFN { /* ofn */
    DWORD    lStructSize;
    HWND     hwndOwner;
    HANDLE   hInstance;
    LPSTR    lpstrFilter;
    LPSTR    lpstrCustomFilter;
    DWORD    nMaxCustFilter;
    DWORD    nFilterIndex;
    LPSTR    lpstrFile;
    DWORD    nMaxFile;
    LPSTR    lpstrFileTitle;
    DWORD    nMaxFileTitle;
    LPSTR    lpstrInitialDir;
    LPSTR    lpstrTitle;
    DWORD    Flags;
    WORD     nFileOffset;
    WORD     nFileExtension;
    LPSTR    lpstrDefExt;
    DWORD    lCustData;
    WORD (FAR PASCAL *lpfnHook)(HWND, unsigned, WORD, LONG);
    LPSTR    lpTemplateName;
} OPENFILENAME;
```

For a full description, see TBD.

Return Value   The return value is TRUE if the user specifies the name of a file to save. It is FALSE if the user cancels or closes the dialog box, or if the buffer identified by the **lpstrFile** member of the **OPENFILENAME** structure is too small to contain the selected filename string.

Errors   Use the **CommDlgExtendedError** function to retrieve the error value, which may be one of the following:

> CDERR_FINDRESFAILURE
> CDERR_INITIALIZATION
> CDERR_LOCKRESFAILURE
> CDERR_LOADRESFAILURE
> CDERR_LOADSTRFAILURE

CDERR_MEMALLOCFAILURE
CDERR_MEMLOCKFAILURE
CDERR_NOHINSTANCE
CDERR_NOHOOK
CDERR_NOTEMPLATE
CDERR_STRUCTSIZE

Example

The following code fragment copies file-filter strings into a buffer, initializes an **OPENFILENAME** structure, then creates an save-as file dialog box:

```
OPENFILENAME ofn;
char szDirName[256];                 /* directory name array  */
char szFile[256], szFileTitle[256]; /* file and title arrays */
char *szFilter[] = {
    "Write Files(*.WRI)",
    "*.wri",
    "Word Files(*.DOC)",
    "*.doc",
    ""
    };
HANDLE hFile;
{

    /* Get the system directory name and store in szDirName */

    GetSystemDirectory((LPSTR) szDirName, 255);

    /* Initialize the OPENFILENAME members */

    szFile[0] = '\0';
    ofn.lStructSize = sizeof(OPENFILENAME);
    ofn.hwndOwner = hwnd;
    ofn.lpstrFilter = szFilter[0];
    ofn.lpstrCustomFilter = (LPSTR) NULL;
    ofn.nMaxCustFilter = 0L;
    ofn.nFilterIndex = 0L;
    ofn.lpstrFile= szFile;
    ofn.nMaxFile = sizeof(szFile);
    ofn.lpstrFileTitle = szFileTitle;
    ofn.nMaxFileTitle = sizeof(szFileTitle);
    ofn.lpstrInitialDir = szDirName;
    ofn.lpstrTitle = (LPSTR) NULL;
    ofn.Flags = OFN_SHOWHELP | OFN_OVERWRITEPROMPT;
    ofn.nFileOffset = 0;
    ofn.nFileExtension = 0;
    ofn.lpstrDefExt = (LPSTR)NULL;

    /* Call the GetSaveFilename function */

    if (GetSaveFileName(&ofn)){
        .
        . /* Perform file operations */
        .
    }
    else
        ErrorHandler();
```

See Also   **GetOpenFileName**

■ GetScrollPos

int GetScrollPos(*hWnd, nBar***)**
HWND *hWnd*;
int *nBar*;

This function retrieves the current position of a scroll-bar thumb. The current position is a relative value that depends on the current scrolling range. For example, if the scrolling range is 0 to 100 and the thumb is in the middle of the bar, the current position is 50.

Parameters

hWnd   Identifies a window that has standard scroll bars or a scroll-bar control, depending on the value of the nBar parameter.

nBar   Specifies the scroll bar to examine. It can be one of the following values:

Value	Meaning
SB_CTL	Retrieves the position of a scroll-bar control. In this case, the hWnd parameter must be the window handle of a scroll-bar control.
SB_HORZ	Retrieves the position of a window's horizontal scroll bar.
SB_VERT	Retrieves the position of a window's vertical scroll bar.

Return Value   The return value specifies the current position of the scroll-bar thumb.

See Also   **SetScrollPos, GetScrollRange, GetScrollRange, ScrollWindow, ScrollDC**

■ GetScrollRange

BOOL GetScrollRange(*hWnd, nBar, lpMinPos, lpMaxPos***)**
HWND *hWnd*;
int *nBar*;
LPINT *lpMinPos*;
LPINT *lpMaxPos*;

This function copies the current minimum and maximum scroll-bar positions for the given scroll bar to the locations specified by the *lpMinPos* and *lpMaxPos* parameters. If the given window does not have standard scroll bars or is not a scroll-bar control, then the **GetScrollRange** function copies zero to *lpMinPos* and *lpMaxPos*.

Parameters

hWnd   Identifies a window that has standard scroll bars or a scroll-bar control, depending on the value of the nBar parameter.

nBar   Specifies an integer value that identifies which scroll bar to retrieve. It can be one of the following values:

Value	Meaning
SB_CTL	Retrieves the position of a scroll-bar control; in this case, the hWnd parameter must be the handle of a scroll-bar control.
SB_HORZ	Retrieves the position of a window's horizontal scroll bar.
SB_VERT	Retrieves the position of a window's vertical scroll bar.

lpMinPos   Points to the integer variable that is to receive the minimum position.

lpMaxPos   Points to the integer variable that is to receive the maximum position.

Return Value   TRUE is returned for success, FALSE for failure.

Comments   The default range for a standard scroll bar is 0 to 100. The default range for a scroll-bar control is empty (both values are zero).

See Also   SetScrollRange, GetScrollPos, SetScrollPos

■ GetSecurityDescriptorControl

BOOL GetSecurityDescriptorControl(*SecurityDescriptor, Control, Revision***)**
PSECURITY_DESCRIPTOR *SecurityDescriptor,*
PSECURITY_DESCRIPTOR_CONTROL *Control,*
PULONG *Revision,*

The **GetSecurityDescriptorControl** function retrieves a security descriptor's control and revision information.

Parameters   *SecurityDescriptor*   Pointer to a **SECURITY_DESCRIPTOR** data structure whose control and revision information the function will retrieve.

The **SECURITY_DESCRIPTOR** data structure has the following form:

```
typedef PVOID PSECURITY_DESCRIPTOR;
```

Control   Pointer to a **SECURITY_DESCRIPTOR_CONTROL** data structure that the function will fill with the security descriptor's control information.

The **SECURITY_DESCRIPTOR_CONTROL** data structure has the following form:

Revision   Pointer to a variable that the function will set to the security descriptor's revision value. This value will always be set, even if **GetSecurityDescriptorControl** returns an error.

Return Value   If the function is successful, the return value is TRUE.

If the function fails, the return value is FALSE. Call **GetLastError** for more detailed error information.

See Also   GetSecurityDescriptorGroup, GetSecurityDescriptorDacl, GetSecurityDescriptorLength, GetSecurityDescriptorOwner, GetSecurityDescriptorSacl, InitializeSecurityDescriptor, IsValidSecurityDescriptor, SetSecurityDescriptorDacl, SetSecurityDescriptorGroup, SetSecurityDescriptorOwner, SetSecurityDescriptorSacl

■ GetSecurityDescriptorDacl

BOOL GetSecurityDescriptorDacl(*SecurityDescriptor*, *DaclPresent*, *Dacl*, *DaclDefaulted***)**
PSECURITY_DESCRIPTOR *SecurityDescriptor*;
PBOOL *DaclPresent*;
PACL * *Dacl*;
PBOOL *DaclDefaulted*;

The **GetSecurityDescriptorDacl** function retrieves a security descriptor's discretionary access control list (**ACL**) information.

Parameters

SecurityDescriptor   Pointer to a **SECURITY_DESCRIPTOR** data structure whose discretionary **ACL** information the function will retrieve.

The **SECURITY_DESCRIPTOR** data structure has the following form:

```
typedef PVOID PSECURITY_DESCRIPTOR;
```

DaclPresent   Pointer to a Boolean variable that the function will set to indicate the presence of a discretionary **ACL** in the security descriptor pointed to by *SecurityDescriptor*. If set to TRUE, the security descriptor does contain a discretionary **ACL**, and the remaining output parameters will receive valid values. If set to FALSE, the security descriptor does not contain a discretionary **ACL**, and the remaining output parameters will not receive valid values.

Dacl   Pointer to a pointer to an **ACL** data structure. If the value stored into the variable pointed to by *DaclPresent* is TRUE, the function sets the pointer pointed to by *Dacl* to the address of the security descriptor's discretionary **ACL**. If the value stored into the variable pointed to by *DaclPresent* is FALSE, no value is stored.

If the function stores a null value into the pointer pointed to by *Dacl*, then the security descriptor has a null discretionary **ACL**.

DaclDefaulted   Pointer to a Boolean variable. If the value stored into the variable pointed to by *DaclPresent* is TRUE, the function sets the variable pointed to by *DaclDefaulted* to the value of the security descriptor's **DaclDefaulted** control flag. If the value stored into the variable pointed to by *DaclPresent* is FALSE, no value is set.

Return Value

If the function is successful, the return value is TRUE.

If the function fails, the return value is FALSE. Call **GetLastError** for more detailed error information.

See Also

GetSecurityDescriptorGroup, GetSecurityDescriptorControl, GetSecurityDescriptorLength, GetSecurityDescriptorOwner, GetSecurityDescriptorSacl, InitializeSecurityDescriptor, IsValidSecurityDescriptor, SetSecurityDescriptorDacl, SetSecurityDescriptorGroup, SetSecurityDescriptorOwner, SetSecurityDescriptorSacl

■ GetSecurityDescriptorGroup

BOOL GetSecurityDescriptorGroup(*SecurityDescriptor, Group, GroupDefaulted***)**
PSECURITY_DESCRIPTOR *SecurityDescriptor*,
PSID * *Group*;
PBOOL *GroupDefaulted*;

The **GetSecurityDescriptorGroup** function retrieves the primary group information of a security descriptor.

Parameters

SecurityDescriptor   Pointer to a **SECURITY_DESCRIPTOR** data structure whose primary group information the function will retrieve.

The **SECURITY_DESCRIPTOR** data structure has the following form:

```
typedef PVOID  PSECURITY_DESCRIPTOR;
```

Group   Pointer to a pointer to an **SID** data structure. If the security descriptor does not currently contain a primary group, the function will set the pointer pointed to by *Group* to NULL, and will ignore the remaining output parameter, *GroupDefaulted*. If the security descriptor does contain an owner, the function will set the pointer pointed to by *Group* to the address of the security descriptor's group **SID**, and will provide a valid value for the variable pointed to by *GroupDefaulted*.

The **SID** data structure has the following form:

```
typedef PVOID * PSID;
```

GroupDefaulted   Pointer to a Boolean variable. If the value stored into the variable pointed to by *Group* is not NULL, the function sets the variable pointed to by *GroupDefaulted* to the value of the security descriptor's **GroupDefaulted** control flag. If the value stored into the variable pointed to by *Group* is NULL, no value is set.

Return Value

If the function is successful, the return value is TRUE.

If the function fails, the return value is FALSE. Call **GetLastError** for more detailed error information.

See Also

GetSecurityDescriptorControl, GetSecurityDescriptorDacl, GetSecurityDescriptorLength, GetSecurityDescriptorOwner, GetSecurityDescriptorSacl, InitializeSecurityDescriptor, IsValidSecurityDescriptor, SetSecurityDescriptorDacl, SetSecurityDescriptorGroup, SetSecurityDescriptorOwner, SetSecurityDescriptorSacl

■ GetSecurityDescriptorLength

ULONG GetSecurityDescriptorLength(*SecurityDescriptor***)**
PSECURITY_DESCRIPTOR *SecurityDescriptor*,

The **GetSecurityDescriptorLength** function returns the length, in bytes, of a structurally valid **SECURITY_DESCRIPTOR**. The length includes the length of all associated data structures, such as **SID**s and **ACL**s.

The minimum length of a security descriptor is SECURITY_DESCRIPTOR_MIN_LENGTH. Such a minimal security descriptor has no associated **SID**s or **ACL**s.

Parameters   *SecurityDescriptor*   Pointer to the **SECURITY_DESCRIPTOR** data structure whose length the function will return. The **SECURITY_DESCRIPTOR**'s structure is assumed to be valid.

The **SECURITY_DESCRIPTOR** data structure has the following form:

```
typedef PVOID PSECURITY_DESCRIPTOR;
```

Return Value   If the function is successful, the return value is the length in bytes of the **SECURITY_DESCRIPTOR**.

If the **SECURITY_DESCRIPTOR**'s structure is invalid, the return value is undefined.

See Also   GetSecurityDescriptorGroup, GetSecurityDescriptorControl, GetSecurityDescriptorDacl, GetSecurityDescriptorOwner, GetSecurityDescriptorSacl, InitializeSecurityDescriptor, IsValidSecurityDescriptor, SetSecurityDescriptorDacl, SetSecurityDescriptorGroup, SetSecurityDescriptorOwner, SetSecurityDescriptorSacl

■ GetSecurityDescriptorOwner

BOOL GetSecurityDescriptorOwner(*SecurityDescriptor, Owner, OwnerDefaulted***)**
PSECURITY_DESCRIPTOR *SecurityDescriptor*,
**PSID * ** *Owner*;
PBOOL *OwnerDefaulted*;

The **GetSecurityDescriptorOwner** function retrieves a security descriptor's owner.

Parameters   *SecurityDescriptor*   Pointer to a **SECURITY_DESCRIPTOR** data structure whose owner the function will retrieve.

The **SECURITY_DESCRIPTOR** data structure has the following form:

```
typedef PVOID PSECURITY_DESCRIPTOR;
```

Owner   Pointer to a pointer to an **SID** data structure. If the security descriptor does not currently contain an owner, the function will set the pointer pointed to by *Owner* to NULL, and will ignore the remaining output parameter, *OwnerDefaulted*. If the security descriptor does contain an owner, the function will set the pointer pointed to by *Owner* to the address of the security descriptor's owner **SID**, and will provide a valid value for the variable pointed to by *OwnerDefaulted*.

The **SID** data structure has the following form:

```
typedef PVOID * PSID;
```

OwnerDefaulted   Pointer to a Boolean variable. If the value stored into the variable pointed to by *Owner* is not NULL, the function sets the variable pointed to by *OwnerDefaulted* to the value of the security descriptor's **OwnerDefaulted** control flag. If the value stored into the variable pointed to by *Owner* is NULL, no value is set.

Return Value

If the function is successful, the return value is TRUE.

If the function fails, the return value is FALSE. Call **GetLastError** for more detailed error information.

See Also

GetSecurityDescriptorGroup, GetSecurityDescriptorControl, GetSecurityDescriptorDacl, GetSecurityDescriptorLength, GetSecurityDescriptorSacl, InitializeSecurityDescriptor, IsValidSecurityDescriptor, SetSecurityDescriptorDacl, SetSecurityDescriptorGroup, SetSecurityDescriptorOwner, SetSecurityDescriptorSacl

GetSecurityDescriptorSacl

BOOL GetSecurityDescriptorSacl(*SecurityDescriptor, SaclPresent, Sacl, SaclDefaulted***)**
PSECURITY_DESCRIPTOR *SecurityDescriptor*;
PBOOL *SaclPresent*;
PACL * *Sacl*;
PBOOL *SaclDefaulted*;

The **GetSecurityDescriptorDacl** function retrieves a security descriptor's system access control list (**ACL**) information.

Parameters

SecurityDescriptor   Pointer to a **SECURITY_DESCRIPTOR** data structure whose system **ACL** information the function will retrieve.

The **SECURITY_DESCRIPTOR** data structure has the following form:

```
typedef PVOID PSECURITY_DESCRIPTOR;
```

SaclPresent   Pointer to a Boolean variable that the function will set to indicate the presence of a system **ACL** in the security descriptor pointed to by *SecurityDescriptor*. If set to TRUE, the security descriptor does contain a system **ACL**, and the remaining output parameters will receive valid values. If set to FALSE, the security descriptor does not contain a system **ACL**, and the remaining output parameters will not receive valid values.

Sacl   Pointer to a pointer to an **ACL** data structure. If the value stored into the variable pointed to by *SaclPresent* is TRUE, the function sets the pointer pointed to by *Sacl* to the address of the security descriptor's system **ACL**. If the value stored into the variable pointed to by *SaclPresent* is FALSE, no value is stored.

If the function stores a null value into the pointer pointed to by *Sacl*, then the security descriptor has a null system **ACL**.

SaclDefaulted   Pointer to a Boolean variable. If the value stored into the variable pointed to by *SaclPresent* is TRUE, the function sets the variable pointed to by *SaclDefaulted* to the value of the security descriptor's **SaclDefaulted** control flag. If the value stored into the variable pointed to by *SaclPresent* is FALSE, no value is set.

Return Value   If the function is successful, the return value is TRUE.

If the function fails, the return value is FALSE. Call **GetLastError** for more detailed error information.

See Also   **GetSecurityDescriptorGroup, GetSecurityDescriptorControl, GetSecurityDescriptorDacl, GetSecurityDescriptorLength, GetSecurityDescriptorOwner, InitializeSecurityDescriptor, IsValidSecurityDescriptor, SetSecurityDescriptorDacl, SetSecurityDescriptorGroup, SetSecurityDescriptorOwner, SetSecurityDescriptorSacl**

■ GetSidIdentifierAuthority

PSID_IDENTIFIER_AUTHORITY GetSidIdentifierAuthority(*Sid***)**
PSID *Sid*;

The **GetSidIdentifierAuthority** function returns the address of an **SID**'s IdentifierAuthority field.

Parameters   *Sid*   Pointer to the **SID** data structure whose IdentifierAuthority field address the function will return.

The **SID** data structure is an opaque data structure of variable length, defined as follows:

```
typedef PVOID * PSID;
```

Return Value   If the function is successful, the return value is the address of the specified **SID**'s IdentifierAuthority field.

If the function fails, the return value is undefined. The function will fail if the **SID** pointed to by *Sid* is invalid. Call **GetLastError** for more detailed error information.

See Also   **CopySid, EqualSid, GetLengthSid, InitializeSid, IsValidSid, GetSidLengthRequired, GetSidSubAuthority, GetSidSubAuthorityCount**

■ GetSidLengthRequired

ULONG GetSidLengthRequired(*SubAuthorityCount***)**
ULONG *SubAuthorityCount*;

The **GetSidLengthRequired** function returns the length, in bytes, required to store a **SID** security identifier having a specified number of sub-authorities.

Parameters   *SubAuthorityCount*   Specifies the number of sub-authorities to be stored in the **SID**.

Return Value   If the function is successful, the return value is the length in bytes required to store the **SID**.

This function can't fail. It just calculates a value based on the *SubAuthorityCount* parameter.

See Also   **CopySid, EqualSid, GetLengthSid, InitializeSid, IsValidSid, GetSidIdentifierAuthority, GetSidSubAuthority, GetSidSubAuthorityCount**

■ GetSidSubAuthority

PULONG GetSidSubAuthority(*Sid, SubAuthority***)**
PSID *Sid*;
ULONG *SubAuthority*;

The **GetSidSubAuthority** function returns the address of a sub-authority array element of an **SID** security identifier.

Parameters   *Sid*   Pointer to the **SID** data structure whose sub-authority array element address the function will return.

The **SID** data structure is an opaque data structure of variable length, defined as follows:

```
typedef PVOID * PSID;
```

SubAuthority   An index value that specifies the sub-authority array element whose address the function will return.

The function performs no validation tests on this value.

Return Value   If the function is successful, the return value is the address of the specified **SID** sub-authority array element.

If the function fails, the return value is undefined. The function will fail if the specified **SID** is invalid, or if the *SubAuthority* index value is out of bounds.

See Also   **CopySid, EqualSid, GetLengthSid, InitializeSid, IsValidSid, GetSidIdentifierAuthority, GetSidLengthRequired, GetSidSubAuthorityCount**

■ GetSidSubAuthorityCount

PUCHAR GetSidSubAuthorityCount(*Sid***)**
PSID *Sid*;

The **GetSidSubAuthorityCount** function returns the address of the sub-authority count field of an **SID** security identifier.

Parameters   *Sid*   Pointer to the **SID** data structure whose count field address the function will return.

The **SID** data structure is an opaque data structure of variable length, defined as follows:

```
typedef PVOID * PSID;
```

Return Value   If the function is successful, the return value is the address of the sub-authority count field of the specified **SID**.

If the **SID** passed to the function is invalid, the return value is undefined.

See Also   **CopySid, EqualSid, GetLengthSid, InitializeSid, IsValidSid, GetSidIdentifierAuthority, GetSidLengthRequired, GetSidSubAuthority**

■ GetStartupInfo

VOID APIENTRY GetStartupInfo(*lpStartupInfo***)**
LPSTARTUPINFO *lpStartupInfo*;

The **GetStartupInfo** function retrieves the startup information for the current process.

The **GetStartupInfo** function may be used as either a wide-character function (where text arguments must use Unicode) or an ANSI function (where text arguments must use characters from the Windows 3.x character set installed).

Parameters   *lpStartupInfo*   Specifies a pointer to a **STARTUPINFO** structure that will be filled in by the API. The pointer fields of the structure will point to static strings.

Here is an overview of the **STARTUPINFO** data structure:

```
typedef struct _STARTUPINFO {
    DWORD   cb;
    LPTSTR  lpReserved;
    LPTSTR  lpDesktop;
    LPTSTR  lpTitle;
    DWORD   dwX;
    DWORD   dwY;
    DWORD   dwXSize;
    DWORD   dwYSize;
    DWORD   dwFlags;
    WORD    wShowWindow;
    WORD    cbReserved2;
    LPBYTE  lpReserved2;
} STARTUPINFOA, *LPSTARTUPINFOA;
```

For detailed information on this data structure, see **STARTUPINFO**.

Return Value   This function does not return a value.

See Also   GetCommandLine, CreateProcess, GetEnvironmentVariable,
SetEnvironmentVariable, STARTUPINFO

■ GetStdHandle

HANDLE GetStdHandle(*nStdHandle***)**
DWORD *nStdHandle*;

The handles for StdIn, StdOut, and StdErr can be retrieved by calling
GetStdHandle.

Parameters   *nStdHandle*   Supplies the std handle to be retrieved.

Value	Meaning
STD_INPUT_HANDLE	return the StdIn handle
STD_OUTPUT_HANDLE	return the StdOut handle
STD_ERROR_HANDLE	return the StdErr handle

Return Value   The return value is a handle if the function is successful. Otherwise it is −1
(0xFFFFFFFF) in which case extented error information can be retrieved by
calling the **GetLastError** function.

Applications that wish to read from or write to the console should pass the handle
returned by **GetStdHandle** to **ReadFile** or **WriteFile**.

See Also   SetStdHandle

■ GetStockObject

HANDLE GetStockObject(*iIndex***)**
int *iIndex*;

The **GetStockObject** function retrieves a handle to one of the predefined stock
pens, brushes, fonts, or palette.

Parameters   *iIndex*   Specifies the type of stock object desired. It can be any one of the
following values:

Value	Meaning
BLACK_BRUSH	Black brush
DKGRAY_BRUSH	Dark gray brush
GRAY_BRUSH	Gray brush
HOLLOW_BRUSH	Hollow brush
LTGRAY_BRUSH	Light gray brush
NULL_BRUSH	Null brush
WHITE_BRUSH	White brush
BLACK_PEN	Black pen

Value	Meaning
NULL_PEN	Null pen
WHITE_PEN	White pen
ANSI_FIXED_FONT	ANSI fixed width system font
ANSI_VAR_FONT	ANSI variable width system font
DEVICE_DEFAULT_FONT	Device-dependent font
OEM_FIXED_FONT	Device-dependent fixed width font
SYSTEM_FONT	The system font. By default, Windows uses the system font to draw menus, dialog-box controls, and other text. This is the same as ANSI_VAR_FONT.
SYSTEM_FIXED_FONT	This is the same as ANSI_FIXED_FONT.
DEFAULT_PALETTE	Default color palette. This palette consists of the 20 static colors always present in the system palette for matching colors in the logical palettes of background windows.

Return Value   The return value is the handle of the desired logical object if the function is successful. Otherwise, it is 0.

■ GetStretchBltMode

int GetStretchBltMode(*hDC***)**
HDC *hDC*;

The **GetStretchBltMode** function retrieves the current stretching mode. The stretching mode defines how information is to be added or removed from bitmaps that are stretched or compressed by using the **StretchBlt** function.

Parameters   *hDC*   Identifies the device context.

Return Value   The return value specifies the current stretching mode. It is 0 if an error occured.

For more information, see the **SetStretchBltMode** function.

See Also   **StretchBlt, SetStretchBltMode**

■ GetSubMenu

HMENU GetSubMenu(*hMenu, nPos***)**
HMENU *hMenu*;
int *nPos*;

This function retrieves the menu handle of a pop-up menu.

Parameters	*hMenu* Identifies the menu.
	nPos Specifies the position in the given menu of the pop-up menu. Position values start at zero for the first menu item. The pop-up menu's integer ID cannot be used in this function.
Return Value	The return value identifies the given pop-up menu. It is NULL if no pop-up menu exists at the given position.
See Also	**GetMenu, CreatePopupMenu**

■ GetSysColor

DWORD GetSysColor(*nIndex***)**
int *nIndex*;

This function retrieves the current color of the display element specified by the *nIndex* parameter. Display elements are the various parts of a window and the Windows display that appear on the system display screen.

Parameters	*nIndex* Specifies the display element whose color is to be retrieved. For a list of the index values, see the SetSysColor function, later in this chapter.
Return Value	The return value specifies an RGB color value that names the color of the given element.
Comments	System colors for monochrome displays are usually interpreted as various shades of gray.
See Also	**SetSysColors**

■ GetSystemDir

WORD GetSystemDir(*szAppDir, lpBuffer, nSize***)**
LPSTR *szAppDir,*
LPSTR *lpBuffer,*
int *nSize*;

The **GetSystemDir** function returns the pathname of the Windows system subdirectory in *lpBuffer*. The system subdirectory contains such files as Windows libraries, drivers, and font files.

This function exists only in the static-link version of the version library. Applications that are not installing software should use **GetSystemDirectory** to determine the Windows directory.

Parameters	*szAppDir* Specifies the directory where the software is being installed. This directory corresponds to the current working directory in a search for Windows files.

lpBuffer   Points to the buffer that is to receive the null-terminated string containing the pathname.

nSize   Indicates the size of the buffer, in bytes, pointed to by *lpBuffer*.

Return Value

The return value is the length of the string copied to *lpBuffer*, including the terminating null character. If the return value is greater than *nSize*, the return value is the size of the buffer required to hold the pathname. The return value is zero if the function failed, in which case extended error information is available from the **GetLastError** function.

Comments

This function exists only in the static link version of the version library.

The pathname retrieved by this function does not end with a backslash unless the Windows system directory is the root directory. For example, if the system directory is named WINDOWS\SYSTEM on drive C:, the pathname of the system subdirectory retrieved by this function is C:\WINDOWS\SYSTEM.

See Also

GetWindowsDir, **GetSystemDirectory**

■ GetSystemDirectory

```
DWORD GetSystemDirectory(lpBuffer, dwSize)
LPTSTR lpBuffer;    /* buffer to receive the system path  */
DWORD dwSize;       /* size of the buffer                 */
```

The **GetSystemDirectory** function obtains the pathname of the Windows system subdirectory. The system subdirectory contains such files as Windows libraries, drivers, and font files.

The **GetSystemDirectory** function may be used as either a wide-character function (where text arguments must use Unicode) or an ANSI function (where text arguments must use characters from the Windows 3.x character set installed).

Parameters

lpBuffer   Points to the buffer that is to receive the null-terminated string containing the pathname.

dwSize   Specifies the maximum size (in bytes) of the buffer. This value should be set to at least MAX_PATH to allow sufficient room in the buffer for the pathname.

Return Value

The return value is the length in bytes of the string copied to *lpBuffer*, not including the terminating null character. Note that an ANSI-ASCII null character uses one byte, a Unicode null character uses two bytes. If the return value is greater than *dwSize*, the return value is the size of the buffer required to hold the pathname. The return value is zero if the function failed, in which case extended error information is available from the **GetLastError** function.

Comments

The pathname retrieved by this function does not end with a backslash unless the system directory is the root directory. For example, if the system directory is named WINDOWS\SYSTEM on drive C:, the pathname of the system subdirectory retrieved by this function is C:\WINDOWS\SYSTEM.

See Also   GetWindowsDirectory, GetCurrentDirectory, SetCurrentDirectory

■ GetSystemInfo

VOID GetSystemInfo (*lpSystemInfo***)**
LPSYSTEM_INFO *lpSystemInfo*;

The **GetSystemInfo** function returns information about the current system. This information includes the processor type, page size, oem id, and other interesting pieces of information.

Parameters   *lpSystemInfo*   Points to a SYSTEM_INFO data structure whose fields this function will fill in order to provide information about the current system.

The SYSTEM_INFO data structure has the following form:

```
typedef struct _SYSTEM_INFO {
    DWORD dwOemId;
    DWORD dwPageSize;
    LPVOID lpMinimumApplicationAddress;
    LPVOID lpMaximumApplicationAddress;
    DWORD dwActiveProcessorMask;
    DWORD dwNumberOfProcessors;
    DWORD dwProcessorType;
    DWORD dwProcessorRevision;
    DWORD dwProcessorOptions;
} SYSTEM_INFO, *LPSYSTEM_INFO;
```

For detailed descriptions of this structure's members, see **SYSTEM_INFO**.

Return Value   This function does not return a value.

See Also   **SYSTEM_INFO**

■ GetSystemMenu

HMENU GetSystemMenu(*hWnd, bRevert***)**
HWND *hWnd*;
BOOL *bRevert*;

This function allows the application to access the System menu for copying and modification.

Parameters   *hWnd*   Identifies the window that will own a copy of the System menu.

bRevert   Specifies the action to be taken.

If *bRevert* is FALSE, the **GetSystemMenu** returns a handle to a copy of the System menu currently in use. This copy is initially identical to the System menu, but can be modified.

If *bRevert* is a non-zero value, and the system menu has been modified, **GetSystemMenu** destroys the copy of the system menu and returns NULL. If *bRevert* is a non-zero value, and the system menu hasn't been modified, **GetSystemMenu** returns the handle of the current copy of the system menu.

Return Value   The return value identifies the System menu if *bRevert* is nonzero and the System menu has been modified. If *bRevert* is nonzero and the System menu has *not* been modified, the return value is NULL. If *bRevert* is zero, the return value identifies a copy of the System menu.

Comments   Any window that does not use the **GetSystemMenu** function to make its own copy of the System menu receives the standard System menu.

The handle returned by the **GetSystemMenu** function can be used with the **AppendMenu, InsertMenu** or **ModifyMenu** functions to change the System menu. The System menu initially contains items identified with various ID values such as SC_CLOSE, SC_MOVE, and SC_SIZE. Menu items on the System menu send WM_SYSCOMMAND messages. All predefined System-menu items have ID numbers greater than 0xF000. If an application adds commands to the System menu, it should use ID numbers less than F000.

Windows automatically grays items on the standard System menu, depending on the situation. The application can carry out its own checking or graying by responding to the WM_INITMENU message, which is sent before any menu is displayed.

See Also   **AppendMenu, InsertMenu, ModifyMenu, GetMenu**

■ GetSystemMetrics

int GetSystemMetrics(*nIndex***)**
int *nIndex*;

This function retrieves the system metrics. The system metrics are the widths and heights of various display elements of the Windows display. The **GetSystemMetrics** function can also return flags that indicate whether the current version is a debugging version, whether a mouse is present, or whether the meaning of the left and right mouse buttons have been exchanged.

Parameters   *nIndex*   Specifies the system measurement to be retrieved. All measurements are given in pixels. The system measurement must be one of the following values:

Index	Meaning
SM_CXBORDER	Width of window frame that cannot be sized.
SM_CYBORDER	Height of window frame that cannot be sized.
SM_CYCAPTION	Actual caption height plus SM_CYBORDER.
SM_CXCURSOR	Width of cursor.
SM_CYCURSOR	Height of cursor.
SM_CXDLGFRAME	Width of frame when window has WS_DLGFRAME style.

Index	Meaning
SM_CYDLGFRAME	Height of frame when window has WS_DLGFRAME style.
SM_CXDOUBLECLK	Width (in pixels) of the rectangle around the location of the first click in a double-click sequence. The second click must occur within this rectangle for the system to consider the two clicks a double click.
SM_CYDOUBLECLK	Height (in pixels) of the rectangle around the location of the first click in a double-click sequence. The second click must occur within this rectangle for the system to consider the two clicks a double click.
SM_CXFRAME	Width of window frame that can be sized.
SM_CYFRAME	Height of window frame that can be sized.
SM_CXFULLSCREEN	Width of window client area for full-screen window.
SM_CYFULLSCREEN	Height of window client area for full-screen window (equivalent to the height of the screen minus the height of the window caption).
SM_CXHSCROLL	Width of arrow bitmap on horizontal scroll bar.
SM_CYHSCROLL	Height of arrow bitmap on horizontal scroll bar.
SM_CXICON	Width of icon.
SM_CYICON	Height of icon.
SM_CXICONSPACING	Width of the rectangles that Program Manager uses to position tiled icons.
SM_CYICONSPACING	Height of the rectangles that Program Manager uses to position tiled icons.
SM_CYKANJIWINDOW	Height of Kanji window.
SM_CYMENU	Height of single-line menu bar minus SM_CYBORDER.
SM_CXMIN	Minimum width of window.
SM_CYMIN	Minimum height of window.
SM_CXMINTRACK	Minimum tracking width of window.
SM_CYMINTRACK	Minimum tracking height of window.
SM_CXSCREEN	Width of screen.
SM_CYSCREEN	Height of screen.

Index	Meaning
SM_CXSHADOWDEPTH	Specifies the width of the shadow, specified in multiples of SM_CXBORDER.
SM_CYSHADOWDEPTH	Specifies the height of the shadow, specified in mutliples of SM_CYBORDER.
SM_CXSIZE	Width of bitmaps contained in the title bar.
SM_CYSIZE	Height of bitmaps contained in the title bar.
SM_CXVSCROLL	Width of arrow bitmap on vertical scroll bar.
SM_CYVSCROLL	Height of arrow bitmap on vertical scroll bar.
SM_CXHTHUMB	Width of thumb box on horizontal scroll bar.
SM_CYVTHUMB	Height of thumb box on vertical scroll bar.
SM_DEBUG	Nonzero if Windows debugging version.
SM_MENUDROPALIGHMENT	Alignment of popup menus. If this value is 0, the left side of a popup menu is aligned with the left side of the corresponding menu-bar item. If this value is nonzero, the left side of a popup menu is aligned with the right side of the corresponding menu-bar item.
SM_MOUSEPRESENT	Nonzero if mouse hardware installed.
SM_SWAPBUTTON	Nonzero if left and right mouse buttons swapped.

Return Value   The return value specifies the requested system metric.

Comments   System metrics depend on the system display and may vary from display to display.

■ GetSystemPaletteEntries

UINT GetSystemPaletteEntries(*hDC, iStartIndex, nNumEntries, lpPaletteEntries*)
HDC *hDC*;
UINT *iStartIndex*;
UINT *nNumEntries*;
LPPALETTEENTRY *lpPaletteEntries*;

The **GetSystemPaletteEntries** function retrieves a range of palette entries from the palette currently realized for the surface associated with *hDC*.

Parameters   *hDC*   Identifies the device context.

iStartIndex   Specifies the first entry in the palette to be retrieved.

nNumEntries   Specifies the number of entries in the palette to be retrieved.

lpPaletteEntries   Points to an array of **PALETTEENTRY** structures to receive the palette entries. The array must contain at least as many data structures as specified by the *nNumEntries* parameter. If this parameter is NULL, the function will return the total number of entries in the palette.

Return Value   The return value is the number of entries retrieved from the palette. It is ERROR if the function failed.

■ GetSystemPaletteUse

UINT GetSystemPaletteUse(*hDC***)**
HDC *hDC*;

The **GetSystemPaletteUse** function determines whether an application has access to the full physical palette of the device. By default, the physical palette contains 20 static colors which are not changed when an application realizes its logical palette. An application can gain access to most of these colors by calling the **SetSystemPaletteUse** function.

The *hDC* parameter must refer to a device that supports color palettes.

Parameters   *hDC*   Identifies the device context.

Return Value   The return value specifies the current use of the physical palette. It is any of the following values:

Value	Meaning
SYSPAL_NOSTATIC	System palette contains no static colors except black and white.
SYSPAL_STATIC	System palette contains static colors which will not change when an application realizes its logical palette.
SYSPAL_ERROR	The *hDC* is invalid or refers to a non-palette capable device.

See Also   **SetSystemPaletteUse**

■ GetSystemTime

VOID GetSystemTime(*lpSystemTime***)**
LPSYSTEMTIME *lpSystemTime*;

The **GetSystemTime** function retrieves the current system time and date.

Parameters   *lpSystemTime*   Points to a **SYSTEMTIME** structure that receives the current system date and time: The **SYSTEMTIME** structure has the following form:

```
typedef struct _SYSTEMTIME {
    WORD wYear;
    WORD wMonth;
```

```
            WORD wDayOfWeek;
            WORD wDay;
            WORD wHour;
            WORD wMinute;
            WORD wSecond;
            WORD wMilliseconds;
        } SYSTEMTIME;
        typedef SYSTEMTIME *PSYSTEMTIME;
        typedef SYSTEMTIME *LPSYSTEMTIME;
```

Return Value   This function does not return a value.

See Also   **SetSystemTime**

■ GetTabbedTextExtent

DWORD GetTabbedTextExtent(*hDC, lpString, nCount, nTabPositions, lpnTabStopPositions***)**

HDC *hDC*;	/* device-context handle */
LPTSTR *lpString*;	/* pointer to string */
int *nCount*;	/* number of characters in string */
int *nTabPositions*;	/* number of tab positions */
LPINT *lpnTabStopPositions*;	/* pointer to array of tab positions */

The **GetTabbedTextExtent** function computes the width and height of a character string. If the string contains one or more tab characters, the width of the string is based upon the tab stops specified by the *lpnTabStopPositions* parameter. The **GetTabbedTextExtent** function uses the currently selected font to compute the dimensions of the string.

The **GetTabbedTextExtent** function may be used as either a wide-character function (where text arguments must use Unicode) or an ANSI function (where text arguments must use characters from the Windows 3.x character set installed).

Parameters   *hDC*   Identifies the device context.

lpString   Points to a character string.

nCount   Specifies the number of bytes in the text string.

nTabPositions   Specifies the number of tab-stop positions in the array pointed to by the *lpnTabStopPositions* parameter.

lpnTabStopPositions   Points to an array containing the tab-stop positions (in device units). The tab stops must be sorted in increasing order; the smallest *x*-value should be the first item in the array.

Return Value   The return value specifies the dimensions of the string (in logical units). The height is in the high-order word and the width is in the low-order word.

Comments   The current clipping region does not affect the width and height returned by the **GetTabbedTextExtent** function.

Since some devices do not place characters in regular cell arrays (that is, they kern the characters), the sum of the extents of the characters in a string may not be equal to the extent of the string.

If the *nTabPositions* parameter is zero and the *lpnTabStopPositions* parameter is NULL, tabs are expanded to eight times the average character width.

If *nTabPositions* is 1, the tab stops are separated by the distance specified by the first value in the array to which *lpnTabStopPositions* points.

See Also   **GetTextExtent, HIWORD, LOWORD, TabbedTextOut**

■ GetTempDrive

The **GetTempDrive** function has been replaced by the **GetTempPath** function.

See Also   **GetTempPath**

■ GetTempFileName

WORD GetTempFileName(*lpPathName, lpPrefixString, wUnique, lpTempFileName***)**
LPTSTR *lpPathName*;
LPTSTR *lpPrefixString*;
WORD *wUnique*;
LPTSTR *lpTempFileName*;

The **GetTempFileName** function creates a temporary filename.

The **GetTempFileName** function may be used as either a wide-character function (where text arguments must use Unicode) or an ANSI function (where text arguments must use characters from the Windows 3.x character set installed).

Parameters   *lpPathName*   Specifies the null terminated pathname of the directory to create the temporary file within.

UNC paths that are valid at the time of the call are acceptable.

lpPrefixString   Points to a null-terminated string to be used as the temporary filename prefix. This is limited to three characters.

wUnique   Specifies an unsigned short integer. If this parameter is zero, a unique number will be returned by the function.

lpTempFileName   Points to the buffer that is to receive the temporary filename. This string consists of characters in the OEM-defined character set. This buffer should be at least MAX_PATH bytes in length to allow sufficient room for the pathname.

Return Value   The return value specifies a unique numeric value used in the temporary filename. If a nonzero value was given for the *wUnique* parameter, the return value specifies this same number.

Comments   To avoid problems resulting from converting an OEM character string to an ANSI string, an application should call the **_lopen** function to create the temporary file.

If the *wUnique* parameter is zero, **GetTempFileName** attempts to form a unique number based on the current system time. If a file with the resulting filename exists, the number is increased by one and the test for existence is repeated. This continues until a unique filename is found; **GetTempFileName** then creates a file by that name and closes it. No attempt is made to create and open the file when *wUnique* is nonzero.

An application can call **GetTempPath** to obtain a value for *lpPathName*.

An existing relative path can be used for *lpPathName*.

See Also   **OpenFile, GetTempPath**

■ GetTempPath

DWORD GetTempPath(*nBufferLength, lpBuffer*)
DWORD *nBufferLength*;
LPTSTR *lpBuffer*;

The **GetTempPath** function obtains the pathname of the directory that should be used to create temporary files.

The **GetTempPath** function may be used as either a wide-character function (where text arguments must use Unicode) or an ANSI function (where text arguments must use characters from the Windows 3.x character set installed).

Parameters   *nBufferLength*   Specifies the size in bytes of the string buffer pointed to by *lpBuffer*.

lpBuffer   Pointer to a string buffer that the function will fill with the temporary file pathname.

Return Value   The return value is the length in bytes of the string copied to *lpBuffer*, not including the terminating null character. If the return value is greater than *nBufferLength*, the return value is the size of the buffer required to hold the pathname. The return value is zero if the function failed.

See Also   **GetTempFileName**

■ GetTextAlign

UINT GetTextAlign(*hDC*)
HDC *hDC*;

The **GetTextAlign** function retrieves the status of the text alignment flags. The text alignment flags determine how the **TextOut** and **ExtTextOut** functions align a string of text in relation to the string's reference point, which is provided to **TextOut** or **ExtTextOut**.

Parameters   *hDC*   Identifies the device context.

Return Value   The return value specifies the status of the text alignment flags. The return value
is a combination of one or more of the following values. The bounding rectangle
is a rectangle bounding all the character cells and has the size returned by
GetTextExtent.

Value	Meaning
TA_BASELINE	The reference point will be on the baseline of the text.
TA_BOTTOM	The reference point will be on the bottom edge of the bounding rectangle.
TA_TOP	The reference point will be on the top edge of the bounding rectangle.
TA_CENTER	The reference point will be aligned horizontally with the center of the bounding rectangle.
TA_LEFT	The reference point will be on the left edge of the bounding rectangle.
TA_RIGHT	The reference point will be on the right edge of the bounding rectangle.
TA_NOUPDATECP	The current position is not updated after each text output call.
TA_UPDATECP	The current position is updated after each text output call.

When the current font has a vertical default baseline, e.g. as with Kanji, then the
following values will be used instead of TA_BASELINE and TA_CENTER.

Value	Meaning
VTA_BASELINE	The reference point will be on the baseline of the text.
VTA_CENTER	The reference point will be aligned vertically with the center of the bounding rectangle.

If an error occurs, the value ERROR is returned.

Comments   The text alignment flags are not necessarily single bit flags and may be equal to
zero.

The flags must be examined in groups of related flags, shown in the following list:

- TA_LEFT, TA_RIGHT, and TA_CENTER.
- TA_BOTTOM, TA_TOP, and TA_BASELINE.
- TA_NOUPDATECP and TA_UPDATECP.

If the current font has a vertical default baseline, the related flags are instead:

- TA_LEFT, TA_RIGHT, and VTA_BASELINE.
- TA_BOTTOM, TA_TOP, and VTA_CENTER.
- TA_NOUPDATECP and TA_UPDATECP.

To verify that a particular flag is set in the return value of this function, the application must perform the following steps:

1   Apply the bitwise OR operator to the flag and its related flags.

2   Apply the bitwise AND operator to the result and the return value.

3   Test for the equality of this result and the flag.

The following example shows a method for determining which horizontal alignment flag is set:

```
switch ((TA_LEFT | TA_RIGHT | TA_CENTER) & GetTextAlign(hDC))
{
case TA_LEFT:
    .
    .
    .
case TA_RIGHT:
    .
    .
    .
case TA_CENTER:
    .
    .
    .
}
```

See Also   **ExtTextOut, SetTextAlign, TextOut**

■ GetTextCharacterExtra

int GetTextCharacterExtra(*hDC***)**
HDC *hDC*;

The **GetTextCharacterExtra** function retrieves the current intercharacter spacing. The intercharacter spacing defines the extra space, in logical units along the baseline, that the **TextOut** or **ExtTextOut** functions add to each character as a line is written. The spacing is used to expand lines of text.

Parameters   *hDC*   Identifies the device context.

Return Value   The return value specifies the current intercharacter spacing. Upon error, the return value is INVALID_WIDTH.

See Also   **ExtTextOut, TextOut**

■ GetTextColor

COLORREF GetTextColor(*hDC***)**
HDC *hDC*;

The **GetTextColor** function retrieves the current text color. The text color defines the foreground color of characters drawn by using the **TextOut** or **ExtTextOut** functions.

Parameters	*hDC* Identifies the device context.
Return Value	The return value specifies the current text color as a COLORREF value. It is CLR_INVALID if an error occures.
See Also	**ExtTextOut, TextOut**

■ GetTextExtentPoint

BOOL GetTextExtentPoint(*hDC, lpString, nCount, lpSize***)**
HDC *hDC*;
LPTSTR *lpString*;
int *nCount*;
LPSIZE *lpSize*;

The **GetTextExtentPoint** function computes the width and height of the line of text pointed to by the *lpString* parameter. The **GetTextExtentPoint** function uses the currently selected font to compute the dimensions of the string. The width and height, in logical units, are computed without considering any clipping.

The **GetTextExtentPoint** function may be used as either a wide-character function (where text arguments must use Unicode) or an ANSI function (where text arguments must use characters from the Windows 3.x character set

Parameters	*hDC* Identifies the device context.
	lpString Points to a text string.
	nCount Specifies the number of bytes in the text string.
	lpSize Points to a **SIZE** data structure. The dimensions of the string are returned here.
Return Value	The return value is TRUE if the function is successful or FALSE if an error occurs.
Comments	Since some devices do not place characters in regular cell arrays, that is they carry out kerning, the sum of the extents of the characters in a string may not be equal to the extent of the string.
	The calculated width takes into account the intercharacter spacing set by **SetTextCharacterExtra**.
See Also	**SetTextCharacterExtra**

GetTextExtentPointEx

DWORD GetTextExtentPointEx(*hdc, lpszString, cbString, nMaxExtent, lpnFit, alpDx***)**
HDC *hdc*;   /* device-context handle   */
LPSTR *lpszString*;   /* pointer to string   */
int *cbString*;   /* number of bytes in string   */
int *nMaxExtent*;   /* maximum width for formatted string   */
LPINT *lpnFit*;   /* pointer to int for chars fitting in max extent */
LPINT *alpDx*;   /* pointer to array for partial string widths */

The **GetTextExtentPointEx** function retrieves the number of characters in a specified string that will fit within a given space and fills an array with text extents for those characters. Each text extent gives the distance between the beginning of the space and each character that will fit in the space. This information is useful for word-wrapping calculations.

Parameters

hdc   Identifies the device context.

lpszString   Points to a null-terminated string for which extents are retrieved.

cbString   Specifies the number of bytes in the string pointed to by the *lpszString* parameter.

nMaxExtent   Specifies the maximum width (in logical units) for the formatted string.

lpnFit   Points to an integer specifying, when the function returns, the number of characters that will fit in the space given by the *nMaxExtent* parameter. When the *lpnFit* parameter is NULL, the *nMaxExtent* parameter is ignored.

alpDx   Points to an array of integers that contains partial string extents when the function returns. Each element in the array gives the distance (in logical units) between the beginning of the string and one of the characters that fits in the space specified by the *nMaxExtent* parameter. Although this array should have at least as many elements as characters specified by the *cbString* parameter, the function fills the array with extents only for as many characters as are given by the *lpnFit* parameter. If *alpDx* is NULL, the function does not compute partial string widths.

Return Value

The return value specifies the dimensions of the string (in logical units). The height is in the high-order word and the width is in the low-order word.

Comments

If both the *lpnFit* and *alpDx* parameters are NULL, the **GetTextExtentPointEx** function is equivalent to **GetTextExtentPoint**.

See Also

GetTextExtentPoint

GetTextFace

int GetTextFace(*hDC, nCount, lpFaceName***)**
HDC *hDC*;
int *nCount*;
LPTSTR *lpFaceName*;

The **GetTextFace** function copies the typeface name of the selected font into a buffer pointed to by the *lpFaceName* parameter. The typeface name is copied as a null-terminated character string. The *nCount* parameter specifies the maximum number of bytes to be copied. If the name is longer than the number of bytes specified by *nCount*, it is truncated.

The **GetTextFace** function may be used as either a wide-character function (where text arguments must use Unicode) or an ANSI function (where text arguments must use characters from the Windows 3.x character set

Parameters

hDC   Identifies the device context.

nCount   Specifies the size of the buffer in bytes.

lpFaceName   Points to the buffer that is to receive the typeface name. If this parameter is NULL, the function returns the number of bytes in the name, counting the null-terminator.

Return Value

The return value specifies the actual number of bytes copied to the buffer. It is 0 if an error occurs.

See Also

GetTextAlign, GetTextColor, GetTextExtentPoint, GetTextMetrics

■ GetTextMetrics

BOOL GetTextMetrics(*hDC, lpMetrics***)**
HDC *hDC*;
LPTEXTMETRIC *lpMetrics*;

The **GetTextMetrics** function fills the buffer pointed to by the *lpMetrics* parameter with the metrics for the currently selected font.

Parameters

hDC   Identifies the device context.

lpMetrics   Points to the **TEXTMETRIC** structure that is to receive the metrics.

Return Value

The return value is TRUE if the function is successful. Otherwise, it is FALSE.

■ GetThreadContext

BOOL GetThreadContext(*hThread, lpContext***)**
HANDLE *hThread*;
LPCONTEXT *lpContext*;

The context of a specified thread can be retreived using GetThreadContext.

Parameters

hThread   Supplies an open handle to a thread whose context is to be retreived. The handle must have been created with THREAD_GET_CONTEXT access to the thread.

lpContext   Supplies the address of a context structure that receives the appropriate context of the specified thread. The value of the ContextFlags field of this structure specifies which portions of a threads context are to be retreived. The context structure is highly machine specific. There are currently two versions of the context structure. One version exists for x86 processors, and another exists for MIPS processors.

Return Value   The return value is TRUE if the function is successful or FALSE if an error occurs.

Comments   This function is used to retreive the context of the specified thread. The API allows selective context to be retrieved based on the value of the **ContextFlags** member of the context structure. The specified thread does not have to be being debugged in order for this API to operate. The caller must simply have a handle to the thread that was created with THREAD_GET_CONTEXT access.

The current format of the context structure is:

```
//
// The Context structure for the x86 is defined as follows
//

//
// The following flags control
// the contents of the CONTEXT structure.
//

#define CONTEXT_i386 0x00010000 // this assumes that i386 and
#define CONTEXT_i486 0x00010000 // i486 have identical context records

#define CONTEXT_CONTROL           (CONTEXT_i386 | 0x00000001L)
      // SS:SP, CS:IP, FLAGS, BP
#define CONTEXT_INTEGER           (CONTEXT_i386 | 0x00000002L)
      // AX, BX, CX, DX, SI, DI
#define CONTEXT_SEGMENTS          (CONTEXT_i386 | 0x00000004L)
      // DS, ES, FS, GS
#define CONTEXT_FLOATING_POINT    (CONTEXT_i386 | 0x00000008L)
      // 387 state
#define CONTEXT_DEBUG_REGISTERS   (CONTEXT_i386 | 0x00000010L)
      // DB 0-3,6,7

#define CONTEXT_FULL (CONTEXT_CONTROL | CONTEXT_INTEGER |\
                      CONTEXT_SEGMENTS | CONTEXT_FLOATING_POINT)

#define SIZE_OF_80387_REGISTERS      80

typedef struct _FLOATING_SAVE_AREA {
    DWORD    ControlWord;
    DWORD    StatusWord;
    DWORD    TagWord;
    DWORD    ErrorOffset;
    DWORD    ErrorSelector;
    DWORD    DataOffset;
    DWORD    DataSelector;
    UCHAR    RegisterArea[SIZE_OF_80387_REGISTERS];
} FLOATING_SAVE_AREA;

typedef FLOATING_SAVE_AREA *PFLOATING_SAVE_AREA;

//
// Context Frame
//
//  This frame has a several purposes: 1) it is used as an argument to
//  NtContinue, 2) is is used to constuct a call frame for APC delivery,
//  and 3) it is used in the user level thread creation routines.
```

```
//
//  The layout of the record conforms to a standard call frame.
//

typedef struct _CONTEXT {

    //
    // The flags values within this flag control the contents of
    // a CONTEXT record.
    //
    // If the context record is used as an input parameter, then
    // for each portion of the context record controlled by a flag
    // whose value is set, it is assumed that that portion of the
    // context record contains valid context. If the context record
    // is being used to modify a threads context, then only that
    // portion of the threads context will be modified.
    //
    // If the context record is used as an IN OUT parameter to capture
    // the context of a thread, then only those portions of the thread's
    // context corresponding to set flags will be returned.
    //
    // The context record is never used as an OUT only parameter.
    //

    DWORD ContextFlags;

    //
    // This section is specified/returned if the
    // ContextFlags word contians the flag CONTEXT_FLOATING_POINT.
    //

    FLOATING_SAVE_AREA FloatSave;

    //
    // This section is specified/returned if the
    // ContextFlags word contians the flag CONTEXT_SEGMENTS.
    //

    DWORD   SegGs;
    DWORD   SegFs;
    DWORD   SegEs;
    DWORD   SegDs;

    //
    // This section is specified/returned if the
    // ContextFlags word contians the flag CONTEXT_INTEGER.
    //

    DWORD   Edi;
    DWORD   Esi;
    DWORD   Ebx;
    DWORD   Edx;
    DWORD   Ecx;
    DWORD   Eax;

    //
    // This section is specified/returned if the ContextFlags word contains
    // the flag CONTEXT_DEBUG_REGISTERS. Note that on set context, the
    // G bits in Dr7 are always cleared.
    //

    DWORD   Dr0;
    DWORD   Dr1;
    DWORD   Dr2;
    DWORD   Dr3;
```

```
        DWORD    Dr6;
        DWORD    Dr7;

        //
        // This section is specified/returned if the
        // ContextFlags word contians the flag CONTEXT_CONTROL.
        //

        DWORD    Ebp;
        DWORD    Eip;
        DWORD    SegCs;                   // MUST BE SANITIZED
        DWORD    EFlags;                  // MUST BE SANITIZED
        DWORD    Esp;
        DWORD    SegSs;

}CONTEXT;

//
// The Context structure for the MIPS is defined as follows
//


//
// The following flags control the contents of the CONTEXT structure.
//

#define CONTEXT_CONTROL         0x00000001L
#define CONTEXT_FLOATING_POINT  0x00000002L
#define CONTEXT_INTEGER         0x00000004L

#define CONTEXT_FULL (CONTEXT_CONTROL | \
                      CONTEXT_FLOATING_POINT | \
                      CONTEXT_INTEGER)


typedef struct _CONTEXT {

        //
        // This section is always present and is used as an argument build
        // area.
        //

        ULONG Argument[4];

        //
        // This section is specified/returned if the ContextFlags word contains
        // the flag CONTEXT_FLOATING_POINT.
        //

        ULONG FltF0;
        ULONG FltF1;
        ULONG FltF2;
        ULONG FltF3;
        ULONG FltF4;
        ULONG FltF5;
        ULONG FltF6;
        ULONG FltF7;
        ULONG FltF8;
        ULONG FltF9;
        ULONG FltF10;
        ULONG FltF11;
        ULONG FltF12;
        ULONG FltF13;
        ULONG FltF14;
        ULONG FltF15;
        ULONG FltF16;
```

```
        ULONG FltF17;
        ULONG FltF18;
        ULONG FltF19;
        ULONG FltF20;
        ULONG FltF21;
        ULONG FltF22;
        ULONG FltF23;
        ULONG FltF24;
        ULONG FltF25;
        ULONG FltF26;
        ULONG FltF27;
        ULONG FltF28;
        ULONG FltF29;
        ULONG FltF30;
        ULONG FltF31;

        //
        // This section is specified/returned if the ContextFlags word contains
        // the flag CONTEXT_INTEGER.
        //
        // N.B. The registers gp, sp, and ra are defined in this section, but
        //  are considered part of the control context rather than part of the
        //  integer context.
        //
        // N.B. Register zero is not stored in the frame.
        //

        ULONG IntZero;
        ULONG IntAt;
        ULONG IntV0;
        ULONG IntV1;
        ULONG IntA0;
        ULONG IntA1;
        ULONG IntA2;
        ULONG IntA3;
        ULONG IntT0;
        ULONG IntT1;
        ULONG IntT2;
        ULONG IntT3;
        ULONG IntT4;
        ULONG IntT5;
        ULONG IntT6;
        ULONG IntT7;
        ULONG IntS0;
        ULONG IntS1;
        ULONG IntS2;
        ULONG IntS3;
        ULONG IntS4;
        ULONG IntS5;
        ULONG IntS6;
        ULONG IntS7;
        ULONG IntT8;
        ULONG IntT9;
        ULONG IntK0;
        ULONG IntK1;
        ULONG IntGp;
        ULONG IntSp;
        ULONG IntS8;
        ULONG IntRa;
        ULONG IntLo;
        ULONG IntHi;

        //
        // This section is specified/returned if the ContextFlags word contains
        // the flag CONTEXT_FLOATING_POINT.
```

```
        //

        ULONG Fsr;

        //
        // This section is specified/returned if the ContextFlags word contains
        // the flag CONTEXT_CONTROL.
        //
        // N.B. The registers gp, sp, and ra are defined in the integer section,
        //   but are considered part of the control context rather than part of
        //   the integer context.
        //

        ULONG Fir;
        ULONG Psr;

        //
        // The flags values within this flag control the contents of
        // a CONTEXT record.
        //
        // If the context record is used as an input parameter, then
        // for each portion of the context record controlled by a flag
        // whose value is set, it is assumed that that portion of the
        // context record contains valid context. If the context record
        // is being used to modify a thread's context, then only that
        // portion of the threads context will be modified.
        //
        // If the context record is used as an IN OUT parameter to capture
        // the context of a thread, then only those portions of the thread's
        // context corresponding to set flags will be returned.
        //
        // The context record is never used as an OUT only parameter.
        //

        ULONG ContextFlags;

        ULONG Fill[2];
    } CONTEXT, *PCONTEXT;
```

See Also	**SetThreadContext**

■ GetThreadDesktop

HANDLE GetThreadDesktop(*dwThread***)**
DWORD *dwThread*;

This api returns the actual desktop handle associated with **dwThread**.

Parameters   *dwThread*   This uniquely identifies a thread in the system whose desktop is being queried. **GetCurrentThread** may be called to reference the currently running thread.

Return Value   Returns the same desktop handle associated with **dwThread**.

■ GetThreadPriority

int GetThreadPriority(*hThread***)**
HANDLE *hThread*;

The specified thread's priority can be read using **GetThreadPriority**.

Parameters   *hThread*   Supplies a handle to the thread whose priority is to be set. The handle must have been created with THREAD_QUERY_INFORMATION access.

Return Value   The return value is the thread's current priority if the function is successful. Otherwise it is THREAD_PRIORITY_ERROR_RETURN in which case extended error information is available from the **GetLastError** function.

A thread's current priority may be read using **GetThreadPriority**.

See Also   **SetThreadPriority**

■ GetThreadSelectorEntry

BOOL GetThreadSelectorEntry (*hThread, dwSelector, lpSelectorEntry*)
HANDLE *hThread*;
DWORD *dwSelector*;
LPLDT_ENTRY *lpSelectorEntry*;

This function is used to return a descriptor table entry for the specified thread corresponding to the specified selector.

Parameters   *hThread*   Supplies a handle to the thread that contains the specified selector. The handle must have been created with THREAD_QUERY_INFORMATION access.

dwSelector   Supplies the selector value to look up. The selector value may be a global selector or a local selector.

lpSelectorEntry   If the specified selector is contained within the thread's descriptor tables, its descriptor table entry is copied into the data structure pointed to by this parameter. This data can be used to compute the linear base address that segment relative addresses refer to.

Return Value   The return value is TRUE if the operation was successful. In that case, the data structure pointed to by *lpSelectorEntry* receives a copy of the specified descriptor table entry.

The return value is FALSE or NULL if the operation failed. In that case, more detailed information is available using **GetLastError**.

Comments   This API is only functional on x86 based systems. For non-x86 based systems a value of FALSE is returned.

This API is used by a debugger so that it can convert segment relative addresses to linear virtual address (since this is the only format supported by ReadMemoryProcess and WriteMemoryProcess).

A descriptor table entry has the following structure:

```
//
// descriptor table entry data structure...
//

typedef struct _LDT_ENTRY {
```

```
WORD     LimitLow;
WORD     BaseLow;
union {
    struct {
        BYTE     BaseMid;
        BYTE     Flags1;      // Declare as bytes to
        BYTE     Flags2;      // avoid alignment Problems.
        BYTE     BaseHi;
    } Bytes;
    struct {
        DWORD    BaseMid : 8;
        DWORD    Type : 5;
        DWORD    Dpl : 2;
        DWORD    Pres : 1;
        DWORD    LimitHi : 4;
        DWORD    Sys : 1;
        DWORD    Reserved_0 : 1;
        DWORD    Default_Big : 1;
        DWORD    Granularity : 1;
        DWORD    BaseHi : 8;
    } Bits;
} HighWord;
} LDT_ENTRY, *PLDT_ENTRY;
```

■ GetTickCount

DWORD GetTickCount(VOID)

This function obtains the number of milliseconds that have elapsed since the system was started.

This function has no parameters.

Return Value   The return value specifies the number of milliseconds that have elapsed since the system was started.

■ GetTokenInformation

BOOL GetTokenInformation(_TokenHandle, TokenInformationClass, TokenInformation, TokenInformationLength, ReturnLength_**)**
HANDLE _TokenHandle_;
TOKEN_INFORMATION_CLASS _TokenInformationClass_;
PVOID _TokenInformation_;
ULONG _TokenInformationLength_;
PULONG _ReturnLength_;

The **GetTokenInformation** function retrieves various types of information about a specified token. The caller must have appropriate access privileges to obtain the information, as noted below in the discussion of the _TokenInformation_ parameter

Parameters   _TokenHandle_   Handle to the token whose information the function will retrieve.

TokenInformationClass   Specifies the type of token information the function will retrieve and put into the buffer pointed to by _TokenInformation_.

TOKEN_INFORMATION_CLASS is an enumerated type. Possible values are listed in the discussion of the *TokenInformation* parameter.

TokenInformation   Pointer to a buffer that the function will fill with the requested information. The buffer must be aligned on at least a longword boundary. The type of data structure put into the buffer depends upon the type of information specified by the *TokenInformationClass* parameter, as shown in this list:

Token Information Class	Structure Returned

TokenUser	**TOKEN_USER** data structure. TOKEN_QUERY access is needed to retrieve this information about a token.
	
	The **TOKEN_USER** data structure has the following form:
	
	<pre>typedef struct tagTOKEN_USER {
	    SID_AND_ATTRIBUTES User;
	} TOKEN_USER ;</pre>

TokenGroups	**TOKEN_GROUPS** data structure. TOKEN_QUERY access is needed to retrieve this information about a token.
	
	The **TOKEN_GROUPS** data structure has the following form:
	
	<pre>typedef struct tagTOKEN_GROUPS {
	    ULONG GroupCount;
	    SID_AND_ATTRIBUTES Groups[];
	} TOKEN_GROUPS ;</pre>

TokenPrivileges	**TOKEN_PRIVILEGES** data structure. TOKEN_QUERY access is needed to retrieve this information about a token.
	
	The **TOKEN_PRIVILEGES** data structure has the following form:
	
	<pre>typedef struct tagTOKEN_PRIVILEGES {
	    ULONG PrivilegeCount;
	    LUID_AND_ATTRIBUTES Privileges[];
	} TOKEN_PRIVILEGES ;</pre>

TokenOwner	**TOKEN_OWNER** data structure. TOKEN_QUERY access is needed to retrieve this information about a token.

Token Information Class	Structure Returned
	The **TOKEN_OWNER** data structure has the following form: ```\ntypedef struct tagTOKEN_OWNER {\n PSID Owner;\n} TOKEN_OWNER ;\n```
TokenPrimaryGroup	**TOKEN_PRIMARY_GROUP** data structure. TOKEN_QUERY access is needed to retrieve this information about a token. The **TOKEN_PRIMARY_GROUP** data structure has the following form: ```\ntypedef struct tagTOKEN_PRIMARY_GROUP {\n PSID PrimaryGroup;\n} TOKEN_PRIMARY_GROUP ;\n```
TokenDefaultDacl	**TOKEN_DEFAULT_DACL** data structure. TOKEN_QUERY access is needed to retrieve this information about a token. The **TOKEN_DEFAULT_DACL** data structure has the following form: ```\ntypedef struct tagTOKEN_DEFAULT_DACL {\n PACL DefaultDacl;\n} TOKEN_DEFAULT_DACL ;\n```
TokenSource	**TOKEN_SOURCE** data structure. TOKEN_QUERY_SOURCE access is needed to retrieve this information about a token. The **TOKEN_SOURCE** data structure has the following form: ```\ntypedef struct tagTOKEN_SOURCE {\n CHAR SourceName[8];\n LUID SourceIdentifier;\n} TOKEN_SOURCE ;\n```
TokenType	**TOKEN_TYPE** data structure. TOKEN_QUERY access is needed to retrieve this information about a token.

Token Information Class	Structure Returned
	The **TOKEN_TYPE** data structure has the following form:

```
typedef enum tagTOKEN_TYPE {
    TokenPrimary = 1,
    TokenImpersonation
} TOKEN_TYPE ;
```

Token Information Class	Structure Returned
TokenImpersonationLevel	**SECURITY_IMPERSONATION_LEVEL** data structure. TOKEN_QUERY access is needed to retrieve this information about a token. STATUS_INVALID_INFO_CLASS status is returned if the token type is not ImpersonationToken.
	The **SECURITY_IMPERSONATION_LEVEL** data structure has the following form:
TokenStatistics	**TOKEN_STATISTICS** data structure. TOKEN_QUERY access is needed to retrieve this information about a token.
	The **TOKEN_STATISTICS** data structure has the following form:

```
typedef struct tagTOKEN_STATISTICS {
    LUID            TokenId;
    GUID            AuthenticationId;
    TIME            ExpirationTime;
    TOKEN_TYPE      TokenType;
    SECURITY_IMPERSONATION_LEVEL
                    ImpersonationLevel;
    ULONG           DynamicCharged;
    ULONG           DynamicAvailable;
    ULONG           GroupCount;
    ULONG           PrivilegeCount;
    LARGE_INTEGER ModifiedId;
} TOKEN_STATISTICS ;
```

TokenInformationLength　　Specifies the size in bytes of the buffer pointed to by *TokenInformation*.

ReturnLength　　Pointer to a variable that the function will set to the actual size in bytes of the requested information. If this value is larger than the value specified by *TokenInformationLength*, then the buffer pointed to by *TokenInformation* is too small, and the function stores no data into the buffer.

If the value of *TokenInformationClass* is TokenDefaultDacl, and the token has no default, the function sets the variable pointed to by *ReturnLength* to zero, and stores no data into the buffer.

Return Value　　If the function is successful, the return value is TRUE.

If the function fails, the return value is FALSE. Call **GetLastError** for more detailed error information.

See Also **AdjustTokenGroups, AdjustTokenPrivileges, OpenProcessToken, OpenThreadToken, SetTokenInformation**

■ GetTopWindow

HWND GetTopWindow(*hWnd*)
HWND *hWnd*;

This function searches for a handle to the top-level child window that belongs to the parent window associated with the *hWnd* parameter. If the window has no children, this function returns NULL.

Parameters *hWnd* Identifies the parent window.

If *hWnd* is NULL, **GetTopWindow** will return the first top-level window on the desktop (the desktop window's first child window).

Return Value The return value identifies a handle to the top-level child window in a parent window's linked list of child windows. If no child windows exist, it is NULL.

See Also **GetWindow, GetNextWindow**

■ GetUpdateRect

BOOL GetUpdateRect(*hWnd, lpRect, bErase*)
HWND *hWnd*;
LPRECT *lpRect*;
BOOL *bErase*;

This function retrieves the coordinates of the smallest rectangle that completely encloses the update region of the given window. If the window was created with the CS_OWNDC style and the mapping mode is not MM_TEXT, the **GetUpdateRect** function gives the rectangle in logical coordinates. Otherwise, **GetUpdateRect** gives the rectangle in client coordinates. If there is no update region, **GetUpdateRect** makes the rectangle empty (sets all coordinates to zero).

The *bErase* parameter specifies whether **GetUpdateRect** should erase the background of the update region. If *bErase* is TRUE and the update region is not empty, the background is erased. To erase the background, **GetUpdateRect** sends a WM_ERASEBKGND message to the given window.

Parameters *hWnd* Identifies the window whose update region is to be retrieved.

lpRect Points to the **RECT** structure that is to receive the client coordinates of the enclosing rectangle.

bErase Specifies whether the background in the update region is to be erased.

Return Value	The return value specifies the status of the update region of the given window. It is nonzero if the update region is not empty. Otherwise, it is zero.
Comments	The update rectangle retrieved by the **BeginPaint** function is identical to that retrieved by the **GetUpdateRect** function.
	BeginPaint automatically validates the update region, so any call to **GetUpdateRect** made immediately after the **BeginPaint** call retrieves an empty update region.
See Also	**BeginPaint, GetUpdateRgn**

■ GetUpdateRgn

```
int GetUpdateRgn(hWnd, hRgn, bErase)
HWND hWnd;
HRGN hRgn;
BOOL bErase;
```

This function copies a window's update region into a region identified by the *hRgn* parameter. The coordinates of this region are relative to the upper-left corner of the window (client coordinates).

Parameters   *hWnd*   Identifies the window that contains the region to be updated.

hRgn   Identifies the update region.

bErase   Specifies whether or not the window background should be erased and nonclient areas of child windows should be drawn. If it is zero, no drawing is done.

Return Value   The return value indicates the type of resulting region. It can be any one of the following values:

Value	Meaning
COMPLEXREGION	The region has overlapping borders.
ERROR	No region was created.
NULLREGION	The region is empty.
SIMPLEREGION	The region has no overlapping borders.

Comments   **BeginPaint** automatically validates the update region, so any call to **GetUpdateRgn** made immediately after the **BeginPaint** call retrieves an empty update region.

See Also   **BeginPaint, GetUpdateRect**

■ GetUserObjectSecurity

BOOL GetUserObjectSecurity (*ObjectDescriptor, SecurityInformation, ResultantDescriptor, DescriptorLength, ReturnLength*)
PSECURITY_DESCRIPTOR *ObjectDescriptor;*
PSECURITY_INFORMATION *SecurityInformation;*
PSECURITY_DESCRIPTOR *ResultantDescriptor;*
ULONG *DescriptorLength;*
PULONG *ReturnLength;*

The **GetUserObjectSecurity** function retrieves information from an existing security descriptor on an existing server application's object. The existing security descriptor must be in self-relative format.

This function does no access checking. Do all access checking before calling this function. An access check should include, as appropriate, checks for READ_CONTROL privilege and the privilege to assign a system **ACL**.

Parameters
ObjectDescriptor Pointer to a pointer to a **SECURITY_DESCRIPTOR** data structure. This is the security descriptor the function will retrieve information from.

The **SECURITY_DESCRIPTOR** data structure has the following form:

```
typedef PVOID PSECURITY_DESCRIPTOR;
```

SecurityInformation Pointer to a **SECURITY_INFORMATION** data structure that specifies the security information being requested.

The **SECURITY_INFORMATION** data structure has the following form:

```
typedef ULONG SECURITY_INFORMATION;
```

ResultantDescriptor Pointer to a buffer into which the function will store the resultant security descriptor. The resultant security descriptor will contain all information specified by the *SecurityInformation* parameter.

DescriptorLength Specifies the length in bytes of the buffer pointed to by *ResultantDescriptor*.

ReturnLength Pointer to a variable that the function will set to the actual number of bytes needed to store the requested information. If the value returned is greater than the value specified by *DescriptorLength*, the function returns the value STATUS_BUFFER_TOO_SMALL and stores no information into the buffer.

Return Value
If the function is successful, the return value is TRUE.

If the function fails, the return value is FALSE. Call **GetLastError** for more detailed error information.

See Also
AbsoluteToSelfRelativeSD, CreateUserObjectSecurity, DestroyUserObjectSecurity, SelfRelativeToAbsoluteSD, SetUserObjectSecurity

■ GetVersion

DWORD GetVersion(VOID)

The **GetVersion** function specifies the current version number of Windows, and the current version number of the operating system.

This function has no parameters.

Return Value   The return value specifies the major and minor version numbers of Windows, and the major and minor version numbers of the operating system. The high-order byte of the low-order word specifies the minor version number of Windows; the low-order byte of the low-order word specifies the major version number of Windows. The high-order byte of the high-order word specifies the major version number of the operating system; the low-order byte of the high-order word specifies the minor version number of the operating system.

■ GetViewportExtEx

BOOL GetViewportExtEx(*hDC, lpSize*)
HDC *hDC*;
LPSIZE *lpSize*;

The **GetViewportExtEx** function retrieves the x and y extents of the device context's viewport.

Parameters   *hDC*   Identifies the device context.

lpSize   Points to a **SIZE** structure. The x and y extents (in device units) are placed in this structure.

Return Value   The return value is TRUE if the function is successful. Otherwise, it is FALSE.

■ GetViewportOrgEx

BOOL GetViewportOrgEx(*hDC, lpPoint*)
HDC *hDC*;
LPPOINT *lpPoint*;

The **GetViewportOrgEx** function retrieves the x and y coordinates of the origin of the viewport associated with the specified device context.

Parameters   *hDC*   Identifies the device context.

lpPoint   Points to a **POINT** structure. The origin of the viewport (in device coordinates) is placed in this structure.

Return Value   The return value is TRUE if the function is successful. Otherwise, it is FALSE.

■ GetVolumeInformation

BOOL GetVolumeInformation(*lpRootPathName, lpVolumeNameBuffer, nVolumeNameSize,*
lpVolumeSerialNumber, lpMaximumComponentLength, lpFileSystemFlags,
*lpFileSystemNameBuffer, nFileSystemNameSize***)**
LPTSTR *lpRootPathName;*
LPTSTR *lpVolumeNameBuffer;*
DWORD *nVolumeNameSize;*
LPDWORD *lpVolumeSerialNumber;*
LPDWORD *lpMaximumComponentLength;*
LPDWORD *lpFileSystemFlags;*
LPTSTR *lpFileSystemNameBuffer;*
DWORD *nFileSystemNameSize;*

The **GetVolumeInformation** function returns information about the file system whose root directory is specified.

The **GetVolumeInformation** function may be used as either a wide-character function (where text arguments must use Unicode) or an ANSI function (where text arguments must use characters from the Windows 3.x character set installed).

Parameters

lpRootPathName An optional parameter, that if specified, supplies the root directory of the file system that information is to be returned about. If this parameter is not specified, then the root of the current directory is used.

lpVolumeNameBuffer An optional parameter that if specified returns the name of the specified volume.

nVolumeNameSize Supplies the length in bytes of the volume name buffer. This parameter is ignored if the volume name buffer is not supplied.

lpVolumeSerialNumber An optional parameter that if specified points to a pair of DWORDS. The first DWORD contains the low order 32-bits of the volume serial number. The second dword contains the high order 32-bits of the volume serial number. If the file system does not support 64-bit volume serial numbers, then the high order 32-bits are zero.

lpMaximumComponentLength An optional parameter that if specified returns the maximum length in bytes of a filename component supported by the specified file system. A filename component is that portion of a filename between pathname seperators.

lpFileSystemFlags An optional parameter that if specified returns flags associated with the specified file system. It can be any combination of the following flags:

Value	Meaning
FS_CASE_IS_PRESERVED	Indicates that the case of file names is preserved when the name is placed on disk.
FS_CASE_SENSITIVE	Indicates that the file system supports case sensative file name lookup.

Value	Meaning
FS_UNICODE_STORED_ON_DISK	Indicates that the file system supports unicode in file names as they appear on disk.

lpFileSystemNameBuffer   An optional parameter that if specified returns the name for the specified file system (e.g. FAT, HPFS...).

nFileSystemNameSize   Supplies the length of the file system name buffer. This parameter is ignored if the file system name buffer is not supplied.

Return Value   The return value is TRUE if ALL the REQUESTED information was retrieved, or FALSE if an error occurred.

■ GetWindow

```
HWND GetWindow(hWnd, wCmd)
HWND hWnd;
UINT wCmd;
```

This function searches for a handle to a window from the window manager's list. The window-manager's list contains entries for all top-level windows, their associated child windows, and the child windows of any child windows. The *wCmd* parameter specifies the relationship between the window identified by the *hWnd* parameter and the window whose handle is returned.

Parameters   *hWnd*   Identifies the original window.

wCmd   Specifies the relationship between the original window and the returned window. It may be one of the following values:

Value	Meaning
GW_CHILD	Identifies the window's first child window.
GW_HWNDFIRST	Returns the first sibling window for a child window. Otherwise, it returns the first top-level window in the list.
GW_HWNDLAST	Returns the last sibling window for a child window. Otherwise, it returns the last top-level window in the list.
GW_HWNDNEXT	Returns the window that follows the given window on the window manager's list.
GW_HWNDPREV	Returns the previous window on the window manager's list.
GW_OWNER	Identifies the window's owner.

Return Value   The return value identifies a window. It is NULL if it reaches the end of the window manager's list or if the *wCmd* parameter is invalid.

See Also   **GetTopWindow, GetActiveWindow, GetNextWindow**

■ GetWindowBufferAttributes

BOOL GetWindowBufferAttributes(*hWnd, lphBitmap, lpX, lpY, lpnFlushRate, lpFlags*)
HWND *hWnd*;
LPHBITMAP *lphBitmap*;
LPINT *lpX*;
LPINT *lpY*;
LPDWORD *lpnFlushRate*;
LPDWORD *lpFlags*;

This function allows an application to get the bitmap buffering parameters associated with hwnd.

Parameters   *hWnd*   Window to get buffering attributes of.

lphBitmap   Pointer to a bitmap handle. If non-NULL, the handle of the bitmap currently being used for buffering will be returned through this parameter. This is NOT a copy of the bitmap, but the real handle being used. If this bitmap is to be used in any operation, either buffering needs to be turned off or the buffer flush rate needs to be set to 0 so that the window manager will not need this bitmap simultaneously.

lpX   Pointer to an integer. If non-NULL, the x coordinate of the bitmap origin will be returned through this parameter.

lpY   Pointer to an integer. If non-NULL, the y coordinate of the bitmap origin will be returned through this parameter.

lpnFlushRate   Pointer to a dword use for the buffer flush rate. If non-NULL, the buffer flush rate is returned through this parameter.

lpFlags   Pointer to a dword of flags. If non-NULL, the bitmap buffering flags will be returned through this parameter.

Return Value   TRUE is returned for success, FALSE for failure.

See Also   **SetWindowBufferAttributes BeginWindowBuffer EndWindowBuffer**

■ GetWindowDC

HDC GetWindowDC(*hWnd*)
HWND *hWnd*;

This function retrieves the display context for the entire window, including caption bar, menus, and scroll bars. A window display context permits painting anywhere in a window, including the caption bar, menus, and scroll bars, since the origin of the context is the upper-left corner of the window instead of the client area.

GetWindowDC assigns default attributes to the display context each time it retrieves the context. Previous attributes are lost.

Parameters   *hWnd*   Identifies the window whose display context is to be retrieved.

Return Value   The return value identifies the display context for the given window if the function is successful. Otherwise, it is NULL.

Comments   The **GetWindowDC** function is intended to be used for special painting effects within a window's nonclient area. Painting in nonclient areas of any window is not recommended.

The **GetSystemMetrics** function can be used to retrieve the dimensions of various parts of the nonclient area, such as the caption bar, menu, and scroll bars.

After painting is complete, the **ReleaseDC** function must be called to release the display context. Failure to release a window display context will have serious effects on painting requested by applications.

See Also   **GetSystemMetrics, ReleaseDC, GetDC**

■ GetWindowExtEx

BOOL GetWindowExtEx(*hDC, lpSize***)**
HDC *hDC*;
LPSIZE *lpSize*;

This function retrieves the *x* and *y* extents of the window associated with the specified device context.

Parameters   *hDC*   Identifies the device context.

lpSize   Points to a **SIZE** structure. The *x* and *y* extents (in logical units) are placed in this structure.

Return Value   The return value is TRUE if the function is successful. Otherwise, it is FALSE.

■ GetWindowLong

LONG GetWindowLong(*hWnd, nIndex***)**
HWND *hWnd*;
int *nIndex*;

This function retrieves information about the window identified by the *hWnd* parameter.

Parameters   *hWnd*   Identifies the window.

nIndex   Specifies the byte offset of the value to be retrieved. It can also be one of the following values:

Value	Meaning
GWL_EXSTYLE	Extended window style.
GWL_STYLE	Window style
GWL_WNDPROC	Long pointer to the window function

Value	Meaning
GWL_HMODULE	Module handle of the module that owns the window.
GWL_HWNDPARENT	Handle of the parent window, if any. The **SetParent** function changes the parent window of a child window. An application should not call the **SetWindowLong** function to change the parent of a child window.
GWL_ID	Control ID of the child window.
GWL_USERDATA	This index can be used to access a LONG that is reserved in every window structure. This LONG is reserved specifically for applications. In general an application should not store values in this LONG if the associated window was created by some other application.

Return Value   The return value specifies information about the given window.

Comments   To access any extra four-byte values allocated when the window-class structure was created, use a positive byte offset as the index specified by the *nIndex* parameter, starting at zero for the first four-byte value in the extra space, 4 for the next four-byte value and so on.

See Also   **SetWindowLong, GetWindowWord, SetWindowWord**

■ GetWindowOrgEx

BOOL GetWindowOrgEx(*hDC, lpPoint***)**
HDC *hDC*;
LPPOINT *lpPoint*;

This function retrieves the *x* and *y* coordinates of the origin of the window associated with the specified device context.

Parameters   *hDC*   Identifies the device context.

lpPoint   Points to a **POINT** structure. The origin of the window (in logical coordinates) is placed in this structure.

Return Value   The return value is TRUE if the function is successful. Otherwise, it is FALSE.

■ GetWindowRect

BOOL GetWindowRect(*hWnd, lpRect***)**
HWND *hWnd*;
LPRECT *lpRect*;

This function copies the dimensions of the bounding rectangle of the specified window into the structure pointed to by the *lpRect* parameter. The dimensions are given in screen coordinates, relative to the upper-left corner of the display screen, and include the caption, border, and scroll bars, if present.

Parameters   *hWnd*   Identifies the window.

lpRect   Points to a **RECT** structure that contains the screen coordinates of the upper-left and lower-right corners of the window.

Return Value   Returns TRUE for success, FALSE for failure.

See Also   **GetClientRect**

■ GetWindowRgn

HRGN GetWindowRgn(*hWnd*)
HWND *hWnd*;

The **GetWindowRgn** function is used to return the window clipping region associated with *hWnd*.

Parameters   *hWnd*   Specifies the window which contains the window clipping region.

Return Value   If no window clipping region is associated with *hWnd*, NULL is returned. Otherwise the window clipping region is returned (not a copy of it, but the actual handle).

See Also   **SetWindowRgn**

■ GetWindowsDir

WORD GetWindowsDir(*szAppDir*, *lpBuffer*, *nSize*)
LPSTR *szAppDir*;
LPSTR *lpBuffer*;
int *nSize*;

The **GetWindowsDir** function returns the pathname of the Windows directory in *lpBuffer*. The Windows directory contains such files as Windows applications, initialization files, and help files.

This function exists only in the static-link version of the version library. Applications that are not installing software should use **GetWindowsDirectory** to determine the Windows directory.

Parameters   *szAppDir*   Specifies the directory where the software is being installed. This directory corresponds to the current working directory in a search for Windows files.

lpBuffer   Points to the buffer that is to receive the null-terminated string containing the pathname.

nSize   Indicates the size of the buffer, in bytes, pointed to by *lpBuffer*.

Return Value   The return value is the length of the string copied to *lpBuffer*, including the terminating null character. If the return value is greater than *nSize*, the return value is the size of the buffer required to hold the pathname. The return value is zero if the function failed, in which case extended error information is available from the **GetLastError** function.

Comments   This function exists only in the static link version of the version library.

The pathname retrieved by this function does not end with a backslash unless the Windows directory is the root directory. For example, if the Windows directory is named WINDOWS on drive C:, the pathname of the Windows directory retrieved by this function is C:\WINDOWS. If Windows was installed in the root directory of drive C:, the pathname retrieved by this function is C:\.

See Also   **GetSystemDir, GetWindowsDirectory**

■ GetWindowsDirectory

DWORD GetWindowsDirectory(*lpBuffer, dwSize***)**
LPTSTR *lpBuffer*,
DWORD *dwSize*;

The **GetWindowsDirectory** function obtains the pathname of the Windows directory. The Windows directory contains such files as Windows applications, initialization files, and help files.

The **GetWindowsDirectory** function may be used as either a wide-character function (where text arguments must use Unicode) or an ANSI function (where text arguments must use characters from the Windows 3.x character set installed).

Parameters   *lpBuffer*   Points to the buffer that is to receive the null-terminated string containing the pathname.

dwSize   Specifies the maximum size (in bytes) of the buffer. This value should be set to at least 144 to allow sufficient room in the buffer for the pathname.

Return Value   The return value is the length (in bytes) of the string copied to *lpBuffer*, not including the terminating null character. If the return value is greater than *dwSize*, the return value is the size of the buffer required to hold the pathname. The return value is zero if the function failed, in which case extended error information is available from the **GetLastError** function.

Comments   The pathname retrieved by this function does not end with a backslash unless the Windows directory is the root directory. For example, if the Windows directory is named WINDOWS on drive C:, the pathname of the Windows directory retrieved by this function is C:\WINDOWS. If Windows was installed in the root directory of drive C:, the pathname retrieved by this function is C:\.

See Also   **GetSystemDirectory, GetCurrentDirectory**

■ GetWindowStationAttrs

WORD GetWindowStationAttrs(*hWindowStation*, *lpWindowStation*, *cbWindowStation*, *lpWinStaAttrs***)**
HANDLE *hWindowStation*;
LPTSTR *lpWindowStation*;
WORD *cbWindowStation*;
LPWINSTAATTRS *lpWinStaAttrs*;

The **GetWindowStationAttrs** function obtains information about a windowstation.

The **GetWindowStationAttrs** function may be used as either a wide-character function (where text arguments must use Unicode) or an ANSI function (where text arguments must use characters from the Windows 3.x character set installed).

Parameters:

hWindowStation   Handle that specifies the windowstation whose information the function will retrieve.

lpWindowStation   Pointer to a buffer that the function will fill with the windowstation's name.

cbWindowStation   Specifies the size in bytes of the buffer pointed to by *lpWindowStation*.

lpWinStaAttrs   Pointer to a **WINSTAATTRS** structure that the function will fill with information about the windowstation. The **cb** field of the **WINSTAATTRS** structure must be set to the structure's size before calling **GetWindowStationAttrs**.

The **WINSTAATTRS** data structure has the following form:

```
typedef struct tagWINSTAATTRS {
    DWORD   cb;
    DWORD   cPhysicalDisplays;
    DWORD   dwReserved;
} WINSTAATTRS ;
```

Return Value

If the function is successful, the return value is the number of bytes copied into the buffer pointed to by *lpWindowStation*.

If the function fails, the return value is 0. Call **GetLastError** for more detailed error information.

If the function returns *cbWindowStation*, the function may have truncated the windowstation name stored into the buffer pointed to by *lpWindowStation*.

See Also

GetProcessWindowStation, SetProcessWindowStation, OpenWindowStation, CloseWindowStation, EnumWindowStations

■ GetWindowTask

The **GetWindowTask** function is now obsolete. It has been replaced by the **GetWindowThreadProcessId** function.

GetWindowTask is macroed onto the **GetWindowThreadProcessId** function to maintain compatibility for older applications. They may continue to call **GetWindowTask** as previously documented. New Windows32 applications should use **GetWindowThreadProcessId** .

Comments   **GetWindowTask** was defined as returning a HANDLE. **GetWindowThreadProcessId** returns a DWORD. The macro that maps **GetWindowTask** onto **GetWindowThreadProcessId** includes a cast to a HANDLE.

This is how **GetWindowTask** is macroed onto **GetWindowThreadProcessId**:

```
#define GetWindowTask(hWnd)\
        ((HANDLE)GetWindowThreadProcessId(hWnd, NULL))
```

See Also   **GetWindowThreadProcessId**

■ GetWindowText

int GetWindowText(*hWnd*, *lpString*, *nMaxCount***)**
HWND *hWnd*;
LPTSTR *lpString*;
int *nMaxCount*;

This function copies the given window's caption title (if it has one) into the buffer pointed to by the *lpString* parameter. If the *hWnd* parameter identifies a control, the **GetWindowText** function copies the text within the control instead of copying the caption.

The **GetWindowText** function may be used as either a wide-character function (where text arguments must use Unicode) or an ANSI function (where text arguments must use characters from the Windows 3.x character set

Parameters   *hWnd*   Identifies the window or control whose caption or text is to be copied.

lpString   Points to the buffer that is to receive the copied string.

nMaxCount   Specifies the maximum number of bytes to be copied to the buffer. If the string is longer than the number of bytes specified in the *nMaxCount* parameter, it is truncated.

Return Value   The return value specifies the length (in bytes) of the copied string. It is zero if the window has no caption or if the caption is empty.

Comments   This function causes a WM_GETTEXT message to be sent to the given window or control.

See Also   **SetWindowText, GetWindowTextLength**

■ GetWindowTextLength

int GetWindowTextLength(*hWnd*)
HWND *hWnd*;

This function returns the length in bytes of the given window's caption title. If the *hWnd* parameter identifies a control, the **GetWindowTextLength** function returns the length in bytes of the text within the control instead of the caption.

Parameters   *hWnd*   Identifies the window or control.

Return Value   The return value specifies the text length in bytes. It is zero if no such text exists.

See Also   **GetWindowText, SetWindowText**

■ GetWindowThreadProcessId

DWORD GetWindowThreadProcessId(*hWnd*, *lpdwProcessId*)
HWND *hWnd*;
LPDWORD *lpdwProcessId*;

This function lets you obtain identifiers for the thread and process that created a window.

Parameters   *hWnd*   Identifies the window of interest.

lpdwProcessId   Points to a DWORD where the function will store the process id of the process that created the window *hWnd*.

Return Value   The return value is the thread id of the thread that created the window *hWnd*. If *lpdwProcessId* is not NULL, the function puts the process id of the process that created *hWnd* into the DWORD *lpdwProcessId* points to.

Comments   Windows 3 used the API function **GetWindowTask** to obtain an hTask task handle for the task that created a window. New Windows 32 applications should use **GetWindowThreadProcessId** instead of **GetWindowTask**.

GetWindowTask is now obsolete. For compatibility, it is macroed on top of **GetWindowThreadProcessId** as follows:

```
#define GetWindowTask(hWnd)\
        ((HANDLE)GetWindowThreadProcessId(hWnd, NULL))
```

... with hTasks mapped to thread ids. Since **GetWindowTask** returned a handle in Win3, the macro casts the **GetWindowThreadProcessId** return value to a HANDLE. This handle is really the thread id of the thread that created hWnd.

■ GetWindowWord

DWORD GetWindowWord(*hWnd*, *nIndex*)
HWND *hWnd*;
int *nIndex*;

This function retrieves information about the window identified by *hWnd*.

Parameters   *hWnd*   Identifies the window.

nIndex   Specifies the byte offset of the value to be retrieved. See the following "comments" section for other values.

Return Value   The return value specifies information about the given window.

Comments   To access any extra two-byte values allocated when the window-class structure was created, use a positive byte offset as the index specified by the *nIndex* parameter, starting at zero for the first two-byte value in the extra space, 2 for the next two-byte value and so on. The return value will contain the retrieved two-byte value in its low-order word, with zero in its high-order word.

The following values for *nIndex* are supported for backwards compatibility. The preferred way to obtain the corresponding values is with the **GetWindowLong** function.

Value	Meaning
GWW_HMODULE	Module handle of the module that owns the window.
GWW_HWNDPARENT	Handle of the parent window, if any. The **SetParent** function changes the parent window of a child window. An application should not call the **SetWindowLong** function to change the parent of a child window.
GWW_HWNDPARENT	Parent window of hwnd

GetWindowWord stores and retrieves LONGs only when supporting the backward compatibility cases documented above. GetWindowWord stores and retrieves WORDs in all other cases. For this reason, applications that store their own handles into private window word indexes should beware: this won't work.

See Also   **SetWindowWord, GetWindowLong, SetWindowLong, SetParent, GetParent**

■ GetWinFlags

The **GetWinFlags** function has been deleted because its values were specific to the x86 hardware. A new function has been defined, called **GetSystemInfo**, that returns information about the hardware environment that the caller is running on.

See Also   **GetSystemInfo**

■ GetWorldTransform

BOOL GetWorldTransform(*hDC*, *lpXform***)**
HDC *hDC*;
LPXFORM *lpXform*;

The **GetWorldTransform** function returns the current World transform.

Parameters

hDC   Specifies the device context from which to get the transform.

lpXform   This is a pointer to the **XFORM** structure where the transform will be written.

Return Value

The return value is TRUE if the function succeeds, otherwise it is FALSE.

Comments

The World transform is stored internally in a higher precision format than **float**. This means that if **ModifyWorldTransform** is used, the transform returned by **GetWorldTransform** could have truncated precision.

See Also

SetWorldTransform, ModifyWorldTransform

■ GlobalAddAtom

ATOM GlobalAddAtom(*lpString*)
LPTSTR *lpString*;   /* string to add */

The **GlobalAddAtom** function adds a string to the system atom table and returns a unique value identifying the string. If the string already existed in the system atom table, the atom for the existing string will be returned, and the atom's reference count will be incremented by one. The string associated with the atom will not be deleted from memory until its reference count is zero (see the description of the **GlobalDeleteAtom** function).

The **GlobalAddAtom** function may be used as either a wide-character function (where text arguments must use Unicode) or an ANSI function (where text arguments must use characters from the Windows 3.x character set installed).

Parameters

lpString   Points to the null-terminated string to be added. The case of the first string added is preserved and returned by the **GlobalGetAtomName** function. Strings that differ only in case are considered identical.

Return Value

The return value identifies the the string if the function is successful. Otherwise, it is zero.

Comments

Global atoms are not automatically deleted when the application terminates. For every call to the **GlobalAddAtom** function, there must be a corresponding call to the **GlobalDeleteAtom** function.

The **GlobalAddAtom** function stores no more than one copy of a given string in the atom table. If the string is already in the table, the function returns the existing atom value and increases the string's reference count by one. The string's reference count is a number that specifies the number of times **GlobalAddAtom** has been called for a particular string.

The atom values returned by **GlobalAddAtom** are within the range 0xC000 to 0xFFFF. Atoms are case insensitive. If GlobalAddAtom is passed a string of the form "#1234" then it will return the atom value that is the 16-bit representation of the decimal number specified in the string (e.g. 0x04D2 in this case). If the decimal value specified is 0x0000 or 0xC000 through 0xFFFF then this function will return NULL to indicate an error. If the pointer to the string is within the range 0x0001 through 0xBFFF then this function will return the low order portion of the pointer as the atom value.

See Also   **AddAtom, GlobalDeleteAtom, GlobalGetAtomName**

■ GlobalAlloc

HANDLE GlobalAlloc(*dwFlags***,** *dwBytes***)**
DWORD *dwFlags*;
DWORD *dwBytes*;

The **GlobalAlloc** function allocates the number of bytes of memory specified by the *dwBytes* parameter from the global heap. The memory can be fixed or movable, depending on the memory type specified by the *dwFlags* parameter. The function returns a 32-bit handle.

Parameters   *dwFlags*   Specifies one or more flags that tell the **GlobalAlloc** function how to allocate the memory. It can be one or more of the following values:

Value	Meaning
GMEM_DDESHARE	Allocates sharable memory. This is used for dynamic data exchange (DDE) memory that is globally accessible to all Windows applications running in the current memory domain. Applications must specify this bit if the memory will be used in a DDE interchange with another Windows application.
	If this bit is specified, none of the remaining discardable memory bits are relevant, as shared memory is automatically visible to all Windows applications and therefore cannot be discardable. Also, shared memory is not automatically deallocated upon process termination. It must be explicitly freed when it is no longer needed.
GMEM_DISCARDABLE	Allocates discardable memory.
GMEM_FIXED	Allocated fixed memory.
GMEM_MOVEABLE	Allocates movable memory. Cannot be used with GMEM_FIXED.
GMEM_ZEROINIT	Initializes memory contents to zero. This flag is not required in 32-bit Windows; Windows always initializes the memory contents to zero.

Choose GMEM_FIXED or GMEM_MOVEABLE, and then combine others as needed by using the bitwise OR operator.

dwBytes   Specifies the number of bytes to be allocated.

Return Value

The return value identifies the allocated global memory if the function is successful. Otherwise, it is NULL, in which case an extended error status is available using the **GetLastError** function.

For non-discardable memory, the successful return value is the virtual address of the allocated memory. Since NULL is used to indicate an error, this implies that virtual address zero is never allocated. This is by design, as it makes detecting storing through NULL pointers easy. Most implementations of the Windows 32-bit Base API actually reserve the first 64KB of each process as no access, so that any reference to the first 64KB of memory will raise an access violation exception.

For discardable and/or moveable memory, the successful return value is a handle that must be translated into a virtual address by calling the **GlobalLock** function. The handle value is a 32-bit quantity. Handles values are private to the process that created them.

Comments

All memory is created with execute access, so no special call is required to execute dynamically generated code.

Some implementations of the Windows 32-bit Base API may ignore the discardable memory flag.

Memory allocated with this function will automatically be freed when the process that allocated it terminates. The one exception to this rule is if the memory was allocated with the GMEM_DDESHARE flag. In this case it is the responsibility of the caller to explicitly free the memory when it is no longer needed. Failure to do this will result in memory leaks.

Memory allocated with this function is guaranteed to be aligned on a 16 byte boundary.

See Also

GlobalSize

■ GlobalCompact

The **GlobalCompact** function is implemented by a macro that returns 0x100000L.

■ GlobalDeleteAtom

ATOM GlobalDeleteAtom(*nAtom***)**
ATOM *nAtom*;   /* specifies the atom to delete */

The **GlobalDeleteAtom** function decreases the reference count of a global atom by one. If the atom's reference count becomes zero, the string associated with the atom is removed from the system atom table.

An atom's reference count specifies the number of times the string has been added to the atom table. The **GlobalAddAtom** function increases the reference count each time it is called with a string that already exists in the system atom table.

Parameters

atom   Identifies the atom to be deleted.

Return Value

The return value is zero if the reference count was decreased (whether or not the associated string was deleted). The return value is zero if the atom passed in the *atom* parameter did not exist.

See Also

DeleteAtom, GlobalAddAtom

■ GlobalDiscard

HANDLE GlobalDiscard(*hMem***)**
HANDLE *hMem*,

The **GlobalDiscard** function discards a global memory block specified by the *hMem* parameter. The lock count of the memory block must be zero.

The global memory block is removed from memory, but its handle remains valid. An application can subsequently pass the handle to the **GlobalReAlloc** function to allocate another global memory block identified by the same handle.

Parameters

hMem   Identifies the global memory block to be discarded. This handle must have been created by a previous call to the **GlobalAlloc** or **GlobalReAlloc** function.

Return Value

The return value identifies the discarded block if the function is successful. Otherwise, it is zero.

Comments

The **GlobalDiscard** function discards only global objects that an application allocated with the GMEM_DISCARDABLE flag set. The function fails if an application attempts to discard a locked object.

See Also

GlobalReAlloc

■ GlobalDosAlloc

The **GlobalDosAlloc** function is deleted because it returns x86 specific segment values.

■ GlobalDosFree

The **GlobalDosFree** function is deleted because it accepts x86 specific segment values.

■ GlobalFindAtom

ATOM GlobalFindAtom(*lpString***)**
LPTSTR *lpString*;

The **GlobalFindAtom** function searches the atom table for the character string pointed to by the *lpString* parameter and retrieves the global atom associated with that string. (A global atom is an atom that is available to all Windows applications.)

The **GlobalFindAtom** function may be used as either a wide-character function (where text arguments must use Unicode) or an ANSI function (where text arguments must use characters from the Windows 3.x character set installed).

Parameters	*lpString* Points to the character string to be searched for. The string must be a null-terminated string.
Return Value	The return value identifies the global atom associated with the given string. It is NULL if the string is not in the table.
See Also	**AddAtom, DeleteAtom, FindAtom, GetAtomName, GlobalAddAtom, GlobalDeleteAtom, GlobalGetAtomName, InitAtomTable**

■ GlobalFix

This function is implemented as a macro that returns the input parameter.

■ GlobalFlags

DWORD GlobalFlags(*hMem***)**
HANDLE *hMem*;

The **GlobalFlags** function returns information about the global memory block specified by the *hMem* parameter.

Parameters	*hMem* Identifies the global memory block. This handle must have been created by a previous call to the **GlobalAlloc** or **GlobalReAlloc** function.
Return Value	If *hMem* is a valid handle, the return value specifies a memory-allocation flag in the high byte of the low word of the DWORD. The flag will be one of the following values:

Value	Meaning
GMEM_DDESHARE	The block can be shared. This is used for dynamic data exchange (DDE) only.
GMEM_DISCARDABLE	The block of memory can be discarded.
GMEM_DISCARDED	The block of memory has been discarded.

The low byte of the low word of the DWORD return value contains the lock count of the block. Use the GMEM_LOCKCOUNT mask to retrieve the lock-count value from the return value.

If *hMem* is invalid, **GlobalFlags** will return GMEM_INVALID_HANDLE.

Comments   To test whether or not an object can be discarded, AND the return value of **GlobalFlags** with GMEM_DISCARDABLE.

See Also   **GlobalLock, GlobalUnlock**

■ GlobalFree

LPVOID GlobalFree(*hMem***)**
HANDLE *hMem;*

The **GlobalFree** function frees the global memory block identified by the *hMem* parameter and invalidates the virtual addresses of the memory block. Any attempt to examine or modified memory after it has been freed will result in undefined behavior. The exception to this is if the memory has been allocated again with **GlobalAlloc** by some thread in the process.

Parameters   *hMem*   Identifies the global memory block to be freed.

Return Value   The return value identifies the outcome of the function. It is NULL if the function is successful. Otherwise, it is equal to *hMem*, in which case extended error information is available by using the **GetLastError** function.

Comments   The **GlobalFree** function must not be used to free a locked memory block, that is, a memory block with a lock count greater than zero. See the description of the **GlobalFlags** function for a list of the functions that affect the lock count.

See Also   **GlobalFlags, GlobalAlloc**

■ GlobalGetAtomName

DWORD GlobalGetAtomName(*nAtom, lpBuffer, dwSize***)**
ATOM *nAtom;*
LPTSTR *lpBuffer;*
DWORD *dwSize;*

The **GlobalGetAtomName** function retrieves a copy of the character string associated with the *nAtom* parameter and places it in the buffer pointed to by the *lpBuffer* parameter. The *dwSize* parameter specifies the maximum size in bytes of the buffer. (A global atom is an atom that is available to all Windows applications.)

The **GlobalGetAtomName** function may be used as either a wide-character function (where text arguments must use Unicode) or an ANSI function (where text arguments must use characters from the Windows 3.x character set installed).

Parameters	*nAtom* Identifies the character string to be retrieved.
	lpBuffer Points to the buffer that is to receive the character string.
	dwSize Specifies the maximum size (in bytes) of the buffer.
Return Value	The return value specifies the actual number of bytes copied to the buffer. It is zero if the specified global atom is not valid.
See Also	**GlobalFindAtom, GlobalDeleteAtom, GlobalAddAtom**

■ GlobalHandle

HANDLE GlobalHandle(*lpMem***)**
LPSTR *lpMem*;

The **GlobalHandle** function can be used to translate backwards from a pointer value to the handle that contains that pointer. The *lpMem* parameter must point to the first byte of an allocated memory block.

Parameters	*lpMem* Identifies a global memory block.
Return Value	The return value is the handle that describes the global memory block pointed to by the *lpMem* parameter if the function is successful. Otherwise it is NULL, in which case extended error information can be retrieved by calling the **GetLastError** function.
See Also	**GlobalLock**

■ GlobalLock

LPSTR GlobalLock(*hMem***)**
HANDLE *hMem*;

The **GlobalLock** function retrieves a pointer to the global memory block specified by the *hMem* parameter.

Locked memory is not subject to movement or discarding except when the memory block is being reallocated by the **GlobalReAlloc** function. The block will not be moved or discarded from memory until its lock count is decreased to zero. It will be pageable always.

Each time an application calls **GlobalLock** for an object, it must eventually call **GlobalUnlock** for the object. The GlobalUnlock function decreases the lock count for the object if **GlobalLock** increased the lock count for the object.

Parameters	*hMem* Identifies the global memory block to be locked.
Return Value	The return value points to the first byte of memory in the global block if the function is successful. If the object has been discarded or an error occurs, the return value is NULL, in which case extended error information can be obtained by using the **GetLastError** function.

Comments	Discarded objects always have a lock count of zero.
See Also	**GlobalFlags, GlobalReAlloc, GlobalUnlock**

■ GlobalLRUNewest

HANDLE GlobalLRUNewest(*hMem***)**
HANDLE *hMem*;

The **GlobalLRUNewest** function moves the global memory object identified by *hMem* to the newest least-recently-used (LRU) position in memory. This greatly reduces the likelihood that the object will be discarded soon, but does not prevent the object from eventually being discarded.

Parameters   *hMem*   Identifies the global memory object to be moved. This handle must have been created previously by a call to the **GlobalAlloc** or **GlobalReAlloc** function.

Return Value   The return value is NULL if the *hMem* parameter does not specify a valid handle.

Comments   This function is useful only if *hMem* is discardable.

■ GlobalLRUOldest

HANDLE GlobalLRUOldest(*hMem***)**
HANDLE *hMem*;

This routine moves the global memory object identified by *hMem* to the oldest least-recently-used (LRU) position in memory and, in so doing, makes it the next candidate for discarding.

Parameters   *hMem*   Identifies the global memory object to be moved. This handle must have been created previously by a call to the **GlobalAlloc** or **GlobalReAlloc** function.

Return Value   The return value is NULL if the *hMem* parameter does not specify a valid handle.

Comments   The **GlobalLRUOldest** function is useful only if *hMem* is discardable.

■ GlobalMemoryStatus

VOID GlobalMemoryStatus(*lpBuffer***)**
LPMEMORYSTATUS *lpBuffer*;

This function obtains information about the availability of memory on the current machine. The information returned is volatile and there is no guarantee that two sequential calls to this function will return the same values. Applications can use the function to determine how aggressive they can be about allocating memory without severely impacting other applications.

Parameters	*lpBuffer* A pointer to a data structure that is filled in by this function with advisory information about the current usage of the memory resources on the machine.

MEMORYSTATUS Structure:

Member	Description
DWORD *dwLength*	size of this structure. Caller should set this field prior to calling this function.
DWORD *dwMemoryLoad*	number between 0 and 100 that gives a general idea of how busy memory is, where 0 is not busy at all, and 100 is extremely busy.
DWORD *dwTotalPhys*	total number of bytes of physical memory.
DWORD *dwAvailPhys*	number of bytes of available physical memory (basically the number of pages on the free page list).
DWORD *dwTotalPageFile*	total number of bytes that can be stored in the paging file.
DWORD *dwAvailPageFile*	number of bytes that are currently unused in the paging file.
DWORD *dwTotalVirtual*	total number of bytes that can be described in the user mode portion of the virtual address space.
DWORD *dwAvailVirtual*	number of bytes that are currently unused in the user mode portion of the virtual address space.

Return Value	No return value.

■ GlobalNotify

The **GlobalNotify** function was deleted, since it is not possible to call out to application code in one process when the discard occurs in another process context.

■ GlobalPageLock

The **GlobalPageLock** function has been deleted.

■ GlobalPageUnlock

The **GlobalPageUnLock** function has been deleted.

■ GlobalReAlloc

HANDLE GlobalReAlloc(*hMem, dwBytes, dwFlags***)**
HANDLE *hMem*;
DWORD *dwBytes*;
DWORD *dwFlags*;

The **GlobalReAlloc** function changes the size of the global memory block specified by the *hMem* parameter by increasing or decreasing its size to the number of bytes specified by the *dwBytes* parameter, or changes the attributes of the specified memory block.

Parameters

hMem   Identifies the global memory block to be modified. This handle must have been created previously by a call to the **GlobalAlloc** or **GlobalReAlloc** function.

dwBytes   Specifies the new size (in bytes) of the memory block. If this size causes the memory block to grow past a multiple of 64KB then the memory block will be moved to a new location in order to satisfy the request. This parameter is ignored if the GMEM_MODIFY flag is set.

dwFlags   Specifies how to reallocate or modify the global block. Use one or more of the following flags, joined by the bitwise OR operator.

Value	Meaning
GMEM_MODIFY	Memory flags are modified. The *dwBytes* parameter is ignored. Use to modify the memory flags of a block without changing its size. Use GMEM_DISCARDABLE and GMEM_MOVEABLE to select the new flags.
GMEM_MOVEABLE	Memory is movable. If *dwBytes* is zero, this flag causes an object previously allocated as movable and discardable to be discarded if the object's lock count is zero. If *dwBytes* is nonzero and the object specified by *hMem* is fixed, this flag allows the reallocated object to be moved to a new fixed location. If *dwBytes* is nonzero and the object specified by *hMem* is movable, this flag allows the object to be moved. This may occur even if the object is currently locked by a previous call to **GlobalLock**. (Note that in this case the handle returned by the **GlobalReAlloc** function may be different from the handle passed to the function.) Use this flag with GMEM_MODIFY to make a fixed memory object movable.
GMEM_DISCARDABLE	Memory can be discarded. Block must be movable. Use only with GMEM_MODIFY.
GMEM_NODISCARD	Objects will not be discarded in order to satisfy the allocation request. This flag is ignored if the GMEM_MODIFY flag is set.

Value	Meaning
GMEM_ZEROINIT	If the block is growing, the additional memory contents are initialized to zero. This flag is ignored if the GMEM_MODIFY flag is set.

Return Value

The return value identifies the reallocated global memory if the function is successful. The return value is NULL if the block cannot be reallocated, in which case extended error information is available by calling the **GetLastError** function.

If the function is successful, the return value is always identical to the *hMem* parameter, unless the object is grown past a multiple of 64K bytes or GMEM_MOVEABLE is specified without GMEM_MODIFY.

See Also

GlobalLock

■ GlobalSize

DWORD GlobalSize(*hMem***)**
HANDLE *hMem*;

The **GlobalSize** function retrieves the current size (in bytes) of the global memory block specified by the *hMem* parameter.

Parameters

hMem   Identifies the global memory block. This handle must have been created previously by a call to the **GlobalAlloc** or **GlobalReAlloc** function.

Return Value

The return value specifies the actual size (in bytes) of the specified memory block. It is zero if the given handle is not valid or if the object has been discarded, in which case extended error information is available by calling the **GetLastError** function.

Comments

The actual size of a memory block is sometimes larger than the size requested when the memory was allocated.

An application should call the **GlobalFlags** function prior to calling the **GlobalSize** function in order to verify that the specified memory block was not discarded. If the memory block were discarded, the return value for **GlobalSize** would be meaningless.

See Also

GlobalFlags

■ GlobalUnfix

This function is implemented as a macro that returns TRUE if the input parameter is non-zero, and FALSE if the input parameter is zero.

■ GlobalUnlock

BOOL GlobalUnlock(*hMem***)**
HANDLE *hMem*;

The **GlobalUnlock** function unlocks the global memory block specified by the *hMem* parameter.

If the block is moveable and/or discardable, **GlobalUnlock** decreases the block's lock count by one. The block is completely unlocked and subject to movement and/or discarding if the lock count is decreased to zero.

In all cases, each time an application calls **GlobalLock** for an object, it must eventually call **GlobalUnlock** for the object.

Parameters   *hMem*   Identifies the global memory block to be unlocked. This handle must have been created previously by a call to the **GlobalAlloc** or **GlobalReAlloc** function.

Return Value   The return value specifies the outcome of the function. It is FALSE if the block's lock count was decreased to zero. Otherwise, the return value is TRUE. An application should not rely on the return value to determine the number of times it must subsequently call **GlobalUnlock** for the memory block.

See Also   **GlobalFlags, GlobalLock**

■ GlobalUnWire

The **GlobalUnWire** function is implemented by a macro that returns TRUE.

■ GlobalWire

The **GlobalWire** function is implemented by a macro that returns the input parameter.

■ GrayString

BOOL GrayString(*hDC, hBrush, lpOutputFunc, lpData, nCount, X, Y, nWidth, nHeight***)**
HDC *hDC*;
HBRUSH *hBrush*;
FARPROC *lpOutputFunc*;
DWORD *lpData*;
int *nCount*;
int *X*;
int *Y*;
int *nWidth*;
int *nHeight*;

This function draws gray text at the given location. The **GrayString** function draws gray text by writing the text in a memory bitmap, graying the bitmap, and then copying the bitmap to the display. The function grays the text regardless of the selected brush and background. **GrayString** uses the font currently selected for the device context specified by the *hDC* parameter.

If the *lpOutputFunc* parameter is NULL, GDI uses the **TextOut** function, and the *lpData* parameter is assumed to be a pointer to the character string to be output. If the characters to be output cannot be handled by **TextOut** (for example, the string is stored as a bitmap), the application must supply its own output function.

Parameters

hDC   Identifies the device context.

hBrush   Identifies the brush to be used for graying.

lpOutputFunc   Is the procedure-instance address of the application-supplied function that will draw the string, or, if the **TextOut** function is to be used to draw the string, it is a NULL pointer. See the following Comments section for details.

lpData   Specifies a pointer to data to be passed to the output function. If the *lpOutputFunc* parameter is NULL, *lpData* must be a pointer to the string to be output.

nCount   Specifies the number of bytes to be output. If the *nCount* parameter is zero, **GrayString** calculates the length of the string (assuming that *lpData* is a pointer to the string). If *nCount* is −1 and the function pointed to by *lpOutputFunc* returns FALSE, the image is shown but not grayed.

X   Specifies the device *x*-coordinate of the starting position of the rectangle that encloses the string.

Y   Specifies the device *y*-coordinate of the starting position of the rectangle that encloses the string.

nWidth   Specifies the width (in device units) of the rectangle that encloses the string. If the *nWidth* parameter is zero, **GrayString** calculates the width of the area, assuming *lpData* is a pointer to the string.

nHeight   Specifies the height (in device units) of the rectangle that encloses the string. If the *nHeight* parameter is zero, **GrayString** calculates the height of the area, assuming *lpData* is a pointer to the string.

Return Value

The return value specifies the outcome of the function. It is TRUE if the string is drawn. A return value of FALSE means that either the **TextOut** function or the application-supplied output function returned FALSE, or there was insufficient memory to create a memory bitmap for graying.

Comments

An application can draw grayed strings on devices that support a solid gray color, without calling the **GrayString** function. The system color COLOR_GRAYTEXT is the solid-gray system color used to draw disabled text. The application can call the **GetSysColor** function to retrieve the color value of COLOR_GRAYTEXT. If the color is other than zero (black), the application can call the **SetTextColor** to set the text color to the color value and then draw the string directly. If the retrieved color is black, the application must call **GrayString** to gray the text.

Callback Function

BOOL APIENTRY *OutputFunc*(*hDC, lpData, nCount*)
HDC *hDC*;
DWORD *lpData*;
int *nCount*;

OutputFunc is a placeholder for the application-supplied callback function name.

Parameters
hDC　Identifies a memory device context with a bitmap of at least the width and height specified by the nWidth and nHeight parameters, respectively.

lpData　Points to the character string to be drawn.

nCount　Specifies the number of bytes to be output.

Return Value
The return value must be TRUE to indicate success. Otherwise, it is FALSE.

Comments
This output function (*OutputFunc*) must draw an image relative to the coordinates (0,0) rather than (*X,Y*).

See Also
GetSysColor, SetTextColor, TextOut, DrawText, TabbedTextOut

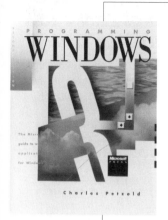
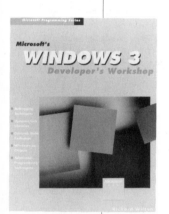